CANADIAN HISTORY: A READER'S GUIDE
VOLUME 1: BEGINNINGS TO CONFEDERATION

EDITED BY M. BROOK TAYLOR

Canadian History: A Reader's Guide Volume 1: Beginnings to Confederation

UNIVERSITY OF TORONTO PRESS
Toronto Buffalo London

© University of Toronto Press Incorporated 1994
Toronto Buffalo London
Printed in Canada

ISBN 0-8020-5016-6 (cloth)
ISBN 0-8020-6826-X (paper)

Canadian Cataloguing in Publication Data

Main entry under title:
Canadian history : a reader's guide

Includes index.
Contents: v. 1. Beginnings to Confederation /
edited by M. Brook Taylor – v. 2. Confederation
to the present / edited by Doug Owram.
ISBN 0-8020-5016-6 (v. 1 : bound)
ISBN 0-8020-6826-X (v. 1 : pbk.)
ISBN 0-8020-2801-2 (v. 2 : bound)
ISBN 0-8020-7676-9 (v. 2 : pbk.)

1. Canada – History – To 1763 (New France) –
Bibliography. 2. Canada – History – 1763– –
Bibliography.* I. Taylor, M. Brook (Martin Brook),
1951– . II. Owram, Douglas, 1947– .

Z1382.C35 1994   016.971   C94-930029-2

To our students

Contents

PREFACE xiii
ABBREVIATIONS xvii

Beginnings to 1600   *Ralph T. Pastore* 3
Methodological Problems 3
Reference Works and Bibliographies 6
Periodicals 9
The Land and the Sea 10
First Peoples in the Prehistoric Period 12
European Expansion 13
The Early Contact Period 22
Conclusion 31

Canada and the *Pays d'en haut*, 1600–1760   *Thomas Wien* 33
The State of the Field 33
Bibliographies, Reference Works, and Surveys 36
Published Documents 41
Periodicals 43
Historiography 44
The Region and Its Inhabitants 48
Population 51
Economy 57
Society 64
Politics and War 71
Conclusion 74

Acadia and Old Nova Scotia to 1784   *Barry Moody* 76
Bibliographies and Reference Works 76
Periodicals 77
General Works 79
Early European Settlement 79
Evolution and Growth of the Acadians 81
Ile Saint-Jean (Prince Edward Island) 87
Louisbourg 88
Native Studies 94
British Nova Scotia 96
The Expulsion of the Acadians 100
New England Planters 102
Nova Scotia and the American Revolution 108
The Great Awakening 109
Conclusion 111

Quebec / Lower Canada   *James H. Lambert* 112
Bibliographies and Reference Works 113
Published Documents 114
Periodicals 116
Historiography 116
Economic and Social History 122
    General Economic and Social Histories 122
    The Rural Economy and Society 124
    Agriculture 131
    Business 133
    Resource Industries 136
    Manufacturing and Industry 138
    Finance 139
    Transportation 140
    Social Structure 141
    Material Culture and Traditional Society 144
    Women's History 145
    Native Studies 147
    Demography and Migration 149
    Urban and Regional History 153
    Medicine 156
Political and Military History 158
Legal and Judicial History 166
Religious History 168

Culture, Science, and Education 173
Conclusion 182

Upper Canada *Bryan D. Palmer* 184
Historiography 185
General Works 186
Bibliographies and Published Documents 188
Periodicals 189
The Upper Canadian Economy 190
Native Peoples: Displacement and Dispossession 196
The Making of a Settler Society: Immigrants, Ideas, and Social
   Structure 200
A Sense of Place 207
Social Differentiation 210
   The Elites 210
   Artisans and Labourers 213
   Gender and Women 215
Regulation and the Social Order 219
Church and State / Institution and Faith 227
The Political Economy of Protest and the Administration of Order:
   Politics, Insurrection, and Government 229

The Maritime Colonies, 1784 to Confederation *Ian Ross Robertson* 237
Bibliographies and Reference Works 237
Periodicals 238
General Texts 239
Aboriginal Peoples 240
Loyalists 242
Immigrants from the United Kingdom 245
Blacks 248
Acadians 249
Women 251
Economic History 254
Nova Scotia 256
Cape Breton Island 262
New Brunswick 263
Prince Edward Island 268
Confederation 276
Conclusion 278

x   Contents

Newfoundland and the International Fishery   *Olaf Uwe Janzen* 280
Bibliographies and Reference Works 281
Published Documents 282
Periodicals 283
Historiography 283
The Fishery in the Sixteenth Century 285
The Fishery in the Seventeenth and Eighteenth Centuries 286
The European Settling of Newfoundland 292
Beothuk and Micmac 302
The Anglo-French Competition for Newfoundland 305
The Fishery in the Nineteenth Century 310
Newfoundland Politics to 1869 312
Social History 317
Labrador 320
Conclusion 323

The Northwest and the North   *Kerry Abel* 325
Bibliographies and General Works 325
Published Documents 327
Periodicals 328
Historiography 329
Ancient History 332
European Exploration 333
The Fur Trade 336
Mission History 341
First Nations 344
Métis 347
Red River Settlement 352
Conclusion 354

The Pacific Coast   *Tina Loo* 356
General Works 357
Bibliographies and Reference Works 358
Periodicals 360
Historiography 360
Native Peoples Precontact 362
European Exploration and the Maritime Fur Trade 364
The Land-Based Fur Trade 370
Vancouver Island 376
British Columbia 382
Conclusion 392

British North America in Its Imperial and International Context
  J.M. Bumsted 394
Reference Works and Documentary Collections 397
Military History 399
External Affairs 408
British North America and the Constitution of the British Empire 413
Trade and Commerce 425
Emigration/Immigration 428
The Transfer of British Institutions 439
Conclusion 447

CONTRIBUTORS 449
AUTHOR INDEX 453
SUBJECT INDEX 489

Preface

The Canadian historical profession is in the process of reorientation. There was a time when – at least in the retelling – scholars typically adopted a relatively coherent national standpoint (French Canada having its own variant), focused on elites, and employed narrative and biographical approaches. The social and political ferment of the 1960s, coupled with the proliferation of graduate schools, spawned a succession of challenges to the traditional picture of Canadian history. New generations of historians enlarged the canvas to include regional identities, the working class, women, Native peoples, and ethnic minorities. Along the way they adopted innovative methodologies, often drawn from the social sciences. While the new wave initially focused primarily on the post-Confederation era, perceptions of pre-Confederation Canada have been altered too, particularly in the multidisciplinary field of Native studies. This reorientation is not over. While old certainties have been dismantled or are under reconsideration, no new edifice has been constructed in its place. Indeed, there is some disagreement over the wisdom of synthesis or even the possibility of harmony. For the moment, then, Canadian historiography is particularly difficult to comprehend.

The purpose of this volume is to chart these potentially disorienting waters. The contributors, after establishing basic reference works and journals, provide a selective, critical guide to the present state of scholarship in their respective fields. No two chapters are alike, but they all grapple with similar problems of legitimate subject matter and appropriate methodology. What do the historians of pre-Confederation Canada think worthy of study? How do they conduct their studies? Occasionally contributors even hazard a guess about why historians make the choices they do. Differences are not resolved, but relationships are clarified.

As will become obvious, those seeking a new synthesis will find pre-Confederation history and historiography particularly intractable. The difficulty stems primarily from the fact that human activity down to 1867 relied, for the most part, on the exploitation of natural resources and was therefore heavily influenced by geography. Variations in climate and physiography created distinctive ecological regions, each of which was answered by different social structures, both among Native communities prior to contact and among colonists thereafter. One has only to consider the gulf separating the Native civilizations of the Atlantic and Pacific regions, or the outports of Newfoundland and the agricultural communities of the St Lawrence Valley, to gauge the significance of the problem. Distance in turn helped to preserve distinctions and stagger the spread of colonization. The timing of Native-European contact, for example, varied widely across the continent. As late as Confederation there were relatively few points where economic activity had pushed beyond close reliance on natural resources or technological innovation had overcome distance. It still remained easier to think of the nation to be as plural rather than singular.

It is not surprising that historians, even in the heyday of the national vision, found the search for unity among the colonies of British North America heavy going. Nevertheless, several 'theses' were proposed to suggest lines of common interpretation, if not of development: the staples thesis of Harold Adams Innis, the Laurentian thesis of Donald Grant Creighton, the frontier thesis of the American Frederick Jackson Turner as applied to Canada by Arthur R.M. Lower and S.D. Clark, and, more recently, the metropolitan thesis of J.M.S. Careless. As the contributors to this volume make clear, none of these theses survives today as a credible basis on which to build a case for unity. The Laurentian and frontier theses have come in for particularly pointed criticism, the former as a manifestation of central Canadian imperialism and the latter as an inappropriate foreign import. The staples and the metropolitan theses have proved more resilient, but in forms that usually explain unbalanced growth, having different effects in different regions at different times, with consequent complications of political control. Indeed, few historians now appear to be employed in the search for a unifying interpretive vision for the pre-Confederation period.

The structure of this volume, therefore, says a great deal about the present state of scholarship relating to the pre-Confederation period. It is chronological, and the chapter divisions are, with two exceptions, regional. The fragmentary nature of colonial development in British North America and before, as well as the regionally specialized nature of the historiography itself, makes this the only reasonable approach. Preparation of the author index brought home the extent to which historical writing on the pre-Confederation period is a regional activity. It was not often that the name of a practising scholar appeared in more than one chapter. Indeed, apart from the authors of such basic survey texts as those on Native peoples (J.R. Miller and Olive Patricia Dickason), women (Alison Prentice et al.), the economy (Douglas Owram and Kenneth Norrie), and so on, there were very few names mentioned in more than two.

Yet this division is itself deceptive, for while most historians of the pre-Confederation period have regional horizons, their studies generally pursue themes that have counterparts in colonies beyond. Historians in the Maritimes who approach their region by analysing family farm economies, for example, may well follow paths trod by historians pursuing a similar theme for Upper Canada or even New France. The same could be said for those interested in the history of Native peoples, law, women, medicine, or any number of lines of inquiry. The potential exists, then, if not for synthesis, at least for some measure of cross-regional integration along thematic lines. Readers of this volume will discover, however, how rare it is to find scholars reaching out and making such links. The linguistic gulf separating French- and English-speaking historians is particularly wide. (In this regard, it was sobering to discover how few of the French titles Jim Lambert identifies as vital contributions to the history of Lower Canada are available at any of the university libraries in Halifax.) And too often titles that suggest comprehensiveness turn out to be a good deal less or, worse, assume the experience of one region mirrors that of all. As a variation on this theme, Ian Robertson notes how often Maritime historians fail to include Prince Edward Island in their calculations, and, on a broader scale, Jack Bumsted regrets the reluctance of historians of the pre-Confederation period to situate their work more firmly in the experience of the North Atlantic and the Empire.

While the structure of this volume accepts the present regional bias of pre-Confederation historiography, the subject index is intended to help readers pursue themes across chapters. Indeed, it is purposively selective in its focus on issues that permit comparative analyses. The chapter subheadings listed in the table of contents may also prove useful in this regard. Certainly the potential for inter-regional studies exists. If exploited, perhaps a successor to this volume published ten or fifteen years from now will be organized on entirely different lines.

A word about format. Based on the assumption that few are likely to read a reference work like this from cover to cover, each chapter was designed to stand alone. This means that titles are given in full the first time they are cited in each chapter, short titles thereafter. Similarly, the first time an author is cited in each chapter the common full name is used – whether in the form of C.P. Stacey, Carl Berger, J. Murray Beck, John G. Reid, or Ian Ross Robertson – thereafter, initials and last name only: the author index should help alleviate any confusion.

A vexing problem was the issue of reprinted publications. Given the many series of Canadian historical reprints and the extraordinary number of excellent essay collections now available for use in both Canadian survey and more specialized courses, which imprint should be cited? Selections were ultimately made on the subjective basis of likely availability in the library of a small undergraduate university, say that of Mount Saint Vincent University in Halifax. In the case of monographs, the reprinted version was often the most accessible and therefore cited, whereas in the case of articles the original publication was preferred if it was in a source generally available (for example, the *Canadian Historical Review*). Whenever a reprinted version was used, every attempt was made to ensure that the date of the original publication was provided. Accessibility, or lack thereof, was also the reason contributors were discouraged from referring to such unpublished sources as MA and PhD theses.

In conclusion, I would like to thank the ten contributors to this volume, who bore my questions and recommendations as well as my frequent ignorance with patience and good humour. All editors should be so favoured. Thanks too, in turn, to our editor at the University of Toronto Press, Laura Macleod, who always seemed to know when to tighten a loose rein, and to our copy editor, Audrey Hlady, who saved us from many an error. The manuscript was prepared with the aid of an internal grant from Mount Saint Vincent University, where my colleague Ken Dewar was particularly supportive.

M. BROOK TAYLOR
BRIDGEWATER, NOVA SCOTIA

Abbreviations

PLACE OF PUBLICATION

CH	Charlottetown
E	Edmonton
F	Fredericton
H	Halifax
K	Kingston
L	London
M	Montreal
NY	New York
O	Ottawa
P	Paris
Q	Quebec City
R	Regina
SJ	St John's
T	Toronto
TR	Trois-Rivières
V	Vancouver
VI	Victoria
W	Winnipeg

PUBLISHERS

AP	Acadiensis Press
BE	Boréal Express
BKW	Breakwater Press
CC	Copp Clark

CCP	Copp Clark Pitman
CHA	Canadian Historical Association
CPRC	Canadian Plains Research Centre
CS	Champlain Society
CUP	Carleton University Press
HBJ	Harcourt Brace Jovanovich
HBRS	Hudson's Bay Record Society
HRW	Holt, Rinehart and Winston
IQRC	Institut québécois de recherche sur la culture
MAC	Macmillan
MHR	McGraw-Hill Ryerson
MQUP	McGill-Queen's University Press
M&S	McClelland and Stewart
OHS	Ontario Historical Society
OS	Osgoode Society
OUP	Oxford University Press
PH	Prentice-Hall
PUL	Les Presses de l'Université Laval
PUM	Les Presses de l'Université de Montréal
PUO	Les Presses de l'Université d'Ottawa
PUQ	Les Presses de l'Université du Québec
RP	Ryerson Press
SPT	Septentrion
UAP	University of Alberta Press
UBCP	University of British Columbia Press
UMP	University of Manitoba Press
UTP	University of Toronto Press
WPPB	Western Producer Prairie Books

JOURNALS AND SERIALS

BCHQ	*British Columbia Historical Quarterly*
BCS	*BC Studies*
CCHA	Canadian Catholic Historical Association (*Report*, *Study Sessions*, and *Historical Studies*)
CHA *AR*	Canadian Historical Association, *Annual Report*
CHA *HP*	Canadian Historical Association, *Historical Papers*
CHR	*Canadian Historical Review*
CJEPS	*Canadian Journal of Economics and Political Science*

CPRH	*Canadian Papers in Rural History*, ed. Donald H. Akenson (Gananoque, Ont.: Langdale Press 1978–)
DCB	*Dictionary of Canadian Biography*
DR	*Dalhousie Review*
ENL	*Encyclopedia of Newfoundland and Labrador*
HAC	*Historical Atlas of Canada*
HS/SH	*Histoire sociale/Social History*
IM	*Island Magazine*
JCCHS	*Journal of the Canadian Church Historical Society*
JCHA	*Journal of the Canadian Historical Association*
JCS	*Journal of Canadian Studies*
JICH	*Journal of Imperial and Commonwealth History*
L/LT	*Labour/Le Travail*
MHB	*Material History Bulletin*
MHR	*Material History Review*
NQ	*Newfoundland Quarterly*
NS	*Newfoundland Studies*
NSHR	*Nova Scotia Historical Review*
NSHS	Nova Scotia Historical Society (*Collections*)
OH	*Ontario History*
QQ	*Queen's Quarterly*
RHAF	*Revue d'histoire de l'Amérique française*
RS	*Recherches sociographiques*
SCHEC	Société canadienne d'histoire de l'Eglise catholique (*Rapport, Sessions d'étude*, and *Etudes d'histoire religieuse*)
TRSC	*Transactions of the Royal Society of Canada*
WMQ	*William and Mary Quarterly*

CANADIAN HISTORY: A READER'S GUIDE
VOLUME 1: BEGINNINGS TO CONFEDERATION

RALPH T. PASTORE

Beginnings to 1600

The purpose of this chapter is to provide a brief bibliographic guide to the Native peoples of Canada on the brink of European contact, the environments within which those First Nations lived, the expansion of Europeans into North America, and the history of Native-European relations in the sixteenth century. Since the study of peoples who did not leave written records requires going beyond historical literature, this chapter draws upon the disciplines of linguistics, anthropology, and, especially, archaeology. Accordingly, an attempt has also been made to explain the methodological problems inherent in interdisciplinary studies of this sort.

METHODOLOGICAL PROBLEMS

Archaeology is a branch of anthropology that studies past human activity largely through the physical remains left behind by people. In the absence of written documents, it is the primary method by which the processes of Native history before Columbus can be revealed. Furthermore, without the analyses of prehistoric Native cultures that archaeology can produce, it would not be possible to understand the changes that occurred after European contact. Archaeologists, however, employ a specialized language that the uninitiated may find daunting. As well, many of the questions addressed by archaeologists may appear, at first, to be of little interest or value to the non-specialist. Nonetheless, the student who persists will find much of value in the archaeological record. For an introduction to the disciplines of archaeology and anthropology, it is advisable to turn to elementary surveys, of which there are many. One of the best archaeological textbooks is Colin Renfrew and Paul Bahn, *Archaeology: Theories, Methods, and Practice* (NY: Thames and Hudson 1991). It is up-to-date, clearly written, and has a very useful glossary and bibliography. For anthropology, a valuable survey is Conrad Phillip Kottak, *Anthropology: The Exploration of Human Diversity* (4th ed., NY: Random House 1987).

Once equipped with a rudimentary understanding of archaeological and anthropological theory and method, one can begin to acquire a rather different perspective of Canadian history. Perhaps the most important contribution that archaeology can provide for the historian of the sixteenth century is the realization that Native societies were not static prior to European arrival. While the pace of change may have accelerated in the 1500s, the prehistoric era saw the migrations and disappearances of whole peoples, the adoption of agriculture in certain regions, the spread of belief systems over huge areas, and the development of new technologies such as the bow and arrow.

At a lower level of examination, archaeologists are concerned with understanding the day-to-day lives of Canada's First Nations. For example, a frequent goal of archaeological researchers is to determine the varieties of foods used by Native peoples. One of the best methods of doing so is through the analysis of faunal and floral remains from archaeological sites. Such evidence can indicate when a site was occupied (migratory birds, for example, can be taken only at specific times of the year); it can also, by the frequency and condition of fur-bearer remains, suggest whether a Native group was participating in a fur trade. Mortuary evidence – that recovered from graves – can also reveal much about past Native populations. Skeletal remains can directly demonstrate the health of a local society; analysis of pathological conditions can indicate the presence of new diseases; and the demographics of a cemetery's population can be evidence of a past epidemic. Native burials that lack the attributes common to earlier interments can sometimes reveal the behaviour of a society under stress. Analysis of entire living sites is another technique that can produce significant results. The presence or absence of fortifications can indicate the state of relations between a site's inhabitants and its neighbours; the movement together of formerly separate villages can sometimes be evidence of the emergence of a new socio-political organization; and the placement of early historic summer living sites near locations known to be frequented by European fishermen-traders can suggest a change in a settlement pattern stemming from an attempt to participate in a seasonal trade.

Although some historians may think that archaeological reconstructions of the past lack the precision associated with specific dates and recorded events, archaeological inferences can be of considerable value. For example, in the seventeenth century the Hurons (an Iroquoian people) became trading partners with the French, but archaeological evidence indicates that in the prehistoric period Ontario Iroquoians were already trading with neighbouring Algonkian peoples. Thus, when the French came to the St Lawrence lowlands, the Hurons were able to fit them into a pre-existing trade network. To cite another example, the people known as the St Lawrence Iroquoians, who once lived along the St Lawrence from Lake Ontario to the Quebec City region, became extinct in the sixteenth century, and it has long been supposed that their demise was somehow connected with the arrival of the Europeans. More recently, however, it has been suggested that a number of St Lawrence Iroquoian communities were destroyed by Huron groups from the west prior to European contact. Archaeologists have drawn this inference on the basis of a combination of observed behaviour and archaeological data. From observation, it is known that in most societies of a certain complexity, pottery is made mainly by women. From the ceramic evidence, archaeologists have correlated the appearance of distinctive St Lawrence Iroquoian pottery at Huron sites in Ontario with the disappearance of St Lawrence Iroquoian villages west of Montreal. The fact that this pottery was made of local, rather than exotic, clays indicates that these vessels were not acquired through trade, but were made by captive St Lawrence Iroquoian women living among the Hurons. (Historically, the practice among Iroquoian victors was to adopt conquered women and children.) Thus, on the basis of material evidence interpreted with the aid of historical analogy, archaeologists were able to conclude that a number of St Lawrence Iroquoian groups had been defeated and absorbed by the Hurons before European contact. The knowledge that the process of St Lawrence Iroquoian disintegration had begun this early adds an invaluable dimension to the perspective of the historian of the sixteenth century.

Of course the interpretative problems of the historian do not cease even after the arrival of Europeans in the New World. Although hundreds of sixteenth-century European fishermen, traders, and explorers visited the shores of what would later become Canada, few of them left written accounts of their observations. The lack of records may be explained by the sort of Europeans who crossed the Atlantic in that century. With the exception of a few well-known explorers, most made the arduous voyage and spent several hard-working months in the New World with the goal of making a profit, not producing detailed descriptions of new lands and new peoples. Indeed, given the widespread illiteracy of the period, the majority of those Europeans could not have left behind reports of their observations even if they had wished to do so. Thus, accounts of North American Native peoples are rare, and, even if they do exist, often frustrating. It is not always possible, for instance, to determine which Native groups were described or even the regions in which they were living. Sixteenth-century terms such as 'Terre Neuve,' 'Terra Nova,' and the 'New-Found-Land,' for example, do not always refer to the present-day island of Newfoundland, and were used on occasion for southern Labrador, the Quebec Lower North Shore, Cape Breton, and elsewhere. A reference to Natives of the New Found Land, therefore, might not necessarily mean the Beothuks, the island's aboriginal inhabitants.

Other difficulties are involved in interpreting sixteenth-century documents. Europeans, as has often been noted, viewed indigenous peoples through a European prism. Like most observers, sixteenth-century Europeans tended to see alien cultures in familiar terms. Coming as they did from hierarchical, state-level societies, for example, Europeans looked for 'chiefs' in egalitarian, band-level societies and may have perceived some individuals as leaders with considerable powers when in fact they may have been little more than spokespersons. We cannot even be sure that European descriptions of Native clothing, housing, and band size were accurate. European visitors, it must be remembered, saw Native peoples only during the warmer months. Native groups in Atlantic Canada frequently followed a seasonal round that involved movement in winter away from places where they had met Europeans in the summer. The size of Native groups in the summer, as well as their clothing and housing, may have varied considerably from what they were in winter.

All these limitations mean that the scholar studying the sixteenth century has to learn to use other forms of evidence as well as written records. Linguists, for example, have begun to produce some inferences about sixteenth-century Native-European interaction that could not have been made by traditional historians. Archaeologists have been even more productive. European trade beads, copper kettles, and iron knives, recovered from sixteenth-century sites, for instance, can provide information about the nature and extent of Native-European contact that is simply unavailable in the historical record.

REFERENCE WORKS AND BIBLIOGRAPHIES

The starting-point for students of the Canadian past is *Historical Atlas of Canada*, vol. 1, *From the Beginning to 1800*, ed. R. Cole Harris (T: UTP [1987]). It consists of expert plates which graphically depict the environment, prehistory, and history of Canada, each with an appended bibliography. Plates 1, 4, and 17 trace Canada's changing environment from 18,000

BC to AD 1500, while plates 2, 5, 6, 7, 8, and 9 deal with Canada's cultural history from 9500 BC to European contact. In addition, more specialized plates examine southern Ontario circa 8600 BC (plate 3), the bison hunters of the plains (plate 10), the cultural history of the Arctic (plate 11), Iroquoian agricultural settlement (plate 12), and the Tsimshian of the British Columbia coast around AD 1750 (plate 13). Plate 14 delineates prehistoric trade patterns throughout the country, and plate 18 displays Canadian Native linguistic, population, and subsistence information. One plate even presents Native belief systems (plate 15). The arrival of the Europeans is dealt with in plates that depict the Norse (plate 16), the Atlantic region and its first European explorers (plates 19 and 20), as well as the sixteenth- and seventeenth-century fisheries (plates 21, 22, and 23).

Equally valuable for the student of early Canadian history and prehistory is the multivolume *Handbook of North American Indians*, under the general editorship of William C. Sturtevant (Washington, DC: Smithsonian Institution 1978–). Volume 15, *Northeast*, ed. Bruce G. Trigger (1978), covers the region from Lake Superior to Newfoundland. Although a great deal of information has appeared since the publication of this work, it remains basic to the study of the Native peoples of the region. The *Northeast* contains articles by leading scholars on the prehistory of the region as well as the history and linguistics of the Beothuk, Micmac, Maliseet (also spelled Malecite), Abenaki, St Lawrence Iroquoian, Algonkin, Huron, Petun, Neutral, and the Nipissing and Ojibwa. The volume also includes an essay on early Native-European contacts and a comprehensive bibliography. For the Innu (Naskapi-Montagnais), Attikamek, northern Ojibwa, Cree, Chipewyan, Yellowknife, Dogrib, Slavey, Beaver, Carrier, Chilcotin, Sekani, Kaska, Tsetsaut, Tahltan, Inland Tlingit, Tagish, Mountain Indian, and Hare, there is volume 6, *Subarctic*, ed. June Helm (1981). The standard reference for the prehistory and history of the Inuit and their predecessors is volume 5, *Arctic*, ed. David Damas (1984). For the remarkable peoples of the British Columbia coast, there is volume 7, *Northwest Coast*, ed. Wayne Suttles (1990), which provides a summary of the prehistory of the region as well as the ethnohistory of the Tlingit, Nishga, Haida, Gitksan, Tsimshian, Haisla, Haihais, Bella Coola, Oowekeeno, Nootka, and Salish. The *Subarctic*, *Arctic*, and *Northwest Coast* volumes of the *Handbook* include valuable articles on the relevant environments in addition to histories of the research (archaeological, linguistic, anthropological, and historical) of the regions. Also of considerable value is Shepard Krech III, *Native Canadian Anthropology and History: A Selected Bibliography* (W: Rupert's Land Research Centre 1986). This guide deserves to be better known. It encompasses the entire country and includes both prehistoric and historical material. It also lists bibliographies and other reference works and published primary sources.

The arrival of Europeans in the New World signals the appearance of the first documentary references to Canada's Native peoples. The most valuable guide to those documents, both printed and manuscript, is David Beers Quinn, *Sources for the Ethnography of Northeastern North America to 1611* (O: National Museums of Canada 1981). The work covers the area from what is now New York State to the eastern Canadian Arctic. The sources are organized chronologically, and Quinn has provided brief summaries of the material. Somewhat older but still very useful is Bernard G. Hoffman, *Cabot to Cartier: Sources for a Historical Ethnography of Northeastern North America, 1497–1550* (T: UTP 1961), which analyses in detail maps and accounts pertinent to the earliest Native-European contacts in the Northeast. It should be supplemented with William Francis Ganong, *Crucial Maps in the Early Cartography and Place-Nomenclature of the Atlantic Coast of Canada* (T: UTP 1964). Volume 1 of the *Dictionary of Canadian Biography* (T: UTP 1966) is still of value, both for its bibliography and for its biographical entries, although the biographies must be used with caution. Alan E. Day, *Search for the Northwest Passage: An Annotated Bibliography* (NY: Garland 1986), is a comprehensive guide to the literature of European attempts to find a northwest passage to Asia that covers the period from John Cabot to the twentieth century. Although most of the citations in Sylvie Vincent and Jean-René Proulx, eds., *Review of Ethnohistorical Research on the Native Peoples of Quebec*, 5 vols. (Q: Direction régionale du Nouveau-Québec et service aux Autochtones, Ministère des Affaires culturelles du Québec 1985), are to sources dealing with subjects later than the sixteenth century, the *Review* is helpful because so much work on sixteenth-century Native peoples is based on inferences drawn from later periods. Robert S. Allen and Mary A.T. Tobin, *Native Studies in Canada: A Research Guide* (3rd ed., O: Treaties and Historical Research Centre 1989), should also be consulted. For the early ethnohistory of the Atlantic region there is Ralph T. Pastore, 'Native History in the Atlantic Region during the Colonial Period,' *Acadiensis* 20/1 (Autumn 1990): 200–25.

By far the most valuable collection of sixteenth-century primary material is D.B. Quinn, ed., *New American World: A Documentary History of North America to 1612*, 5 vols. (NY: Arno Press 1979). Volumes 1, 3, and 4 are particularly useful for Canada. In the late sixteenth and early seventeenth centuries, the Oxford scholar Richard Hakluyt promoted British expansion by collecting and publishing accounts of British explorers, a number of whom visited Canada's shores. Perhaps the most accessible of those editions are

Richard Hakluyt, *The Principal Navigations, Voyages, Traffiques, and Discoveries of the English Nation*, 12 vols. (NY: AMS Press 1965), and Hakluyt, *The Principal Navigations*, 8 vols., Everyman's Library (NY: Dutton 1907). Henry Percival Biggar, ed., *The Voyages of Jacques Cartier* (O: Public Archives of Canada 1924), long the standard edition of Cartier's observations, has now been supplanted by Ramsay Cook, ed., *The Voyages of Jacques Cartier* (T: UTP 1993), which includes a superb introduction by its editor, and by Michel Bideaux, ed., *Jacques Cartier Relations* (M: PUM 1986). Still essential, however, are Biggar's editions *A Collection of Documents Relating to Jacques Cartier and the Sieur de Roberval* (O: Public Archives of Canada 1930) and *The Precursors of Jacques Cartier, 1497–1534* (O: Public Archives of Canada 1911).

PERIODICALS

Among journals the pre-eminent vehicle for Canadian archaeologists is the *Canadian Journal of Archaeology* (1977–), but *Ontario Archaeology* (1954–) also has articles of value pertaining to the protohistoric period, when Native peoples were affected by a European presence, but not in contact with them. *American Antiquity* (1935–), the most important journal for American archaeologists, sometimes contains material of interest for students of the sixteenth century. Much more useful in this regard is *Man in the Northeast* (1971–), retitled *Northeast Anthropology* in 1993, which publishes articles by both archaeologists and ethnohistorians, as does *Etudes inuit/Inuit Studies* (1977–), a journal devoted to the study of the Inuit. Indispensable for the study of Quebec's Native peoples is *Recherches amérindiennes au Québec* (1971–), which includes both archaeological and ethnohistorical studies. For the rest of the country, the following regional archaeological journals should be consulted: Ontario Archaeology Society, *Arch Notes* (1962–), *Ontario Archaeology* (1954–), *Manitoba Archaeological Quarterly* (1977–), *Saskatchewan Archaeology* (1980–), *Occasional Papers of the Archaeological Survey of Alberta* (1976–), and *BC Studies* (1968–).

Basic for all historians of Native peoples is *Ethnohistory* (1954–), the journal of the American Society for Ethnohistory. A number of anthropological journals should also be kept in mind, particularly *Anthropologica* (1955–), which occasionally carries ethnohistorical works, as does *Culture* (1981–), the journal of the Canadian Ethnology Society. The *Western Canadian Journal of Anthropology* (1969–) should be consulted for archaeological and ethnohistorical works pertaining to the West as should the *Great Plains Journal* (1960–) and *Plains Anthropologist* (1955–). Arctic concerns are well served by *Arctic* (1948–), the journal of the Arctic Institute of North America, which contains articles ranging from arctic exploration history to arctic anthropology and archaeology. The interested reader should also be aware of *Arctic Anthropology* (1962–) and the *Musk-Ox* (1967–).

Among the historical periodicals, the *Canadian Historical Review* (1920–) and the *Revue d'histoire de l'Amérique française* (1947–) are the leading Canadian journals, although, with respect to the sixteenth century, both are generally more useful for their book reviews than for their articles. *The Beaver* (1920–), a journal aimed at a popular audience, occasionally contains articles by leading authorities on Canada's early history. *Acadiensis* (1971–), the journal of the Atlantic region, has also published material of relevance to the sixteenth century. *Terrae Incognitae* (1969–) is devoted to studies of European exploration and often contains articles on sixteenth-century Canada. For articles dealing with maritime history, especially the history of technical developments, see *The Mariner's Mirror* (1911–). Information on Newfoundland's indigenous people, especially the Beothuks, often appears in *Newfoundland Studies* (1985–). For information on Ontario see *Ontario History* (1899–). *The Canadian Geographer* (1950–) also occasionally has articles of value to the history student.

Most of these scholarly journals are of use not only for their articles, but also for their book reviews. As well, the historical – although not usually the anthropological and archaeological – journals offer listings of current publications of interest to students in the field.

THE LAND AND THE SEA

A good starting-place for an understanding of the environment that was the home of Canada's First Nations is J.H. McAndrews and G.C. Manville, 'Ecological Regions, ca AD 1500' and 'Descriptions of Ecological Regions,' in *HAC*, vol. 1, plates 17 and 17A. Other useful plates in *HAC*, vol. 1, are J.H. McAndrews et al., 'Environmental Change after 9000 BC,' plate 4; and Conrad E. Heidenreich and James V. Wright, 'Population and Subsistence,' plate 18. The Canadian climate is thoroughly described in F. Kenneth Hare and Morley K. Thomas, *Climate Canada* (2nd ed., T: J. Wiley & Sons 1979). For more specialized works on the environments of the regions see Ian Brookes, 'The Physical Geography of the Atlantic Provinces,' in Alan G. Macpherson, ed., *The Atlantic Provinces* (T: UTP 1972); A.G. Macpherson and Joyce Brown Macpherson, eds., *The Natural Environment of Newfoundland, Past and Present* (SJ: Memorial University of Newfoundland 1981); and James S. Gardner, 'General Environment,' in J. Helm, ed.,

Subarctic. In the same volume see also Edward S. Rogers and James G.E. Smith, 'Environment and Culture in the Shield and Mackenzie Borderlands,' and Catharine McClellan and Glenda Denniston, 'Environment and Culture in the Cordillera.' Similarly, D. Damas, ed., *Arctic*, contains John K. Stager and Robert J. McSkimming, 'Physical Environment.' The environment of southern Quebec and southern Ontario is dealt with in a number of works: see especially James A. Tuck, 'Regional Cultural Development, 3000 to 300 B.C.,' in B.G. Trigger, ed., *Northeast*; and the United States Environmental Protection Agency and Environment Canada, *The Great Lakes: An Environmental Atlas and Resource Book* (T: Environment Canada 1987). For the environment in which the early Hurons lived, C.E. Heidenreich, *Huronia: A History and Geography of the Huron Indians, 1600–1650* (T: M&S 1971), part 2, 'The Physical Geography of Huronia,' is especially good. The Prairie provinces each have published fine atlases, which should be consulted for an introduction to the environments of that region. In this regard turn to Thomas R. Weir, ed., *Atlas of Manitoba* (W: Department of Natural Resources 1983); J. Howard Richards, ed., *Atlas of Saskatchewan* (Saskatoon, Sask.: University of Saskatchewan 1969); and Department of Geography, University of Alberta, comp., *Atlas of Alberta* (E: UAP 1969). For British Columbia see W. Suttles, 'Environment,' in Suttles, ed., *Northwest Coast*.

With the exception of the Iroquoian horticulturalists, the majority of Canada's Native peoples drew their sustenance from the animals of the land and water. Some useful guides to these resources are A.W.F. Banfield, *The Mammals of Canada* (T: UTP 1974); Ernest S. Burch, Jr, 'The Caribou/ Wild Reindeer as a Human Resource,' *American Antiquity* 37/3 (July 1972): 339–68; Arthur E. Spiess, *Reindeer and Caribou Hunters: An Archaeological Study* (San Francisco, CA: Academic Press 1979); W. Earl Godfrey, *The Birds of Canada* (rev. ed., O: National Museums of Canada 1986); Erhard Rostlund, *Freshwater Fish and Fishing in Native North America* (Berkeley and Los Angeles, CA: University of California Press 1952); Alexander Henry Lein and William Beverley Scott, *Fishes of the Atlantic Coast of Canada* (O: Fisheries Research Board of Canada 1966); and W.B. Scott and Mildred Grace Scott, *Atlantic Fishes of Canada* (T: UTP 1988). Marcel Moussette, *Fishing Methods Used in the St. Lawrence River and Gulf* (O: Parks Canada 1979), is a comprehensive account of Native and European fishing techniques, based on archaeological, ethnographic, and historical evidence.

Regional works include Norman Clermont, 'Le contrat avec les animaux Bestiaire sélectif des Indiens nomades du Québec au moment du contact,' *Recherches amérindiennes au Québec* 10/1–2 (1980): 91–109, a study of human-animal relationships among Quebec hunter-gatherers at the time of contact. For northern Ontario there is Bruce Winterhalder, 'History and Ecology of the Boreal Zone in Ontario,' in A. Theodore Steegmann, Jr, ed., *Boreal Forest Adaptations: The Northern Algonkians* (NY: Plenum Press 1983). The animals exploited by subarctic hunter-gatherers are described in Beryl C. Gillespie, 'Major Fauna in the Traditional Economy,' in J. Helm, ed., *Subarctic*. D. Damas, ed., *Arctic*, should be consulted for Milton M.R. Freeman, 'Arctic Ecosystems.' A readable account of the mainstay of prairie hunters is Francis Haines, *The Buffalo* (NY: Thomas Y. Crowell 1970). For the salmon fishery, which was the basis of the impressive West Coast Native cultures, see Gordon W. Hewes, 'Indian Fisheries Productivity in Pre-contact Times in the Pacific Salmon Area,' *Northwest Anthropological Research Notes* 7/2 (Fall 1973): 133–55, and Randall F. Schalk, 'The Structure of an Anadramous Fish Resource,' in Lewis R. Binford, ed., *For Theory Building in Archaeology: Essays on Faunal Remains, Aquatic Resources, Spatial Analysis, and Systematic Modeling* (NY: Academic Press 1977).

FIRST PEOPLES IN THE PREHISTORIC PERIOD

For the non-specialist, the Canadian Museum of Civilization has produced a series of books that is an excellent beginning for the study of the archaeology of Canada. The starting-point in that series is Robert McGhee, *Ancient Canada* (O: Canadian Museum of Civilization 1989), which is a collection of essays on the major cultural traditions of prehistoric Canada. A more detailed general introduction to Canadian prehistory (and ethnohistory) is Alan D. McMillan, *Native Peoples and Cultures of Canada: An Anthropological Overview* (V: Douglas & McIntyre 1988). Turning to the prehistory of specific regions, the reader will find a good introduction to the prehistory of the Arctic in R. McGhee, *Canadian Arctic Prehistory* (T: Van Nostrand Reinhold 1978). McGhee has also published 'Thule Prehistory of Canada,' in D. Damas, ed., *Arctic*, a shorter, more up-to-date version of his older work. For those in need of more technical information there is Moreau S. Maxwell, *Prehistory of the Eastern Arctic* (Orlando, FL: Academic Press 1985), which contains a useful chapter on the arctic environment as well as material on the historic Inuit and their ancestors. For the prehistory of Labrador see William W. Fitzhugh, 'Indian and Eskimo/Inuit Settlement History in Labrador: An Archaeological View,' in Carol Brice-Bennett, ed., *Our Footprints Are Everywhere: Inuit Land Use and Occupancy in Labrador* (Nain, Lab.: Labrador Inuit Association 1977), and his 'Winter Cove 4 and the Point Revenge Occupation of the Central Labrador Coast,' *Arctic*

Anthropology 15/2 (1978): 146–74, an archaeological investigation of what are the probable ancestors of today's Innu. The ancestors of those same Innu, among other groups, are also treated in J.V. Wright, 'Prehistory of the Canadian Shield,' in J. Helm, ed., *Subarctic*. For the western subarctic there is Donald W. Clark, *Western Subarctic Prehistory* (O: National Museums of Canada 1991). The starting-point for Newfoundland's prehistory is still J.A. Tuck, *Newfoundland and Labrador Prehistory* (O: National Museums of Canada 1976), and for the Maritimes there is his *Maritime Provinces Prehistory* (O: National Museums of Canada 1984), which should be supplemented by his 'Prehistoric Archaeology in Atlantic Canada since 1975,' *Canadian Journal of Archaeology* 6 (1982): 201–18.

Quebec prehistory is covered in Charles A. Martijn, 'Etat de la recherche en préhistoire du Québec,' *Revue de géographie de Montréal* 28/4 (1974): 429–41; Claude Chapdelaine, ed., *Images de la préhistoire du Québec* (M: Recherches amérindiennes au Québec 1978); J.V. Wright, *Quebec Prehistory* (T: Van Nostrand Rinehold 1979); and N. Clermont, 'Quebec Prehistory Goes Marching In,' *Canadian Journal of Archaeology* 6 (1982): 195–200. For Ontario see J.V. Wright, *Ontario Prehistory: An Eleven-Thousand-Year Archaeological Outline* (O: National Museums of Canada 1972), and William C. Noble, 'Potsherds, Potlids, and Politics: An Overview of Ontario Archaeology during the 1970's,' *Canadian Journal of Archaeology* 6 (1982): 167–94. The prehistory of the Prairie provinces is examined in Leo F. Pettipas, ed., *Introducing Manitoba Prehistory* (W: Manitoba Department of Cultural Affairs and Historical Resources 1983); Ian Dyck, 'The Prehistory of Southern Saskatchewan,' in Henry T. Epp and Dyck, eds., *Tracking Ancient Hunters: Prehistoric Archaeology in Saskatchewan* (R: Saskatchewan Archaeological Society 1983); and J. Roderick Vickers, *Alberta Plains Prehistory: A Review* (E: Archaeological Survey of Canada 1986). Knut R. Fladmark, *British Columbia Prehistory* (O: National Museums of Canada 1986), is a readable, beautifully illustrated introduction to the prehistory of that province; it complements his 'An Introduction to the Prehistory of British Columbia,' *Canadian Journal of Archaeology* 6 (1982): 95–156.

EUROPEAN EXPANSION

In the sixteenth century Atlantic Canada was invaded by a growing number of explorers, fishermen, whalers, and fur traders. The best general survey of the activities of these newcomers is D.B. Quinn, *North America from Earliest Discovery to First Settlements: The Norse Voyages to 1612* (NY: Harper & Row 1977). Its chapters on the background to European exploration, as well as those on the exploration and exploitation of Canada's Atlantic coasts, the St Lawrence lowlands, and the search for a northwest passage, will remain the standard in the field for a long time. The work also includes a valuable, but now dated, bibliographical essay. Present-day scholars may object to some of Samuel Eliot Morison, *The European Discovery of America: The Northern Voyages, A.D. 500–1600* (NY: OUP 1971), especially his treatment of Native peoples, but the book remains a lively, if occasionally personal and idiosyncratic, treatment of the first European explorers and settlers to North America. For the student of Canadian history, there are lengthy chapters on the Norse, Cabot, the Portuguese explorers, Cartier, Sir Martin Frobisher, Sir Humphrey Gilbert, and John Davis, as well as on the European background. Morison's treatment of ships, sailing techniques, and navigational devices is especially helpful. The chapters include lengthy bibliographical essays, which, although now dated, are good points from which to begin bibliographic research. Also useful are William Patterson Cumming, R.A. Skelton, and D.B. Quinn, *The Discovery of North America* (T: M&S 1971), and the first part of Carl O. Sauer, *Sixteenth Century North America: The Land and the People As Seen by the Europeans* (Berkeley and Los Angeles, CA: University of California Press 1971). Part 1 of D.W. Meinig, *The Shaping of America: A Geographical Perspective on 500 Years of History*, vol. 1, *Atlantic America, 1492–1800* (New Haven, CT: Yale University Press 1986), is a geographer's interpretation of the beginnings of Europe's construction of the Atlantic world. Alan Cooke and Clive Holland, *The Exploration of Northern Canada, 500 to 1920: A Chronology* (T: Arctic History Press 1978) (in which northern Canada is defined as north of New Brunswick), is a detailed chronology with an extensive bibliography.

Fredi Chiappelli, ed., *First Images of America: The Impact of the New World on the Old*, 2 vols. (Berkeley and Los Angeles, CA: University of California Press 1976), is a wide-ranging collection of essays analysing the effect of early perceptions of the New World on the Old, and see too the provocative analysis in Wayne Franklin, *Discoverers, Explorers, Settlers: The Diligent Writers of Early America* (Chicago, IL: University of Chicago Press 1979). R. McGhee's aptly named *Canada Rediscovered* (O: Canadian Museum of Civilization 1991) is a well-written, beautifully produced, popular history of the first Europeans in Canada. Incorporating the latest scholarship, both historical and archaeological, the work touches on the Native peoples of Canada, Irish and Norse explorations of the North Atlantic, and the subsequent discovery and early exploitation of the resources of sixteenth-century Newfoundland and the Canadian mainland. It should serve for a long time as an introduction to the history of the first Europeans to reach Canada.

To understand why this expansion occurred when it did it is necessary to understand the background from which these Europeans came. A good introduction to the process by which Europe came to dominate so much of the world is Eric Wolf's ground-breaking study, *Europe and the People without History* (Berkeley and Los Angeles, CA: University of California Press 1982), which, within a Marxist framework, analyses the world – both that of the Europeans and that of 'the people without history' – as a total system. For a more narrowly focused work on the preconditions of European expansion see Immanuel Wallerstein, *The Modern World System*, vol. 1, *Capitalist Agriculture and the Origins of the European World-Economy in the Sixteenth Century* (NY: Academic Press 1974). Other useful general works covering the social and economic background of European exploration include John Huxtable Elliott, *The Old World and the New, 1492–1650* (Cambridge, Eng.: Cambridge University Press 1970); Ralph Davis, *The Rise of the Atlantic Economies* (Ithaca, NY: Cornell University Press 1973); and Fernand Braudel, *Capitalism and Material Life, 1400–1800* (NY: Harper & Row 1973), and his magisterial *Civilization and Capitalism, 15th–18th Century*, 3 vols. (NY: Harper & Row 1981–4).

For an analysis of the impact of the discovery of the New World on the world-view of Europe there is J.H. Elliott, 'Renaissance Europe and America: A Blunted Impact?' in F. Chiappelli, ed., *First Images of America*. Three works by J.H. Parry are essential for an understanding of the maritime expansion of Europe in the early modern age: *The Age of Reconnaissance* (L: Weidenfeld and Nicolson 1963); *Europe and a Wider World, 1415–1715* (3rd ed., L: Hutchinson 1966); and *The Discovery of the Sea* (NY: Dial Press 1974). The technical developments that helped make these transatlantic expeditions possible are outlined in Carlo M. Cipolla, *Guns, Sails and Empires: Technological Innovation and the Early Phases of European Expansion, 1400–1700* (NY: Pantheon Books 1965). More specialized are Romola Anderson and R.C. Anderson, *The Sailing-Ship: Six Thousand Years of History* (1926; rev. ed., NY: Norton 1963), and David W. Waters, *The Art of Navigation in England in Elizabethan and Early Stuart Times*, 3 vols. (2nd ed., Greenwich, Eng.: National Maritime Museum 1978).

In recent years historians have come to understand the momentous ecological consequences that European contact with the New World initiated. A general work which also examines the export of European pathogens to the New World is William H. McNeill, *Plagues and Peoples* (Garden City, NY: Anchor Books 1976). Two volumes that deal with the exchange of European fauna and flora between the Old World and the New are Alfred W. Crosby, *The Columbian Exchange: Biological and Cultural Consequences of*

1492 (Westport, CT: Greenwood Press 1972), and his important and wide-ranging *Ecological Imperialism: The Biological Expansion of Europe, 900–1900* (NY: Cambridge University Press 1986).

Five groups of Europeans met Canada's Native peoples in the Middle Ages and the sixteenth century. They were the Norse, the English, the French, the Portuguese, and the Spanish. Much of what we now know about the Norse in North America is the result of work done at L'Anse aux Meadows, Newfoundland, the only verified pre-Columbian European site in North America. It was excavated initially by Helge Ingstad and Anne Stine Ingstad and then by Parks Canada. The results of the first excavations are dealt with in Anne Stine Ingstad, *The Norse Discovery of America*, vol. 1, *Discovery of a Norse Settlement in America* (Oslo: Norwegian University Press 1985). The background to the Norse enterprise that was responsible for L'Anse aux Meadows is examined in Helge Ingstad, *The Norse Discovery of America*, vol. 2, *The Historical Background and the Evidence of the Norse Settlement Discovered in Newfoundland* (Oslo: Norwegian University Press 1985). For a preliminary report on the Parks Canada excavations see Birgitta Linderoth Wallace, 'The L'Anse aux Meadows Site,' in Gwyn Jones, *The Norse Atlantic Saga* (2nd ed., NY: OUP 1986). Wallace offers the convincing explanation that the Norse abandoned their settlement in North America simply because everything that the settlers could get from North America, they could also get – and more – from Europe. Jones's *Norse Atlantic Saga* is perhaps the best general introduction to Norse involvement in North America, and it includes translations of the relevant sagas, but see also R. McGhee, 'Northern Approaches: Before Columbus: Early European Visitors to the New World,' *The Beaver* 72/3 (June/July 1992): 6–23. McGhee also analyses the various claims for contact between Native peoples and the Norse in 'Contact between Native North Americans and the Medieval Norse: A Review of the Evidence,' *American Antiquity* 49/1 (Jan. 1984): 4–26, which examines both saga and archaeological evidence. A convenient translation of the sagas is to be found in Magnus Magnusson and Harmann Palsson, *The Vinland Sagas: The Norse Discovery of America* (Baltimore, MD: Penguin 1965). The sixth chapter in the first volume of D.B. Quinn, ed., *New American World*, also contains relevant documentation pertaining to the Vinland voyages of the eleventh century.

In 1965 Yale scholars produced an early-fifteenth-century map that depicted a region called Vinland and showed Greenland as an island – both concepts thought by modern scholars to be outside the knowledge of fifteenth-century cartographers. The map and its background are explained in R.A. Skelton, Thomas E. Marston, and George D. Painter, eds., *The Vin-*

land Map and the Tartar Relation (New Haven, CT: Yale University Press 1965). In the 1970s chemical analysis appeared to prove the map a forgery; however, more recent sophisticated analysis seems to have borne out the map's legitimacy. See R. McGhee, *Canada Rediscovered*, for an account of the map's varying fortunes.

The maps of the sixteenth century are essential for an understanding of the growing European knowledge of Atlantic and arctic Canada, but the cartographic history of the period is particularly intricate. The best guides to that history are B.G. Hoffman, *Cabot to Cartier*; S.E. Morison, *European Discovery of America*; and D.B. Quinn, *North America from Earliest Discovery*. Among the most useful collections of maps and commentaries are: Map Division, Public Archives of Canada, comp., *Sixteenth-Century Maps Relating to Canada; A Check-list and Bibliography* (O: Public Archives of Canada 1956), and W.F. Ganong, *Crucial Maps*, as well as Henry Harrisse, *The Discovery of North America* (L: Henry Stevens & Son 1892; repr. Amsterdam: N. Israel 1961), and his *Découverte et évolution cartographique de Terre-Neuve et des pays circonvoisins, 1497–1501–1769* (P: H. Welter 1900; repr. Ridgewood, NJ: Gregg 1968). Despite their age, Harrisse's works should not be ignored. They are concerned with more than just cartographic history, and they contain information not found elsewhere.

Only a selection can be made from the considerable number of general works dealing with sixteenth-century England. Among the best introductions to the social and economic conditions that form the background of English exploration are Leslie A. Clarkson, *The Pre-Industrial Economy in England, 1500–1750* (NY: Schocken Books 1972); W.G. Hoskins, *The Age of Plunder: King Henry's England, 1500–1547* (NY: Longman 1976); Kenneth R. Andrews, *Trade, Plunder, and Settlement: Maritime Enterprise and the Genesis of the British Empire, 1480–1630* (Cambridge, Eng.: Cambridge University Press 1984); Joyce A. Youings, *Sixteenth-Century England* (L: Allen Lane 1984); and D.M. Palliser, *The Age of Elizabeth: England under the Later Tudors, 1547–1603* (2nd ed., NY: Longman 1992).

There is a rich body of literature dealing with early English exploration of Maritime Canada. The best introduction is D.B. Quinn's collection of essays, *England and the Discovery of America, 1481–1620* (NY: Knopf 1974), a work which also explores the possibility that Bristol fishermen reached North America before Cabot and Columbus. That question is addressed as well by Alwyn A. Ruddock, 'John Day of Bristol and the English Voyages across the Atlantic before 1497,' *Geographical Journal* 132/2 (June 1966): 225–33, and by Patrick McGrath, 'Bristol and America, 1480–1631,' in K.R. Andrews et al., eds., *The Westward Enterprise: English Activities in Ire-*

land, the Atlantic and America, 1480–1650 (Detroit, MI: Wayne State University Press 1979). The Day letter, with its suggestion of an English pre-Columbian landfall in North America, is translated and printed in L.-A. Vigneras, 'The Cape Breton Landfall: 1494 or 1497? Note on a Letter from John Day,' *CHR* 38/3 (Sept. 1957): 219–28. For the Cabots, James Alexander Williamson, *The Cabot Voyages and Bristol Discovery under Henry VII* (Cambridge, Eng.: Hakluyt 1962), and A.A. Ruddock, 'The Reputation of Sebastian Cabot,' *Bulletin of the Institute of Historical Research* 47/115 (May 1974): 95–9, are still useful. Paul Fuson, 'The John Cabot Mystique,' in Stanley H. Palmer and Dennis Reinhartz, eds., *Essays on the History of North American Discovery and Exploration* (College Station, TX: Texas A&M Press 1988), calls into question both Cabots' accomplishments and the historians who have celebrated them.

Primary printed documents relating to early-sixteenth-century English and other explorations are to be found in D.B. Quinn, ed., *New American World*, vol. 1, as well as H.P. Biggar, ed., *Precursors of Jacques Cartier*. For those wishing to read the collections of Richard Hakluyt as they were originally published, there is *The Principall Navigations, Voiages and Discoveries of the English Nation*, imprinted at London in 1589, facsimile edition with introduction by D.B. Quinn and R.A. Skelton, 2 vols. (Cambridge, Eng.: Hakluyt 1965). Formats more accessible to the modern reader are cited in the section 'Reference Works and Bibliographies.' Hakluyt and other sixteenth-century English historians of European exploration are assessed in Myron P. Gilmore, 'The New World in French and English Historians of the Sixteenth Century,' in F. Chiappelli, ed., *First Images of America*. See also the collection of essays in D.B. Quinn, ed., *The Hakluyt Handbook*, 2 vols. (L: Hakluyt 1974). For the latter part of the sixteenth century, published documents relating to English exploratory voyages are found in D.B. Quinn, ed., *The Voyages and Colonising Enterprises of Sir Humphrey Gilbert*, 2 vols. (L: Hakluyt 1940; repr. NY: Kraus 1967), which also includes a useful biography of Gilbert; Quinn, ed., *New American World*, vols. 3–4; Vilhjalmur Stefansson, ed., *The Three Voyages of Martin Frobisher in Search of a Passage to Cathay and India by the North-West, A.D. 1576–8*, 2 vols. (L: Argonaut 1938); and A.H. Markham, ed., *The Voyages and Works of John Davis, the Navigator* (L: Hakluyt 1880). Some archaeological investigation of Frobisher's voyages has been undertaken, the beginnings of which are outlined in Walter Andrew Kenyon, *Tokens of Possession: The Northern Voyages of Martin Frobisher* (T: Royal Ontario Museum 1975).

Almost all sixteenth-century illustrations of Native peoples are deficient because their makers saw New World inhabitants through European eyes.

The result was often a depiction of Native people who looked like Europeans. An exception was John White, whose representations contain a wealth of accurate detail. He accompanied Martin Frobisher on the latter's second exploratory voyage in 1577, and his drawings of Canadian Inuit are found in Paul Hulton and D.B. Quinn, *The American Drawings of John White, 1577–1590*, 2 vols. (Chapel Hill, NC: University of North Carolina Press 1964). Because of the expense and limited printing of this work, it may not be readily available. P. Hulton, *America, 1585: The Complete Drawings of John White* (Chapel Hill, NC: University of North Carolina Press 1984), is an acceptable substitute, although its reproductions of White's drawings fall below those of the 1964 edition. W.C. Sturtevant, 'First Visual Images of Native America,' in F. Chiappelli, ed., *First Images of America*, is an invaluable comprehensive listing and analysis of sixteenth-century depictions of New World Native people.

The Portuguese were among the first Europeans to reach the Gulf of St Lawrence, but disappointingly little has been written about their presence in the North Atlantic. Of some help as studies of the background of Portuguese exploration and exploitation are C.R. Boxer, *The Portuguese Seaborne Empire, 1415–1825* (NY: Knopf 1969), and Bailey W. Diffie and George D. Winius, *Foundations of the Portuguese Empire, 1415–1580* (Minneapolis, MN: University of Minnesota Press 1977), especially Diffie's contribution which examines the Atlantic voyages and discoveries. Lucien Campeau, 'Découvertes portugaises en Amérique du Nord,' *RHAF* 20/2 (sept. 1966): 171–227, is a good overview of Portuguese exploration of North America. Primary source material on the Portuguese in Canadian waters can be found in H.P. Biggar, ed., *Precursors of Jacques Cartier*, and D.B. Quinn, ed., *New American World*, vols. 1 and 4.

While Spanish fishermen were working off the coasts of Newfoundland early in the sixteenth century, Spanish exploration was directed toward more southerly regions. Only one Spanish explorer, the Portuguese-born Estevão Gomes (in Spanish, Esteban Gómez), who sailed along the shores of Nova Scotia and Newfoundland in 1525, is known to have visited Canadian waters in the sixteenth century. Documentation relative to that voyage is available in H. Harrisse, *Discovery of North America*; H.P. Biggar, ed., *Precursors of Jacques Cartier*; and D.B. Quinn, ed., *New American World*, vol. 1, ch. 20; and L.-A. Vigneras offers a brief account of the Gomes expedition in 'The Voyage of Esteban Gómez from Florida to the Baccalaos,' *Terrae Incognitae* 2 (1970): 25–8. Where general works on sixteenth-century Spain deal with the Spanish presence overseas, the emphasis is invariably on Spanish possessions in Latin America and the Pacific, not their more mundane fishing and whaling enterprises in Atlantic Canada. Nonetheless, the following works provide a good introduction to the Spain from which Gomes and so many fishermen and whalers sailed: R. Trevor Davies, *The Golden Century of Spain, 1501–1621* (1937; repr. L: MAC 1967); J.H. Elliott, *Imperial Spain, 1469–1716* (L: E. Arnold 1963); J.H. Parry, *The Spanish Seaborne Empire* (NY: Knopf 1966); John Lynch, *Spain under the Habsburgs*, vol. 1, *Empire and Absolutism, 1516–1598* (2nd ed., NY: OUP 1981); and Elliott, *Spain and Its World, 1500–1700: Selected Essays* (New Haven, CT: Yale University Press 1989).

The Cartier-Roberval voyages of 1534–43 were major efforts backed by the French monarchy to explore and settle the St Lawrence. The background to the France of Francis I, who supported Cartier and Roberval, is covered especially well in J.H.M. Salmon, *Society in Crisis: France in the Sixteenth Century* (NY: St Martin's Press 1975), and R.J. Knecht, *Francis I* (Cambridge, Eng.: Cambridge University Press 1982). For the latter part of the sixteenth century, D.B. Quinn, 'Henri Quatre and New France,' *Terrae Incognitae* 22 (1990): 13–28, should be consulted. The most useful surveys of French activity in Canada in the sixteenth century are still two works by Marcel Trudel, *Histoire de la Nouvelle-France*, vol. 1, *Les vaines tentatives, 1524–1603* (M: Fides 1963), and *The Beginnings of New France, 1524–1663* (T: M&S 1973). For an analysis of French claims to North America in the sixteenth century, see Brian Slattery, 'French Claims in North America, 1500–59,' *CHR* 59/2 (June 1978): 139–69, which argues that before 1560 France made no definite claim to any part of North America and recognized Native peoples as independent nations exercising sovereignty over their lands. A different view of this question is provided by Olive Patricia Dickason, 'Old World Law, New World Peoples, and Concepts of Sovereignty,' in S.H. Palmer and D. Reinhartz, eds., *Essays on the History of North American Discovery and Exploration*.

One of the first relatively full accounts of early French exploration resulted from a voyage undertaken in 1529 by a French sea captain, probably one Jean Parmentier, who visited Nova Scotia and Newfoundland. His voyage was recorded, probably by Pierre Crignon, whose relation contains an intriguing, if brief, account of the region's Native peoples. That report and an accompanying analysis are in B.G. Hoffman, 'Account of a Voyage Conducted in 1529 to the New World, Africa, Madagascar, and Sumatra, Translated from the Italian, with Notes and Comments,' *Ethnohistory* 10/1 (Winter 1963): 1–79. But from a Canadian perspective clearly the most significant of the French exploratory voyages of the first half of the sixteenth century were the Cartier-Roberval expeditions of 1534–43. André Thevet

(1504–92), the court cosmographer of France in the last half of the six-teenth century, collected material from Cartier and others, and although his later works are marred with a great deal of fiction, his earlier ones are of some value. Thevet's works are most accessible in Roger Schlesinger and Arthur P. Stabler, eds., *André Thevet's North America: A Sixteenth-Century View* (K&M: MQUP 1986). For an examination of Thevet within the wider context of contemporary French historical writing about the New World, there is M.P. Gilmore, 'The New World in French and English Histories of the Sixteenth Century,' in F. Chiappelli, ed., *First Images of America. Le monde de Jacques Cartier: l'aventure au XVIe siècle* (M: Libre Expression 1984), is a lavishly produced collection of essays by a number of authorities on Cartier and the background of St Malo and France, as well as the peoples and lands he encountered. Yves Jacob, *Jacques Cartier: de Saint-Malo au Saint-Laurent* (P: Editions Maritimes & d'Outre-Mer 1984), should also be consulted. Essential source material is located in H.P. Big-ger, ed., *Collection of Documents Relating to Jacques Cartier and the Sieur de Roberval*; M. Bideaux, ed., *Jacques Cartier Relations*; and R. Cook, ed., *The Voyages of Jacques Cartier*.

Beginning possibly before Columbus, English fishermen had begun to exploit the rich waters off the coast of Newfoundland, and by the early six-teenth century they had been joined by the French, Spanish, and Portu-guese. Printed primary sources illustrative of the European cod and whale fisheries are to be found in D.B. Quinn, ed., *New American World*, vol. 4. Surprisingly, no general history of the European fishery has yet superseded Harold Adams Innis, *The Cod Fisheries: The History of an International Econ-omy* (1940; rev. ed., T: UTP 1954). Although primarily concerned with the seventeenth century, Gillian T. Cell, *English Enterprise in Newfoundland, 1577–1660* (T: UTP 1969), is valuable. Despite its age, H.A. Innis's 'The Rise and Fall of the Spanish Fishery in Newfoundland,' *TRSC* ser. 3, 25 (1931), sec. ii, 51–70, reprinted in Mary Q. Innis, ed., *Essays in Canadian Economic History* (T: UTP 1956), is still useful, mainly because so little has been published on the Spanish fishery. The same is true of the Portuguese fishery – a subject largely ignored, even by Portuguese historians. The French fishery has been much more satisfactorily dealt with. Although it mostly covers a later period, Charles de La Morandière, *Histoire de la pêche française de la morue dans l'Amérique septentrionale*, 3 vols. (P: Maisonneuve et Larose 1962–6), is still the best overall study of the French fishery. For a more specialized study see Jacques Bernard, *Navires et gens de mer à Bor-deaux (vers 1400–vers 1550)*, 3 vols. (P: SEVPEN 1968). Laurier Turgeon, 'Pour redécouvrir notre 16e siècle: les pêches à Terre-Neuve d'après les archives notariales de Bordeaux,' *RHAF* 39/4 (printemps 1986): 523–49, is a distillation of his work on the sixteenth-century French fishery as reflected in the notarial archives of Bordeaux.

The role of the French and Spanish Basques as cod fishermen and whalers in the Gulf of St Lawrence is just beginning to be explored. An early pioneer of an investigation of that presence is René Bélanger, *Les Basques dans l'estuaire du Saint-Laurent, 1535–1635* (M: PUQ 1971). A good introduction to the whaling industry in the North Atlantic is Jean-Pierre Proulx, *Whaling in the North Atlantic from Earliest Times to the Mid-19th Century* (O: Parks Canada 1986). For a historical treatment of the Basque whalers of southern Quebec–Labrador, there is Selma Barkham, 'The Documentary Evidence for Basque Whaling Ships in the Strait of Belle Isle,' in G.M. Story, ed., *Early European Settlement and Exploitation in Atlantic Canada: Selected Papers* (SJ: Memorial University of Newfoundland 1982). J.A. Tuck and Robert Grenier, *Red Bay, Labrador: World Whaling Capital, A.D. 1550–1600* (SJ: Atlantic Archaeology 1989), is a popular account by two archaeologists of the best known of the Basque whaling sites. Tuck, who directed the land archaeology at Red Bay, and Grenier, who led the underwater team, also produced 'A 16th-Century Basque Whaling Station in Labrador,' *Scientific American* 245/5 (Nov. 1981): 180–4, 186–8, 190. On the French Basques and their relations with the Native peoples of the Gulf, see L. Turgeon, 'Pêcheurs basques et indiens des côtes du Saint-Laurent au XVIe siècle: perspectives de recherches,' *Etudes canadiennes/Canadian Studies* 13 (1982): 9–14, and his 'Basque-Amerindian Trade in the Saint Lawrence during the Sixteenth Century: New Documents, New Perspectives,' *Man in the Northeast* 40 (Fall 1990): 81–7.

THE EARLY CONTACT PERIOD

The works referred to in this section deal only with those Canadian Native peoples who either encountered Europeans in the sixteenth century or acquired European goods. These include the Inuit, the Innu (Naskapi-Montagnais), the Beothuks, the Micmacs and Maliseets, and the St Lawrence Iroquoians, all of whom had direct contact with Europeans. The Hurons and other Iroquoian peoples of Ontario, and possibly some of the northern Algonkian neighbours of the Hurons, did acquire a limited amount of European trade goods, but apparently did not meet Europeans face-to-face.

For a general overview of the first Native-European contacts refer to Ted J. Brasser, 'Early Indian-European Contacts,' in B.G. Trigger, ed.,

Northeast, and James Axtell, 'At the Water's Edge: Trading in the Sixteenth Century,' in Axtell, *After Columbus: Essays in the Ethnohistory of Colonial North America* (NY: OUP 1988). Trigger, 'Early Native North American Responses to European Contact: Romantic versus Rationalistic Interpretations,' *Journal of American History* 77/4 (Mar. 1991): 1195–1215, argues persuasively that not long after initial contact with Europeans Native traders were guided more by universal rational considerations than by the constraints of a traditional belief system. George R. Hamell, using archaeological, historical, and folkloric evidence, has also attempted to understand the world-view of Native peoples who participated in the first trading encounters with Europeans. His work is most accessible in 'Strawberries, Floating Islands, and Rabbit Captains: Mythical Realities and European Contact in the Northeast during the Sixteenth and Seventeenth Centuries,' *JCS* 21/4 (Winter 1986–7): 72–94; 'Mythical Realities and European Contact in the Northeast during the Sixteenth and Seventeenth Centuries,' *Man in the Northeast* 33 (1987): 63–87; and with Christopher L. Miller, 'A New Perspective on Indian-White Contact: Cultural Symbols and Colonial Trade,' *Journal of American History* 73/2 (Sept. 1986): 311–28.

Students should also be aware of the controversy surrounding Calvin Martin, *Keepers of the Game: Indian-Animal Relationships and the Fur Trade* (Berkeley and Los Angeles, CA: University of California Press 1978), in which Martin charged that as a result of epidemic disease brought by Europeans Native peoples declared 'war' on animals and overhunted them drastically. For a convincing alternative to the Martin thesis there are the essays in S. Krech III, ed., *Indians, Animals and the Fur Trade: A Critique of 'Keepers of the Game'* (Athens, GA: University of Georgia Press 1981). Of particular relevance are the articles by Dean R. Snow, Charles A. Bishop, and B.G. Trigger. In '*Keepers of the Game* and the Nature of Explanation,' Snow argued that although the Abenaki, for example, believed that animals could cause disease, only specific animals, who were shamans in disguise, could do such a thing. Snow was also highly sceptical that an ideology such as that posited by Martin could be such a 'dysfunctional prime mover' for very long. In 'Northeastern Indian Concepts of Conservation and the Fur Trade: A Critique of Calvin Martin's Thesis,' Bishop noted that it was illogical to argue, as Martin had done, that the war against animals was the result of Native rejection of traditional ideology when an alleged onslaught against the animal world would itself have been the result of that ideology. Bishop also rejected Martin's assertion that Native peoples had first abandoned their belief system and then later resurrected it.

The argument for a Native population at the time of contact much larger than previously suspected has been presented in its most extreme form by Henry F. Dobyns, *Their Number Become Thinned: Native American Population Dynamics in Eastern North America* (Knoxville, TN: University of Tennessee Press 1983). A much more balanced estimate is to be found in Douglas H. Ubelaker, 'North American Indian Population Size, A.D. 1500 to 1985,' *American Journal of Physical Anthropology* 77/3 (Nov. 1988): 289–94. The question of the timing and the effects of the first European epidemics to strike the peoples of the Northeast has been equally heated. *Their Number Become Thinned* argues for a number of pandemics in the sixteenth century which affected the Native peoples of the Northeast. This position is challenged in David Henige, 'Primary Source by Primary Source? On the Role of Epidemics in New World Depopulation,' *Ethnohistory* 33/3 (Summer 1986): 293–312, which is highly critical of Dobyns's use of sources, and D.R. Snow and Kim M. Lanphear, 'European Contact and Indian Depopulation in the Northeast: The Timing of the First Epidemics,' *Ethnohistory* 35/1 (Winter 1988): 15–33, which maintains that there were no serious epidemics of European disease in the Northeast until the seventeenth century. The argument is continued in Dobyns, Henige, and Snow and Lanphear, 'Commentary on Native American Demography,' *Ethnohistory* 36/3 (Summer 1989): 285–307.

In sixteenth-century North America contact between Europeans and Inuit occurred, for the most part, in Labrador and on Baffin Island. A few printed primary sources relating to those contacts exist, most notably those found in V. Stefansson, ed., *Three Voyages of Martin Frobisher*, and Hakluyt, *The Principal Navigations*. Of the secondary literature devoted to early European–Labrador Inuit contact north of the Strait of Belle Isle, there is J. Garth Taylor, 'Historical Ethnography of the Labrador Coast,' in D. Damas, ed., *Arctic*, and Susan A. Kaplan, 'European Goods and Socio-Economic Change in Early Labrador Inuit Society,' in W.W. Fitzhugh, ed., *Cultures in Contact: The Impact of European Contacts on Native American Cultural Institutions, A.D. 1000–1800* (Washington, DC: Smithsonian Institution 1985), which traces the history of the Labrador Inuit from their initial prehistoric settlement of Labrador in the fifteenth century to the middle of the eighteenth century. For a summary of the evidence on contacts between the Norse and the Inuit or their predecessors, as well as possible contacts between the Norse and Indian groups, see R. McGhee's previously cited 'Contact between Native North Americans and the Medieval Norse,' *American Antiquity* (1984), and W.W. Fitzhugh, 'Early Contacts North of Newfoundland before A.D. 1600: A Review,' in Fitzhugh, ed., *Cultures in Contact*.

In the sixteenth century contact between the Inuit and Europeans in Labrador took place mainly on the southern Quebec–Labrador side of the Strait of Belle Isle. While François Trudel, 'Les Inuit face à l'expansion commerciale européenne dans la region du Détroit de Belle-isle aux XVIe et XVIIe siècles,' *Recherches amérindiennes au Québec* 7/3–4 (1978): 49–58, touches briefly on Inuit-European relations in that area in the sixteenth century, *Etudes inuit/Inuit Studies* devoted an entire issue, 4/1–2 (1980), including an extensive bibliography, to the question of the nature and extent of the Inuit presence in the Strait of Belle Isle, and many of its articles are essential to the study of sixteenth-century European-Inuit interaction. Of particular value is N. Clermont, 'Les Inuit du Labrador méridional avant Cartwright' (147–66), which argues that in the last half of the sixteenth century a small group of Inuit gradually began to occupy southern Labrador. This point is disputed by J.G. Taylor in 'The Inuit of Southern Quebec–Labrador: Reviewing the Evidence' (185–94), and supported by C.A. Martijn in 'La présence inuit sur la Côte-Nord du golfe St-Laurent à l'époque historique' (105–26) and 'The Inuit of Southern Quebec–Labrador: A Rejoinder to J. Garth Taylor' (194–8). The few extant references to Inuit-Basque relations are explicated in S. Barkham, 'A Note on the Strait of Belle Isle during the Period of Basque Contact with Indians and Inuit' (51–8). On the question of contact between Labrador Inuit and Europeans, there is W.C. Sturtevant, 'The First Inuit Depiction by Europeans' (47–50), which is a gloss on a reproduction of a woodcut advertising the exhibition of a kidnapped Labrador Inuit woman and child in Augsburg, Germany, in 1567. The European explorers' practice of kidnapping Native people was all too prevalent in the sixteenth century – see, for example, the case of the English explorer Martin Frobisher who captured three Inuit in 1577. The story of those captives' lives in England is told in Neil Cheshire et al., 'Frobisher's Eskimos in England,' *Archivaria* 10 (Summer 1980): 23–50.

The other Native group encountered by early European visitors to the Quebec Lower North Shore were the Innu (Naskapi-Montagnais). There are a few scattered references to sixteenth-century Innu in printed primary sources, notably in H.P. Biggar's two compilations, *Voyages of Jacques Cartier* and *Collection of Documents Relating to Jacques Cartier and the Sieur de Roberval*. The first three chapters of Christian Pouyez and Yolande Lavoie, *Les Saguenayens: introduction à l'histoire des populations du Saguenay, XVIe–XXe siècles* (Sillery, Que.: PUQ 1983), are also valuable.

For Newfoundland's aboriginal people, the Beothuks, James P. Howley's *The Beothucks, or Red Indians: The Aboriginal Inhabitants of Newfoundland*

(Cambridge, Eng.: Cambridge University Press 1915; repr. T: Coles 1980) is indispensable. Howley's work contains most of the primary sources relating to the Beothuks. Although written in 1622, Sir Richard Whitbourne's *A Discourse and Discovery of New-Found-Land* covers events of the late sixteenth century and has been reprinted in G.T. Cell, ed., *Newfoundland Discovered: English Attempts at Colonization, 1610–1630* (L: Hakluyt 1982). R.T. Pastore, 'The Collapse of the Beothuk World,' *Acadiensis* 19/1 (Fall 1989): 52–71, outlines the prehistoric use of the island and southern Quebec–Labrador by the ancestors of the Beothuks and describes the role played by successive groups of invaders – Europeans, Micmacs, and Inuit – in contributing to the demise of the Beothuks by denying them access to vitally needed resources. Ingeborg Marshall, 'Beothuk and Micmac: Reexamining Relationships,' *Acadiensis* 17/2 (Spring 1988): 52–82, argues that the Micmacs played a direct role in exterminating the Beothuks. Douglas T. Robbins, 'Regards archéologiques sur les Béothuks de Terre-Neuve,' *Recherches amérindiennes au Québec* 19/2–3 (automne 1989): 21–32, makes the case that the ancestors of the Beothuks had failed to establish the sort of trade relations with other groups that might have prevented their final outcome. The tragedy of Beothuk extinction is also placed within the larger context of Newfoundland's prehistory in J.A. Tuck and R.T. Pastore, 'A Nice Place to Visit, but ... Prehistoric Human Extinctions on the Island of Newfoundland,' *Canadian Journal of Archaeology* 9/1 (1985): 69–80, which concludes that the impoverished Newfoundland environment was responsible for the extinction of a number of the island's prehistoric peoples.

Works of history dealing with the Beothuks have been concerned primarily with the central problem of their extinction, but most touch, at least briefly, on the sixteenth century. Frederick W. Rowe, *Extinction: The Beothucks of Newfoundland* (T: MHR 1977), offers a balanced overview of the Beothuk experience, while Leslie F.S. Upton, 'The Extermination of the Beothucks of Newfoundland,' *CHR* 58/2 (June 1977): 133–53, and I. Marshall, 'Disease as a Factor in the Demise of the Beothuk Indians,' *Culture* 1/1 (1981): 71–7, reprinted in Carol Wilton, ed., *Change and Continuity: A Reader on Pre-Confederation Canada* (T: MHR 1992), stress the role of disease as the major cause of their demise. R.T. Pastore, 'Fishermen, Furriers, and Beothuks: The Economy of Extinction,' *Man in the Northeast* 33 (Spring 1987): 47–62, suggests that the Beothuks did not engage in a fur trade because they were able to acquire desirable iron goods, particularly nails, by pilfering from seasonally abandoned fishing premises. As a result they did not develop trading relationships with the Europeans, who otherwise might have had a stake in their continued existence.

Although the Micmacs were one of the first of Canada's Native peoples to be contacted by Europeans, most of the documentary material pertaining to them was the creation of seventeenth-century observers. Sixteenth-century Micmacs were described by Jacques Cartier, however, and these accounts are to be found in R. Cook, ed., *The Voyages of Jacques Cartier*, as well as H.P. Biggar's collections, *Voyages of Jacques Cartier* and *Collection of Documents Relating to Jacques Cartier and the Sieur de Roberval*. There is also a valuable portrayal of late-sixteenth-century Micmac-European relations in D.B. Quinn, 'The Voyage of Etienne Bellenger to the Maritimes in 1583: A New Document,' *CHR* 43/4 (Dec. 1962): 328–43.

Currently the starting-point for researchers in Micmac history and prehistory is C.A. Martijn, ed., *Les Micmacs et la mer* (M: Recherches amérindiennes au Québec 1986). The volume includes essays on historic and prehistoric Micmac use of the lands and seas of the Gulf of St Lawrence. N. Clermont, 'L'adaptation maritime au pays des Micmacs,' stresses the unusual (in the context of northeastern Algonkian peoples) maritime adaptation of the Micmacs; and I. Marshall, 'Le canot de haute mer des Micmacs,' describes the central place of the canoe in Micmac culture and outlines its construction and use from the prehistoric to the late historic period. Three essays deal with the Micmacs and the Magdalen Islands: Pierre Dumais and Gilles Rousseau, 'Menagoesenog, ou les îles de la Madeleine: contexte environnemental,' which describes the terrain, vegetation, geology, and faunal resources of the islands; Moira T. McCaffrey, 'La préhistoire des îles de la Madeleine: bilan préliminaire,' which surveys the prehistory of the islands; and Martijn, 'Les Micmacs aux îles de la Madeleine: visions fugitives et glanures ethnohistoriques,' which examines Micmac use of the Magdalens from the sixteenth to the twentieth centuries. And in a key essay, 'Voyages des Micmacs dans la vallée du Saint-Laurent, sur la Côte-Nord et à Terre-Neuve,' Martijn argues that the Micmacs created a network of trade, diplomacy, war, and resource exploitation over a large area of the Gulf of St Lawrence. The precise boundaries of this interaction sphere changed from the sixteenth to the nineteenth century as a result of demographic, economic, political, social, and religious factors.

C.A. Martijn called for more archaeological investigation in the Maritimes to illuminate the Micmac past, but a great deal of work remains to be done before there are definitive answers to some of the most significant questions posed by students of the sixteenth century. Even at this early date, however, archaeologists have begun to call into question some beliefs that have been long held by historians. The portrayal of the Micmacs as a people who lived on the coast in the summer and in the interior in the winter has been challenged in such works as David V. Burley, 'Proto-Historic Ecological Effects of the Fur Trade on Micmac Culture in Northeastern New Brunswick,' *Ethnohistory* 28/3 (Summer 1981): 203–16; David Sanger, 'Changing Views of Aboriginal Seasonality and Settlement in the Gulf of Maine,' *Canadian Journal of Anthropology* 2/2 (Spring 1982): 195–203; and Frances L. Stewart, 'Seasonal Movements of Indians in Acadia as Evidenced by Historical Documents and Vertebrate Faunal Remains from Archaeological Sites,' *Man in the Northeast* 38 (Fall 1989): 55–77. The question of the size of the Micmac population at the time of contact is addressed by Virginia P. Miller, 'The Decline of Nova Scotia Micmac Population, A.D. 1600–1850,' *Culture* 2/3 (1982): 107–20, who posits a contact population larger than what most researchers accept. For a lower estimate see D.R. Snow, *The Archaeology of New England* (NY: Academic Press 1980). For different views on the level of Micmac socio-political complexity, there are V.P. Miller, 'Social and Political Complexity on the East Coast: The Micmac Case,' and R.G. Matson, 'Intensification and the Development of Cultural Complexity: The Northwest versus the Northeast Coast,' both in Ronald J. Nash, ed., *The Evolution of Maritime Cultures on the Northeast and the Northwest Coasts of America* (V: Department of Archaeology, Simon Fraser University 1983).

The beginnings of European contact with the Micmacs were first dealt with, masterfully, by Alfred Goldsworthy Bailey, *The Conflict of European and Eastern Algonkian Cultures, 1504–1700: A Study in Canadian Civilization* (2nd ed., T: UTP 1969). Originally published in 1937, this work by Canada's first ethnohistorian has held up well in the face of new evidence. Some of that new evidence has been provided by scholars such as Bruce J. Bourque and Ruth Holmes Whitehead, whose 'Tarrentines and the Introduction of European Trade Goods in the Gulf of Maine,' *Ethnohistory* 32/4 (Dec. 1985): 327–41, concludes that in the late sixteenth century Micmac middlemen were trading European goods to people to the south – continuing a trade pattern that had existed in the prehistoric period. Much of that trade may have been with Basque fishermen, and the result appears to have been the emergence of a Basque-Micmac pidgin language, a subject explored in Peter Bakker, 'Basque Pidgin Vocabulary in European-Algonquian Trade Contacts,' in William Cowan, ed., *Papers of the Nineteenth Algonquian Conference* (O: CUP 1988).

The Cartier-Roberval expeditions of 1535–6 and 1541–3 to the Montreal–Quebec City region brought back to Europe what was probably the first account of an Iroquoian people who were then living along the banks of the St Lawrence. These people, called the St Lawrence Iroquoians by archaeologists and ethnohistorians, disappeared in the late sixteenth century, a fact which has occasioned considerable investigation by both historians and archaeologists. The ancestry of these people is examined in C. Chapdelaine, 'L'ascendance culturelle des Iroquoiens du Saint-Laurent,' *Recherches amérindiennes au Québec* 10/3 (1980): 145–52. It should be supplemented by Chapdelaine's more recent 'The Mandeville Site and the Definition of a New Regional Group within the Saint Lawrence Iroquoian World,' *Man in the Northeast* 39 (Spring 1990): 53–63; William Engelbrecht, Earl Sidler, and Michael Walko, 'The Jefferson County Iroquoians,' *Man in the Northeast* 39 (Spring 1990): 65–77; James F. Pendergast, 'Emerging Saint Lawrence Iroquoian Settlement Patterns,' *Man in the Northeast* 40 (Fall 1990): 17–30; and N. Clermont, 'Why Did the Saint Lawrence Iroquoians Become Horticulturalists?' *Man in the Northeast* 40 (Fall 1990): 75–9. Printed primary sources referring to the St Lawrence Iroquoians are to be found primarily in R. Cook, ed., *The Voyages of Jacques Cartier*, and H.P. Biggar's collections, *Voyages of Jacques Cartier* and *Collection of Documents Relating to Jacques Cartier and the Sieur de Roberval*.

There is a continuing debate about the complicated question of the ultimate fate of the St Lawrence Iroquoians. B.G. Trigger, 'The St Lawrence Valley, 16th Century,' in *HAC*, vol. 1, plate 33, graphically presents two versions of their demise, one suggesting internal warfare followed by attacks from Iroquois south of Lake Ontario, the other arguing for attack and dispersal by the Hurons. In *Natives and Newcomers: Canada's 'Heroic Age' Reconsidered* (K&M: MQUP 1985) and *The Indians and the Heroic Age of New France*, CHA Historical Booklet no. 30 (rev. ed., O: 1989), Trigger argues that a substantial number of the St Lawrence Iroquoians were absorbed by other groups, perhaps the Hurons, in the prehistoric period. The remaining St Lawrence Iroquoians encountered by Cartier and Roberval in the area between Montreal and Quebec City may have been weakened by epidemics, environmental change, and Micmac attacks before they were destroyed by Iroquois from what is now New York State. For a somewhat different view see J.B. Jamieson, 'Trade and Warfare: The Disappearance of the Saint Lawrence Iroquoians,' *Man in the Northeast* 39 (Spring 1990): 79–86, which argues that the St Lawrence Iroquoians, over a long period of time, were dispersed by Five Nations Iroquois from New York and took refuge with allied Algonkian and Ontario Iroquoian groups. Peter George Ramsden, 'Saint Lawrence Iroquoians in the Upper Trent River Valley,' *Man in the Northeast* 39 (Spring 1990): 87–95, suggests that the sixteenth-century St Lawrence Iroquoian dispersal was the result of a number of factors including European disease, traditional warfare, climatic change, and possibly 'European-Canadian interaction.' Some of the remaining St Lawrence Iroquoian refugees, he posits, may have taken refuge with the Trent Valley Hurons. Investigations at a possible sixteenth-century St Lawrence Iroquoian site are the subject of J.F. Pendergast and B.G. Trigger, *Cartier's Hochelaga and the Dawson Site* (M: MQUP 1972), and a detailed discussion of the nature and extent of the St Lawrence Iroquoian occupation of the region is to be found in C.A. Martijn, 'The Iroquoian Presence in the Estuary and Gulf of the Saint Lawrence River Valley: A Reevaluation,' *Man in the Northeast* 40 (Fall 1990): 45–63, which concludes that although the St Lawrence Iroquoians had been seasonally using the St Lawrence River estuary since perhaps AD 1000, it is possible that their presence in the Strait of Belle Isle was the result of their trade with Europeans and may have lasted only from about 1536 to about 1580.

Although sixteenth-century Europeans apparently never traded directly with the Hurons, European goods had by then begun to reach them. In fact, it is possible that in the sixteenth century Huron groups from further south clustered together in the region between Lakes Huron and Simcoe in order to get easier access to the European trade goods which their northern Algonkian neighbours were bringing from Tadoussac on the St Lawrence by way of Lake Nipissing. The social and political changes that resulted from this concentration of thousands of people in a relatively small area are still a matter of conjecture, but it is possible that one result was that confederacy itself. The classic study of the Huron confederacy is B.G. Trigger, *The Children of Aataentsic: A History of the Huron People to 1660*, 2 vols. (M: MQUP 1976). Based on both archaeological and historical evidence, it remains a model of ethnohistorical scholarship. It is especially valuable because it reveals that the history of the Hurons prior to European contact was not static, but rather showed considerable cultural change over time. It also serves as a useful corrective to the notion that most of the major patterns associated with the early historic period were the result of interaction with Europeans. Trigger's later work *Natives and Newcomers* contains information about the Hurons not available at the time *The Children of Aataentsic* was published, and thus should also be consulted. Although primarily concerned with the seventeenth century, C.E. Heidenreich's *Huronia* offers a geographer's perspective on the Hurons.

Much less research has been done on the other Iroquoian peoples of Ontario, but the place to begin is B.G. Trigger, ed., *Northeast*, particularly Charles Garrad and C.E. Heidenreich, 'Khionontateronon (Petun),' and Marian E. White, 'Neutral and Wenro.' Because of the lack of contact between Europeans and the non-Huron Ontario Iroquoians, researchers are dependent upon archaeological investigation for information about these relatively little known groups. Among archaeological studies of the Neutral are Milton J. Wright, *The Walker Site*, and Paul Anthony Lennox, *The Hamilton Site: A Late Historic Neutral Town*, both in Archaeological Survey of Canada, Paper no. 103 (O: National Museums of Canada 1981); William R. Fitzgerald, *Lest the Beaver Run Loose: The Early 17th Century Christianson Site and Trends in Historic Neutral Archaeology*, Archaeological Survey of Canada, Paper no. 111 (O: National Museums of Canada 1982); and Rosemary Prevec and W.C. Noble, 'Historic Neutral Iroquois Faunal Utilization,' *Ontario Archaeology* 39 (1983): 41–56. The Petuns are the subject of C. Garrad, 'Petun Pottery,' in Charles F. Hayes III, ed., *Proceedings of the 1979 Iroquois Pottery Conference*, Rochester Museum and Science Center, Research Records no. 13 (Rochester, NY: Rochester Museum and Science Center 1980), and are briefly mentioned in P.G. Ramsden, *A Refinement of Some Aspects of Huron Ceramic Analysis*, Archaeological Survey of Canada, Paper no. 63 (O: National Museums of Canada 1977).

The immediate northern Algonkian neighbours of the Hurons during the protohistoric period are referred to in J.V. Wright, *Ontario Prehistory*; Wright, *Quebec Prehistory*; J. Helm, E.S. Rogers, and J.G.E. Smith, 'Intercultural Relations and Cultural Change in the Shield and Mackenzie Borderlands,' in Helm, ed., *Subarctic*; and Gérard E. McNulty and Louis Gilbert, 'Attikamek (Tête de Boule),' in the same volume. The first volume of B.G. Trigger's *The Children of Aataentsic* comments on prehistoric trade patterns between the Hurons and the Algonkian peoples to the north, as does the third chapter of his *Natives and Newcomers*.

CONCLUSION

This survey of recent prehistoric and historical works suggests that researchers are increasingly adopting an interdisciplinary approach to the study of Canada's Native peoples. Ethnohistorians are drawing upon the work of archaeologists, while archaeologists themselves have come to rely heavily upon biologists, botanists, and geologists, among others. This is as it should be. While specialization can be a powerful tool, most scholars have now come to realize that the past is not rigidly divided into disciplinary categories. Another point that has emerged has to do with the way in which (largely non-Native) researchers view Canada's early past. No longer is the story of European exploration and settlement regarded as a heroic tale in which Native peoples appear only as part of the background. A number of recent works attempt to present the past from the Native viewpoint – a very rare approach even twenty years ago. Similarly, present-day scholars are much more aware of the dynamic past of Canadian Native peoples prior to European contact. The older European perception of aboriginal societies as a 'people without history' has almost vanished. While still in existence, the line between prehistory and history has been redefined. Many scholars now regard that division as resulting primarily from the difference in techniques (archaeological as opposed to historical) required to gather the data, rather than as a real division signalling the entry of Native peoples into 'history' in the European sense.

The pace of this academic change is accelerating; even as this volume goes to press, new works are appearing. It is hoped that this chapter will provide students with the information needed to discover these new works.

THOMAS WIEN

Canada and the *Pays d'en haut*, 1600–1760

This chapter surveys historical work on the inhabitants of the seigneurial zone of the St Lawrence Valley, the lands to the north and south, and the *pays d'en haut* in the Great Lakes region.[1] It covers the years when Canada, as the eastern part of the valley was known, was a colony of France. Two populations, the one composed largely of French immigrants and their descendants, and the other of Native peoples whose ancestors had arrived much earlier, co-existed in this enlarged drainage basin between 1600 and 1760. The region can thus be said to have two distinct, albeit interconnected, histories. Until quite recently, only one, that of the colonists, received much attention from historians. That imbalance is now being corrected. At the same time, our understanding of the colonial past is being broadened and renewed.

THE STATE OF THE FIELD

Conjuring up images of orderly, weed-free cultivation, the notion of a field of study dates from a time when historians still agreed on their professional task: to chronicle, and to celebrate, the formation of the nation and its state.

While assuming full responsibility for all remaining error, I would like to thank Toby Morantz for her comments on an earlier draft of this chapter. Thanks are also due to Paul Aubin of the Institut québécois de recherche sur la culture for sending me a computer printout, taken from a not yet published volume of the *Bibliography of the History of Quebec and Canada*, of titles covering the French regime that appeared from 1986 to 1990.

1 Contemporary French-speakers applied the term *pays d'en haut* to the territory situated upstream from Montreal and north of the Illinois country, and about which they had reasonably precise geographical knowledge. As the network of trading posts supplied from Montreal expanded westward, the *pays d'en haut* came to include part of the region northwest of Lake Superior surveyed in the chapter 'The Northwest and the North.'

By that measure, the historians of our region and period have all but abandoned the old agriculture in favour of a particularly anarchic form of land clearance. In current work, analyses of groups and of dimensions of experience, which were of peripheral interest at best a few decades ago, have largely supplanted the blow-by-blow accounts of the rise and fall of New France (or of the Iroquois, for that matter). In the place of a history emphasizing not just military events but also military relationships, seeing peasants chiefly as militiamen and Native peoples mainly as allies or enemies, have emerged two histories – and several subhistories – seeking to reconstitute as many facets as possible of their subjects' lives. In the kind of population they study, the sources and the methods they use, the extent of their debt to other disciplines, and their amenability to synthesis, the two are quite different, of course, but they have followed parallel trajectories all the same. To quote the title of a recent reader, both the common people of the colony and their Native contemporaries of all social ranks have recently emerged 'out of the background' of scholarly historical consciousness.

The problems of the two histories reflect the rapid pace of historiographical renewal during the last three decades. They include the challenge of finding and adapting for our arcane purposes evidence that contemporaries assembled for reasons of their own, covering equitably both periods and social groups, and synthesizing new work and integrating it with the old.

All these problems take a particular form depending upon which population one studies. The most important differences result from the nature of the records describing colonists and Natives. In the documentary sources of the period, the French do the writing, while Native people are only quoted or paraphrased. Granted, many ordinary *Canadiens* were no more literate than most of their Native neighbours, but a busy swarm of notaries, priests, and other record-keepers regularly described some of their actions. It is true, on the other hand, that the missionaries left descriptions of the Native peoples' way of life that have no parallel in the annals of the colony, and the parish records of some Native missions have survived. On the whole, though, the documents, like a microscope with two lenses of different power, offer a higher degree of resolution for the colonial population than for the aboriginal one. Hence arises a difference that no amount of archaeological or ethnographic research into the history of Native peoples will be able to surmount: documents pertaining to the *Canadiens* are much more likely than those describing Native peoples to name names. Historians of the colony can use a technique that ethnohistorians studying Native peoples of the period can rarely, if ever, employ: assembling the mentions of individuals in several kinds of records into aggregate studies of considerable precision. While students of French Canada's history are emulating the ethnohistorians in their use of archaeological and ethnographic information, such issues as the reliability of oral traditions or of particular artifacts as indicators of change cannot have the same urgency when a relatively well documented population is being discussed.

It is also partly for documentary reasons that some periods have received less attention than others and have been interpreted from different perspectives. If the growing population and an increasingly complex society are more important than the volume and variety of sources in explaining colonial historians' tendency to focus on the century after 1663, the availability of seventy-three volumes of *Jesuit Relations* dealing mostly with the earlier period certainly helps account for the temporal imbalance in the study of the region's Native inhabitants. And while it is true that the eighteenth century saw the Native peoples of the Great Lakes region much more caught up than before in the rivalries of the colonizing powers, one wonders whether the history of the *pays d'en haut* during this period would be quite as political and military if administrative correspondence, French and Anglo-American, did not loom so large among written sources.

Biased in the angle of approach, the documents evidently play favourites geographically as well, favouring those areas where French record-keepers stayed longest or gathered their first impressions. Again thanks to the *Relations*, for example, we can study Hurons much more thoroughly than we can the Neutrals, an Iroquoian group whom the missionaries visited infrequently.

Unequal coverage of another sort arises out of the colony's social complexity. While historians usually follow anthropological precedent in seeing Native societies whole, they tend to give the more stratified and better-documented colonial one piecemeal treatment. Some pieces have so far received much more attention than others. We know more about Canadian peasants than about artisans, for example, and more about a few individual merchants and nobles than about either category as a social group. If such fragmentation permits detailed study and helps explain the sheer volume of work on the colonial past, it also encourages us to elude the crucial question of the relationship of the pieces to one another. The state, which was once omnipresent in accounts of the French regime and certainly a power to be reckoned with, thus receives short shrift in most recent work on the colony's social history. So, usually, do the constraints imposed by another, less visible form of absolutism, the colonial economy.

These examples point to the wider problem of synthesis that currently bedevils us. Recent surveys may well survey, but rarely do they synthesize the disparate strands of the colonial experience into a coherent interpretation of development. A similar difficulty intervenes at the regional level. Native history has resurrected the independent actors hidden behind the stereotypical Indian, but in analysing Franco-Native relations, it is not always willing to make the same effort with regard to the French. Colonial history, meanwhile, has only partly absorbed the implications of the new work on Native peoples. Surely, if we are to understand the nature and the extent of the connections between the two histories, the historians who write them will have to take each other's work into account.

BIBLIOGRAPHIES, REFERENCE WORKS, AND SURVEYS

The logical starting-point for research on the period 1600–1760 is the *Bibliography of the History of Quebec and Canada*, published under the auspices of the Institut québécois de recherche sur la culture. It has so far listed works published over the years 1946–85 in four two-volume instalments (Q: IQRC 1981–90); the volumes covering 1966–75 were compiled by Paul Aubin and the others by Aubin and Louis-Marie Côté. A fifth set will soon add a further five years of listings. References to older work can be gleaned from Jean-Jacques Messier, comp., *Bibliographie relative à la Nouvelle-France* (M: L'Aurore 1979), and Claude Thibault, comp., *Bibliographia Canadiana* (Don Mills, Ont.: Longman 1973). In addition, there are three useful annotated bibliographies. Jacques Mathieu and John A. Dickinson, in their contributions to Jacques Rouillard, ed., *Guide d'histoire du Québec du Régime français à nos jours: bibliographie commentée* (M: Méridien 1991), concentrate on recent work on both French and Native peoples. Cornelius J. Jaenen, 'Canada during the French Régime,' in D.A. Muise, ed., *A Reader's Guide to Canadian History*, vol. 1, *Beginnings to Confederation* (T: UTP 1982), is the best place to look for older references, notably to the colonial church and Franco-Native relations. W.J. Eccles's pithily annotated bibliography in his *France in America* (1972; rev. ed., Markham, Ont.: Fitzhenry and Whiteside 1990) takes a chronological approach. Strong on imperial and military history and on reference works, it is idiosyncratic in its selection and evaluation of studies of the economic and social realms.

To obtain a sense of the range of materials available, readers can consult the reference sections of volumes 1 through 4 of the *Dictionary of Canadian Biography* (T: UTP 1966–79), which include lists of primary sources, manuscript and printed, as well as secondary ones. Even wider ranging is the survey of research tools by Jacqueline Roy et al., in *Guide du chercheur en histoire canadienne* (Q: PUL 1986). Among the specialized bibliographies,

Jack Warwick's discussion of contemporary accounts in 'New France, Writing in,' in William Toye, gen. ed., *The Oxford Companion to Canadian Literature* (T: OUP 1983), and Joanne Burgess et al., *Clés pour l'histoire de Montréal: bibliographie* (M: BE 1992), are particularly noteworthy.

In the biographical section of the reference shelf, the *DCB* of course holds pride of place. Volumes 1 through 4 cover, in increasing detail, individuals who died between 1600 and 1800. Users may find the *Index* (T: UTP 1981) to these four volumes, which includes a listing by profession, more helpful than the volume indexes and the more recent *Index* to volumes 1 through 12 (T: UTP 1991), which do not. For the French population, several genealogical compilations permit the industrious researcher to begin to compensate for the *DCB*'s inevitable predilection for the better-documented part of the area's population. René Jetté, *Dictionnaire généalogique des familles du Québec: des origines à 1730* (M: PUM 1983), is both accurate and easy to use but stops thirty years before the Conquest. Cyprien Tanguay's classic *Dictionnaire généalogique des familles canadiennes depuis la fondation de la colonie jusqu'à nos jours*, 7 vols. (1871–90; repr. M: Elysée 1975), is also user-friendly and traces many family lines to 1760, but it is far from error-free. The Université de Montréal's Programme de recherche en démographie historique, for its part, has published a *Répertoire des actes de baptême, mariage, sépulture et des recensements du Québec ancien*, 47 vols. (M: PUM 1980–90), summarizing the contents of all the colony's parish registers and nominal censuses. Several index volumes permit the persevering researcher to reconstitute families.

Among the atlases, the *Historical Atlas of Canada*, vol. 1, *From the Beginning to 1800*, ed. R. Cole Harris (T: UTP [1987]), devotes nearly a third of its seventy-odd plates to the period and area that interest us. Drawing on much new work, notably on Native peoples, and summarizing the old, it is an indispensable research aid and will be referred to repeatedly below. Marcel Trudel's older *An Atlas of New France* (Q: PUL 1968) is still invaluable for its reproductions of contemporary maps. A few of the latter are also reproduced in R. Louis Gentilcore and C. Grant Head, eds., *Ontario's History in Maps* (T: UTP 1984), but here readers would do well to consult Conrad E. Heidenreich's two articles on the cartography of the Great Lakes region: 'Mapping the Great Lakes: The Period of Exploration, 1603–1700,' *Cartographica* 17/3 (Autumn 1980): 32–64, and 'Mapping the Great Lakes: The Period of Imperial Rivalries, 1700–1760,' *Cartographica* 18/3 (Autumn 1981): 74–109. Montreal now has its historical atlas: Jean-Claude Robert, ed., *Atlas historique de Montréal* (M: Libre Expression 1993). Quebec City deserves similar treatment.

As a source of general information, M. Trudel's handbook *Introduction to New France* (T/M: HRW 1968) requires updating. Two more specialized reference works shed light on the measures of another time: currency exchange rates are tabulated in John J. McCusker, *Money and Exchange in Europe and America, 1600–1775: A Handbook* (Chapel Hill, NC: University of North Carolina Press 1978); and Ronald Zupko presents the Parisian weights and measures that more often than not were used in the colony in *French Weights and Measures before the Revolution: A Dictionary of Provincial and Local Units* (Bloomington, IN: Indiana University Press 1978).

Bibliographies listing work in various disciplines on the history of the area's Native inhabitants are quite numerous, and are usually annotated. The best general compilation is Shepard Krech III, ed., *Native Canadian Anthropology and History: A Selected Bibliography* (W: Rupert's Land Research Centre 1986). A second edition is in press. Also useful are the annotated listings, classified by tribe, in the Newberry Library series of regional bibliographies published by Indiana University Press at Bloomington: Elisabeth Tooker, ed., *The Indians of the Northeast: A Critical Bibliography* (1978); June Helm, ed., *The Indians of the Subarctic: A Critical Bibliography* (1976); and Helen Hornbeck Tanner, ed., *The Ojibwas: A Critical Bibliography* (1976). Research on the Native peoples of Quebec, and also of neighbouring areas, is given the same treatment in Richard Dominique and Jean-Guy Deschênes, eds., *Cultures et sociétés autochtones du Québec: bibliographie critique* (Q: IQRC 1985). Donald B. Smith, *Le Sauvage: The Native People in Quebec Historical Writing on the Heroic Period (1534–1663) of New France* (O: National Museums of Canada 1974), includes a useful historical bibliography on the Native peoples of southern Quebec. Finally, Robert J. Surtees devotes some fifteen pages to the French regime in his *Canadian Indian Policy: A Critical Bibliography* (Bloomington, IN: Indiana University Press 1982).

The most inclusive reference works remain two regional volumes of the multivolume *Handbook of North American Indians*, gen. ed. William C. Sturtevant (Washington, DC: Smithsonian Institution 1978–): vol. 15, *Northeast*, ed. Bruce G. Trigger (1978), and vol. 6, *Subarctic*, ed. J. Helm (1981). Both contain tribal histories as well as topical ones, in addition to voluminous bibliographies. Readers might also consult the more recent vol. 4, *History of Indian-White Relations*, ed. Wilcomb E. Washburn (1988), which places within a North American context the interaction of French traders, missionaries, and soldiers with Native peoples. H.H. Tanner, *Atlas of Great Lakes Indian History* (Norman, OK: University of Oklahoma Press 1987), complements *HAC*, vol. 1, in its particular subject area, and also contains an extensive bibliography.

There is no shortage of surveys of the history of either colonists or Native peoples during the French regime. The shelf life of overviews of colonial history has shortened considerably as the pace of research accelerates, so that many older works are now mainly of historiographical or even literary interest. Although the distinction is never clear-cut, it is useful to differentiate the more thematic histories emphasizing economic and social phenomena from the narratives highlighting political and military aspects of the colony's history. Among the former, J. Mathieu, *La Nouvelle-France: les Français en Amérique du Nord, XVIe–XVIIIe siècle* (P/Q: Belin/PUL 1991), is a compromise between an undergraduate-level survey and a handbook. Concentrating on Canada despite its title, it summarizes much recent research, notably on the history of colonization. J.A. Dickinson places more emphasis on social conflict and Franco-Native relations in the first sections of Brian Young and Dickinson, *A Short History of Quebec* (1988; 2nd ed., T: CCP 1993). Part of the Canadian Centenary Series, Dale Miquelon's careful, thorough *New France, 1701–1744: 'A Supplement to Europe'* (T: M&S 1987) strikes a balance between the two approaches in its account of the first half of the eighteenth century. For hurried readers, Christopher Moore's chapter, 'Colonization and Conflict: New France and Its Rivals, 1600–1760,' in Craig Brown, ed., *The Illustrated History of Canada* (T: Lester & Orpen Dennys 1987), is a highly concentrated introduction to the period.

To add balance, two complementary surveys of women's history should be consulted: Alison Prentice et al., *Canadian Women: A History* (T: HBJ 1988), notable among other things for its coverage of Native women, and Micheline Dumont et al. (Le Collectif Clio), *Quebec Women: A History* (T: Women's Press 1987). Those with the choice should use the new French edition, *L'histoire des femmes au Québec depuis quatre siècles* (1982; 2nd ed., M: Le Jour 1992), which takes into account the latest developments in this fast-moving field.

Several studies more narrative than thematic now show their age, but can still serve as guides to chronology and policy. Three of them round out the Centenary Series. M. Trudel's *The Beginnings of New France, 1524–1663* (T: M&S 1973) summarizes the early volumes of his meticulously descriptive *Histoire de la Nouvelle-France*, vol. 1, *Les vaines tentatives, 1524–1603* (M: Fides 1963), and vol. 2, *Le comptoir, 1604–1627* (M: Fides 1966), but is partly superseded by vol. 3, *La seigneurie des Cent-Associés, 1627–1663*, part 1, *Les événements* (M: Fides 1979), and the thematic part 2, *La société* (M: Fides 1983). W.J. Eccles takes up the story in *Canada under Louis XIV, 1663–1701* (T: M&S 1964), while George F.G. Stanley carries the torch to the Conquest in *New France, 1744–1760: The Last Phase* (T: M&S 1968).

Based on primary research, unlike Stanley's account, Guy Frégault's *Canada: The War of the Conquest* (T: OUP 1969), first published in French in 1955, charts the final phase of French rule with great narrative verve.

As for the broader context, which sometimes disappears from view in the colonial histories, W.J. Eccles's recently revised but still romantic *France in America* has the merit of presenting the history of French activity on a continental scale. The imperially-minded can also delve into Pierre Pluchon's vast *Histoire de la colonisation française*, vol. 1, *Le premier empire colonial, des origines à la Restauration* (P: Fayard 1991), which, however, as its title suggests, is a better history of French colonization than of French colonies. R.C. Harris writes from a geographer's perspective in 'France in North America,' in Robert D. Mitchell and Paul A. Groves, eds., *North America: The Historical Geography of a Changing Continent* (Totowa, NJ: Rowman and Littlefield 1987). This article updates the same author's more narrowly focused contribution to Harris and John Warkentin, *Canada before Confederation: A Study in Historical Geography* (T: OUP 1974). On the development of Anglo-American colonies see Harry M. Ward's capacious survey, *Colonial America, 1607–1763* (Englewood Cliffs, NJ: PH 1991). Pierre Goubert fills in the French background in *The Ancien Régime: French Society, 1600–1750* (NY: Harper and Row 1973). Readers of French will prefer the more recent and more sociocultural *Les Français et l'Ancien Régime*, 2 vols. (P: Armand Colin 1984), by Goubert and Daniel Roche.

What will surely become the benchmark history of the Native peoples of Canada, Olive Patricia Dickason, *Canada's First Nations: A History of Founding Peoples from Earliest Times* (T: M&S 1992), accords generous coverage to the century and a half after 1600 and contains an extensive, up-to-date bibliography. J.R. Miller, *Skyscrapers Hide the Heavens: A History of Indian-White Relations in Canada* (1989; rev. ed., T: UTP 1991), focuses more on later periods, but also bears perusal. The contributors to R. Bruce Morrison and C. Roderick Wilson, eds., *Native Peoples: The Canadian Experience* (T: M&S 1986), view the area's tribal groups from an anthropological perspective, paying explicit attention to the French regime, as does Alan D. McMillan's more condensed *Native Peoples and Cultures of Canada: An Anthropological Overview* (V: Douglas & McIntyre 1988).

Several works on particular periods offer greater detail. B.G. Trigger, *Natives and Newcomers: Canada's 'Heroic Age' Reconsidered* (K&M: MQUP 1985), authoritatively surveys the history, archaeology, and the historians of the years up to 1663. Trigger provides a convenient précis in *The Indians and the Heroic Age of New France*, CHA Historical Booklet no. 30 (rev. ed., O: 1989); and Denys Delâge, an empathetic complement in *Bitter Feast:*

Amerindians and Europeans in Northeastern North America, 1600–64 (V: UBCP 1993), first published in French in 1985. Richard White's ambitious *The Middle Ground: Indians, Empires, and Republics in the Great Lakes Region, 1650–1815* (Cambridge, Eng.: Cambridge University Press 1991) covers the history of the Great Lakes region during the period indicated.

PUBLISHED DOCUMENTS

The publication of documents relating to the history of the French regime in Canada began before the Conquest and has continued intermittently ever since. The early interest in the period's documentary legacy means that many important sources – and some less important ones – have been printed. But much of this wealth is widely scattered, and some of it is now in the last phases of decomposition as acidic paper gets on with its labour of self-destruction. If the microfiches of the Canadian Institute for Historical Microreproductions often permit the reader to get around the latter problem, there remains the more intractable one of the unreliability of some of the early transcriptions and translations.

A few of the more important series deserve special mention; others will be cited later. Among the most voluminous is the annual report of the Quebec Archives. Under the successive titles *Rapport de l'archiviste de la province de Québec* (1920–59), *Rapport des Archives du Québec* (1960–9), and *Rapport des Archives nationales du Québec* (1970–5), there is scarcely a volume among the fifty-three that does not contain something of interest to the historian of the French colony before 1760. The documents in volumes 1 through 42 can be found using the *Table des matières des rapports des Archives du Québec* (Q: Roch Lefebvre 1965). In addition to calendaring a vast array of official and notarial documents, the Protean first provincial archivist, Pierre-Georges Roy, also published a goodly number separately. On the federal side, the *Report* of the Public (now National) Archives of Canada, published since 1872, contains more calendars but fewer documents than its Quebec counterpart. It can be consulted with the aid of Françoise Caron-Houle, *Guide to the Reports of the Public Archives of Canada, 1872–1972* (O: Information Canada 1975). During its heroic period before the First World War, the Public Archives also published separately a few documentary collections. Other multivolume compilations of official documents include *Edits, ordonnances royaux, déclarations et arrêts du Conseil d'Etat du roi concernant le Canada*, 3 vols. (2nd ed., Q: E.R. Fréchette 1854–6); *Collection de manuscrits contenant lettres, mémoires, et autres documents historiques relatifs à la Nouvelle-France*, 4 vols. (Q: A. Côté 1883–5); *Jugements et délibérations du Conseil Sou-*

verain de la Nouvelle-France (1663–1716), 6 vols. (Q: A. Côté 1885–91); and Edouard-Zotique Massicotte, ed., *Montréal sous le Régime français: répertoire des arrêts, édits, mandements, ordonnances et règlements conservés dans les Archives du Palais de Justice de Montréal, 1640–1760* (M: G. Ducharme 1919). Notable among the military collections are Henri-Raymond Casgrain, ed., *Collection des manuscrits du maréchal de Lévis*, 12 vols. (Q: L.-J. Demers 1889–95), and, for the documents but not for the rest, Arthur George Doughty and G.W. Parmelee, *The Siege of Quebec and the Battle of the Plains of Abraham*, 6 vols. (Q: Dussault & Proulx 1901).

A half-dozen contemporary accounts are worth taking along to a desert island: Henry Percival Biggar, gen. ed., *The Works of Samuel de Champlain*, 6 vols. (T: CS 1922–36); Pierre Boucher, *Histoire véritable et naturelle des moeurs et productions du pays de la Nouvelle-France vulgairement dite le Canada* (1664; repr. Boucherville, Que.: Société historique de Boucherville 1964); Pierre-François-Xavier de Charlevoix, *History and General Description of New France*, ed. John Gilmary Shea, 6 vols. (1866–72; repr. Chicago, IL: Loyola University Press 1962); Charlevoix, *Journal of a Voyage to North-America: Undertaken by Order of the French King*, ed. Louise Phelps Kellogg, 2 vols. (Chicago, IL: Caxton Club 1923); a translation from the Swedish of the account of Pehr (Peter) Kalm, *The America of 1750: Peter Kalm's Travels in North America*, ed. Adolph B. Benson, 2 vols. (1937; repr. NY: Dover 1966), or, for readers of French, a new translation of the Canadian portion of his voyage in Jacques Rousseau and Guy Béthune, eds., *Voyage de Pehr Kalm au Canada en 1749* (M: Cercle du livre français 1977); and Marie-Elisabeth Rocbert de La Morandière, veuve Bégon de La Cour, 'Correspondance de Mme Bégon,' *Rapport de l'archiviste de la province de Québec* (1934–5). All should be read critically, bearing in mind the profession, origin, and social class of the author.

Many of these works contain observations on Native peoples, but a few series are particularly rich. Among the numerous publications of missionaries' reports and correspondence, Reuben Gold Thwaites's edition and translation of *The Jesuit Relations and Allied Documents*, 73 vols. (1896–1901; repr. NY: Pageant 1959), heads the list. The recent, definitive collection of Jesuit relations, letters, and other documents, grouped together under the title *Monumenta Novae Franciae* and edited by Lucien Campeau, now contains six volumes. Volumes 2 through 6 (Q: PUL 1979, 1987; M: Bellarmin 1989, 1990, 1992) cover Jesuit activities in the region from 1616 to 1646. Finally, the editorial practices of Edmund Bailey O'Callaghan and his co-editors in *Documents Relative to the Colonial History of the State of New-York*, 15 vols. (Albany, NY: Weed, Parsons 1853–87), do not meet current standards, but the collection remains the point of departure for work on the Iroquois, along with James Sullivan et al., eds., *The Papers of Sir William Johnson*, 14 vols. (Albany, NY: University of the State of New York 1921–65). Outside of these collections, a short list of ethnographic accounts describing the tribes coming into contact with the French might include Joseph-François Lafitau, *Customs of the American Indians Compared with the Customs of Primitive Times*, ed. William N. Fenton and Elizabeth L. Moore, 2 vols. (T: CS 1974–7); Nicolas Perrot, *Mémoire sur les moeurs, coustumes et relligion des sauvages de l'Amérique septentrionale* (1864; repr. M: Elysée 1973); Gabriel Sagard, *Sagard's Long Journey to the Country of the Hurons*, ed. George M. Wrong (T: CS 1939); and Louis-Armand de Lom d'Arce, Baron de Lahontan, *New Voyages to North-America*, ed. R.G. Thwaites, 2 vols. (Chicago, IL: A.C. McClurg 1905), or, for readers of French, the complete works edited by Réal Ouellet with Alain Beaulieu, *Lahontan: oeuvres complètes*, 2 vols. (M: PUM 1990).

The Champlain Society and the Presses de l'Université de Montréal, with the Bibliothèque du Nouveau Monde, have ongoing programs of critical editions of contemporaries' accounts of early Canada and parts westward.

PERIODICALS

Although no journal specializes in the history of the colony under French rule, the *Revue d'histoire de l'Amérique française* (1947–) is the next best thing. It regularly publishes articles on the subject, in addition to book reviews, archives notes, and a running bibliography. The *Canadian Historical Review* (1920–) rarely includes articles on the period, but keeps abreast of recent publications with book reviews and a bibliography. *Histoire sociale/Social History* (1968–) occasionally publishes relevant articles and reviews as well as an annual list of recent publications in historical demography, some of which pertain to the French regime. Relevant articles may also be found in the Canadian Historical Association, *Annual Report* (1922–65), retitled *Historical Papers* (1966–89), and now *Journal of the Canadian Historical Association* (1990–). There is also the occasional article in the *William and Mary Quarterly* of interest to specialists of the period. Contributions to the annual *Cahiers des Dix* (1936–) sometimes cast light on points of detail. So, in its inimitable way, does the antiquarian *Bulletin des recherches historiques* (1895–1969), a hodgepodge of biographies, *petite histoire*, and documents, founded by P.-G. Roy.

The pronounced interdisciplinary character of the study of the past of the Native peoples makes for a scattered periodical literature. Among the historical journals, the *CHR* and *RHAF* have reflected the rise of Native history both in their selection of articles and in their running bibliographies and reviews, as has, where articles and reviews are concerned, the *WMQ*. Two more specialized periodicals should be consulted first, however: *Ethnohistory* (1954–), which often publishes articles and reviews on the region and the period, and *Recherches amérindiennes au Québec* (1971–), a multidisciplinary journal with a historical bent ranging well beyond Quebec. William Cowan, ed., *Papers of the ... Algonquian Conference* (O: CUP 1970–), an annual publication, occasionally contains papers relevant to our period. Of the numerous anthropological journals, *Man in the Northeast* (1971–), retitled *Northeast Anthropology* in 1993, focuses most directly on the region.

HISTORIOGRAPHY

Until recently, historians of the period between 1600 and 1760 rarely took more than a sidelong glance at the founding peoples, so preoccupied were they with the fate of the missionaries, officers, merchants, and settlers who had come from France. It is thus appropriate to begin with the history of these latecomers before turning to that of the region's first inhabitants.

Specialists of the history of the French regime in Canada have approached their subject in new ways over the past few decades. In this they are, of course, not alone. But if the change has taken the same general direction as in other national histories, moving from political chronicles to attempts to explain change in many areas of past experience, it has followed an itinerary that reflects the period's special place in the histories of Quebec and Canada. In fact, so special is that place that many historians have viewed the French regime not just as a period, but as a civilization. For scholars paying homage to national symbols, whether these be fleurs-de-lis, crosses, maple leaves, or even roses and thistles, the French regime was particularly rich in possibilities. Abruptly separated from what came after by the Conquest, and from what came before by Champlain's first portentous step ashore at Quebec, it was certainly well defined. It was apparently simple as well: not only were the Canadian French seen to be *maîtres chez eux* in their corner of the continent between 1608 and 1760 (or 1763), but they were still tied to their original metropole. Here was a period bereft of what most historians writing before the 1960s saw as the only conflict worth mentioning, the struggle of the two nations warring in the bosom of a single state. Instead, the enemies, Iroquois, Anglo-Americans, or British, threatened from outside. Equally important in determining historians' perceptions of the embattled colony was its position at the beginning of the national chronicle. To most, New France embodied the original phase of national history, or at least the first that counted in a view of the past that made little room for Native peoples. Not only did it lay the groundwork for the later phases, but it postulated an alternative to them, in the form of a French regime that might have continued well beyond 1763 and ended in independence, not conquest and accommodation with the British. Pregnant with two presents, one that was and one that might have been, this apparently uncomplicated period like no other invited historians to indulge their propensity for projection. It invited them to find under the French regime signs of what their nation could be, should be, or, for those who thought that the Conquest was a good thing, should not be.

Many accepted the invitation, and this explains the bewildering variety of French regimes one finds in the older literature. Generalizations on the essence of the period tend to cluster near two extremes, positive and negative, paradise and purgatory. National origin only partly explains the difference, for scholars writing in English or in French can be found in either camp. At one extreme, historians saw the colony as the theatre of papist despotism, or as a fragment of feudal France cast adrift in the New World, or as a backward place where the state and its client nobility stifled enterprise. At the other, Canada under the French regime was seen more positively, as the incarnation of rural virtues (piety first among them), an economically dynamic society, an outpost of empire aglow with aristocratic benevolence, or even an egalitarian frontier society.

Granted, this history often made much of social groups, but only by reducing them to archetypes. Historians tended to single out a particular class, not for close study, but as a screen on which to project the national character as they perceived it. This tendency links the idealized peasantry of the clerico-nationalist historians, the energetic but ill-defined bourgeoisie of some participants in the debate on the Conquest, and even the paternalistic aristocrats of W.J. Eccles. Taken together, these interpretations perhaps gave some inkling of the complexity of colonial society, but they hardly constituted social or economic history. Mutually exclusive, they were based mostly on the contradictory, superficial observations of colonial administrators and contemporary travellers.

How, then, did a new history of the French regime emerge? It was already taking form in the passionate discussion among Quebec historians concerning the impact of the Conquest that marked the years just before and just after the event's bicentennial. Here, two nationalisms impelled by the Quiet Revolution collided with great polemical force. The issue was not new, but the idiom, borrowed to a much greater extent than before from the social sciences, was. Most of the new work that arose out of the debate concerned the period after 1760, but the discussion did prompt a partial, hesitant re-evaluation of the French regime.

Eventually, it also prompted a reaction against the easy generalizations and the presentism of the 1960s. By the middle of the next decade, a more careful history attacked in earnest the task of unearthing the social complexity of the French regime. We have since learned much, from various disciplinary angles, about the colony. The plurality of approaches has ensured that, whatever the explanatory schemata behind it, our knowledge of behaviour is more precise, as neglected sources (notarial records) begin to be exploited or familiar ones (parish records and even the official correspondence) are read in new ways. The history of the French regime is now more open, to other disciplines, to more explicit comparisons with France, and, less systematically, with the Anglo-American colonies. The result has been a wealth of research, as yet not fully assimilated, into such hitherto-neglected aspects of colonial life as popular religion, women's experience, criminality, and land settlement.

The Native peoples of the region, of course, number among the redis-covered groups. To an even greater extent than ordinary *Canadiens*, they were the victims of stereotypes in much of the old history, unless they were simply ignored. Even sympathetic historians rarely treated them as more than aboriginal appendages – allies, enemies, trading partners, catechumens – of the French. Those who went further, such as Alfred Goldsworthy Bailey or Léo-Paul Desrosiers, received little notice from a profession interested in another history altogether.

All the same, sooner or later historians of the colony investigating what went on outside the colonial power centres would have reached the Native peoples. In the event, scholars from other fields, notably the various subdis-ciplines of anthropology, met them more than halfway. Increasingly inter-ested in cultural change and its determinants, and spurred on by Native land claims research and the increasing dynamism of the Native-rights movement, they too set about constructing a Native past. The result of this encounter of the disciplines is throwing new light on colonial history as well.

Given its special significance, the historiography of Canada under the French regime has attracted much critical scrutiny, although the work of the past fifteen years has yet to receive the attention it deserves. Authorita-tive on the early phases of historiography in French is Serge Gagnon, *Quebec and Its Historians, 1840 to 1920* (M: Harvest House 1982). M. Brook

Taylor, *Promoters, Patriots, and Partisans: Historiography in Nineteenth-Century English Canada* (T: UTP 1989), serves as a foil to Gagnon's work in briefly tracing the fortunes of the notion of the providential Conquest in English-Canadian historical writing. In *The Writing of Canadian History: Aspects of English-Canadian Historical Writing since 1900* (1976; 2nd ed., T: UTP 1986), Carl Berger analyses twentieth-century English-Canadian historiography, a literature mostly concerned with other periods of Canadian history. Broader in scope than its title would suggest, Yves F. Zoltvany's *The Government of New France: Royal, Clerical, or Class Rule?* (Scarborough, Ont.: PH 1971) covers writing on the colony from the early nineteenth century to the 1960s.

Several authors have chronicled the twentieth-century acceleration in Québécois writing on the period. Jean Blain elegantly analyses historians' and sociologists' work in a series of articles, marked by the impatience of the early 1970s, entitled 'Economie et société en Nouvelle-France': 'Le cheminement historiographique dans la première moitié du XXe siècle,' *RHAF* 26/1 (juin 1972): 3–31; 'L'historiographie des années 1950–1960: Guy Frégault et l'école de Montréal,' *RHAF* 28/2 (sept. 1974): 163–86; and 'L'historiographie au tournant des années 1960: la réaction à Guy Frégault et à l'école de Montréal, la voie des sociologues,' *RHAF* 30/3 (déc. 1976): 323–62. S. Gagnon also surveys the crucial years of the Quiet Revolution in 'The Historiography of New France, 1960–1974: Jean Hamelin to Louise Dechêne,' *JCS* 13/1 (Spring 1978): 80–99, reprinted in his *Quebec and Its Historians: The Twentieth Century* (M: Harvest House 1985). Louise Dechêne herself takes the measure of progress in economic and social history in 'Coup d'oeil sur l'historiographie de la Nouvelle-France,' *Etudes canadiennes/Canadian Studies* 3 (1977): 45–57, as does, from a French perspective, Robert Mandrou, in 'L'historiographie canadienne française: bilan et perspectives,' *CHR* 51/1 (Mar. 1970): 5–20. Alfred Dubuc, 'The Influence of the *Annales* School in Quebec,' *Review of the Fernand Braudel Center* 1/3–4 (Winter–Spring 1978): 123–46, briefly discusses some historians of the French regime.

Of the more recent historiographical pieces, Roberta Hamilton's *Feudal Society and Colonization: The Historiography of New France* (Gananoque, Ont.: Langdale Press 1988) is the most ambitious. It would be a telling enough Marxist analysis of the historiography of the period did the author not attempt, on the basis of the non-Marxist secondary literature, to do history as well. Matteo Sanfilippo, in a deft critique that could apply to Hamilton, convincingly argues that earlier armchair Marxists' choice of furniture does a disservice to historical materialism: 'Du féodalisme au capitalisme? Essai d'interprétation des analyses marxistes de la Nouvelle-France,' *HS/SH* 18/ 35 (May 1985): 85–98. S. Dale Standen takes a brief look at the Conquest controversy, now in historiographic eclipse, in 'The Debate on the Social and Economic Consequences of the Conquest: A Summary,' a 1985 article most accessible in R. Douglas Francis and D.B. Smith, eds., *Readings in Canadian History*, vol. 1, *Pre-Confederation* (3rd ed., T: HRW 1990). In an implied critique of recent writing on the period before the Conquest, Gérard Bouchard attempts to breathe life into the frontier thesis: 'L'historiographie du Québec rural et la problématique nord-américaine avant la Révolution tranquille: étude d'un refus,' *RHAF* 44/2 (automne 1990): 199– 222. Fernand Ouellet, a specialist of colonial history after the Conquest, takes students of the previous period to task for neglecting social classes in his polemic first published in French in 1981 and now translated as 'The Formation of a New Society in the St. Lawrence Valley: From Classless Society to Class Conflict,' in his *Economy, Class, & Nation in Quebec: Interpretive Essays* (T: CCP 1991). More constructive is Catherine Desbarats's review of recent work in colonial rural history in 'Agriculture within the Seigneurial Régime of Eighteenth-Century Canada: Some Thoughts on the Recent Literature,' *CHR* 73/1 (Mar. 1992): 1–29.

Surveys of the fate of the Native peoples at the hands of historians have accorded considerable space to the French period. The standard work on the Quebec literature is D.B. Smith's exhaustive but largely descriptive *Le Sauvage*. More recently, B.G. Trigger has devoted a chapter of his *Natives and Newcomers* to historiography in both languages. He extends his analysis in 'The Historians' Indian: Native Americans in Canadian Historical Writing from Charlevoix to the Present,' *CHR* 67/3 (Sept. 1986): 315–42. Attentive to the historiography of the French regime, James W.StG. Walker's two-part *j'accuse* is still worth reading: 'The Indian in Canadian Historical Writing,' CHA *HP* (1971): 21–47, and 'The Indian in Canadian Historical Writing, 1972–1982,' in Ian A.L. Getty and Antoine S. Lussier, eds., *As Long As the Sun Shines and Water Flows: A Reader in Canadian Native Studies* (V: UBCP 1983). D. Peter MacLeod reflects on Native historical traditions in 'The Anishinabeg Point of View: The History of the Great Lakes Region to 1800 in Nineteenth-Century Mississauga, Odawa, and Ojibwa Historiography,' *CHR* 73/2 (June 1992): 194–210.

THE REGION AND ITS INHABITANTS

The people of the region, be they Native or French, adapted to the local physical environment. J.H. McAndrews and G.C. Manville, in 'Ecological

Regions, ca AD 1500' and 'Descriptions of Ecological Regions,' *HAC*, vol. 1, plates 17 and 17A, bring together much information on the climate, terrain, vegetation, and fauna of the Great Lakes, the St Lawrence Valley, and adjoining lands a century before the beginning of our period. Ralph T. Pastore lists the relevant work on fauna in the preceding chapter, 'Beginnings to 1600.' More precise data on the recent climate can be gathered from Cynthia V. Wilson, *The Climate of Quebec*, part 1, *Climatic Atlas* (O: Information Canada 1971), and the United States Environmental Protection Agency and Environment Canada, *The Great Lakes: An Environmental Atlas and Resource Book* (T: Environment Canada 1987). Concerning the historic climate in Quebec see Louise Filion, 'Le cadre climatique au Québec pendant la période historique,' in *Proceedings of the Eleventh Annual Meeting of the French Colonial Historical Society (May 1985)* (Lanham, MD: University Press of America 1987).

For reasons mentioned earlier, historians have long been interested in the character of the colonial social formation, although most detailed studies date from after 1960. Scholars from other disciplines were the first to examine closely past Native societies of the region; lately, ethnohistorians have contributed more precise notions of the timing, causes, and nature of change during the period. We shall begin with a few general works – to which should be added the recent surveys discussed above – before covering more specialized ones. These last are classified, sometimes arbitrarily, under the rubrics population, economy, society, and politics and war.

Once again, the best introduction to the history of the region's Native peoples is the collection of tribal studies in J. Helm, ed., *Subarctic*, and B.G. Trigger, ed., *Northeast*, volumes 6 and 15 respectively of the *Handbook of North American Indians*. These present production and material culture, exchange, social organization, and belief and leadership systems in their many variations. Readers in search of a more detailed analysis of continuity and change in the seventeenth and eighteenth centuries can consult the ethnohistorians. Owing to the state of the sources and scholarly priorities, some tribes and confederacies have been covered more thoroughly than others. Among the agriculturalists, the Hurons, dispersed by the early 1650s, have received the most attention. In the past thirty years, scholars have approached them from various perspectives: E. Tooker in *An Ethnography of the Huron Indians, 1615–1649* (1964; repr. Syracuse, NY: University of Syracuse Press 1991); C.E. Heidenreich in *Huronia: A History and Geography of the Huron Indians, 1600–1650* (T: M&S 1971); and, most systematically, B.G. Trigger in *The Huron: Farmers of the North* (1969; 2nd ed., Fort Worth, TX: HRW 1990) and, above all, in *The Children of Aataentsic: A His-*

tory of the Huron People to 1660, 2 vols. (M: MQUP 1976; repr. in 1 vol., 1987). James W. Bradley, *Evolution of the Onondaga Iroquois: Accommodating Change, 1500–1655* (Syracuse, NY: Syracuse University Press 1987), and now Daniel K. Richter, *The Ordeal of the Longhouse: The Peoples of the Iroquois League in the Era of European Colonization* (Chapel Hill, NC: University of North Carolina Press 1992), cover the Iroquois. For a general perspective on the region's non- or less agricultural groups see, notably, the ethnohistorical overviews of the Ojibwas and the Montagnais: A.G. Bailey, *The Conflict of European and Eastern Algonkian Cultures, 1504–1700: A Study in Canadian Civilization* (1937; 2nd ed., T: UTP 1969); Edward S. Rogers, 'Cultural Adaptations: The Northern Ojibwa of the Boreal Forest, 1670–1800,' in A. Theodore Steegmann, Jr, ed., *Boreal Forest Adaptations: The Northern Algonkians* (NY: Plenum Press 1983); and Harold Hickerson, *The Chippewa and Their Neighbors: A Study in Ethnohistory* (1970; rev. ed., Prospect Heights, IL: Waveland Press 1988), the editors of the revised edition, Jennifer S.H. Brown and Laura L. Peers, providing an excellent review of work published since the first edition. Also on the Montagnais, a published document, *Le missionnaire, l'apostat, le sorcier: relation de 1634 de Paul Lejeune*, ed. Guy Laflèche (M: PUM 1973), translated into English in R.G. Thwaites, ed., *The Jesuit Relations*, vols. 6–7, is fundamental.

Among the early studies of the colonial social formation, Emile Salone, *La colonisation de la Nouvelle-France: étude sur les origines de la nation canadienne française* (1906; repr. TR: BE 1970), which mines the official correspondence, is still serviceable. Alice Jean E. Lunn's 1942 PhD thesis, recently published in French, repeats the exercise for the eighteenth century with more statistics in *Développement économique de la Nouvelle-France, 1713–1760* (M: PUM 1986). *Les origines économiques du Canada: l'oeuvre de la France* (Mamers, Fr.: G. Enault 1928), Paul-Emile Renaud's sketch of colonial economic development, contains a tantalizing mixture of perceptive observations and errors. More scholarly, more readable, but inclined to emphasize the idyllic aspects of the thirty years' peace, is G. Frégault, *La civilisation de la Nouvelle-France, 1713–1744* (1944; repr. M: Bibliothèque québécoise 1990). Jean Hamelin's more pessimistic *Economie et société en Nouvelle-France* (Q: PUL 1960) asked innovative questions, but answered them in traditional fashion with the complaints of the colonial officials, for whom the colony never developed quickly enough. L. Dechêne's investigation of Montreal Island under Louis XIV, *Habitants et marchands de Montréal au XVIIe siècle* (P: Plon 1974), now translated under the title *Habitants and Merchants in Seventeenth-Century Montreal* (K&M: MQUP 1992), marked the real sea change in colonial historiography. In this regional study on the French model, Dechêne analysed unfamiliar sources with great respect for seventeenth-century constraints, challenging the received wisdom concerning many aspects of economy and society in town and countryside.

POPULATION

In studying the origins of immigrants and the vital rhythms of Canadian families, among other things, demographers and historians have thrown new light on the colonial population. Demography has indeed become one of the strong points of work on the colony, thanks in large measure to the computerized population register compiled over the last twenty years by the Programme de recherche en démographie historique of the Université de Montréal. Since the efforts of such pioneers as Georges Langlois, whose *Histoire de la population canadienne-française* (M: Albert Lévesque) appeared in 1934, much new information has accumulated concerning the demographic behaviour of the *anciens Canadiens* and their immigrant forebears. Students of the Native population, for their part, struggle with a paucity of sources and a momentous problem: measuring the disastrous effects of European disease on the region's original inhabitants.

Given the extent of the disaster that befell Native peoples, it is not surprising that Native demography of the period has been studied mostly through the prism of mortality. Discussion of the 'virgin soil epidemics' introduced by Europeans has centred on the work of Henry F. Dobyns, and notably on *Their Number Become Thinned: Native American Population Dynamics in Eastern North America* (Knoxville, TN: University of Tennessee Press 1983). This attempt at measuring the impact of disease and others are reviewed in John D. Daniels, 'The Indian Population of North America in 1492,' *WMQ* 3rd ser., 49/2 (Apr. 1992): 298–320. A volume currently in preparation for the *Handbook of North American Indians* will no doubt contribute much additional information. In the meantime, regional estimates made for this publication can be found in Douglas H. Ubelaker, 'North American Indian Population Size, A.D. 1500 to 1985,' *American Journal of Physical Anthropology* 77/3 (Nov. 1988): 289–94. These figures notwithstanding, decline may not be the only theme of the region's population history before 1760. Drawing on contemporary estimates and censuses, some of which have been tabulated in H.H. Tanner, *Atlas of Great Lakes Indian History*, scholars have detected signs of a population recovery after 1700 in certain western parts. For one such analysis and references to others see Jeanne Kay, 'The Fur Trade and Native American Population Growth,'

Ethnohistory 31/4 (Fall 1984): 265–87. On Native strategies to cope with contagion see D.P. MacLeod, 'Microbes and Muskets: Smallpox and the Participation of the Amerindian Allies of New France in the Seven Years' War,' *Ethnohistory* 39/1 (Winter 1992): 42–64.

The logical place to begin a discussion of the more fortunate French-speaking population is, of course, immigration. Here was a predicable target for the old history's generalizations, drawing together as it did two traditional themes, colonial origins and the character of the population. But the quality of immigrants did not monopolize historians' attention; quantitative considerations intervened as well. Scholars were wont to lament lost opportunities, faulting the French colonizers for not shipping out more settlers. Only recently have the determinants of emigration other than royal or church policy received closer scrutiny.

The royal measures designed to spur population growth in the colony are usefully summarized in Hubert Charbonneau and Yves Landry, 'La politique démographique en Nouvelle-France,' *Annales de démographie historique* (1979): 29–57. The economic and social background, of course, often counteracted state designs. On the French demographic context and the broader pattern of emigration, Jacques Dupâquier, ed., *Histoire de la population française*, vol. 2, *De la Renaissance à 1789* (P: Presses universitaires de France 1988), is an authoritative recent survey. A discussion of the points of departure of the seventeenth-century migrants can be found in R.C. Harris's 1972 article 'The French Background of Immigrants to Canada before 1700,' reprinted in J.M. Bumsted, ed., *Interpreting Canada's Past*, vol. 1, *Before Confederation* (T: OUP 1986; 2nd ed., 1993). The French origins and the decennial frequency of arrival of emigrants who stayed in the colony are presented for the whole period in H. Charbonneau and Normand Robert, 'The French Origins of the Canadian Population, 1608–1759,' *HAC*, vol. 1, plate 45.

We now know that these figures describe only the tip of the iceberg, for a majority of the French who set foot in the colony departed again without founding a family. Mario Boleda calculates the colony's low retention rate of immigrants in 'Trente mille Français à la conquête du Saint-Laurent,' *HS/SH* 23/45 (May 1990): 153–77. The role of kinship in attracting migrants to Canada and in keeping them there is studied in J. Mathieu and Lina Gouger, 'Transferts de population,' *Annales de Bretagne et des pays de l'Ouest* 95/4 (1988): 337–45, and in André Guillemette and Jacques Légaré, 'The Influence of Kinship on Seventeenth-Century Immigration to Canada,' *Continuity and Change* 4/1 (1989): 79–102.

Studies of immigration to the colony tend to concentrate on the seventeenth century, when the cohorts of immigrants who would make a crucial contribution to population growth arrived. M. Trudel takes a close look at those who came before 1663 in his *Histoire de la Nouvelle-France*, especially in vol. 3, *La seigneurie des Cent-Associés*, part 2, *La société*. He has also published the file of individuals on which this work is based, *Catalogue des immigrants, 1632–1662* (M: Hurtubise HMH 1983). On the initial adaptations see Ramsay Cook, 'Cabbages Not Kings: Towards an Ecological Interpretation of Early Canadian History,' *JCS* 25/4 (Winter 1990–1): 5–16.

Other scholars have singled out particular categories of French immigrants. On the young women sent out at the king's expense, Y. Landry, *Orphelines en France, pionnières au Canada: les Filles du roi au XVIIe siècle* (M: Leméac 1992), supersedes all earlier work on the subject. Landry studies another group of immigrants, those in uniform, in 'Mortalité, nuptialité et canadianisation des troupes françaises de la guerre de Sept Ans,' *HS/SH* 12/24 (Nov. 1979): 298–315. Immigrant fishermen are the subject of Alain Laberge, 'Communautés rurales et présence étrangère au Canada au 18e siècle: les Granvillais sur la Côte-du-Sud (1730–1770),' in G. Bouchard and Joseph Goy, eds., *Famille, économie et société rurale en contexte d'urbanisation (17e–20e siècles)* (Chicoutimi, Que./P: Centre interuniversitaire SOREP/Ecole des hautes études en sciences sociales 1990). The fate of a fourth group, the indentured servants, or *engagés*, is traced in several studies. On the mechanisms of indentured servitude, L. Dechêne's *Habitants and Merchants* remains an essential reference. Fragmentary sources hamper the attempt to count the *engagés*. Gabriel Debien has spent the most time combing through French notarial archives in search of engagement contracts for Canada. For a sample of the results see his 'Les engagés pour le Canada partis de Nantes (1725–1732),' *RHAF* 33/4 (mars 1980): 583–6. Peter N. Moogk draws on this and his own research to compile a chronological series of engagements in 'Reluctant Exiles: Emigrants from France in Canada before 1760,' *WMQ* 3rd ser., 46/3 (July 1989): 463–505. Extending his analysis to other types of emigrants as well, the author stresses the importance of cultural factors in explaining the comparatively small flow of immigrants to Canada. Leslie P. Choquette emphasizes the role of the Canadian climate in discouraging immigration in 'Recruitment of French Emigrants to Canada, 1600–1760,' in Ida Altman and James Horn, eds., *'To Make America': European Emigration in the Early Modern Period* (Berkeley and Los Angeles, CA: University of California Press 1991), and 'French and British Emigration to the North American Colonies: A Comparative View,' in Peter Benes, ed., *New England/New France, 1600–1850*, Dublin Seminar for New England Folklife, Annual Proceedings 1989 (Boston, MA: Boston University 1992).

Other migrants, of course, did not need to cross the Atlantic. Among them were a goodly number of Anglo-Americans, who came as captives in the colonial wars. Listed some years ago in Emma Lewis Coleman, *New England Captives Carried to Canada between 1677 and 1760*, 2 vols. (Portland, ME: Southworth Press 1925), they are now being studied more closely. For statistics see Alden T. Vaughan and D.K. Richter, 'Crossing the Cultural Divide: Indians and New Englanders, 1605–1763,' *Proceedings of the American Antiquarian Society* 90 (1980): 23–99. Two recent articles deal with the experience of female captives in particular: Barbara E. Austen, 'Captured ... Never Came Back: Social Networks among New England Female Captives in Canada, 1689–1763,' and Alice N. Nash, 'Two Stories of New England Captives: Grizel and Christine Otis of Dover, New Hampshire,' both in P. Benes, ed., *New England/New France*. The views of migrants who returned to tell the tale are surveyed in J.M. Bumsted, '"Carried to Canada!" Perceptions of the French in British Colonial Captivity Narratives, 1690–1760,' *American Review of Canadian Studies* 13/1 (Spring 1983): 79–96.

War also brought the colony another cohort of immigrants, the Acadians. For a brief introduction to Acadian history see Naomi E.S. Griffiths, *The Contexts of Acadian History, 1686–1784* (K&M: MQUP 1992). The overall pattern is depicted in Jean Daigle and Robert LeBlanc, 'Acadian Deportation and Return,' *HAC*, vol. 1, plate 30.

Other migrants were Native people who settled in the colony or, as they often saw it, on the edge of their own territory. These migrations should be viewed in the broader context of tribal movements, over which there is considerable scholarly disagreement. The tribal histories contained in B.G. Trigger, ed., *Northeast*, and J. Helm, ed., *Subarctic*, volumes 15 and 6 respectively of the *Handbook of North American Indians*, chart migration patterns. So too, in a more general way, do the series of plates in *HAC*, vol. 1: C.E. Heidenreich has reconstructed tribal populations in the eastern Great Lakes region about 1700 with James V. Wright in 'Population and Subsistence,' plate 18; the impact of wars and epidemics on the region's inhabitants in the first half of the seventeenth century in 'The Great Lakes Basin, 1600–1653,' plate 35; and later tribal territories with Françoise Noël in plates 37 through 40.

On the history of the Indian settlements in Canada, B.G. Trigger, 'Native Resettlement, 1635–1800,' *HAC*, vol. 1, plate 47, is a good place to begin, but see also G.F.G. Stanley, 'The First Indian "Reserves" in Canada,' *RHAF* 4/2 (oct. 1950): 178–210. On Iroquois migrations see D. Delâge, 'Les Iroquois chrétiens des "réductions," 1667–1770: migration et rapports avec les Français,' *Recherches amérindiennes au Québec* 21/1–2

(1991): 59–70; on those of the Abenakis, Gordon M. Day, *The Identity of the Saint Francis Indians* (O: National Museums of Canada 1981). C.J. Jaenen analyses Franco-Native intermarriage in 'Miscegenation in Eighteenth Century New France,' in Barry M. Gough and Laird Christie, eds., *New Dimensions in Ethnohistory: Papers of the Second Laurier Conference on Ethnohistory and Ethnology* (Hull, Que.: Canadian Museum of Civilization 1991). For statistics see Bertrand Desjardins, 'Homogénéité ethnique de la population québécoise sous le Régime français,' *Cahiers québécois de démographie* 19/1 (printemps 1990): 63–76.

Migration in the other direction, that of French-speakers to the lands of Native people, is difficult to follow precisely, as much of it, particularly early on, involved clandestine traders or *coureurs de bois*, who had no interest in appearing in too many written records. The principal French settlements in the *pays d'en haut* are presented in C.E. Heidenreich et al., 'French Interior Settlements, 1750s,' *HAC*, vol. 1, plate 41. Patterns of migration from the Canadian countryside to Detroit and the Illinois country have been studied in the previously cited J. Mathieu and L. Gouger, 'Transferts de population,' *Annales de Bretagne et des pays de l'Ouest* (1988), and Mathieu, 'Mobilité et sédentarité: stratégies familiales en Nouvelle-France,' *RS* 28/2–3 (1987): 211–27. Jacqueline Peterson discusses intermarriage between French and Native peoples at posts and missions of the Great Lakes region in 'Many Roads to Red River: Métis Genesis in the Great Lakes Region, 1680–1815,' in Peterson and J.S.H. Brown, eds., *The New Peoples: Being and Becoming Métis in North America* (W: UMP 1985). Readers wishing to take a closer look at these scattered communities can consult several volumes of published documents: Leopold Lamontagne, ed., *Royal Fort Frontenac* (T: CS 1958); Ernest J. Lajeunesse, ed., *The Windsor Border Region, Canada's Southernmost Frontier: A Collection of Documents* (T: CS 1960); and the parish registers published by Marthe F. Beauregard in *La population des forts français d'Amérique (XVIIIe siècle)*, 2 vols. (M: Bergeron 1982–4). For early eastern counterparts to this last publication see Léonidas Larouche, *Le second registre de Tadoussac, 1662–1700* (M: PUQ 1972), and Léo-Paul Hébert, ed., *Le troisième registre de Tadoussac: miscellaneorum liber* (M: PUQ 1976).

Once established in Canada, most immigrants who stayed formed families, if they had not arrived *en famille*. The definitive analysis of this process for the seventeenth-century French contingent is H. Charbonneau et al., *Naissance d'une population: les Français établis au Canada au XVIIe siècle* (P/M: Presses universitaires de France/PUM 1987), now available in English as *The First French Canadians: Pioneers in the St. Lawrence Valley* (Newark, NJ: University of Delaware Press 1993). Y. Landry and J. Légaré have presented additional results from this study in 'The Life Course of Seventeenth-Century Immigrants to Canada,' *Journal of Family History* 12/1–3 (1987): 201–12.

There is no single source of up-to-date information at the moment on the demographic behaviour of the immigrants and their descendants over the whole period. Jacques Henripin's classic *La population canadienne au début du XVIIIe siècle: nuptialité, fécondité, mortalité infantile* (P: Presses universitaires de France 1954) can still be read with profit, as can H. Charbonneau's meticulous *Vie et mort de nos ancêtres: étude démographique* (M: PUM 1975). The data in Henripin and Yves Péron, 'The Demographic Transition of the Province of Quebec,' in D.V. Glass and Roger Revelle, eds., *Population and Social Change* (L: Edward Arnold 1972), are far less precise than Charbonneau's, but have the advantage of situating the birth, death, and marriage rates of the French regime in the context of the long-term evolution of the colonial population. Charbonneau and Jean-Pierre Bardet, for their part, have compared demographic behaviour in the metropole and in the colony in 'Cultures et milieux en France et en Nouvelle-France,' in J. Goy and Jean-Pierre Wallot, eds., *Evolution et éclatement du monde rural: structures, fonctionnement et évolution différentielle des sociétés françaises et québécoises, XVIIe–XIXe siècles* (P/M: Ecole des hautes études en sciences sociales/ PUM 1986). A systematic comparison with the Anglo-American colonies has yet to be made, but see Robert V. Wells, 'Marriage Seasonals in Early America: Comparisons and Comments,' *Journal of Interdisciplinary History* 18/2 (Autumn 1987): 299–307.

Several scholars have isolated demographic behaviour in particular contexts. Lorraine Gadoury et al. reviewed the evidence for urban-rural differences in 'Démographie différentielle en Nouvelle-France: villes et campagnes,' *RHAF* 38/3 (hiver 1985): 357–78. Since then, scholars have taken a closer look at both the urban and the rural populations. Danielle Gauvreau's sensitive study of the colonial capital, *Québec, une ville et sa population au temps de la Nouvelle-France* (Sillery, Que.: PUQ 1991), based on a complete family reconstitution, is an indispensable introduction to the demography of urban Canada, but see also L. Dechêne's analysis, first published in French in 1973, of the lack of dynamism of one town's population, in 'The Growth of Montreal in the Eighteenth Century,' in J.M. Bumsted, ed., *Canadian History before Confederation: Essays and Interpretations* (2nd ed., Georgetown, Ont.: Irwin-Dorsey 1979), reprinted in Angus D. Gilbert et al., eds., *Reappraisals in Canadian History*, vol. 1, *Pre-Confederation* (Scarborough, Ont.: PH 1993). Much thorough research on the demography of the countryside slumbers in unpublished theses; until this has been synthesized, a chapter in Allan Greer's study of the Richelieu Valley, *Peasant, Lord, and Merchant: Rural Society in Three Quebec Parishes, 1740–1840* (T: UTP 1985), will remain the best concise overview of the rural demographic regime. Other scholars have isolated particular social groups. On the nobles see L. Gadoury, *La noblesse de Nouvelle-France: familles et alliances* (Ville La Salle, Que.: Hurtubise HMH 1992), and her 'Comportements démographiques et alliances de la noblesse de Nouvelle-France,' *Annales de démographie historique* (1990): 259–83; on merchants see José E. Igartua, 'Le comportement démographique des marchands de Montréal vers 1760,' *RHAF* 33/3 (déc. 1979): 427–45; and on servants in the fur trade see H. Charbonneau et al., 'Le comportement démographique des voyageurs sous le Régime français,' *HS/SH* 11/21 (May 1978): 120–33.

Beyond all these tendencies and counter-tendencies, averages and exceptions to the rule, one thing is certain – the colonial population grew rapidly. A surprising number of colonial censuses have been published or at least recapitulated, notably in *Census of Canada, 1870–71*, vol. 4 (O: I.B. Taylor 1876), and in various volumes of the *Rapport de l'archiviste de la province de Québec* and of the *Répertoire des actes de baptême, mariage, sépulture et des recensements*. Historians have gradually come to realize that few of these sources were absolutely reliable. Leaving nothing to chance, M. Trudel simply used all the available documentation to reconstitute the known population in 1663 in *La population du Canada en 1663* (M: Fides 1973). On the *recensements généraux* of later years see Richard Lalou and M. Boleda, 'Une source en friche: les dénombrements sous le Régime français,' *RHAF* 42/1 (été 1988): 47–72. In 'Essai sur l'évolution démographique du Québec de 1534 à 2034,' *Cahiers québécois de démographie* 13/1 (avril 1984): 5–21, H. Charbonneau draws on earlier critical work to take a long-term view of Quebec's population, be it of European origin or Native.

ECONOMY

Once a story of policy or of trade, colonial economic history has come to concentrate more on the conditions of production. A similar trend is evident in studies of the Native past, where the broader context of production is lending depth to studies of the fur trade. We begin with a mainstay of the Native peoples' subsistence cycles and an important element in the Canadian economy, the fisheries.

The region's Native peoples relied heavily on the fisheries of the Great Lakes, the St Lawrence, and the Gulf, and sometimes came into conflict with European and *Canadien* users of the resource. Marcel Moussette presents the techniques of both Native and colonial fishermen in *Fishing Methods Used in the St. Lawrence River and Gulf* (O: Parks Canada 1979). Charles A. Martijn studies Micmac use of the river in 'Voyages des Micmacs dans la vallée du Saint-Laurent, sur la Côte-Nord et à Terre-Neuve,' in Martijn, ed., *Les Micmacs et la mer* (M: Recherches amérindiennes au Québec 1986). Conflict between the Inuit and the French over access to the Labrador fishery is the subject of François Trudel, 'Les Inuit du Labrador méridional face à l'exploitation canadienne et française des pêcheries (1700–1760),' *RHAF* 31/4 (mars 1978): 481–99. On the Great Lakes fishery see Charles E. Cleland, 'The Inland Shore Fishery of the Northern Great Lakes: Its Development and Importance in Prehistory,' *American Antiquity* 47/4 (Oct. 1982): 761–84.

European fishermen had, of course, been landing on the North Shore and the Gaspé Peninsula long before 1600. French ones in particular continued to do so; increasingly, they were apt to encounter confrères based at Quebec as well as Native fishermen. Much work has been done on the French fishery using these shores since Harold Adams Innis described it in *The Cod Fisheries: The History of an International Economy* (1940; rev. ed., T: UTP 1954). For a brief survey see Laurier Turgeon, 'Le temps des pêches lointaines: permanences et transformations (vers 1500–vers 1850),' in Michel Mollat, ed., *Histoire des pêches maritimes en France* (Toulouse, Fr.: Privat 1987). For a longer, less recent one see Charles de La Morandière, *Histoire de la pêche française de la morue dans l'Amérique septentrionale*, 3 vols. (P: Maisonneuve et Larose 1962–6). The Gaspé fishery figures prominently in Jean-François Brière's recent *La pêche française en Amérique du Nord au XVIIIe siècle* (Saint-Laurent, Que.: Fides 1990). Closer to shore, Mario Mimeault focuses on the Gaspé fishery supplied from Quebec in 'Les enterprises de pêche à la morue de Joseph Cadet, 1751–1758,' *RHAF* 37/4 (mars 1984): 557–72. Mario Lalancette maps the St Lawrence and Gaspé fisheries in 'Exploitation of the Gulf of St Lawrence,' *HAC*, vol. 1, plate 54. On the river fishery for beluga see A. Laberge, 'Etat, entrepreneurs, habitants et monopole: le "privilège" de la pêche au marsouin dans le Bas Saint-Laurent, 1700–1730,' *RHAF* 37/4 (mars 1984): 543–56.

Once a by-product of the fishery, the fur trade provided the colony with its main export commodity until well after 1760. It has since provided Canadian economic history with an exportable idea, in the form of the staples approach that H.A. Innis worked out in *The Fur Trade in Canada: An Introduction to Canadian Economic History* (1930; rev. ed., T: UTP 1970). For all its importance, the book is not for the faint of heart. Most will eschew its clumsy prose and prefer to take their Innis in more distilled form, such as the foreword to Murray G. Lawson, *Fur: A Study in English Mercantilism, 1700–1775* (T: UTP 1943). Sixty years on, Innis's ability to link apparently unrelated phenomena still dazzles, but not enough to obscure the extent to which he misinterpreted the trade of the French regime in order to make it fit into his model of competition. This was already apparent by 1947, when E.R. Adair first published 'Anglo-French Rivalry in the Fur Trade during the 18th Century,' reprinted in J.M. Bumsted, ed., *Canadian History before Confederation*, an understated critique partly based on J. Lunn's research. Some thirty years later, W.J. Eccles added further corrections and more emphasis in 'A Belated Review of Harold Adams Innis, *The Fur Trade in Canada*,' *CHR* 60/4 (Dec. 1979): 419–41.

Meanwhile, much new information has accumulated on the actual workings of the fur-merchandise trade in the *pays d'en haut* as well as in the colony (we still know very little about the European phases of the trade). The study of Native participation in the trade has seen the most striking progress. Referring intermittently to the larger debate among anthropologists concerning the nature of exchange in non-state societies, and paying heed alternately to Hudson's Bay Company traders' testimony and that of French administrators and missionaries, the discussion has meandered over the years and cannot be summarized in detail here. Suffice it to say that if Innis saw Natives as little more than a canoe-borne profit motive, later students of the trade have greatly qualified, if not rejected out of hand, that judgment. Rather, they have shown the extent to which Native peoples imposed their own priorities in the trade. These varied according to time and place; they usually included hunting for subsistence and a need for military security as well as access to a steady supply of selectively consumed European trade goods. The principal way stations on the road leading to this conclusion are E.E. Rich's 1960 article 'Trade Habits and Economic Motivation among the Indians of North America,' reprinted in J.R. Miller, ed., *Sweet Promises: A Reader on Indian-White Relations in Canada* (T: UTP 1991); Abraham Rotstein, 'Innis: The Alchemy of Fur and Wheat,' *JCS* 12/5 (Winter 1977): 6–31, based on his 1967 PhD thesis; Arthur J. Ray and Donald B. Freeman, *'Give Us Good Measure': An Economic Analysis of Relations between the Indians and the Hudson's Bay Company before 1763* (T: UTP 1978); Daniel Francis and Toby Morantz, *Partners in Furs: A History of the Fur Trade in Eastern James Bay, 1600–1870* (K&M: MQUP 1983); and R. White, *The Middle Ground*. For an enlightening case study see also Daniel Castonguay, 'Les impératifs de la subsistance chez les Montagnais de la Traite de Tadoussac (1720–1750),' *Recherches amérindiennes au Québec* 19/1 (1989): 17–30.

These discussions have encouraged us to view Native peoples as producers and not just as traders or 'middlemen.' Hunting has received the most attention, notably in a long-running anthropological controversy concerning the age of northern Algonkian hunting territories. For evidence of such territories before 1760 see 'Who Owns the Beaver? Northern Algonquian Land Tenure Reconsidered,' *Anthropologica* n.s. 28/1–2 (1986), a special issued edited by Charles A. Bishop and T. Morantz, and the latter's 'Colonial French Insights into Early Eighteenth-Century Algonquians of Central Quebec,' in W. Cowan, ed., *Papers of the Twenty-Second Algonquian Conference* (O: CUP 1991). Several scholars have investigated the tendency of some Native peoples to overkill fur-bearers. Calvin Martin proposed a complicated cultural explanation in *Keepers of the Game: Indian-Animal Relationships and the Fur Trade* (Berkeley and Los Angeles, CA: University of California Press 1978), while his critics tended to adopt a simpler socioeconomic one in S. Krech III, ed., *Indians, Animals and the Fur Trade: A Critique of 'Keepers of the Game'* (Athens, GA: University of Georgia Press 1981). On the importance of Native women's work, notably on the products of the hunt, see A. Prentice et al., *Canadian Women*, and Sylvia Van Kirk's programmatic 'Toward a Feminist Perspective in Native History,' in W. Cowan, ed., *Papers of the Eighteenth Algonquian Conference* (O: CUP 1987). D. Wayne Moodie assesses the role of Native agriculture, usually a woman's pursuit, in provisioning the fur trade in 'Agriculture and the Fur Trade,' in Carol M. Judd and A.J. Ray, eds., *Old Trails and New Directions: Papers of the Third North American Fur Trade Conference* (T: UTP 1980).

The Canadian fur trade is a tangle of ephemeral monopolies, merchants in various combinations, and all too colourful voyageurs. The first monopolies are the subject of H.P. Biggar, *The Early Trading Companies of New France: A Contribution to the History of Commerce and Discovery in North America* (1901; repr. NY: Argonaut 1965). M. Trudel chronicles the ups and downs of the monopolies during the colony's heroic age in his *Histoire de la Nouvelle-France*. G. Frégault's 1960 study 'La Compagnie de la Colonie,' reprinted in his *Le XVIIIe siècle canadien: études* (M: Hurtubise HMH 1968), should now be read in tandem with D. Miquelon, *New France, 1701–1744*. Thomas Wien examines the activities of the Compagnie des Indes, sole official beaver exporter after 1720, in 'Selling Beaver Skins in North America and Europe, 1720–1760: The Uses of Fur-Trade Imperialism,' *JCHA* 1 (1990): 293–317.

The monopolists notwithstanding, small *sociétés* linking merchants, traders, and at times military officers managed the colonial fur trade throughout most of the period. L. Dechêne devotes two chapters of *Habitants and Mer-*

chants to these key figures (as well as to the canoemen they employed), and explains the changes in the division of labour among them during the reign of Louis XIV. J.E. Igartua has studied the merchants working under the altered conditions of the last decade of French rule in 'The Merchants of Montreal at the Conquest: Socio-Economic Profile,' *HS/SH* 8/16 (Nov. 1975): 275–93; for a retrospective view see his 'A Change in Climate: The Conquest and the *Marchands* of Montreal,' CHA *HP* (1974): 115–34. Lilianne Plamondon studies a Quebec merchant widow active in the fur trade in a 1977 article, translated as 'A Businesswoman in New France: Marie-Anne Barbel, the Widow Fornel,' in Veronica Strong-Boag and Anita Clair Fellman, eds., *Rethinking Canada: The Promise of Women's History* ([1st ed.], T: CCP 1986). Several merchants and traders also number among the subjects of the *DCB*. The thorny problem of the relationship between officers and merchants in the eighteenth-century trade is addressed in Gratien Allaire, 'Officiers et marchands: les sociétés de commerce des fourrures, 1715–1760,' *RHAF* 40/3 (hiver 1987): 409–28. Allaire has also studied the servants, or *engagés*, who manned the canoes and worked at the posts. For a digest of his findings see C.E. Heidenreich et al., 'French Interior Settlements, 1750s,' *HAC*, vol. 1, plate 41. Heidenreich and F. Noël chart the expansion of the post network that explains the increase in the number of *engagés* in plates 37 through 40. On exploration, intimately linked to this expansion, see Richard I. Ruggles and Heidenreich's convenient synthesis 'French Exploration,' plate 36.

The fur trade and the other branches of commerce that gradually grew up beside it were connected to Atlantic markets. James S. Pritchard has charted the changing volume of shipping sent to the colony from France in 'The Pattern of French Colonial Shipping to Canada before 1760,' *Revue française d'histoire d'outre-mer* 63/231 (2e trimestre 1976): 189–210. On the metropolitan merchant communities involved in the colonial trade see John F. Bosher, *The Canada Merchants, 1713–1763* (NY: OUP 1987). In *Dugard of Rouen: French Trade to Canada and the West Indies, 1729–1770* (M: MQUP 1978), D. Miquelon analyses the operations of a Rouen business partnership that sent ships to Canada, to the West Indies, and on triangular voyages. This brings us to the other Canada trade, which after 1720 linked Quebec with Louisbourg and the Antilles. J. Mathieu has studied its workings in *Le commerce entre la Nouvelle-France et les Antilles au XVIIIe siècle* (M: Fides 1981). J. Lunn introduces the trade between Montreal and Albany, New York, in 'The Illegal Fur Trade out of New France, 1713–60,' CHA *AR* (1939): 61–79. T. Wien and J.S. Pritchard map overseas trade patterns in 'Canadian North Atlantic Trade,' *HAC*, vol. 1, plate 48. Principally through military expenditures, the Crown helped right the colony's adverse balance of trade. W.J. Eccles makes this important point in 'The Social, Economic, and Political Significance of the Military Establishment in New France,' *CHR* 52/1 (Mar. 1971): 1–22.

Once inclined to reduce colonial economic history to men and goods moving westward and furs moving eastward, historians have come to realize that by the later seventeenth century most Canadian families lived on farms and were less and less likely to send men to the *pays d'en haut*. Historians approached the rural economy obliquely at first, through the study of that peculiar institution, the seigneury. The apparent incongruity of finding a pillar of feudalism in the clearings of the New World had already excited comment in the nineteenth century. Early in the twentieth, William Bennett Munro took the first close look at the institution in *The Seigniorial System in Canada: A Study in French Colonial Policy* (Cambridge, MA: Harvard University Press 1907), based on the sources printed in his *Documents Relating to the Seigniorial Tenure in Canada* (T: CS 1908). Taking his cue from the seigneurs' own defence of their institution a century earlier, M. Trudel cast the seigneur in the role of a colonizer and the seigneury in that of a shield of the nation in his *The Seigneurial Regime*, CHA Historical Booklet no. 6 (O: 1956). A decade later, the geographer R.C. Harris, in *The Seigneurial System in Early Canada: A Geographical Study* (1966; 2nd ed., K&M: MQUP 1984), broke with tradition by concluding that the system made no great difference to a society whose basic structures were North American and egalitarian. This was to neglect the seigneury's role as a surplus appropriation mechanism and general encumbrance, countered L. Dechêne five years later, on the basis of a detailed examination of the administration of the seigneury of Montreal: 'L'évolution du régime seigneurial au Canada: le cas de Montréal aux XVIIe et XVIIIe siècles,' *RS* 12/2 (mai–août 1971): 143–83. Work published since on other seigneuries tends to bear out these conclusions while stressing the system's adaptability to local circumstances. On our period see Sylvie Dépatie and M. Lalancette's chapters in Dépatie et al., *Contributions à l'étude du régime seigneurial canadien* (Ville La Salle, Que.: Hurtubise HMH 1987). L. Dechêne maps patterns of seigneurial ownership in 'The Seigneuries,' *HAC*, vol. 1, plate 51.

Once viewed as a wasteful by-activity, Canadian agriculture has received more sympathetic treatment recently. In *The Seigneurial System*, R.C. Harris took a decisive step away from the denunciations of the older literature in finding reasons other than sloth for the habitants' extensive practices. Delving deeper into the sources and bringing a detailed knowledge of metropolitan conditions to bear, L. Dechêne's *Habitants and Merchants* portrayed a New World incarnation of the peasantry caught up in the logic of old practices and old constraints. In *Peasant, Lord, and Merchant*, a book devoted mostly to the period after 1760, A. Greer confirmed this judgment but placed more emphasis on the feudal burden. Returning to a less-studied constraint on productivity, T. Wien examines the effects of climate in '"Les travaux pressants": calendrier agricole, assolement et productivité au Canada au XVIIIe siècle,' *RHAF* 43/4 (printemps 1990): 535–58. Another approach to the rural economy draws on the ethnological tradition, incarnated notably in Robert-Lionel Séguin's work. In *La civilisation traditionnelle de l'habitant' aux 17e et 18e siècles: fonds matériel* (2nd ed., M: Fides 1973) and the posthumous *L'équipement aratoire et horticole du Québec ancien* (*XVIIe, XVIIIe et XIXe siècles*), 2 vols. (M: Guérin 1989), Séguin spared no efforts to catalogue rural Canadians' material culture, but failed to explain change and evaluate the representativity of the objects mentioned. A study by Bernard Audet and Raymond Létourneau, *Avoir feu et lieu dans l'Ile d'Orléans au XVIIe siècle: étude de culture matérielle* (Q: PUL 1990), is more firmly rooted in place and time. Historians have since analysed the objects listed in post-mortem inventories as indicators of wealth, lifestyle, and technological change. See, for example, Christian Dessureault and J.A. Dickinson, 'Farm Implements and Husbandry in Colonial Quebec, 1740–1840,' in P. Benes, ed., *New England/New France*.

Other historians studying the later years of the period, when an export market for farm products opened up episodically, have focused on commercialization. Of the published work, 'Un marchand rural en Nouvelle-France: François-Augustin Bailly de Messein, 1709–1771,' *RHAF* 33/2 (sept. 1979): 215–62, Louis Michel's study of a rural merchant, is most relevant to the years before 1760. In an article covering a later countryside but with important implications for the French regime, C. Dessureault analyses self-sufficiency, surpluses, and inequality: 'L'égalitarisme paysan dans l'ancienne société rurale de la vallée du Saint-Laurent: éléments pour une ré-interprétation,' *RHAF* 40/3 (hiver 1987): 373–407.

Since Joseph-Noël Fauteux wrote his still-useful study *Essai sur l'industrie au Canada sous le Régime français*, 2 vols. (Q: Ls.-A. Proulx 1927), historians and ethnologists have looked more closely at several trades and occupations as well as the royal shipyards and the Saint-Maurice ironworks. J. Mathieu examines the former in *La construction navale royale à Québec, 1739–1759* (Q: Société historique de Québec 1971), while Luce Vermette, *Domestic Life at Les Forges du Saint-Maurice* (O: Parks Canada 1982), and Cameron Nish, *François-Etienne Cugnet, 1719–1751: entrepreneur et entreprises en Nouvelle-France* (M: Fides 1975), respectively, concentrate on the workers and the founder of the latter. Most occupational studies emphasize social as well as economic aspects. See notably Réal N. Brisson's imaginative study of shipwrights, *Les 100 premières années de la charpenterie navale à Québec, 1663–1763* (Q: IQRC 1983). The leather trades are the subject of Marise Thivierge, 'Les artisans du cuir du temps de la Nouvelle-France: Québec, 1660–1760,' in Jean-Claude Dupont and J. Mathieu, eds., *Les métiers du cuir* (Q: PUL 1981), while P.N. Moogk examines construction in *Building a House in New France: An Account of the Perplexities of Client and Craftsmen in Early Canada* (T: M&S 1977). Studies concentrating on artisan life include Jean-Pierre Hardy, 'Quelques aspects du niveau de richesse et de la vie matérielle des artisans de Québec et de Montréal, 1740–1755,' *RHAF* 40/3 (hiver 1987): 339–72, and Hardy's contribution to his and David-Thiery Ruddel's *Les apprentis artisans à Québec, 1660–1815* (M: PUQ 1977). Gilles Proulx looks at soldiers, an important source of labour, in *The Garrison of Quebec from 1748 to 1759* (O: National Historic Sites, Parks Service 1991). On slaves see M. Trudel, *L'esclavage au Canada français* (Q: PUL 1960), and his *Dictionnaire des esclaves et de leurs propriétaires au Canada français* (M: Hurtubise HMH 1990).

To take the measure of all this activity, readers can consult the attempts to apply to the colony the techniques of the new economic history. Robert Armstrong surveys the period from this vantage point in *Structure and Change: An Economic History of Quebec* (T: Gage 1984). Morris Altman, for his part, relies on figures from the colony's general censuses to calculate the growth rate in 'Economic Growth in Canada, 1695–1739: Estimates and Analysis,' *WMQ* 3rd ser., 45/4 (Oct. 1988): 684–711.

SOCIETY

Colonial society is profitably divided into rural and urban spheres. After much generalizing on the social implications of seigneurialism at the forest's edge – for one particularly delirious example see Sigmund Diamond, 'An Experiment in "Feudalism": French Canada in the Seventeenth Century,' *WMQ* 3rd ser., 18/1 (Jan. 1961): 3–34 – scholars have begun to take a closer look at social relations in the countryside. Social reproduction is the central theme of recent work in rural family history; how did parents give their children a start in life, and how did family strategies merge in migration and settlement patterns on the frontier of colonization? Two programmatic articles originally published in French in 1983 attest to the influence of other disciplines in the discussion: sociology and demography in the case of G. Bouchard, 'Transmission of Family Property and the Cycle of Quebec Rural

Society from the Seventeenth to the Twentieth Century,' in Bettina Bradbury, ed., *Canadian Family History: Selected Readings* (T: CCP 1992), and
geography in that of Serge Courville, 'Space, Territory, and Culture in New
France: A Geographical Perspective,' in Graeme Wynn, ed., *People, Places,
Patterns, Processes: Geographical Perspectives on the Canadian Past* (T: CCP
1990). J. Mathieu and his students have carried out much of the research on
the French regime, summarized in Mathieu's previously cited 'Mobilité et
sédentarité,' *RS* (1987). Louis Lavallée's sensitive local study, *La Prairie en
Nouvelle-France (1647–1760): étude d'histoire sociale* (K&M: MQUP 1992),
focuses notably on marriage patterns. S. Dépatie, for her part, has taken an
important step in combining the economic and social approaches in 'La
transmission du patrimoine dans les terroirs en expansion: un exemple canadien au XVIIIe siècle,' *RHAF* 44/2 (automne 1990): 171–98. One of the
sources that sheds light on settlement has recently been published in abbreviated form in J. Mathieu and A. Laberge, eds., *L'occupation des terres dans la
vallée du Saint-Laurent: les aveux et dénombrements, 1723–1745* (Sillery, Que.:
SPT 1991). M. Trudel has assembled much the same kind of information in
Le terrier du Saint-Laurent en 1663 (O: PUO 1973).

Even the general studies of the colonial towns tend to emphasize social
phenomena. André Lachance, *La vie urbaine en Nouvelle-France* (M: BE
1987), introduces the reader to urban society, while Marc Lafrance and
André Charbonneau cover the spatial aspects in 'The Towns,' *HAC*, vol. 1,
plate 49. John Hare, M. Lafrance, and D.-T. Ruddel devote some one hundred pages to the economy, population, society, environment, institutions,
and cultural life of the colonial capital in their *Histoire de la ville de Québec,
1608–1871* (M/O: BE/Canadian Museum of Civilization 1987). Pitched to
a general audience and copiously illustrated, Y. Landry, ed., *Pour le Christ et
le Roi: la vie au temps des premiers Montréalais* (M: Libre Expression/Art Global 1992), portrays daily life under the French regime in Ville Marie/Mon-
treal. M. Trudel reconstructs the first phase of that town's development in
Montréal: la formation d'une société, 1642–1663 (M: Fides 1976), summarized
in a 1969 article translated as 'The Beginnings of a Society: Montreal,
1642–1663,' in Michael S. Cross and Gregory S. Kealey, eds., *Readings in
Canadian Social History*, vol. 1, *Economy and Society during the French Regime
to 1759* (T: M&S 1983). L. Dechêne draws broader conclusions concerning
the second phase in *Habitants and Merchants*. With Marie Baboyant, Trudel
has also edited François Dollier de Casson's contemporary history of the
town's early years, *Histoire du Montréal* (M: Hurtubise HMH 1992), which
can also be consulted in English translation as *A History of Montreal, 1642–
1672*, ed. Ralph Flenley (L: Dent 1928).

There is a considerable amount of work on more general social themes. For two approaches to childhood see P.N. Moogk, '*Les petits sauvages*: The Children of Eighteenth-Century New France,' in Joy Parr, ed., *Childhood and Family in Canadian History* (T: M&S 1982), and Denise Lemieux, *Les petits innocents: l'enfance en Nouvelle-France* (Q: IQRC 1985). Women's roles are the subject of Jan Noel's 1981 article 'New France: les femmes favorisées,' most accessible in V. Strong-Boag and A.C. Fellman, eds., *Rethinking Canada*. Noel's argument should be considered in the light of M. Dumont, 'Les femmes de la Nouvelle-France étaient-elles favorisées?' *Atlantis* 8/1 (Autumn 1982): 118–24. Marie-Aimée Cliche has studied the lives of a particularly *défavorisée* category of women in a 1988 article translated as 'Unwed Mothers, Families, and Society during the French Regime,' in B. Bradbury, ed., *Canadian Family History*. Francine Barry investigates the universe of female domestic servants in 'Familles et domesticité féminine au milieu du XVIIIe siècle,' in Nadia Fahmy-Eid and M. Dumont, eds., *Maîtresses de maison, maîtresses d'école: femmes, famille et éducation dans l'histoire du Québec* (M: BE 1983). Sylvie Savoie examines divorce in 'La rupture du couple en Nouvelle-France: les demandes de séparation aux XVIIe et XVIIIe siècles,' *Canadian Woman Studies* 7/4 (Winter 1986): 58–63. C. Nish, *Les bourgeois-gentilshommes de la Nouvelle-France, 1729–1748* (M: Fides 1968), offers an early glimpse of marriage strategies among the colony's privileged classes; D. Gauvreau, *Québec, une ville et sa population*, and L. Gadoury, *La noblesse de Nouvelle-France*, have since taken up the subject but not the interpretive framework. Maureen Molloy, 'Considered Affinity: Kinship, Marriage, and Social Class in New France, 1640–1729,' *Social Science History* 14/1 (Spring 1990): 1–26, attempts to analyse choice of marriage partners as an aspect of class formation.

The considerable variations in Native peoples' social organization are best approached initially through the various volumes of the *Handbook of North American Indians*. On women's experience in Native societies see notably Eleanor Burke Leacock, *Myths of Male Dominance: Collected Articles on Women Cross-Culturally* (NY: Monthly Review Press 1981). In *Chain Her by One Foot: The Subjection of Women in Seventeenth-Century New France* (L: Routledge 1991), Karen Anderson presents the first half-century of contact as a metaphor for the subjugation of women in general. James Axtell, ed., *The Indian Peoples of Eastern America: A Documentary History of the Sexes* (NY: OUP 1981), is a useful collection of texts and commentary.

The sociocultural realm has attracted increasing interest recently. Diet (as well as provisioning) in the colony is the subject of François Rousseau's study of hospital fare, *L'oeuvre de chère en Nouvelle-France: le régime des malades à l'Hôtel-Dieu de Québec* (Q: PUL 1983). Connoisseurs of applied history will wish to test the modernized recipes in M. Lafrance and Yvon Desloges, *A Taste of History: The Origins of Quebec's Gastronomy* (M: Editions de la Chenelière 1989). Another form of nourishment is presented in Antonio Drolet, *Les bibliothèques canadiennes, 1604–1960* (M: Cercle du livre de France 1965), while J.A. Dickinson offers a glimpse of book-owning habits in 'Un aperçu de la vie culturelle en Nouvelle-France: l'examen de trois bibliothèques privées,' *University of Ottawa Quarterly* 44/4 (Oct.–Dec. 1974): 453–66. On writers and their work, see the first sections of Maurice Lemire, ed., *La vie littéraire au Québec*, vol. 1, *1764–1805* (Sainte-Foy, Que.: PUL 1991). Roger Magnuson, *Education in New France* (K&M: MQUP 1992), is the most recent survey of its subject, but see also Louis-Philippe Audet, 'Society and Education in New France,' in J. Donald Wilson et al., eds., *Canadian Education: A History* (Scarborough, Ont.: PH 1970). M. Dumont, *Girls' Schooling in Quebec, 1639–1960*, CHA Historical Booklet no. 49 (O: 1990), and N. Fahmy-Eid, 'L'éducation des filles chez les Ursulines de Québec sous le Régime français,' in Fahmy-Eid and Dumont, eds., *Maîtresses de maison, maîtresses d'école*, analyse girls' education.

On literacy toward the end of the period and beyond see A. Greer, 'L'alphabétisation et son histoire au Québec: état de la question,' in Yvan Lamonde, ed., *L'imprimé au Québec: aspects historiques (18e–20e siècles)* (Q: IQRC 1983), and Michel Verrette, 'L'alphabétisation de la population de la ville de Québec de 1750 à 1849,' *RHAF* 39/1 (été 1985): 51–76. Marthe Faribault offers a concise introduction to the French spoken before 1760 in 'Un parler parisien,' in Y. Landry, ed., *Pour le Christ et le Roi*. The victory of French over patois is the subject of Philippe Barbaud, *Le choc des patois en Nouvelle-France: essai sur l'histoire de la francisation au Canada* (Sillery, Que.: PUQ 1984); H. Charbonneau has since contributed more precise figures on the proportion of French-speaking immigrants in 'Le caractère français des pionniers de la vallée laurentienne,' *Cahiers québécois de démographie* 19/1 (printemps 1990): 49–62. Another form of speech has received a surprising amount of attention in A. Lachance, 'Une étude de mentalité: les injures verbales au Canada au XVIIIe siècle (1712–1748),' *RHAF* 31/2 (sept. 1977): 229–38, and P.N. Moogk, '"Thieving Buggers" and "Stupid Sluts": Insults and Popular Culture in New France,' *WMQ* 3rd ser., 36/4 (Oct. 1979): 524–47. The best introduction to Native linguistics remains Victor Egon Hanzeli, *Missionary Linguistics in New France: A Study of Seventeenth- and Eighteenth-Century Descriptions of American Indian Languages* (The Hague: Mouton 1969).

Colonial science is surveyed in Luc Chartrand et al., *Histoire des sciences au Québec* (M: BE 1987). Toby Gelfand, 'Medicine in New France,' in Ronald L. Numbers, ed., *Medicine in the New World: New Spain, New France, and New England* (Knoxville, TN: University of Tennessee Press 1987), is a summary of the secondary literature and emphasizes institutions, while Renald Lessard, *Health Care in Canada during the Seventeenth and Eighteenth Centuries* (Hull, Que.: Canadian Museum of Civilization 1990), takes a social approach. On mental illness see André Cellard, *Histoire de la folie au Québec de 1600 à 1850: 'le désordre'* (M: BE 1991). Hélène Laforce's study of midwives, *Histoire de la sage-femme dans la région de Québec* (Q: IQRC 1985), briefly summarized in 'The Different Stages of the Elimination of Midwives in Quebec,' in Katherine Arnup et al., eds., *Delivering Motherhood: Maternal Ideologies and Practices in the 19th and 20th Centuries* (L: Routledge 1990), takes a close look at the period before 1760.

Colonial music and music-making are examined in Helmut Kallmann et al., eds., *Encyclopedia of Music in Canada* (1981; 2nd ed., T: UTP 1992), under the names of the two colonial towns. Madeleine Béland, *Chansons de voyageurs, coureurs de bois et forestiers* (Q: PUL 1982), includes six authentic voyageur songs. Dennis Reid, *A Concise History of Canadian Painting* (1973; 2nd ed., T: OUP 1988), and François-Marc Gagnon and Nicole Cloutier, *Premiers peintres de la Nouvelle-France*, 2 vols. (Q: Ministère des Affaires culturelles 1976), present colonial painting and painters. Some of the more striking archival art illustrates André Vachon, *Dreams of Empire: Canada before 1700* and, with Victorin Chabot, *Taking Root: Canada from 1700 to 1760* (O: Public Archives of Canada 1982–5). Jean Trudel, dir., *Le grand héritage*, vol. 1, *L'Eglise catholique et les arts au Québec* (Q: Musée du Québec 1984), serves as a concise introduction to religious art. Jean Palardy, *The Early Furniture of French Canada* (2nd ed., T: MAC 1965), is still the best survey of its subject. On architecture see Luc Noppen et al., *Québec: trois siècles d'architecture* (3rd ed., M: Libre Expression 1989); Jean-Claude Marsan, *Montreal in Evolution: Historical Analysis of the Development of Montreal's Architecture and Urban Environment* (K&M: MQUP 1981); and Georges-Pierre Léonidoff, 'The House, 1660–1800' and 'The Wooden House,' *HAC*, vol. 1, plates 55 and 56. Many of the surviving originals are lovingly presented in *Les chemins de la mémoire: monuments et sites historiques du Québec*, 2 vols. (Q: Publications du Québec 1990–2).

On changes to Native material culture, the overview by archaeologist George I. Quimby, *Indian Culture and European Trade Goods: The Archaeology of the Historic Period in the Western Great Lakes* (Madison, WI: University of Wisconsin Press 1966), remains valuable. Just how Native people, especially women, incorporated European goods and influences into their material culture can be seen in objects from the later eighteenth century presented in Ruth B. Phillips, 'Like a Star, I Shine: Northern Woodlands Artistic Traditions,' in Julia D. Harrison et al., *The Spirit Sings: Artistic Traditions of Canada's First Peoples* (T: M&S/Glenbow Museum 1987). On the influence of another new substance, alcohol, A. Vachon, 'L'eau-de-vie dans la société indienne,' CHA *AR* (1960): 22–32, would bear updating. On the cultural significance of European objects early in contact see George R. Hamell, 'Strawberries, Floating Islands, and Rabbit Captains: Mythical Realities and European Contact in the Northeast during the Sixteenth and Seventeenth Centuries,' *JCS* 21/4 (Winter 1986–7): 72–94. The same article contains an hypothesis on the timing of certain rituals, and brings us to the spiritual realm.

Conversion, assimilation, and persistence of Native beliefs in the face of the missionary offensive are treated in a vast body of literature. For a sample of ethnological work on Native spirituality see Christopher Vecsey, *Traditional Ojibwa Religion and Its Historical Changes* (Philadelphia, PA: American Philosophical Society 1983), and E. Tooker, ed., *Native North American Spirituality of the Eastern Woodlands* (NY: Paulist Press 1979). The best survey of French missionary activity is John Webster Grant, *Moon of Wintertime: Missionaries and the Indians of Canada in Encounter since 1534* (T: UTP 1984). J. Axtell adds a third party, the Anglo-Americans, to the equation in *The Invasion Within: The Contest of Cultures in Colonial North America* (NY: OUP 1985). The wider ramifications of conversion are the subject of Kenneth M. Morrison, 'Baptism and Alliance: The Symbolic Mediations of Religious Syncretism,' *Ethnohistory* 37/4 (Fall 1990): 416–37, and D. Delâge, 'La religion dans l'alliance franco-amérindienne,' *Anthropologie et sociétés* 15/1 (1991): 55–87. A. Beaulieu has examined conversion among the Montagnais and Algonkins in *Convertir les fils de Caïn: jésuites et Amérindiens nomades en Nouvelle-France, 1632–1642* (M: Nuit Blanche 1990). F.-M. Gagnon surveys missionary techniques in *La conversion par l'image: un aspect de la mission des jésuites auprès des Indiens du Canada au XVIIe siècle* (M: Bellarmin 1975), as does Dominique Deslandres, 'Séculiers, laïcs, jésuites: épistémés et projets d'évangélisation et d'acculturation en Nouvelle-France. Les premières tentatives, 1604–1613,' *Mélanges de l'Ecole française de Rome. Italie et Méditerranée* 101/2 (1989): 751–88. Alain Croix draws revealing parallels in 'Missions, Hurons et Bas-Bretons au XVIIe siècle,' *Annales de Bretagne et des pays de l'Ouest* 95/4 (1988): 487–98. Education dispensed to Native children is the subject of C.J. Jaenen, 'Education for Francization: The Case of New France in the Seventeenth Century,' a revised version of a 1983 article, published in Jean Barman et al., eds., *Indian Education in Can-*

ada, vol. 1, *The Legacy* (V: UBCP 1986), and D. Deslandres, 'L'éducation des Amérindiennes d'après la correspondance de Marie Guyart de l'Incarnation,' *Studies in Religion/Sciences religieuses* 16/1 (1987): 91–110.

On the mental schemata that accompanied and grew out of French interaction with Natives see C.J. Jaenen, *Friend and Foe: Aspects of French-Amerindian Cultural Contact in the Sixteenth and Seventeenth Centuries* (T: M&S 1976), an analysis extended to the eighteenth century in 'Les sauvages amériquains: Persistence into the Eighteenth Century of Traditional French Concepts and Constructs for Comprehending Amerindians,' *Ethnohistory* 29/1 (Winter 1982): 43–56, and O.P. Dickason, *The Myth of the Savage and the Beginnings of French Colonialism in the Americas* (E: UAP 1984). F.-M. Gagnon analyses the engravings illustrating Champlain's *Voyages* in *Ces hommes dits sauvages: l'histoire fascinante d'un préjugé qui remonte aux premiers découvreurs du Canada* (M: Libre Expression 1984). The Native viewpoint is explored in C.J. Jaenen, 'Amerindian Views of French Culture in the Seventeenth Century,' *CHR* 55/3 (Sept. 1974): 261–91.

Canadian popular religion has also attracted scholarly attention. M.-A. Cliche, *Les pratiques de dévotion en Nouvelle-France: comportements populaires et encadrement ecclésial dans le gouvernement de Québec* (Q: PUL 1988), is the essential reference. On devotional confraternities also see Brigitte Caulier, 'Bâtir l'Amérique des dévôts: les confréries de dévotion montréalaises depuis le Régime français,' *RHAF* 46/1 (été 1992): 45–66. More speculative is Jonathan L. Pearl, 'Witchcraft in New France in the Seventeenth Century: The Social Aspect,' *Historical Reflections* 4/2 (Winter 1977): 191–205. On the French background of the early church see Elizabeth Rapley, *The Dévotes: Women and Church in Seventeenth-Century France* (K&M: MQUP 1990), which presents, among other cases, Marguerite Bourgeoys; and Charles Frostin, 'Vogue canadienne et milieu métropolitain de soutien à la mission lointaine au XVIIe siècle: "l'épopée mystique" de la Nouvelle-France,' in J. Goy and J.-P. Wallot, eds., *Evolution et éclatement du monde rural*. On the colonial church, C.J. Jaenen, *The Role of the Church in New France* (T: MHR 1976), summarized under the same title in CHA Booklet no. 40 (O: 1985), is still useful, as is the standard reference, Auguste Gosselin, *L'Eglise du Canada depuis Mgr de Laval jusqu'à la Conquête*, 3 vols. (Q: Laflamme & Proulx 1911–14).

More specialized studies have focused on religious institutions, and through them have presented the life of nuns. Among them are Micheline D'Allaire, *L'Hôpital-Général de Québec, 1692–1764* (M: Fides 1971) and *Les dots de religieuses au Canada français, 1639–1800: étude économique et sociale* (M: Hurtubise HMH 1986); Michel Allard et al., *L'Hôtel-Dieu de Montréal*,

1642–1973 (M: Hurtubise HMH 1973); and F. Rousseau, *La croix et le scalpel: histoire des Augustines et de l'Hôtel-Dieu de Québec (1639–1989)*, vol. 1, *1639–1892* (Sillery, Que.: SPT 1989).

POLITICS AND WAR

Most of the general works cited earlier trace changes in Native leadership structures. On Algonkians see in particular T. Morantz, 'Northern Algonquian Concepts of Status and Leadership Reviewed: A Case Study of the Eighteenth-Century Trading Captain System,' *Canadian Review of Sociology and Anthropology* 19/4 (Nov. 1982): 482–501. Jean-Marie Therrien, *Parole et pouvoir: figure du chef amérindien en Nouvelle-France* (M: L'Hexagone 1986), contains useful information but is more descriptive.

The colonial administration should be considered in the light of the metropolitan one, presented in considerable detail in Roland Mousnier, *The Institutions of France under the Absolute Monarchy, 1598–1789*, 2 vols. (Chicago, IL: University of Chicago Press 1978–84). The colony's government is concisely described in A. Vachon, 'The Administration of New France,' *DCB*, vol. 2 (T: UTP 1969). Jacques-Yvan Morin has since analysed the division of powers in 'L'évolution constitutionnelle du Canada et du Québec de 1534 à 1867,' in Morin and José Woehrling, *Les constitutions du Canada et du Québec: du Régime français à nos jours* (M: Thémis 1992), which also contains a selection of documents. On colonial power struggles see S.D. Standen, 'Politics, Patronage, and the Imperial Interest: Charles de Beauharnais's Disputes with Gilles Hocquart,' *CHR* 60/1 (Mar. 1979): 19–40, and G. Frégault, 'Politique et politiciens,' in his *Le XVIIIe siècle canadien*. J.F. Bosher argues that peculation was inevitable under the Ancien Régime in 'Government and Private Interests in New France,' *Canadian Public Administration* 10/2 (June 1967): 244–57. The colony's last intendant, portrayed as a scoundrel in G. Frégault, *François Bigot, administrateur français*, 2 vols. (M: Institut d'histoire de l'Amérique française 1948), went beyond the call of duty in this respect.

The biographical file on other leading officials has thickened in recent years, thanks namely to the *DCB*, but also to several full-length works. W.J. Eccles continued the tradition of critical biographies inaugurated by G. Frégault with his *Frontenac: The Courtier Governor* (T: M&S 1959). Later portraits include Jean-Claude Dubé, *Claude-Thomas Dupuy: intendant de la Nouvelle-France, 1678–1738* (M: Fides 1969); Y.F. Zoltvany, *Philippe de Rigaud de Vaudreuil: Governor of New France, 1703–1725* (T: M&S 1974); M. D'Allaire, *Montée et déclin d'une famille noble: les Ruette d'Auteuil (1617–1737)*

(Ville La Salle, Que.: Hurtubise HMH 1980); Dubé, *Les intendants de la Nouvelle-France* (M: Fides 1984), a prosopography notable for its analysis of clienteles; and Dubé and Pierre-Julien Laferrière, *Les Bigot, du XVIe siècle à la Révolution: évolution d'un lignage* (M: Fides 1988).

Colonial justice has attracted much interest in recent years. The colony's legal code is discussed in Y.F. Zoltvany, 'Esquisse de la coutume de Paris,' *RHAF* 25/3 (déc. 1971): 365–84. André Morel, 'Réflexions sur la justice criminelle canadienne, au 18e siècle,' *RHAF* 29/2 (sept. 1975): 241–53, is still useful concerning one branch of judicial activity. A. Lachance has treated the subject in greater depth, first in his institutional history, *La justice criminelle du roi au Canada au XVIIIe siècle: tribunaux et officiers* (Q: PUL 1978), and then in *Crimes et criminels en Nouvelle-France* (M: BE 1984). In 'Women and Crime in Canada in the Early Eighteenth Century, 1712–1759,' first published in 1981 and reprinted in R.C. Macleod, ed., *Lawful Authority: Readings on the History of Criminal Justice in Canada* (T: CCP 1988), Lachance focuses on a particular category of criminals. M.-A. Cliche traces the long-term incidence of one form of crime in 'L'infanticide dans la région de Québec (1660–1969),' *RHAF* 44/1 (été 1990): 31–59. Jean-François Leclerc examines assault and battery in 'Justice et infra-justice en Nouvelle-France: les voies de fait à Montréal entre 1700 et 1760,' *Criminologie* 18/1 (1985): 25–39. In *Justice et justiciables: la procédure civile à la Prévôté de Québec, 1667–1759* (Q: PUL 1982), J.A. Dickinson analyses civil justice as dispensed by the provost court of Quebec. The same author explores Ancien Régime terminology in 'Réflexions sur la police en Nouvelle-France,' *McGill Law Journal* 32/3 (1987): 496–522, and studies the activities of the best-documented seigneurial court in 'La justice seigneuriale en Nouvelle-France: le cas de Notre-Dame-des-Anges,' *RHAF* 28/3 (déc. 1974): 323–46. L. Lavallée has recently shed new light on another rural institution, the *communauté des habitants*, in *La Prairie en Nouvelle-France*. On popular resistance see Terence A. Crowley, '"Thunder Gusts": Popular Disturbances in Early French Canada,' *CHA HP* (1979): 11–32. Colin Coates broaches the delicate subject of authority in 'Authority and Illegitimacy in New France: The Burial of Bishop Saint-Vallier and Madeleine de Verchères vs. the Priest of Batiscan,' *HS/SH* 22/43 (May 1989): 65–90.

War is, of course, a major theme in the history of both societies. In Native lands and in historical accounts, the Iroquois wars overshadow all the rest. George T. Hunt, *The Wars of the Iroquois: A Study in Intertribal Trade Relations* (Madison, WI: University of Wisconsin Press 1940), initially attributed the seventeenth-century Iroquois attacks to economic motives, but several studies have since placed more emphasis on cultural factors. In particular see

D.K. Richter, 'War and Culture: The Iroquois Experience,' *WMQ* 3rd ser., 40/4 (Oct. 1983): 528–59. One of the reasons, the adoption of slaves, is explained in William A. Starna and Ralph Watkins, 'Northern Iroquoian Slavery,' *Ethnohistory* 38/1 (Winter 1991): 34–57. Francis Jennings surveys relations between the Iroquois and the Anglo-Americans in *The Ambiguous Iroquois Empire: The Covenant Chain Confederation of Indian Tribes with English Colonies, from Its Beginnings to the Lancaster Treaty of 1744* (NY: Norton 1984) and *Empire of Fortune: Crowns, Colonies, and Tribes in the Seven Years War in America* (NY: Norton 1988). The studies collected in D.K. Richter and James H. Merrell, eds., *Beyond the Covenant Chain: The Iroquois and Their Neighbors in Indian North America, 1600–1800* (Syracuse, NY: Syracuse University Press 1987), shift the focus away from the colonies and toward the Indian nations. In the same vein, Leroy V. Eid, 'The Ojibwa-Iroquois War: The War the Five Nations Did Not Win,' *Ethnohistory* 26/4 (Fall 1979): 297–324, draws attention to a conflict that colonial officials scarcely noticed. J.A. Dickinson examines the demographic consequences for the colony of the early Iroquois attacks in 'La guerre iroquoise et la mortalité en Nouvelle-France, 1608–1666,' *RHAF* 36/1 (juin 1982): 31–54. The peace of 1701 is seen as a diplomatic event but also as a ceremony in Gilles Havard, *La grande paix de Montréal de 1701: les voies de la diplomatie franco-amérindienne* (M: Recherches amérindiennes au Québec 1992). On the Franco-Native alliance see K.M. Morrison, *The Embattled Northeast: The Elusive Ideal of Alliance in Abenaki-Euramerican Relations* (Berkeley and Los Angeles, CA: University of California Press 1984); Colin G. Calloway, *The Western Abenakis of Vermont, 1600–1800: War, Migration, and the Survival of an Indian People* (Norman, OK: University of Oklahoma Press 1990); Peter S. Schmalz, *The Ojibwa of Southern Ontario* (T: UTP 1991); and R. White, *The Middle Ground*. C.J. Jaenen discusses sovereignty in a 1986 article, 'French Sovereignty and Native Nationhood during the French Régime,' most accessible in J.R. Miller, ed., *Sweet Promises*.

For an overview of colonial wars see Ian K. Steele, *Guerillas and Grenadiers: The Struggle for Canada, 1689–1760* (T: RP 1969). On the French side, J.S. Pritchard, *Louis XV's Navy, 1748–1762: A Study of Organization and Administration* (K&M: MQUP 1987), helps explain the difficulties of defending Canada. The fortifications of the colonial towns are well studied in A. Charbonneau, Y. Desloges, and M. Lafrance, *Quebec, the Fortified City: From the 17th to the 19th Century* (O: Parks Canada 1982), and in the catalogue, edited by Phyllis Lambert and Alan Stewart, of a memorable exhibition, *Montréal, ville fortifiée au XVIIIe siècle* (M: Canadian Centre for Architecture 1992).

The final wars have received much attention in the older surveys, as well as from W.J. Eccles, who in reaction notably to C.P. Stacey, *Quebec, 1759: The Siege and the Battle* (T: MAC 1959), criticizes the generalship of both sides in 'The Battle of Quebec: A Reappraisal,' first published in 1978 and most accessible in his *Essays on New France* (T: OUP 1987). He has, with Susan L. Laskin, mapped the military operations of the Conquest in 'The Seven Years' War' and 'The Battles for Québec, 1759 and 1760,' *HAC*, vol. 1, plates 42 and 43. The standard work on military organization is Lee Kennett, *The French Armies in the Seven Years' War: A Study in Military Organization and Administration* (Durham, NC: Duke University Press 1967), but see also W.J. Eccles, 'The French Forces in North America during the Seven Years' War, *DCB*, vol. 3 (T: UTP 1974). Relations between colonial and French officers are the subject of D.P. MacLeod, 'The Canadians against the French: The Struggle for Control of the Expedition to Oswego in 1756,' *OH* 80/2 (June 1988): 143–57, and Martin L. Nicolai, 'A Different Kind of Courage: The French Military and the Canadian Irregular Soldier during the Seven Years' War,' *CHR* 70/1 (Mar. 1989): 53–75. On the effects of the Seven Years' War on the civilian population, John Knox is not always accurate but sometimes eloquent in *An Historical Journal of the Campaigns in North America for the Years 1757, 1758, 1759, and 1760*, ed. A.G. Doughty, 3 vols. (T: CS 1914–16).

The view from the Anglo-American side is covered in several works. Overall strategy is examined in Richard Middleton, *The Bells of Victory: The Pitt-Newcastle Ministry and the Conduct of the Seven Years' War, 1757–1762* (Cambridge, Eng.: Cambridge University Press 1985), while the armies are the subject of Douglas E. Leach, *Roots of Conflict: British Armed Forces and Colonial Americans, 1677–1763* (Chapel Hill, NC: University of North Carolina Press 1986), and C.P. Stacey, 'The British Forces in North America during the Seven Years' War,' *DCB*, vol. 3. Fred Anderson studies the Massachusetts militia in *A People's Army: Massachusetts Soldiers and Society in the Seven Years' War* (Chapel Hill, NC: University of North Carolina Press 1984). Finally, Richard I. Melvoin, *New England Outpost: War and Society in Colonial Deerfield* (NY: Norton 1989), and Harold E. Selesky, *War and Society in Colonial Connecticut* (New Haven, CT: Yale University Press 1990), describe the effects of Canadian-Native raids on neighbouring colonies.

CONCLUSION

Research on the French regime has deepened and broadened in recent years to include hitherto-neglected groups, notably the region's Native peoples. At the moment, our view of the first phase of colonial development is long on aspects and short on overarching themes. One hopes that a new synthesis will eventually strike a balance between the interconnections and the separateness of colonial and Native history. Meanwhile, as an essential first step, the civilization has become a period ... *pas comme les autres*, to be sure, but a period all the same.

BARRY MOODY

Acadia and Old Nova Scotia to 1784

During the past twenty years there has been a renaissance in interest in the history of the Maritime provinces before 1784. Historians have re-examined some of the old issues and arrived at exciting new conclusions, while some previously unexplored topics have begun to receive the attention that they deserve. New approaches to the past have also been tried, with archaeologists and those interested in material culture shedding new light on this period.

Beginnings have been made toward a better understanding of the history of the Native peoples, as well as their relations with the incoming Europeans. Interest in, and understanding of, the French settlers of the region – the Acadians – has continued and deepened, with the focus shifting from the expulsion of 1755 to the life of the Acadians both before and after that tragic event. The scholarly activity spawned by the reconstruction of Fortress Louisbourg has added immeasurably to our knowledge of eighteenth-century life and has set exacting standards for others to follow. The English-speaking settlers who followed the Acadians have also attracted much attention, with the interest focusing first on the religious revival of the 1770s, and more recently on the many aspects of life in Nova Scotia immediately before and during the American Revolution.

The researcher who wishes to explore this rich period will thus find many excellent aids to assist the inquirer, but there is also the challenge of many unanswered questions and unexplored areas.

BIBLIOGRAPHIES AND REFERENCE WORKS

A number of bibliographies are available to help students through the maze of books and articles, old and new, that are waiting to be perused. For the

Acadians, *Index général des sources documentaires sur les Acadiens*, 3 vols. (Moncton, NB: Les éditions d'Acadie 1975–6), is now somewhat dated but still very helpful. It should be supplemented by Claude Potvin, comp., 'Recent Acadiana: An Annotated List,' *APLA [Atlantic Provinces Library Association] Bulletin* 46 (Sept. 1982): 18–20; 47 (Jan. 1983): 39–41; and Hélène Harbec, ed., *Guide bibliographique de l'Acadie, 1976–1987* (Moncton, NB: Centre d'études acadiennes 1988). Glenn E. Conrad and Carl A. Brasseaux, *A Selected Bibliography of Scholarly Literature on Colonial Louisiana and New France* (Lafayette, LA: Center for Louisiana Studies, University of Southwestern Louisiana 1982), is useful in following those Acadians who eventually make their way to what is now the southern United States.

For the period after 1755 the best single bibliographic source is *A Checklist of Secondary Sources for Planter Studies*, compiled by Daniel C. Goodwin and Steven Bligh McNutt ([Wolfville, NS]: Planter Studies Committee, Acadia University 1990). This publication focuses on books, articles, and theses dealing specifically with the New England settlement of the Maritime region, but it also includes works on other settlement groups in the last half of the eighteenth century. *Baptists in Canada, 1760–1990: A Bibliography of Selected Printed Resources in English*, prepared by Philip G.A. Griffin-Allwood, George A. Rawlyk, and Jarold K. Zeman (Hantsport, NS: Lancelot 1989), is useful in identifying sources for the early New Light and Baptist movements. Shirley B. Elliott, comp., 'Travel in the Maritime Provinces, 1750–1867: A Bibliography,' *APLA Bulletin* 46 (May 1983): 70–1, provides information on a more specialized subject.

Our understanding of the seventeenth- and eighteenth-century Maritimes would be much the poorer were it not for the impressive *Dictionary of Canadian Biography* (T: UTP 1966–). There is virtually no subject in the history of this period that can be approached adequately without reference to this crucial series. The well-researched and well-written biographies of the important and not-so-important men and women of this period are arranged by volume according to date of death. For example, those who died before the close of 1700 are found in volume 1. The biographies relevant for the study of the period before 1784 are thus in the first seven volumes. A useful bibliography is included at the end of each entry.

PERIODICALS

Unquestionably the best journal on the Atlantic region is *Acadiensis* (1971–), published by the University of New Brunswick. Its articles and review essays are invariably first-rate, although the bulk of the articles to date have dealt with the nineteenth and twentieth centuries. An index to the first twenty volumes, *The Acadiensis Index, 1971–1991* (F: AP 1992), is available. Two collections of pre-Confederation articles drawn from the journal have been published, which contain some articles relevant to Acadia and early Nova Scotia: Phillip A. Buckner and David Frank, eds., *The Acadiensis Reader*, vol. 1, *Atlantic Canada before Confederation* (F: AP 1985; 2nd ed., 1990). Since the spring 1975 issue, *Acadiensis* has provided an invaluable service to its readers by including in most issues a section entitled 'Recent Publications Relating to the Atlantic Provinces.' This convenient list, arranged by province and, further, by author, allows a researcher to discover easily what has been published recently on any given topic.

The *Nova Scotia Historical Review* (1981–) publishes a number of articles of interest for the period under consideration, although in general they tend to be somewhat less scholarly than those appearing in *Acadiensis*. The same comments hold true for the *Island Magazine* (1976–), published by the Prince Edward Island Museum and Heritage Foundation. *Cahiers*, published by La Société historique acadienne, has since its beginnings in 1961 frequently contained helpful articles on the Acadian experience; most appear in French. Journals published elsewhere in Canada, such as the *Canadian Historical Review* (1920–), *Histoire sociale/Social History* (1968–), and *Journal of Canadian Studies* (1966–), only infrequently contain articles on this early period of Maritime history. Each issue of the *CHR* does, however, include a section entitled 'Recent Publications Relating to Canada.'

The Nova Scotia Historical Society, *Collections*, which appears irregularly, often contains articles of interest and considerable scholarly merit. The Department of the Environment, Canadian Parks Service, publishes two very useful series. The first, History and Archaeology, usually contains reports on basic research, especially archaeological, and is often narrowly focused with little emphasis on the work's broader application. The second, Canadian Historic Sites: Occasional Papers in Archaeology and History, is a forum for monographs by Parks researchers, which usually deal with one or more of Canada's National Historic Parks.

In 1979 a series of monographs and document reprints, entitled the Baptist Heritage in Atlantic Canada, was launched under the sponsorship of Acadia Divinity College and the Baptist Historical Committee based in Wolfville, Nova Scotia. The resulting volumes make available to the researcher a number of the documents necessary for an understanding of Nova Scotia's early Protestant religious history. Acadia University also provides a home for the Planter Studies Committee, which recently commenced a series of its own. Thus far two significant volumes have been published, each containing some of the papers given at conferences focusing on the Planters, the six to seven thousand New Englanders who settled many parts of Nova Scotia and New Brunswick in the 1760s. Specific articles in *They Planted Well: New England Planters in Maritime Canada* (F: AP 1988) and *Making Adjustments: Change and Continuity in Planter Nova Scotia, 1759–1800* (F: AP 1991), both edited by Margaret Conrad, will be referred to in the thematic sections later in the chapter.

GENERAL WORKS

In spite of the work already done on this period, we still lack a comprehensive survey of the Maritime provinces either collectively or individually. W.S. MacNutt, *The Atlantic Provinces: The Emergence of Colonial Society, 1712–1857* (T: M&S 1965), serves well for part of the period under consideration, although it is now somewhat dated, especially for the Planter and Revolutionary sections. John Bartlet Brebner, *New England's Outpost: Acadia before the Conquest of Canada* (NY: Columbia University Press 1927), and G.A. Rawlyk, *Nova Scotia's Massachusetts: A Study of Massachusetts–Nova Scotia Relations, 1630 to 1784* (M: MQUP 1973), provide overviews, but both present the area's history largely in terms of its relationship with the nearby colony of Massachusetts. Andrew Hill Clark, *Acadia: The Geography of Early Nova Scotia to 1760* (Madison, WI: University of Wisconsin Press 1968), is of great value in understanding the period, but as the title suggests, the author is concerned with the geographic and demographic changes in Acadia. The same approach was taken by the author in his *Three Centuries and the Island: A Historical Geography of Settlement and Agriculture in Prince Edward Island, Canada* (T: UTP 1959), the first part of which is useful for an understanding of the early history of Prince Edward Island. George MacBeath's introductory essay to the first volume of the *DCB* (1966), 'The Atlantic Region,' is brief but helpful.

Older surveys of Maritime history are of limited use, providing some good factual material but being very weak on the interpretive side. The work by John G. Leefe and Peter McCreath, *A History of Early Nova Scotia* (Tantallon, NS: Four East Publications 1982), is more recent but is largely a narrative of the main events of the period.

EARLY EUROPEAN SETTLEMENT

Surprisingly little that is really useful has been written about the period of early European settlement in the Maritime region. The life of the first permanent settlement, that at Port Royal in 1605–13, is the subject of a very good study by Elizabeth Jones, *Gentlemen and Jesuits: Quests for Glory and Adventure in the Early Days of New France* (T: UTP 1986). While focusing on the conflict between the colony's founders and the Jesuit Order, the rest of the life at the settlement is also brought under close scrutiny. The best short analysis of the significance of the first decade of the seventeenth century is John G. Reid, 'The 1600s: Decade of Colonization,' in his *Six Crucial Decades: Times of Change in the History of the Maritimes* (H: Nimbus 1987), reprinted in J.M. Bumsted, ed., *Interpreting Canada's Past*, vol. 1, *Pre-Confederation* (2nd ed., T: OUP 1993). The author argues that the real power was held by the Native peoples and that it was they who determined the direction of events by tolerating and offering support for the newly arrived Europeans. Reid's *Acadia, Maine, and New Scotland: Marginal Colonies in the Seventeenth Century* (T: UTP 1981) is the most important longer study of settlement in seventeenth-century Acadia/Nova Scotia. He does an excellent job in examining the colonizing activities of France, England, and Scotland, and is one of the few historians to use a richly comparative approach in dealing with the region. In 'European Expectations of Acadia and the Bermudas, 1603–1624,' *HS/SH* 20/40 (Nov. 1987): 319–35, Reid extends his comparative approach to include the Islands of Bermuda. In *1492 and All That: Making a Garden out of a Wilderness* (T: Robarts Centre for Canadian Studies, York University 1993), Ramsay Cook explores the important distinctions Europeans made between 'garden' and 'wilderness,' 'civilization' and 'savagery,' as they encountered Acadia and its inhabitants.

Much can be learned about the first few decades of European settlement in the Maritimes by examining the lives of individuals involved in the process. The early chapters of Morris Bishop, *Champlain: The Life of Fortitude* (NY: Knopf 1948; repr. T: M&S 1963), and Joe C.W. Armstrong, *Champlain* (T: MAC 1987), focus on the Port Royal experiment. Important insights are given into the reasons for the settlement and the character of its principal founder. Armstrong's book is particularly useful for its wonderful maps.

A good understanding of this early period can be gained only by reference to the *DCB*. First-volume entries 'Jean de Biencourt de Poutrincourt et de Saint-Just,' 'Samuel de Champlain,' 'Pierre Du Gua de Monts,' and 'François Gravé du Pont' shed much light on the founding of French settlements in Acadia/Nova Scotia. The entry 'Sir Samuel Argall' gives a brief glimpse of the man responsible for the temporary destruction of the French presence there.

The first volume of the *DCB* also contains 'Marc Lescarbot,' a biography of the poet and playwright who laid the foundation of Maritime literature during his brief sojourn at Port Royal. For a discussion of his play see Hannah Fournier, 'Lescarbot's "Théâtre de Neptune": New World Pageant, Old World Polemic,' *Canadian Drama* 7/1 (Spring 1981): 3–11, and Eugene Benson, 'Marc Lescarbot and "The Theatre of Neptune,"' *Canadian Drama* 8/1 (Spring 1982): 84–5.

Many of the most important documents of this early period of settlement have been reprinted in translation. Samuel de Champlain, *Works*, gen. ed. Henry Percival Biggar, 6 vols. (T: CS 1922–36); Marc Lescarbot, *The History of New France*, ed. William Lawson Grant, 3 vols. (T: CS 1907–14); Nicolas Denys, *The Description and Natural History of the Coasts of North America (Acadia)*, ed. William Francis Ganong (T: CS 1908); and the relevant sections of the first three volumes of Reuben Gold Thwaites, ed., *The Jesuit Relations and Allied Documents*, 73 vols. (Cleveland, OH: Burrows 1896–1901), make fascinating and rewarding reading.

The brief but interesting activities of the Scots in Nova Scotia in the 1620s and 1630s have attracted little scholarly interest as yet. David S. Macmillan, 'Scottish Enterprise and Influence in Canada, 1620–1900,' in R.A. Cage, ed., *The Scots Abroad: Labour, Capital, Enterprise, 1750–1914* (L: Croom Helm 1985), gives a brief overview. The work of J.G. Reid is the most significant for this topic. His articles 'Styles of Colonisation and Social Disorders in Early Acadia and Maine: A Comparative Approach,' *Cahiers* 7/3 (sept. 1976): 106–17, reprinted in J.M. Bumsted, ed., *Interpreting Canada's Past*, vol. 1, *Before Confederation* ([1st ed.], T: OUP 1986), and 'The Scots Crown and the Restitution of Port Royal, 1629–1632,' *Acadiensis* 6/2 (Spring 1977): 39–63, contain a number of the insights that are developed to a greater extent in his longer study *Acadia, Maine, and New Scotland*. An article by Naomi E.S. Griffiths and J.G. Reid, 'New Evidence on New Scotland, 1629,' *WMQ* 3rd ser., 49/3 (July 1992): 492–508, provides the reader with a recently discovered document that forces a reassessment of some aspects of the Scottish presence in Nova Scotia. The biographies 'Sir William Alexander' and 'Sir William Alexander the younger' in the *DCB*, vol. 1, give useful views of the characters of the men primarily responsible for the Scottish colonizing efforts. The tangled web of claims to Acadia/Nova Scotia resulting from the brief Scottish occupation can be partially followed by reference to the biographies 'William Crowne' and 'Sir Thomas Temple' in the same source.

EVOLUTION AND GROWTH OF THE ACADIANS

The best work on the Acadians before the expulsion is unquestionably that by N.E.S. Griffiths. Although lamentably short, her book *The Acadians: Creation of a People* (T: MHR 1973) is still the best single source on the topic. It provides an important overview of their development from the founding of the colony to the end of the eighteenth century, with a few comments on the later period. A shorter account by Griffiths, 'The Acadians,' is to be found as an introductory essay to the *DCB*, vol. 4 (1979). Her more recent work, *The Contexts of Acadian History, 1686–1784* (K&M: MQUP 1992), sets the French settlement of Acadia and the evolution of the Acadians in the proper European and North American framework and is essential reading for an understanding of this period.

Jean Daigle, 'Acadia, 1604-1763: An Historical Synthesis,' in Daigle, ed., *The Acadians of the Maritimes: Thematic Studies* (Moncton, NB: Centre d'études acadiennes 1982), provides a useful survey of the period. Joan Dawson, 'Colonists or Birds of Passage? A Glimpse of the Inhabitants of LaHave, 1632–1636,' *NSHR* 9/1 (June 1989): 42–61, examines the short-lived French settlement on Acadie's south shore. Brenda Dunn, *The Acadians of Minas* (O: Parks Canada 1985; repr. 1990), looks at the settlers of the best-known Acadian community.

On the topics of demography and settlement patterns, Gisa I. Hynes, 'Some Aspects of the Demography of Port Royal, 1650–1755,' *Acadiensis* 3/1 (Autumn 1973): 3–17, is a provocative overall analysis. More basic information can be found in a number of sources. The first part of Muriel K. Roy's article 'Settlement and Population Growth in Acadia,' in J. Daigle, ed., *The Acadians of the Maritimes*, is a good place to start, for it provides much useful information and a number of graphs and tables. Still, A.H. Clark's older *Acadia* remains essential reading for this topic, filled as it is with valuable statistics well-situated within a sound historical framework. Students can also now turn to the *Historical Atlas of Canada*, vol. 1, *From the Beginning to 1800*, ed. R. Cole Harris (T: UTP [1987]). Of particular interest are plates 29, 'Acadian Marshland Settlement,' and 30, 'Acadian Deportation and Return.' The first graphically shows the expansion of the Acadian community and the utilization of low-lying marshlands, which became a hallmark of the Acadian form of settlement. The second plots the location of Acadian settlements and their approximate sizes in 1750 and thus provides the necessary data for a proper understanding of the expulsion. Finally, students should also be aware that beginning in 1963 the surviving church records of the Acadian period have appeared in printed form, and contain much useful information about marriage, birth, and death patterns in Acadia. See David M. Rieder and Norma Gaudet Rieder, eds., *Acadian Church Records*, vols. 1–5 (Mobile, AL, and Metairie, LA: 1963–83).

For an understanding of the period of virtual civil war in Acadia in the mid-seventeenth century see M.A. MacDonald, *Fortune & La Tour: The Civil War in Acadia* (T: Methuen 1983). It should be supplemented by the relevant sections of J.B. Brebner, *New England's Outpost*, and G.A. Rawlyk, *Nova Scotia's Massachusetts*. For excellent analyses of the lives of the major protagonists in this quarrel consult entries in the *DCB*, vol. 1, including 'Françoise-Marie Jacqueline,' 'Charles de Menou d'Aulnay,' 'Jeanne Motin,' and 'Charles de Saint-Etienne de La Tour.' In examining this conflict one should be careful to avoid the romantic and sentimental tales that have been woven around it over the centuries.

The confusion over rival French claims to the region was complicated during this first century of settlement by several successful attacks by the English/New Englanders. The *DCB* entries 'Robert Sedgwick' and 'Sir William Phips,' vol. 1, and French governor 'Louis-Alexandre Des Friches de Meneval,' vol. 2 (1969), among others, provide useful insights into the ongoing struggle for control of the colony. Even the Dutch were active for a brief time in attempts to capture the region, as the entries 'Jurriaen Aernoutsz' and 'John Rhoades,' vol. 1, reveal.

More specialized studies of aspects of the Acadian experience are beginning to appear, which greatly broaden our understanding of this period and these people. J.G. Reid, for example, examines the position of Acadia vis-à-vis the larger French colony of the period in 'Acadia and the Acadians: In the Shadow of Quebec,' *The Beaver* 67/5 (Oct.–Nov. 1987): 26–31. Rose Mary Babitch brings the training of a linguist to bear on the topic in 'The English of Acadians in the Seventeenth Century,' Atlantic Provinces Linguistic Association, *Papers* (1981): 96–115. In spite of the importance of the family in Acadian life, little has been written as yet on the subject. J. Alphonse Deveau, 'Quelques aspects de la famille en Acadie de 1670 à 1714,' *Revue de l'Université Sainte-Anne* (1981): 3–11, is a start, and N.E.S. Griffiths, 'Mating and Marriage in Early Acadia,' *Renaissance and Modern Studies* 35 (1992): 109–27, raises provocative new questions about the Acadian family, but there is obviously much that remains to be done. Deveau's 'L'architecture acadienne avant l'expulsion,' *Revue de l'Université Sainte-Anne* (1982): 40–3, is a beginning in the re-evaluation of Acadian housing, but it has been largely superseded by the reports (discussed later in the chapter) of archaeologists working in the 1980s at Acadian sites. Jeanne Arseneault, 'Le costume traditionnel français en Acadie,' in René Bouchard, ed., *La vie quotidienne au Québec: histoire, métiers, techniques et traditions* (Sillery, Que.: PUQ 1983), adds to our meagre understanding of the daily lives of the Acadians. In general we are lacking studies of specific Acadian communities. An exception is Joan Bourque Campbell, 'The Acadian Seigneury of St-Mathieu at Cobequid,' *NSHR* 9/2 (Dec. 1989): 74–88.

The relationship between Acadia and New England has been thoroughly explored by several historians. J.B. Brebner, *New England's Outpost*, and G.A. Rawlyk, *Nova Scotia's Massachusetts*, both see New England's domination of the region as the crucial factor in the evolution of the colony of Acadia/Nova Scotia, although they differ somewhat in their analyses. Both, however, tend to view Acadian society from the outside in, and from the top down, rather than focusing on the internal developments of the ordinary people of the colony.

The major breakthrough in understanding the Acadians has taken place in the past ten years not as the result of delving in the archives but rather by digging in the ground. For the first time archaeologists have looked seriously at the life of Acadians in the seventeenth and eighteenth centuries. The results have forced a major re-evaluation of the culture of these French settlers, and have posed as yet unanswered questions about the evolution of this people and their ongoing relationships to both the French and the English governments.

Archaeological work at military and domestic sites throughout Acadia reveals the richness of the material culture of the inhabitants and tells us much about the way of life and trading patterns in the region. Much of the following material is in the form of reports by the archaeologists involved in the excavations; in some cases the results of a summer's work are merely reported, while in others the significance of the finds is analysed and interpreted. Alaric Faulkner, 'Maintenance and Fabrication at Fort Pentagoet, 1634–1654: Products of an Acadian Armorer's Workshop,' *Historical Archaeology* 20/1 (1986): 63–94, gives an interesting insight into the workings of an important profession in the military life of Acadia, and, with Gretchen Faulkner, his *The French at Pentagoet, 1635–1674: An Archaeological Portrait of the Acadian Frontier* (Augusta, ME: Maine Historic Preservation Commission 1987) is a fine report on a part of Acadia that is now in the state of Maine. Jeanne Alyluia, *Eighteenth-Century Container Glass from the Roma Site, Prince Edward Island* (O: Parks Canada 1981), and Denise Hansen, *Seventeenth-Century Ceramics from Nicholas Denys' Fort Saint Pierre, St. Peter's, Nova Scotia* (O: Canadian Parks Service 1989), illustrate the richness of the material waiting to be found, and reveal a far more complex way of life at trading post and fort than previously realized. The way in which the material provided by the archaeologist can be used to expand our knowledge of life in seventeenth- and eighteenth-century Acadia is shown in Jean-François Blanchette's important study *The Role of Artifacts in the*

Study of Foodways in New France, 1720–60 (O: Parks Canada 1981), which deals with the Roma site in Prince Edward Island.

Although these volumes provide insights into the milieu in which the Acadians themselves evolved, the excavations in specifically Acadian village sites have removed all doubt as to the extent that the Acadians themselves were influenced by the material culture around them. The reports of archaeologist David J. Christianson on the results of excavations at Belleisle, Nova Scotia, in the early 1980s, *Belleisle, 1983: Excavations at a Pre-Expulsion Acadian Site* (H: Nova Scotia Museum 1984), and 'Acadian Archaeological Research at Belleisle, Nova Scotia,' Nova Scotia Museum, *The Occasional* 8/3 (Spring 1984): 16–21, conclusively destroyed the myth of the Acadians as a poverty-stricken peasantry. His work was re-enforced and amplified by that carried out by Parks Canada archaeologists at the Melanson site at Port Royal, Nova Scotia. In *The Melanson Settlement: An Acadian Farming Community (ca. 1664–1755)* (O: Environment Canada Parks 1986), archaeologist Andrée Crepeau and historian B. Dunn do an excellent job of interpreting Acadian life on the basis of the evidence that both the ground and the archives have yielded. It is the most complete picture yet produced of life in a small Acadian community.

One of the most profitable ways the average student of history can examine the Acadians is by looking at the lives of individuals. For this, the first three volumes of the *DCB* are indispensable. French fur traders and colonizers, governors and rogues, settlers, soldiers, and priests, and many more have found their way into the pages of this important work. In volume 1 are biographies of the seigneur 'Alexandre Le Borgne de Belle-Isle,' and settler 'Charles Melanson.' Chronicled in volume 2 are the lives of 'Guillaume Blanchard,' early settler on the Petticodiac River; 'Jacques Bourgeois,' surgeon and founder of Beaubassin; and 'Pierre Maisonnat *dit* Baptiste,' shipmaster and privateer, among a host of others. The women of Acadia have not been well served by historians, but something can be learned by an examination of these entries in the *DCB*: 'Madame de Brice,' vol. 1, an early teacher in Acadia; 'Francoise-Marie Jacquelin,' vol. 1, long a heroine of early Acadia; 'Agathe de Saint-Etienne de La Tour,' vol. 2, a shrewd woman of business; and 'Marie-Madelaine Maisonnat' (Madame Winniett), vol. 3 (1974), another person who forcefully took her future into her own hands.

The role of the Roman Catholic Church in the lives of the Acadians has not as yet been the subject of extensive historical research. J. Brian Hanington, *Every Popish Person: The Story of Roman Catholicism in Nova Scotia and the Church of Halifax, 1604–1984* (H: Archdiocese of Halifax 1984), gives a brief summary of developments during this early period. Cornelius J. Jaenen, *The Role of the Church in New France* (T: MHR 1976), while focusing mainly on Quebec, is still useful for understanding the church in Acadia. Luca Codignola, 'Rome and North America: The Interpretive Framework,' *Rivista Storia Nord Americana* 1/1 (1984): 5–33, as the title suggests, provides the broad context within which the work in Acadia must be seen. For more specific information on the church in Acadia, once again the *DCB* comes to the rescue, providing much-needed information on the early priests to the Acadians. See, for example, the short but insightful entries on these little-known figures: 'Louis-Pierre Thury,' vol. 1; 'Louis Geoffroy' and 'Louis Petit,' vol. 2; and 'Justinien Durand' and 'Jean-Baptiste de Gay Desenclaves,' vol. 3. For a survey of the work being done on this topic see Fernand Arsenault, 'L'Eglise catholique en Acadie: état de la recherche,' *Revue de l'Université de Moncton* 15/1 (janv.–mars 1982): 105–17.

Material is much more readily available on the Catholic missions to the Native peoples of the Maritime region. E. Vaucheret, 'Marc Lescarbot et la conversion des Indiens d'Acadie au début du XVIIe siècle,' *Etudes canadiennes/Canadian Studies* 13 (1982): 173–88, looks at the beginnings of the attempts to convert the Native peoples to Christianity. Katherine J. Brooks, 'The Effect of the Catholic Missionaries on the Micmac Indians of Nova Scotia, 1610–1986,' *NSHR* 6/1 (June 1986): 107–15, deals with the results of the efforts at conversion over a long period of time, while Helen Ralston, 'Religion, Public Policy and the Education of Micmac Indians of Nova Scotia, 1605–1872,' *Canadian Review of Sociology and Anthropology* 18/4 (Nov. 1981): 470–98, examines a specific aspect of the church's role among the Native peoples. The first part of John Webster Grant, *Moon of Wintertime: Missionaries and the Indians of Canada in Encounter since 1534* (T: UTP 1984), sheds light on the situation in both Acadia and Canada during this formative period.

The most controversial, and colourful, missionary to the Micmac was Jean-Louis Le Loutre. Norman McLeod Rogers, 'The Abbé Le Loutre,' *CHR* 11/2 (June 1930): 105–28, is still the best single source for an understanding of this complex individual, as well as the hard choices facing French Roman Catholic priests in a British Protestant colony. It should be supplemented by the entry 'Jean-Louis Le Loutre,' *DCB*, vol. 4. Gérard Finn, 'Jean-Louis Le Loutre vu par les historiens,' *Cahiers* 8/3 (sept. 1977): 108–47, reviews the way in which historians have presented this controversial character. The *DCB* should also be consulted for studies of other priests who, while less well known than Le Loutre, were probably more important in the conversion process. See, among others, 'Antoine Gaulin' and 'Sébastien Rale,' vol. 2; 'Charles de La Goudalie,' 'Félix Pain,' and especially 'Pierre Maillard,' vol. 3; and 'Jean-Pierre de Miniac,' vol. 4.

A surprising amount of work has been done in recent years on the mapping of the Maritime region in the colonial period. We now know much more than ever before about how the region was perceived, and what the early settlers actually knew about the colonies they were to occupy. Much of the useful work of exploring and analysing the early maps of Acadia/Nova Scotia has been done by J. Dawson. Her *The Mapmaker's Eye: Nova Scotia through Early Maps* (H: Nimbus 1988) looks at cartography in the Maritime region and is filled with marvellous coloured illustrations. More specialized are her articles 'The Mapping of LaHave and Lunenburg, 1604–1754,' Nova Scotia Museum, *The Occasional* 8/3 (Spring 1984): 8–15; 'L'Acadie en 1632: la carte d'Isaac de Razilly,' *Cahiers* 15/4 (déc. 1984): 127–37; 'Putting Acadia on the Map: The "Transitional" Cartography of Nova Scotia, 1600–1755,' *Cartographica* 22/2 (Summer 1985): 79–91; and 'Beyond the Bastions: French Mapping of Cape Breton Island, 1713–1758,' *NSHR* 10/2 (Dec. 1990): 6–30. Conrad E. Heidenreich and Edward H. Dahl, in 'The French Mapping of North America, 1700–1760,' *The Map Collector* 19 (June 1982): 2–7, provide a somewhat broader perspective, expanded in their book *The French Mapping of North America, 1600–1760* (Berkhampstead, Eng.: Map Collector 1982).

ILE SAINT-JEAN (PRINCE EDWARD ISLAND)

Because of the comparatively late settlement of the island by Europeans, and the very limited numbers of settlers during the time under consideration, little has been written about the early history of this region of the Maritimes. A.H. Clark, *Three Centuries and the Island*, is the best place to begin in attempting to understand the island during this period. Nicolas de Jong, 'The French Regime, 1534–1758,' in Francis W.P. Bolger, ed., *Canada's Smallest Province: A History of P.E.I.* (CH: Prince Edward Island 1973 Centennial Commission 1973), supplies a quick introduction to the period. Daniel Cobb Harvey's much older *The French Régime in Prince Edward Island* (New Haven, CT: Yale University Press 1926; repr. NY: AMS Press 1970) is still valuable. Several studies have been done of the beginnings of Acadian settlement on the island, although all leave something to be desired. J.-Henri Blanchard, *The Acadians of Prince Edward Island, 1720–1964* (CH: Blanchard 1964; repr. 1976), and two works by Georges

Arsenault, 'The Acadian Experience in Prince Edward Island,' *Cahiers* 14/2 (juin 1983): 59–72, and *The Island Acadians, 1720–1980* (CH: Ragweed 1989), can be examined with profit.

Few early-eighteenth-century island figures have found their way into the *DCB*, but those who have are well worth looking at for the light their lives shed on this rather misty period. The first parish priest for the island, 'René-Charles Breslay,' military officers 'Jacques d'Espiet de Pensens' and 'Robert-David Gotteville de Belile,' vol. 2, and 'Claude-Elisabeth Denys de Bonnaventure,' vol. 3, colonizer 'Jean-Pierre Roma,' vol. 3, and settler 'Michel Haché-Gallant,' vol. 2, all played their roles in the attempts to create a French colony on the island in the first half of that tumultuous century.

LOUISBOURG

Few areas in Canadian colonial history have witnessed as dramatic a rise in interest and scholarly activity as has Louisbourg. The decision by the federal government in the early 1960s to reconstruct the French fortress in Cape Breton has led to an outpouring of reports, articles, and books on a vast array of subjects. The rich documentary sources available, added to the information obtained by extensive archaeological work, have made possible the reconstruction not merely of part of the physical fortress itself – fortifications, houses, barracks, and so forth – but also of the way of life of the period, often down to the smallest of details. No other colonial community in Canada, and few in North America, has been subject to such close scrutiny. The work carried out by Canadian Parks Service has immeasurably enriched our understanding of life in North America in the first half of the eighteenth century. The student of this topic is provided with an exciting variety of subjects and approaches, more so than for any other single area of Canadian history.

J.S. McLennan, *Louisbourg: From Its Foundation to Its Fall, 1713–1758* (L: MAC 1918; 3rd ed., Sydney, NS: Fortress Press 1969), although an early account, is still the best introduction to the history of the fortress and is a good starting-place for understanding Louisbourg's evolution. The popularized account by Fairfax Downey, *Louisbourg: Key to a Continent* (Englewood Cliffs, NJ: PH 1965), seems readily available but has been completely superseded by later work and should be avoided. Similarly, John Fortier and Owen Fitzgerald's *Fortress of Louisbourg* (T: OUP 1979) is designed for the general reader and should be used with caution. *Canada: An Historical Magazine* 1/4 (June 1974) devoted an entire issue to Louisbourg, which contains general articles on its reconstruction, buildings, economy, and social life. Terry A. Crowley, *Louisbourg: Atlantic Fortress and Seaport*, CHA Historical Booklet no. 48 (O: 1990), provides a brief but succinct overview. A good assessment of the literature published before 1981 is to be found in the same author's 'Monuments to Empire: Atlantic Forts and Fortifications,' *Acadiensis* 10/2 (Spring 1981): 167–72.

Terry MacLean, 'Historical Research at Louisbourg: A Case Study in Museum Research and Development,' in Kenneth Donovan, ed., *Cape Breton at 200: Historical Essays in Honour of the Island's Bicentennial, 1785–1985* (Sydney, NS: University College of Cape Breton Press 1985), focuses on the approaches used and the problems encountered in exploring the history of this vast fortress. A number of articles and reports are available on the archaeological work which has been such an essential aspect of reconstructing the buildings and social life of this community. While these reports are often fairly technical, much can be learned about the fortress by their examination. Edward McM. Larrabee, 'Archaeological Research at the Fortress of Louisbourg, 1961–1965,' *Canadian Historic Sites: Occasional Papers in Archaeology and History*, no. 2 (1971): 8–43, looks at the beginnings of modern archaeological work at Louisbourg. In the same volume is a shorter article by Bruce W. Fry, 'A Rescue Excavation at the Princess Half-Bastion, Fortress of Louisbourg' (pp. 46–54), which deals with a specific structure. In no. 12 (1975) of the same series, Charles S. Lindsay, 'Louisbourg Guardhouses' (pp. 47–100), shows how historical research, archaeological investigation, and examination of eighteenth-century French buildings are brought together to produce an accurate reconstruction.

Studies are available on very detailed topics, but these are usually more specialized than the general student of this period will find useful. Paul McNally, *French Table Glass from the Fortress of Louisbourg, Nova Scotia* (O: Parks Canada 1979), and Kenneth James Barton, *Coarse Earthenwares from the Fortress of Louisbourg* (O: Parks Canada 1981), among others, are found in the highly technical History and Archaeology series produced by Parks Canada. Iain C. Walker, 'An Archaeological Study of Clay Pipes from the King's Bastion, Fortress of Louisbourg,' *Canadian Historic Sites: Occasional Papers in Archaeology and History*, no. 2 (1971): 55–100, is the type of specialized but often informative article published in that series, also by Parks Canada.

On the construction of the original fortress, B.W. Fry, *'An Appearance of Strength': The Fortifications of Louisbourg*, 2 vols. (O: Parks Canada 1984), looks at the myth and the reality, as well as the consequences of the gap between the two. The physical growth of Louisbourg is nicely presented in

'Ile Royale, 18th Century,' *HAC*, vol. 1, plate 24. Blaine Adams, 'The Construction and Occupation of the Barracks of the King's Bastion at Louisbourg,' *Canadian Historic Sites: Occasional Papers in Archaeology and History*, no. 18 (1978): 59–147, provides a detailed discussion of the building of the barracks and the life of the soldiers who occupied it, weaving together the material and social history with the military. The daily life of the soldier at Louisbourg is further explored by Allan Greer in *The Soldiers of Isle Royale, 1720–45* (O: Parks Canada 1979), and in his more focused study 'Mutiny at Louisbourg, December 1744,' *HS/SH* 10/20 (Nov. 1977): 305–36, reprinted in J.M. Bumsted, ed., *Interpreting Canada's Past*, vol. 1, 2nd ed. A.J.B. Johnston examines another important theme in the life of the soldier in 'The Men of the Garrison: Soldiers and Their Punishments at Louisbourg, 1751–53,' *NSHR* 10/2 (Dec. 1990): 45–62.

No understanding of the New England attack on Louisbourg in 1745 is possible without some insight into the nature and extent of trade relations binding Louisbourg and Boston. The best work on this topic is to be found in William G. Godfrey, *Pursuit of Profit and Preferment in Colonial North America: John Bradstreet's Quest* (Waterloo, Ont.: Wilfrid Laurier University Press 1982), and in his 'John Bradstreet at Louisbourg: Emergence or Re-emergence?' *Acadiensis* 4/1 (Autumn 1974): 100–20. See also Donald F. Chard, 'The Price and Profits of Accommodation: Massachusetts-Louisbourg Trade, 1713–1744,' in *Seafaring in Colonial Massachusetts* (Boston, MA: Colonial Society of Massachusetts 1980).

Of the two sieges of Louisbourg, 1745 and 1758, the former has received the bulk of the attention by historians, primarily because of the important part played by the New Englanders. G.A. Rawlyk, *Yankees at Louisbourg* (Orono, ME: University of Maine Press 1967), is still undoubtedly the best single source on the 1745 capture of the fortress. Raymond F. Baker, 'A Campaign of Amateurs: The Siege of Louisbourg, 1745,' *Canadian Historic Sites: Occasional Papers in History and Archaeology*, no. 18 (1978): 5–57, adds nothing new to our understanding of the events, but provides a reasonably good summary. J.M. Bumsted, 'Sermon Literature and the 1745 Louisbourg Campaign,' *DR* 63/2 (Summer 1983): 264–76, gives a provocative assessment of an important element of the New England background to the expedition. S.E.D. Shortt, 'Conflict and Identity in Massachusetts: The Louisbourg Expedition of 1745,' *HS/SH* 5/10 (Nov. 1972): 165–85, provides further insights into the complex situation in Massachusetts that led to the expedition. Douglas E. Leach, 'Brothers in Arms? Anglo-American Friction at Louisbourg, 1745–1746,' *Proceedings of the Massachusetts Historical Society* 89 (1977): 36–54, examines a topic of considerable significance during and immediately after the siege. Some of the New England documents dealing with the siege were reprinted in Louis Effingham DeForest, ed., *Louisbourg Journals, 1745* (NY: Society of Colonial Wars 1932). For a contemporary French account see George M. Wrong, ed., *Louisbourg in 1745: The Anonymous 'Lettre d'un habitant de Louisbourg,'* University of Toronto Studies, History, 2nd ser., vol. 1 (1897).

The commanding officer of the New England forces has been the subject of a recent biography by Neil Rolde, *Sir William Pepperrell of Colonial New England* (Brunswick, ME: Harpswell Press 1982), but Byron Fairchild's older *Messrs. William Pepperrell: Merchants at Piscataqua* (Ithaca, NY: Cornell University Press 1954) is still worth consulting. Pepperrell's French counterpart, Governor Louis Du Pont Duchambon, has not been similarly dealt with apart from a fine entry in the *DCB*, vol. 4. Indeed the third and fourth volumes of the *DCB* cover all the major and many of the minor figures involved on both sides of the conflict. In addition to the entry on Du Pont Duchambon, for instance, in volume 3 see 'Jean-Baptiste-Louis Le Prévost Duquesnel,' 'Jeremiah Moulton,' 'William Vaughan,' 'Samuel Waldo,' and 'Sir Richard Warren.' In volume 4 are to be found the biographies 'Philippe-Joseph d'Allard de Saint-Marie' and 'Jacques Prevost de La Croix.' Julian Gwyn, *The Enterprising Admiral: The Personal Fortune of Admiral Sir Peter Warren* (K&M: MQUP 1974), is a good study of the British naval officer whose assistance was vital in the capture of Louisbourg, but its focus is primarily on his financial concerns rather than his contribution to the 1745 expedition.

The 1758 siege has not fared as well at the hands of the historians, the events of that year perhaps overshadowed by the larger conflict that raged in North America and the dramatic fall of Quebec the following year. Michel Wyczynski, 'The Expedition of the Second Battalion of the Combis Regiment to Louisbourg, 1758,' *NSHR* 10/2 (Dec. 1990): 95–110, is one of the few detailed examinations of an aspect of that siege. J. Gwyn, 'French and British Naval Power at the Two Sieges of Louisbourg: 1745 and 1758,' *NSHR* 10/2 (Dec. 1990): 63–94, looks at both attacks, focusing on an aspect of the conflict that is sometimes overlooked or downplayed – naval power.

Much fine work has appeared lately dealing with life in the fortress, military and civilian. Our understanding of Canadian eighteenth-century social history has been greatly enhanced by the work of the Louisbourg historians. A.J.B. Johnston, *The Summer of 1744: A Portrait of Life in 18th-Century Louisbourg* (O: Parks Canada 1983), is a good glimpse of a frozen moment of time, well researched and well written, provocative yet comprehensible to the novice. Christopher Moore, *Louisbourg Portraits: Life in an Eighteenth-*

Century Garrison Town (T: MAC 1982), was a daringly innovative approach to biography, which comes off remarkably well. Moore paints verbal portraits of five actual residents of the city, based on primary documents, but he is also ready to make calculated assumptions and attribute probable thoughts and emotions to his characters. The result is a wonderfully alive portrayal of a tumultuous and memorable city.

Articles now regularly appear on a variety of subjects dealing with everyday life in the fortress. K. Donovan has written 'Communities and Families: Family Life and Living Conditions in Eighteenth-Century Louisbourg,' *MHB* 15 (Summer 1982): 33–47, and 'Inflation at Louisbourg, 1757,' *Canadian Collector* 18/1 (Jan.–Feb. 1983): 20–2. Rosemary Hutchison, 'Furnishing the Fortress,' *Canadian Collector* 20/2 (Mar.–Apr. 1985): 37–41, covers the physical surroundings of the inhabitants of the city, while Florence MacIntyre, 'Clothes Make the Man: Fashions and Fabrics in 18th Century Louisbourg,' *Canadian Collector* 20/2 (Mar.–Apr. 1985): 45–7, examines the issue of what people wore and how clothing was made.

A topic often neglected by historians is one that must have been vital in the daily lives of colonial Maritimers. The rich documentary and archaeological evidence at Louisbourg has allowed the beginning of an understanding of gardening and gardens during this time period. Once again, the need of Parks Canada to re-create an accurate milieu for its National Historic Park has spawned useful articles in a long-ignored area. Anne O'Neill, 'Discipline and Beauty: The Orderly Gardens of 18th-Century Louisbourg,' *Canadian Collector* 20/2 (Mar.–Apr. 1985): 42–4, and 'The Gardens of 18th-Century Louisbourg,' *Journal of Garden History* 3 (July/Sept. 1983): 176–8, have considerably broadened our knowledge of this subject.

The role played by the Roman Catholic Church in the lives of the residents of the fortress has also come under close scrutiny, and the result is a series of studies that greatly outstrips the work yet done on the church in Acadia. A.J.B. Johnston, *Religion in Life at Louisbourg, 1713–1758* (K&M: MQUP 1984), is a fine study of the topic, carefully researched and well written. It may be augmented by two very useful articles by T.A. Crowley, 'The Inroads of Secularization in Eighteenth-Century New France: Church and People at Louisbourg,' *CCHA*, *Historical Studies* (1984): 5–27, and 'Religion in New France: Church and State at Louisbourg,' French Colonial Historical Society, *Proceedings* (1987): 139–60.

The economy of Ile Royale during the French regime has not been the subject of as much interest by historians. Harold Adams Innis, 'Cape Breton Island during the French Regime,' *TRSC* ser. 3, 29 (1935), sec. ii, 51–87, can still be consulted, although it is now somewhat dated. A.H. Clark, 'New

England's Role in the Underdevelopment of Cape Breton Island during the French Regime, 1713–1758,' *Canadian Geographer* 9/1 (1965): 1–12, reprinted in Don Macgillivray and Brian Tennyson, eds., *Cape Breton Historical Essays* (Sydney, NS: College of Cape Breton Press 1980), provides a valuable overview of the topic. C. Moore, 'The Other Louisbourg: Trade and Merchant Enterprise in Ile Royale, 1713–58,' *HS/SH* 12/23 (May 1979): 79–96, shifts the focus of attention at least temporarily away from the military aspects of the colony. B.A. Balcom, *The Cod Fishery of Isle Royale, 1713–58* (O: Parks Canada 1984), brings to the fore the vital issue of the fisheries, one of the economic pillars of the island, the existence of which was inexorably intertwined with that of Louisbourg itself. A.J.B. Johnston, 'The Fishermen of Eighteenth-Century Cape Breton: Numbers and Origins,' *NSHR* 9/1 (June 1989): 62–72, takes a careful look at the men involved in this essential industry. John Robert McNeil, *Atlantic Empires of France and Spain: Louisbourg and Havana, 1700–1763* (Chapel Hill, NC: University of North Carolina Press 1985), uses the two communities to examine the evolving economic and military empires of these European powers.

Work has only really just begun on the topic of the life of women in the society of Ile Royale, but some relevant studies have already appeared. Two significant articles have shed much light on the female experience at Louisbourg: A.J.B. Johnston, 'Education and Female Literacy at Eighteenth-Century Louisbourg: The Work of the Soeurs de la Congrégation de Notre-Dame,' in J. Donald Wilson, ed., *An Imperfect Past: Education and Society in Canadian History* (V: Faculty of Education, University of British Columbia 1984); and Catherine Rubinger, 'Marriage and the Women of Louisbourg,' *DR* 60/3 (Autumn 1980): 445–61.

The study of disease, health, and medicine, while a fascinating topic, is still in its infancy for the early colonial period, but some work has been done. The ravages of one of the dread diseases of the eighteenth century in Louisbourg has been explored in George Burns, 'Smallpox at Louisbourg, 1713–1758,' *NSHR* 10/2 (Dec. 1990): 31–44. A.J.B. Johnston has looked at medical care in 'The Frères de la charité and the Louisbourg Hôpital du Roi,' CCHA, *Study Sessions* (1981): 5–25. We clearly need to know a great deal more about disease, medicine, and death in order to understand more fully the lives of these early Maritimers.

The Louisbourg project, with all its resulting books, reports, and articles, has been immensely stimulating for both eighteenth-century and Maritime studies. The reconstructed fortress itself is a wonderful learning tool, giving us insights into eighteenth-century life not available anywhere else in Canada.

NATIVE STUDIES

In addition to the work done on the Roman Catholic missions to the Native peoples, noted previously, historians are beginning to look at the history of these people in their own right. The major shifts in North American perceptions and understanding of the first inhabitants of this continent have greatly influenced approaches to this subject in the Maritime region as well, although much remains to be done. In a recent and excellent review article, 'Native History in the Atlantic Region during the Colonial Period,' *Acadiensis* 20/1 (Autumn 1990): 200–25, Ralph T. Pastore has examined much of the recent literature in this field.

Alfred Goldsworthy Bailey's classic *The Conflict of European and Eastern Algonkian Cultures, 1504–1700: A Study in Canadian Civilization* (1937; 2nd ed., T: UTP 1969), although now superseded by more recent literature on the subject, is still worthy of a close look by the inquiring student. Leslie F.S. Upton's fine study *Micmacs and Colonists: Indian-White Relations in the Maritimes, 1713–1867* (V: UBCP 1979) carries the examination of the two cultures forward from where Bailey left off. Olive Patricia Dickason produced two works that focus on a shorter time span and more specific topics: *Louisbourg and the Indians: A Study in Imperial Race Relations, 1713–1760* (O: Parks Canada 1976) and 'Amerindians between French and English in Nova Scotia, 1713–1760,' *American Indian Culture and Research Journal* 10/4 (1986): 31–56, reprinted in J.R. Miller, ed., *Sweet Promises: A Reader on Indian-White Relations in Canada* (T: UTP 1991). Harold Franklin McGee, Jr, ed., *The Native Peoples of Atlantic Canada: A History of Indian-European Relations* (O: CUP 1983), provides a good series of articles on the subject.

O.P. Dickason, *The Myth of the Savage and the Beginnings of French Colonialism in the Americas* (E: UAP 1984), establishes a broad interpretative framework in which one may place a study of the Maritime situation, while C.J. Jaenen, *The French Relationship with the Native Peoples of New France and Acadia* (O: Indian and Northern Affairs Canada 1984), deals more expressly with Native-European relations during the French period. Bruce J. Bourque looks at a relevant issue in 'Ethnicity on the Maritime Peninsula, 1600–1759,' *Ethnohistory* 36/3 (Summer 1989): 257–84. Virginia P. Miller, 'The Decline of Nova Scotia Micmac Population, A.D. 1600–1850,' *Culture* 2/3 (1982): 107–20, examines population numbers during 250 years of Native-European interaction. Comparative work with a quite different region of Canada is undertaken in Dickason, 'Frontiers in Transition: Nova Scotia, 1713–1763, compared to the North West, 1869–1885,' in F. Laurie

Barron and James B. Waldram, eds., *1885 and After: Native Society in Transition* (R: CPRC 1986).

Ellice B. Gonzalez, *Changing Economic Roles for Micmac Men and Women: An Ethnohistorical Analysis* (O: National Museums of Canada 1981), looks at a crucial issue in the evolution of Micmac society. Frances L. Stewart, 'Seasonal Movements of Indians in Acadia as Evidenced by Historical Documents and Vertebrate Faunal Remains from Archaeological Sites,' *Man in the Northeast* 38 (Fall 1989): 55–77, shows how the work of archaeologists can shed light on our understanding of the rhythm of life of the Native peoples.

Treaties and land rights have become topics of considerable interest in recent years, and literature that elucidates these issues is beginning to appear. Andrea Bear Nicholas, 'Maliseet Aboriginal Rights and Mascarene's Treaty, not Drummer's Treaty,' in William Cowan, ed., *Actes du dix-septième congrès des algonquinistes* (O: CUP 1986), deals with an important treaty between the Native peoples and the British government, while Bill Wickens, 'Mi'kmaq Land in Southwestern Nova Scotia, 1771–1823,' in M. Conrad, ed., *Making Adjustments*, examines the fate of Native land claims in the face of a rapidly expanding European population.

Some work has been done in the fascinating area of Native material culture, about which there is obviously much more to learn. An important beginning is provided by Ruth Holmes Whitehead, in *Elitekey: Micmac Material Culture from 1600 A.D. to the Present* (H: Nova Scotia Museum 1980) and her more substantial *Micmac Quillwork: Micmac Indian Techniques Of Porcupine Quill Decoration, 1600–1950* (H: Nova Scotia Museum 1982). Both are well researched and beautifully illustrated. The same author has also compiled a valuable sourcebook that gathers together documents and oral traditions, *The Old Man Told Us: Excerpts from Micmac History, 1500–1950* (H: Nimbus 1991). Still, the best source for Micmac legends remains Silas Tertius Rand, *Legends of the Micmacs* (NY: Longmans, Green 1894), a classic in its field. Many of the legends have been turned into children's stories, and have often been substantially altered in the process. The serious student should avoid such 'popularized' versions, as they can badly misrepresent this aspect of the Indian legacy. Even the original printed versions must be used with care; the reader must not forget that these legends have been translated into French or English, and have been filtered through European minds.

Important aspects of the Native experience during the colonial period can be examined by looking at the lives of individuals. One should remember, however, that even the best of these biographies are based on sources generated by Europeans and that even this type of material is scanty. The early volumes of the *DCB* provide the most readily accessible biographical material. In volume 1 see the entry 'Membertou,' the Micmac chief who befriended the French at Port Royal, making possible the peaceful settlement of Europeans in that area. Abenaki chiefs 'Mog,' 'Wenemouet,' and 'Wowurna' are included in volume 2, along with the first two generations of the Abbadie de Saint-Castin family in Acadia, Bernard-Anselme and Jean-Vincent. These two men, along with another Abbadie de Saint-Castin, Joseph, in volume 3, played key roles in the evolving relationship between French and Native in the region, intermarrying with the Abenaki and serving as chiefs of their tribe. The lives of such eighteenth-century Micmac warriors as 'Etienne Bâtard,' 'Jean-Baptiste Cope,' 'Paul Laurent,' and 'Jacques Padanuques,' vol. 3, show that, while often acting as allies of the French in the struggle for Acadia/Nova Scotia, the Native peoples of the region were no mere dupes of the European powers but carefully pursued their own objectives. As late as the Revolutionary War, the Native peoples of the region, and particularly of present-day New Brunswick, were still a potent factor in military affairs, as the biographies of such men as the Malecites 'Nicholas Akomápis,' 'Ambroise Saint-Aubin,' and 'Pierre Tomah,' and Micmac 'Jean-Baptiste Arimph,' vol. 4, indicate.

BRITISH NOVA SCOTIA

The period of British rule following the acquisition of the colony of Acadia/ Nova Scotia in 1713 has received very little attention from historians in recent years. What is still lacking is a major re-evaluation of the critical period between the capture of Port Royal in 1710 and the expulsion of the Acadians in 1755. For the moment J.B. Brebner, *New England's Outpost*, and G.A. Rawlyk, *Nova Scotia's Massachusetts*, provide the best framework within which to examine the period, while A.H. Clark, *Acadia*, remains essential for understanding the shifting demography and geography of the region and supplies a good narrative of events. Less useful is Robert Rumilly, *L'Acadie anglaise, 1713–1755* (M: Fides 1983).

George M. Waller, *Samuel Vetch: Colonial Enterpriser* (Chapel Hill, NC: University of North Carolina Press 1960), looks at the varied and controversial career of one of the key players in the 1710 conquest, and a man who would play a significant role in the first decade of British rule in the colony. A shorter version of Vetch's life by the same author is to be found in the *DCB*, vol. 2, along with entries on many other military leaders in this time of conflict. One could consult with profit, in the same volume, the entries

'Francis Nicholson,' the British commanding officer, and 'Daniel d'Auger de Subercase,' the valiant defender of Port Royal. A view of Nicholson in a quite different North American context is presented in Bruce T. McCully, 'Governor Francis Nicholson, Patron *Par Excellence* of Religion and Learning in Colonial America,' *WMQ* 3rd ser., 39/2 (Apr. 1982): 310–33. A good firsthand account of the siege of Port Royal is given in the 'Journal of Colonel Nicholson at the Capture of Annapolis, 1710,' NSHS, *Collections* 1 (1878): 59–104, reprinted in *Collections of the Nova Scotia Historical Society for the Years 1878–1884* (Belleville, Ont.: Mika 1976). Malcolm MacLeod, 'The First American Conquest: Acadia, 1710–1760,' *NSHR* 1/2 (Dec. 1981): 64–73, places the 1710 conquest in a broader context, and James D. Alsop, 'The Age of the Projectors: British Imperial Strategy in the North Atlantic in the War of Spanish Succession,' *Acadiensis* 21/1 (Autumn 1991): 30–53, traces the development of British strategy during this war that was so crucial for Acadia/Nova Scotia.

The beginnings of British governmental and judicial structures and policies in Nova Scotia may be examined by reference to the first part of J. Murray Beck, *Politics of Nova Scotia*, vol. 1, *1710–1896* (Tantallon, NS: Four East Publications 1985). The difficulties of establishing British justice in a colony with a very weak government and a mixed population are nicely outlined in Thomas Garden Barnes, '"The Dayly Cry for Justice": The Juridical Failure of the Annapolis Royal Regime, 1713–1749,' in Philip Girard and Jim Phillips, eds., *Essays in the History of Canadian Law*, vol. 3, *Nova Scotia* (T: OS 1990). Students of this period are fortunate that the Public Archives of Nova Scotia has published many of the relevant original documents. *Nova Scotia Archives*, vol. 3, *Original Minutes of His Majesty's Council at Annapolis Royal, 1720 to 1739*, ed. Archibald M. MacMechan (H: 1908), and vol. 4, *Minutes of His Majesty's Council at Annapolis Royal, 1736 to 1749*, ed. Charles Bruce Fergusson (H: 1967), show the workings of the infant government at Annapolis, the erratic attempts to deal with the Acadians, the faint beginnings of the legal system, and the indifference of the British government; and vol. 2, *A Calendar of Two Letter-Books and One Commission-Book in the Possession of the Government of Nova Scotia, 1713–1741*, ed. A.M. MacMechan (H: 1900), provides a useful synopsis of many of the official letters from governors of the period, which, with the minutes of council, provide quite a good insight into the government of the infant colony.

Once again the *DCB* is indispensable for understanding the personalities and the problems of this period. Especially important are the studies 'Richard Philipps,' vol. 3, governor of Nova Scotia for most of the period under review; 'Lawrence Armstrong,' vol. 2, frequent administrator of the colony and commanding officer of the garrison until his strange death in 1739; and 'Paul Mascarene,' vol. 3, commanding officer and administrator during the turbulent 1740s and sympathizer of the Acadian plight. The Mascarene entry should be supplemented by the older but still informative article by J.B. Brebner, 'Paul Mascarene of Annapolis Royal,' *DR* 8/4 (Jan. 1929): 501–16, reprinted in G.A. Rawlyk, ed., *Historical Essays on the Atlantic Provinces* (T: M&S 1967). The biographies of many of the early English inhabitants of the colony – merchants, soldiers, and officials – are to be found in the *DCB*, especially the second and third volumes, and a study of their lives does much to flesh out the picture of this rather neglected period.

Recent archaeological work in the only other British settlement of this period, Canso, has shed a great deal of light on the lifestyle of a prosperous merchant. The reports and articles on the excavations of Edward How's home and business on Grassy Island allow us an interesting glimpse into quite another aspect of pre-expulsion Nova Scotia. Some of the raw data are provided in Robert Ferguson et al., *Report on the 1979 Field Season at Grassy Island, Nova Scotia* (O: Parks Canada 1981). Anita Campbell, 'The How Household: A Colonial Merchant's Life-Style in 18th Century Canso,' *Canadian Collector* 20/2 (Mar.–Apr. 1985): 54–7, gives an excellent overview, while D. Hansen provides much more detail on specific elements in *Eighteenth Century Fine Earthenwares from Grassy Island* (O: Parks Canada 1986) for those wishing to pursue the subject further. Together, these reports paint the earliest picture available of domestic life in English Nova Scotia.

A survey of this period's continuing conflict between French and English is given in Robert Sauvageau, *Acadie: la guerre de cent ans des français d'Amérique aux Maritimes et en Louisiane, 1670–1769* (P: Berger-Levrault 1987), and in J.B. Brebner, *New England's Outpost*, and G.A. Rawlyk, *Nova Scotia's Massachusetts*. Bernard Pothier recounts the events of the French attack on the British capital of the colony in 'The Siege of Annapolis Royal, 1744,' *NSHR* 5/1 (June 1985): 59–71. Pothier is also editor of *Course à l'Acadie: journal de campagne de François Du Pont Duvivier en 1744* (Moncton, NB: Les éditions d'Acadie 1982), which puts in the hands of the student a firsthand account of the attack, as well as providing considerable insight into the difficulties of the French in mobilizing the Acadians. Once again, many neglected aspects of this period can be at least partially covered by reference to the *DCB*. See 'Arthur Noble,' 'Edward How,' and 'Jean-Baptiste-Louis-Frédéric de La Rochefoucauld de Roye, Marquis de Roucy, Duc d'Anville,' vol. 3; and 'Joseph Goreham' and 'Jean-François Bourdon de Dombourg,' vol. 4.

N.E.S. Griffiths, 'The Golden Age: Acadian Life, 1713–1748,' *HS/SH*

17/33 (May 1984): 21–34, reprinted in R. Douglas Francis and Donald B. Smith, eds., *Readings in Canadian History*, vol. 1, *Pre-Confederation* (3rd ed., T: HRW 1990), is absolutely essential for an understanding of Acadian life during the period of British administration. Neil Boucher, 'Paul Mascarene et les Acadiens, 1710–1748,' *Revue de l'Université Sainte-Anne* (1984–5): 14–22, looks at the relationship between the Acadians and the most sympathetic of the British administrators of the period. B. Pothier, 'Acadian Emigration to Ile Royal after the Conquest of Acadia,' *HS/SH* 3/6 (Nov. 1970): 116–31, examines those Acadians who chose to leave the colony rather than accommodate themselves to the British presence. Some of the relevant documents concerning the relationship between the Acadians and the colonial government have been reprinted in Thomas Beamish Akins, ed., *Nova Scotia Archives*, vol. 1, *Selections from the Public Documents of the Province of Nova Scotia* (H: Charles Annand 1869). In using these documents, however, it must be remembered that only one side of the picture is being presented.

The founding in 1749 and early development of Halifax have received little attention from historians in recent years. The best source is still W.S. MacNutt, 'Why Halifax Was Founded,' *DR* 12/4 (Jan. 1933): 524–32, which may be supplemented by the first part of Thomas H. Raddall, *Halifax: Warden of the North* (1948; rev. ed., 1968; repr. T: M&S 1971). Once again much valuable information and interpretation are given in the *DCB*, where biographies of all the key figures in the capital's founding appear, including the founding governor, 'Edward Cornwallis,' vol. 4. A firsthand account of the settling of Halifax is provided in Ronald Rompkey, ed., *Expeditions of Honour: The Journal of John Salusbury in Halifax, Nova Scotia, 1749–53* (Newark, NJ: University of Delaware Press 1982). The 1750s is dealt with in an excellent essay, 'The 1750s: Decade of Expulsion,' in J.G. Reid, *Six Crucial Decades*. Donald H. Fleck, 'Early Money in Nova Scotia: A Short History of Currency, Exchange and Finance,' *NSHR* 1/2 (Dec. 1981): 4–15, focuses on money and finance during the French and British periods, while *Documents Relating to Currency, Exchange and Finance in Nova Scotia, with Prefatory Documents, 1675–1758*, ed. Adam Shortt (O: King's Printer 1933), provides some of the basic documents that allow one to examine the subject firsthand.

The best single source on the coming to Nova Scotia in the mid-eighteenth century of immigrants from central Europe is Winthrop Pickard Bell, *The 'Foreign Protestants' and the Settlement of Nova Scotia* (T: UTP 1961), which was recently reprinted with an introduction by L.D. McCann (Sackville, NB: Centre for Canadian Studies, Mount Allison University 1990). This pioneering work should be supplemented by Gertrud Waseem,

'German Settlement in Nova Scotia,' in *German Canadian Studies: Critical Approaches*, ed. Peter Liddell (V: Canadian Association of University Teachers of German 1983), and Terrence M. Punch, 'Montbeliard: An Unknown Homeland,' *NSHR* 5/2 (Dec. 1985): 75–92. Richard Henning Field has begun examining the material culture of these central Europeans. See, for example, his 'Proxemic Patterns: Eighteenth Century Lunenburg-German Domestic Furnishings and Interiors,' *MHB* 22 (Fall 1985): 40–8, and 'Claiming Rank: The Display of Wealth and Status by Eighteenth-Century Lunenburg, Nova Scotia, Merchants,' *MHR* 35 (Spring 1992): 1–20. Deborah Trask, *'Hier Ruhet In Gott*: Germanic Gravestones in Nova Scotia,' in M. Conrad, ed., *Making Adjustments*, uses eighteenth-century gravestones to examine attitudes and values among the Germanic settlers.

THE EXPULSION OF THE ACADIANS

Although much has been written about this event, there is still relatively little available that the serious student can use with safety and profit. Strongly biased accounts (from either the British or the Acadian perspective) abound but add little to a real understanding of the events of 1755 and the years that immediately followed. N.E.S. Griffiths, ed., *The Acadian Deportation: Deliberate Perfidy or Cruel Necessity?* (T: CC 1969), which gathered and classified the various interpretations of this controversial and complex event, is still the best place to begin. J.B. Brebner, *New England's Outpost*, and G.A. Rawlyk, *Nova Scotia's Massachusetts*, both provide the broader context and examine the uncertain role of New England in the events of 1755. C.B. Fergusson, 'The Expulsion of the Acadians,' *DR* 35/2 (Summer 1955): 127–35, reprinted in Angus D. Gilbert et al., eds., *Reappraisals in Canadian History*, vol. 1, *Pre-Confederation* (Scarborough, Ont.: PH 1993), is dated but still one of the few overviews we have. Highly romanticized versions of the event should be avoided, although it is possible to examine Henry Wadsworth Longfellow's epic poem *Evangeline* (1847) with profit, provided that it is remembered that Longfellow was not a historian but a poet. The poem is essential reading for understanding the growth of the myths that have come to surround the expulsion. T.G. Barnes, 'Historiography of the Acadians' *Grand Dérangement, 1755,*' *Québec Studies* 7 (1988): 74–86, provides a historiographic framework in which to view the expulsion of the Acadians, one that is useful for unilingual English students in that it provides translations from the most significant French sources.

There has been little scholarly work done on one of the key players in this event – acting governor Charles Lawrence. The best insights into his character are to be found in the entry in *DCB*, vol. 3. On the other hand, a number of primary documents relevant to the expulsion have been reprinted. For example, the 'Journal of Colonel John Winslow of the Provincial Troops, While Engaged in the Siege of Fort Beausejour, in the Summer and Autumn of 1755,' NSHS, *Collections* 4 (1884): 113–246, sheds light on the military events of 1755 in which the Acadians are quickly embroiled. Similarly, for a firsthand account of the deportation of the Acadians from the Grand Pré area, consult the 'Journal of Colonel John Winslow, of the Provincial Troops, While Engaged in Removing the Acadian French Inhabitants from Grand Pré, and the Neighbouring Settlements, in the Autumn of the Year 1755,' NSHS, *Collections* 3 (1882–3): 71–196. Both Winslow journals were reprinted in the volume *Collections of the Nova Scotia Historical Society for the Years 1878–1884*. These two journals contain not only Winslow's own observations, but also many of the letters and military orders of that crucial summer.

While little that is new has been written in recent years about the expulsion itself, such is not the case when one looks at the fate of the Acadians immediately after the event. There has been much interest in tracing the paths of the expelled Acadians, and in attempting to understand the impact that expulsion had on these people. N.E.S. Griffiths has done excellent work in this area: 'The Acadians Who Had a Problem in France,' *Canadian Geographic* 101/4 (Aug.–Sept. 1981): 40–5, and 'The Acadians of Belle-Ile-en-Mer,' *Natural History* 90/1 (Jan. 1981): 48–56, look at the Acadians who ended up in France; and 'Acadians in Exile: The Experiences of the Acadians in the British Seaports,' *Acadiensis* 4/1 (Autumn 1974): 67–84, follows those who went into exile, at least temporarily, in Britain. Bona Arsenault, 'Les Acadiens réfugiés à la baie des Chaleurs en 1758,' *Cahiers* 17/3 (juillet–sept. 1986): 89–93, examines some of those who escaped deportation by fleeing to northern New Brunswick; Michel Poirier, *Les Acadiens aux îles Saint-Pierre et Miquelon, 1758–1828* (Moncton, NB: Les éditions d'Acadie 1984), those who eventually settled on the French islands in the Gulf of St Lawrence; and Jean Gaudette, 'Des réfugiés acadiens à Québec en 1757,' *Cahiers* 17/4 (oct.–déc. 1986): 144–9, those who made it to Quebec. Even those Acadians who settled in the Lesser Antilles have been the subject of scholarly interest in Gabriel Debien, 'Les Acadiens réfugiés aux petites Antilles (1761–1791),' *Cahiers* 15/3 (juin–sept. 1984): 57–99.

More ambitious is the work of C.A. Brasseaux, who has examined the movement of Acadians to Louisiana and the establishment of an Acadian culture there. His 'A New Acadia: The Acadian Migrations to South Louisiana, 1764–1803,' *Acadiensis* 15/1 (Autumn 1985): 123–32, is greatly expanded in *The Founding of New Acadia: The Beginnings of Acadian Life in Louisiana, 1765–1803* (Baton Rouge, LA: Louisiana State University Press 1987). Brasseaux's work has the advantage of allowing the student to compare the evolution of Acadian life in the Maritimes with that in distant Louisiana.

Rather surprisingly, there has been less work done on those Acadians who returned to Nova Scotia, or who escaped deportation altogether. E. Roy Officer has looked at an important aspect of the Acadian experience in what is now New Brunswick in 'Crown Land Grants to Acadians in New Brunswick, 1760–1848,' *Cahiers* 12/4 (déc. 1981): 128–42, while N. Boucher, 'The Doucets of Saint Mary's Bay: Community Leaders amongst an Uprooted People,' *NSHR* 5/1 (June 1985): 43–58, examines an Acadian family that settled in Nova Scotia. Thomas R. Berger, 'The Acadians: Expulsion and Return,' in his *Fragile Freedoms: Human Rights and Dissent in Canada* (T: Clarke, Irwin 1981) places the events of 1755 and the return of the Acadians in a somewhat different context. The complex wanderings and settlement of the post-1755 Acadians are made easier to follow by the very helpful maps in *HAC*, vol. 1, plate 30, 'Acadian Deportation and Return.'

One of the best ways of understanding the impact that the forced removal of the Acadians had on the people themselves is through the examination of individual lives. The *DCB*, in short but revealing biographies, sheds much light on the hardships imposed on the ordinary people of the colony. The varying impacts that expulsion had is shown in the entries 'Pierre Doucet' and 'Pierre Le Blanc,' vol. 4. 'Michel Bastarache, *dit* Basque,' 'Cécile Boudreau,' 'Pierre Cormier,' 'Amable Doucet,' and 'Jean-Baptiste Robichaux,' vol. 5 (1986), are representative of those whose lives were totally disrupted by this event.

NEW ENGLAND PLANTERS

Second only to the attention devoted to Louisbourg in the past twenty years is the scholarly interest shown in the New England settlers who moved to the old colony of Nova Scotia in the 1760s, providing the region with its first permanent English-speaking population. The work of the Planter Studies Committee, based at Acadia University, has done much to stimulate activity in this area, and articles have appeared recently on many aspects of this topic.

Despite new work, the classic study of the period from 1760 to 1783 remains J.B. Brebner, *The Neutral Yankees of Nova Scotia: A Marginal Colony during the Revolutionary Years* (1937; repr., intro. W.S. MacNutt, T: M&S

1969). While some aspects of it have been superseded by more recent studies, overall it is still required reading for the period. G.A. Rawlyk, 'J.B. Brebner and Some Recent Trends in Eighteenth-Century Maritime Historiography,' in M. Conrad, ed., *They Planted Well*, revised and reprinted in Stephen J. Hornsby et al., eds., *The Northeastern Borderlands: Four Centuries of Interaction* (F: AP 1989), looks at the Brebner legacy and the challenges to it in recent years. J.G. Reid, 'Change and Continuity in Nova Scotia, 1758–1775,' in M. Conrad, ed., *Making Adjustments*, examines more recent interpretations of the era and places Planter Nova Scotia in a broader North American context. James E. Candow, *The New England Planters in Nova Scotia* (O: Parks Canada 1986), reprinted as an article in R.D. Francis and D.B. Smith, eds., *Readings in Canadian History*, vol. 1, provides a comprehensive, recent overview of the Planter experience. Plate 31, 'Pre-Loyalist Nova Scotia,' *HAC*, vol. 1, gives much helpful information about the origin of settlers, settlement patterns, and land distribution. Much of the best work done on Planter Nova Scotia since the mid-1980s has appeared in the two volumes edited by M. Conrad, *They Planted Well* and *Making Adjustments*. Only some of the articles published there will be referred to directly, but a thorough study of both books is required for a good understanding of this period.

The politics of the early Planter period has been dealt with by a number of historians, both in its own right and as the necessary prelude to an understanding of the Nova Scotian response to the American Revolution. J.M. Beck, *The Government of Nova Scotia* (T: UTP 1957) and *Politics of Nova Scotia*, vol. 1, provide an overview. John Garner, *The Franchise and Politics in British North America, 1755–1867* (T: UTP 1969), while casting a very broad net, is still useful for an understanding of these issues in pre-Revolutionary Nova Scotia. W.S. MacNutt, 'The Beginnings of Nova Scotia Politics, 1758–1766,' *CHR* 16/1 (Mar. 1935): 41–53, although written many years ago, is still worth a careful look. D.C. Harvey, 'The Struggle for the New England Form of Township Government in Nova Scotia,' CHA *AR* (1933): 15–22, deals with the crucial issues of Planter expectations and disappointments concerning the form of government adopted for Nova Scotia. J.M. Bumsted, 'Church and State in Maritime Canada, 1749–1807,' CHA *AR* (1967): 41–58, provides the best study we have of the intimate relationship between these two aspects of life in the colonies. Norah Story, 'The Church and State "Party" in Nova Scotia, 1749–1851,' NSHS, *Collections* 27 (1947): 33–57, examines the evolving union of religion and politics in Nova Scotia. The biographies of individual politicians and officials shed much light on the complexities of the period. Of particular use are the *DCB* entries 'Michael Franklin,' 'Francis Legge,' and 'Joshua Mauger,' vol. 4; and 'Jonathan Belcher,' vol. 5.

Historians have begun to move away from a concentration on the political aspects of the era, and, among other topics, the literary and cultural activities of the Planters have started to attract attention. E. Jennifer Monaghan, 'Literacy in Eighteenth-Century New England: Some Historiographical Reflections on Issues of Gender,' in *Making Adjustments*, provides an excellent review of the New England context of Planter literacy in this very fine essay. Nancy Vogan, 'The Musical Traditions of the Planters and "Mary Miller Her Book,"' in the same volume, is one of the first to examine seriously the role of secular music and the singing school in this period of Nova Scotia's development. Margaret A. Filshie, 'Sacred Harmonies: The Congregational Voice in Canadian Protestant Worship, 1750–1850,' in William Westfall et al., eds., *Religion/Culture: Comparative Canadian Studies* (O: Association for Canadian Studies 1985), presents a fine article on music as a part of the religious experience of Canadians.

Interest in the material culture of the Planters and other Nova Scotians has greatly expanded in recent years as well. Archaeological excavations, archives, cemeteries, museums, and private collections of artifacts have yielded a great deal of information about how the people of Nova Scotia lived, giving us insights into the period that were not possible before. The kind of information available from professionally conducted archaeological digs is presented in Marc Lavoie, 'Archaeological Evidence of Planter Material Culture in New Brunswick and Nova Scotia,' in *Making Adjustments*. M.A. MacDonald, 'Artifact Survivals from Pre-Loyalist English-speaking Settlers of New Brunswick,' *MHB* 26 (Fall 1987): 27–9, and MacDonald with Robert S. Elliot, 'New Brunswick's "Early Comers": Lifestyles through Authenticated Artifacts, a Research Project,' in *They Planted Well*, show how articles used by a people – furniture, dishes, tools, clothing, and so forth – reveal much about their way of life, and even their values and concerns. R.H. Field, 'The Material Lives of the Yeoman Planters of Kings County, Nova Scotia: A Preliminary Survey Based on Probate Inventories, 1761–1797,' in *Making Adjustments*, utilizes wills and other probate records to come to some rather startling conclusions about the daily lives of this group of settlers. Field compares Planter and German material culture in 'Domestic Life in Eighteenth-Century Nova Scotia: A Rural Perspective Based on Lunenburg County and Kings County Yeoman Probate Records,' *MHR* 35 (Spring 1992): 47–54. Yet another form of artifact was used by D. Trask in her quest for understanding of the Planters – gravestones. In *Life How Short, Eternity How Long: Gravestone Carving and Carvers in Nova Scotia*

(H: Nova Scotia Museum 1978) and, with Debra McNabb, 'Carved in Stone: Material Evidence in the Graveyards of Kings County, Nova Scotia,' *MHB* 23 (Spring 1986): 35–42, the memorial stones and the attitudes they reveal are examined.

Far larger, but very useful, 'artifacts' are the remaining Planter buildings, both public and private, which provide an excellent opportunity for analysing values, lifestyles, level of prosperity, attitudes, and influences in the Planter community. The first key article on the subject was Alan Gowans, 'New England Architecture in Nova Scotia,' *The Art Quarterly* (Detroit) 25/ 1 (Spring 1962): 7–33. The topic is pursued in an excellent article by Peter Ennals, 'The Yankee Origins of Bluenose Vernacular Architecture,' *American Review of Canadian Studies* 12/2 (Summer 1982): 5–21, and enlarged upon by Ennals and Deryck Holdsworth in 'Vernacular Architecture and the Cultural Landscape of the Maritime Provinces – A Reconnaissance,' *Acadiensis* 10/2 (Spring 1981): 86–106. Allen Penney, *The Simeon Perkins House: An Architectural Interpretation, 1767–1987* (H: Nova Scotia Museum 1987), looks at one of the most significant and best documented of the surviving Planter houses. See also his article 'A Planter House: The Simeon Perkins House, Liverpool, Nova Scotia,' in *They Planted Well*. In the same volume is Heather Davidson, 'Private Lives from Public Artifacts: The Architectural Heritage of Kings County Planters,' which uses six extant Planter-period buildings in Kings County, Nova Scotia, to explore this important dimension of these settlers' lives. The early houses of worship in Nova Scotia, Planter and otherwise, are examined in an important work by Allan F. Duffus et al., *Thy Dwellings Fair: Churches of Nova Scotia, 1750–1830* (Hantsport, NS: Lancelot 1982).

Case studies of Planter settlements can be a valuable way of learning about this period. Esther Clark Wright began this process fifty years ago in her pioneering 'Cumberland Township: A Focal Point of Early Settlement on the Bay of Fundy,' *CHR* 17/1 (Mar. 1946): 27–32. D. McNabb examines one key element of the Planter experience in 'The Role of the Land in Settling Horton Township, Nova Scotia, 1766–1830,' in *They Planted Well*; Elizabeth Mancke uses the Planter townships of Liverpool and Machias in 'Corporate Structure and Private Interest: The Mid-Eighteenth Century Expansion of New England,' in the same volume; and Barry Moody, 'Land, Kinship and Inheritance in Granville Township, 1760–1800,' in *Making Adjustments*, studies these interlocking themes. Alan R. MacNeil looks primarily at the economies of two townships in 'Early American Communities on the Fundy: A Case Study of Annapolis and Amherst Townships, 1767–1827,' *Agricultural History* 63/2 (Spring 1989): 101–19, and at the head start

Acadian efforts gave Planters in Annapolis Township in 'The Acadian Legacy and Agricultural Development in Nova Scotia, 1760–1861,' in Kris Inwood, ed., *Farm, Factory and Fortune: New Studies in the Economic History of the Maritime Provinces* (F: AP 1993).

The religious life of the Planters (see also 'The Great Awakening' later in the chapter) has been dealt with by a number of historians. Baptist beginnings may be examined by reference to George Levy's excellent study *The Baptists of the Maritime Provinces, 1753–1946* (Saint John, NB: Barnes-Hopkins 1946), and Maurice W. Armstrong's 'Elder Moulton and the Nova Scotia Baptists,' *DR* 24/3 (Oct. 1944): 320–3. Also useful is Robert G. Gardner, 'Early Maritime Baptists,' *NSHR* 4/2 (Nov. 1984): 25–37. The origins of Presbyterianism in the Maritimes are explored by M.W. Armstrong in 'The First Protestant Ordination in Canada,' *DR* 27/1 (Apr. 1947): 53–9. Frank Baker, 'The Trans-Atlantic Triangle: Relations between British, Canadian, and American Methodism during Wesley's Lifetime,' United Church of Canada Committee on Archives and History, *Bulletin* 28 (1979): 5–21, presents the Maritime experience in its broader context, and the first part of Goldwin S. French, *Parsons & Politics: The Rôle of Wesleyan Methodists in Upper Canada and the Maritimes from 1780 to 1855* (T: RP 1962), deals with the rise of the denomination during the American Revolution. J.W. Grant, 'Methodist Origins in Atlantic Canada,' and G.A. Rawlyk, 'William Black, Henry Alline, and Nova Scotia's First Great Awakening,' both in Charles H.H. Scobie and Grant, eds., *The Contribution of Methodism to Atlantic Canada* (K&M: MQUP 1992), are the most recent examinations of the beginnings of this important denomination in the Maritime colonies. Allen B. Robertson, in 'To Declare and Affirm: Quaker Contributions to Planter Nova Scotia,' in *Making Adjustments*, has provided an interesting insight into a little-known sect in Nova Scotia during this time. I.G. Mackinnon, *Settlement and Churches in Nova Scotia* (M: Walker House 1932), is now somewhat dated but is still a valuable overview. The vital issue of religious toleration in the colony is the focus of M.W. Armstrong, 'Backgrounds of Religious Liberty in Nova Scotia,' NSHS, *Collections* 27 (1947): 17–32.

The geographer Graeme Wynn has contributed significantly to our understanding of the economic aspects of Planter Nova Scotia. In 'A Region of Scattered Settlements and Bounded Possibilities: Northeastern North America, 1775–1800,' and 'A Province Too Much Dependent on New England,' *Canadian Geographer* 31/2,4 (Summer, Winter 1987): 98–113, 319–38, Wynn places the region in its North American context. His 'Late Eighteenth-Century Agriculture on the Bay of Fundy Marshlands,'

Acadiensis 8/2 (Spring 1979): 80–9, examines the Planter use of the former Acadian lands. J. Gwyn has written a very useful article on the impact of war on the Maritime economy, 'Economic Fluctuations in Wartime Nova Scotia, 1755–1815,' in *Making Adjustments*.

Some of the documents concerning the Planter experience in Nova Scotia have been published. Undoubtedly the most important is the massive diary of a Liverpool Planter, which is a vast treasure house of information on almost all aspects of community and family life: *The Diary of Simeon Perkins*, 5 vols. (with various editors), published by the Champlain Society (T: 1948–78). Some of the eighteenth-century census data have also been published. See, for example, 'A Census of Yarmouth and Barrington Townships, 1762,' *NSHR* 1/1 (June 1981): 73–8.

The Planters and the Acadians are not the only groups of settlers to the region that have attracted the attention of historians. Aside from the Germans mentioned earlier, good work has also been done on several other groups which made Nova Scotia their home during this period. Bernard Bailyn, *Voyagers to the West: A Passage in the Peopling of America on the Eve of the Revolution* (NY: Knopf 1986), gives some comment on Nova Scotia specifically and provides a wonderful general context. The Ulster-Irish migration in particular is the subject of Carol Campbell's provocative 'A Scots-Irish Plantation in Nova Scotia: Truro, 1760–1775,' in *Making Adjustments*, while the *DCB*, vol. 5, provides the biography 'Alexander McNutt,' the chief colonizer involved in the Ulster migrations to Nova Scotia. Background to the movement is to be found in R.J. Dickson, *Ulster Emigration to Colonial America, 1718–1775* (L: Routledge & Kegan Paul 1966), and Kerby A. Miller, *Emigrants and Exiles: Ireland and the Irish Exodus to North America* (NY: OUP 1985).

Peter Latta, 'Eighteenth Century Immigrants to Nova Scotia: The Yorkshire Settlers,' *MHB* 28 (Fall 1988): 46–51, looks at a small but significant English migration just prior to the American Revolution. A representative Yorkshire settler can be seen in the life of 'Charles Dixon,' *DCB*, vol. 5. Blacks in pre-Loyalist Nova Scotia have not yet received all the attention warranted, but some work has been done on the subject. The most recent study is Gary Hartlen, 'Bound for Nova Scotia: Slaves in the Planter Migration, 1759–1800,' in *Making Adjustments*.

Donald MacKay, *Scotland Farewell: The People of the Hector* (T: MHR 1980), examines the arrival of the first group of Scottish settlers to Nova Scotia. Details of the lives of some of these Scottish settlers are to be found in the *DCB* entries 'John Harris,' 'William Pagan,' and 'Robert Patterson,' vol. 5. J.M. Bumsted has done excellent work on Scottish migration to the

Maritime provinces, and the early parts of his 'Scottish Emigration to the Maritimes, 1770–1815: A New Look at an Old Theme,' *Acadiensis* 10/2 (Spring 1981): 65–85, and *The People's Clearance: Highland Emigration to British North America, 1770–1815* (Edinburgh/W: Edinburgh University Press/UMP 1982), are essential reading for this topic. Also useful are the first chapters of Douglas Campbell and R.A. MacLean, *Beyond the Atlantic Roar: A Study of the Nova Scotia Scots* (T: M&S 1974).

Little has yet been done in the field of women's studies for this period. The narrative of a Planter woman has been reprinted with an introduction by M. Conrad: 'Mary Bradley's Reminiscences: A Domestic Life in Colonial New Brunswick,' *Atlantis* 7/1 (Fall 1981): 92–101. Thomas B. Vincent has examined literary images of women in 'The Image and Function of Women in the Poetry of Affection in Eighteenth-Century Maritime Canada,' in *Making Adjustments*.

NOVA SCOTIA AND THE AMERICAN REVOLUTION

With the exception of the expulsion of the Acadians and Fortress Louisbourg, few topics in Maritime history have excited as much interest by historians as Nova Scotia's response to the American Revolution. Unfortunately, these historians have at times been concerned primarily with explaining why the colony did not join the Revolution, rather than with attempting to understand and delineate the full range of responses present in Nova Scotia.

Both J.B. Brebner, *Neutral Yankees of Nova Scotia*, and G.A. Rawlyk, *Nova Scotia's Massachusetts*, provide important interpretations of the colony's response to the Revolution. Rawlyk also edited *Revolution Rejected: 1775–1776* (Scarborough, Ont.: PH 1968), which brings together excerpts from some of the key documents and the major interpretations published to that date. It is a good place to begin the study of this topic but should be supplemented by his articles on the subject: 'The American Revolution and Nova Scotia Reconsidered,' *DR* 43/3 (Autumn 1963): 379–94, and 'Nova Scotia and the American Revolution,' in Owen Edwards and George Shepperson, eds., *Scotland, Europe and the American Revolution* (NY: St Martin's Press 1976). A recent article by Donald Desserud, 'Nova Scotia and the American Revolution: A Study of Neutrality and Moderation in the Eighteenth Century,' in *Making Adjustments*, examines Nova Scotia's response from the vantage point of Enlightenment thought. The abortive 'invasion' of Nova Scotia in 1776 and its aftermath can be approached through the *DCB* entries 'Joseph Goreham' and 'Allan Maclean,' vol. 4; and 'John

Allan,' 'Jonathan Eddy,' 'William Hazen,' 'Seth Noble,' and 'Israel Perley,' vol. 5.

Several studies have appeared which focus on the Revolution in specific communities in Nova Scotia. Mary Ellen Wright, 'Of a Licentious and Rebellious Disposition: The Cobequid Townships and the American Revolution,' NSHS, *Collections* 42 (1986): 27–40, and Ernest A. Clarke, 'Cumberland Planters and the Aftermath of the Attack on Fort Cumberland,' in *They Planted Well*, both look at the situation in eastern Nova Scotia. Lewis R. Fischer, 'Revolution without Independence: The Canadian Colonies, 1749–1775,' in Ronald Hoffman et al., eds., *The Economy of Early America: The Revolutionary Period, 1763–1790* (Charlottesville, VA: University Press of Virginia 1988), provides a larger, and primarily economic, perspective for the period.

THE GREAT AWAKENING

Interest in the religious revival, the Great Awakening, which occurred almost simultaneously with the Revolution, began as an offshoot of the interest in the military event, but has since taken on a life of its own. A number of important studies have appeared in recent years, and most of the key documents of the revival are now in print.

M.W. Armstrong greatly stimulated interest in the subject with *The Great Awakening in Nova Scotia, 1776–1809* (Hartford, CT: American Society of Church History 1948), which is still well worth reading. J.M. Bumsted, *Henry Alline, 1748–1784* (T: UTP 1971; repr. Hantsport, NS: Lancelot 1984), provides a readable and provocative study of the prime mover of the revival. G.A. Rawlyk and Gordon T. Stewart examined the interaction of the revival and the Revolution, challenging some of Armstrong's earlier arguments, in 'Nova Scotia's Sense of Mission,' *HS/SH* 1/2 (Nov. 1968): 5–17, and *A People Highly Favoured of God: The Nova Scotia Yankees and the American Revolution* (T: MAC 1972). Stewart developed the work further with a case study, 'Socio-economic Factors in the Great Awakening: The Case of Yarmouth, Nova Scotia,' *Acadiensis* 3/1 (Autumn 1973): 18–34, and in 'Charisma and Integration: An Eighteenth Century North American Case,' *Comparative Studies in Society and History* 16/2 (Mar. 1974): 138–49, which used the Great Awakening to examine the societal impact of charismatic movements.

G.A. Rawlyk has continued to work in the period as well, although he has come to question some of his earlier views. He has also linked the Awakening with ongoing trends in the religious and social history of the Maritime provinces. The student of the Awakening should consult his 'New Lights, Baptists and Religious Awakenings in Nova Scotia, 1776–1843: A Preliminary Probe,' *JCCHS* 25/2 (Oct. 1983): 43–73, reprinted in Mark G. McGowan and David B. Marshall, eds., *Prophets, Priests, and Prodigals: Readings in Canadian Religious History, 1608 to Present* (T: MHR 1992). Some of these themes are explored much further in his *Ravished by the Spirit: Religious Revivals, Baptists, and Henry Alline* (K&M: MQUP 1984).

Other scholars have examined additional aspects of the revival and the revivalist. David G. Bell, 'The Death of Henry Alline: Some Contemporary Reactions,' and Frederick C. Burnett, 'Henry Alline's "Articles & Covenant of a Gospel Church,"' both in *NSHR* 4/2 (Nov. 1984): 7–12, 13–24, provide insights into the revivalist and the churches he founded. Jamie S. Scott, '"Travels of My Soul": Henry Alline's Autobiography,' *JCS* 18/2 (Summer 1983): 70–90, takes a provocative look at one of the principal documents of the Awakening. T.B. Vincent, 'Henry Alline: Problems of Approach and Reading the *Hymns* as Poetry,' in M. Conrad, ed., *They Planted Well*, examines Alline as poet.

Our understanding of the Awakening has been considerably amplified by the appearance in print during the past ten years of many of the key documents of the event. These documents, together with the introductions and explanatory footnotes, provide further clarification, but more importantly allow the student of the period to develop his or her own conclusions concerning this controversial event. Many of Henry Alline's writings have been republished and are readily available. G.A. Rawlyk has edited Alline's *New Light Letters and Spiritual Songs, 1778–1793* (Hantsport, NS: Lancelot 1983) and *The Sermons of Henry Alline* (Hantsport, NS: Lancelot 1986). He has also published *Henry Alline: Selected Writings* (NY: Paulist Press 1987). In addition to the Alline collections edited by Rawlyk, students may turn to: James Beverley and B. Moody, eds., *The Life and Journal of the Rev. Mr. Henry Alline* (Hantsport, NS: Lancelot 1982); T.B. Vincent, ed., *Selected Hymns and Spiritual Songs of Henry Alline* (K: Loyal Colonies Press 1982); and J.M. Bumsted, ed., *Hymns and Spiritual Songs by Henry Alline* (Sackville, NB: Ralph Pickard Bell Library, Mount Allison University 1987).

The most significant body of church records extant for this subject are those of Chebogue (Yarmouth), Nova Scotia. These, along with other documents, including parts of Alline's journal, were edited with an introduction by G.T. Stewart in *Documents Relating to the Great Awakening in Nova Scotia, 1760–1791* (T: CS 1982). The church records themselves have been published in the more readily available *The Records of the Church of Jebogue in Yarmouth, 1766–1851*, ed. Gwen G. Trask and Stuart Trask (Yarmouth,

NS: Stoneycroft 1992). The journal of Alline's chief protagonist in Nova Scotia, the Yarmouth minister Jonathan Scott, has also been reprinted: Henry E. Scott, ed., *The Journal of the Reverend Jonathan Scott* (n.p.: New England Historic Genealogical Society 1980).

CONCLUSION

Our understanding of many aspects of the history of seventeenth- and eighteenth-century Acadia/Nova Scotia has been substantially altered and enlarged during the past two decades. Historians now ask many more, and different, questions than they did little more than a generation ago. As can be seen from the preceding material, more varied sources are now consulted than was usual before, greatly broadening the picture of the past. In these developments, the historiography of the region has been immensely influenced by recent developments in Canada, the United States, and Europe. In pursuing any of the topics just discussed, it might also be very useful to see what historians elsewhere are saying about similar issues in other parts of the new world or Europe. There has been little such comparative work done thus far, but this approach seems to hold out great hope of enlarging our understanding of the history of this region.

As yet we still lack the synthesis of the entire period that is so essential in gaining an overview of the history of the Maritimes. Greater understanding of some aspects of the story is still necessary, for example, the area of family and the role of women, as well as the relations between Europeans and Native peoples. The work that has already been done, and the unexplored areas that remain, make the study of the history of this region in the seventeenth and eighteenth centuries an exciting and challenging field for professionals and amateurs alike.

JAMES H. LAMBERT

Quebec/Lower Canada

Historical writing is not about absolutes; it reflects the personal biases of the historians who undertake it and the collective perceptions and preoccupations of their times. Similarly, those who read history expect to find in it some link with their own experience of life. This questioning of the past in terms of the present gives meaning to historical writing and explains in part why more recent works tend to replace older ones. Thus, while historical writing improves as methodology is refined, recent works also seem better because they speak more directly to contemporary concerns. Those works from the past that retain more than historiographical significance do so to the extent that they address subjects and use approaches that reflect preoccupations of their period which in some way correspond to those of our own. The writing of the history of Quebec between the Conquest and Confederation proves no exception to this rule of historical relevance.

Presently, the historiography of Quebec and Lower Canada by French-language historians reflects two major influences: the concern of contemporary Quebec primarily with matters economic and social, and the development of the historical profession in Quebec after 1947 but more specifically after the publication in 1966 of Fernand Ouellet's landmark *Histoire économique et sociale du Québec, 1760–1850: structures et conjoncture* (M: Fides). The dominance in recent historical writing of economic and social history, either through the study of the economy and society or as an approach to other fields, is overwhelming. Many historians prefer quantitative methods and now limit the scope of their work to case and regional studies, indispensable to the emergence of new syntheses. On the other hand, in religious and cultural history new syntheses have emerged. Women's and Native studies show only modest progress, while legal history remains hampered by the complexity of judicial records.

BIBLIOGRAPHIES AND REFERENCE WORKS

Bibliographie de bibliographies québécoises (Q: Bibliothèque nationale du Québec 1979; 2 supplements 1980–1), although somewhat dated, is still useful, particularly for specialized bibliographies. The *Bibliographie du Québec* (M: Bibliothèque nationale du Québec 1968–) is the most exhaustive retrospective and current bibliography of publications on Quebec. It consists of three distinct publications: *Laurentiana parus avant 1821* (1976), *Bibliographie du Québec, 1821–1967* (1980), and *Bibliographie du Québec*, covering current publications since 1968. A good general research guide for students of Canadian history, Jacqueline Roy et al., *Guide du chercheur en histoire canadienne* (Q: PUL 1986), provides a relatively up-to-date bibliography as well as references to older ones. It also offers sections on related disciplines such as archives, genealogy, archaeology, numismatics, geography, climatology, demography, economics, political science, sociology, anthropology, ethnology, folklore, social psychology, and law, as well as chapters on history as a discipline and the historian's use of the computer. In addition, it provides references to European studies for comparative purposes. Alan F.J. Artibise, ed., *Interdisciplinary Approaches to Canadian Society: A Guide to the Literature* (K&M: MQUP 1990), refers to major works in the fields of labour, religious, immigration, ethnic, and Native studies. By treating Quebec historiography in a fashion parallel with that of the rest of Canada, it invites comparisons between the two. More specific to Quebec is Jacques Mathieu, ed., *Les dynamismes de la recherche au Québec* (Q: PUL 1991), which reflects the interdisciplinary approach that now characterizes the study of Quebec society generally.

The most complete bibliography of historical writing since 1946 on Quebec is Paul Aubin and Louis-Marie Côté, comps., *Bibliography of the History of Quebec and Canada*, 8 vols. (Q: IQRC 1981–90). For publications prior to 1946 see Claude Thibault, comp., *Bibliographia Canadiana* (Don Mills, Ont.: Longman 1973). Claudette Cardinal, *The History of Quebec: A Bibliography of Works in English* (M: Centre for the Study of Anglophone Quebec, Concordia University, 1981), was conceived for those who do not read French. Two recent bibliographies on the period 1760–1867 are Gérald Bernier and Robert Boily, *Le Québec en transition, 1760–1867: bibliographie thématique* (M: Association canadienne-française pour l'avancement des sciences 1987), and Pierre Tousignant and Jean-Pierre Wallot, 'Le Régime britannique (1760–1867),' in Jacques Rouillard, ed., *Guide d'histoire du Québec du Régime français à nos jours: bibliographie commentée* (M: Méridien 1991). The former offers a bibliography of Quebec political and constitutional history from a global perspective that takes into account economic and social history and reflects a theoretical commitment to the view that Quebec's status as a British colony stunted what would otherwise have been its 'normal' development. The latter provides a more recent listing and a broader, less theory-driven perspective along with summary historiographical analyses. Indispensable are the current bibliographies found in the *Revue d'histoire de l'Amérique française* and *Canadian Historical Review*, each stronger in the historiography of its language of publication.

Two major reference works are the multivolume *Dictionary of Canadian Biography* (T: UTP 1966–) and the *Historical Atlas of Canada*, vol. 1, *From the Beginning to 1800*, ed. R. Cole Harris (T: UTP [1987]); specific biographies from the one and plates from the other are cited in the appropriate thematic sections later in the chapter. The *DCB*'s biographies knit together through cross-references to constitute a veritable study of Quebec's and Lower Canada's history from a biographical perspective, while the graphs, charts, and maps of the *HAC* offer an innovative and striking perspective on historical development. The general and specific bibliographies in both works are also extremely useful.

PUBLISHED DOCUMENTS

Students of Quebec/Lower Canada are particularly well served by several excellent guides to published primary materials. A good place to start is the general bibliographies of volumes 3 to 12 of the *DCB*, where section 2, 'Printed Primary Sources,' provides short lists of key items relevant to the history of this period. Many printed works listed therein are available on microfiche: see *Canada, the Printed Record: A Bibliographic Register with Indexes to the Microfiche Series of the Canadian Institute for Historical Microreproductions* (O: Canadian Institute for Historical Microreproductions 1990). Furthermore, excellent annotated bibliographies of the imprints of Quebec and Lower Canada exist: see, in particular, Frances M. Staton and Marie Tremaine, eds., *A Bibliography of Canadiana, Being Items in the Public Library of Toronto, Canada, Relating to the Early History and Development of Canada* (T: Toronto Public Library 1934; repr. 1965; 2 supplements 1959–89); Tremaine, ed., *A Bibliography of Canadian Imprints, 1751–1800* (T: UTP 1952); John Hare and J.-P. Wallot, *Les imprimés dans le Bas-Canada, 1801–1840: bibliographie analytique*, vol. 1, *1801–1810* (M: PUM 1967), which provides abundant contextual and critical comment; Jean Hamelin et al., eds., *Brochures québécoises, 1764–1972* (Q: Ministère des Communications, Direction générale des publications governementales 1981); and Milada

Vlach and Yolande Buono, *Catalogue collectif des impressions québécoises, 1764–1820* (Q: Bibliothèque nationale du Québec 1984), which also includes valuable statistics and can be approached through several types of index.

Although there are no substantial general collections of published documents on Quebec and Lower Canada, modest volumes issued as teaching aids do exist. They usually provide either complete documents or extended citations organized by theme or around specific issues, often with a commentary establishing the historical or historiographical context. A list of such works can be found in J. Roy et al., *Guide du chercheur en histoire canadienne.* Documentary collections relating to specific fields are cited in the following thematic sections, but particular mention should be made of J. Hare and J.-P. Wallot, eds., *Ideas in Conflict: A Selection of Texts on Political, Economic and Social Questions in Lower Canada, 1806–1810* (TR: BE 1970); Bruce G. Wilson, ed., *Colonial Identities: Canada from 1760 to 1815*, and George Bolotenko, ed., *A Future Defined: Canada from 1849 to 1873* (O: National Archives of Canada 1988, 1992); and Robert Hébert, ed., *L'Amérique française devant l'opinion étrangère, 1756–1960: anthologie* (M: L'Hexagone 1989), a collection of reflections by European intellectuals, well chosen and presented with an excellent annotated bibliography.

Certain published travel accounts of Lower Canada are especially useful for obtaining an idea of the flavour of life in the colony. C. Thibault, comp., *Bibliographia Canadiana*, and Elizabeth Waterston et al., comps., *The Travellers: Canada to 1900: An Annotated Bibliography of Works Published in English from 1577* (Guelph, Ont.: University of Guelph 1989), provide lists. Of all surveys and travelogues, the works of Joseph Bouchette are the most fertile source of information on the physical and human geography of Lower Canada: see *A Topographical Description of the Province of Lower Canada* (1815; repr. Saint-Lambert, Que.: Canada East Reprints 1973), *The British Dominions in North America*, 2 vols. (L: Colburn and Bentley 1831), and *A Topographical Dictionary of the Province of Lower Canada* (L: Colburn and Bentley 1831). The entry on Bouchette in *DCB*, vol. 7 (1988), places his work in context and provides an excellent bibliography.

Newspapers first appeared in Quebec after the Conquest. Early papers are more interesting historically for their advertisements than for their news. In the nineteenth century, however, they become more firmly rooted in colonial soil and consequently the vehicles of competing ideologies. An exhaustive list with informative historical notices on each newspaper is found in André Beaulieu and J. Hamelin, eds., *La presse québécoise, des origines à nos jours*, vols. 1–2 (Q: PUL 1973–5).

PERIODICALS

Most vanguard historical writing in all fields appears in *RHAF* (1947–), which also provides excellent book reviews. On the evolution of the journal see Fernand Harvey and Paul-André Linteau, 'L'évolution de l'historiographie dans la *Revue d'histoire de l'Amérique française*, 1947–1972: aperçus quantitatifs,' *RHAF* 26/2 (sept. 1972): 163–83, and Jean-Paul Coupal, 'Les dix dernières années de la *Revue d'histoire de l'Amérique française*, 1972–1981,' *RHAF* 36/4 (mars 1983): 553–67. The *CHR* (1920–) publishes an occasional, invariably valuable article on Quebec or Lower Canada and is useful for its book reviews.

Relevant articles may also be found in the Canadian Historical Association, *Annual Report* (1922–65), retitled *Historical Papers* (1966–89), and now *Journal of the Canadian Historical Association* (1990–), and more recently in *Québec Studies* (1983–). *Histoire sociale/Social History* (1968–) is an excellent source of articles from a social perspective, and new approaches are proposed from time to time in the *Cahiers de géographie du Québec* (1978–), formerly *Cahiers de géographie de Québec*, and the *Material History Bulletin* (1977–90), now *Material History Review* (1991–). The *Bulletin des recherches historiques* (1895–1969) contains much anecdotal but also useful material; it should be used with caution, however. The *Transactions of the Royal Society of Canada* (1882–) and the *Cahiers des Dix* (1936–) contain articles by recognized senior historians but rarely break new ground methodologically. *Livres et auteurs québécois* (1969–82) offered annual reviews of the year's historical production.

HISTORIOGRAPHY

Studies of the writing of Canadian history have proliferated in the last twenty-five years. For summary historiographical treatments see D.A. Muise, ed., *A Reader's Guide to Canadian History*, vol. 1, *Beginnings to Confederation* (T: UTP 1982), and J. Rouillard, ed., *Guide d'histoire du Québec du Régime français à nos jours*. Older but still useful are Serge Gagnon, 'Historiographie canadienne ou les fondements de la conscience nationale,' in A. Beaulieu et al., *Guide d'histoire du Canada* (Q: PUL 1969), and a number of historiographical essays in Ramsay Cook, *Canada and the French-Canadian Question* (T: MAC 1966; repr. T: CCP 1986) and *The Maple Leaf Forever: Essays on Nationalism and Politics in Canada* (1971; 3rd ed., T: CCP 1986). In J. Roy et al., *Guide du chercheur en histoire canadienne*, a more exhaustive and more recent list of studies of historiographical trends, first generally and then by subject, will be found. F. Ouellet, *The Socialization of Quebec Historiography since 1960* (T: Robarts Centre for Canadian Studies, York University 1988), is a wide-ranging, critical study that illuminates the main directions of research but does not always escape oversimplification. References to more specialized historiographies will be made in this section as appropriate and in the various thematic sections.

Early-nineteenth-century English-Canadian historiography of Lower Canada largely reflects the attachment of the authors to British constitutional principles and political institutions as the foundations for the sound political development of the colony within the British Empire. Generally speaking it also represents the British-Canadian view of the time, which saw French-Canadian society as politically authoritarian, economically feudal, and socially dominated by the Roman Catholic clergy. According to this historiography, the Conquest, by importing British political institutions, freed New France from the grip of French absolutism, and, by permitting trade with Britain, introduced prosperity through the efforts of a dynamic British middle class. For treatments of the works in English of this period, placing their authors in economic, social, political, and intellectual context, see M. Brook Taylor, *Promoters, Patriots, and Partisans: Historiography in Nineteenth-Century English Canada* (T: UTP 1989), and the *DCB* entries 'John Fleming,' vol. 6 (1987); 'John George Lambton, 1st Earl of Durham,' and 'William Smith,' vol. 7; and 'Robert Christie,' vol. 8 (1985).

The works of English-language authors provoked French-language intellectuals. François-Xavier Garneau, *Histoire du Canada, depuis sa découverte jusqu'à nos jours*, 4 vols. (Q&M: Aubin, Fréchette and Lovell 1845–52), struck a sensitive cord among French Canadians by its romantically inspired portrayal of the Conquest as a tragic event and of the subsequent history of the colony as the heroic struggle of a people to survive in the face of great odds. The *Histoire* went through many editions and various aspects of its nationalism were echoed in all subsequent nineteenth- and early-twentieth-century French-Canadian historiography. Indeed, Garneau's nationalism was perpetuated, albeit in a modified form, down to the Quiet Revolution in the 1960s, especially by Lionel Groulx, professor at the Université de Montréal. Exercising an influence equal to that of Garneau himself, Groulx strongly promoted French, Catholic, and rural traditions and values as bulwarks against the encroachments of Anglo-Saxon materialism on a small, beleaguered, French-Canadian population. An indispensable analysis of French-Canadian historiography from Garneau through Groulx, placing historians in their historical and ideological context, is S. Gagnon, *Quebec and Its Historians, 1840 to 1920* (M: Harvest House 1982). Unfortunately, it does not contain a bibliography. Other useful studies are 'François-Xavier Garneau,' *DCB*, vol. 9 (1976); Jean-Paul Gaboury, *Le nationalisme de Lionel Groulx: aspects idéologiques* (O: PUO 1970); Susan Mann Trofimenkoff, ed., *Abbé Groulx: Variations on a Nationalist Theme* (T: CC 1973); and 'Lionel Groulx: 100e anniversaire de sa naissance, 1878–1978 [Numéro spécial],' *RHAF* 32/3 (déc. 1978). Michael Oliver, *The Passionate Debate: The Social and Political Ideas of Quebec Nationalism, 1920–1945* (M: Véhicule Press 1991), is of contextual interest.

Meanwhile, at the turn of the century the first generation of English-language professional historians, while retaining the nation-building approach of their amateur predecessors, introduced to Canada a positivist empiricist methodology and expanded the scope of inquiry to include economic factors. From the 1930s fairly distinct schools began to emerge. Harold Adams Innis argued that the driving force behind national development was a succession of economic staples, natural products the trade in which structured a national economy, the underpinning of national existence. Building on Innis, Donald Grant Creighton advanced the thesis that the staples of fur, timber, and wheat were developed by an entrepreneurial and progressive British commercial bourgeoisie, who, in their exploitation of the St Lawrence waterway and the markets of the British Empire, laid the foundations for a transcontinental economy in the face of obstacles placed in their way by an inward-looking, feudal, and agricultural French-Canadian society. Creighton's work, most notably *The Commercial Empire of the St. Lawrence, 1760–1850* (T: RP 1937), reprinted as *The Empire of the St. Lawrence* (T: MAC 1956), established the conceptual framework of what became known as the Laurentian school. A parallel liberal school saw nation-building as a process combining emergence from colonial status, rejection of the north-south pull of continental geography, and a reconciliation of the antithetical cultures of French and English Canada. Its best-known advocate, Arthur R.M. Lower, expressed the views of this school most clearly in *Colony to Nation: A History of Canada* (T: Longmans, Green 1946). The standard study of twentieth-century English-language historiography is Carl Berger, *The Writing of Canadian History: Aspects of English-Canadian Historical Writing since 1900* (1976; 2nd ed., T: UTP 1986).

The professionalization of French-Canadian historians occurred in the late 1940s with the establishment of departments of history at the Université de Montréal and Université Laval. They gave rise to sharply opposed schools of interpretation, but rooted in a new common approach to history. As had English-Canadian professional historians, those in Quebec now saw the economy, or politically rooted changes to it, as the major influence on national development. At the Université de Montréal, the neo-nationalist school carried on the nationalist tradition of Garneau and Groulx but rejuvenated it in the context of the industrialization and modernization of Quebec. Its intellectual leader was Maurice Séguin, who in his 1947 doctoral dissertation, later published as *La 'nation canadienne' et l'agriculture (1760– 1850): essai d'histoire économique* (TR: BE 1970), and in *L'idée d'indépendence au Qùébec: genèse et historique* (TR: BE 1977) adopted (while reinterpreting) Groulx's notions of the centrality and tragic nature of the Conquest. For Séguin, the Conquest closed the door of trade to French Canadians, forcing them into agriculture and stunting their 'normal' economic and hence social and political development. Séguin's *normes*, or guidelines, taught year after year to his students, constituted the influential framework of neo-nationalist interpretation and methodology. On Séguin see R. Comeau, ed., *Maurice Séguin, historien du pays québécois vu par ses contemporains* (M: VLB Editeur 1987), which includes the *normes*. Michael D. Behiels, *Prelude to Quebec's Quiet Revolution: Liberalism versus Neo-Nationalism, 1945–1960* (K&M: MQUP 1985), establishes the context in which the neo-nationalist school developed.

Michel Brunet, a younger colleague of Séguin at the Université de Montréal, took Séguin's thesis into the political sphere. In such works as *Canadians et Canadiens: études sur l'histoire et la pensée des deux Canadas* (M: Fides 1954), *La présence anglaise et les Canadiens: études sur l'histoire et la pensée des deux Canadas* (M: Beauchemin 1958), *French Canada in the Early Decades of British Rule, 1760–1791*, CHA Historical Booklet no. 13 (O: 1963), and *Les Canadiens après la Conquête, 1759–1775: de la révolution canadienne à la révolution américaine* (M: Fides 1969), he argued that the Conquest had decapitated French-Canadian society economically, depriving it of its commercial class, and thus weakened it politically. The void left in the lay leadership was filled by a nationalist professional bourgeoisie, which, however, was emasculated politically by the Rebellions of 1837–8. The new vacuum was filled by an ultramontanist clergy, and Lower Canada was thereafter forced into dangerous political unions with English Canada.

The neo-nationalist interpretation was contested by what became known as the Quebec school, based in the Institut d'histoire at Université Laval. Strongest in opposition was F. Ouellet, who, while agreeing that Lower Canada and Quebec had not developed 'normally,' argued that the crucial absence of a commercial middle class was largely a result of French colonial policy before 1760 rather than of British policy after. Writing during the Quiet Revolution in the context of the liberal reaction to the conservative nationalism of Maurice Duplessis, Ouellet also affirmed that the roots of

Quebec's economic inferiority lay primarily in the conservative mentality of its leaders and people, largely unattuned to a market economy. In two major works, *Histoire économique et sociale du Québec*, translated as *Economic and Social History of Quebec, 1760–1850: 'Structures' and 'Conjunctures'* (T: MAC 1980), and *Le Bas-Canada, 1791–1840: changements structuraux et crise* (O: PUO 1976), translated in an abridged and revised form as *Lower Canada, 1791–1840: Social Change and Nationalism* (T: M&S 1980), he argued that the Conquest had less impact on the subsequent development of Lower Canada than a crisis in agriculture at the beginning of the nineteenth century which had major social and economic consequences, including the Rebellions of 1837–8. The crisis, Ouellet maintained, following the general interpretive lines of D.G. Creighton, was largely due to the inability of a conservative, inward-looking, nationalist leadership and people to work with a progressive British commercial bourgeoisie in adapting the colony to a changing western economy.

In the long run, Ouellet's conclusions, which today are widely contested, have been less important than the epistemological and methodological revolution he introduced into Quebec historiography. By writing a global history – economic, social, and political – on the basis of a quantitative study of the colonial economy, Ouellet led historians into the field of quantitative economic and social history – pioneered in France by the *Annales* school. Alfred Dubuc, 'L'influence de l'école des Annales au Québec,' *RHAF* 33/3 (déc. 1979): 357–86, provides a contextual and critical study of the impact of that school on Quebec historiography. More specifically on the work of Ouellet see S. Gagnon, *Quebec and Its Historians: The Twentieth Century* (M: Harvest House 1985), which demonstrates how the historian's ideology affects his use of quantitative methods.

J.-P. Wallot, initially within the neo-nationalist conceptual framework, but later (often in collaboration with Gilles Paquet) revising the neo-nationalist position, has contested Ouellet's postulate of an agricultural crisis and its roots in an inability to modernize that was specific to French-Canadian society. Instead, expanding the methodology introduced by Ouellet, he has worked over the past twenty years through numerous books and articles toward a different global interpretation of Lower Canadian society, one that is rooted in the 'normal' development of Quebec in the 1970s and 1980s. He sees in French Lower Canada a 'normal' dynamic, entrepreneurial society in the process of economic and social reconstruction and modernization, open to the social and political revolutions going on in the Atlantic world, increasingly affected by the market economy that produces ever more clearly defined social groups. This dynamic French-Canadian society, with its local views of the colony's economic, social, and political destiny, collides with a conservative British colonial business community operating in an imperial perspective. Politically, the protagonists clash within a semi-parliamentary system that allows each to express its views dominantly in one or the other of the two chambers; the inability of either to overcome the other generates frustration and ultimately ignites the Rebellions of 1837–8. This interpretation is most concisely expressed in G. Paquet and J.-P. Wallot, *Lower Canada at the Turn of the Nineteenth Century: Restructuring and Modernization*, CHA Historical Booklet no. 45 (O: 1988). Ronald Rudin, 'Revisionism and the Search for a Normal Society: A Critique of Recent Quebec Historical Writing,' *CHR* 73/1 (Mar. 1992): 30–61, argues that revisionists have tried too hard to portray Lower Canadian society as integrated into the development of western society and have understated the seriousness of ethnic conflict. However, he largely ignores Wallot's school, which gives prominence to that question. As well, Rudin's assimilation of Ouellet with the 'traditionalist' historiography is a gross oversimplification, but his suggestion of parallels between Quebec and Irish historiography is intriguing.

The nationalist component in Québécois ideology is so constant and intense that even Marxist historical studies, normally based on the class struggle, were profoundly influenced by it. In the fertile matrix of the Quiet Revolution Marxist historiography emerged from the strong left-wing ideology that characterized much of sociological thought in Montreal intellectual circles. Gilles Bourque, *Question nationale et classes sociales au Québec, 1760–1840* (M: Parti Pris 1970), gave fullest expression to the synthesis of Marxism and nationalism constituted by the concept of the ethnic class. Bourque argued that the Conquest had inflicted on Quebec a double, ethnically based class structure; the French-Canadian class structure had no top and the British no base so that all subsequent class conflict was also governed by ethnic differences. This work and Bourque's subsequent studies are long on hypothesis and analysis, but short on empirical demonstration. The Marxist approach had declined along with radical left-wing ideology in contemporary Quebec society, which since the late 1970s has consistently moved in a capitalist, entrepreneurial direction better represented in historical interpretations by J.-P. Wallot, his students, and others. However, socialist historiography was recently rejuvenated by G. Bernier and Daniel Salée in *The Shaping of Québec Politics and Society: Colonialism, Power, and the Transition to Capitalism in the 19th Century* (NY: Crane Russak 1992). They reject analysis of the development of Lower Canada in terms of a national conflict or of an economic metropolitan-colonial dynamic, and instead argue that the problems in Lower Canada must be viewed in terms of the internal colonial dynamic of a society in transition from feudalism to capitalism. This approach, which promises to renew once again the historiography of Lower Canada, is already echoed, for example, in the field of judicial history by the work of Jean-Marie Fecteau.

Some recent general works bring together the major contemporary historiographical trends. S.M. Trofimenkoff, *The Dream of Nation: A Social and Intellectual History of Quebec* (T: MAC 1982), synthesizes work in French and English to that point, adding a women's perspective (albeit limited for the period 1760 to 1850) to explain to English Canadians how the dream of nation took root in post-Conquest Quebec. Brian Young and John A. Dickinson's *A Short History of Quebec* (1988; 2nd ed., T: CCP 1993) succeeds admirably and innovatively by employing a periodization based on economic rather than political developments. The work of R. Douglas Francis et al., *Origins: Canadian History to Confederation* (2nd ed., T: HRW 1992), is useful but less original. Two original studies which look at the past from the perspective of the formation of collective memory and national identity are Heinz Weinmann, *Du Canada au Québec: généalogie d'une histoire* (M: L'Hexagone 1987), and J. Mathieu and Jacques Lacoursière, *Les mémoires québécoises* (Q: PUL 1991).

ECONOMIC AND SOCIAL HISTORY

In the past decade the majority of studies on Quebec and Lower Canada have been economic or social or have approached other fields, such as politics, religion, or culture, from a socio-economic perspective. F. Ouellet, *Socialization of Quebec Historiography*, reveals the scope of this trend, while J.A. Dickinson and B. Young, in 'Periodization in Quebec History: A Reevaluation,' *Québec Studies* 12 (Spring/Summer 1991): 1–10, argue that the impact is such that historians ought to abandon the politically based periodization generally employed to date.

It being virtually impossible in contemporary historical approaches to separate the economy and society, this section will be by far the largest of the thematic divisions. An effort, inevitably frustrating, has been made to reduce this vast field to more comprehensible but still meaningful subdivisions.

General Economic and Social Histories

While rejecting neither H.A. Innis's staples theory nor, generally speaking,

D.G. Creighton's Laurentian perspective, F. Ouellet's *Economic and Social History of Quebec* broadened Innis's and Creighton's perspectives to include the French-Canadian economy and society, which they had largely neglected. It studied a number of quantitative series, such as grain prices, production, and export volumes, in order to determine the economic underpinnings of the social and political development of the colony. In subsequent books, *Eléments d'histoire sociale du Bas-Canada* (M: Hurtubise HMH 1972) (a collection of essays) and *Lower Canada, 1791–1840*, as well as in numerous articles, Ouellet sought to confirm his hypothesis of a crisis in agriculture that was in large part a result of a cultural mentality-based rejection by the French-speaking farmer of British technological innovations and the market economy. Ouellet's development of his position in the 1980s, in large part in response to new interpretations of many of the phenomena that he had studied earlier, is revealed in a major collection of translated and reprinted articles entitled *Economy, Class, & Nation in Quebec: Interpretive Essays*, ed. and trans. Jacques A. Barbier (T: CCP 1991). Of particular interest is 'Ruralization, Regional Development, and Industrial Growth before 1850,' especially written for the volume, which, after a survey of the most recent literature, maintains his original views.

In numerous articles since the late 1960s G. Paquet and J.-P. Wallot have contested Ouellet's interpretation. On the basis of their own studies of quantitative serial indices as well as a vast research into notarial records, they have argued that the Lower Canadian economy functioned well in the early nineteenth century, restructuring and modernizing under market influences. Rather than becoming poorer, they assert, the Canadian farmer improved his financial and social lot. This interpretation has been expressed most recently in Paquet and Wallot, *Lower Canada at the Turn of the Nineteenth Century*. In *The Shaping of Québec Politics and Society*, G. Bernier and D. Salée see in political and institutional resistance to the transition from a feudal to a capitalist society the primary source of political and social tension in the colony. An earlier expression of their views was ably criticized by Claude Couture, 'The Conquest of 1760 and the Problem of the Transition to Capitalism,' in Angus D. Gilbert et al., eds., *Reappraisals in Canadian History*, vol. 1, *Pre-Confederation* (Scarborough, Ont.: PH 1993), first published in French in 1986.

Mention must be made also of the voluminous and original work of Serge Courville, who, along with Jean-Claude Robert and Normand Séguin, is currently directing a vast study of the Laurentian axis, focusing on economic, social, and geographic factors involved in the transformation of pre-industrial Quebec society. Reference will be made later to specific publications by these authors; however, a general sense of the scope, direction, and initial results of the work of their research group can be gleaned from *Le pays laurentien au XIXe siècle, cahier 1* (Q/M/TR: Université Laval/ Université du Québec à Montréal/Université du Québec à Trois-Rivières 1992).

Robert Armstrong, in *Structure and Change: An Economic History of Quebec* (T: Gage 1984), adopts the staples theory as his basic explanatory model down to 1850, but also incorporates the work of Ouellet, Paquet and Wallot, Courville, and John McCallum, among others, into a global view of the economy. He argues that language and cultural differences after 1760 slowed the modernization of Quebec's agriculture but that the mentality of the French-speaking habitant was not a deciding factor as Ouellet advanced. Armstrong's approach is strongly criticized in José E. Igartua, 'Le Québec de Pangloss: *Structure and Change: An Economic History of Quebec*,' *RHAF* 39/2 (automne 1985): 253–61. The best general economic history of the period after 1850 is still J. Hamelin and Yves Roby, *Histoire économique du Québec, 1851–1896* (M: Fides 1971). Finally, the work of Kenneth Norrie and Douglas Owram, *A History of the Canadian Economy* (T: HBJ 1990), provides a useful summary of the debate on the question of the economy as revealed in English-language publications. Its failure to consider the breadth and depth of the literature in French, however, prevents it from rendering satisfactorily the richness and complexity of the controversy.

The Rural Economy and Society

Much of recent work has concentrated on rural life, a neglected field prior to the publication of F. Ouellet's *Histoire économique et sociale du Québec*. Treatments of the historiography will be found in J.-P. Wallot, 'L'historiographie canadienne et l'histoire de la société rurale québécoise,' in Joseph Goy and Wallot, eds., *Etude comparative de la société rurale de la France de l'Ouest et du Québec (XVIIIe–XXe siècles)* (M: Université de Montréal 1981), and J. Rouillard, ed., *Guide d'histoire du Québec du Régime français à nos jours*. Catherine Desbarats, 'Agriculture within the Seigneurial Régime of Eighteenth-Century Canada: Some Thoughts on the Recent Literature,' *CHR* 73/1 (Mar. 1992): 1–29, is an excellent critical study, largely applicable as well to the literature of the early nineteenth century. One should also consult Jacques Cochetière and Louis Dupont, 'Genèse des structures d'habitat dans les seigneuries du Québec: une bibliographie sélective,' *Cahiers de géographie du Québec* 28/73-4 (avril–sept. 1984): 317–27, and the bibliography in S. Courville, *Entre ville et campagne: l'essor du village dans les seigneuries du Bas-Canada* (Q: PUL 1990). Gérard Bouchard, 'La dynamique communautaire et l'évolution des sociétés rurales québécoises aux 19e et 20e siècles: construction d'un modèle,' *RHAF* 40/1 (été 1986): 51–71, argues that historians should concentrate their efforts more on the study of certain constants in rural social dynamics.

A number of reference works have grown out of this preoccupation with rural society while aspiring to strengthen the foundation on which more solid analysis can be constructed. The evolution of the territorial organization of Lower Canada into parishes, towns, fiefs, and seigneuries is a vital factor in quantitative studies of data relating to clearly defined geographical units in time. This evolution is detailed in S. Courville et al., *Seigneuries et fiefs du Québec: nomenclature et cartographie* (Q: CELAT/Commission de toponymie 1988), and Courville et al., *Paroisses et municipalités de la région de Montréal au XIXe siècle (1825–1861): répertoire documentaire et cartographique* (Q: PUL 1988). These two valuable works will further advance one major trend in Lower Canadian historiography in the last decade: detailed case studies, focused on specific historiographical issues, in small, clearly de-limited geographical areas. Christian Dessureault, 'Crise ou modernisation: la société rurale maskoutaine durant le premier tiers du XIXe siècle,' *RHAF* 42/3 (hiver 1989): 359–87, is a regional case study that finds confirmation of the general interpretation of G. Paquet and J.-P. Wallot.

Another major trend in the last decade is the flowering of comparative history. J.I. Little has produced several studies comparing different aspects of French-Canadian and Anglo-American agriculture in the Eastern Town-ships, culminating in his *Crofters and Habitants: Settler Society, Economy, and Culture in a Quebec Township, 1848–1881* (K&M: MQUP 1991), a compari-son of the Scottish and French-Canadian settlement experiences in Win-slow Township. G. Bouchard, 'L'historiographie du Québec rural et la problématique nord-américaine avant la Révolution tranquille: étude d'un refus,' *RHAF* 44/2 (automne 1990): 199–222, and Béatrice Craig, 'Pour une approche comparative de l'étude des sociétés rurales nord-américaines,' *HS/SH* 23/46 (Nov. 1990): 249–70, argue forcefully that the study of rural Quebec requires the perspective provided by comparison with other North American rural societies. In 'Un nouvel espace historiographique: la dynamique inter-régionale et le cycle de la société rurale québécoise du 17e au 20e siècle,' in Philip P. Boucher, ed., *Proceedings of the Eleventh Meeting of the French Colonial Historical Society, May 1985* (NY: University Press of America 1987), G. Bouchard also argues in favour of comparative studies within the French-Canadian experience.

Much work in the last decade, however, has concentrated on the comparison of rural society in Lower Canada and in the west of France, from where most Lower Canadian families originated. Several works containing original empirical research are to be found in the published proceedings of a number of symposia: J. Goy and J.-P. Wallot, eds., *Société rurale dans la France de l'Ouest et au Québec (XVIIe–XXe siècles)* ([M/P]: Université de Montréal/Ecole des hautes études en sciences sociales 1981); Goy and Wallot, eds., *Evolution et éclatement du monde rural: structures, fonctionnement et évolution différentielle des sociétés françaises et québécoises, XVIIe–XXe siècles* (P/M: Ecole des hautes études en sciences sociales/PUM 1986); François Lebrun and N. Séguin, eds., *Sociétés villageoises et rapports villes-campagnes au Québec et dans la France de l'Ouest, XVIIe–XXe siècles* (TR: Centre de recherche en études québécoises, Université du Québec à Trois-Rivières 1987); 'Les dynamismes culturels en France et au Québec: colloque France-Québec, Rennes, 2 et 3 juin 1988,' a special issue of *Annales de Bretagne et des pays de l'Ouest* 95/4 (1988); and G. Bouchard and Goy, eds., *Famille, économie et société rurale en contexte d'urbanisation (17e–20e siècles)* (Chicoutimi, Que./P: Centre interuniversitaire SOREP/Ecole des hautes études en sciences sociales 1990). These collective works are as interesting for the comparison of methodologies used by Québécois and French historians as for the results. For all their interest these studies are not without weaknesses, most notably a lack of direction and focus and a tendency to produce parallel rather than truly comparative results. Claire Dolan, 'Nouveaux besoins, nouvelles cibles? L'histoire rurale et la coopération France-Québec,' *RHAF* 42/4 (printemps 1989): 589–96, and Hubert Watelet, 'Ombres et lumières d'un vaste projet: l'histoire rurale comparée de la France de l'Ouest et du Québec,' *RHAF* 43/2 (automne 1989): 233–45, provide perceptive assessments.

Meanwhile, the study of the dynamics within Lower Canadian rural society begun in the 1960s has continued apace in the last decade. S. Courville, in particular, in numerous articles, has studied various facets and dynamics of Quebec rural society between 1815 and 1850 from the perspective of a historical geographer. His perception of Lower Canada is of a society in transition broadly but not uniformly influenced by market forces – local more than imperial – and tending to a form of rural urbanization, that is, the development of villages, with consequent economic and social distinctions, which form the link between the local and urban economies. Courville's views are presented succinctly in S. Courville and N. Séguin, *Rural Life in Nineteenth-Century Quebec*, CHA Historical Booklet no. 47 (O: 1989), and developed more fully in *Entre ville et campagne*. In the latter he weaves together geographic, demographic, ethnographic, economic, and social aspects of Quebec rural society generally to explain the emergence, social composition, and functions of rural villages, and their relationship with their hinterlands.

Courville is not alone in furthering rural analyses. J.-C. Robert, 'Aperçu sur les structures socio-professionnelles des villages de la région nord de Montréal durant la première moitié du XIXe siècle,' *Cahiers de géographie du Québec* 28/73–4 (avril–sept. 1984): 63–72, studies the roles of villages, while his 'Activités agricoles et urbanisation dans la paroisse de Montréal, 1820–1840,' in F. Lebrun and N. Séguin, eds., *Sociétés villageoises et rapports villes-campagnes*, analyses farmers' adjustment to the Montreal market and the urban influence on agricultural land use. Lise St-Georges, 'Transformations de la société rurale dans l'espace périurbain montréalais: Pointe-aux-Trembles, 1781–1871,' in G. Bouchard and J. Goy, eds., *Famille, économie et société rurale*, outlines the *problématique* of a doctoral thesis that constitutes a case study in rural change. Allan Greer, *Peasant, Lord, and Merchant: Rural Society in Three Quebec Parishes, 1740–1840* (T: UTP 1985), is as interesting for its conceptual framework and multidisciplinary approach as for its empirical results. Much more than a case study of three parishes in the Richelieu Valley, this work demonstrates from within how rural society adjusted to changing circumstances and, better than any other study, how and to what extent it was connected to the broader commercial economy.

An integral part of rural society, the seigneurial system, has attracted attention for much longer than has that society as a whole. An indispensable reference work is S. Courville et al., *Seigneuries et fiefs du Québec*, while a graphic synthesis of seigneurial development in the late eighteenth century is provided in Louise Dechêne, 'The Seigneuries,' *HAC*, vol. 1, plate 51. Numerous studies in the past by Georges Baillargeon, Jacques Boucher, F. Ouellet, M. Séguin, and J.-P. Wallot (see G. Bernier and R. Boily, *Le Québec en transition, 1760–1867: bibliographie thématique*) have examined the economic impact of the seigneurial system and analysed the reasons for its abolition. Corinne Beutler, 'Les moulins à farine du Séminaire de Saint-Sulpice à Montréal (1658–1840): essai d'analyse économique d'une prérogative du régime seigneurial,' CHA *HP* (1983): 184–207, studies the economic impact of the seigneurs' right to grind grain, while her 'Le rôle des moulins banaux du Séminaire de Saint-Sulpice à Montréal entre la campagne et la ville, 1790–1840,' in J. Goy and J.-P. Wallot, eds., *Evolution et éclatement du monde rural*, portrays the seigneurial grist mill as a linchpin between the rural and urban economies.

Some of the best work in this field focuses on the experience of individual seigneuries. Sylvie Dépatie, Mario Lalancette, and C. Dessureault, *Con-*

tributions à l'étude du régime seigneurial canadien (Ville La Salle, Que.: Hurtubise HMH 1987), through three case studies inspired by the work of L. Dechêne, scrutinize the seigneurial system in the light of current historiographical preoccupations. By studying particularly the seigneurial dues as the heart of the system, they conclude that it was essentially feudal and exploitive. Claude Baribeau, *La seigneurie de la Petite-Nation, 1801–1854: le rôle économique et social du seigneur* (Hull, Que.: Asticou 1983), arrives at similar conclusions. Françoise Noël, *The Christie Seigneuries: Estate Management and Settlement in the Upper Richelieu Valley, 1760–1854* (K&M: MQUP 1992), synthesizes the results of a number of excellent articles that she has contributed in recent years on the manner in which certain seigneurs adapted their management to different economic and geographic circumstances. And S. Courville, 'Rente déclarée payée sur la censive de 90 arpents au recensement nominatif de 1831: méthodologie d'une recherche,' *Cahiers de géographie du Québec* 27/70 (avril 1983): 43–61, although essentially a methodological exposé of considerable interest, nevertheless also concludes from a study of rents paid that seigneurs adapted the rents they composed in such a manner as to obtain maximum profits from their situation. Richard Chabot, 'Les terriers de Nicolet: une source importante pour l'histoire rurale du Québec au début du XIXe siècle,' *Les cahiers nicolétains* 6/3 (sept. 1984): 114–26, and Alain Laberge, 'Seigneur, censitaires et paysage rural: le papier-terrier de la seigneurie de la Rivière-Ouelle de 1771,' *RHAF* 44/4 (printemps 1991): 567–87, demonstrate the possibilities and limitations of the seigneurial estate rolls as a documentary source. Michael B. Percy and Rick Szostak, in 'The Political Economy of the Abolition of Seigneurial Tenure in Canada East,' *Explorations in Economic History* 29/1 (Jan. 1992): 51–68, argue that the timing and manner of the commutation of seigneurial to freehold tenure in 1854 reflect politico-financial rather than socio-economic factors.

Various aspects of the functioning of rural society have been explored by historians in an effort to determine how (and how well) that society adjusted to changing economic conditions. One of these is the accumulation, exploitation, and transmission of property, which is studied in Louis Michel, 'Varennes et Verchères, des origines au milieu du XIXe siècle: état d'une enquête,' in J. Goy and J.-P. Wallot, eds., *Evolution et éclatement du monde rural*, and G. Paquet and Wallot, 'Stratégie foncière de l'habitant: Québec (1790–1835),' *RHAF* 39/4 (printemps 1986): 551–81, as well as in essays by Paquet and Wallot, M. Lalancette, and C. Dessureault in F. Lebrun and N. Séguin, eds., *Sociétés villageoises et rapports ville-campagnes*. All are interesting methodological studies as well. G. Bouchard, 'Transmission of Family

Property and the Cycle of Quebec Rural Society from the Seventeenth to the Twentieth Century,' in Bettina Bradbury, ed., *Canadian Family History: Selected Readings* (T: CCP 1992), sees social reproduction through property transmission as the basis of social structure and transformation and argues that the cycle of transformation of Quebec rural society completed two revolutions – one in the St Lawrence Valley and one in interior frontier regions – from the seventeenth to the twentieth centuries.

The transmission of wealth through inheritance and inheritance practices themselves and their consequences are the subjects of several specialized analyses: Dominique Joulia, 'Pratiques successorales en milieu rural, 1795–1820: étude comparative de cas France de l'Ouest – Québec,' in J. Goy and J.-P. Wallot, eds., *Société rurale dans la France de l'Ouest et au Québec*; Katherine Macklem, 'Patterns of Inheritance in Early Mid-Nineteenth Century French Canada,' *The Register* 2/1 (1981): 1–25; and B. Craig, 'La transmission des patrimoines fonciers dans le Haut-Saint-Jean au XIXe siècle,' *RHAF* 45/2 (automne 1991): 207–28. Luce Vermette, 'Les donations: activités domestiques et genre de vie, 1800–1820 et 1850–1870,' in J. Goy and J.-P. Wallot, eds., *Evolution et éclatement du monde rural*, shows how, concerned about their old age in an uncertain economic climate, elderly parents contracted for their upkeep with their children in return for bequeathing their property. And Michel Verdon, 'Autour de la famille souche: essai d'anthropologie conjecturale,' *Anthropologie et sociétés* 11/1 (1987): 137–60, is a speculative article that supports F. Ouellet's thesis of an agricultural crisis on the grounds that such a crisis would account for changes in inheritance practices and the appearance of stem families.

Another measure of economic and social development in rural society much studied in recent years is the accumulation of wealth or debt as revealed by the payment of seigneurial dues, spending patterns in rural stores, and property estates. G. Paquet and J.-P. Wallot, 'Crédit et endettement en milieu rural bas-canadien,' in G. Bouchard and J. Goy, eds., *Famille, économie et société rurale*, provides a historiographical survey of the subject and argues that debt accumulation, as a corollary of the extension of credit, is an indication of the penetration of market mechanisms into rural Lower Canada rather than of peasant impoverishment. L. Michel, 'Endettement et société rurale dans la région de Montréal au dix-huitième siècle: premières approches et éléments de réflexion,' in F. Lebrun and N. Séguin, eds., *Société villageoises et rapports villes-campagnes*, had earlier argued in that vein.

A key source for the study of wealth and debt accumulation is the estate inventory, the value and uses of which are assessed in G. Paquet and J.-P.

Wallot, 'Les inventaires après décès à Montréal au tournant du XIXe siècle: préliminaires à une analyse,' *RHAF* 30/2 (sept. 1976): 163–221, and 'Les inventaires après décès: source riche pour l'étude de la culture matérielle et des genres de vie dans le Bas Canada,' *Annales de Bretagne et des pays de l'Ouest* 95/4 (1988): 389–400. Yvan Morin, 'La représentativité de l'inventaire après décès – l'étude d'un cas: Québec au début du XIXe siècle,' *RHAF* 34/4 (mars 1981): 515–33; C. Dessureault, 'L'inventaire après décès et l'agriculture bas-canadienne,' *MHB* 17 (Spring 1983): 127–38; Lorraine Gadoury, 'Les stocks des habitants dans les inventaires après décès,' *MHB* 17 (Spring 1983): 139–47; and C. Beutler, 'L'outillage agricole dans les inventaires paysans de la région de Montréal: reflète-t-il une transformation de l'agriculture entre 1792 et 1835?' in F. Lebrun and N. Séguin, eds., *Sociétés villageoises et rapports villes-campagnes*, demonstrate historical uses of this source for the analysis of agricultural practices as an indication of changes (or stability) in wealth. On the other hand, the essay by Martine Cardin and J.A. Dickinson, 'Les inventaires de biens après décès et la civilisation matérielle dans les plaines de Caen et de Montréal 1740–1780,' also in the Lebrun and Séguin volume, is an interesting methodological study on the limits and usefulness of the inventory for comparative history. Dickinson, 'Niveau de vie des paysans normands et québécois au 18e siècle,' in G. Bouchard and J. Goy, eds., *Famille, économie et société rurale*, looks at the use of a standard of living index derived from data in estate inventories. Evaluating another source, M. Cardin and Guy Desmarais, in 'Les contrats de mariage au Bas-Canada: étude préliminaire,' *Cahiers d'histoire* 3/2 (printemps 1983): 45–63, render a qualified verdict on the utility of marriage contracts for determining levels of wealth but affirm their general usefulness for economic and social history.

Others use merchants' accounts to determine the degree of penetration of the market economy from consumer patterns: L. Michel, 'Le livre de compte (1784–1792) de Gaspard Massue, marchand à Varennes,' *HS/SH* 13/26 (Nov. 1980): 369–98; Claude Desrosiers, 'Un aperçu des habitudes de consommation de la clientèle de Joseph Cartier, marchand général à Saint-Hyacinthe à la fin du XVIIIe siècle,' *CHA HP* (1984): 91–110; and Desrosiers, 'La clientèle d'un marchand général en milieu rural à la fin du XVIIIe siècle: analyse des comportements de consommation,' in F. Lebrun and N. Séguin, eds., *Sociétés villageoises et rapports villes-campagnes*, all look at the end of the eighteenth century, a period of economic difficulty.

Studies of property transmission and spending patterns fuel discussions about the stratification of rural society as evidence of social development. For F. Ouellet that means difficult economic conditions leading to political crisis, and for G. Paquet and J.-P. Wallot it signifies the penetration of market forces. For examples of these approaches see the works of Ouellet already cited; Paquet and Wallot, 'Structures sociales et niveaux de richesse dans les campagnes de Québec, 1792–1812,' *MHB* 17 (Spring 1983): 25–44; and C. Dessureault, 'L'égalitarisme paysan dans l'ancienne société rurale de la vallée du Saint-Laurent: éléments pour une ré-interprétation,' *RHAF* 40/ 3 (hiver 1987): 373–407, which considers social differentiation inherent in pre-industrial rural society. Michel Monette, 'Groupes dominants et structure locale de pouvoir à Deschambault et Saint-Casimir, comté de Portneuf (1829–1870),' *Cahiers de géographie du Québec* 28/73–4 (avril–sept. 1984): 73–88, analyses the emergence of local power struggles in a context of rural social restructuring. Tiphaine Barthelemy de Saizieu, 'Les alliances matrimoniales à Neuville à la fin du XVIIIe siècle,' in J. Goy and J.-P. Wallot, eds., *Evolution et éclatement du monde rural*, obtained equivocal results in an attempt to discern social stratification in marriage strategies.

Agriculture

With notable exceptions, agriculture was a neglected subject until the 1960s. Works that, because of their historiographical significance, still bear reading are W.H. Parker, 'A New Look at Unrest in Lower Canada in the 1830's,' *CHR* 40/3 (Sept. 1959): 209–17, which, by linking the Rebellions of 1837–8 to bad harvests in the years preceding them, foreshadows the work of F. Ouellet; and M. Séguin, *La 'nation canadienne' et l'agriculture*, which, in finding French-Canadian agricultural practices comparable to those of contemporary Americans and Upper Canadians, established a school of thought that rejected a backward, feudal mentality as the explanation for the agricultural crisis. It is F. Ouellet, however, who brought agriculture to the forefront of historical study, through previously mentioned books and numerous articles, such as 'Les prix agricoles dans les villes et les campagnes du Québec d'avant 1850: aperçus quantitatifs,' *HS/SH* 15/29 (May 1982): 83–127, written with J. Hamelin and R. Chabot.

Ouellet has his antagonists. G. Paquet and J.-P. Wallot expressed their view in 'The Agricultural Crisis in Lower Canada, 1802–12: *mise au point*. A Response to T.J.A. Le Goff,' *CHR* 56/2 (June 1975): 133–61. As study of the subject advanced, others intervened. T.J.A. Le Goff, 'The Agricultural Crisis in Lower Canada, 1802–12: A Review of a Controversy,' *CHR* 55/1 (Mar. 1974): 1–31, rather supported Ouellet. L. Dechêne, 'Observations sur l'agriculture du Bas-Canada au début du XIXe siècle,' in J. Goy and J.-P. Wallot, eds., *Evolution et éclatement du monde rural*, sees more difficulties than progress before 1837. S. Courville, 'La crise agricole du Bas-Canada, éléments d'une réflexion géographique [deux parties],' *Cahiers de géographie du Québec* 24/62–3 (sept.–déc. 1980): 193–223, 385–428, supports Paquet and Wallot. R.M. McInnis, 'A Reconsideration of the State of Agriculture in Lower Canada in the First Half of the Nineteenth Century,' *CPRH*, vol. 3 (1982), and C. Beutler, 'Le marché du blé et les prix céréaliers à Montréal à la fin du régime seigneurial (1790–1840),' in Liliane Mottu-Webber and Dominique Zumkeller, eds., *Mélanges d'histoire économique offerts au Professeur Anne-Marie Pinz* (Genève: ISTEC/Université de Genève 1989), offer interpretations contradicting Ouellet. Robert Lavertue, 'L'histoire de l'agriculture québécoise au XIXe siècle: une schématisation des faits et des interprétations,' *Cahiers de géographie du Québec* 28/73–4 (avril–sept. 1984): 275–87, is a useful summary comparison of the major interpretations to that date.

J. McCallum's excellent comparative study, *Unequal Beginnings: Agriculture and Economic Development in Quebec and Ontario until 1870* (T: UTP 1980), credits the thesis of a crisis in Lower Canadian agriculture but attributes it to competition from Upper Canada and the United States, where rich, new soils rather than technological superiority made the production of wheat and other produce more profitable. Lower Canadian agriculture restructured itself in consequence, more or less successfully, diversifying its production and concentrating on local markets. The lack of a strong commercially based agriculture prevented the growth of villages, which in turn hobbled the development of a manufacturing sector and forced farmers to migrate to Montreal and Quebec or to the United States or to remain on the land as cheap labour. McCallum has been criticized for underestimating the importance of technology and of cultural factors and institutions – particularly the seigneurial system – in hampering French-Canadian agriculture: see, for example, R. Armstrong's review in *RHAF* 35/2 (sept. 1982): 281–4. His assertion that there was little growth of villages in the countryside has been challenged by S. Courville, *Entre ville et campagne*. Nevertheless, McCallum's work is an impressive empirical study that goes well beyond description to seek the mechanisms behind growth and development. Thomas Wien, 'Visites paroissiales et production agricole au Canada vers la fin du XVIIIe siècle,' in F. Lebrun and N. Séguin, eds., *Sociétés villageoises et rapports villes-campagnes*, assesses payment of the tithe as an indicator of agricultural production, while R.C. Harris, 'The Agricultural Economy,' *HAC*, vol. 1, plate 53, provides an excellent graphic survey of eighteenth-century agriculture in Quebec.

Central to the debate over agriculture is the efficiency of Lower Canadian farmers and the role of culture and technology in agricultural productivity. In addition to being discussed in a number of works already mentioned, these questions have specifically formed the subject of a number of studies, notably, Frank D. Lewis and Marvin McInnis, 'The Efficiency of the French-Canadian Farmer in the Nineteenth Century,' *Journal of Economic History* 40/3 (Sept. 1980): 497–514, and 'Agricultural Output and Efficiency in Lower Canada, 1851,' *Research in Economic History* 9 (1984): 45–87. These economic studies call into question earlier findings that Anglo-American farmers were more efficient than their francophone counterparts and that there was an agricultural crisis in the 1830s. R. Armstrong, 'The Efficiency of Quebec Farmers in 1851,' *HS/SH* 17/33 (May 1984): 149–63, disputes the findings of Lewis and McInnis on the basis of weaknesses in their data. McInnis, 'Some Pitfalls in the 1851–1852 Census of Agriculture of Lower Canada,' *HS/SH* 14/27 (May 1981): 219–31, and J.I. Little, 'Agricultural Progress in Canada East/Quebec: Problems in Measuring Relative Productivity during the Grain-Dairy Transition Period,' *HS/SH* 18/36 (Nov. 1985): 425–31, provide salutary warnings about the limitations of the sources for and the complexity of the subject of such studies. In the essentially ethnographic study, *L'équipement aratoire et horticole du Québec ancien (XVIIe, XVIIIe, et XIXe siècles)*, 2 vols. (M: Guérin 1989), Robert-Lionel Séguin analyses the relative roles of geography, climate, culture, and politics, among others, in the choice, adaptation, and transmission of agricultural equipment. See also C. Beutler, 'La modernisation de l'équipement agricole dans la région de Montréal: recherches sur l'origine des nouveaux modèles de charrue d'après les inventaires après décès, 1792–1835,' in G. Bouchard and J. Goy, eds., *Famille, économie et société rurale*.

Business

Although it was one of the first sectors of economic history to be explored, business has been eclipsed by agriculture in the last decade. The study of business history has tended to be divided into sectors: imperial versus internal trade, and Montreal versus Quebec; recently there has been a trend to searching for the links between small and large commercial operations. The historiography of Lower Canadian business in general (specific sectors will be discussed later) begins with D.G. Creighton's study of the Montreal big business community, *The Commercial Empire of the St. Lawrence*. Its influence on historiography has been strong, but the book has now been surpassed. The previously cited works of F. Ouellet do examine both local and imperial trade as well as the Montreal and Quebec business communities but not in depth. The Scottish merchants, who dominated the imperial trade, have been studied in David S. Macmillan, 'The "New Men" in Action: Scottish Mercantile and Shipping Operations in the North American Colonies, 1760–1825,' in Macmillan, ed., *Canadian Business History: Selected Studies, 1497–1971* (T: M&S 1972). More recently Michael Bliss, *Northern Enterprise: Five Centuries of Canadian Business* (T: M&S 1987), has synthesized English-Canadian historiography from a business perspective but added little that is original and virtually ignored studies in French on local businessmen. T. Wien and James S. Pritchard's 'Canadian North Atlantic Trade,' *HAC*, vol. 1, plate 48, provides a revealing comparison of trade from Quebec as a French and as a British colony in the eighteenth century. George Bervin, 'Les sources archivistiques: leur utilisation dans l'étude de la bourgeoisie marchande bas-canadienne (1800–1830),' *RHAF* 38/2 (automne 1984): 203–22, is an excellent introduction to the primary sources on which recent studies have been based.

Bervin's own work, especially *Québec au XIXe siècle: l'activité économique des grands marchands* (Sillery, Que.: SPT 1991), gives the fullest picture to date of the business community at Quebec in the early nineteenth century, its British business and colonial military connections, credit network, financial structure, and role in the development of steam navigation. It concludes that the Quebec businessman of this time, engaging as he did in a multiplicity of activities, was a transitional figure between the commercial merchant of the eighteenth century and the manufacturing entrepreneur of the later nineteenth century. It is not a synthesis, however, since connections with retailers and rural suppliers, among other subjects, are little explored. The book does provide an excellent bibliography.

As for Montreal, C. Beutler analyses the mechanics of that city's wheat trade in 'Approvisionnement et commerce des blés à Montréal au tournant du XIXe siècle,' in J. Goy and J.-P. Wallot, eds., *Etude comparative de la société rurale*, and 'Le rôle du blé à Montréal sous le régime seigneurial,' *RHAF* 36/2 (sept. 1982): 241–62. B. Young, *In Its Corporate Capacity: The Seminary of Montreal as a Business Institution, 1816–1876* (K&M: MQUP 1986), is a solidly documented, innovative, analytic study of an influential institution but unfortunately excludes consideration of the seminary's religious and teaching vocations in studying its business performance during a period of transition from feudalism to capitalism.

G. Bernier and D. Salée's *The Shaping of Québec Politics and Society*, a largely interpretive essay written from a Marxist perspective, argues that because business at this time was still based mainly on trade and landownership rather than production, it was essentially feudal rather than capitalist in nature. Evelyn Kolish, 'L'introduction de la faillite au Bas-Canada: conflit social ou national?' *RHAF* 40/2 (automne 1986): 215–35, studies the nature of a conflict over the introduction of bankruptcy laws that aggravated already difficult relations between the British business community and the French-Canadian professional bourgeoisie.

Study of the small rural merchants is a new, largely unexplored field. Apart from A. Greer, *Peasant, Lord, and Merchant*, S. Courville, *Entre ville et campagne*, and the previously mentioned studies by L. Michel and C. Desrosiers, see L. St-Georges, 'Commerce, crédit et transactions foncières: pratiques de la communauté marchande du bourg de l'Assomption, 1748–1791,' *RHAF* 39/3 (hiver 1986): 323–43; Claude Pronovost and St-Georges, 'L'identification des marchands ruraux dans six paroisses de la plaine de Montréal, 1831 à 1861,' *RHAF* 42/2 (automne 1988): 241–51; and Pronovost, 'Marchands et crédit marchand au début du XIXe siècle,' in G. Bouchard and J. Goy, eds., *Famille, économie et société rurale*. Even less explored is the place of itinerant peddlars in the rural economy. Serge Jaumain, 'Contribution à l'histoire comparée: les colporteurs belges et québécois au XIXe siècle,' *HS/SH* 20/39 (May 1987): 49–77, is an excellent study of the question.

Major works on individuals and families are also rare. Shirley E. Woods, *The Molson Saga, 1763–1983* (T: Doubleday 1983), is largely descriptive. The *DCB* biographies 'John Molson, Sr,' vol. 7; 'John Molson,' vol. 8; and 'Thomas Molson,' vol. 9, correspond more to current historiographical trends. Charlotte Thibault, *Samuel Brooks, entrepreneur et homme politique de Sherbrooke, 1793–1849* (Sherbrooke, Que.: Université de Sherbrooke 1985), is a rare scholarly study of a local businessman. See also the following discussions on the various business activities.

The volumes of the *DCB* are particularly valuable because they provide studies of individuals and their activities based on hitherto little exploited notarial records and other primary sources, and because collectively they reveal much of business community networks. As well, the biographical approach has the advantage of revealing the connections among the multifarious activities – commercial, financial, manufacturing, political, social, and cultural – that characterized the careers of the colony's early businessmen. For Quebec see the *DCB* entries 'Thomas Ainslie,' 'George Allsopp,' 'François Baby,' 'John Craigie,' 'Alexandre Dumas,' 'Louis Dunière,' 'William Grant,' 'Robert Lester,' 'Pierre Marcoux,' 'Alexander Munn,' 'James Tod,' and 'John Young,' vol. 5 (1983); 'James McCallum' and 'John Mure,' vol. 6; 'Mathew Bell,' vol. 7; 'John Henry Dunn,' 'John Munn,' and 'Peter

Patterson,' vol. 8; 'James Bell Forsyth' and 'William Price,' vol. 9; 'Guillaume-Eugène Chinic' and 'Louis-Adélard Senécal,' vol. 11 (1982); and 'Timothy Hibbard Dunn' and 'Isidore Thibaudeau,' vol. 12 (1990). Collectively, these biographies show that most early businessmen at Quebec diversified to spread the risk of failure, although almost all engaged in the import-export trade.

The *DCB* entries for Montreal businessmen show that they specialized more. For Montreal see 'James Dunlop,' 'Alexander Ellice,' 'Pierre Foretier,' 'Joseph Frobisher,' 'Pierre Guy,' 'James McGill,' 'Simon McTavish,' 'Nicholas Montour,' and 'Isaac Todd,' vol. 5; 'David David,' 'John Fleming,' and 'John Richardson,' vol. 6; 'Austin Cuvillier' and 'Joseph Masson,' vol. 7; 'Peter De Witt' and 'Peter McGill,' vol. 8; 'John Anthony Donegani,' 'George Moffatt,' and 'John Redpath,' vol. 9; 'John Alfred Poor' and 'John Young,' vol. 10 (1972); and 'Sir Francis Hincks,' vol. 11.

Some merchants represent regional economic activities: among prominent country merchants see 'Jacques Cartier,' vol. 5; and 'Pierre Casgrain' and 'Pierre Guerout,' vol. 6; and one should not neglect the eccentric but shrewd Trois-Rivières businessman 'Moses Hart,' vol. 8.

Resource Industries

One of the earliest and most-studied business activities is the fur trade from Montreal, but it has fallen out of favour of late. A solid, recent general work is D.S. Macmillan's previously cited 'The "New Men" in Action,' in Macmillan, ed., *Canadian Business History*. Good regional studies of the fur trade in Quebec are Elaine Allan Mitchell, *Fort Timiskaming and the Fur Trade* (T: UTP 1977); Daniel Francis and Toby Morantz, *Partners in Furs: A History of the Fur Trade in Eastern James Bay, 1600–1870* (K&M: MQUP 1983); and Diane Caron, *Les postes de traite de fourrure sur la Côte-Nord et dans l'Outaouais* (Q: Ministère des Affaires culturelles 1984).

There are also a number of more focused analytical studies. The impact of the Conquest on the fur trade is explored in J.E. Igartua, 'A Change in Climate: The Conquest and the *marchands* of Montreal,' CHA *HP* (1974): 115–34. Ann Carlos, 'The Causes and Origins of the North American Fur Trade Rivalry, 1804–1810,' *Journal of Economic History* 41/4 (Dec. 1981): 777–94, and 'The Birth and Death of Predatory Competition in the North American Fur Trade, 1810–1821,' *Explorations in Economic History* 19/2 (Apr. 1982): 156–83, investigate the nature, causes, and dynamics of the competition between the Hudson's Bay Company and the North West Company. F. Ouellet, 'Economic Dualism and Technological Change in

Quebec, 1760–1790,' in his *Economy, Class, & Nation in Quebec,* and A. Greer, 'Fur-Trade Labour and Lower Canadian Agrarian Structures,' CHA *HP* (1981): 197–214, study aspects of the relationship between agriculture and fur-trade labour. Specific economic and political aspects of the trade from Montreal are discussed in a series of articles in Bruce G. Trigger, T. Morantz, and L. Dechêne, eds., *'Le Castor Fait Tout': Selected Papers of the Fifth North American Fur Trade Conference, 1985* (M: Lake St Louis Historical Society 1987), as well as previously cited *DCB* entries for François Baby, Alexander Ellice, Simon McTavish, Joseph Frobisher, Nicholas Montour, James McGill, and Isaac Todd.

While interest in the fur trade based in the colony has faded recently, the fisheries have always been a neglected aspect of its economic historiography. Under the circumstances H.A. Innis's important work *The Cod Fisheries: The History of an International Economy* (1940; rev. ed., T: UTP 1954) remains the only general study. M. Lalancette, 'Exploitation of the Gulf of St Lawrence,' *HAC*, vol. 1, plate 54, provides an excellent synthesis of commercial activities in the Gulf of St Lawrence in the later eighteenth century and the demographic development that resulted. Considerable research has been conducted in recent years into the operations of fishing firms on the Gaspé coast. More specifically researchers have studied fishing and drying techniques and the firms' role in impoverishing the economy and population, in part through a truck system that made the fishermen virtually indentured slaves. On these points see David Lee, *The Robins in Gaspé, 1766 to 1825* (T: Fitzhenry and Whiteside 1984); Roch Samson, *Fishermen and Merchants in 19th Century Gaspé* (O: Parks Canada 1984); and Mario Mimeault, 'La continuité de l'emprise des compagnies de pêche françaises et jersiaises sur les pêcheurs au XVIIIe siècle: le cas de la compagnie Robin,' *HS/SH* 18/35 (May 1985): 59–74. Rosemary E. Ommer, *From Outpost to Outport: A Structural Analysis of the Jersey-Gaspé Cod Fishery, 1767–1886* (K&M: MQUP 1991), while not disagreeing fundamentally with the conclusions of these studies, expands the *problématique* by recasting the staples theory as a commodity-trade model and examining structure and process in the management, production, and marketing functions within the context of the British colonial system. It must be considered the new standard study of the subject, notwithstanding a virulent critique by André Lepage in *RHAF* 45/4 (printemps 1992): 617–21. M. Lalancette, 'Description et analyse du rapport pêche/seigneurie à l'Ile-aux-Coudres au XVIIIe siècle,' in J. Goy and J.-P. Wallot, eds., *Evolution et éclatement du monde rural,* examines a neglected aspect of seigneurial life and the fishing industry, while A. Lepage, 'Une transition technique: les "pêches" au loup-marin sur la côte du

Labrador depuis le début du XVIIIe siècle,' *Anthropologie et sociétés* 13/2 (1989): 55–78, is an interesting study in technical change. Previously cited *DCB* entries for William Grant and Pierre Marcoux tie the North Shore fishery to the Quebec economy.

The timber trade was the colony's economic motor from early in the nineteenth century until Confederation. The pioneering works of A.R.M. Lower, although now dated in their interpretation based on the frontier thesis, are still a useful starting-point: see, for example, *Great Britain's Woodyard: British America and the Timber Trade, 1763–1867* (M: MQUP 1973). F. Ouellet, *Economic and Social History of Quebec* and *Lower Canada, 1791–1840,* and G. Paquet and J.-P. Wallot, 'Le Bas-Canada au début du XIXe siècle: une hypothèse,' *RHAF* 25/1 (juin 1971): 39–61, tie the trade into Quebec's economic and social history. L. Dechêne, 'Les entreprises de William Price, 1810–1850,' *HS/SH* 1/1 (Apr. 1968): 16–52, and John Keyes, 'La diversification de l'activité économique de Timothy Hibbard Dunn, commerçant de bois à Québec, 1850–1898,' *RHAF* 35/3 (déc. 1981): 323–36, discuss two barons of the trade. For aspects of the conduct of the trade in the Ottawa Valley see Sandra J. Gillis, *The Timber Trade in the Ottawa Valley, 1806–54* (O: Parks Canada 1975); in the Lac Saint-Jean area, N. Séguin, *La conquête du sol au 19e siècle* (Sillery, Que.: BE 1977); and in the Eastern Townships, J.I. Little, *Nationalism, Capitalism, and Colonization in Nineteenth-Century Quebec: The Upper St Francis District* (K&M: MQUP 1989). Guy Gaudreau, *L'exploitation des forêts publiques au Québec, 1842–1905* (Q: IQRC 1986), furnishes an interesting methodological tool, based on statistics from the Crown Lands Department, for a renewed 'assault' on the history of the forest industry, which, in fact, has been quiet in recent years. Previously cited *DCB* entries for William Price and Timothy Hibbard Dunn, as well as 'Archibald McMillan,' vol. 6; 'George Hamilton,' vol. 7; and 'Peter McLeod,' vol. 8, provide excellent concise points of entry into the subject.

Manufacturing and Industry

The historiography of manufacturing has benefited to some extent from the recent intense study of rural society. For examples see David Schulze, 'Rural Manufacture in Lower Canada: Understanding Seigneurial Privilege and the Transition in the Countryside,' *Alternate Routes* 7 (1984): 134–67, and S. Courville, J.-C. Robert, and N. Séguin, 'The Spread of Rural Industry in Lower Canada, 1831–1851,' *JCHA* 2 (1991): 43–70, which argue that the appearance of rural industry is a sign of capitalist penetration of the countryside. D. Salée, 'Seigneurial Landownership and the Transition to Capitalism in Nineteenth-Century Quebec,' *Québec Studies* 12 (Spring/ Summer 1991): 21–32, disputes that interpretation. See also the section on urban and regional history later in the chapter.

There are relatively few analyses of individual industries. Pierre Dufour, 'La construction navale à Québec, 1760–1825: sources inexplorées et nouvelles perspectives de recherches,' *RHAF* 35/2 (sept. 1981): 231–51, constitutes an excellent introduction to the little-known shipbuilding industry, to which now must be added Eileen Marcil, *The Charley-Man: The History of Wooden Ship Building at Quebec, 1763–1893* (K: Quarry Press 1993). The previously cited *DCB* entries for Alexander and John Munn provide rare case studies. As for textiles, David-Thiery Ruddel, 'The Domestic Textile Industry in the Region and City of Quebec, 1792–1835' and 'Consumer Trends, Clothing, Textiles, and Equipment in the Montreal Area, 1792–1835,' *MHB* 17 (Spring 1983): 95–125, and 32 (Fall 1990): 45–64, examine the factors, particularly colonial policy and British imports, affecting local textile production. In 'Domestic Textile Production in Colonial Quebec, 1608–1840,' *MHB* 31 (Spring 1990): 39–49, Ruddel demonstrates how the ethnographers' study of traditional society (see 'Material Culture and Traditional Society' later in the chapter) can be valuable to historians of domestic production in the colonial economy and particularly of women's contribution to that production.

One regional industry, the Saint-Maurice ironworks, has received considerable attention. Louise Trottier, *Les Forges du Saint-Maurice: Their Historiography* (O: Parks Canada 1980), is an excellent introduction. See also L. Vermette, *Domestic Life at Les Forges du Saint-Maurice* (O: Parks Canada 1982), and R. Samson, 'Une industrie avant l'industrialisation: le cas des Forges du Saint-Maurice,' *Anthropologie et sociétés* 10/1 (1986): 85–107, which studies the transition from proto-industrial to industrial production. Concise descriptions of the forges are provided in the previously cited *DCB* entry for Mathew Bell and in 'Pierre de Sales Laterrière,' vol. 5. A paper by Paul Craven and Tom Traves, 'Canadian Railways as Manufacturers, 1850–1880,' *CHA HP* (1983): 254–81, demonstrates the importance of the Grand Trunk Railway as a manufacturer in Montreal through its building and maintenance of locomotives and cars.

Finance

The field of money, banking, and finance has been an attractive one for historians. For a good guide to general histories on currency and banking prior to Confederation see the bibliography for chapter 6 of M. Bliss, *Northern Enterprise*. Allan B. McCullogh, *Money and Exchange in Canada to 1900* (T: Dundern 1984), discusses the complicated question of currency. Mention has been made of recent work on the indebtedness of rural farmers, which historians have tended to treat as the workings of a rural credit system. G. Paquet and J.-P. Wallot, *Le système financier bas-canadien au tournant du XIXe siècle* (O: Faculty of Administration, University of Ottawa 1983), looks at the factors and conflicts involved in efforts to establish a formal financial structure in Quebec and Montreal. The informal credit system that existed at Quebec and the formation of the Quebec Bank are discussed in G. Bervin, *Québec au XIXe siècle*. Also excellent is Donald G. Paterson and Ronald A. Shearer, 'Terminating Building Societies in Quebec City, 1850–1864,' *Business History Review* 63/2 (Summer 1989): 384–415. Merrill Denison, *Canada's First Bank: A History of the Bank of Montreal*, 2 vols. (T: M&S 1966–7), remains the fullest treatment of that subject, and R. Rudin, *Banking en français: The French Banks of Quebec, 1835–1925* (T: UTP 1985), breaks new ground.

The role of public finance in economic development attracted the attention of D.G. Creighton and Helen Taft Manning in the 1930s and 1940s and generated a debate over the significance of the control of the civil list. Julian Gwyn, 'The Impact of British Military Spending on the Colonial American Money Markets, 1760–1783,' CHA *HP* (1980): 77–99, asserts that, to the extent military spending had an impact in the late eighteenth century, it was negative for local British merchants. G. Paquet and J.-P. Wallot, *Patronage et pouvoir dans le Bas-Canada, 1794–1812: un essai d'économie historique* (M: PUQ 1973), and G. Bervin, *Québec au XIXe siècle*, argue that patronage favoured local British over French-Canadian interests in the early nineteenth century.

Transportation

The historiography of transportation in Quebec before 1867 is patchy. G.P. de T. Glazebrook, *A History of Transportation in Canada*, 2 vols. (1938; repr. T: M&S 1964), is still the basic work. For river transportation Gerald Tulchinsky, *The River Barons: Montreal Businessmen and the Growth of Industry and Transportation, 1837–53* (T: UTP 1977), is essential reading. It deals well with the coming of steam on the St Lawrence, introduced by the Molsons (see previous mentions of them), as does A. Dubuc's updated 'Montréal et les débuts de la navigation à vapeur sur le Saint-Laurent,' in Marcel Bellavance, ed., *La grande mouvance* (Sillery, Que.: SPT 1990). G. Bervin,

Québec au XIXe siècle, examines steamboats from the Quebec perspective. Hélène Espesset, 'History of Quebec Canals: A Review of the Literature,' Environment Canada–Parks, *Research Bulletin* (1987), is a helpful guide to the excellent research undertaken by the historians of Parks Canada. An article by S. Courville, J.-C. Robert, and N. Séguin, 'Le Saint-Laurent, artère de vie: réseau routier et métiers de la navigation au XIXe siècle,' *Cahiers de géographie du Québec* 34/92 (sept. 1990): 181–96, introduces a broad inquiry into the St Lawrence as a stimulator of settlement and an integrator of local and regional economies. Jean Leclerc, *Le Saint-Laurent et ses pilotes, 1805–1860* (M: Leméac 1990), is a solid study of a little-known subject. For navigation on the Richelieu see P.-André Sévigny, 'Le commerce du blé et la navigation dans le bas-Richelieu avant 1849,' *RHAF* 38/1 (été 1984): 5–21, which argues convincingly that poor navigability on the river constituted a major restriction on the wheat trade.

Railway historiography is slight despite the growing impact of railways on politics and economic development, in particular, capital accumulation, manufacturing, trade, and communications, all centring on Montreal. Excellent studies from different perspectives are B. Young, *Promoters and Politicians: The North-Shore Railways in the History of Quebec, 1854–85* (T: UTP 1978); Henry C. Klassen, 'Luther Holton: Mid-Century Montreal Railwayman,' *Revue de l'Université d'Ottawa* 52 (1982): 316–39; and François Cinq-Mars, *L'avènement du premier chemin de fer au Canada, Saint-Jean-Laprairie, 1836* (Saint-Jean-sur-Richelieu, Que.: Editions Mille-Roches 1982).

Social Structure

Out of economic activity develops social structure. The bibliography by G. Bernier and R. Boily, *Le Québec en transition, 1760–1867: bibliographie thématique*, is good, while F. Ouellet, 'Les classes dominantes au Québec, 1760–1840: bilan historiographique,' *RHAF* 38/2 (automne 1984): 223–43, and chapter 6 of J. Rouillard, ed., *Guide d'histoire du Québec du Régime français à nos jours*, authored by J.-P. Wallot, provide overviews of the subject. General works by Ouellet, Paquet and Wallot, and the Marxist historians G. Bernier, G. Bourque, and A. Dubuc, have all dealt with social stratification.

Work on the rural farmers and the business class has already been mentioned. The seigneurial class has been the subject of several biographical publications in recent years, in addition to the studies of seigneuries mentioned previously. For an inside, albeit romanticized, view of the life of the seigneur see *A Man of Sentiment: The Memoirs of Philippe-Joseph Aubert de Gaspé, 1786–1871*, originally published in 1866 and recently translated, with excellent editorial commentaries, by Jane Brierley (M: Véhicule Press 1988). It may be complemented by Jacques Castonguay, *Philippe Aubert de Gaspé: seigneur et homme de lettres* (Sillery, Que.: SPT 1991). Raymonde Litalien, 'Jean-Baptiste-Nicolas Roch de Ramezay et sa famille, au Canada et en France, après 1760,' *RHAF* 37/4 (mars 1984): 603–10, and Andrée Desilets, *Louis-Rodrigue Masson: un seigneur sans titres* (M: BE 1985), are more analytical. Excellent *DCB* biographies are 'Gabriel Christie,' vol. 4 (1979); and 'Barthélemy Joliette,' 'Joseph Papineau,' and 'Louis Proulx,' vol. 7. G. Bervin profiles the official class in 'Environnement matériel et activités économiques des conseillers exécutifs et législatifs à Québec, 1810–1830,' *MHB* 17 (Spring 1983): 45–62.

The professional bourgeoisie has been studied abundantly in the works of F. Ouellet and Gérard Parizeau. See also Robert Gagnon, 'Capital culturel et identité sociale: les fonctions sociales du discours sur l'encombrement des professions libérales au XIXe siècle,' *Sociologie et sociétés* 21/2 (oct. 1989): 129–46, and later sections for the medical and legal professions. A word of warning, however: L. Gadoury and Jean-François Leclerc, 'Profil de quelques bourgeois de Montréal, 1820–1825,' *Cahiers d'histoire* 5/2 (printemps 1985): 7–23, studied early-nineteenth-century usage of the term 'bourgeois' and concluded that it covered such a broad socio-economic range that it could constitute a trap for historians. On the other hand, B. Young, *George-Etienne Cartier: Montreal Bourgeois* (K&M: MQUP 1981), an excellent study of a later period, considers that Cartier and others like him can best be understood as 'bourgeois' despite the vagueness of the term.

Artisans and workers have been much studied since 1970. For the historiography prior to that date see H. Espessat, Jean-Pierre Hardy, and D.-T. Ruddel, 'Le monde du travail au Québec au XVIIIe et au XIXe siècles: historiographie et état de la question,' *RHAF* 25/4 (mars 1972): 499–539. For a more recent and general historiography see Jacques Ferland, Gregory S. Kealey, and Bryan D. Palmer, 'Labour Studies,' in A.F.J. Artibise, ed., *Interdisciplinary Approaches to Canadian Society*. An interesting interpretive work, which must be used cautiously, however, is H. Clare Pentland, *Labour and Capital in Canada, 1650–1860*, ed. and intro. Paul Phillips (T: James Lorimer 1981); to place it in historical and historiographical perspective see John Willis's critical review in *RHAF* 38/2 (automne 1984): 245–53, and Donald Harman Akenson, *Being Had: Historians, Evidence, and the Irish in North America* (Port Credit, Ont.: P.D. Meany 1985). A good, recent work is B.D. Palmer, *Working-Class Experience: Rethinking the History of Canadian*

Labour, 1800–1991 (T: Butterworth 1983; 2nd ed., T: M&S 1992), which approaches the subject from a Marxist perspective. So too do the excellent articles of Robert Tremblay, 'La formation matérielle de la classe ouvrière à Montréal entre 1790 et 1830,' *RHAF* 33/1 (juin 1979): 39–50, and 'Un aspect de la consolidation du pouvoir d'Etat de la bourgeoisie coloniale: la législation anti-ouvrière dans le Bas-Canada, 1800–50,' *L/LT* 8–9 (Autumn–Spring 1981–2): 243–52.

For descriptions of the working class and working conditions see J.-P. Hardy and D.-T. Ruddel, *Les apprentis artisans à Québec, 1660–1825* (M: PUQ 1977); Jean-Pierre Kesteman, 'Les travailleurs à la construction du chemin de fer dans la région de Sherbrooke (1851–1853),' *RHAF* 31/4 (mars 1978): 525–45; Claire-Andrée Fortin, 'Profil de la main-d'oeuvre forestière en Mauricie d'après le recensement de 1861' and 'Notes sur les conditions de vie et de travail des bûcherons en Mauricie au 19e siècle,' *MHB* 13 (Fall 1981): 75–81 and 83–95; Claudette Lacelle, *Urban Domestic Servants in 19th-Century Canada* (O: Environment Canada 1987); and Ruddel, 'La main-d'oeuvre en milieu urbain au Bas-Canada: conditions et relations de travail,' *RHAF* 41/3 (hiver 1988): 389–402. Of particular interest relative to early strikes are Margaret Heap, 'La grève des charretiers à Montréal, 1864,' *RHAF* 31/3 (déc. 1977): 371–95; Raymond Boily, *Les Irlandais et le canal de Lachine: la grève de 1843* (M: Leméac 1980); and R. Tremblay, 'The Strike of Workers in the Quebec Shipyards (1840),' in Carol Wilton, ed., *Change and Continuity: A Reader on Pre-Confederation Canada* (T: MHR 1992). Michael S. Cross, 'The Shiners' War: Social Violence in the Ottawa Valley in the 1830s,' *CHR* 54/1 (Mar. 1973): 1–26, is a much-reprinted study of class struggle and ethnic violence within the working class. On the other hand, Peter Bischoff, 'Des Forges du Saint-Maurice aux fonderies de Montréal: mobilité géographique, solidarité communautaire et action syndicale des mouleurs, 1829–1881,' *RHAF* 43/1 (été 1989): 3–29, studies the role of solidarities – families, friendships, and union ties – in workers' mobility and adaptability to changing industrial contexts. Judith Fingard, 'The Winter's Tale: The Seasonal Contours of Pre-Industrial Poverty in British North America, 1815–1860,' CHA *HP* (1974): 65–94, looks at winter living conditions of the working class in Quebec, while B. Bradbury, *Working Families: Age, Gender, and Daily Survival in Industrializing Montreal* (T: M&S 1993), portrays the daily struggle in all seasons. J.-M. Fecteau, *Un nouvel ordre des choses: la pauvreté, le crime et l'Etat au Québec, de la fin du XVIIIe siècle à 1840* (M: VLB Editeur 1989), emphasizes the increasing role given to the state in the social management of poverty as Lower Canada moved from a feudal to a capitalist socio-economy. Donald

Fyson, 'Du pain au madère: l'alimentation à Montréal au début du XIXe siècle,' *RHAF* 46/1 (été 1992): 67–90, explores a new dimension of class stratification by comparing the diets of Montreal canal workers and the city's elites. The *DCB* biography 'Joseph Laurin,' vol. 11, is an excellent profile of an early union leader. Joanne Burgess, 'The Growth of a Craft Labour Force: Montreal Leather Artisans, 1815–1831,' CHA *HP* (1988): 48–62, calls into question conclusions respecting the complexion of the leather artisans' trade in Montreal based only on census statistics.

Material Culture and Traditional Society

Only relatively recently has the social historian seen in material culture and traditional practices indicators of economic and social conditions and changes. J.-P. Hardy et al., 'Material Conditions and Society in Lower Canada, 1792–1835,' *MHB* 17 (Spring 1983): 1–7, sets down the justification and methodology for a vast study of the socio-material history of Lower Canada. For years material culture has been studied by ethnographers; recently their approach has met up with that of the social historian, as in the work of Marcel Moussette, *Le chauffage domestique au Canada des origines à l'industrialisation* (Q: PUL 1983); Jean-Claude Dupont, *Exercices des métiers du bois* and *Exercices des métiers de la pierre et de l'argile* (Q: CELAT 1986 and 1988); and Jean Provencher, *Les quatre saisons dans la vallée du Saint-Laurent* (M: BE 1988), a descriptive study, season by season, of traditional life in early-nineteenth-century rural Lower Canada. See also Sophie-Laurence Lamontagne, *L'hiver dans la culture québécoise (XVIIe–XIXe siècles)* (Q: IQRC 1983), and Thérèse Beaudoin, *L'été dans la culture québécoise (XVIIe–XIXe siècles)* (Q: IQRC 1987), which offer longer term perspectives.

With respect to material culture, archaeology can be employed profitably: see M. Moussette, 'Archéologie et changements matériels, XVIIe–XIXe siècles,' *Annales de Bretagne et des pays de l'Ouest* 95/4 (1988): 369–77, and *Under the Boardwalk in Quebec: Archaeology in the Courtyard and Gardens of the Château Saint-Louis* (Sillery, Que.: SPT 1990). The benefits to be derived from the contributions of ethnography, architectural history, and historical human geography are evident in J.-C. Dupont, ed., *Habitation rurale au Québec* (M: Hurtubise HMH 1978); and Georges-Pierre Léonidoff, 'The House, 1660–1800' and 'The Wooden House,' *HAC*, vol. 1, plates 55 and 56. John R. Porter, 'L'objet matériel et ses contextes: le cas du meuble de l'époque victorienne au Québec,' *Annales de Bretagne et des pays de l'Ouest* 95/4 (1988): 379–88, demonstrates how an object can be read like a document. J.-P. Hardy, 'Niveaux de richesse et intérieurs domestiques dans le quartier Saint-Roch à Québec, 1820–1850,' *MHB* 17 (Spring 1983): 63–94, looks at the economic and social impact of the lumber and shipbuilding industries through a comparative analysis of the material culture of three social groups in an essentially working-class district. Studies of the rural habitant were mentioned previously. Material culture as social history is a specialty of Parks Canada and the Museum of Man and almost all the studies done under their auspices bear the stamp of that approach.

Women's History

Since, as a field, women's history cuts across traditional historiographic lines, studies that might have been described in other historiographical contexts will be found here, while important aspects of women's history will be found in several other sections of this chapter. Most works mentioned here are distinguished by their focus on women.

A study of women's history in Quebec begins with Denise Lemieux and Lucie Mercier, *La recherche sur les femmes au Québec: bilan et bibliographie* (1982; 2nd ed., Q: IQRC 1990), an indispensable thematic guide. Gail Cuthbert Grant, 'Postmodern Patchwork: Some Recent Trends in the Writing of Women's History in Canada,' *CHR* 72/4 (Dec. 1991): 441–70, places women's historiography in Quebec in the Canadian context. The author finds troublesome the persistence of an early tendency to write women's history in parallel to 'men's,' as does Rosemary R. Gagan, 'Putting Humpty Together Again: The Challenge of Canadian Women's History,' *British Journal of Canadian Studies* 4/2 (1989): 276–95, which, however, largely ignores Quebec. An excellent brief review is Andrée Lévesque, 'Historiography: History of Women in Quebec since 1985,' *Québec Studies* 12 (Spring/Summer 1991): 83–91, which identifies four poles of research: work, motherhood, education, and politics. It points out that the period 1760 to 1867 has been neglected.

Le Collectif Clio (Micheline Dumont, Michèle Jean, Marie Lavigne, and Jennifer Stoddart), *L'histoire des femmes au Québec depuis quatre siècles* (1982; 2nd ed., M: Le Jour 1992), synthesizes the writing on women's history, employing a periodization based on women's historical experience while placing that experience in the broader historical context as interpreted through it. *Quebec Women: A History* (T: Women's Press 1987) is a translation of the 1982 edition and does not take into account the historiography of the last decade. The work by Alison Prentice et al., *Canadian Women: A History* (T: HBJ 1988), is sketchy on Lower Canada.

Studies of interest focusing on work performed by women are D. Suzanne Cross, 'The Neglected Majority: The Changing Role of Women in 19th-Century Montréal,' *HS/SH* 6/12 (Nov. 1973): 202–23; B. Bradbury, 'Women and Wage Labour in a Period of Transition: Montreal, 1861–1881,' *HS/SH* 17/33 (May 1984): 115–31; and B. Young, 'Getting around Legal Incapacity: The Legal Status of Married Women in Trade in Mid-Nineteenth-Century Lower Canada,' in Peter A. Baskerville, ed., *Canadian Papers in Business History*, vol. 1 (VI: Public History Group, University of Victoria 1989).

Although education is another pole of research identified by A. Lévesque, publications on it pass quickly over Lower Canada. Such is the case with Nadia Fahmy-Eid and M. Dumont, eds., *Maîtresses de maison, maîtresses d'école: femmes, famille et éducation dans l'histoire du Québec* (M: BE 1983); Dumont and Fahmy-Eid, *Les Couventines: l'éducation des filles au Québec dans les congrégations religieuses enseignantes, 1840–1960* (M: BE 1986); and Dumont, *Girls' Schooling in Quebec, 1639–1960*, CHA Historical Booklet no. 49 (O: 1990).

With respect to women and the church see Marta Danylewycz's influential *Taking the Veil: An Alternative to Marriage, Motherhood and Spinsterhood in Quebec, 1840–1920* (T: M&S 1987). Denise Robillard, *Emilie Tavernier Gamelin* (M: Méridien 1988), argues that women, excluded from influence in the institutions of the church, created, through their social work, a parallel network of services in Montreal that protected the poor from the abuses of a nineteenth-century liberal economy, but that this network was taken over by the establishment under Bishop Ignace Bourget. Raymond Courcy, 'Les communautés religieuses du Québec au XIXème siècle: servantes diocésaines idéales ou femmes québécoises en devenir?' in Pierre Guillaume, ed., *Le diocèse au Québec et en France au XIX et XXèmes siècles* (n.p.: Maison des Sciences de l'Homme d'Aquitaine 1990), takes a similar line, adding a feminist perspective inspired by M. Dumont and similar to that of Danylewycz.

A few recent studies of particular interest into other aspects of women's history are Hélène Laforce, *Histoire de la sage-femme dans la région de Québec* (Q: IQRC 1985); B. Bradbury, 'Surviving as a Widow in 19th-Century Montreal,' *Urban History Review* 17/3 (Feb. 1989): 148–60, which examines survival strategies in the 1860s and after; and A. Greer, 'La république des hommes: les Patriotes de 1837 face aux femmes,' *RHAF* 44/4 (printemps 1991): 507–28, which argues that the Patriotes' conception of women's domestic role isolated women from their cause. Constance Backhouse, *Petticoats and Prejudice: Women and Law in Nineteenth-Century Canada* (T: OS/

Women's Press 1991), struggles with a limited historiography for Lower Canada. Of interest as well are the *DCB* biographies 'Marie-Catherine Delezenne,' vol. 6; and 'Maria Monk,' vol. 7.

Women have also been studied in the context of different relationships. See, in particular, W. Peter Ward, *Courtship, Love, and Marriage in Nineteenth-Century English Canada* (K&M: MQUP 1990), and Ward, ed., *A Love Story from 19th Century Quebec: The Diary of George Stephen Jones* (Peterborough, Ont.: Broadview Press 1989), both of which look at the private and social factors influencing courtship and marriage; Danielle Gauvreau and Mario Bourque, '"Jusqu'à ce que la mort nous sépare": le destin des femmes et des hommes mariés au Saguenay avant 1930,' *CHR* 71/4 (Dec. 1990): 441–61, a historical demographical approach to the differing fates of men and women in marriage; S. Gagnon, *Plaisir d'amour et crainte de Dieu: sexualité et confession au Bas-Canada* (Q: PUL 1990), which notes differences in the attitudes of and about men and women in sexual relations; and Peter Gossage, 'Family Formation and Age at Marriage in Saint-Hyacinthe, Québec, 1854–1891,' *HS/SH* 24/1 (May 1991): 61–84. Indeed, shifts in the relationships between men and women constitute the *problématique* of feminist historians who see a parallel 'women's history' as more or less sterile and call instead for an exploration of 'gender history.' For an example see Lykke de la Cour et al., 'Gender Regulation and State Formation in Nineteenth-Century Canada,' in A. Greer and Ian Radforth, eds., *Colonial Leviathan: State Formation in Mid-Nineteenth-Century Canada* (T: UTP 1992), and B. Bradbury, *Working Families*.

Native Studies

Native studies have not been a preoccupation of mainstream Lower Canadian historiography, which they traditionally entered, if at all, through Native peoples' participation in the fur trade (see the section 'Resource Industries'), a field now in fallow. Fortunately anthropologists and ethnohistorians have to some extent filled the void. For a comprehensive bibliography and a historical overview of the major Native nations see Richard Dominique and Jean-Guy Deschênes, eds., *Cultures et sociétés autochtones du Québec: bibliographie critique* (Q: IQRC 1985). D. Francis, *A History of the Native Peoples of Quebec* (O: Department of Northern and Indian Affairs 1984), provides a brief general history. See too the new survey by Olive Patricia Dickason, *Canada's First Nations: A History of Founding Peoples from the Earliest Times* (T: M&S 1992). B.G. Trigger, 'Native Resettlement, 1635–1800,' *HAC*, vol. 1, plate 47, traces settlement patterns, population trends, and age and sex profiles following sustained contact with Europeans.

The story of relations with non-Natives is traced in J.R. Miller, *Skyscrapers Hide the Heavens: A History of Indian-White Relations in Canada* (1989; rev. ed., T: UTP 1991), a synthesis of the literature in English rather than an original study. It divides that history into three phases, cooperation, coercion, and confrontation, and situates after the War of 1812 the separation between the first two periods. An interesting study by Jacqueline Beaulieu, Christiane Cantin, and Maurice Ratelle, 'La Proclamation royale de 1763: le droit refait l'histoire,' *La Revue du Barreau* 49/1 (jan.–fév. 1989): 317–43, written by a geographer, a historian, and a lawyer, claims to re-establish the geographical and historical 'true facts' about the Royal Proclamation of 1763, a key document in Native land claims, in the face of recent legal interpretations that 'rewrite history' to achieve a desired goal.

The establishment of, and life on, the reserves are treated in Gérard L. Fortin and Jacques Frenette, 'L'Acte de 1851 et la création de nouvelles réserves indiennes au Bas-Canada en 1853,' *Recherches amérindiennes au Québec* 19/1 (printemps 1989): 31–7, and Hélène Bédard, *Les Montagnais et la réserve de Betsiamites, 1850–1900* (Q: IQRC 1988). The Montagnais are also studied in J. Frenette, *Mingan au 19e siècle: cycles annuels des Montagnais et politiques commerciales de la Compagnie de la Baie d'Hudson* (O: Musée canadien des civilisations 1986), and José Mailhot, 'Beyond Everyone's Horizon Stand the Naskapi,' *Ethnohistory* 33/4 (Fall 1986): 384–418. Histories written from the 'inside' of two major Native protagonists are Marguerite Vincent Tehariolina and Pierre-H. Savignac, *La nation huronne: son histoire, sa culture, son esprit* (Q: Éditions du Pélican 1984), and Daniel K. Richter and James H. Merrell, eds., *Beyond the Covenant Chain: The Iroquois and Their Neighbors in Indian North America, 1600–1800* (Syracuse, NY: Syracuse University Press 1987), which explores the cultural, social, and political motivations and objectives behind the Iroquois' relations with their Native neighbours. Robert J. Surtees, 'The Iroquois in Canada,' in Francis Jennings et al., eds., *The History and Culture of Iroquois Diplomacy: An Interdisciplinary Guide to the Treaties of the Six Nations and Their League* (Syracuse, NY: Syracuse University Press 1985), provides an excellent, brief overview. See also Charles A. Martijn, ed., *Les Micmacs et la mer* (M: Recherches amérindiennes au Québec 1986).

T. Morantz has studied extensively and effectively the relations between Native peoples (particularly the Cree) and fur traders in the James Bay area: see *Partners in Furs* (with D. Francis); *An Ethnohistoric Study of Eastern James Bay Cree Social Organization, 1700–1850* (O: National Museums of Canada

1983); '"Not Annual Visitors": The Drawing in to Trade of Northern Algonquian Caribou Hunters,' in William Cowan, ed., *Actes du quatorzième congrès des algonquinistes* (O: CUP 1983); 'Economic and Social Accommodation of the James Bay Inlanders to the Fur Trade,' in Shepard Krech III, ed., *The Subarctic Fur Trade: Native Social and Economic Adaptations* (V: UBCP 1984); and '"So Evil a Practice": A Look at the Debt System in the James Bay Fur Trade,' in R.E. Ommer, ed., *Merchant Credit and Labour Strategies in Historical Perspective* (F: AP 1990). François Trudel has studied the Inuit in a similar context in 'Albert One-Eye, un Inuk à l'emploi de la Compagnie de la Baie d'Hudson (1841–1849),' *Recherches amérindiennes au Québec* 19/1 (printemps 1989): 52–62, and 'Un recensement des Inuit à Petite rivière de la Baleine, 1858,' *Cahiers québécois de démographie* 18/2 (automne 1989): 379–92. His 'Les relations entre Indiens et Inuit dans l'est de la Baie d'Hudson,' in W. Cowan, ed., *Papers of the Twenty-First Algonquian Conference* (O: CUP 1990), is also useful. Léo-Paul Hébert has conducted an original and detailed study of a missionary to Native peoples, *Histoire ou légende? Jean-Baptiste de La Brosse* (M: Bellarmin 1984). The *DCB*, vol. 4, contains interesting biographies of Indian agents 'John Campbell,' 'Joseph Chew,' 'Christian Daniel Claus,' 'Sir William Johnson,' and 'Luc de La Corne,' which, along with Earle Thomas, *Sir John Johnson: Loyalist Baronet* (T: Dundurn 1986), provide a good account of the British administration of Indian affairs. The *DCB* also has entries for such Native people as 'Atiatoharongwen,' vol. 5; 'Nicolas Vincent,' vol. 7; and 'Peter McLeod,' vol. 8.

Demography and Migration

The absence of reliable and comparable censuses between 1760 and 1831 has been a major obstacle for demographic and settlement historians, who have, consequently, tended to concentrate on the periods before and after that. For general studies see F. Ouellet, 'L'accroissement naturel de la population catholique québécoise avant 1850: aperçus historiographiques et quantitatifs,' *L'actualité économique* 59/3 (sept. 1983): 402–22; and Jacques Henripin and Yves Péron, 'The Demographic Transition of the Province of Quebec,' in W.P. Ward, ed., *The Social Development of Canada: Readings* (Richmond, BC: Open Learning Institute 1983). These should be supplemented by Hubert Charbonneau and R.C. Harris, 'Resettling the St Lawrence Valley'; L. Dechêne, 'The Town of Québec, 18th Century' and 'The Seigneuries'; and Harris, 'The Agricultural Economy,' *HAC*, vol. 1, plates 46, 50, 51, and 53. F. Ouellet, *Lower Canada, 1791–1840*, linked strong population growth to the agricultural crisis. This position is contested in S. Courville, J.-C. Robert, and N. Séguin, 'Population et espace rural au Bas-Canada: l'exemple de l'axe laurentien dans la première moitié du XIXe siècle,' *RHAF* 44/2 (automne 1990): 243–62, which argues that much of the growth was absorbed by villages. Marie-Aimée Cliche, 'L'infanticide dans la région de Québec (1660–1969),' *RHAF* 44/1 (été 1990): 31–59, and Patricia A. Thornton, Sherry Olson, and Quoc Thuy Thach, 'Dimensions sociales de la mortalité infantile à Montréal au milieu du XIXe siècle,' *Annales de démographie historique* (1988): 299–325, relate types of infant mortality to social conditions and values. P. Gossage, 'Les enfants abandonnés à Montréal au 19e siècle: la Crèche d'Youville des Soeurs Grises, 1820–1871,' *RHAF* 40/4 (printemps 1987): 537–59, takes a similar approach with the phenomenon of child abandonment.

Two regions settled during the period have been the subject of intense study. The older of the two, the Eastern Townships, became an area of competition between English- and French-speaking colonizers. In *Nationalism, Capitalism, and Colonization*, J.I. Little examines the political and economic considerations of promoters influencing settlement projects in one part of the Townships. Although well documented and argued, the series of discrete chapters that compose the book, rather tenuously united by the conclusion, do not constitute a monograph. On the other hand, the cohesion of his *Crofters and Habitants*, conceived as a monograph, lends greater weight to the conclusions that he draws from its comparative study of French-Canadian and Scottish settlements in Winslow Township. Winslow's distinctive situation, however, make generalizations from it difficult.

Various aspects of French-Canadian colonization efforts have been portrayed in Little, 'The Parish and French Canadian Migrants to Compton County, Quebec, 1851–1891,' *HS/SH* 11/21 (May 1978): 134–43; Gilles Parent, *Deux efforts de colonisation française dans les Cantons de l'Est, 1848 et 1851* (Sherbrooke, Que.: Groupe de recherche en histoire régionale, Université de Sherbrooke 1980); Michel Morin, 'La pensée colonisatrice de Calixte Marquis,' *Les cahiers nicolétains* 3/3 (sept. 1981): 78–111; and Little, 'The Catholic Church and French-Canadian Colonization of the Eastern Townships, 1821–51,' *Revue de l'Université d'Ottawa* 52 (1982): 142–65.

The second major area of study, the Saguenay region, was settled in the decades immediately before Confederation. A general survey is Christian Pouyez and Yolande Lavoie, *Les Saguenayens: introduction à l'histoire des populations du Saguenay, XVIe–XXe siècles* (Sillery, Que.: PUQ 1983), which incorporates much of the work done to that date by Pouyez, G. Bouchard, and others. More recent and focused studies on the origins of the population are Marc St-Hilaire, 'Origines et destins des familles pionnières d'une paroisse saguenayenne au XIXe siècle,' *Cahiers de géographie du Québec* 32/85 (avril 1988): 5–26; G. Bouchard and Jeannette Larouche, 'Dynamique des populations locales: la formation des paroisses rurales au Saguenay (1840–1911),' *RHAF* 41/3 (hiver 1988): 363–88; and Bouchard and Lise Bergeron, 'Aux origines d'une population régionale: mythes et réalités démographiques et sociales,' *RHAF* 42/3 (hiver 1989): 389–409. Russel Bouchard, *Le pays du Lac-Saint-Jean: esquisse historique de la colonisation* (2nd ed., Chicoutimi-Nord, Que.: Russel Bouchard 1988), is a largely descriptive and popular, but still useful, study of a neighbouring region.

The Saguenay area has also been the focus of study in the new field of genetic history. Initial settlement and subsequent demographic factors such as marriages and migratory movements determine the specific genetic profile of a region and can be used practically in the management of genetic disorders. In G. Bouchard and Marc De Braekeleer, eds., *Histoire d'un génome: population et génétique dans l'est du Québec* (Sillery, Que.: PUQ 1990), an interdisciplinary group of researchers from Université Laval, Université du Québec à Chicoutimi, and McGill University present the results of studies on settlement and migratory patterns, demographics, family reproduction, and genetic epidemiology of the Saguenay and Charlevoix regions as well as the legal and ethical parameters of historical demographic and genetic research. In 'Homogénéité ou diversité? L'histoire de la population du Québec revue à travers ses gènes,' *HS/SH* 23/46 (Nov. 1990): 325–61, Bouchard and De Braekeleer summarize the latest findings in genetic historical research and their historiographical ramifications.

Internal migration from the countryside to the village is a general theme of S. Courville, *Entre ville et campagne*. The role of family ties in migration has been studied in Daniel Maisonneuve, 'Structure familiale et exode rural: le cas de Saint-Damase, 1852–1861,' *Cahiers québécois de démographie* 14/2 (oct. 1985): 231–40, and in France Gagnon, 'Parenté et migration: le cas des Canadiens-français à Montréal entre 1845 et 1875,' CHA *HP* (1988): 63–85, which calls into question the hypothesis that most migrants to urban centres were non-inheriting sons.

Emigration to the United States prior to Confederation, formerly a neglected field, now attracts attention as historians explore the effects of economic changes. Bruno Ramirez, 'Emigration et Franco-Américanie: bilan des recherches historiques,' in Dean Louder, ed., *Le Québec et les francophones de la Nouvelle-Angleterre* (Q: PUL 1991), is a useful guide to the literature. Y. Roby, *Les Franco-Américains de la Nouvelle-Angleterre (1776–1930)* (Sillery, Que.: SPT 1990), is the most recent survey, but see also Claire Quintal, ed., *L'émigrant québécois vers les Etats-Unis, 1850–1920* (Q:

Vie française 1982). Betsy Beatty, 'Opportunity across the Border: The Burlington Area Economy and the French Canadian Worker in 1850,' *Vermont History* 55/3 (Summer 1987): 133–52, looks at a specific case.

Problems of studying migration through censuses have been underlined in C. Pouyez, R. Roy, and François Martin, 'The Linkage of Census Name Data: Problems and Procedures,' *Journal of Interdisciplinary History* 14/1 (Summer 1983): 129–52, which uses the censuses of 1851 and 1861 in the Saguenay area as an example.

Immigration to Quebec has a venerable historiography. The first immigrants were political refugees, the Loyalists, who are best served by Wallace Brown and Hereward Senior, *Victorious in Defeat: The Loyalists in Canada* (T: Methuen 1984). After opportunistic 'late' Loyalists came economic refugees from the four 'nations' of the British Isles. Still useful for their study are Norman Macdonald, *Canada, 1763–1841, Immigration and Settlement: The Administration of the Imperial Land Regulations* (L: Longmans, Green 1939), and his *Canada: Immigration and Colonization, 1841–1903* (T: MAC 1966); Helen I. Cowan, *British Emigration to British North America: The First Hundred Years* (1928; rev. ed., T: UTP 1961); and Hugh J.M. Johnston, *British Emigration Policy, 1815–1830: 'Shovelling Out Paupers'* (Oxford: Clarendon Press 1972). A recent, useful research tool is Normand Robert and Michel Thibault, *Catalog of Catholic Immigrants from the British Isles before 1825* (M: Société de recherche historique Archiv-Histo 1988).

The bulk of British immigration was from Ireland, for whom Kerby A. Miller, *Emigrants and Exiles: Ireland and the Irish Exodus to North America* (NY: OUP 1985), is the best general survey. For the Canadian experience, Donald MacKay, *Flight from Famine: The Coming of the Irish to Canada* (T: M&S 1990), provides a descriptive, popular history, while Cecil J. Houston and William J. Smyth, in *Irish Emigration and Canadian Settlement: Patterns, Links, and Letters* (T: UTP 1990), employ an original historical geographical approach. An excellent shorter synthesis of the Irish experience is J. Willis, 'Le Québec, l'Irlande et les migrations de la grande famine: origine, contexte et dénouement,' in M. Bellavance, ed., *La grande mouvance*. Bruce S. Elliott's *Irish Migrants in the Canadas: A New Approach* (K&M: MQUP 1988) lives up to its title by employing genealogical techniques to demonstrate the importance of family and friendship relations in the migration process. For Scottish immigration see J.M. Bumsted, *The People's Clearance: Highland Emigration to British North America, 1770–1815* (Edinburgh/W: Edinburgh University Press/UMP 1982).

Once they arrived, the immigrants became ethnic minorities in their new land. S. Courville, *Entre ville et campagne*, and Marcelle Cinq-Mars, 'Représentations et stratégies sociales d'un marchand étranger à Québec: le journal de Johann Heinrich Juncken (septembre 1788–mai 1789),' *RHAF* 44/4 (printemps 1991): 549–66, examine their reception and mechanisms of integration.

For study of the English-language minority, Brendan O'Donnell, comp., *Printed Sources for the Study of English-Speaking Quebec* (Lennoxville, Que.: Bishop's University 1985), provides a comprehensive bibliography to 1980. Honorius Provost, *Les premiers Anglo-Canadiens à Québec: essai de recensement, 1759–1775* (Q: IQRC 1983), documents the beginnings of this community. The subsequent history of that population has been surveyed in R. Rudin, *The Forgotten Quebecers: A History of English-Speaking Quebec, 1759–1980* (Q: IQRC 1985). Lynda Price, *Introduction to the Social History of the Scots in Quebec, 1780–1840* (O: National Museum of Man 1981), is a short, useful synthesis of the literature on that group.

The Jewish minority has been much studied. The work by David Rome, Judith Nefsky, and Paule Obermeir, *Les Juifs du Québec: bibliographie rétrospective annotée* (Q: IQRC 1981), is a good starting-point. Rome has produced a number of useful documentary studies in a series entitled Canadian Jewish Archives. Michael Brown, *Jew or Juif? Jews, French Canadians, and Anglo-Canadians, 1759–1914* (Philadelphia, PA: Jewish Publication Society 1987), is a scholarly analysis of the historical roots of Jewish identification with the English- rather than the French-speaking population. G. Tulchinsky, '"Said to Be a Very Honest Jew": The R.G. Dun Credit Reports and Jewish Business Activity in Mid-19th Century Montreal,' *Urban History Review* 18/3 (Feb. 1990): 200–9, looks at the contours of Jewish business activities and concludes that, notwithstanding its existence, anti-Semitism did not affect the assessment of the creditworthiness of Jewish businessmen.

Jean-Pierre Wilhelmy, *German Mercenaries in Canada* (Beloeil, Que.: Maison des Mots 1986), throws light on a little-known but not insignificant subject. For Black history see Daniel Gay, *Des empreintes noires sur la neige blanche: les Noirs au Québec, 1750–1900* (Q: Conseil québécois de la recherche sociale 1988). Marcel Trudel, *Dictionnaire des esclaves et de leurs propriétaires au Canada français* (M: Hurtubise HMH 1990), helps to establish the dimensions of slavery to about 1810; however, the identification of slaves is not always certain. The *DCB* entry 'Joe,' vol. 4, puts a human face on slavery.

Urban and Regional History

Cutting across economic sectors and social categories are urban and regional histories. A good introduction is A.F.J. Artibise and Gilbert A. Stelter, comps., *Canada's Urban Past: A Bibliography to 1980 and Guide to Canadian Urban Studies* (V: UBCP 1981). Of the two main urban centres in Quebec, Quebec City is the most studied but much of the historiography dates only from the last decade. The standard work is now J. Hare, Marc Lafrance, and D.-T. Ruddel, *Histoire de la ville de Québec, 1608–1871* (M/O: BE/Canadian Museum of Civilization 1987), a model global history that synthesizes a decade of intense research rooted in economic and social history. It can be supplemented by Ruddel's more specialized and interpretive *Quebec City, 1765–1832: The Evolution of a Colonial Town* (O: Canadian Museum of Civilization 1987), which studies the effects of colonial status on urban development. The review *Cap-aux-Diamants*, now devoted to popularizing the history of the province, formerly specialized in the history of the city of Quebec. See also L. Dechêne, 'Quelques aspects de la ville de Québec au XVIIIe siècle d'après les dénombrements paroissiaux,' *Cahiers de géographie du Québec* 28/75 (déc. 1984): 485–505, an excellent analytic and methodological study that grew out of research for 'The Town of Québec, 18th Century,' *HAC*, vol. 1, plate 50.

Different aspects of Quebec's urban life have been addressed in recent publications. Michael McCulloch, 'Most Assuredly Perpetual Motion: Police and Policing in Quebec City, 1838–58,' *Urban History Review* 19/1 (Oct. 1990): 100–12, studies influences on the nature and structure of the police force. André Charbonneau, Yvon Desloges, and M. Lafrance, *Quebec, the Fortified City: From the 17th to the 19th Century* (O: Parks Canada 1982), is an impressive study of the development of Quebec as a fortified garrison city and the consequences of that status. J. Mathieu et al., *The Plains of Abraham: The Search for the Ideal* (Sillery, Que.: SPT 1993), traces the different vocations – from battlefield to playground – and influence of an extraordinary urban green space. J. Fingard's excellent *Jack in Port: Sailortowns of Eastern Canada* (T: UTP 1982) focuses on Quebec's status as a port city; although well documented, it is essentially impressionistic.

The port was the focus of activity of Lower Town Quebec, the heart of which was Place Royal. In the last decade historical and archaeological studies have been carried out there, and the resulting reports are interesting not only for their contents but for their combination of archaeological and historical evidence. Each report comprises a synthesis and appendices, presenting (with analysis) selected or comprehensive data from the original sources. Such detailed study of an urban quarter is unique in Canadian historiography. To date Monique Lagrenade-Meunier, J. Provencher, Réal N. Brisson, G. Bervin, Yves Laframboise, and Serge Saint-Pierre have published syntheses on ways of life, social organization, and the residential and commercial functions there (Q: Gouvernement du Québec 1985–92).

Montreal has been much studied in the last decade – as is reflected in an excellent selective bibliography edited by J. Burgess et al., *Clés pour l'histoire de Montréal: bibliographie* (M: BE 1992). The groundwork is currently being laid for a new general history, as evidenced in P.-A. Linteau and J.-C. Robert, 'Montréal au 19e siècle: bilan d'une recherche,' *Urban History Review* 13/3 (Feb. 1985): 207–23, and Robert Sweeny, 'Un passé en mutations: bilan et perspectives pour une histoire socio-économique de Montréal au XIXe siècle,' in J.-R. Brault, ed., *Montréal au XIXe siècle: des gens, des idées, des arts, une ville* (M: Leméac 1990). The latter volume also contains other interesting articles on various aspects of life in nineteenth-century Montreal. See also David B. Hanna, 'Creation of an Early Victorian Suburb in Montreal,' *Urban History Review* 9/2 (Oct. 1980): 38–64; Robert D. Lewis, 'The Development of an Early Suburban Industrial District: The Montreal Ward of Saint-Ann, 1851–71,' *Urban History Review* 19/3 (Feb. 1991): 166–80; Lucia Ferretti, *Entre voisins, la société paroissiale en milieu urbain: Saint-Pierre-Apôtre de Montréal, 1848–1930* (M: BE 1992); and Pauline Desjardins and Geneviève Duguay, *Pointe-à-Callières: l'aventure montréalaise* (Sillery, Que.: SPT 1992), a revealing archaeological study. On Trois-Rivières see Guy Trépanier, *Arrondissement historique et vieux port de Trois-Rivières: étude historique et de potentiel archéologique* (TR: Ville de Trois-Rivières 1988). Yves Bergeron, 'Les premières places de marché au Québec,' *MHR* 35 (Spring 1992): 21–34, examines the role and evolution of an institution common to all urban centres, the market.

Regional history has been stimulated tremendously in the last decade by research conducted under the auspices of the Institut québécois de recherche sur la culture. It has produced, to date, nearly a dozen comprehensive regional bibliographies and three regional histories characterized less by their originality and analysis than by their thorough synthesis of the best historiography. With their corresponding regional bibliographies, these histories constitute excellent points of departure for work in regional history. Published to date are Jules Bélanger et al., *Histoire de la Gaspésie* (1981); Serge Laurin, *Histoire des Laurentides* (1989); and Camil Girard and Normand Perron, *Histoire du Saguenay-Lac-Saint-Jean* (1989). *Saguenayensia* (1959–) is a journal devoted to regional history. For the Gaspé see Maryse Grandbois, 'Le développement des disparités régionales en Gaspésie, 1760–1960, '*RHAF* 36/4 (mars 1983): 483–506. For the Outaouais, Chad Gaffield, 'The New Regional History: Rethinking the History of the Outaouais,' *JCS* 26/1 (Spring 1991): 64–81, argues for combining the differing anglophone and francophone approaches to regional history and refers to some of the historiography. René Hardy and N. Séguin's *Forêt et société en Mauricie: la formation de la région de Trois-Rivières, 1830–1930* (M: BE 1984) is excellent; the regional historical journal, *Les cahiers nicolétains* (1979–90) contains interesting articles of an empirical descriptive nature.

Medicine

Closely related to social history is the history of medicine, a field that has seen much excellent work done in recent years. André Paradis, 'L'histoire de la médecine: une porte ouverte sur l'histoire sociale,' *RHAF* 42/1 (été 1988): 73–83, an extended review of Marcel Fournier, Yves Gingras, and Othmar Keel, eds., *Sciences et médecine au Québec: perspectives sociohistoriques* (Q: IQRC 1987), hypothesizes on the conditions that have enabled medical history to become an element of social history. Denis Goulet and Paradis, in *Trois siècles d'histoire médical au Québec: chronologie des institutions et des pratiques (1639–1939)* (M: VLB Editeur 1992), translate this approach into a useful reference work with an excellent introduction and bibliography. S.E.D. Shortt, ed., *Medicine in Canadian Society: Historical Perspectives* (M: MQUP 1981), in addition to containing two fine texts illustrating the social approach to medical history, has an excellent historiographical study by the editor.

Leading the way in rejuvenating medical historiography has been Jacques Bernier, whose articles in the last decade have been synthesized into what must now be considered the standard work on the medical profession and its practices, *La médecine au Québec: naissance et évolution d'une profession* (Q: PUL 1989), which also provides a complete bibliography. Another major contributor to the socializing of medical historiography is Barbara R. Tunis: see 'Medical Licensing in Lower Canada: The Dispute over Canada's First Medical Degree,' *CHR* 55/4 (Dec. 1974): 489–504, reprinted in Shortt's anthology, and 'Medical Education and Medical Licensing in Lower Canada: Demographic Factors, Conflict and Social Change,' *HS/SH* 14/27 (May 1981): 67–91. Continuing in this vein are O. Keel and Peter Keating, 'Autour du *Journal de médecine de Québec/Quebec Medical Journal* (1826–1827): programme scientifique et programme de médicalisation,' in Richard A. Jarrell and Arnold E. Roos, eds., *Critical Issues in the History of Canadian Science, Technology and Medicine* (Thornhill, Ont.: HSTC [History of Science and Technology in Canada] Publications 1983); George Weisz, 'The Geographical Origins and Destinations of Medical Graduates in Quebec, 1834–1939,' *HS/SH* 19/37 (May 1986): 93–119; and A. Paradis, 'Un bilan de l'évolution de l'intérêt des médecins québécois pour les maladies infectieuses dans les périodiques médicaux (1826–1899),' *RHAF* 43/1 (été 1989): 63–91. J.-C. Robert, 'The City of Wealth and Death: Urban Mortality in Montreal, 1821–1871,' in Wendy Mitchinson and Janice Dickin McGinnis, eds., *Essays in the History of Canadian Medicine* (T: M&S 1988), concludes that among the social factors explaining differing mortality rates among ethnic groups are the groups' attitudes toward death. Sylvio Leblond, *Médecine et médecins d'autrefois: pratiques traditionnelles et portraits québécois* (Q: PUL 1986), containing articles published between 1951 and 1983, is more traditional and descriptive but informative and well written. Good institutional histories of hospitals are rare; François Rousseau, *La croix et le scalpel: histoire des Augustines et de l'Hôtel-Dieu de Québec (1639–1989)*, vol. 1, *1639–1892* (Sillery, Que.: SPT 1989), is a model study.

Geoffrey Bilson, *A Darkened House: Cholera in Nineteenth-Century Canada* (T: UTP 1980), treats the appearance of cholera as a crisis that reveals the character of a social period as any crisis would that of an individual. Thus it not only describes the fight against cholera, but above all analyses what that struggle shows about the political, administrative, social, medical, and even cultural structures of the time. How these structures, as well as popular attitudes toward cholera and its victims, were altered as a result are also examined. Réjean Lemoine, 'Les brochures publiées au XIXe siècle afin de lutter contre le choléra: essai bibliographique,' *Les Cahiers du livre ancien du Canada français* 1 (1984): 35–41, is a helpful survey of a major primary source.

The work of A. Paradis et al., *Essais pour une préhistoire de la psychiatrie au Canada (1800–1885)* (TR: Université du Québec à Trois-Rivières 1977), is a pioneering effort at viewing psychiatry and the treatment of the insane as a reflection of changing social, economic, and political values. Michel Clement, *L'aire du soupçon: contributions à l'histoire de la psychiatrie au Québec* (M: Triptyche 1990), ch. 1, provides an excellent analysis of the recent historiography. André Cellard, *Histoire de la folie au Québec de 1600 à 1850: 'le désordre'* (M: BE 1991), shows how the diagnosis and treatment of mental disorder reveal the values of a society. In this it also has affinities with the work of G. Bilson and of J.-M. Fecteau on social marginalism and deviance (see 'Legal and Judicial History' later in the chapter). Its multidimensional approach – medical, sociological, and ideological – represents a new trend in social historiography. Indeed, it demonstrates as well how the social values of historians colour their assessments of the practices and values of other periods. See also P. Keating, *La science du mal: l'institution de la psychiatrie au Québec, 1800–1814* (M: BE 1993).

A number of excellent biographies in the *DCB* also reflect the rejuvenation of medical history. See, in particular, 'Philippe-Louis-François Badelard' and 'George Longmore,' vol. 5; 'François Blanchet,' 'William Holmes,' 'John Mervin Nooth,' and 'Charles-Norbert Perrault,' vol. 6; 'Daniel Arnoldi,' vol. 7; and 'Edward Dagge Worthington,' vol. 12.

POLITICAL AND MILITARY HISTORY

Once as attractive as economic and social history now is, the study of constitutional, political, administrative, and military history has fallen on hard times in the last decade. A consensus now exists among Quebec historians that political and administrative structures stand on economic and social foundations and should be studied from that perspective. This approach is not often shared, however, by English-speaking historians outside Quebec. An excellent guide to historiographical currents and the literature is P. Tousignant's chapter 5 in J. Rouillard, ed., *Guide d'histoire du Québec du Régime français à nos jours*. Particularly strong on the literature in this field is G. Bernier and R. Boily, *Le Québec en transition, 1760–1867: bibliographie thématique*. Government printed records of particular value are the Lower Canadian House of Assembly, Legislative Council, and Special Council journals and their appendices, 1792–1841; and the Province of Canada Legislative Assembly and Legislative Council journals, 1841–67. Also of value are Arthur George Doughty et al., eds., *Documents Relating to the Constitutional History of Canada*, 3 vols. (O: Public Archives of Canada 1907–35); Elizabeth [Nish] Gibbs, ed., *Debates of the Legislative Assembly of United Canada, 1841–1867*, 12 vols. to date (M: Presses de l'Ecole des hautes études commerciales 1970–); and Jacques-Yvan Morin and José Woehrling, *Les constitutions du Canada et du Québec: du Régime français à nos jours* (M: Thémis 1992). An indispensable research tool is the *Dictionnaire des parlementaires du Québec, 1792–1992* (Sainte-Foy, Que.: PUL 1993), which supplements but also owes a great debt to the *DCB*.

Denis Monière and André Vachet, *Les idéologies au Québec: bibliographie* (3rd ed., M: Bibliothèque nationale du Québec 1980), is useful, and Monière, *Ideologies in Quebec: The Historical Development* (T: UTP 1981), is the best synthesis of that subject. Louis Balthazar, *Bilan du nationalisme au Québec* (M: L'Hexagone 1986), draws a useful but rather too sharp distinction between the 'modern' French-Canadian nationalism of the period 1791–1840, influenced by the French Revolution and liberal movements in Europe, and the 'traditional' or conservative nationalism that developed after 1840.

For the period from the Conquest to the Constitutional Act of 1791,

Alfred LeRoy Burt, *The Old Province of Quebec* (T: RP 1933; repr., intro. Hilda Neatby, 2 vols., T: M&S 1968), and H. Neatby, *Quebec: The Revolutionary Age, 1760–1791* (T: M&S 1966), still constitute the most comprehensive surveys, while M. Brunet, *Les Canadiens après la Conquête*, presents the neo-nationalist argument. They should be supplemented for interpretive purposes by P. Tousignant, 'The Integration of the Province of Quebec into the British Empire, 1763–91. Part 1, From the Royal Proclamation to the Quebec Act,' *DCB*, vol. 4. There is an abundant and contradictory literature on the Quebec Act, conveniently sampled in H. Neatby, *The Quebec Act: Protest and Policy* (Scarborough, Ont.: PH, 1972), which also includes the act and a selection of extracts from other documents. Philip Lawson rejuvenates the long historiography on the subject by portraying the metropolitan response to the acquisition of Quebec and the Quebec Act as a radical revision of British constitutional thinking in *The Imperial Challenge: Quebec and Britain in the Age of the American Revolution* (K&M: MQUP 1989).

Several works tell the story of the assault on Quebec during the American Revolution and its implications. Gustave Lanctôt, *Canada and the American Revolution, 1774–1783* (Cambridge, MA: Harvard University Press 1967), is a solidly documented, analytical treatment of the subject, while George F.G. Stanley, *Canada Invaded, 1775–1776* (T: Hakkert 1973), and Robert McConnell Hatch, *Thrust for Canada: The American Attempt on Quebec in 1775–1776* (Boston, MA: Houghton Mifflin 1979), provide more descriptive treatments. Various interpretations of the significance of the American Revolution for Quebec are given an airing in George A. Rawlyk, ed., *Revolution Rejected, 1775–1776* (Scarborough, Ont.: PH 1968). Roch Legault, 'L'organisation militaire sous le Régime britannique et le rôle assigné à la gentilhommerie canadienne (1760–1815),' *RHAF* 45/2 (automne 1991): 229–49, looks at an old subject from a new, social perspective.

The bicentenary of the French Revolution produced a number of collective works: see, in particular, Pierre-H. Boulle and Richard-A. Lebrun, eds., *Le Canada et la Révolution française* (M: Centre interuniversitaire d'études européennes 1989); Michel Grenon, ed., *L'image de le Révolution française au Québec, 1789–1989* (M: Hurtubise HMH 1989); and Sylvain Simard, ed., *La Révolution française au Canada français* (O: PUO 1991). For the period leading up to the Constitutional Act of 1791 see P. Tousignant, 'Problématique pour une nouvelle approche de la constitution de 1791,' *RHAF* 27/2 (sept. 1973): 181–234, and David Milobar, 'Conservative Ideology, Metropolitan Government, and the Reform of Quebec, 1782–1791,' *International History Review* 12/1 (Feb. 1990): 45–64.

The 1760–91 period is well served biographically by the *DCB*. The biographies of the major figures are all strong and their bibliographies lead to fuller treatments. See, in particular, governors James Murray (vol. 4), Guy Carleton, 1st Baron Dorchester (vol. 5), and Sir Frederick Haldimand, (vol. 5, appendix); American Revolutionary army officers Richard Montgomery (vol. 4) and Benedict Arnold (vol. 5); Clément Gosselin and Moses Hazen (vol. 4); and legislative councillors Hector Theophilus Cramahé and Luc de La Corne (vol. 4), and Francis Maseres (vol. 6).

The major general works covering the period following the Constitutional Act to the Act of Union in 1841 are F. Ouellet, *Economic and Social History of Quebec* and *Lower Canada, 1791–1840*; J.-P. Wallot, *Un Québec qui bougeait: trame socio-politique du Québec au tournant du XIXe siècle* (TR: BE 1973); and G. Paquet and Wallot, *Lower Canada at the Turn of the Nineteenth Century*. H.T. Manning, *The Revolt of French Canada, 1800–1835* (T: MAC 1962), remains serviceable.

Several interpretive articles have appeared more recently. James Sturgis, in 'Anglicisation as a Theme in Lower Canadian History, 1807–1843,' *British Journal of Canadian Studies* 3/2 (1988): 210–29, first published in 1979, argues the necessity to distinguish intended from incidental effects, and, in a short sequel, 'Afterthoughts on Anglicisation' (pp. 230–3), makes comparisons with South Africa and urges a return to considering humans as having free will rather than as agents of impersonal economic and social forces. G. Bernier and D. Salée, 'Social Relations and the Exercise of State Power in Lower Canada (1791–1840): Elements for an Analysis,' *Studies in Political Economy* 22 (Spring 1987): 101–43, and Bernier, 'Landownership and Access to Political Power in Lower Canada, 1791–1838,' *Québec Studies* 7 (1988): 87–97, argue that political power in the colony reflected Britain's own political situation in which aristocracy sought to defend its hegemony from the challenges of the middle class. See also Richard LaRue, 'Allégeance et origine: contribution à l'analyse de la crise politique au Bas-Canada,' *RHAF* 44/4 (printemps 1991): 529–48.

The technical functioning of the new constitution is analysed in Henri Brun, *La formation des institutions parlementaires québécoises, 1791–1838* (Q: PUL 1970), and its political functioning, in André Garon, 'La fonction politique et sociale des chambres hautes canadiennes, 1791–1841,' *HS/SH* 3/5 (Apr. 1970): 66–87, and J. Hare, 'L'Assemblée législative du Bas-Canada, 1792–1814: députation et polarisation politique,' *RHAF* 27/3 (déc. 1973): 361–95. P. Tousignant, 'La première campagne électorale des Canadiens en 1792,' *HS/SH* 8/15 (May 1975): 120–48, examines ethnic and social divisions in the early electoral process. European influences are studied in Claude Galarneau, *La France devant l'opinion canadienne, 1760–1815* (Q/P: PUL/Armand Colin 1970); 'La légende napoléonienne au Québec,' in Fernand Dumont and Yves Martin, eds., *Imaginaire social et représentations collectives: mélanges offerts à Jean-Charles Falardeau* (Q: PUL 1982); and 'Les Canadiens en France (1815–1855),' *Cahiers des Dix* 44 (1989): 135–81; as well as J. Hare, *La pensée socio-politique au Québec, 1784–1812: analyse sémantique* (O: PUO 1977); and J.-P. Wallot, 'Frontière ou fragment du système atlantique: des idées étrangères dans l'identité bas-canadienne au début du XIXe siècle,' CHA *HP* (1983): 1–29. The article by Mark Olsen and Louis-Georges Harvey, 'Computers in Intellectual History: Lexical Statistics and the Analysis of Political Discourse,' *Journal of Interdisciplinary History* 18/3 (Winter 1988): 449–64, is an original methodological study of ideology using pre- and post-French Revolutionary Quebec as an example. Results of their study are given in 'French Revolutionary Forms in French-Canadian Political Language, 1805–35,' *CHR* 68/3 (Sept. 1987): 374–92.

The War of 1812 has been described solidly, if traditionally, in G.F.G. Stanley, *The War of 1812: Land Operations* (T: MAC/National Museums of Canada 1983), the bibliography of which leads to an abundant literature. Michelle Guitard, *The Militia of the Battle of Châteauguay: A Social History* (O: Parks Canada 1984), fills a hole in Stanley's study, the role of the militia.

The war had imposed a fragile political consensus between, on the one hand, British merchants and office-holders entrenched in the appointed Legislative and Executive councils, and, on the other, a French-Canadian nationalist professional bourgeoisie, which dominated the elected House of Assembly. By 1820 this consensus was dissolving and in the next two decades a struggle for power led to the Rebellions of 1837–8. Apart from the general works mentioned previously, a number of recent studies examine aspects of this growing conflict. See André Lefebvre, *La 'Montreal Gazette' et le nationalisme canadien, 1835–1842* (M: Guérin 1970 [i.e. 1971]); France Galarneau, 'L'élection partielle du quartier-ouest de Montréal en 1832: analyse politico-sociale,' *RHAF* 32/4 (mars 1979): 565–84; Philippe Reid, 'L'émergence du nationalisme canadien-français: l'idéologie du *Canadien*, 1806–1842,' *RS* 21/1–2 (jan.–août 1980): 11–53; E. Kolish, 'Le Conseil législatif et les bureaux d'enregistrement (1836),' *RHAF* 35/2 (sept. 1981): 217–30; G. Bernier, 'Le Parti patriote, 1827–1838,' in Vincent Lemieux, ed., *Personnel et partis politiques au Québec: aspects historiques* (M: BE 1982); and David De Brou, 'The Rose, the Shamrock and the Cabbage: The Battle for Irish Voters in Upper-Town Quebec, 1827–1836,' *HS/SH*

24/48 (Nov. 1991): 305–34. M. McCulloch, 'The Death of Whiggery: Lower-Canadian British Constitutionalism and the *tentation de l'histoire parallèle*,' *JCHA* 2 (1991): 195–213, examines the whig foundations of the Constitutionalist party's position in the 1830s and their erosion in a new political and economic context in the following decade.

The development of French-Canadian political ideology can also be followed through studies of the views of the political leaders. Of particular interest in this respect is Pierre-Stanislas Bédard, the early leader-theoretician of the Canadian party; see the *DCB* entry in vol. 6, and John L. Finlay, 'The State of a Reputation: Bédard as Constitutionalist,' *JCS* 20/4 (Winter 1985): 60–76. But also of interest is the tortuous career of Bédard's successor, Sir James Stuart, whose *DCB* entry is in vol. 8. The career of the leader of the increasingly nationalist Patriote party in the 1820s and 1830s, Louis-Joseph Papineau, is the subject of considerable scholarly debate but few satisfactory biographies. Robert Rumilly, *Papineau et son temps*, 2 vols. (M: Fides 1977), is the fullest account. The entry for Papineau by F. Ouellet in *DCB*, vol. 10, is intriguing and controversial. Biographies of other major figures are D. Monière, *Ludger Duvernay et la révolution intellectuelle au Bas-Canada* (M: Québec/Amérique 1987); 'Ludger Duvernay,' *DCB*, vol. 8; G. Parizeau, *La vie studieuse et obstinée de Denis-Benjamin Viger, 1774–1861* (M: Fides 1980); and 'Denis-Benjamin Viger,' *DCB*, vol. 9.

The imperial government's attempts to manage the growing crisis are the subject of Phillip A. Buckner's iconoclastic and important *The Transition to Responsible Government: British Policy in British North America, 1815–1850* (Westport, CT: Greenwood Press 1985). Buckner's introductory essay to *DCB*, vol. 8, 'The Colonial Office and British North America, 1801–50,' is essential reading for an understanding of the functioning, and misfunctioning, of that office. British attitudes – official, popular, and historiographical – toward the colony are discussed in Peter Burroughs, *British Attitudes towards Canada, 1822–1849* (Scarborough, Ont.: PH 1971), as well as in Mark Francis's interestingly eccentric *Governors and Settlers: Images of Authority in the British Colonies, 1820–60* (L: MAC 1992).

The *DCB* presents the complete spectrum of ideological positions through a number of biographies in addition to those already mentioned. The development of the radical Patriote position is well illustrated by Louis Bourdages (vol. 6) and the moderate nationalist position by Jean-Antoine Panet (vol. 5), John Neilson (vol. 7), Jacques Viger (vol. 8), and Joseph-Rémi Vallières de Saint-Réal (vol. 7). Jean-Marie Mondelet (vol. 7) struggled to stay neutral, and Pierre-Amable De Bonne (vol. 5) represents the French-Canadian office-holder. The most informative biographies of British politicians and office-holders are John Craigie (vol. 5), Hugh Finlay (vol. 5), Herman Witsius Ryland (vol. 7), Jonathan Sewell (vol. 7), John Young (vol. 5), and John Richardson (vol. 6). Finally, the British government's position is well represented by excellent biographies of the governors, notably Sir George Prevost (vol. 5), Sir John Coape Sherbrooke (vol. 6), George Ramsay, 9th Earl of Dalhousie (vol. 7), Sir James Kempt (vol. 8), and Archibald Acheson, 2nd Earl of Gosford (vol. 7).

There is a vast historiography of the Rebellions of 1837–8. Jean-Paul Bernard, *Les rébellions de 1837–1838: les Patriotes du Bas-Canada dans la mémoire collective et chez les historiens* (M: BE 1983), is an indispensable aid to sorting it out. Bernard has also brought together the speeches of the Patriotes and their opponents in the rebellion period in *Assemblées publiques, résolutions et déclarations de 1837–1838* (M: VLB Editeur 1988). In addition to the interpretations of the rebellions in Bernard, see A. Greer, 'La dimension ville-campagne de l'insurrection de 1837,' in F. Lebrun and N. Séguin, eds., *Sociétés villageoises et rapports villes-campagnes*, and, with Léon Robichaud, 'La rébellion de 1837–1838 au Bas-Canada: une approche géographique,' *Cahiers de géographie du Québec* 33/90 (déc. 1989): 345–77, which disputes the linkage of rebellion and agrarian distress made by Ouellet and others before him.

Gérard Filteau's venerable and partisan *Histoire des Patriotes*, 3 vols. (1937–42; repr. in 1 vol., M: L'Aurore 1975), the most detailed account of the rebellions, can now be supplemented by Elinor Kyte Senior's more balanced and solid *Redcoats and Patriotes: The Rebellions in Lower Canada, 1837–38* (Stittsville, Ont.: Canada's Wings/National Museums of Canada 1985). Senior, *British Regulars in Montreal: An Imperial Garrison, 1832–1854* (M: MQUP 1981), and Denis Racine, *Répertoire des officiers de milice du Bas-Canada, 1830–1848* (Sainte-Foy, Que.: Société de généalogie de Québec 1986), shed light on two hitherto little-known groups before and after the rebellions. A number of excellent *DCB* biographies of Patriotes help place the rebellions in a broader perspective: see especially 'Joseph-Narcisse Cardinal,' 'Jean-Olivier Chénier,' 'Amury Girod,' and 'Chevalier de Lorimier,' vol. 7; 'Jean-Joseph Girouard,' 'Timothée Kimber,' 'Siméon Marchessault,' and 'Louis-Michel Viger,' vol. 8; and 'Robert Nelson,' vol. 10.

For the post-rebellion period see the works of P. Burroughs and P.A. Buckner as well as the *DCB* entries 'John George Lambton, 1st Earl of Durham' and 'Charles Edward Poulett Thomson, 1st Baron Sydenham,' vol. 7. Janet Ajzenstat, *The Political Thought of Lord Durham* (K&M: MQUP 1988), has been strongly contested for failing to consider historical context but is an interesting example of a political philosophy approach to history.

A special issue of the *JCS*, 25/1 (Spring 1990), is devoted entirely to Durham. Ruth L. White, *Louis-Joseph Papineau et Lamennais: le chef des Patriotes canadiens à Paris, 1839–1845, avec correspondance et documents inédits* (M: Hurtubise HMH 1983), is a fascinating glimpse of the most celebrated exile, and F. Murray Greenwood translated and edited *Land of a Thousand Sorrows: The Australian Prison Journal, 1840–1842, of the Exiled Canadien Patriote, François Maurice Lepailleur* (V: UBCP 1980), a sympathetic look at the painful life in exile of the uncelebrated. I. Radforth, 'Sydenham and Utilitarian Reform,' in A. Greer and Radforth, eds., *Colonial Leviathan*, argues, contrary to a certain historiographical consensus, that Sydenham's administration had a major and enduring impact on state formation.

There exist a number of excellent general studies of the period from the Act of Union to Confederation, but few have been published in the last fifteen years. English-language historians consider the period crucial to the birth of Canada. For example, see W.L. Morton, *The Critical Years: The Union of British North America, 1857–1873* (T: M&S 1964); J.M.S. Careless, *The Union of the Canadas: The Growth of Canadian Institutions, 1841–1857* (T: M&S 1967); Jacques Monet, *The Last Cannon Shot: A Study of French-Canadian Nationalism, 1837–1850* (T: UTP 1969); and P.A. Buckner, *Transition to Responsible Government*. Paul G. Cornell, *The Alignment of Political Groups in Canada, 1841–1867* (T: UTP 1962), remains a useful monograph.

There are also a number of more focused works. Eric Ross, *Full of Hope and Promise: The Canadas in 1841* (K&M: MQUP 1991), is a useful snapshot of life in the Canadas at the Union. Michael J. Piva, 'Government Finance and the Development of the Canadian State,' in A. Greer and I. Radforth, eds., *Colonial Leviathan*, looks at the role of the development of financial policy in state formation. Trade relations with the United States as an aspect of political development – typified by the annexation movement of 1849 and the Reciprocity Treaty of 1854 – have long been a matter of historiographical consideration. Ben Forster, *A Conjunction of Interests: Business, Politics, and Tariffs, 1825–1879* (T: UTP 1986), is a recent, original look at the subject as a reflection of the changing motivations and weight of interest groups. See also articles by Ged Martin, Ralph C. Nelson et al., and Peter J. Smith in Martin, ed., *The Causes of Canadian Confederation* (F: AP 1990).

With J. Monet, contemporary French-language historians have concentrated their efforts on the study of competing nationalist currents within Canada East. Apart from the works of D. Monière and L. Balthazar mentioned earlier, see Georges Vincenthier, ed., *Histoire des idées au Québec: des troubles de 1837 au référendum de 1980* (M: VLB Editeur 1983), which includes formerly unpublished texts illustrating the elites' reactions to changes in society. Yvan Lamonde, *Gens de parole: conférences publiques, essais et débats à l'Institut canadien de Montréal, 1845–1871* (M: BE 1990), offers a broadly based presentation of the form and substance of liberal thought. J.-P. Bernard, *Les Rouges: libéralisme, nationalisme et anticléricalisme au milieu de XIXe siècle* (M: PUQ 1971), remains unsurpassed, however, as a study of liberal nationalism in action. The liberals were opposed by conservative ultramontanes. In addition to the works on their ideology mentioned in the section 'Religious History,' see M. Bellavance, *Le Québec et la Confédération: un choix libre? Le clergé et la constitution de 1867* (Sillery, Que.: SPT 1992), a quantitatively based study which argues that the church's intervention in favour of Confederation effectively eliminated freedom of choice. As for the attitudes of French Canadians in general toward the project, see Jean-Charles Bonenfant, *The French Canadians and the Birth of Confederation*, CHA Historical Booklet no. 21 (O: 1966), and *La naissance de la Confédération* (M: Leméac 1969), as well as Arthur I. Silver, *The French-Canadian Idea of Confederation, 1864–1900* (T: UTP 1982).

A number of excellent *DCB* entries offer a panorama of the nationalist political spectrum from radical liberal to conservative ultramontane. See, in particular, 'Jean-Baptiste-Eric Dorion,' 'Sir Louis-Hippolyte La Fontaine,' 'Augustin-Norbert Morin,' and 'Sir Etienne-Paschal Taché,' vol. 9; 'Gonzalve Doutre' and 'Médéric Lanctôt,' vol. 10; 'Joseph-Edouard Cauchon,' 'Pierre-Joseph-Olivier Chauveau,' 'Joseph Doutre,' and 'Louis-Victor Sicotte,' vol. 11; and 'Louis-Antoine Dessaulles' and 'Sir Antoine-Aimé Dorion,' vol. 12. The biographies of English-speaking politicians 'Lewis Thomas Drummond,' 'Sir Francis Hincks,' and 'Lucius Seth Huntington,' vol. 11, complete the picture. Also see B. Young, *George-Etienne Cartier*.

The standard history of public administration is J.E. Hodgetts, *Pioneer Public Service: An Administrative History of the United Canadas, 1841–1867* (T: UTP 1955). Works of particular interest on specific aspects of public administration are Marc-André Bédard, 'Le greffier sous le régime de l'Union [parties 1 et 2],' *Bulletin de la bibliothèque de l'Assemblée nationale du Québec* 14/1 (1984): 47–60; 15/1 (1985): 21–52; and Alain Baccigalupo, *Les administrations municipales québécoises, des origines à nos jours: anthologie administrative*, 2 vols. (M: Agence d'ARC 1984). The *DCB* entries 'Hugh Finlay' and 'Samuel Johannes Holland,' vol. 5; and 'Joseph Bouchette,' and 'Herman Witsius Ryland,' vol. 7, offer insights into various aspects of the early provincial administration.

Finally, popular reactions to various situations throughout the period 1760–1867, inevitably difficult to measure, are studied in J.-P. Wallot,

Intrigues françaises et américaines au Canada, 1800–1802 (M: Leméac 1965); Terence A. Crowley, '"Thunder Gusts": Popular Disturbances in Early French Canada,' CHA *HP* (1979): 11–32; and Stephen Kenny, '"Cahots" and Catcalls: An Episode of Popular Resistance in Lower Canada at the Outset of the Union,' *CHR* 65/2 (June 1984): 184–208, which recalls J.-M. Fecteau's work on the social regulation of deviance in the following section.

LEGAL AND JUDICIAL HISTORY

Legal and judicial historiography was hampered by the state of Quebec's judicial archives which are voluminous, complex, and rich in content but formerly difficult of access. However, progress has been made in organizing them: see 'Archives judiciaires,' *Archives* 22/4 (été 1991): 2–118. There are two useful reference works: Pierre-E. Audet, *Les officiers de justice des origines de la colonie jusqu'à nos jours* (M: Wilson et Lafleur 1986), and G. Blaine Baker et al., *Sources in the Law Library of McGill University for a Reconstruction of the Legal Culture of Quebec, 1760–1890* (M: McGill University 1987).

Like other historical fields, legal and judicial history has been marked by economic and social history. J.-M. Fecteau, *Un nouvel ordre des choses*, synthesizes a number of his articles written from the perspective of social regulation, the effort by those in power to manage the twin threats of poverty and crime in a period of transition from a feudal to a capitalist society. Methodologically and historiographically this work marks a new departure in Quebec toward the study of social marginalism and criminality and is essential reading. Jacques Laplante, *Prison et ordre social au Québec* (O: PUO 1989), an interpretive work based on the publications of legal historians and others, adopts a similar approach by viewing the prison in its economic, social, and ideological contexts as an instrument for the management of poverty. A. Greer, 'The Birth of the Police in Canada,' in Greer and I. Radforth, eds., *Colonial Leviathan*, takes a similar tack: the state formed police forces in order to appropriate a social control formerly exercised by civil society. D. Owen Carrigan, *Crime and Punishment in Canada: A History* (T: M&S 1991), is weak on Lower Canada but offers a source of comparison with the other British colonies.

Two recent studies examine influences on the evolution of Lower Canadian civil law and procedure: Jean-Maurice Brisson, *La formation d'un droit mixte: l'évolution de la procédure civile de 1774 à 1867* (M: Thémis 1986), and E. Kolish, 'The Impact of the Change in Legal Metropolis on the Development of Lower Canada's Legal System: Judicial Chaos and Legislative Paralysis in the Civil Law, 1791–1838,' in *Papers Presented at the 1987 Canadian Law in History Conference Held at Carleton University, Ottawa, June 8–10, 1987* ([O: Carleton University] 1987), vol. 1. The relationship between the law and business has been the subject of some recent research. G.B. Baker, 'Law Practice and Statecraft in Mid-Nineteenth-Century Montreal: The Torrance-Morris Firm, 1848 to 1868,' in C. Wilton, ed., *Essays in the History of Canadian Law*, vol. 4, *Beyond the Law: Lawyers and Business in Canada, 1830 to 1930* (T: OS/UTP 1990), explores relations among lawyers, legislators, and businessmen in the establishment of social control and of Montreal's legal and commercial hinterland. In the same volume, B. Young, 'Dimensions of a Law Practice: Brokerage and Ideology in the Career of George-Etienne Cartier,' looks at the direction of Cartier's reform of the civil law and the influences that moulded it. J.-M. Fecteau, 'Les "petites républiques": les compagnies et la mise en place du droit corporatif moderne au Québec au milieu du 19e siècle,' *HS/SH* 25/49 (May 1992): 35–56, is an examination of the creation and application of corporate law as an expression of the relationship between business and government. From a broader perspective, Fecteau, 'Etat et associationnisme au XIXe siècle québécois: éléments pour une problématique des rapports Etat/société dans la transition au capitalisme,' and B. Young, 'Positive Law, Positive State: Class Realignment and the Transformation of Lower Canada, 1815–1866,' both in A. Greer and I. Radforth, eds., *Colonial Leviathan*, look at the changing relationships within civil society and between it and the state, mediated through the law and legal forms in a period of economic transition to capitalism.

Useful studies of the workings of the law and the judicial system under the successive constitutional regimes are Douglas Hay, 'The Meanings of the Criminal Law in Quebec, 1764–1774,' in Louis A. Knafla, ed., *Crime and Criminal Justice in Europe and Canada* (Waterloo, Ont.: Wilfrid Laurier University Press 1981); H. Neatby, *The Administration of Justice under the Quebec Act* (L: OUP 1937); F.M. Greenwood, 'L'insurrection appréhendée et l'administration de la justice au Canada: le point de vue d'un historien,' *RHAF* 34/1 (juin 1980): 57–93; and Greenwood, 'The General Court Martial of 1838–39 in Lower Canada: An Abuse of Justice,' in W. Wesley Pue and Barry Wright, eds., *Canadian Perspectives on Law and Society: Issues in Legal History* (O: CUP 1988).

Finally, the *DCB* biographies of a number of lawyers and judges present, when combined, the judicial system in its social and political contexts and with a human face. See, in particular, 'Pierre Du Calvet,' 'François-Joseph Cugnet,' and 'William Smith,' vol. 4; 'David Lynd,' 'Pierre-Louis Panet,' and 'Jenkin Williams,' vol. 5; 'Sir James Monk,' vol. 6; 'Jonathan Sewell' and 'Joseph-Rémi Vallières de Saint-Réal,' vol. 7; and 'Sir James Stuart,' vol. 8.

RELIGIOUS HISTORY

Like all other fields, religious history has been transformed by the accent on economic and social history. Indeed, the shift from an institutional to a social perspective is the dominant characteristic of religious historiography in the last fifteen years. That historiography has been well delineated in articles by Guy Laperrière: 'Religion populaire, religion de clercs? Du Québec à la France, 1972 à 1982,' in Benoît Lacroix and Jean Simard, eds., *Religion populaire, religion de clercs?* (Q: IQRC 1984); 'L'histoire religieuse du Québec: principaux courants, 1978–1988,' *RHAF* 42/4 (printemps 1989): 563–78; and, with William Westfall, 'Religious Studies,' in A.F.J. Artibise, ed., *Interdisciplinary Approaches to Canadian Society*. Another useful research tool is the annual bibliography in the Canadian Catholic Historical Association, *Report* (1933–65), *Study Sessions* (1966–83), and now *Historical Studies*. The French equivalent, Société canadienne d'histoire de l'Eglise catholique, *Rapport* (1933–65), *Sessions d'étude* (1966–89), and now *Etudes d'histoire religieuse*, increasingly contains articles of professional quality. Luca Codignola, *Guide to Documents Relating to French and British North America in the Archives of the Sacred Congregation 'de Propaganda Fide' in Rome, 1622–1799* (O: National Archives of Canada 1991), provides an excellent introduction to a major source for the writing of post-Conquest religious history.

Lucien Lemieux, Philippe Sylvain, and Nive Voisine, *Histoire du catholicisme québécois, les XVIIIe et XIXe siècles*, vol. 1, *Les années difficiles (1760–1839)*; vol. 2, *Réveil et consolidation (1840–1898)* (M: BE 1989–91), now constitute the standard general history of Catholicism in Quebec during this period, incorporating all the latest research and approaches. J. Simard, dir., *Le grand héritage*, vol. 2, *L'Eglise catholique et la société du Québec* (Q: Musée du Québec 1984), an exhibition catalogue, contains a helpful, well-illustrated, shorter synthesis. The institutional history of the church is solidly documented in L. Lemieux, *L'établissement de la première province ecclésiastique au Canada, 1783–1844* (M: Fides 1968), and Jacques Grisé, *Les conciles provinciaux de Québec et l'Eglise canadienne, 1851–1886* (M: Fides 1979). *L'Eglise de Montréal, 1836–1986: aperçus d'hier et d'aujourd'hui* (M: Fides 1986) presents various aspects, from institutional to social, of the history of the Diocese of Montreal. Over the past decade *Les cahiers nicolétains* has published several articles of interest on the religious life of the Mauricie–Bois-Francs region.

The church's ideology, a subject of intense study in the 1970s, no longer attracts much research. P. Sylvain, 'Libéralisme et ultramontanisme au Canada français: affrontement idéologique et doctrinal (1840–1865),' in W.L. Morton, ed., *The Shield of Achilles: Aspects of Canada in the Victorian Age* (T: M&S 1968), and N. Fahmy-Eid, *Le clergé et le pouvoir politique au Québec: une analyse de l'idéologie ultramontaine au milieu du XIXe siècle* (M: Hurtubise HMH 1978), are solid studies from quite different perspectives. N. Voisine, 'L'ultramontanisme canadien-français au XIXe siècle,' in Voisine and J. Hamelin, eds., *Les ultramontains canadiens-français* (M: BE 1985), provides a useful synthesis.

The Catholic episcopacy has been the subject of several biographies. Guy-Marie Oury, *Mgr Briand, évêque de Québec, et les problèmes de son époque* (Sainte-Foy, Que.: La Liberté 1985), is a traditional study that does not eclipse André Vachon's 'Jean-Oliver Briand,' *DCB*, vol. 4. No full-length biography yet exists of Joseph-Octave Plessis, but James H. Lambert's entry on him in the *DCB*, vol. 6, summarizes a doctoral thesis; see also Lambert, 'L'apprivoisement du pouvoir: l'apprentissage épiscopal de Pierre Denaut et de Joseph-Octave Plessis,' SCHEC, *Sessions d'étude* 51 (1984): 9–17. Gilles Chaussé, *Jean-Jacques Lartigue, premier évêque de Montréal* (M: Fides 1980); N. Voisine, *Louis-François Laflèche, deuxième évêque de Trois-Rivières*, vol. 1, *Dans le sillage de Pie IX et de Mgr Bourget, 1818–1878* (Saint-Hyacinthe, Que.: Edisem 1980); and Léon Pouliot, *Monseigneur Bourget et son temps*, 3 vols. (M: Beauchemin 1955–72), are the fullest treatments of their subjects. And, of course, there is the *DCB*: see 'Joseph Signay,' vol. 7; 'Jean-Charles Prince,' vol. 8; and 'Ignace Bourget,' vol. 11.

On the lower clergy, an article by S. Gagnon and Louise Lebel-Gagnon, 'Le milieu d'origine du clergé québécois, 1775–1840: mythes et réalités,' *RHAF* 37/3 (déc. 1983): 373–97, is a solid examination of that subject. R. Chabot tackles the issue of religious fervour and clerical influence in *Le curé de campagne et la contestation locale au Québec de 1791 aux troubles de 1837–38* (M: Hurtubise HMH 1975). See also R. Hardy, 'L'activité sociale du curé de Notre-Dame de Québec: aperçu de l'influence du clergé au milieu du XIXe siècle,' *HS/SH* 3/6 (Nov. 1970): 5–32, and 'Ce que sacrer veut dire: à l'origine du juron religieux au Québec,' *Mentalités* 2 (1989): 99–125. Christine Hudon, 'Carrières et vie matérielle du clergé du Richelieu-Yamaska (1790–1840),' *RHAF* 45/4 (printemps 1992): 573–94, is an interesting case study showing that the effects of the shortage of clergy of the time on the quality of clerical life were not all negative, but it gives only incidental consideration to episcopal administrative policies and objectives.

A major event in asserting clerical influence was a religious revival conducted in the early 1840s. Concerning it see Louis Rousseau, 'A l'origine d'une société maintenant perdue: le réveil religieux montréalais de 1840,' in Yvon Desrosiers, ed., *Religion et culture au Québec: figures contemporaines du sacré* (M: Fides 1986); 'Les missions populaires de 1840–42: acteurs principaux et conséquences,' SCHEC, *Sessions d'étude* 53 (1986): 7–21; and 'Les rapports entre le "réveil" et la réorganisation ecclésiale dans le Québec du 19ème siècle,' in P. Guillaume, ed., *Le diocèse au Québec et en France*. See as well C. Galarneau, 'Monseigneur de Forbin-Janson au Québec en 1840–1841,' in N. Voisine and J. Hamelin, eds., *Les ultramontains canadiens-français*; and Huguette Lapointe-Roy, 'Le renouveau religieux à Montréal au XIXe siècle, et le rôle des Sulpiciens dans le domaine de l'éducation chrétienne,' SCHEC, *Sessions d'étude* 53 (1986): 51–62. L.-P. Hébert, ed., *Le Québec de 1850 en lettres détachées* (Q: Ministère des Affaires culturelles 1985), presents perceptions of Quebec by French members of the community of the Clercs de Saint-Viateur as revealed in their correspondence home from 1847 to 1877; although the letters are interesting, a critical reading is necessary to distinguish observation from prejudice.

There are a few valuable biographies of lower clergy. Jacqueline Lefebvre, *L'abbé Philippe Desjardins: un grand ami du Canada, 1753–1833* (Q: Société historique de Québec 1982), is a solid treatment of a discreetly influential figure. *DCB* biographies of clergy have not been its strength, but there are exceptions: 'Etienne Chartier,' 'Jean-Baptiste Kelly,' 'Thomas Maguire,' and 'Joseph-Vincent Quiblier,' vol. 8; 'Louis-Jacques Casault,' vol. 9; and 'Charles-Félix Cazeau' and 'François Pilote,' vol. 11.

During this period two institutions trained clergy. Noël Baillargeon, *Le Séminaire de Québec de 1760 à 1800* (Q: PUL 1981), is a solid study of one; Rolland Litalien, ed., *Le Grand Séminaire de Montréal de 1840 à 1990: 150 années au service de la formation des prêtres* (M: Editions du Grand Séminaire de Montréal 1990), is useful, despite a rather outdated approach.

A study of the religious communities begins with Henri-Bernard Boivin, Claire Jean, and Réal Bosa, *Histoire des communautés religieuses au Québec: bibliographie* (M: Bibliothèque nationale du Québec 1984). Several articles in SCHEC, *Sessions d'étude* 57 (1990), provide an excellent historiographical introduction. Robert Lahaise, *Les édifices conventuels du Vieux-Montréal: aspects ethno-historiques* (M: Hurtubise HMH 1980), looks at the physical development of communities. Female communities have been studied of late from the perspective of women's history. Although the work of Diane Bélanger and Lucie Rozon, *Les religieuses au Québec* (M: Libre Expression 1982), is largely descriptive, Micheline D'Allaire, *Les dots de religieuses au Canada français, 1639–1800: étude économique et sociale* (M: Hurtubise HMH

1986); M. Danylewycz, *Taking the Veil*; and R. Courcy, 'Les communautés religieuses du Québec au XIXème siècle,' in P. Guillaume, ed., *Le diocèse au Québec et en France*, are analytic and interpretive. F. Rousseau, *La croix et le scalpel: histoire des Augustines et de l'Hôtel Dieu*, is an exceptional history of a female community.

Male religious communities were re-established in Quebec only from the 1840s after having been allowed to die out following the Conquest. Gabriel Dussault and Gilles Martel's *Charisme et économie: les cinq premières communautés masculines établies au Québec sous le Régime anglais (1837-1870)* (Q: Faculté des sciences sociales, Université Laval 1981) is an excellent example of sociological methodology applied to historical analysis. On the other hand, N. Voisine, *Les Frères des écoles chrétiennes au Canada*, vol. 1, *La conquête de l'Amérique, 1837-1880* (Q: Anne Sigier 1987), is a model study using classic historical methodology, sympathetic to its subject (it is a commissioned history) but rigorous. *Les prêtres de Saint-Sulpice: grandes figures de leur histoire* (Sainte-Foy, Que.: PUL 1992), written largely from within the Catholic institutional historiographical tradition, offers new information on members of one of the most influential religious institutions of the period, without, however, renewing the subject. Nevertheless, it completes the picture provided in B. Young, *In Its Corporate Capacity*.

A number of recent works look at the vehicles and modes of transmission of religious faith and clerical influence. André Laganière, 'Le missionnaire et son rôle de pasteur ...,' a series of articles in *Les cahiers nicolétains* 10–12 (1988–90), describes the complete range of them as used by nineteenth-century missionaries in the Mauricie–Bois-Francs region. Raymond Brodeur, ed., *Les catéchismes au Québec, 1702-1963* (Q/P: PUL/Centre national de la recherche scientifique 1990), is an indispensable research tool that offers elements of analysis and includes political and other catechisms. Articles by Brodeur and René Dubeau-Legentil in Brodeur and Jean-Paul Rouleau, eds., *Une inconnue de l'histoire de la culture: la production des catéchismes en Amérique française* (Sainte-Foy, Que.: Anne Sigier 1986), constitute solid interpretive studies of a little-known subject. L. Rousseau, *La prédication à Montréal de 1800 à 1830: approche religiologique* (M: Fides 1975), and N. Voisine, 'Jubilés, missions paroissiales et prédication au XIXe siècle,' in F. Dumont and Y. Martin, eds., *Imaginaire social et représentations collectives*, are rare examinations of preaching and its impact. S. Gagnon and R. Hardy, in *L'Eglise et le village au Québec, 1850-1930: l'enseignement des cahiers de prône* (M: Leméac 1979), use the parish priests' weekly announcements from the pulpit to study the dialectic between popular and institutional religion. This tension is also the subject of B. Lacroix and J. Simard, eds., *Religion popu-*

laire, religion de clercs? which introduces the insights of ethnographic studies. See also Brigitte Caulier, 'Les confréries de dévotion traditionnelles et le réveil religieux à Montréal au XIXe siècle,' SCHEC, *Sessions d'étude* 53 (1986): 23–41. An excellent annotated guide to the varied literature on popular religion is B. Lacroix et al., eds., *La piété populaire: répertoire bibliographique. Canada*, vol. 1, *Le Québec* (Turnhout, Belgium/M: Brepols/ Bellarmin 1991). The church's presence through control of social assistance is well documented in H. Lapointe-Roy, *Charité bien ordonnée: le premier réseau de lutte contre la pauvreté à Montréal au 19e siècle* (M: BE 1987), a descriptive rather than analytic or interpretive work, sympathetic to the church's action but nevertheless very useful. On this subject see also B. Bradbury, 'Mourir chrétiennement: la vie et la mort dans les établissements catholiques pour personnes agées à Montréal au XIXe siècle,' *RHAF* 46/1 (été 1992): 143–75, a sociologico-historical treatment of the urban Catholic institutional context of ageing and dying, which at once contrasts with and complements in terms of methodology and subject S. Gagnon's work mentioned in the next paragraph. L. Ferretti, *Entre voisins*, a well-documented, analytical study of a Montreal parish demonstrates how the church acted as an agency of acculturation for rural French Canadians who moved to the city.

The most recent historiographical trend seeks to discern rather than measure the influence of religion on social behaviour. J.-P. Wallot, 'Religion and French-Canadian Mores in the Early Nineteenth Century,' *CHR* 52/1 (Mar. 1971): 51–94, broke new ground but reads rather too much of secularized contemporary Quebec into Lower Canadian society. S. Gagnon has produced two remarkable, impressionistic studies: *Mourir, hier et aujourd'hui: de la mort chrétienne dans la campagne québécoise au XIXe siècle à la mort technicisée dans la cité sans Dieu* (Q: PUL 1987) and *Plaisir d'amour et crainte de Dieu*. Contrary to Wallot's study, and more realistically, they underline the gulf in mentalities between early-nineteenth- and late-twentieth-century Quebec. On the other hand, the third volume in his trilogy on religion and mores in Lower Canada, *Mariage et famille au temps de Papineau* (Sainte-Foy, Que.: PUL 1993), acknowledges the inroads made by advancing secularism in the management of the institution of marriage. See also Jacques Paul Couturier, 'La religion de François Roy, de Catherine Valade et des autres: analyse exploratoire des clauses religieuses de testaments montréalais, 1790–1840,' *Cahiers d'histoire* 5/1 (automne 1984): 67–79, which tends to support Wallot while recognizing the limitations of the article's documentary base.

Little has been written of late on the Protestant denominations in Quebec. Thomas R. Millman's *DCB* entries 'Jacob Mountain,' vol. 6, and 'Charles James Stewart,' vol. 7, update his earlier monograph-length studies of two Anglican bishops, to which may be added the *DCB* entries 'John Brooke,' vol. 4, and 'David-François de Montmollin,' vol. 5. Similarly, the *DCB* entries 'Clark Bentom' and 'Alexander Spark,' vol. 5, provide starting-points into the historiography of the Presbyterian and Congregational churches, particularly at Quebec. For Montreal see Jane Greenlaw, 'Choix pratiques et choix des pratiques: le non-conformisme protestant à Montréal (1825–1842),' *RHAF* 46/1 (été 1992): 91–113. Surprisingly, Protestant missionary work has attracted some attention of late. For different aspects of it see F. Noël, *Competing for Souls: Missionary Activity and Settlement in the Eastern Townships, 1784–1851* (Sherbrooke, Que.: Université de Sherbrooke 1988), a 1976 MA thesis that would have benefited from updating before publication, and R.M. Black, 'Different Visions: The Multiplication of Protestant Missions to French-Canadian Roman Catholics, 1834–1855,' in John S. Moir and C. Thomas McIntire, eds., *Canadian Protestant and Catholic Missions, 1820s–1920s: Historical Essays in Honour of John Webster Grant* (NY: Peter Lang 1988).

CULTURE, SCIENCE, AND EDUCATION

Unlike elsewhere in Canada, culture has always been viewed in Quebec as a reflection of the national soul, the 'Anglo-Saxon' world, by contrast, having been perceived as wedded to materialism. This perception remained elitist and ideological, however, until in the 1960s such sociologists as Jean-Charles Falardeau and F. Dumont demonstrated that culture was rooted in social perceptions and reflected the collective imagination and memory. Initially engulfed, like other fields, in the wave of socio-economic history that followed, cultural history resurfaced in the 1980s as part of that wave. Today cultural historians examine the socio-economic more than the aesthetic aspects of the different modes of culture.

Y. Lamonde, *Territoires de la culture québécoise* (Q: PUL 1991), testifies to this trend in articles on methodology and historiography as well as in case studies. On the matter of language see Danièle Noël, *Les questions de langue au Québec, 1759–1850: étude* (Q: Conseil de la langue française 1990), an historical-sociological study.

The culture of the printed word has been the subject of intense study from a social perspective in the last decade. Even though it was recently published, Manon Brunet et al., *Bibliographie des études québécoises sur l'imprimé, 1970–1987* (M: Bibliothèque nationale du Québec 1991), is now somewhat dated. For bibliographies of printed works themselves see the section 'Published Documents' earlier in this chapter. Y. Lamonde, 'La recherche récente en histoire de l'imprimé au Québec,' and C. Galarneau, 'Livre et société à Québec (1760–1859): état des recherches,' both in Lamonde, ed., *L'imprimé au Québec: aspects historiques (18e–20e siècles)* (Q: IQRC 1983), examine historiographical and methodological trends. Other studies in the same volume address various aspects of the book industry as do several very good articles in C. Galarneau and Maurice Lemire, eds., *Livre et lecture au Québec (1800–1850)* (Q: IQRC 1988).

Two excellent studies examine the relationship between books and politics in a time of growing political conflict: Jean-Louis Roy, *Edouard-Raymond Fabre, libraire et patriote canadien (1799–1854)* (M: Hurtubise HMH 1974), and Gilles Gallichan, *Livre et politique au Bas-Canada, 1791–1849* (Sillery, Que.: SPT 1991). Although the latter work studies books mainly in the parliamentary context, the bulk of research in the last decade has concentrated on the different mechanisms of, and control on, the diffusion of books in Lower Canadian society. Y. Lamonde, *Les bibliothèques de collectivités à Montréal, 17e–19e siècles: sources et problèmes* (M: Bibliothèque nationale du Québec 1979), is a useful bio-bibliography of private institutional libraries. Marcel Lajeunesse, *Les Sulpiciens et la vie culturelle à Montréal au XIXe siècle* (M: Fides 1982), looks at the war of libraries between the church and the liberal Institut canadien de Montréal. See also Y. Lamonde, 'La bibliothèque de l'Institut canadien de Montréal (1852–1876): pour une analyse multidimensionnelle,' *RHAF* 41/3 (hiver 1988): 335–61, which proposes a methodology combining quantitative and qualitative analyses. Ginette Bernatchez, 'La Société littéraire et historique de Québec (The Literary and Historical Society of Quebec), 1824–1890,' *RHAF* 35/2 (sept. 1981): 179–92, studies that organization from a sociocultural perspective. See also M. Lajeunesse, 'Meilleur, Chauveau, and Libraries in Mid-Nineteenth Century Quebec,' *Journal of Library History* 18/3 (Summer 1983): 255–73, an interesting article showing the influence of the church in the substitution of parish for public libraries in Lower Canada.

Much attention has also been paid to the diffusion of books according to the law of supply and demand. Respecting supply see Y. Lamonde, *La librairie et l'édition à Montréal, 1776–1920* (M: Bibliothèque nationale du Québec 1991), which examines the conditions necessary for publishing to become economically viable; J.-L. Roy, *Edouard-Raymond Fabre*; Roy, 'La librairie Crémazie,' in Réjean Robidoux and Paul Wyczynski, eds., *Crémazie et Nelligan: recueil d'études* (M: Fides 1981); and C. Galarneau and M. Lemire, eds., *Livre et lecture au Québec*. As for demand, historians look for answers in the contents of personal libraries. The reference work by Y. Lamonde and Daniel Olivier, *Les bibliothèques personnelles au Québec: inventaire analytique et préliminaire des sources* (M: Bibliothèque nationale du Québec 1983), is helpful, although incomplete. Y. Morin, 'Les bibliothèques privées à Québec d'après les inventaires après décès (1800–1819),' in Y. Lamonde, ed., *L'imprimé au Québec,* is a very interesting study.

Literature has been a much-examined aspect of the culture of the printed word, from the perspectives of both literary criticism and sociocultural history. In an interesting historiographical survey, M. Brunet, 'Faire l'histoire de la littérature française du XIXe siècle québécois,' *RHAF* 38/4 (printemps 1985): 523–47, asserts that methodological weaknesses have prevented it from moving to the forefront of historical study in Quebec. Mary Lu MacDonald, 'Nineteenth-Century Canadian Literature as a Primary Source for the Study of Canadian Social and Intellectual History,' *Canadian Issues/Thèmes canadiens* 10/5 (1988): 5–16, proposes quantitative content analysis of literary works as a valid method in the study of social and intellectual history and offers conclusions based on her use of it for Lower Canada between 1817 and 1850. The article is suggestive but does not provide the evidence in support of its conclusions. The *Dictionnaire des oeuvres littéraires du Québec,* vol. 1, *Des origines à 1900* (M: Fides 1978), is the basic reference work. It can now be supplemented by Sylvie Tellier, *Chronologie littéraire du Québec, 1760–1960* (Q: IQRC 1982), and M. Lemire et al., *La vie littéraire au Québec,* vol. 1, *1764–1805*; vol. 2, *1806–1839* (Sainte-Foy, Que.: PUL 1991-2), the new standard synthesis for the period it covers, which includes a very full bibliography. M. Lemire, *Formation de l'imaginaire littéraire au Québec, 1764–1867* (M: L'Hexagone, 1993), is an interpretive work based on a study of the dialectic in Lower Canadian writing between the great myths of traditional literature and the popular culture of the colony. René Dionne, ed., *Le Québécois et sa littérature* (Sherbrooke, Que.: Naaman 1984), contains a broad overview. Lucie Robert, *L'institution du littéraire au Québec* (Q: PUL 1989), is an interpretive examination of the perception of the literary. Pierre Rajotte, 'Les pratiques associatives et la constitution du champ de production littéraire au Québec (1760–1867),' *RHAF* 45/4 (printemps 1992): 545–72, shows how political, religious, and other factors contributed to defining the literary mode and structuring its development.

There are excellent monographs on literary genres, most notably the novel: Jeanne Lafrance, *Les personnages dans le roman canadien-français, 1837–1862* (Sherbrooke, Que.: Naaman 1977); Guildo Rousseau, *L'image des Etats-Unis dans la littérature québécoise, 1775–1930* (Sherbrooke, Que.:

Naaman 1981); Michel Lord, *En quête du roman gothique québécois, 1837–1860: tradition littéraire et imaginaire romanesque* (Q: Université Laval 1985); and Réjean Beaudoin, *Naissance d'une littérature: essai sur le messianisme et les débuts de la littérature canadienne française, 1850–1890* (M: Boréal 1989). The collective work edited by M. Lemire, *Le romantisme au Canada* (Q.: Nuit Blanche Editeur 1993), affirms that the romantic movement was known in Lower Canada while it was popular in France but was largely rejected as irrelevant to the Canadian context. All of these works explore facets of the relationship between society and literary culture. In *'Jean Rivard' ou l'art de réussir: idéologie et utopie dans l'oeuvre d'Antoine Gérin-Lajoie* (Q: PUL 1991), Robert Major offers yet another example of the social interpretation of literature, one that also typifies the revisionist reinterpretation of Quebec history in terms of the 'normal' development of North American society. Rejecting the long-standing perception of Gérin-Lajoie's classic *Jean Rivard, le défricheur canadien* (1862) as the literary expression of traditionalist agriculturalist ideology, he makes a strong case for interpreting it as a French-Canadian expression of the American ideal of the self-made man. Two other early novelists have received particular attention: Frances Brooke (Moore), an eighteenth-century writer, who is the subject of Lorraine McMullen, *An Odd Attempt in a Woman: The Literary Life of Frances Brooke* (V: UBCP 1983); and P.-J. Aubert de Gaspé, mentioned earlier.

Poetry has been a particularly well studied literary genre. Both *Les textes poétiques du Canada français, 1606–1867*, 5 vols. (M: Fides 1987–92), which seeks to be exhaustive, and Laurent Mailhot and Pierre Nepveu, comps., *La poésie québécoise: des origines à nos jours* (2nd ed., M: L'Hexagone 1986), which is selective on literary grounds, are valuable sourcebooks. J. d'A. Lortie, *La poésie nationaliste au Canada français (1606–1867)* (Q: PUL 1975), is still the best synthesis on the subject. Octave Crémazie was the greatest poet of this period; his works have been re-edited by Odette Condemine in *Octave Crémazie: oeuvres*, 2 vols. (M: Editions du Fleuve 1989), which has a very full introduction. See also R. Robidoux and P. Wyczynski, eds., *Crémazie et Nelligan*.

The theatre, too, has been much studied from a sociocultural perspective. Baudouin Burger, *L'activité théâtrale au Québec, 1765–1825* (M: Parti pris 1974), is still an interesting interpretive study but should be supplemented by more recent works, such as Jean Laflamme and Rémi Tourangeau, *L'Eglise et le théâtre au Québec* (M: Fides 1979), and Leonard E. Doucette, *Theatre in French Canada: Laying the Foundations, 1606–1867* (T: UTP 1984).

The press, and to a lesser extent journalism, is one of the most-studied aspects of written culture. Most of the collective works mentioned in this section have articles dealing with it. The basic reference work is A. Beaulieu and J. Hamelin, eds., *La presse québécoise*, vols. 1–2. J.-P. de Lagrave, *Fleury Mesplet, 1734–1794: diffuseur des Lumières au Québec* (M: Patenaude 1985), and Lagrave and Jacques-G. Ruelland, *Premier journaliste de langue française au Canada: Valentin Joutard, 1736–1787* (Sainte-Foy, Que.: Le Griffon d'Argile 1988), are useful studies of two early democratic printer-journalists. See also César Rouban, 'Propagande antiphilosophique dans les gazettes de Montréal et de Québec après la fin du Régime français,' *Revue de l'Université d'Ottawa* 54 (1984): 79–98, and the studies mentioned previously by P. Reid (*Le Canadien*), A. Lefebvre (*Montreal Gazette*), and D. Monière (Ludger Duvernay). Peter G. Goheen, 'The Impact of the Telegraph on the Newspaper in Mid-Nineteenth Century British North America,' *Urban Geography* 11/2 (Mar.–Apr. 1990): 107–29, looks at patterns of communication generated by the introduction of the telegraph and the relationship between technology and geography. The *DCB* contains many entries of interest for the history of the written word; see, for example, 'William Brown,' vol. 4; 'Joseph Quesnel,' vol. 5; 'Robert-Anne d'Estimauville,' vol. 6; 'John Neilson,' vol. 7; 'Georges-Barthélemi Faribeault,' vol. 9; and 'Napoléon Aubin,' vol. 11.

For painting J. Russell Harper, *Painting in Canada: A History* (1966; 2nd ed., T: UTP 1977), is a serviceable mainstream survey but of limited historiographical value. Barry Lord, *The History of Painting in Canada: Toward a People's Art* (T: NC Press 1974), offers a left-wing nationalist interpretation. Mario Béland, ed., *Painting in Québec, 1820–1850* (Q: Musée du Québec 1992), is a rich book, visually as well as historiographically, with a very full bibliography. Dennis Reid, *'Our Own Country Canada,' Being an Account of the National Aspirations of the Principal Landscape Artists in Montreal and Toronto, 1860–1890* (O: National Gallery of Canada 1979), relates artistic production to nation-building. A recent work on an important artist of the period, William Berczy, is Rosemary L. Tovell, ed., *Berczy* (O: National Gallery of Canada 1991). Mary Allodi, *Printmaking in Canada: The Earliest Views and Portraits* and *An Engraver's Pilgrimage: James Smillie in Quebec, 1821–1830* (T: Royal Ontario Museum 1980, 1989), are excellent, well-illustrated studies.

Louise Saint-Pierre, *Bibliographie québécoise de l'artisanat et des métiers d'art, 1689–1985* (Q: Centre de formation et de consultation en métiers d'art 1986), is a good point from which to launch into the abundant and uneven historiography on that field. J.R. Porter and Jean Bélisle, in *La sculpture ancienne au Québec: trois siècles d'art religieux et profane* (M: Editions de l'Homme 1986), provide the best introduction to that subject. For an excellent, well-illustrated study of religious art in general see Jean Trudel, dir., *Le grand héritage*, vol. 1, *L'Eglise catholique et les arts au Québec* (Q: Musée du Québec 1984). On the gold and silversmith trades see the *DCB* entries 'Ignace-François Delezenne,' vol. 4, and 'François Ranvoyzé,' vol. 5.

The literature on architecture is growing in volume and sophistication. For church architecture see Luc Noppen, *Les églises du Québec (1600–1850)* (Q/M: Editeur officiel du Québec/Fides 1977), and Robert Caron, *Un couvent du XIXe siècle: la maison des Soeurs de la charité de Québec* (M: Libre Expression 1980), the latter an interesting case study. Jean-Claude Marsan, *Montreal in Evolution: Historical Analysis of the Development of Montreal's Architecture and Urban Environment* (K&M: MQUP 1981), is the best general treatment of architecture there. Guy Pinard, *Montréal: son histoire, son architecture*, 4 vols. (M: La Presse/Méridien 1987–91), offers well-researched, popularly written 'biographies' of numerous buildings from the pre-Confederation period, while the popular study by Michèle Benoît and Roger Gratton, *Pignon sur rue: les quartiers de Montréal* (M: Guérin 1991), brings out the architectural distinctiveness of the various parts of the city by relating the architecture of each sector to its economic and social development. Raymond Montpetit, 'La construction de l'Eglise Notre-Dame de Montréal: quelques pistes pour une interprétation socio-historique,' in J.-R. Brault, ed., *Montréal au XIXe siècle*, offers a socio-economic approach to the study of architectural style. The best synthesis of architecture in Quebec City is L. Noppen et al., *Québec: trois siècles d'architecture* (3rd ed., M: Libre Expression 1989). It can be supplemented by A.J.H. Richardson et al., *Quebec City: Architects, Artisans, and Builders* (O: National Museum of Man and Parks Canada 1984), an excellent reference work; Christina Cameron and Monique Trépanier, *Vieux Québec: son architecture intérieure* (O: National Museum of Man 1986); Hélène Bourque, *La maison du faubourg: l'architecture domestique des faubourgs Saint-Jean et Saint-Roch avant 1845* (Q: PUL 1991), which studies a hitherto-unknown aspect of architecture; and C. Cameron, *Charles Baillairgé: Architect and Engineer* (K&M: MQUP 1989), which revises the previously standard treatment of Baillairgé, the principal architect of the period, as established by Gérard Morisset. The *DCB* has a number of excellent biographies of architects: 'Jean Baillairgé,' vol. 5; 'François Baillairgé,' vol. 6; 'Victor Bourgeau' and 'George Browne,' vol. 11; and 'John Ostell,' vol. 12.

The history of music, the poor relation in cultural historiography, is an open field. The standard reference work is Helmut Kallmann et al., eds.,

Encyclopedia of Music in Canada (1981; 2nd ed., T: UTP 1992). The most acceptable syntheses currently are Kallmann, *A History of Music in Canada, 1534–1914* (T: UTP 1960), and Willy Antmann, *La musique au Québec, 1600–1875* (M: Editions de l'Homme 1976). Preliminary research for a new synthesis has so far produced Juliette Bourassa-Trépanier and Lucien Poirier, eds., *Répertoire des données musicales de la presse québécoise, Tome 1, Canada*, vol. 1, *1764–1799* (Q: PUL 1990), a research tool with introductory articles on the various social forums for musical performances. The work by Maurice Carrier and Monique Vachon, comps., *Chansons politiques du Québec*, 2 vols. (M: Leméac 1977–9), reveals popular political views through songs. See also the *DCB* entry 'Théodore-Frédéric Molt,' vol. 8.

Various aspects of popular culture are presented in recent publications. Aurélien Boivin, ed., *Le conte fantastique québécois au XIXe siècle* (M: Fides 1987), introduces the 'unofficial literature' of a largely 'illiterate' population, the oral folk-tale. Simonne Voyer, *La danse traditionnelle dans l'est du Canada: quadrilles et cotillons* (Q: PUL 1986); Donald Guay, *Introduction à l'histoire des sports au Québec* (M: VLB Editeur 1987); and M. Lafrance and Y. Desloges, 'Au carrefour de trois cultures: la restauration au Québec au XIXe siècle,' in Alain Huetz de Lemps and Jean-Robert Pitte, eds., *Les restaurants dans le monde et à travers les âges* (Grenoble, Fr.: Editions Glenat 1990), explore undeveloped fields of sociocultural research.

The history of science and technology is a developing sector of Quebec historiography. An essential research tool is R. Alan Richardson and Bertram H. Macdonald, eds., *Science and Technology in Canadian History: A Bibliography of Primary Sources to 1914* (Thornhill, Ont.: HSTC Publications 1987). Raymond Duchesne, 'Historiographie des sciences et des techniques au Canada,' *RHAF* 35/2 (sept. 1981): 193–215, is a helpful survey of the literature, which again testifies to the ubiquity of economic and social preoccupations in recent years. Progress has been steady in the decade since Duchesne's article. He himself, with Luc Chartrand and Y. Gingras, has published the most satisfactory synthesis in the field, *Histoire des sciences au Québec* (M: BE 1987).

Several articles by R.A. Jarrell argue that nationalist preoccupations and ideological struggles delayed development of a scientific culture in Quebec: 'The Rise and Decline of Science at Quebec, 1821–1844,' *HS/SH* 10/19 (May 1977): 77–91; 'Differential National Development and Science in the Nineteenth Century: The Problems of Quebec and Ireland,' in Nathan Riengold and Marc Rothenberg, eds., *Scientific Colonialism: A Cross-Cultural Comparison* (Washington, DC: Smithsonian Institution 1987); and 'L'ultramontantism et la science au Canada français,' in M. Fournier et al., eds., *Sci-*

ences et médecine au Québec. In 'The Social Functions of the Scientific Society in Nineteenth Century Canada,' in Jarrell and A.E. Roos, eds., *Critical Issues in the History of Canadian Science, Technology and Medicine,* Jarrell asserts that supposedly scientific societies in the nineteenth century had a greater social than scientific function, reflecting that society's attachment to culture and entertainment. R. Duchesne and Paul Carle, 'L'ordre des choses: cabinets et musées d'histoire naturelle au Québec (1824–1900),' *RHAF* 44/1 (été 1990): 3–30, and Hervé Gagnon, 'Du cabinet de curiosités au musée scientifique: le musée italien et la genèse des musées à Montréal dans la première moitié du XIXe siècle,' *RHAF* 45/3 (hiver 1992): 415–30, see middle-class social and cultural interests as the motor for the development of science. On the other hand, Suzanne Zeller, *Inventing Canada: Early Victorian Science and the Idea of a Transcontinental Nation* (T: UTP 1987), demonstrates the influence of progress in science on the development of the popular imagination.

Several works examine specific sciences. R.A. Jarrell, *The Cold Light of Dawn: A History of Canadian Astronomy* (T: UTP 1988), provides a brief overview of that subject for the period 1760–1867 in Quebec. *The St. Lawrence Survey Journals of Captain Henry Wolsey Bayfield, 1829–1853,* ed. Ruth McKenzie, 2 vols. (T: CS 1984–6), is a useful source illustrative of nineteenth-century techniques of hydrography and cartography. Pierre Trépanier, 'Les influences leplaysiennes au Canada français, 1855–1888,' *JCS* 22/1 (Spring 1987): 66–83, is a rare look at the early history of the social sciences in Quebec.

The *DCB* has a few useful articles on scientists, cartographers, and surveyors, particularly, 'Nicolas-Gaspard Boisseau,' 'Samuel Johannes Holland,' and 'André Michaux,' vol. 5; 'Thomas Delvecchio,' vol. 6; 'Joseph Bouchette,' vol. 7; and 'Joseph-Alexandre Crevier,' vol. 11. R. Gagnon, 'Les discours sur l'enseignement pratique au Canada français, 1850–1900,' in M. Fournier et al., eds., *Sciences et médecine au Québec,* links attitudes toward science with the education system.

The historiography of education in Lower Canada goes back to the nineteenth century. Because of the historic denominational nature of education in Quebec, reference must also be had to the section 'Religious History' earlier in the chapter. Many notable works have been produced in the past, but the field is currently begging for development at a time when the importance of education for economic development is increasingly recognized. As a result of this situation, Louis-Philippe Audet's traditionalist studies *Le système scolaire de la province de Québec,* 6 vols. (Q: PUL 1950–6) and *Histoire de l'enseignement au Québec, 1608–1971* (T: HRW 1971) remain useful general works on primary education. A more recent and interpretive overview is provided by Roger Magnuson, *A Brief History of Quebec Education, from New France to Parti Québécois* (M: Harvest House 1980). Jean-Pierre Charland, 'Le réseau d'enseignement public bas-canadien, 1841–1867: une institution de l'Etat libéral,' *RHAF* 40/4 (printemps 1987): 505–35, discusses the use of primary education to spread liberal philosophical views before it became dominated by the clergy. Andrée Dufour, 'Diversité institutionnelle et fréquentation scolaire dans l'île de Montréal en 1825 et en 1835,' *RHAF* 41/4 (printemps 1988): 507–35, reinterprets in terms of availability of schools and economic considerations what has until now been considered indifference toward education on the part of Lower Canadians. C. Galarneau, 'Les écoles privées à Québec (1760–1859),' *Cahiers des Dix* 45 (1990): 95–113, ties the development of urban education to the economic and social expansion of Lower Canada. Several *DCB* biographies of teachers and administrators are illuminating: 'Finlay Fisher' and 'James Tanswell,' vol. 5; 'Louis Labadie' and 'Joseph Langley Mills,' vol. 6; 'Thaddeus Osgood' and 'Daniel Wilkie,' vol. 8; and 'Jean-Baptiste Meilleur,' vol. 10.

A related subject of considerable study in recent years is literacy. A. Greer, 'L'alphabétisation et son histoire au Québec: état de la question,' in Y. Lamonde, ed., *L'imprimé au Québec*, surveys the historiography; to it must be added Michel Verrette, 'L'alphabétisation de la population de la ville de Québec de 1750 à 1849,' *RHAF* 39/1 (été 1985): 51–76, and Claude Lessard, 'L'alphabétisation dans le comté de Nicolet depuis le XVIIe siècle' and 'L'alphabétisation à Trois-Rivières de 1634 à 1939,' *Les cahiers nicolétains* 10/1 (mars 1988): 3–65; 12/3 (sept. 1990): 83–117.

The classical colleges have received much attention in the past two decades. The best survey work is still C. Galarneau, *Les collèges classiques au Canada français* (M: Fides 1978). For early monographs on specific institutions see its bibliography. Two more recent studies are also of interest. C. Lessard, *Le Séminaire de Nicolet, 1803–1869* (TR: Editions du Bien Public 1980), a descriptive study, short on analysis and perspective; and N. Baillargeon, *Le Séminaire de Québec*. For the study of specific disciplines taught in the colleges and seminaries again see the bibliography in Galarneau. To those works must be added Y. Lamonde, *La philosophie et son enseignement au Québec (1665–1920)* (M: Hurtubise HMH 1980), and Marc Chabot et al., *Figures de la philosophie québécoise après les troubles de 1837*, 3 vols. (M: Université du Québec à Montréal 1985–8). The *DCB* biographies 'Charles-François Painchaud,' vol. 7; and 'Jérôme Demers' and 'John Holmes,' vol. 8, are useful contributions to the literature. Finally, Stanley Brice Frost, *McGill University: For the Advancement of Learning*, vol. 1, *1801–1895* (M:

MQUP 1980), is a substantial contribution to the thin historiography on higher education. The *DCB* entry 'Sir John William Dawson,' vol. 10, is also of interest. For Université Laval see J.H. Lambert, '"Le haut enseignement de la religion": Mgr Bourget and the Founding of Laval University,' *Revue de l'Université d'Ottawa* 45 (1975): 278–94.

CONCLUSION

As stated in the introduction, each generation infuses the history it writes with its own preoccupations. Nineteenth-century historians, English- and French-speaking, were concerned in their own time with questions of empire, union, nation-building, survival, and religion, and their historiography tended to centre on matters constitutional, political, and religious. These great preoccupations, once established, did not die, and they remained the inspiration of traditional historiography. In the twentieth century, a more materialistic age, and particularly from the economic and social crisis of the 1930s, economic and social history became the new norm of English-Canadian historiography while national survival and traditional values continued to inspire French-Canadian writing. In time the two historiographies, which had always reflected distinct national agendas, became increasingly influenced by methodological considerations as the writing of history became professionalized. The publication in 1966 of F. Ouellet's *Histoire économique et sociale du Québec* initiated a methodological revolution in Quebec historiography that is still being worked through. Within Quebec, the parallel historiographies are now largely gone; a common agenda, based on economic and social history, seems to govern all fields of historical research and to be followed by historians of both ethnic groups.

Ouellet had expressed the hope that his book would be considered, not as a definitive synthesis, but as a point of departure for analytic studies of the structures and conjunctures that he had discerned. The results have probably exceeded his expectations. His *Histoire* has aged quickly, as he had hoped, and a new generation of historians, largely following an agenda set out by Ouellet's strongest protagonists, G. Paquet and J.-P. Wallot, probes the economic and social life of Lower Canada in the early nineteenth century. The image of French Canada as a clerically dominated, spiritually focused, feudally oppressed, immobile, closed, rural peasant society seeking to survive beside a materialistically focused, capitalist-inspired, dynamic, open, urban, commercial British society is widely rejected. It has largely yielded to that of a French-Canadian society open to the influences of the world around it, sensitive to a considerable degree to changing economic and social circumstances, increasingly assertive politically, and hampered in its economic, social, and political development by a conservative, feudal-commercial British society. Despite the intense research, however, no new substantial synthesis of the scope of Ouellet's work has yet emerged. G. Bernier and D. Salée's *The Shaping of Québec Politics and Society* is the most recent original explanatory and interpretive study of Lower Canadian history, criticizing previous schools (while largely ignoring Wallot) for having exaggerated either the importance of the 'national question' or the completeness of the penetration of a market economy mentality.

On the other hand, the sharply focused study of the economic and social history of early-nineteenth-century Quebec has so preoccupied historians that it has effectively drained attention from the late eighteenth and mid-nineteenth centuries and from other historical fields such as political, religious, and, to a lesser extent, cultural history. Even fields that are emerging elsewhere in Canada and the world, such as Native and women's history, are suffering with respect to Lower Canada. At the same time, however, it must be conceded that these other fields have been to a considerable degree rejuvenated or inspired by methods employed and results obtained in economic and social history. Indeed, it is in these relatively neglected fields that new syntheses have been emerging. On the one hand, one wishes that the attention at present so sharply concentrated on one (admittedly crucial) aspect of Lower Canadian history could be broadened; on the other, it may well be that the present situation masks a movement toward a new general synthesis of Lower Canadian history, comprehensive and cohesive, that starts from an economic and social centre.

BRYAN D. PALMER

Upper Canada

For many on the so-called edges of our country the term 'Upper Canada' is synonymous with Ontario, a designation that conjures up images of privilege and power. It is the site of central Canada, another term weighted down with meaning: more than a geographical expression of location, the centre is also the place of decision-making and ultimate economic and political clout. In the 1990s, however, Ontario is less and less the concentrated locus of advantage and authority. As the traditional economic foundations of central Canadian affluence and might crumble in plant closings, job losses, and recession, its electoral political representatives seemingly out of step with those of the federal government, it is worth reconsidering the image of Upper Canada as a kind of bedrock of centralized and stable power, a point long ago raised in Arthur R.M. Lower, 'Ontario – Does It Exist?' *OH* 60/2 (June 1968): 65–9. For in its original period of consolidation, as well as in its subsequent history, defining the region of Upper Canada was always something of a transitory and fragmented process.

As noted in J.K. Johnson's important bibliographic essay, 'Upper Canada,' in D.A. Muise, ed., *A Reader's Guide to Canadian History*, vol. 1, *Beginnings to Confederation* (T: UTP 1982), upon which this commentary builds, technically Upper Canada existed only as a provincial entity for the half-century from 1791 to 1841. Before this the region was integrated into the Province of Quebec created from the colony of New France, and, in the aftermath of the *Report* of Lord Durham, from 1841 until Confederation in 1867, Upper Canada was merged with Lower Canada in the forced unification of the Province of Canada. Along with the identification Canada West, Upper Canada continued to be used as a loose description of the western reaches of 'the Canadas' in the years 1841–67. The modern province of Ontario, of course, had its beginnings with Confederation, a political project in which Upper Canada and its leading political personalities figured prominently, an interpretive point made with bluntness in Stanley B. Ryerson's early Marxist statement, *Unequal Union: Confederation and the Roots of Conflict in the Canadas, 1815–1873* (T: Progress 1968), part of which deals with Upper Canada. Historians are thus generally in agreement that Upper Canada refers to old Ontario in the years from the British Conquest of 1760 to the union of British North America in 1867.

HISTORIOGRAPHY

The historiography of Upper Canada is, in many ways, a reflection of more general historiographic developments. Writing on Upper Canada is ordered within an interpretive field of force marking out specific oppositions. At its historiographic core a dominant tradition orchestrates the Upper Canadian experience along narrowly political paths, detailing the almost biographical contours of public life. The resulting writings, which exhibit an insular resistance not only to theory but also to a range of insights that might be garnered from the scholarship of other national contexts, tend to follow the paths of previous Upper Canadian scholarship, filling in holes in the interpretive roadway and widening its lanes with expanding empirical data. Around the margins of this historiographic centre-cut oscillates a struggling variety of interpretive challenges, moved by new understandings of what constitutes evidence and different approaches to how history is conceived and written. Signalled by J.M.S. Careless's highly influential '"Limited Identities" in Canada,' *CHR* 50/1 (Mar. 1969): 1–10, and Ramsay Cook's less well known statement 'Canadian Centennial Cerebrations,' *International Journal* 22/4 (Autumn 1967): 659–63, this historiographic turn outward from the political centre of a traditionalist focus is recasting the nature of historical writing on Upper Canada. Marxist and feminist histories of educational experience and state formation, for instance, pose significant, if only yet suggestive, questions about the hegemony of a mainstream historiography dominated by the narrowly empirical and institutional reading of politics. They counterpose to this established depiction a social history, but one that is decidedly hampered by the lack of a fully developed economic history of Upper Canada.

What marks out the writing on Upper Canada, then, is the lack of an integrated synthesis, in which old concerns and new understandings come together in an appreciation of the totality of overlapping histories that were lived, by Upper Canadians, not as separations, but as a whole encompassing the political, the economic, and the social. In the absence of a historiography with this kind of interpretive and empirical range, writings on Upper Canada take on the trappings of a kind of siege mentality: at the core the traditionalist wagons of a dominant political history draw closer together in a defensive encampment as the marginalized threat of new historiographical break-throughs circles the entrenched authorities, firing the odd analytic arrow which is replied to with periodic volleys of retort. Within this field of force there is thus fairly constant motion, but few signs of the kind of movement that would actually recast the historiographic meaning of Upper Canada.

Those looking for an introduction to the nineteenth-century histori-ography of Upper Canada can now consult M. Brook Taylor, *Promoters, Patriots, and Partisans: Historiography in Nineteenth-Century English Canada* (T: UTP 1989). Current writing on Upper Canada can be located within the general methodological and interpretive shifts detailed in the two major texts on the historiography of English-speaking North America. Both Carl Berger, *The Writing of Canadian History: Aspects of English-Canadian Histori-cal Writing since 1900* (1976; 2nd ed., T: UTP 1986), and Peter Novick, *That Noble Dream: The 'Objectivity Question' and the American Historical Pro-fession* (NY: Cambridge University Press 1988), end their accounts contrast-ing the seeming stabilities and continuities of traditional historical writing with the destabilizing ruptures emanating from a host of 'new' histories.

GENERAL WORKS

Nowhere is the dominance of the traditional political history more evident than in the accessible surveys that either include Upper Canada in a broad synthetic sweep of Ontario's development or present the history of Upper Canada in an explicitly political context. Two recent overviews of Ontario contain approaches to Upper Canada. Randall White, *Ontario, 1610–1985: A Political and Economic History* (T: Dundurn 1985), is more comprehensive than Robert Bothwell, *A Short History of Ontario* (E: Hurtig 1986), in which treatment of Upper Canada is somewhat truncated. These texts displace older surveys. The long-established standard account, Gerald M. Craig, *Upper Canada: The Formative Years, 1784–1841* (T: M&S 1963), remains indispensable. For the political aftermath of Craig's account see J.M.S. Careless, *The Union of the Canadas: The Growth of Canadian Institutions, 1841–1857* (T: M&S 1967), a book necessarily branching out beyond Upper Canada. S.J.R. Noel focuses on this explicit concern with politics in his *Patrons, Clients, Brokers: Ontario Society and Politics, 1791–1896* (T: UTP 1990), almost two-thirds of which deals with the Upper Canadian experi-ence. Charting one's way through the maze of Upper Canadian officialdom, from the British Colonial Office down to the clerks of the Customs and Emigrant offices, is made far more manageable with the revised edition of Frederick H. Armstrong, *Handbook of Upper Canadian Chronology* (1967; rev. ed., T: Dundurn 1985).

Those wanting entry into the challenges of new writings will have to find their way through recent collections of essays on Upper Canada. Older edited collections, such as Edith G. Firth, ed., *Profiles of a Province: Studies in the History of Ontario* (T: Ontario Historical Society 1967), and F.H. Armstrong et al., eds., *Aspects of Nineteenth-Century Ontario: Essays Presented to James J. Talman* (T: UTP 1974), never zeroed in directly on Upper Canada. The same could be said for such recent collections as Roger Hall et al., eds., *Patterns of the Past: Interpreting Ontario's History* (T: Dundurn 1988); David Keane and Colin Read, eds., *Old Ontario: Essays in Honour of J.M.S. Careless* (T: Dundurn 1990); and Allan Greer and Ian Radforth, eds., *Colonial Leviathan: State Formation in Mid-Nineteenth-Century Canada* (T: UTP 1992), although all contain essays that open out into new interpretive possibilities with respect to Upper Canada. The only concentrated collections of essays directly on Upper Canada are J.K. Johnson, ed., *Historical Essays on Upper Canada* [hereafter *Historical Essays*, 1st ed.] (T: M&S 1975), and its replacement, Johnson and Bruce G. Wilson, eds., *Historical Essays on Upper Canada: New Perspectives* [hereafter *Historical Essays*, 2nd ed.] (O: CUP 1989). The second of these reflects the small but important recent inroads of feminist, Marxist, and working-class historians as well as the continuities in the dominant historiographic tradition.

Finally, mention should be made of two basic reference works. The *Historical Atlas of Canada*, vol. 1, *From the Beginning to 1800*, ed. R. Cole Harris; vol. 2, *The Land Transformed, 1800–1891*, ed. R. Louis Gentilcore (T: UTP [1987], 1993), presents a wealth of information in cartographic form, often displaying visually the amassed material drawn from much research in statistical sources. Volume 1 contains only sporadic reference to Upper Canada, but the concluding plates 68 and 69 should be consulted by those interested in settlement patterns, economy, and Native peoples at 1800. Volume 2, which at the time of writing has not yet appeared, will be of more comprehensive interest, with specific plates on exploration (2), Loyalism (7), demography (10), Upper Canadian agriculture (14), transportation (25 and 26), the Rebellion of 1837 (23), education (54 and 55), manufacturing (47), and social conflict and early labour organization (57). The ongoing multivolume *Dictionary of Canadian Biography* (T: UTP 1966–), overseen in its English-language version by Francess G. Halpenny and, subsequently, R. Cook, although scaffolded on biography, often presents detail and interpretation on Upper Canadian economic, social, political, and cultural life.

BIBLIOGRAPHIES AND PUBLISHED DOCUMENTS

There has not been appreciable bibliographic advance since J.K. Johnson, 'Upper Canada,' in D.A. Muise, ed., *A Reader's Guide to Canadian History*, vol. 1. William F.E. Morley, comp., *Ontario and the Canadian North* (T: UTP 1978), and Barbara B. Aitken, comp., *Local Histories of Ontario Municipalities, 1951–1977: A Bibliography* (T: Ontario Library Association 1978), are both extremely useful but rather tedious. Olga Bishop's bibliographic compilations *Publications of the Government of the Province of Canada, 1841–1867* (O: National Library 1963) and the two-volume *Bibliography of Ontario History, 1867–1976: Cultural, Economic, Political, Social*, Ontario Historical Studies Series (T: UTP 1980), are probably the place for most students and scholars to start. A broadly conceived approach to urban history means that Alan F.J. Artibise and Gilbert A. Stelter, comps., *Canada's Urban Past: A Bibliography to 1980 and Guide to Canadian Urban Studies* (V: UBCP 1981), contains much of relevance under the chapter heading 'Ontario.' Business history written prior to 1970 is detailed in the general bibliographic statement, F.H. Armstrong, 'Canadian Business History: Approaches and Publications to 1970,' in David S. Macmillan, ed., *Canadian Business History: Selected Studies, 1497–1971* (T: M&S 1972), although the reader will have to separate out the studies relevant to Upper Canada. Similarly, discerning researchers can also benefit from consulting Neil Sutherland et al., eds., *History of Canadian Childhood and Youth: A Bibliography* (Westport, CT: Greenwood Press 1992). *Historical Essays*, 2nd ed., concludes with a useful select bibliography.

Documents pertaining to the legislative, land, and legal histories of Upper Canada were regularly published by the Department of Public Records and Archives (originally the Bureau of Archives of Ontario) in the first third of the twentieth century. Titled *Annual Reports* of these respective Ontario institutions, these publications are not to be confused with an equally valuable source, the *Annual Report* of the National Archives of Canada, which also regularly reprinted documents of relevance to Upper Canadian topics. This latter source is indexed in *Guide to the Reports of the Public Archives of Canada, 1872–1972* (O: Information Canada 1975).

The most ambitious and helpful project reproducing documents pertaining to the history of Upper Canada is the Ontario Series of the Champlain Society, which, while continuing the society's long-standing role in this area, owed much to the support of Premier Leslie Frost in the 1950s. Originally published by the University of Toronto Press, but now appearing in the Carleton Library Series with Carleton University Press, these collections of original sources are now prefaced by lengthy scholarly introductions, themselves invaluable interpretive statements that are often 'books' in their own right. Individual titles are referred to later in the chapter.

PERIODICALS

The starting-point for anyone interested in the history of Upper Canada is the now-quarterly journal of the Ontario Historical Society, *Ontario History*, previously *Papers and Records* (1899–1946). This publication can be indexed through Hilary Bates and Robert Sherman, comps., *Index to the Publications of the Ontario Historical Society, 1899–1972* (T: OHS 1974), superseded, since 1980, by the OHS, *Annual Bibliography of Ontario History*. *OH* has also recently initiated a book review section.

Other scholarly journals regularly publish articles and reviews directly on the Upper Canadian experience or related to it, among them *Labour/Le Travail* (1976–), *Journal of Canadian Studies* (1966–), *Histoire sociale/Social History* (1968–), *Studies in Political Economy* (1978–), and the *Canadian Historical Review* (1920–). Both *L/LT* and the *CHR* produce regular bibliographies that can be scrutinized for Upper Canadian material. Relevant articles may also be found in the Canadian Historical Association, *Annual Report* (1922–65), retitled *Historical Papers* (1966–89), and now *Journal of the Canadian Historical Association* (1990–). Special mention should be made of the ongoing multivolume *Canadian Papers in Rural History*, edited by Donald Harman Akenson (Gananoque, Ont.: Langdale Press 1978–), which has published a series of articles relating to the history of Upper Canadian agriculture. On occasion international scholarly journals, such as *Social History* in England or *Journal of Social History* in the United States, publish an article relating to Upper Canada, but this is rare.

Local historical society publications abound, the best of which is probably *Historic Kingston*. First published in 1952, *Historic Kingston* has been a forum for the interaction of professional and amateur historians. Access to it is facilitated by *Historic Kingston, Volumes 1–20, 1952–1972: Cumulative Index* (K: Kingston Historical Society 1973). The York (Toronto), Guelph, Grimsby, Niagara, London and Middlesex, Lennox and Addington, Simcoe, and Waterloo historical societies, among others, have also, at various times, published particular proceedings, transactions, and notes of interest to those studying Upper Canada.

THE UPPER CANADIAN ECONOMY

There is nothing approaching an adequate economic history of Upper Canada. Such general analyses as there are tend to be older and wedded to the now-outdated staples thesis and the complementary Laurentian thesis. The staples approach, perhaps the most influential and well-known contribution of Canadian economic history, was originally associated with the writings of Harold Adams Innis, such as *The Fur Trade in Canada: An Introduction to Canadian Economic History* (1930; rev. ed., T: UTP 1970). It asserts that Canadian economic life has been driven by the export of a succession of particular staples (fish, fur, timber, grain, minerals, and so forth) to the more advanced economies of France, Great Britain, and the United States. Suggesting that each staple structures rates of settlement and other socio-economic and political matters differentially, the Innisian formulation of the staples thesis also claims that Canada has historically become locked into resource export dependency, thereby stunting the country's industrialization. Donald Grant Creighton's study of Montreal merchants, *The Commercial Empire of the St. Lawrence, 1760-1850* (T: RP 1937), reprinted as *The Empire of the St. Lawrence* (T: MAC 1956), built on the staples approach to create the Laurentian thesis, which argues that mercantile exploitation of the transatlantic and transcontinental possibilities of the St Lawrence River system determined the character and content of Canadian economic life along an east-west axis dominated by central Canada. Students will find fuller descriptions of the staples and Laurentian theses in C. Berger, *The Writing of Canadian History*. A theoretical critique of the staples school appears in David McNally, 'Staple Theory as Commodity Fetishism: Marx, Innis, and Canadian Political Economy,' *Studies in Political Economy* 6 (Autumn 1981): 35-63, while R.T. Naylor provides an irreverent revision of the Laurentian thesis in 'The Rise and Fall of the Third Commercial Empire of the St Lawrence,' in Gary Teeple, ed., *Capitalism and the National Question in Canada* (T: UTP 1972). As will be indicated later, much recent writing in the area of economic history interrogates the staples thesis directly by presenting evidence of a much more diversified and differentiated economy.

The extent to which the staples approach and Laurentian thesis dominate general texts can be gleaned from a cursory examination of W.T. Easterbrook and Hugh G.J. Aitken, *Canadian Economic History* (T: MAC 1956); William L. Marr and Donald G. Paterson, *Canada: An Economic History* (T: MAC 1980); and the major staples-driven edited collection of essays, Easterbrook and M.H. Watkins, eds., *Approaches to Canadian Economic History*

(T: M&S 1967). The same approach informs even the more recent *A History of the Canadian Economy* (T: HBJ 1991) by Kenneth Norrie and Douglas Owram.

Readers can still profit from the dated and much-debated alternative depiction of pre-Confederation economic history in H. Clare Pentland, *Labour and Capital in Canada, 1650–1860*, ed. and intro. Paul Phillips (T: James Lorimer 1981), as well as two important articles by Pentland, 'The Role of Capital in Canadian Economic Development before 1875,' *CJEPS* 16/4 (Nov. 1950): 457–74, and 'The Development of a Capitalistic Labour Market in Canada,' *CJEPS* 25/4 (Nov. 1959): 450–61. The enduring value of Pentland lies in his insistence on integrating structural change in the economy and an appreciation of the human dimensions of this process, a two-sided understanding of historical development almost impossible within the staples paradigm. For a similar statement from historical geographers see the chapter on Ontario in R.C. Harris and John Warkentin, *Canada before Confederation: A Study in Historical Geography* (T: OUP 1974).

Indeed, Pentland's implicit rejection of the staples thesis has been developed much further in the ongoing work of Douglas McCalla and R.M. McInnis, both of whom question rigorously the view of the Upper Canadian economy as driven by the wheat staple. The classic staples account of the centrality of wheat to the Upper Canadian economy was H.A. Innis, 'An Introduction to the Economic History of Ontario from Outpost to Empire,' OHS, *Papers and Records* 30 (1934): 111–23, reprinted in Innis, *Essays in Canadian Economic History*, ed. Mary Q. Innis (T: UTP 1956), and a modified variant of this thesis was presented in John McCallum, *Unequal Beginnings: Agriculture and Economic Development in Quebec and Ontario until 1870* (T: UTP 1980). McCalla's more complex views are presented in 'The Wheat Staple and Upper Canadian Development,' CHA *HP* (1978): 34–46; 'The "Loyalist" Economy of Upper Canada, 1784–1806,' *HS/SH* 16/32 (Nov. 1983): 279–304; and 'The Internal Economy of Upper Canada: New Evidence on Agricultural Marketing before 1850,' *Agricultural History* 59/3 (July 1985): 397–416, reprinted in *Historical Essays*, 2nd ed. These articles are now superseded by McCalla's *Planting the Province: The Economic History of Upper Canada* (T: UTP 1993). McInnis supplies a review of the question as it now stands in 'Perspectives on Ontario Agriculture, 1815–1930,' *CPRH*, vol. 8 (1992).

These revisionist assessments of wheat and the agrarian economy of Upper Canada should be read alongside more traditional treatments, including the only broad account of agriculture, R.L. Jones, *History of Agriculture in Ontario, 1613–1880* (T: UTP 1946), and the more narrowly focused work of Kenneth Kelly, 'The Evaluation of Land for Wheat Culti-vation in Early Nineteenth Century Ontario,' *OH* 62/1 (Mar. 1970): 57–64; 'The Transfer of British Ideas for Improved Farming to Ontario during the First Half of the Nineteenth Century,' *OH* 63/2 (June 1971): 103–11; 'Wheat Farming in Simcoe County in the Mid-Nineteenth Century,' *Canadian Geographer* 15/2 (Summer 1971): 95–112; 'The Impact of Nineteenth Century Agricultural Settlement on the Land,' in J. David Wood, ed., *Perspectives on Landscape and Settlement in Nineteenth Century Ontario* (T: M&S 1975); and 'The Development of Farm Produce Marketing Agencies and Competition between Market Centres in Eastern Simcoe County, 1850–1875,' *CPRH*, vol. 1 (1978).

The importance of lumbering in Upper Canada was considerable and any appreciation of this economic sector begins with the writings of A.R.M. Lower, subject of a chapter in C. Berger, *The Writing of Canadian History*. Like most of Canada's early historians of nationhood, Lower seldom wrote directly on Upper Canada, but his studies always address the region. His most relevant works are *Settlement and the Forest Frontier in Eastern Canada* (T: MAC 1936), *The North American Assault on the Canadian Forest: A History of the Lumber Trade between Canada and the United States* (T: RP 1938), and *Great Britain's Woodyard: British America and the Timber Trade, 1763–1867* (M: MQUP 1973). On this theme see, as well, Peter A. Russell, 'Forest into Farmland: Upper Canadian Clearing Rates, 1822–1839,' *Agricultural History* 57/3 (July 1983): 326–39, reprinted in *Historical Essays*, 2nd ed. There is a useful opening chapter on the relationship of the lumber industry and government in H.V. Nelles, *The Politics of Development: Forests, Mines, and Hydro-Electric Power in Ontario, 1849–1941* (T: MAC 1974), while the Ottawa Valley is surveyed in Sandra J. Gillis, *The Timber Trade in the Ottawa Valley, 1806–54* (O: Parks Canada 1975), and Richard M. Reid, ed., *The Upper Ottawa Valley to 1855: A Collection of Documents* (O: CS/CUP 1990). Among the most useful articles on lumbering are Michael S. Cross, 'The Lumber Community of Upper Canada, 1815–1867,' *OH* 52/4 (Dec. 1960): 213–33; C. Grant Head, 'An Introduction to Forest Exploitation in Nineteenth Century Ontario,' in J.D. Wood, ed., *Perspectives on Landscape and Settlement*; and D. McCalla, 'Forest Products and Upper Canadian Development, 1815–46,' *CHR* 68/2 (June 1987): 159–98, which expands his scepticism concerning the wheat staple into an equally revisionist statement on timber. Finally, students should seek out Robert Peter Gillis's entries 'Henry Franklin Bronson,' 'John Hamilton,' 'James Little,' 'William Goodhue Perley,' and 'James Skead,' in *DCB*, vol. 11 (1982).

The connection between the timber trade and transportation is obvious from a reading of an early treatment of the Calvin enterprise of Garden Island near Kingston, examined in D.D. Calvin, *A Saga of the St. Lawrence: Timber and Shipping through Three Generations* (T: RP 1945), and Christian Norman, 'A Company Community: Garden Island, Upper Canada at Mid-Century,' *CPRH*, vol. 2 (1980). But those looking for a general introduction to transportation can start with plates 25 and 26 in *HAC*, vol. 2, and then turn to G.P. de T. Glazebrook, *A History of Transportation in Canada*, vol. 1, *Continental Strategy to 1867* (1938; repr. T: M&S 1964); H.G.J. Aitken, *The Welland Canal Company* (Cambridge, MA: Harvard University Press 1954); Edwin C. Guillet, *Pioneer Travel in Upper Canada* (T: UTP 1963); and Thomas F. McIlwraith, 'The Adequacy of Rural Roads in the Era before Railways: An Illustration from Upper Canada,' *Canadian Geographer* 14/4 (Winter 1970): 344–60.

Peter A. Baskerville's important essays on the entrepreneur and the transportation system link the steamship and the railway, finances and politics, economy and the state, in what is another historiographic blow to the staples approach. See, for instance, 'Donald Bethune's Steamboat Business: A Study of Upper Canadian Commercial and Financial Practice,' *OH* 67/3 (Sept. 1975): 135–49, reprinted in *Historical Essays*, 2nd ed.; 'The Entrepreneur and the Metropolitan Impulse: James Gray Bethune and Cobourg, 1825–1836,' in Jaroslav Petryshyn et al., eds., *Victorian Cobourg: A Nineteenth Century Profile* (Belleville, Ont.: Mika 1976); 'Professional vs. Proprietor: Power Distribution in the Railroad World of Upper Canada/Ontario, 1850 to 1881,' CHA *HP* (1978): 47–63; 'Entrepreneurship and the Family Compact: York-Toronto, 1822–55,' *Urban History Review* 9/3 (Feb. 1981): 15–34; 'Americans in Britain's Backyard: The Railway Era in Upper Canada, 1850–1880,' *Business History Review* 55/3 (Autumn 1981): 314–36; and 'Transportation, Social Change, and State Formation, Upper Canada, 1841–1864,' in A. Greer and I. Radforth, eds., *Colonial Leviathan*. Other studies of railways and entrepreneurs include F.H. Armstrong, 'Toronto's First Railway Venture, 1834–1838,' *OH* 58/1 (Mar. 1966): 21–42, and D. McCalla, 'Peter Buchanan, London Agent for the Great Western Railway of Canada,' in D.S. Macmillan, ed., *Canadian Business History*.

Railway boosterism, in terms of both the practical promotions of the nineteenth century and the historiographic enthusiasms of the twentieth, still provides a useful point of entry into this era of Upper Canadian transportation. See Thomas C. Keefer, *Philosophy of Railroads and Other Essays* (1849–50; repr., ed. H.V. Nelles, T: UTP 1972); J.M. Trout and E. Trout, *The Railways of Canada* (1871; repr. T: Coles 1970); A.W. Currie, *The Grand Trunk Railway of Canada* (T: UTP 1957); and G.R. Stevens, *Canadian*

National Railways, vol. 1, *Sixty Years of Trial and Error (1836–1896)* (T: Clarke, Irwin 1960). Ken Cruikshank, *Close Ties: Railways, Government, and the Board of Railway Commissioners, 1851–1933* (K&M: MQUP 1991), contains useful information on early state-railway relations, while an essay by Ann Carlos and Frank D. Lewis, 'The Profitability of Early Canadian Railroads: Evidence from the Grant Trunk and Great Western Railway Companies,' in Claudia Goldin and Hugh Rockoff, eds., *Strategic Factors in Nineteenth Century American Economic History: A Volume to Honor Robert W. Fogel* (Chicago, IL: University of Chicago Press 1992), addresses the question of economic viability.

A perspective on the large picture of Canadian business history with some relationship to the Upper Canadian experience can be gleaned from Michael Bliss, *Northern Enterprise: Five Centuries of Canadian Business* (T: M&S 1987), although discerning readers will want to delve deeper into more substantial studies. Among the best are T.W. Acheson, 'John Baldwin: Portrait of a Colonial Entrepreneur,' *OH* 61/3 (Sept. 1969): 153–66; Acheson, 'The Nature and Structure of York Commerce in the 1820s,' *CHR* 50/4 (Dec. 1969): 406–28; R.G. Hoskins, 'Hiram Walker and the Origins and Development of Walkerville, Ontario,' *OH* 64/3 (Sept. 1972): 122–31; M.L. Magill, 'William Allan: A Pioneer Business Executive,' in F.H. Armstrong et al., eds., *Aspects of Nineteenth-Century Ontario*; W.P.J. Millar, 'George P.M. Ball: A Rural Businessman in Upper Canada,' *OH* 66/2 (June 1974): 65–78; J.K. Johnson, 'John A. Macdonald and the Kingston Business Community,' in Gerald Tulchinsky, ed., *To Preserve and Defend: Essays on Kingston in the Nineteenth Century* (M: MQUP 1976); D. McCalla, *The Upper Canada Trade, 1834–1872: A Study of the Buchanans' Business* (T: UTP 1979); Johnson, '"One Bold Operator": Samuel Zimmerman, Niagara Entrepreneur, 1843–1857,' *OH* 74/1 (Mar. 1982): 26–44; B.G. Wilson, *The Enterprises of Robert Hamilton: A Study of Wealth and Influence in Early Upper Canada, 1776–1812* (O: CUP 1983); R.M. Reid, 'The Rosamond Woolen Company of Almonte: Industrial Development in A Rural Setting,' *OH* 75/3 (Sept. 1983): 266–89; and I. Radforth, 'Confronting Distance: Managing Jacques and Hay's New Lowell Operations, 1853–73,' in P.A. Baskerville, ed., *Canadian Papers in Business History*, vol. 1 (VI: Public History Group, University of Victoria 1989). The important agricultural implements industry and its Upper Canadian origins are covered in Merrill Denison, *Harvest Triumphant: The Story of Massey-Harris* (T: M&S 1948), and there are some general comments on this sector in William Gregory Phillips, *The Agricultural Implement Industry in Canada* (T: UTP 1956).

The most accessible account of the complexities of banking and capital resources is now P.A. Baskerville, ed., *The Bank of Upper Canada: A Collection of Documents* (O: CS/CUP 1987), a documentary collection with a long and valuable introduction. To this must be added Angela Redish, 'Why Was Specie Scarce in Colonial Economies? An Analysis of the Canadian Currency, 1796–1830,' *Journal of Economic History* 44/3 (Sept. 1984): 713–28, and Michael J. Piva, *The Borrowing Process: Public Finance in the Province of Canada, 1840–1867* (O: University of Ottawa Press 1992). But students can still consult with profit such older works as H.C. Pentland, 'The Role of Capital in Canadian Economic Development,' *CJEPS* (1950); H.G.J. Aitken, 'A Note on the Capital Resources of Upper Canada,' *CJEPS* 18/4 (Nov. 1952): 525–33; and John Ireland [M.L. Magill], 'John H. Dunn and the Bankers,' *OH* 62/2 (June 1970): 83–100, reprinted in *Historical Essays*, 1st ed.; as well as the more recent Magill, 'The Failure of the Commercial Bank,' in G. Tulchinsky, ed., *To Preserve and Defend*; and P.A. Baskerville, 'The Pet Bank, the Local State and the Imperial Centre, 1850–1864,' *JCS* 20/3 (Fall 1985): 22–46. Two books by E.P. Neufeld, *The Financial System of Canada: Its Growth and Development* (T: MAC 1972) and *Money and Banking in Canada* (T: M&S 1964), remain valuable, the latter an edited collection of documents and commentary.

The development of economic thought, closely associated with this history of banking, capital resources, and finance, is outlined in Craufurd D.W. Goodwin, *Canadian Economic Thought: The Political Economy of a Developing Nation, 1814–1914* (Durham, NC: Duke University Press 1961), and his 'John Rae: Undiscovered Exponent of Canadian Banking,' *The Canadian Banker* 66/3 (Winter 1959): 110–15. Goodwin's work is now supplemented by M.J. Piva, 'Continuity and Crisis: Francis Hincks and Canadian Economic Policy,' *CHR* 66/2 (June 1985): 185–210, and 'Government Finance and the Development of the Canadian State,' in A. Greer and I. Radforth, eds., *Colonial Leviathan*, as well as P.A. Baskerville, 'Imperial Agendas and "Disloyal" Collaborators: Decolonization and the John Sanfield Macdonald Ministries, 1862–1864,' in D. Keane and C. Read, eds., *Old Ontario*. Gilbert N. Tucker, *The Canadian Commercial Revolution, 1845–1851* (1936; repr., ed. H.G.J. Aitken, T: M&S 1964), and Donald C. Masters, *The Reciprocity Treaty of 1854* (1937; repr. T: M&S 1963), are dated accounts of the shifting policies of mid-century. The basic analysis on tariff policy is now Ben Forster, *A Conjunction of Interests: Business, Politics, and Tariffs, 1825–1879* (T: UTP 1986). Such studies do not necessarily focus on Upper Canada, but can be mined to good advantage. An innovative statement on insurance is D. McCalla, 'Fire and Marine Insurance in Upper

Canada: The Establishment of a Service Industry, 1832–68,' in P.A. Baskerville, ed., *Canadian Papers in Business History*, vol. 1.

Early manufacturing is the subject of the still indispensable volume by Jacob Spelt, *Urban Development in South-Central Ontario* (1955; repr. T: M&S 1972), which can be complemented with the sometimes difficult presentation in J.M. Gilmour, *Spatial Evolution of Manufacturing: Southern Ontario, 1851–1891* (T: UTP 1972). Peter G. Goheen, *Victorian Toronto: Pattern and Process of Growth, 1850–1900* (Chicago, IL: Department of Geography, University of Chicago 1970), has much on early Toronto industrialization. An extremely useful statement is Paul Craven and Tom Traves, 'Canadian Railways as Manufacturers, 1850–1880,' CHA *HP* (1983): 254–81. An older statement is M.Q. Innis, 'The Industrial Development of Ontario, 1783–1820,' OHS, *Papers and Records* (1937): 105–13, reprinted in *Historical Essays*, 1st ed. Labour historians addressed the rise of industrial capitalism in the post-1840 years in Bryan D. Palmer, *A Culture in Conflict: Skilled Workers and Industrial Capitalism in Hamilton, Ontario, 1860–1914* (M: MQUP 1979), and Gregory S. Kealey, *Toronto Workers Respond to Industrial Capitalism, 1867–1892* (T: UTP 1980). On the beginnings of competition and markets see B. Forster, 'Finding the Right Size: Markets and Competition in Mid- and Late Nineteenth-Century Ontario,' in R. Hall et al., eds., *Patterns of the Past*.

Taken together these varied writings on the Upper Canadian economy present a more complex picture of trade, commerce, and production than that which emerged out of the staples thesis and its Laurentian offspring. However important specific resource exports were, they alone did not encompass the entirety of people's economic lives. Nor can a staple such as timber be interpreted entirely in terms of its mercantile, export dimension, timber also being used in construction and as a source of fuel. What emerges from recent scholarship on the Upper Canadian economy, then, is a depiction of a society highly influenced by particular staples, but moving toward a more differentiated and industrialized order, a society in which there were not just traders and harvesters, but also emerging capitalists and workers, as well as 'others' whom it was necessary to marginalize and displace.

NATIVE PEOPLES: DISPLACEMENT AND DISPOSSESSION

The fundamental precondition for the economic development and diversification outlined in the historical writing just cited was the displacement and dispossession of Native peoples by European colonization and settlement. The study of this process is attracting increasing attention, and not just by historians. Indeed, a fundamental characteristic of the field is the way in which it combines the findings of archaeologists, anthropologists, ethnologists, geographers, as well as historians. Fortunately, a number of general surveys now exist that provide an introduction to the methodological challenges of Native studies while at the same time setting the Upper Canadian experience in context. While Diamond Jenness, *The Indians of Canada* (7th ed., T/O: UTP/National Museums of Canada 1977), is still useful, students would be better advised to consult Alan D. McMillan, *Native Peoples and Cultures of Canada: An Anthropological Overview* (V: Douglas & McIntyre 1988), J.R. Miller, *Skyscrapers Hide the Heavens: A History of Indian-White Relations in Canada* (1989; rev. ed., T: UTP 1991), and Olive Patricia Dickason, *Canada's First Nations: A History of Founding Peoples from Earliest Times* (T: M&S 1992). Miller has also edited *Sweet Promises: A Reader on Indian-White Relations in Canada* (T: UTP 1991), to which one should add the collection edited by Ian A.L. Getty and Antoine S. Lussier, *As Long As the Sun Shines and Water Flows: A Reader in Canadian Native Studies* (V: UBCP 1983). For a general commentary on the rise of this new field see John A. Price, 'Native Studies,' in A.F.J. Artibise, ed., *Interdisciplinary Approaches to Canadian Society: A Guide to the Literature* (K&M: MQUP 1990).

The Ojibwa, at the time of the Conquest the most powerful Native people in what would become Upper Canada, have drawn the attention of several scholars in recent years. Two in particular stand out, Peter S. Schmalz and Donald B. Smith. Schmalz, *The Ojibwa of Southern Ontario* (T: UTP 1991), provides a general survey based on an interesting amalgam of oral traditions, archaeology, and primary documents. This work supersedes Schmalz's earlier articles, but students should still seek out his *The History of the Saugeen Indians* (T: OHS 1977). Smith's work focuses more narrowly on the Ojibwa along the north shore of Lake Ontario, those known as the Mississauga, but is nonetheless important for that. See his 'Who Are the Mississauga?' *OH* 67/4 (Dec. 1975): 211–22; 'The Dispossession of the Mississauga Indians: A Missing Chapter in the Early History of Upper Canada,' *OH* 73/2 (June 1981): 67–87, reprinted in *Historical Essays*, 2nd ed.; and *Sacred Feathers: The Reverend Peter Jones (Kahkewaquonaby) and the Mississauga Indians* (T: UTP 1987). Both authors provide insightful analyses of the process of dispossession. In addition to the work of Schmalz and Smith, see Charles A. Bishop, *The Northern Ojibwa and the Fur Trade: An Historical and Ecological Study* (T: HRW 1974).

In the wake of the American Revolution, the Ojibwa had to make room for Native, mostly Iroquois, refugees from south of the Great Lakes. These refugees are also the subject of several studies, three in particular by Charles M. Johnston: 'An Outline of Early Settlement in the Grand River Valley,' *OH* 54/1 (Mar. 1962): 43–67, reprinted in *Historical Essays*, 1st ed.; 'Joseph Brant, the Grand River Lands and the Northwest Crisis,' *OH* 55/4 (Dec. 1963): 267–82; and, as editor, *The Valley of the Six Nations: A Collection of Documents on the Indian Lands of the Grand River* (T: CS 1964). Isabel Thompson Kelsay's *Joseph Brant, 1743–1807: Man of Two Worlds* (Syracuse, NY: Syracuse University Press 1984) is a biography of the most famous refugee. Some sense of why so many Iroquoians had to flee north can be gleaned from Jack M. Sosin, 'The Use of Indians in the War of the American Revolution: A Re-Assessment of Responsibility,' *CHR* 46/2 (June 1965): 101–21; S.F. Wise, 'The American Revolution and Indian History,' in John S. Moir, ed., *Character and Circumstance: Essays in Honour of Donald Grant Creighton* (T: MAC 1970); and Barbara Graymont, 'The Six Nations Indians in the Revolutionary War,' in *The Iroquois in the American Revolution: 1976 Conference Proceedings* (Rochester, NY: Rochester Museum and Science Center 1981), reprinted in J.R. Miller, ed., *Sweet Promises*.

The subsequent triangular interplay of Native, British, and American interests from the end of the American Revolution to the War of 1812 has also developed a substantial literature of its own. In addition to the works of P.S. Schmalz and D.B. Smith already cited, see George F.G. Stanley, 'The Indians in the War of 1812,' *CHR* 31/2 (June 1950): 145–65, reprinted in J.R. Miller, ed., *Sweet Promises*; Colin G. Calloway, *Crown and Calumet: British-Indian Relations, 1783–1815* (Norman, OK: University of Oklahoma Press 1987); Richard White, *The Middle Ground: Indians, Empires, and Republics in the Great Lakes Region, 1650–1815* (NY: Cambridge University Press 1991); and Gregory Evans Dowd, *A Spirited Resistance: The North American Indian Struggle for Unity, 1745–1815* (Baltimore, MD: Johns Hopkins University Press 1992). A small scholarly industry has grown up around the role of Shawnee chief Tecumseh in the War of 1812. Carl F. Klinck, ed., *Tecumseh: Fact and Fiction in Early Records* (1961; 2nd ed., O: Tecumseh 1978), suggests how such interest began. For more straightforward approaches see R. David Edmunds, *Tecumseh and the Quest for Indian Leadership* (Boston, MA: Little, Brown 1984), and the entry 'Tecumseh,' *DCB*, vol. 5 (1983).

Treaty-making lay at the heart of European dispossession of Native peoples, and the study of this process – in part because of present relevance – proceeds apace. A good place to start is with the treaties themselves, available in *Indian Treaties and Surrenders from 1680 to 1890*, 3 vols. (O: King's

Printer 1891–1912; repr. T: Coles 1971). For analyses of this process see – again in addition to the works of P.S. Schmalz and D.B. Smith – the studies by Robert J. Surtees: 'The Development of an Indian Reserve Policy in Canada,' *OH* 61/2 (June 1969): 87–98, reprinted in *Historical Essays*, 1st ed.; 'Indian Land Cessions in Upper Canada, 1815–1830,' in I.A.L. Getty and A.S. Lussier, eds., *As Long As the Sun Shines*; and *Indian Land Surrenders in Ontario, 1763–1867* (O: Indian and Northern Affairs Canada 1984); as well as Leo A. Johnson, 'The Mississauga–Lake Ontario Land Surrender of 1805,' *OH* 83/3 (Sept. 1990): 233–53. As for the development of the bureaucracy and policies built to 'administer' Native peoples turn to J.E. Hodgetts, *Pioneer Public Service: An Administrative History of the United Canadas, 1841–1867* (T: UTP 1955); Douglas Leighton, 'The Compact Tory as Bureaucrat: Samuel Peters Jarvis and the Indian Department, 1837–1845,' *OH* 73/1 (Mar. 1981): 40–53; John Leslie, 'The Bagot Commission: Developing a Corporate Memory for the Indian Department,' CHA *HP* (1982): 31–52; and Robert S. Allen, *His Majesty's Indian Allies: British Indian Policy in the Defence of Canada, 1774–1815* (T: Dundurn 1992).

The activities of missionaries, especially in regard to the education of Native peoples, can be approached first through such general surveys as Elizabeth Graham, *Medicine-Man to Missionary: Missionaries as Agents of Change among the Indians of Southern Ontario, 1784–1867* (T: Peter Martin Associates 1975), and John Webster Grant, *Moon of Wintertime: Missionaries and the Indians of Canada in Encounter since 1534* (T: UTP 1984). For more specific analyses see Ruth Bleasdale, 'Manitowaning: An Experiment in Indian Settlement,' *OH* 66/3 (Sept. 1974): 147–57; J. Donald Wilson, '"No Blanket to Be Worn in School": The Education of Indians in Early Nineteenth-Century Ontario,' *HS/SH* 7/14 (Nov. 1974): 293–305; and F. Laurie Barron, 'Alcoholism, Indians, and the Anti-Drink Cause in the Protestant Indian Missions of Upper Canada, 1822–1850,' in I.A.L. Getty and A.S. Lussier, eds., *As Long As the Sun Shines*. Attempts are also being made to see the missionary effort from the Native point of view, as, for example, in Christopher Vecsey, *Traditional Ojibwa Religion and Its Historical Changes* (Philadelphia, PA: American Philosophical Society 1983).

General works on Native peoples in mid-century are James A. Clifton, *A Place of Refuge for All Time: Migration of the American Potawatomi into Upper Canada, 1830 to 1850* (O: National Museums of Canada 1975); D. Leighton, 'The Manitoulin Incident of 1863: An Indian-White Confrontation in the Province of Canada,' *OH* 69/2 (June 1977): 113–24; Kenneth G. Pryke and L.L. Kulisek, eds., *The Western District* (Windsor, Ont.: Essex County Historical Society 1983); and the first chapters of L.A. Johnson, *History of the County of Ontario, 1615–1875* (Whitby, Ont.: Ontario County Council 1973). An important recent statement drawing on much of the established relevant literature is Tony Hall, 'Native Limited Identities and Newcomer Metropolitanism in Upper Canada, 1814–1867,' in D. Keane and C. Read, eds., *Old Ontario*. On art see Dennis Reid and Joan M. Vastokas, *From the Four Quarters: Native and European Art in Ontario, 5000 BC to 1867 AD* (T: Art Gallery of Ontario 1984), and the general statement in Vastokas, 'Native Art as Art History: Meaning and Time from Unwritten Sources,' *JCS* 21/4 (Winter 1986–7): 7–36. Finally, one should not neglect the relevant entries on Natives, missionaries, traders, and bureaucrats in the volumes of the *DCB*.

THE MAKING OF A SETTLER SOCIETY: IMMIGRANTS, IDEAS, AND SOCIAL STRUCTURE

Dispossessing Native peoples was a long, drawn-out, and complex process, but fundamental to its realization, and central to economic development and diversification, was the recruitment of a differentiated white population composed of an elite loyal to the colonial interests of the British Empire and a plebeian mass structured into the various subsistence activities of the settlement frontier and the emerging commercial/urban milieu. A brief conceptual statement on aspects of this process appears in B.D. Palmer, 'Town, Port, and Country: Speculations on the Capitalist Transformation of Canada,' *Acadiensis* 12/2 (Spring 1983): 131–9.

Immigrant settlers arrived in Upper Canada to find the social structure less developed than the ideological hegemony of the Loyalist elite. The United Empire Loyalists who reacted to the American Revolution with settlement in Upper Canada and other areas are the subject of an established literature concerned with the relation of ideas, settlement, and political rule. Many of the most thought-provoking essays on this subject are by S.F. Wise, most of which have been collected in *God's Peculiar Peoples: Essays on Political Culture in Nineteenth-Century Canada*, ed. A.B. McKillop and Paul Romney (O: CUP 1993). Included in the collection is 'Liberal Consensus or Ideological Battleground: Some Reflections on the Hartz Thesis,' originally published in CHA *HP* (1974): 1–14, in which Wise considers the influential argument of Kenneth D. McRae, 'The Structure of Canadian History,' in Louis B. Hartz, ed., *The Founding of New Societies* (NY: Harcourt Brace and World 1964). Other early works still worth consulting are H.V. Nelles, 'Loyalism and Local Power: The District of Niagara, 1792–1837,' *OH* 58/2 (June 1966): 99–114; David V.J. Bell, 'The Loyalist Tradition in Canada,' *JCS* 5/2 (May 1970): 22–33; Terry Cook, 'John Beverley Robinson and the Conservative Blueprint for the Upper Canadian Community,' *OH* 64/2 (June 1972): 79–94, reprinted in *Historical Essays*, 1st ed.; and Darrell A. Norris, 'Household and Transiency in a Loyalist Township: The People of Adolphustown, 1784–1822,' *HS/SH* 13/26 (Nov. 1980): 399–415. Useful documentary collections include Ernest A. Cruikshank, ed., *The Settlement of the United Empire Loyalists on the Upper St. Lawrence and the Bay of Quinte in 1784: A Documentary Record* (T: OHS 1934); James J. Talman, ed., *Loyalist Narratives from Upper Canada* (T: CS 1946); and Leslie F.S. Upton, ed., *The United Empire Loyalists: Men and Myths* (T: CC 1967).

Building on this literature are more recent statements: Howard Temperley, 'Frontierism, Capital, and the American Loyalists in Canada,' *Journal of American Studies* 13/1 (Apr. 1979): 5–27; B.G. Wilson, *As She Began: An Illustrated Introduction to Loyalist Ontario* (T: Dundurn 1981); Dennis Duffy, *Gardens, Covenants, Exiles: Loyalism in the Literature of Upper Canada/Ontario* (T: UTP 1982); George A. Rawlyk, 'Loyalist Military Settlement in Upper Canada,' in R.S. Allen, gen. ed., *The Loyal Americans: The Military Rôle of the Loyalist Provincial Corps and Their Settlement in British North America, 1775–1784* (O: National Museums of Canada 1983); Jane Errington and Rawlyk, 'The Loyalist-Federalist Alliance of Upper Canada,' *American Review of Canadian Studies* 14/2 (Summer 1984): 157–76; Wallace Brown and Hereward Senior, *Victorious in Defeat: The Loyalists in Canada* (T: Methuen 1984); S.F. Wise et al., eds., *'None Was Ever Better ...': The Loyalist Settlement of Ontario* (Cornwall, Ont.: Stormont, Dundas, and Glengarry Historical Society 1984); and Christopher Moore, *The Loyalists: Revolution, Exile, Settlement* (T: MAC 1984). The most useful statements, however, are J. Errington, *The Lion, the Eagle, and Upper Canada: A Developing Colonial Ideology* (K&M: MQUP 1987), and David Mills, *The Idea of Loyalty in Upper Canada, 1784–1850* (K&M: MQUP 1988).

Once established, the Loyalist elite governed, in good part, through its land policy, which many American immigrants after 1792 took advantage of as so-called late Loyalists. For introductions to the administration of colonial lands see Gilbert C. Patterson, *Land Settlement in Upper Canada, 1783–1846* (T: Ontario Archives 1921); Lillian F. Gates, *Land Policies of Upper Canada* (T: UTP 1968); G.A. Wilson, *The Clergy Reserves of Upper Canada: A Canadian Mortmain* (T: UTP 1968); J.D. Wood, ed., *Perspectives on Landscape and Settlement*; R.L. Gentilcore, ed., *Ontario* (T: UTP 1972); Gentilcore and Kate Donkin, 'Land Surveys of Southern Ontario: An Introduction to the Field Notebooks of the Ontario Land Surveyors, 1784–

1859,' *Cartographica*, Monograph no. 8 (1973); and R.C. Harris and J. Warkentin, *Canada before Confederation*. Particular phenomena, such as the Canada Company or the Talbot settlement, are specifically treated in Frederick Coyne Hamil, *Lake Erie Baron: The Story of Colonel Thomas Talbot* (T: MAC 1955); Clarence G. Karr, *The Canada Land Company: The Early Years* (T: OHS 1974); and 'Thomas Talbot,' *DCB*, vol. 8 (1985).

This context of Loyalism and land was central to the experience of immigrant arrival in Upper Canada. Something of the transatlantic crossing, as well as its initial preparations and final outcomes, can be gleaned from E.C. Guillet, *The Great Migration: The Atlantic Crossing by Sailing-Ship since 1770* (1937; 2nd ed., T: UTP 1963), a source that must nevertheless be used with caution. Early general accounts of immigration include Helen I. Cowan, *British Emigration to British North America: The First Hundred Years* (1928; rev. ed., T: UTP 1961); Norman Macdonald, *Canada, 1763–1841, Immigration and Settlement: The Administration of the Imperial Land Regulations* (L: Longmans, Green 1939); and, especially in terms of the American migrants, Fred Landon, *Western Ontario and the American Frontier* (T: RP 1941; repr. T: M&S 1967). Hugh J.M. Johnston, *British Emigration Policy, 1815–1830: 'Shovelling Out Paupers'* (Oxford: Clarendon Press 1972), explores the aims of the state, and Jean Burnet, *Ethnic Groups in Upper Canada* (T: OHS 1972), looks at social differentiation among immigrant groups, relying mainly on travellers' accounts.

Studies dealing with the process of emigration and immigrant settlement include J.K. Johnson, 'The Chelsea Pensioners in Upper Canada,' *OH* 53/4 (Dec. 1961): 273–89; H.J.M. Johnston, 'Immigration to the Five Eastern Townships of the Huron Tract,' *OH* 54/3 (Sept. 1962): 207–24; James M. Cameron, 'Scottish Emigration to Upper Canada, 1815–1855: A Study of Process,' in W. Peter Adams and Frederick M. Helleiner, eds., *International Geography, 1972* (T: UTP 1972); Wendy Cameron, 'The Petworth Emigration Committee: Lord Egremont's Assisted Emigrations from Sussex to Upper Canada, 1832–1837,' *OH* 65/4 (Dec. 1973): 231–45; W. Cameron, 'Selecting Peter Robinson's Irish Emigrants,' *HS/SH* 9/17 (May 1976): 29–46; J.M. Bumsted, *The People's Clearance: Highland Emigration to British North America, 1770–1815* (Edinburgh/W: Edinburgh University Press/ UMP 1982); Marianne McLean, 'Peopling Glengarry County: The Scottish Origins of a Canadian Community,' CHA *HP* (1982): 156–71; C. Moore, 'The Disposition to Settle: The Royal Highland Emigrants and Loyalist Settlement in Upper Canada, 1784,' *OH* 76/4 (Dec. 1984): 306–25, reprinted in *Historical Essays*, 2nd ed.; D.A. Norris, 'Migration, Pioneer Settlement, and the Life Course: The First Families of an Ontario Township,'

CPRH, vol. 4 (1984), reprinted in *Historical Essays*, 2nd ed.; W. Cameron, 'Peter Robinson's Settlers in Peterborough,' in Robert O'Driscoll and Lorna Reynolds, eds., *The Untold Story: The Irish in Canada*, vol. 1 (T: Celtic Arts of Canada 1988); and McLean, *The People of Glengarry: Highlanders in Transition, 1745–1820* (K&M: MQUP 1991). Ernest J. Lajeunesse, ed., *The Windsor Border Region, Canada's Southernmost Frontier: A Collection of Documents* (T: CS 1960), focuses on the francophone settlers of the early 'western' reaches of Upper Canada.

The historiography of Irish immigration is extensive, combative, and influential. Especially innovative for its time was John J. Mannion's *Irish Settlements in Eastern Canada: A Study of Cultural Transfer and Adaptation* (T: UTP 1974). A series of articles have suggested different emphases regarding the Irish settlement in the cities or the countryside. See Frances Morehouse, 'Canadian Migration in the Forties,' *CHR* 9/4 (Dec. 1928): 309–29; Kenneth Duncan, 'Irish Famine Immigration and the Social Structure of Canada West,' *Canadian Review of Sociology and Anthropology* 2/1 (Feb. 1965): 19–40; Joy Parr, 'The Welcome and the Wake: Attitudes in Canada West toward the Irish Famine Migration,' *OH* 66/2 (June 1974): 101–13; R.C. Harris, Pauline Roulston, and Chris de Freitas, 'The Settlement of Mono Township,' *Canadian Geographer* 19/1 (Spring 1975): 1–17; William J. Smyth, 'The Irish In Mid Nineteenth-Century Ontario,' *Ulster Folk Life* 23 (1977): 97–105; Howard T. Pammett, 'The Irish Immigrant Settler in the Pioneer Kawarthas,' *Families* 17 (1978): 154–74; Alan G. Brunger, 'Geographical Propinquity among Pre-Famine Catholic Irish Settlers in Upper Canada,' *Journal of Historical Geography* 8/3 (1982): 265–82; Glenn J. Lockwood, 'Irish Immigrants and the "Critical Years" in Eastern Ontario: The Case of Montague Township, 1821–1881,' *CPRH*, vol. 4, reprinted in *Historical Essays*, 2nd ed.; and A. Gordon Darroch and Michael Ornstein, 'Ethnicity and Class, Transitions over a Decade: Ontario, 1867–1871,' CHA *HP* (1984): 111–37.

These articles have been followed by a virtual deluge of recent books, most of which owe some kind of debt to the polemical zeal of D.H. Akenson, 'Ontario: Whatever Happened to the Irish?' *CPRH*, vol. 3 (1982). Akenson's insistence on rewriting the history of the Irish out of aggregate data that established the quantitative importance of rural settlement over urban experience has reoriented the study of the Irish, not only in Upper Canada, but in Canada as a whole. There have been immense gains in understanding as a consequence, but also a narrowing of vision and a mechanical refusal to consider different questions. As important as the Irish were to the country, they were also critically significant in the cities, to social conflict, and to the emergence of institutions and modes of regulation (such as the prison or pauper relief), as will be apparent in later sections of this essay and as is underscored in D.S. Shea, 'The Irish Immigrant Adjustment to Toronto, 1840–1860,' CCHA, *Study Sessions* 39 (1972): 53–60; H. Senior, *Orangeism: The Canadian Phase* (T: MHR 1972); Michael B. Katz, *The People of Hamilton, Canada West: Family and Class in a Mid-Nineteenth-Century City* (Cambridge, MA: Harvard University Press 1975); and Cecil J. Houston and W.J. Smyth, *The Sash Canada Wore: A Historical Geography of the Orange Order in Canada* (T: UTP 1980). The new approach to the Irish is evident in G.J. Lockwood, *Montague: A Social History of an Irish Ontario Township, 1783–1980* (K: Corporation of the Township of Montague 1980); D.H. Akenson, *The Irish in Ontario: A Study in Rural History* (K&M: MQUP 1984), which is actually a study of the Irish in Leeds and Landsdowne Township; Bruce S. Elliott, *Irish Migrants in the Canadas: A New Approach* (K&M: MQUP 1988); and C.J. Houston and W.J. Smyth, *Irish Emigration and Canadian Settlement: Patterns, Links, and Letters* (T: UTP 1990).

The social structure that developed out of this conjuncture of immigration, ideas, and interest is explored, with differing emphases on the potential for social mobility, in L.A. Johnson, 'Land Policy, Population Growth and Social Structure in the Home District, 1793–1851,' *OH* 63/1 (Mar. 1971): 41–60, reprinted in *Historical Essays*, 1st ed.; G. Teeple, 'Land, Labour, and Capital in Pre-Confederation Canada,' in Teeple, ed., *Capitalism and the National Question*; Johnson, 'The Settlement of the Western District, 1749–1850,' in F.H. Armstrong et al., eds., *Aspects of Nineteenth-Century Ontario*; and J.D. Wood, 'Population Change on an Agricultural Frontier: Upper Canada, 1796 to 1841,' in R. Hall et al., eds., *Patterns of the Past.*

Most important in understanding the Upper Canadian complexity of land settlement, demographic development, speculation, and political rule are the recent writings of David Gagan and geographer John Clarke. Gagan, *Hopeful Travellers: Families, Land, and Social Change in Mid-Victorian Peel County, Canada West* (T: UTP 1981), develops an argument of demographic determinism, contending that the first settlers succeeded, their persistence souring the possibilities for their offspring, whose life chances faded as lack of access to land and overreliance on the wheat staple produced a rural crisis of declining yields, out-migration, and rural depopulation. Many of Gagan's more specialized articles detail the central importance of land in the wielding of social, economic, and political power, an interpretive direction also developed in the studies of Clarke and others. Key references by Gagan are, with Herbert Mays, 'Historical Demography and Canadian Social History: Families and Land in Peel County, Ontario,' *CHR* 54/1 (Mar. 1973): 27–47; 'Property and "Interest": Some Preliminary Evidence of Land Speculation by the "Family Compact" in Upper Canada, 1820–1840,' *OH* 70/1 (Mar. 1978): 64–70; and 'Land, Population, and Social Change: The "Critical Years" in Rural Canada West,' *CHR* 59/3 (Sept. 1978): 293–318. Key references by Clarke are 'The Role of Political Position and Family and Economic Linkage in Land Speculation in the Western District of Upper Canada, 1788–1815,' *Canadian Geographer* 19/1 (Spring 1975): 18–34; 'Aspects of Land Acquisition in Essex County, Ontario, 1790–1900,' *HS/SH* 11/21 (May 1978): 98–119; and 'The Activity of an Early Canadian Land Speculator in Essex County, Ontario: Would the Real John Askin Please Stand Up?' *CPRH*, vol. 3.

In addition to Gagan and Clarke, see also Randy William Widdis, 'Motivation and Scale: A Method of Identifying Land Speculators in Upper Canada,' *Canadian Geographer* 23/4 (Winter 1979): 337–51; P.A. Russell, 'Upper Canada: A Poor Man's Country? Some Statistical Evidence,' *CPRH*, vol. 3; Daniel A. Bilak, 'The Law of the Land: Rural Debt and Private Land Transfer in Upper Canada, 1841–1867,' *HS/SH* 20/39 (May 1987): 177–88; Russell, *Attitudes to Social Structure and Mobility in Upper Canada, 1815–1840* (Queenston, Ont.: Edwin Mellon 1990); J.K. Johnson, 'Land Policy and the Upper Canadian Elite Reconsidered: The Canadian Emigration Association, 1840–1841,' in D. Keane and C. Read, eds., *Old Ontario*; and A.G. Darroch and Lee Soltow, 'Inequality in Landed Wealth in Nineteenth-Century Ontario: Structure and Access,' *Canadian Review of Sociology and Anthropology* 29/2 (May 1992): 167–90.

Among the accessible primary sources that should be consulted in light of the debate developing out of the preceding literature, the most significant is perhaps Robert Fleming Gourlay, *Statistical Account of Upper Canada, Compiled with a View to a Grand System of Emigration*, 2 vols. (L: Simpkin & Marshall 1822), and accompanying *General Introduction* (L: Simpkin & Marshall 1822), which addressed conditions of 1817. Stanley Mealing recently rendered this unwieldy work more accessible and manageable by publishing a much-abridged single-volume version, *Statistical Account of Upper Canada* (T: M&S 1974). Mealing's excellent introduction can be supplemented by reference to the entry 'Robert Fleming Gourlay,' *DCB*, vol. 9 (1976); Gerald Bloch, 'Robert Gourlay's Vision of Agrarian Reform,' *CPRH*, vol. 3; M.B. Taylor, *Promoters, Patriots, and Partisans*, ch. 4; and Robert W. Dimand, 'Political Protest and Political Arithmetic on the Niagara Frontier: Robert Gourlay's "Statistical Account of Upper Canada,"' *Brock Review* 1/1 (1992): 52–63.

Gourlay's work is but the tip of a paper iceberg of travel literature and settler accounts. For a guide to this literature see Elizabeth Waterston et al., comps., *The Travellers: Canada to 1900: An Annotated Bibliography of Works Published in English from 1577* (Guelph, Ont.: University of Guelph 1989). To get a taste of these accounts, primarily the product of 'gentlemen' and 'gentlewomen,' one can turn to G.M. Craig, ed., *Early Travellers in the Canadas, 1791–1867* (T: MAC 1955), or Audrey Y. Morris, *Gentle Pioneers: Five Nineteenth-Century Canadians* (T: Hodder & Stoughton 1968). Brief analyses are provided in the relevant chapters of C.F. Klinck, gen. ed., *Literary History of Canada: Canadian Literature in English* (T: UTP 1965), and Robert S. Dilley, 'British Travellers in Early Canada: A Content Analysis of Itineraries and Images,' *CPRH*, vol. 5 (1986).

Among examples of this writing (in reprinted editions) are: John Howison, *Sketches of Upper Canada* (1821; repr. T: Coles 1970); Edward Allen Talbot, *Five Years Residence in the Canadas* (1824; repr. NY: Johnson Reprint 1968); Catharine Parr Traill [Strickland], *The Backwoods of Canada* (1836; repr. T: Coles 1971); Anna B. Jameson [Murphy], *Winter Studies and Summer Rambles in Canada* (1838; repr. T: Coles 1972); Susanna Moodie [Strickland], *Roughing It in the Bush* (1852; repr. O: Centre for Editing Early Canadian Texts 1988); and Samuel Strickland, *Twenty-Seven Years in Canada West* (1853; repr. E: Hurtig 1970). There are entries in the *DCB* for each of these authors. Also note Terence A. Crowley, '"The Site of Paradise": A Settler's Guide to Becoming a Farmer in Early Upper Canada,' *CPRH*, vol. 6 (1988).

Recent statements that draw on this material to present significant impressions of Upper Canadian life include D. Gagan, '"The Prose of Life": Literary Reflections of the Family, Individual Experience and Social Structure in Nineteenth-Century Canada,' *Journal of Social History* 9/3 (Spring 1976): 367–81, reprinted in J.M. Bumsted, ed., *Interpreting Canada's Past*, vol. 1, *Before Confederation* ([1st ed.], T: OUP 1986); Graeme Wynn, 'Notes on Society and Environment in Old Ontario,' *Journal of Social History* 13/1 (Fall 1979): 49–65; A.G. Darroch, 'Migrants in the Nineteenth Century: Fugitives or Families in Motion?' *Journal of Family History* 6/3 (Fall 1981): 257–77; Allan Smith, 'Farms, Forests and Cities: The Image of the Land and the Rise of the Metropolis in Ontario, 1860–1914,' in D. Keane and C. Read, eds., *Old Ontario*; and W.J. Keith, *Literary Images of Ontario* (T: UTP 1992).

One group always on the margins was the Black population of this White settler society, a point made in global terms in Robert A. Huttenback, *Racism and Empire: White Settlers and Colored Immigrants in the British Self-Gov-*

erning Colonies, 1830–1910 (Ithaca, NY: Cornell University Press 1976). For more specific information see Robin W. Winks, *The Blacks in Canada: A History* (M/New Haven, CT: MQUP/Yale University Press 1971); Ged Martin, 'British Officials and Their Attitude to the Negro Community in Canada, 1833–1861,' *OH* 66/2 (June 1974): 79–88; James W.StG. Walker, *Racial Discrimination in Canada: The Black Experience*, CHA Historical Booklet no. 41 (O: 1985); and Allen P. Stouffer, *The Light of Nature and the Law of God: Antislavery in Ontario, 1833–1877* (K&M: MQUP 1992). A legal case of interest is the subject of Robert C. Reinders, 'The John Anderson Case, 1860–1: A Study in Anglo-Canadian Imperial Relations,' *CHR* 56/4 (Dec. 1975): 393–415, and Patrick Brode, *The Odyssey of John Anderson* (T: OS/UTP 1989). 'Mary Ann Camberton (Cary) Shadd,' *DCB*, vol. 12 (1990), is a rare account of a woman born to a free Black abolitionist family; Shadd taught in interracial schools in Windsor and Chatham and had a close connection with the American antislavery crusader John Brown.

A SENSE OF PLACE

Evident in the preceding citations is an increasing historiographic concern with profiling a sense of place – urban and rural – through recourse to statistical data. While the landmark studies and continuing exploration of place have been concerns of historians, the perspectives and methods of historical geographers have certainly been influential, again, as indicated in the output from this field noted in the last section. The central texts in this historiographic turn grew out of attempts to take particular places and reconstruct their histories through an intensive examination of the routinely generated sources of nineteenth-century public life: the limited surviving material of various census undertakings, urban assessment rolls, land records, and the like. Note, in particular, M.B. Katz, *The People of Hamilton*; D. Gagan, *Hopeful Travellers*; Katz, Michael J. Doucet, and Mark J. Stern, *The Social Organization of Early Industrial Capitalism* (Cambridge, MA: Harvard University Press 1982); and Elizabeth Bloomfield, 'Using the 1871 Census Manuscript Industrial Schedules: A Machine-Readable Source for Social Historians,' *HS/SH* 19/38 (Nov. 1986): 427–41.

The Katz project was notable for the stimulation it gave to Canadian historical methodology, forcing attention away from elites, ideas, and political institutions, and demanding an account of the routine material life experiences of ordinary men, women, and children, whose histories could be partially explored through recourse to routinely generated data. Katz and his colleagues then developed an appreciation of this relatively anonymous experience through insisting that it be understood alongside the socio-economic changes of the mid-to-late nineteenth century, fundamental to which were the development of capitalist relations and the awkward process of class formation in an urban-industrial setting. Never far from sight, moreover, was the central importance of family, and Katz's Hamilton study, like Gagan's of Peel County, moved historians to see more clearly the reciprocal relationships of production and reproduction that would later prove pivotal to an emerging feminist historiography.

Orchestrated by accessibility to the census, these works proved landmarks in scholarship framed by earlier and later texts, such as P.G. Goheen, *Victorian Toronto*, or G.J. Lockwood, *Montague*, but they have not displaced the study of the specificity of place ordered by more traditional and impressionistic methodologies.Useful commentary can be gleaned from edited collections such as J. Petryshyn et al., eds., *Victorian Cobourg*.

Toronto in the Upper Canadian years is treated in three recent volumes. Victor L. Russell, ed., *Forging a Consensus: Historical Essays on Toronto* (T: UTP 1984), contains a number of essays addressing the social history of early Toronto; F.H. Armstrong, *A City in the Making: Progress, People and Perils in Victorian Toronto* (T: Dundurn 1988), draws together most of Armstrong's previously published essays on Toronto; and Chris Raible, *Muddy York Mud: Scandal and Scurrility in Upper Canada* (T: Curiosity House 1993), focuses on a small society's conflicts. Now dated, but still useful, are D.C. Masters, *The Rise of Toronto, 1850–1890* (T: UTP 1947), and G.P. de T. Glazebrook, *The Story of Toronto* (T: UTP 1971). P.G. Goheen, *Victorian Toronto*, prefigured the dovetailing interests of historical geographers and historians that are now central to scholarship. J.M.S. Careless, *Toronto to 1918: An Illustrated History* (T: James Lorimer 1984), devotes half of its pages to the Upper Canadian period, and there is a little to be found in Robert F. Harney, ed., *Gathering Place: Peoples and Neighbourhoods of Toronto, 1834–1945* (T: Multicultural History Society of Ontario 1985). Elmes Henderson, 'Bloor Street, Toronto, and the Village of Yorkville in 1849,' OHS, *Papers and Records* 26 (1930): 445–60, is useful. Toronto also has an abundance of published documents, including the Champlain Society collections edited by E.G. Firth, *The Town of York, 1793–1815: A Collection of Documents of Early Toronto* (T: CS 1962) and *The Town of York, 1815–1834: A Further Collection of Documents of Early Toronto* (T: CS 1966), and Henry Scadding, *Toronto of Old* (1873; repr., ed. F.H. Armstrong, T: Dundurn 1987).

Next to Toronto, Kingston is probably the most-studied locale, with a proliferation of amateur histories and many articles. Some of the most useful appear in G. Tulchinsky, ed., *To Preserve and Defend*. Brian S. Osborne and Donald Swainson, *Kingston: Building on the Past* (Westport, Ont.: Butternut Press 1988), is now the standard narrative account of the city's development, incorporating past writing, and its bibliography is extensive. One can also turn to Richard A. Preston, ed., *Kingston before the War of 1812: A Collection of Documents* (T: CS 1959).

Beyond Toronto and Kingston a scattering of studies exists on other urban centres. Hamilton is particularly well served by the writings of M.B. Katz cited earlier, as well as by Marjorie Freeman Campbell, *A Mountain and a City: The Story of Hamilton* (T: M&S 1966), and John C. Weaver, *Hamilton: An Illustrated History* (T: James Lorimer 1982). For Ottawa/ Nepean see John H. Taylor, *Ottawa: An Illustrated History* (T: James Lorimer 1986), and B.S. Elliott, *The City Beyond: A History of Nepean, Birthplace of Canada's Capital, 1792–1990* (Nepean, Ont.: Corporation of the City of Nepean 1991). Further afield see L.A. Johnson, *History of Guelph, 1827–1927* (Guelph, Ont.: Guelph Historical Society 1977), and F.H. Armstrong and Daniel J. Brock, 'The Rise of London: A Study of Urban Evolution in Nineteenth-Century Southwestern Ontario,' in Armstrong et al., eds., *Aspects of Nineteenth-Century Ontario*. J. Spelt, *Urban Development in South-Central Ontario*, remains helpful in its wide range.

Moving from urban to rural settings, students will find the best township studies focus on the Irish, G.J. Lockwood, *Montague*, and D.H. Akenson, *The Irish in Ontario*, being the most noteworthy. Beyond this, L.A. Johnson, *History of the County of Ontario*, is superb, and William Hugh Graham, *Greenbank: Country Matters in 19th Century Ontario* (Peterborough, Ont.: Broadview Press 1988), is a wonderful evocation of the rural way of life. There are also several interesting collections of documents: E.C. Guillet, ed., *The Valley of the Trent* (T: CS 1957); Florence B. Murray, ed., *Muskoka and Haliburton, 1615–1875: A Collection of Documents* (T: CS 1963); and Elizabeth Arthur, ed., *Thunder Bay District, 1821–1892: A Collection of Documents* (T: CS 1973). These kinds of writings have largely superseded the older county histories written in the late nineteenth and early twentieth centuries, many of which have been reprinted by Mika Publishing of Belleville. J.K. Johnson, 'Upper Canada,' in D.A. Muise, ed., *A Reader's Guide to Canadian History*, vol. 1, lists the most significant of these. Among local studies that deserve mention are F.C. Hamil, *The Valley of the Lower Thames, 1640–1850* (T: UTP 1951; repr. 1973); C.M. Johnston, *The Head of the Lake: A History of Wentworth County* (1958; 2nd ed., Hamilton, Ont.: Wentworth County Council 1967); Gerald E. Boyce, *Historic Hastings* (Belleville, Ont.: Hastings County Council 1967); Johnston, *Brant County:*

A History, 1784–1945 (T: OUP 1967); W.S. Johnston and H.J.M. Johnston, *History of Perth County to 1967* (Stratford, Ont.: Perth County Council 1967); and R. McGillivray and Eric Ross, *A History of Glengarry* (Belleville, Ont.: Mika 1979).

A central influence in the development of the sense of place in Upper Canada is the writing of J.M.S. Careless. Many of his most important studies on this topic and others can be found in his collection *Careless at Work: Selected Canadian Historical Studies* (T: Dundurn 1990), which includes such seminal articles as 'Frontierism, Metropolitanism, and Canadian History' (1954) and 'Some Aspects of Urbanization in Nineteenth-Century Ontario' (1974), as well as a bibliography of his works. More recent still is Careless, *Frontier and Metropolis: Regions, Cities and Identities in Canada before 1914* (T: UTP 1989). For analyses of Careless see C. Berger, *The Writing of Canadian History*; and F.H. Armstrong, 'Maurice Careless,' and Kenneth McNaught, '"Us Old-Type Relativist Historians": The Historical Scholarship of J.M.S. Careless,' in D. Keane and C. Read, eds., *Old Ontario*. More traditional methodologically than M.B. Katz or D. Gagan, and still drawn to features of the staples-Laurentian theses, Careless is attuned to elites rather than to masses in his sense of place. Processes such as class formation and geographical or social mobility appear in Careless as elite, rather than social, phenomena, a hold-over from the Laurentian tendency to see Canada as a 'one-class' society.

SOCIAL DIFFERENTIATION

The Elites

Economic differentiation and the ideological hegemony of a loose tory loyalism culminated in the rough beginnings of a class structure in Upper Canada. At the pinnacle of the social order were various elites or 'compacts,' leading families that combined the attributes of status, wealth, cultural authority, and political rule. Embedded in the distinct regional political economies of an Upper Canada yet to be thoroughly integrated by elaborate transportation and communication networks or drawn into a systematic economic whole, the elites of old Ontario always shared some common features at the same time as they were each shaped in unique ways.

Unfortunately the best treatments of the elites are often in inaccessible unpublished dissertations. Among published sources, J.K. Johnson, *Becoming Prominent: Regional Leadership in Upper Canada, 1791–1841* (K&M: MQUP 1989), is an absolutely indispensable study of 283 Upper Canadians who, through their election to the House of Assembly, left their mark on all aspects of public life. S.J.R. Noel, *Patrons, Clients, Brokers*, is also revealing on the subject of elite formation. F.H. Armstrong, *Handbook of Upper Canadian Chronology*, is invaluable for locating and understanding elite figures. Armstrong has also provided an important statement on ethnicity and the elite in 'Ethnicity in the Formation of the Family Compact: A Case Study in the Growth of the Canadian Establishment,' in Jorgen Dahlie and Tissa Fernando, eds., *Ethnicity, Power and Politics in Canada* (T: Methuen 1981). Some older works are still worth consulting: Robert E. Saunders, 'What Was the Family Compact?' *OH* 49/4 (Dec. 1957): 165–78, reprinted in *Historical Essays*, 1st ed., remains an appropriate interpretive beginning; and D.W.L. Earl, ed., *The Family Compact: Aristocracy or Oligarchy?* (T: CC 1967), is a useful compilation. Interesting, too, is a comparison between D. Gagan, '"Property and Interest,"' *OH* (1978), and H. Pearson Gundy, 'The Family Compact at Work: The Second Heir and Devisee Commission of Upper Canada, 1805–1841,' *OH* 66/3 (Sept. 1974): 129–46.

Among the useful studies of local elites are F.H. Armstrong, 'The Carfrae Family: A Study in Early Toronto Toryism,' *OH* 54/3 (Sept. 1962): 161–81; S.F. Wise, 'Tory Factionalism: Kingston Elections and Upper Canadian Politics, 1820–1836,' *OH* 57/4 (Dec. 1965): 205–25, reprinted in his *God's Peculiar Peoples*; M.S. Cross, 'The Age of Gentility: The Formation of an Aristocracy in the Ottawa Valley,' CHA *HP* (1967): 105–17; Elva M. Richards, 'The Joneses of Brockville and the Family Compact,' *OH* 60/4 (Dec. 1968): 169–84; R.J. Burns, 'God's Chosen People: The Origins of Toronto Society, 1793–1818,' CHA *HP* (1973): 213–28; M.B. Katz, 'The Entrepreneurial Class in a Canadian City: The Mid-Nineteenth Century,' *Journal of Social History* 8/2 (Winter 1975): 1–29, reprinted in J.M. Bumsted, ed., *Interpreting Canada's Past*, vol. 1, 1st ed.; J.K. Johnson, 'The U.C. Club and the Upper Canadian Elite, 1837–1840,' *OH* 69/3 (Sept. 1977): 151–68; Armstrong, 'The Oligarchy of the Western District of Upper Canada, 1788–1841,' CHA *HP* (1977): 87–102; C. Read, 'The London District Oligarchy in the Rebellion Era,' *OH* 72/4 (Dec. 1980): 195–209; Ian Macpherson, *Matters of Loyalty: The Buells of Brockville, 1830–1850* (Belleville, Ont.: Mika 1981); and M.J. Doucet and J.C. Weaver, 'Town Fathers and Urban Continuity: The Roots of Community Power and Physical Form in Hamilton, Upper Canada in the 1830s,' *Urban History Review* 13/2 (Oct. 1984): 75–90, reprinted in *Historical Essays*, 2nd ed.

In the Upper Canadian historiography elite formation is often approached biographically. Here the starting-point is the *DCB*. J.K. Johnson, *Becoming Prominent*, conveniently provides an appendix of the 283 prominent figures he has studied, designating the approximately one-third of these who have been treated in the *DCB*. Among the major biographical studies of elite figures the most noteworthy are S.F. Wise, 'The Rise of Christopher Hagerman,' *Historic Kingston* 14 (1966): 12–23, reprinted in his *God's Peculiar Peoples*; R. Alan Douglas, ed., *John Prince, 1796–1870: A Collection of Documents* (T: CS 1980); Donald R. Beer, *Sir Allan Napier MacNab* (Hamilton, Ont.: Dictionary of Hamilton Biography 1984); and P. Brode, *Sir John Beverley Robinson: Bone and Sinew of the Compact* (T: OS/UTP 1984). Older studies of leading Upper Canadian politicians who went on to be influential in the later development of Ontario and Canada as a whole include D.G. Creighton, *John A. Macdonald*, vol. 1, *The Young Politician* (T: MAC 1952); J.M.S. Careless, *Brown of 'The Globe,'* 2 vols. (T: MAC 1959–63); Bruce W. Hodgins, *John Sandfield Macdonald, 1812–1872* (T: UTP 1971); and Joseph Schull, *Edward Blake*, vol. 1, *The Man of the Other Way, 1833–1881* (T: MAC 1975). The assembled biographies of Upper Canadian government leaders is J.M.S. Careless, ed., *The Pre-Confederation Premiers: Ontario Government Leaders, 1841–1867* (T: UTP 1980).

Many other biographies of elite figures exist, but few are successful. Francis Bond Head, for instance, is poorly treated in S.W. Jackman, *Galloping Head* (L: Phoenix House 1958), while W.H. Graham, *The Tiger of Canada West* (T: Clarke, Irwin 1962), is structured around William Dunlop's eccentricities. Students are better directed to C.F. Klinck's collection of Dunlop's writings, *William 'Tiger' Dunlop, 'Blackwoodian Backwoodsman': Essays by and about Dunlop* (T: RP 1958). The irascible Colonel Thomas Talbot is ironically best served, although he too cries out for new interpretive treatment. Nevertheless, Charles Oakes Zaccheus Ermatinger, *The Talbot Regime – or the First Half Century of the Talbot Settlement* (St Thomas, Ont.: Municipal World 1904), and F.C. Hamil, *Lake Erie Baron*, provide readers with a great deal to grapple with. The closing bibliography of *Historical Essays*, 2nd ed., lists other dated treatments of elite figures for those who truly remain gluttons for biographical punishments.

There are some family histories that deal with elite figures, including D. Gagan, *The Denison Family of Toronto, 1792–1925* (T: UTP 1973). The study of the reform-oriented patrician Baldwins, William Warren and his son Robert, by R.M. Baldwin and Joyce Baldwin, *The Baldwins and the Great Experiment* (Don Mills, Ont.: Longmans 1969), is less useful as are Hamilton Baird Timothy, *The Galts: A Canadian Odyssey*, vol. 1, *John Galt, 1779–1839* (T: M&S 1977); and Anne Wilkinson, *Lions in the Way: A Discursive History of the Oslers* (T: MAC 1956).

High culture was often the terrain of the elite. Carol D. Lowrey charts this relationship in 'The Society of Artists and Amateurs, 1834: Toronto's First Art Exhibition and Its Antecedents,' and her 'The Toronto Society of Arts, 1847–8: Patriotism and the Pursuit of Culture in Canada West,' *Revue de l'art canadienne/Canadian Art Review* 8 (1981): 99–136; 12 (1985): 3–44. Similar connections can be found in D. Reid, *A Concise History of Canadian Painting* (1973; 2nd ed., T: OUP 1988), and Sandra Paikowsky, 'Landscape Painting in Canada,' in K.G. Pryke and Walter C. Soderlund, eds., *Profiles of Canada* (T: CCP 1992). A hint of the elite's role in early sport is given in Alan Metcalfe, *Canada Learns to Play: The Emergence of Organized Sport, 1807–1914* (T: M&S 1987).

Artisans and Labourers

One of the most vibrant developments in recent Canadian historiography is the emergence of working-class history. But the bulk of published work has focused on the late nineteenth and early twentieth centuries, when a modern working class was in the making and trade unions, as the foundation of the labour movement, were being established. General surveys of Canadian labour are weak on Upper Canada, examples being Craig Heron, *The Canadian Labour Movement: A Short History* (T: James Lorimer 1989), and Desmond Morton, *Working People: An Illustrated History of the Canadian Labour Movement* (T: Summerhill 1990). Eugene Forsey, *Trade Unions in Canada, 1812–1902* (T: UTP 1982), is encyclopedic in its content and organization, for which he provides a précis in *The Canadian Labour Movement, 1812–1902*, CHA Historical Booklet no. 27 (O: 1974). Stephen Langdon, *The Emergence of the Canadian Working Class Movement, 1845–1875* (T: New Hogtown Press 1975), gives a brief but more relevant analysis. M.S. Cross, ed., *The Workingman in the Nineteenth Century* (T: OUP 1974), remains a useful documentary collection. H.C. Pentland, *Labour and Capital in Canada*, generally elicits strong negative views, but it is still essential reading. Examples of Pentland bashing include the wild and wonderful D.H. Akenson, 'H. Clare Pentland, the Irish, and the New Canadian Social History,' in his *Being Had: Historians, Evidence, and the Irish in North America* (Port Credit, Ont.: P.D. Meany 1985), and, in Des Morton's words, 'for those who enjoy theological disputation,' A. Greer, 'Wage Labour and the Transition to Capitalism: A Critique of Pentland,' *L/LT* 15 (Spring 1985): 7–22. The only general survey of Canadian workers that addresses the Upper Canadian experience substantively, but again in ways somewhat controversial, is B.D. Palmer, *Working-Class Experience: Rethinking the History of Canadian Labour, 1800–1991* (2nd ed., T: M&S 1992), although the original edition of this text (T: Butterworth 1983) contains some material and appendices (on strikes and riots for instance) deleted from the revised version. Palmer, 'Labour Protest and Organization in Nineteenth-Century Canada, 1820–1890,' *L/LT* 20 (Fall 1987): 61–83, presents material that will appear in cartographic form in *HAC*, vol. 2, plate 57.

Most studies of early Upper Canadian workers have focused on either the independent commodity-producing artisans or the rough unskilled labourers, especially canal navvies and timber workers. Treatments of artisans are especially important conceptually for they point to the existence of independent commodity production and proto-industrialization, calling into question the one-sided emphases of the staples-Laurentian theses, which are capable of obscuring the producing classes in brief allusion to canal labourers and timber workers as mere appendages in the essential business of trade. See F.H. Armstrong, 'Reformer as Capitalist: William Lyon Mackenzie and the Printers' Strike of 1836,' *OH* 59/4 (Dec. 1967): 187–96; M.S. Cross, 'The Shiners' War: Social Violence in the Ottawa Valley in the 1830s,' *CHR* 54/1 (Mar. 1973): 1–26; G.S. Kealey, 'Artisans Respond to Industrialism: Shoemakers, Shoe Factories and the Knights of St. Crispin in Toronto,' CHA *HP* (1973): 137–57; B.D. Palmer, 'Kingston Mechanics and the Rise of the Penitentiary, 1833–1836,' *HS/SH* 13/25 (May 1980): 7–32; R. Bleasdale, 'Class Conflict on the Canals of Upper Canada in the 1840s,' *L/LT* 7 (Spring 1981): 9–39, reprinted in *Historical Essays*, 2nd ed.; L.A. Johnson, 'Independent Commodity Production: Mode of Production or Capitalist Class Formation?' *Studies in Political Economy* 6 (Autumn 1981): 93–112; William N.T. Wylie, 'Poverty, Distress, and Disease: Labour and the Construction of the Rideau Canal, 1826–32,' *L/LT* 11 (Spring 1983): 7–29; J. Parr, 'Hired Men: Ontario Agricultural Wage Labour in Historical Perspective,' *L/LT* 15 (Spring 1985): 91–103; Kealey, 'Work Control, the Labour Process, and Nineteenth-Century Canadian Printers,' in C. Heron and Robert Storey, eds., *On the Job: Confronting the Labour Process in Canada* (K&M: MQUP 1986); Wylie, 'The Blacksmith in Upper Canada, 1784–1850: A Study of Technology, Culture and Power,' *CPRH*, vol. 7 (1990); and Peter Bischoff, '"Traveling the Country 'Round": migrations et syndicalisme chez les mouleurs de l'Ontario et du Québec membres de l'*Iron Molders Union of North America*, 1860 à 1892,' *JCHA* 1 (1990): 37–71. The work of A.G. Darroch has been especially important in demonstrating the persistence of small producers and petty property alongside proletarianization: 'Early Industrialization and Inequality in Toronto, 1861–1899,' *L/LT* 11 (Spring 1983): 31–61; 'Occupational Structure, Assessed Wealth and Homeowning during Toronto's Early Industrialization, 1861–1899,' *HS/SH* 16/32 (Nov. 1983): 381–410; and 'Class in Nine-teenth-Century, Central Ontario: A Reassessment of the Crisis and Demise of Small Producers during Early Industrialization, 1861–1871,' *Canadian Journal of Sociology* 13/1–2 (Winter–Spring 1988): 49–71.

Early attempts to address the social and cultural experience of Upper Canadian workers included M.J. Doucet, 'Working Class Housing in a Small Nineteenth Century Canadian City: Hamilton, Ontario, 1852–1881,' and Harvey J. Graff, 'Respected and Profitable Labour: Literacy, Jobs and the Working Class in the Nineteenth Century,' both in G.S. Kealey and Peter Warrian, eds., *Essays in Working Class History* (T: M&S 1976). Other noteworthy essays are B.D. Palmer, 'Discordant Music: Charivaris and Whitecapping in Nineteenth-Century North America,' *L/LT* 3 (1978): 5–62; and P. Craven and T. Traves, 'Dimensions of Paternalism: Discipline and Culture in Canadian Railway Operations in the 1850s,' in C. Heron and R. Storey, eds., *On the Job*. For an attempt to address the question of class organization, state repression, and migration, albeit briefly, see Allen G. Talbot, 'In Memory of the Tolpuddle Martyrs,' *OH* 62/1 (Mar. 1970): 65–9.

Some of the more exciting recent writing focuses on the law and the reg-ulatory order. Eric Tucker, '"That Indefinite Area of Toleration": Criminal Conspiracy and Trade Unions in Ontario, 1837–77,' *L/LT* 27 (Spring 1991): 15–54, is of fundamental importance, but see also his *Administering Danger in the Workplace: The Law and Politics of Occupational Health and Safety Regulation in Ontario, 1850–1914* (T: UTP 1990). Other relevant works are P. Craven, 'The Law of Master and Servant in Mid-Nineteenth-Century Ontario,' in David H. Flaherty, ed., *Essays in the History of Canadian Law*, vol. 1 (T: OS/UTP 1981); 'Workers' Conspiracies in Toronto, 1854–72,' *L/LT* 14 (Fall 1984): 49–70; and 'The Meaning of Misadventure: The Bap-tiste Creek Railway Disaster of 1854 and Its Aftermath,' in R. Hall et al., eds., *Patterns of the Past*; as well as Bob Russell, *Back to Work: Labour, State, and Industrial Relations in Canada* (Scarborough, Ont.: Nelson 1990), and Barry Wright, 'Sedition in Upper Canada: Contested Legality,' *L/LT* 29 (Spring 1992): 7–57.

Gender and Women

There is very little written on the construction of gender identity in Upper Canada, although this will undoubtedly be a topic of considerable future research. For the most part the Upper Canadian literature reflects a con-cern with elite and literary women. But there are abundant signs that sexuality, domestic relations, and the gendered meaning of various forms of regulation will broaden the content of Upper Canadian studies of gender. For now, however, the literature set within the regional and chronological boundaries of Upper Canada is generally preliminary, the beginnings of a much-needed history of women that will lead to a more wide-ranging appreciation of gender relations.

For a general statement see Joan Wallach Scott, *Gender and the Politics of History* (NY: Columbia University Press 1988), Alison Prentice et al., *Canadian Women: A History* (T: HBJ 1988), and Lykke de la Cour, Cecilia Morgan, and Mariana Valverde, 'Gender Regulation and State Formation in Nineteenth-Century Canada,' in A. Greer and I. Radforth, eds., *Colonial Leviathan*. Note especially D. Swainson, 'Schuyler Shibley and the Underside of Victorian Ontario,' *OH* 65/1 (Mar. 1973): 51–60; G. Martin, 'Sir Francis Bond Head: The Private Side of a Lieutenant-Governor,' *OH* 73/3 (Sept. 1981): 145–70; and M.S. Cross and Robert L. Fraser, '"The Waste That Lies before Me": The Public and Private Worlds of Robert Baldwin," CHA *HP* (1983): 164–83. Historians are unduly and universally impatient with Gary Kinsman, *The Regulation of Desire: Sexuality in Canada* (M: Black Rose 1987), but it can be a stimulating and provocative introduction to meanings and conceptions long suppressed, as well as being the most accessible source on gay history. Unfortunately, the one specific study that should open our interpretive eyes is a classic example of how not to write the history of gendered experience, namely, W. Peter Ward, *Courtship, Love, and Marriage in Nineteenth-Century English Canada* (K&M: MQUP 1990). Readers may prefer the abbreviated and more focused studies from Ward, articles that also have the virtue of being less purposively contentious, for example, 'Unwed Motherhood in Nineteenth-Century English Canada,' CHA *HP* (1981): 34–56, and 'Courtship and Social Space in Nineteenth-Century English Canada,' *CHR* 68/1 (Mar. 1987): 35–62.

Statements that attempt to address the gendered nature of the political economy of Upper Canada include L.A. Johnson, 'The Political Economy of Ontario Women in the Nineteenth Century,' in Janice Acton et al., eds., *Women at Work: Ontario, 1850–1930* (T: Women's Press 1974); J. Errington, 'Pioneers and Suffragists,' in Sandra Burt et al., eds., *Changing Patterns: Women in Canada* (T: M&S 1988); and Marjorie Griffin Cohen, *Women's Work, Markets, and Economic Development in Nineteenth-Century Ontario* (T: UTP 1988). Two documentary collections are also useful: R. Cook and Wendy Mitchinson, eds., *The Proper Sphere: Woman's Place in Canadian Society* (T: OUP 1976); and Beth Light and A. Prentice, eds., *Pioneer and Gen-*

tlewomen of British North America, 1713–1867 (T: New Hogtown Press 1980).

As the site of the regulation of gender relations, law is now one of the most-studied realms. The writing of Constance Backhouse is central here, specifically her many articles, which underscore the extent to which law reinforced the generalized power of men over women and contributed to a pervasive process of gender subordination. Among the most relevant are 'Shifting Patterns in Nineteenth-Century Canadian Custody Law,' in D.H. Flaherty, ed., *Essays in the History of Canadian Law*, vol. 1; 'Nineteenth-Century Canadian Rape Law, 1800–92,' in Flaherty, ed., *Essays in the History of Canadian Law*, vol. 2 (T: OS/UTP 1983); 'Nineteenth-Century Canadian Prostitution Law: Reflection of a Discriminating Society,' *HS/SH* 18/36 (Nov. 1985): 387–423; 'The Tort of Seduction: Fathers and Daughters in Nineteenth Century Canada,' *Dalhousie Law Journal* 10/1 (June 1986): 45–80; 'Pure Patriarchy: Nineteenth-Century Canadian Marriage,' *McGill Law Journal* 31/2 (1986): 264–312; and 'Married Women's Property Law in Nineteenth-Century Canada,' *Law and History Review* 6/2 (Fall 1988): 211–57, reprinted in Bettina Bradbury, ed., *Canadian Family History: Selected Readings* (T: CCP 1992). These articles and others, with revisions, are incorporated in Backhouse, *Petticoats and Prejudice: Women and Law in Nineteenth-Century Canada* (T: OS/Women's Press 1991), which also has a useful bibliography.

In addition to the work of Backhouse on women and the law, see Ruth A. Olson, 'Rape – An "Un-Victorian" Aspect of Life in Upper Canada,' *OH* 68/2 (June 1976): 75–9; Graham Parker, 'The Legal Regulation of Sexual Activity and the Protection of Females,' *Osgoode Hall Law Journal* 21/2 (Oct. 1983): 187–244; and Christine Ball, 'Female Sexual Ideologies in Mid to Later Nineteenth-Century Canada,' *Canadian Journal of Women and the Law* 1/2 (1986): 324–38. Finally, for the highly gendered customary and ritualistic regulatory practices that reached beyond law, turn to Josephine Phelan, 'The Tar and Feather Case, Gore Assizes, August 1827,' *OH* 68/1 (Mar. 1976): 17–23, and B.D. Palmer, 'Discordant Music,' *L/LT* (1978).

Studies of elite women and gentlewomen writers include three items by Katherine M.J. McKenna, 'Anne Powell and the Early York Elite,' in S.F. Wise et al., eds., *'None Was Ever Better ...'*; 'Option for Elite Women in Early Upper Canadian Society: The Case of the Powell Family,' in *Historical Essays*, 2nd ed.; and 'The Role of Women in the Establishment of Social Status in Early Upper Canada,' *OH* 83/3 (Sept. 1990): 179–206; and two by Janice Potter, 'Patriarchy and Paternalism: The Case of Eastern Ontario Loyalist Women,' *OH* 81/1 (Mar. 1989): 3–24, reprinted in Angus D. Gilbert et al., eds., *Reappraisals in Canadian History*, vol. 1, *Pre-Confederation* (Scarborough, Ont.: PH 1993); and, now Potter-MacKinnon, *While the Women Only Wept: Loyalist Refugee Women in Eastern Ontario* (K&M: MQUP 1993), which explains how women's considerable contributions as Loyalists have become obscured in the historical record. Also see Elizabeth Hopkins, 'A Prison-House for Prosperity: The Immigrant Experience of the Nineteenth Century Upper-Class British Woman,' in J. Burnet, ed., *Looking into My Sister's Eyes: An Exploration in Women's History* (T: Multicultural History Society of Ontario 1986), reprinted in J.M. Bumsted, ed., *Interpreting Canada's Past*, vol. 1, *Pre-Confederation* (2nd ed., T: OUP 1993).

A small industry has arisen around the axis of Moodie, Traill, and Jameson: see, for example, George Henry Needler, *Otonabee Pioneers: The Story of the Stewarts, the Stricklands, the Traills, and the Moodies* (T: Burns and MacEachern 1953); Clara Thomas, *Love and Work Enough: The Life of Anna Jameson* (T: UTP 1967); A.Y. Morris, *Gentle Pioneers*; Robin Mathews, 'Susanna Moodie, Pink Toryism, and Nineteenth Century Ideas of Canadian Identity,' *JCS* 10/3 (Aug. 1975): 3–15; and Marion Fowler, *The Embroidered Tent: Five Gentlewomen in Early Canada* (T: Anansi 1982). To these must now be added Helen M. Buss, *Mapping Ourselves: Canadian Women's Autobiography* (K&M: MQUP 1993).

Other studies of importance are C. Lesley Biggs, 'The Case of the Missing Midwives: A History of Midwifery in Ontario from 1795–1900,' *OH* 75/1 (Mar. 1983): 21–35; and the recent writing of W. Mitchinson which, although focused on the later nineteenth-century years, does often touch on the Upper Canada period: 'Historical Attitudes toward Women and Childbirth,' *Atlantis* 4/2 (Spring 1979): 13–34; 'A Medical Debate in Nineteenth-Century English Canada: Ovariotomies,' *HS/SH* 17/33 (May 1984): 133–47; and 'Hysteria and Insanity in Women: A Nineteenth-Century Canadian Perspective,' *JCS* 21/3 (Fall 1986): 87–105. Much of this work is contained in Mitchinson, *The Nature of Their Bodies: Women and Their Doctors in Victorian Canada* (T: UTP 1991), although this book accentuates the post-Confederation period. D.H. Akenson, *At Face Value: The Life and Times of Eliza McCormack/John White* (K&M: MQUP 1990), is a joke. For those who have not yet realized it, they've been had. Gender relations and Native peoples are touched on in Gretchen Green, 'Molly Brant, Catharine Brant, and Their Daughters: A Study in Colonial Acculturation,' *OH* 81/3 (Sept. 1989): 235–50, and Sylvia Van Kirk, *'Many Tender Ties': Women in Fur-Trade Society in Western Canada, 1670–1870* (W: Watson and Dwyer 1980), which, although dealing mainly with the Northwest, remains insightful.

The centrality of gender to the emerging forms of regulation and state formation dictates that those concerned with gender identity in general and women in particular turn to other sections of this bibliography to explore the connections linking the women, men, and social structures in the Upper Canada past. As will be evident in the next section, the question of gender bears directly on a wide range of issues, from schooling to social welfare.

REGULATION AND THE SOCIAL ORDER

Social differentiation conditioned a climate in which emerging antagonisms and tensions demanded attention. The history of a hierarchically ordered society thus develops, over the course of the Upper Canadian years, as an incremental movement toward social regulation, evident in the rise of specific social 'problems' such as trade unions, the poor, crime, and disorder, and the consequent attempts to address the seeming breakdown of harmony and a sense of place (as an understanding of a particular social station within a demarcated social space) with measures that were both institutional and cultural.

H.C. Pentland, *Labour and Capital in Canada*, early called attention to the role of Irish disorder (on the canals and in the countryside) as a factor in the preliminary consolidation of the state and its apparatus of coercion. See, as well, J.K. Johnson, 'Colonel James Fitzgibbon and the Suppression of Irish Riots in Upper Canada,' *OH* 58/3 (Sept. 1966): 139–55. But the use of force in the emerging regulatory order was not unrelated to other, more subtle, modes of constructing and maintaining hegemony. M.B. Katz provides an introduction to the general problem of order directly relevant to Upper Canada in 'The Origins of the Institutional State,' *Marxist Perspectives* 4 (Winter 1978): 6–22. The emerging regulatory order, besides addressing the issues of sexuality and working-class trade unionism, alluded to previously, also necessarily had to deal with poverty, crime, disease, and education, none of which could be entirely separated from processes of class and gender.

Poverty and poor relief can be approached first through the introductory chapters in such broad synthetic accounts of social welfare as Richard B. Splane, *Social Welfare in Ontario, 1791–1893* (T: UTP 1965), and Dennis Guest, *The Emergence of Social Security in Canada* (1980; 2nd ed., V: UBCP 1985). Thereafter the literature is specialized and diverse. Especially useful are Stephen A. Speisman, 'Munificent Parsons and Municipal Parsimony: Voluntary *vs* Public Poor Relief in Nineteenth Century Toronto,' *OH* 65/1 (Mar. 1973): 33–49; Judith Fingard, 'The Winter's Tale: The Seasonal Contours of Pre-Industrial Poverty in British North America, 1815–1860,'

CHA *HP* (1974): 65–94; Patricia Malcolmson, 'The Poor in Kingston, 1815–1850,' in G. Tulchinsky, ed., *To Preserve and Defend*; Dennis Carter-Edwards, 'Cobourg: A Nineteenth-Century Response to the "Worthy" Poor,' in J. Petryshyn et al., eds., *Victorian Cobourg*; Joey Noble, '"Classifying" the Poor: Toronto Charities, 1850–1880,' *Studies in Political Economy* 2 (Autumn 1979): 109–28; Rainer Baehre, 'Paupers and Poor Relief in Upper Canada,' CHA *HP* (1981): 57–80; Baehre, 'Pauper Emigration to Upper Canada in the 1830s,' *HS/SH* 14/28 (Nov. 1981): 339–67; Patricia T. Rooke and R.L. Schnell, 'Childhood and Charity in Nineteenth-Century British North America,' *HS/SH* 15/29 (May 1982): 157–79, reprinted in A.D. Gilbert et al., eds., *Reappraisals in Canadian History*, vol. 1; and Rooke and Schnell, *Discarding the Asylum: From Child Rescue to the Welfare State in English-Canada (1800–1950)* (Lanham, MD: University Press of America 1983).

The literature on crime is now expanding. None interested in this area should ignore Peter Linebaugh, *The London Hanged: Crime and Civil Society in the Eighteenth Century* (Cambridge, Eng.: Cambridge University Press 1992). Canadian studies include J. Jerald Bellomo, 'Upper Canadian Attitudes towards Crime and Punishment,' *OH* 64/1 (Mar. 1972): 11–26; Susan E. Houston, 'Victorian Origins of Juvenile Delinquency: A Canadian Experience,' *History of Education Quarterly* 12/3 (Fall 1972): 254–80; J.M. Beattie, *Attitudes towards Crime and Punishment in Upper Canada, 1830–1850: A Documentary Study* (T: Centre of Criminology, University of Toronto 1977); R. Baehre, 'Origins of the Penitentiary System in Upper Canada,' *OH* 69/3 (Sept. 1977): 185–207; H.J. Graff, 'Crime and Punishment in the Nineteenth Century: A New Look at the Criminal,' *Journal of Interdisciplinary History* 7/3 (Winter 1977): 477–91; C. James Taylor, 'The Kingston, Ontario Penitentiary and Moral Architecture,' *HS/SH* 12/24 (Nov. 1979): 385–408; B.D. Palmer, 'Kingston Mechanics and the Rise of the Penitentiary,' *HS/SH* (1980); John D. Blackwell, 'Crime in the London District, 1828–1837: A Case Study of the Effect of the 1833 Reform in Upper Canadian Penal Law,' *Queen's Law Journal* 6 (1981): 528–59, reprinted in *Historical Essays*, 2nd ed.; Dennis Curtis et al., *Kingston Penitentiary: The First Hundred and Fifty Years, 1835–1985* (O: Correctional Service of Canada 1985); and J.C. Weaver, 'Crime, Public Order, and Repression: The Gore District in Upheaval, 1832–1851,' *OH* 78/3 (Sept. 1986): 175–207.

The study of crime is, of course, intricately related to the development and place of law, a subject addressed here in an earlier section. Among the more interesting of the new legal scholars is P. Romney, whose *Mr. Attorney: The Attorney General for Ontario in Court, Cabinet, and Legislature, 1791–*

1899 (T: OS/UTP 1986) and 'From the Rule of Law to Responsible Government: Ontario Political Culture and the Origins of Canadian Statism,' CHA *HP* (1988): 86–119, are particularly valuable in their placing of legal developments in a wider context than is normally done in histories of case law. The first two volumes of *Essays in the History of Canadian Law*, edited by D.H. Flaherty, contain a number of important studies. From the first volume, for example, see R.C.B. Risk, 'The Law and the Economy in Mid-Nineteenth-Century Ontario: A Perspective,' and J.D. Blackwell, 'William Hume Blake and the Judicature Acts of 1849: The Process of Legal Reform at Mid-Century in Upper Canada'; and, from the second, W.N.T. Wylie, 'Instruments of Commerce and Authority: The Civil Courts in Upper Canada, 1789–1812.' Finally, many of the papers in Carol Wilton, ed., *Essays in the History of Canadian Law*, vol. 4, *Beyond the Law: Lawyers and Business in Canada, 1830 to 1930* (T: OS/UTP 1990), are relevant. R.L. Fraser, ed., *Provincial Justice: Upper Canadian Legal Portraits from the 'Dictionary of Canadian Biography'* (T: OS/UTP 1992), assembles *DCB* entries relating to jurists, lawyers, and those accused of notable crimes.

Most of the literature relating to health and disease is rather dated, as indicated in Charles M. Godfrey, *Medicine for Ontario* (Belleville, Ont.: Mika 1979). But the recent edited collection of W. Mitchinson and Janice Dickin McGinnis, *Essays in the History of Canadian Medicine* (T: M&S 1988), contains essays indicative of new scholarly concerns and orientations which place health and disease firmly in a broad societal context. See, for example, Mitchinson, 'Reasons for Committal to a Mid-Nineteenth-Century Ontario Insane Asylum: The Case of Toronto,' and Heather MacDougall, 'Public Health and the "Sanitary" Idea in Toronto, 1866–1890.' Moreover, this collection has a useful bibliography. Still of value, too, is S.E.D. Shortt, ed., *Medicine in Canadian Society: Historical Perspectives* (M: MQUP 1981), especially for Shortt's survey of the literature, 'Antiquarians and Amateurs: Reflections on the Writing of Medical History of Canada.' Other surveys include Shortt, 'The New Social History of Medicine: Some Implications for Research,' *Archivaria* 10 (Summer 1980): 5–22, and Mitchinson, 'Canadian Medical History: Diagnosis and Prognosis,' *Acadiensis* 12/1 (Autumn 1982): 125–32. No issue looms larger in this field than the cholera epidemics, covered in C.M. Godfrey, *The Cholera Epidemics in Upper Canada, 1832–1866* (T: Seccombe House 1968), now superseded by Geoffrey Bilson, *A Darkened House: Cholera in Nineteenth-Century Canada* (T: UTP 1980). Studies of hospitals include Margaret Angus, *Kingston General Hospital: A Social and Institutional History* (M: MQUP 1973), W.G. Cosbie, *The Toronto General Hospital, 1819–1965: A Chronicle* (T: MAC 1975), and S.E.D.

Shortt, 'The Canadian Hospital in the Nineteenth Century: An Historio-graphic Lament,' *JCS* 18/4 (Winter 1983-4): 3-14. Other useful discussions on diverse topics are M. Angus, 'Health, Emigration and Welfare in Kingston, 1820-1840,' in D. Swainson, ed., *Oliver Mowat's Ontario* (T: MAC 1972); S.E.D. Shortt, 'Physicians, Science, and Status: Issues in the Professionalization of Anglo-American Medicine in the Nineteenth Century,' *Medical History* 27/1 (Jan. 1983): 51-68; W.N.T. Wylie, 'Poverty, Distress, and Disease,' *L/LT* (1983); and R.D. Gidney and W.P.J. Millar, 'The Origins of Organized Medicine in Ontario, 1850-1869,' in Charles G. Roland, ed., *Health, Disease and Medicine: Essays in Canadian History* (T: Hannah Institute for the History of Medicine 1984). Note, as well, Thomas E. Brown, 'The Origins of the Asylum in Upper Canada, 1830-1839,' *Canadian Bulletin of Medical History* 1/1 (Summer 1984): 27-58; Brown, 'Foucault Plus Twenty: On Writing the History of Canadian Psychiatry in the 1980s,' *Canadian Bulletin of Medical History* 2/1 (Summer 1985): 23-49; and, although extending beyond the period, S.E.D. Shortt, *Victorian Lunacy: Richard M. Bucke and the Practice of Late Nineteenth-Century Psychiatry* (NY: Cambridge University Press 1986).

The realm of regulation most studied is that of education, where two decades of scholarship have provided a proliferation of monographs. A. Prentice, *The School Promoters: Education and Social Class in Mid-Nineteenth Century Upper Canada* (T: M&S 1977), early staked out an approach to education that stressed its aim as correcting the tendency to social disorder arising out of the mid-century transition to capitalism and its process of class formation. In partnership with S.E. Houston, Prentice also edited a useful collection of documents, *Family, School and Society in Nineteenth-Century Canada* (T: OUP 1975), and produced the survey *Schooling and Scholars in Nineteenth-Century Ontario* (T: UTP 1988). This burgeoning scholarship on Upper Canadian education was prefaced by two valuable collections of essays, Paul H. Mattingly and M.B. Katz, eds., *Education and Social Change: Themes from Ontario's Past* (NY: New York University Press 1975), and Neil McDonald and Alf Chaiton, eds., *Egerton Ryerson and His Times* (T: MAC 1978). Chad Gaffield, 'Children, Schooling, and Family Reproduction in Nineteenth-Century Ontario,' *CHR* 72/2 (June 1991): 157-91, relates education and wider socio-economic trends.

Bruce Curtis, *Building the Educational State: Canada West, 1836-1871* (Sussex/London, Ont.: Falmer Press/Althouse Press 1988) and *True Government by Choice Men? Inspection, Education, and State Formation in Canada West* (T: UTP 1992), extend beyond A. Prentice's concern with social order and control to address the extent to which the new state bureaucracies and appointed experts aligned with educational reform were part of a larger process of state formation and political centralization in the 1840s. 'Responsible government' thus ironically resulted, not in the 'people' being granted more governmental authority, but in the state concentrating its powers. Aside from Curtis's books, the following selected articles are also indicative of his approach: 'Preconditions of the Canadian State: Educational Reform and the Construction of a Public in Upper Canada, 1837–1846,' *Studies in Political Economy* 10 (Winter 1983): 99–121, reprinted in *Historical Essays*, 2nd ed.; 'Capitalist Development and Educational Reform: Comparative Material from England, Ireland and Upper Canada to 1850,' *Theory and Society* 13/1 (Jan. 1984): 41–68; and 'Policing Pedagogical Space: "Voluntary" School Reform and Moral Regulation,' *Canadian Journal of Sociology* 13/3 (Summer 1988): 283–304. C. Gaffield, *Language, Schooling, and Cultural Conflict: The Origins of the French-Language Controversy in Ontario* (K&M: MQUP 1987), places education within the perennial Canadian question of French-English relations.

More institutional and less theoretical than Curtis is R.D. Gidney: 'The Rev. Robert Murray: Ontario's First Superintendent of Schools,' *OH* 43/4 (Dec. 1971): 191–204; 'Upper Canadian Public Opinion and Common School Improvement in the 1830s,' *HS/SH* 5/9 (Apr. 1972): 48–60; 'Centralization and Education: The Origins of an Ontario Tradition,' *JCS* 7/4 (Nov. 1972): 33–48; and 'Making Nineteenth-Century School Systems: The Upper Canadian Experience and Its Relevance to English Historiography,' *History of Education* 9/2 (June 1980): 101–16. He also published with D.A. Lawr: 'Egerton Ryerson and the Origins of the Ontario Secondary School,' *CHR* 60/4 (Dec. 1979): 442–65; 'Who Ran the Schools? Local Influence on Educational Policy in Nineteenth-Century Ontario,' *OH* 72/3 (Sept. 1980): 131–43; and 'Bureaucracy vs. Community? The Origins of Bureaucratic Procedure in the Upper Canadian School System,' *Journal of Social History* 13/3 (Spring 1981): 438–57, reprinted in *Historical Essays*, 2nd ed.; and with W.P.J. Millar, 'Rural Schools and the Decline of Community Control in Nineteenth-Century Ontario,' Fourth Annual Agricultural History of Ontario Seminar, *Proceedings* (1979); and 'From Voluntarism to State Schooling: The Creation of the Public School System in Ontario,' *CHR* 66/4 (Dec. 1985): 443–73.

Other revisionist articles of note are S.E. Houston, 'Politics, Schools and Social Change in Upper Canada,' *CHR* 53/3 (Sept. 1972): 249–71; J.D. Purdy, 'The English Public School Tradition in Nineteenth-Century Ontario,' and J.D. Wilson, 'The Teacher in Early Ontario,' both in F.H. Armstrong et al., eds., *Aspects of Nineteenth-Century Ontario*; Wilson, '"No

Blanket to Be Worn in School,"' *HS/SH* (1974); D. Calman, 'Postponed Progress: Cobourg Common Schools, 1850–1871,' in J. Petryshyn et al., eds., *Victorian Cobourg*; Marion Royce, 'Education for Girls in Quaker Schools in Ontario,' *Atlantis* 3/1 (Fall 1977): 181–92; Royce, 'Methodism and the Education of Women in Nineteenth Century Ontario,' *Atlantis* 3/2 (Spring 1978): 131–43; James H. Love, 'Cultural Survival and Social Control: The Development of a Curriculum for Upper Canada's Common Schools in 1846,' *HS/SH* 15/30 (Nov. 1982): 357–82; G. Blaine Baker, 'Legal Education in Upper Canada, 1785–1889: The Law Society as Educator,' in D.H. Flaherty, ed., *Essays in the History of Canadian Law*, vol. 2; F.H. Armstrong, 'John Strachan, Schoolmaster, and the Evolution of the Elite in Upper Canada/Ontario,' in J.D. Wilson, ed., *An Imperfect Past: Education and Society in Canadian History* (V: Centre for the Study of Curriculum and Instruction, University of British Columbia 1984); Baker, 'The Juvenile Advocate Society, 1821–1826: Self-Proclaimed Schoolroom for Upper Canada's Governing Class,' CHA *HP* (1985): 74–101; and D.H. Akenson, 'Mass Schooling in Ontario: The Irish and "English Canadian" Popular Culture,' in Akenson, *Being Had*.

Gender figures importantly in A. Prentice, 'The Feminization of Teaching,' in Susan Mann Trofimenkoff and Prentice, eds., *The Neglected Majority: Essays in Canadian Women's History* (T: M&S 1977); C. Gaffield, 'Schooling, the Economy and Rural Society in Nineteenth-Century Ontario,' in J. Parr, ed., *Childhood and Family in Canadian History* (T: M&S 1982); Marta Danylewycz, B. Light, and Prentice, 'The Evolution of the Sexual Division of Labour in Teaching: A Nineteenth-Century Ontario and Quebec Case Study,' *HS/SH* 16/31 (May 1983): 81–109; and Prentice, '"Friendly Atoms in Chemistry": Women and Men at Normal School in Mid-Nineteenth-Century Toronto,' in D. Keane and C. Read, eds., *Old Ontario*.

These recent and often openly revisionist studies should be supplemented by a reading of more standard works, among them: Charles Bruce Sissons, *Egerton Ryerson: His Life and Letters*, 2 vols. (T: Clarke, Irwin 1937–47); Franklin A. Walker, *Catholic Education and Politics in Upper Canada: A Study of the Documentation Relative to the Origin of Catholic Elementary Schools in the Ontario School System* (T: J.M. Dent & Sons 1955); Sissons, *Church and State in Canadian Education: An Historical Study* (T: RP 1959); and J.D. Wilson, Robert M. Stamp, and Louis-Philippe Audet, eds., *Canadian Education: A History* (Scarborough, Ont.: PH 1970). Studies of early universities include C.B. Sissons, *A History of Victoria University* (T: UTP 1952), and Hilda Neatby, *Queen's University, 1841–1917: And Not to Yield* (M: MQUP

1978). See, as well, Richard P. Howard, *Upper Canada College, 1829–1879: Colborne's Legacy* (T: MAC 1979). John George Hodgins early compiled a mass of documentary material that allows students direct access to original sources: *Documentary History of Education in Upper Canada*, 28 vols. (T: Warwick Brothers and Ruter 1894–1910); *The Establishment of Schools and Colleges in Ontario, 1792–1910*, 3 vols. (T: L.K. Cameron 1910); and *Historical and Other Papers and Documents Illustrative of the Educational System of Ontario, 1792–1876*, 6 vols. (T: L.K. Cameron 1911–12). George W. Spragge was perhaps the most prolific early historian of Upper Canadian education. One of the most useful of his many articles is 'John Strachan's Contribution to Education, 1800–1823,' *CHR* 22/2 (June 1941): 147–58.

Less likely to be considered within the context of the regulatory state, but undoubtedly related to this historical development, are the histories of science and architecture. See the important book by Suzanne Zeller, *Inventing Canada: Early Victorian Science and the Idea of a Transcontinental Nation* (T: UTP 1987). Other studies of value include Gerald Killan, *David Boyle: From Artisan to Archaeologist* (T: UTP 1983), Dianne Newell, *Technology on the Frontier: Mining in Old Ontario* (V: UBCP 1986), and E. Arthur, 'Beyond Superior: Ontario's New-Found Land,' in R. Hall et al., eds., *Patterns of the Past*. The role of the built environment in representing and constructing – in both the material and ideological senses – a particular order can be gleaned from Gunter Gad and Deryck Holdsworth, 'Building for City, Region, and Nation: Office Development in Toronto, 1834–1984,' in V.L. Russell, ed., *Forging a Consensus*; Nancy Z. Tausky and Lynne D. DiStefano, *Victorian Architecture in London and Southwestern Ontario: Symbols of Aspiration* (T: UTP 1986); Gad and Holdsworth, 'Streetscape and Society: The Changing Built Environment of King Street, Toronto,' in R. Hall et al., eds., *Patterns of the Past*; and William Westfall and Malcolm Thurlby, 'Church Architecture and Urban Space: The Development of Ecclesiastical Forms in Nineteenth-Century Ontario,' in D. Keane and C. Read, eds., *Old Ontario*; as well as other sources previously cited on crime and those to be cited later on religion.

Beyond regulation lay defence, but the military history of Upper Canada is an underdeveloped realm that at present deals only with such moments of crisis as the War of 1812, the Rebellions and border incursions of 1837–8, and the Fenian raids of the Confederation era. While works on the international environment in which these conflicts took place are covered elsewhere in this volume by J.M. Bumsted, there remains a substantial literature with a primarily Upper Canadian focus. Indeed, there is a tendency among central Canadian scholars to see the first of these conflicts, the War of 1812, as little more than an Upper Canadian affair. This is particularly pronounced in earlier works that verged on hagiography and myth-making, but still lingers in the more recent popular works such as Pierre Berton, *The Invasion of Canada, 1812–1813* and *Flames across the Border, 1813–1814* (T: M&S 1980–1), and even in the scholarly volume by J. Mackay Hitsman, *The Incredible War of 1812: A Military History* (T: UTP 1965), and in G.F.G. Stanley, *The War of 1812: Land Operations* (T: MAC/ National Museums of Canada 1983).

Much of the best work on the war is currently to be found in essay form, often in such collections as Philip P. Mason, ed., *After Tippecanoe: Some Aspects of the War* (T: RP 1963); Morris Zaslow, ed., *The Defended Border: Upper Canada and the War of 1812* (T: MAC 1964); and R. Arthur Bowler, ed., *War along the Niagara: Essays on the War of 1812 and Its Legacy* (Youngstown, NY: Old Fort Niagara Association 1991). In addition see Malcolm MacLeod, 'Fortress Ontario or Forlorn Hope? Simcoe and the Defence of Upper Canada,' *CHR* 53/2 (June 1972): 149–78; J. Errington, 'Friends and Foes: The Kingston Elite and the War of 1812 – A Case Study in Ambivalence,' *JCS* 20/1 (Spring 1985): 58–79; and R.A. Bowler, 'Propaganda in Upper Canada in the War of 1812,' *American Review of Canadian Studies* 18/ 1 (Spring 1988): 11–32, reprinted in J.M. Bumsted, ed., *Interpreting Canada's Past*, vol. 1, 2nd ed. However, the most damaging blows to long-held traditional views often come by way of entries in the *DCB*: in particular see 'Sir Isaac Brock,' vol. 5; and 'Laura Secord [Ingersoll],' vol. 9.

Useful collections of documents on the War of 1812 can be found in the following: E.A. Cruikshank, ed., *Documentary History of the Campaign upon the Niagara Frontier, 1812–1814*, 9 vols. (Welland, Ont.: Lundy's Lane Historical Society 1896–1908); William Wood, ed., *Select British Documents of the Canadian War of 1812*, 3 vols. in 4 (T: CS 1920–8); Milo Quaife, ed., *The John Askin Papers*, 2 vols. (Detroit, MI: Detroit Library Commission 1928–31); and, for newspaper accounts, R.A. Bowler, ed., *The War of 1812* (T: HRW 1973).

The Rebellions and border raids of 1837–8 are handled in the political section to follow, but mention should be made of the narrative in Mary Beacock Fryer, *Volunteers & Redcoats, Raiders & Rebels: A Military History of the Rebellions in Upper Canada* (T: Dundurn 1987). The final military crisis, the Fenian raid of 1866, is the endnote of Upper Canadian military history. W.S. Neidhardt, *Fenianism in North America* (University Park, PA: Pennsylvania State University Press 1975), provides the general picture of this extraordinary Irish movement, while H. Senior, *The Fenians and Canada* (T: MAC 1978), focuses on British North America. Neidhardt has also contributed 'The Fenian Brotherhood and Western Ontario: The Final Years,' *OH* 60/3 (Sept. 1968): 149–61, and 'Fenian Trials in the Province of Canada, 1866–7: A Case Study of Law and Politics in Action,' *OH* 66/1 (Mar. 1974): 23–36. A basic account of the raids themselves is Senior's *The Last Invasion of Canada: The Fenian Raids, 1866–1870* (T: Dundurn 1991). C.P. Stacey, *Canada and the British Army, 1846–1871* (1936; rev. ed., T: UTP 1963) and 'Confederation: The Atmosphere of Crisis,' in E.G. Firth, ed., *Profiles of a Province*, highlight the political implications of the raids.

Otherwise, there is little to be had on the social role of the military in Upper Canadian society; certainly nothing to compare to work done in Lower Canada. Still, one can turn to John Spurr, 'Garrison and Community, 1815–1870,' in G. Tulchinsky, ed., *To Preserve and Defend*, and Peter Burroughs, 'Tackling Army Desertion in British North America,' *CHR* 61/ 1 (Mar. 1980): 28–68.

CHURCH AND STATE / INSTITUTION AND FAITH

Church and state were a paired, if contentious, relation in Upper Canada, and traditional scholarship focused primarily on the political and social accommodations made in response to denominational growth. General surveys of religious life in Canada are a product of this approach and set the Upper Canadian experience in context. For example, see J.S. Moir, *The Church in the British Era: From the British Conquest to Confederation* (T: MHR 1972), or his edited *The Cross in Canada* (T: RP 1966). Moir also provides the basic traditional statements on Upper Canada in *Church and State in Canada West: Three Studies in the Relation of Denominationalism and Nationalism, 1841–1867* (T: UTP 1959); his edited collection *Church and State in Canada, 1627–1867: Basic Documents* (T: M&S 1967); 'The Upper Canadian Religious Tradition,' in E.G. Firth, ed., *Profiles of a Province*; and 'American Influences on the Canadian Protestant Churches before Confederation,' *Church History* 36/4 (Dec. 1967): 440–55.

Beyond this, the basic entryway into the traditional literature is through such denominational histories as J.J. Talman, 'The Position of the Church of England in Upper Canada, 1791–1840,' *CHR* 15/4 (Dec. 1934): 361–75; Stuart Ivison and Fred Rosser, *The Baptists in Upper and Lower Canada before 1820* (T: UTP 1956); Goldwin S. French, *Parsons & Politics: The Rôle of Wesleyan Methodists in Upper Canada and the Maritimes from 1780 to 1855* (T: RP 1962); French, 'The Evangelical Creed in Canada,' in W.L. Morton, ed., *The Shield of Achilles: Aspects of Canada in the Victorian Age* (T: M&S 1968); Arthur G. Dorland, *The Quakers in Canada: A History* (1927; 2nd ed.,

T: RP 1968); and J.S. Moir, *Enduring Witness: A History of the Presbyterian Church in Canada* (T: Presbyterian Publications 1975). Among the more recent contributions to this field are Neil Semple, 'Ontario's Religious Hegemony: The Creation of the National Methodist Church,' *OH* 77/1 (Mar. 1985): 19–42; Elizabeth Cooper, 'Religion, Politics, and Money: The Methodist Union of 1832–1833,' *OH* 81/2 (June 1989): 89–108; and Curtis Fahey, *In His Name: The Anglican Experience in Upper Canada, 1791–1854* (O: CUP 1991). Catholics are understudied, but there are a number of significant essays in Terrence Murphy and Gerald Stortz, eds., *Creed and Culture: The Place of English-Speaking Catholics in Canadian Society, 1750–1930* (K&M: MQUP 1993).

More often than not, Anglican John Strachan and Methodist Egerton Ryerson were at the centre of most denominational rivalries. For Strachan, students can turn to J.L.H. Henderson, ed., *John Strachan: Documents and Opinions* (T: M&S 1969); *John Strachan, 1788–1867* (T: UTP 1969); and 'John Strachan,' *DCB*, vol. 9. Ryerson has recently drawn more attention for his educational role and views than his religious, but see C. Thomas, *Ryerson of Upper Canada* (T: RP 1969); G.S. French, 'Egerton Ryerson and the Methodist Model for Upper Canada,' in N. McDonald and A. Chaiton, eds., *Egerton Ryerson and His Times*, reprinted in *Historical Essays*, 2nd ed.; and 'Egerton Ryerson,' *DCB*, vol. 11. W. Westfall uses the contest between these two men as a key to initiate an analysis of protestant religion that transcends the traditional denominational and biographical approach in *Two Worlds: The Protestant Culture of Nineteenth-Century Ontario* (K&M: MQUP 1989).

Westfall's work represents the best of the recent trend in scholarship to switch emphasis from church and state to religion. While some earlier works took on this task, for example, William H. Elgee, *The Social Teachings of the Canadian Churches: Protestant: The Early Period, before 1850* (T: RP 1964), and S.F. Wise, 'Sermon Literature and Canadian Intellectual History,' originally published in 1965 and reprinted in his *God's Peculiar Peoples*, there now is clearly a concerted focus on the subject of the nature and content of belief. Among the best of the new scholarship are Westfall, 'The Dominion of the Lord: An Introduction to the Cultural History of Protestant Ontario in the Victorian Period,' *QQ* 83/1 (Spring 1976): 47–70; Westfall, 'Order and Experience: Patterns of Religious Metaphor in Early Nineteenth Century Upper Canada,' *JCS* 20/1 (Spring 1985): 5–24; J.W. Grant, *A Profusion of Spires: Religion in Nineteenth-Century Ontario* (T: UTP 1988); Marguerite Van Die, *An Evangelical Mind: Nathanael Burwash and the Methodist Tradition in Canada, 1839–1918* (K&M: MQUP 1989); N. Semple, 'The Quest for the Kingdom: Aspects of Protestant Revivalism in Nineteenth-Century Ontario,' in D. Keane and C. Read, eds., *Old Ontario*; Michael Gauvreau, *The Evangelical Century: College and Creed in English Canada from the Great Revival to the Great Depression* (K&M: MQUP 1991); and David B. Marshall, *Secularizing the Faith: Canadian Protestant Clergy and the Crisis of Belief, 1850–1940* (T: UTP 1992). Closely allied but broader in scope are A.B. McKillop, *A Disciplined Intelligence: Critical Inquiry and Canadian Thought in the Victorian Era* (M: MQUP 1979), C. Berger, *Science, God, and Nature in Victorian Canada* (T: UTP 1983), and S. Zeller, *Inventing Canada*.

THE POLITICAL ECONOMY OF PROTEST AND THE ADMINISTRATION OF ORDER: POLITICS, INSURRECTION, AND GOVERNMENT

Governing Upper Canada has its administrative history and relates directly to the political culmination of protest associated with the reform impulse and its movement toward insurrection in the rebellious activity of 1837–8. Published documents of use in understanding the administrative political history of Upper Canada include E.A. Cruikshank, ed., *The Correspondence of Lieut. Governor John Graves Simcoe*, 5 vols. (T: OHS 1923–31); Cruikshank and A.F. Hunter, eds., *The Correspondence of the Honourable Peter Russell*, 3 vols. (T: OHS 1932–6); Arthur George Doughty, ed., *The Elgin-Grey Papers, 1846–1852*, 4 vols. (O: King's Printer 1937); C.P. Sanderson, ed., *The Arthur Papers*, 3 vols. (T: Toronto Public Library 1957–9); and J.K. Johnson, ed., *The Letters of Sir John A. Macdonald, 1836–1861*, 2 vols. (O: Queen's Printer 1968–9). Paul G. Cornell, *The Alignment of Political Groups in the Province of Canada, 1841–1867* (T: UTP 1962), details the development and personnel of political identities: east/west, reform/conservative, catholic/protestant, and so forth. J.E. Hodgetts, *Pioneer Public Service*, and John Garner, *The Franchise and Politics in British North America, 1755–1867* (T: UTP 1969), are of fundamental importance in understanding the political process in Upper Canada.

A sense of the overall political history of Upper Canada can be gleaned from the three relevant volumes of the Canadian Centenary Series: G.M. Craig, *Upper Canada*; J.M.S. Careless, *The Union of the Canadas*; and W.L. Morton, *The Critical Years: The Union of British North America, 1857–1873* (T: M&S 1964); as well as S.J.R. Noel's attempt at a synthesis, *Patrons, Clients, Brokers*. Aileen Dunham's older *Political Unrest in Upper Canada, 1815–1836* (1927; repr. T: M&S 1963) remains useful. In addition to these basic texts, there are a number of edited collections: Frank H. Underhill, *In Search of Canadian Liberalism* (T: MAC 1960); Craig Brown, ed., *Upper Canadian Politics in the 1850's* (T: UTP 1967); and G.M. Craig, ed., *Discontent in Upper Canada* (T: CC 1974). Local government is a more obscure realm, but see J.H. Aitchinson, 'The Municipal Corporations Act of 1849,' *CHR* 30/2 (June 1949): 107–22; G.P. de T. Glazebrook, 'The Origins of Local Government,' and C.F.J. Whebell, 'Robert Baldwin and Decentralization, 1841–9,' both in F.H. Armstrong et al., eds., *Aspects of Nineteenth-Century Ontario*; and G.M. Betts, 'Municipal Government and Politics, 1800–1850,' in G. Tulchinsky, ed., *To Preserve and Defend*.

Specific treatments of the reform movement and its meaning include G.M. Craig, 'The American Impact on the Upper Canadian Reform Movement before 1837,' *CHR* 29/4 (Dec. 1948): 333–52; Eric Jackson, 'The Organization of Upper Canadian Reformers, 1818–1867,' *OH* 53/2 (June 1961): 95–115, reprinted in *Historical Essays*, 1st ed.; F.C. Hamil, 'The Reform Movement in Upper Canada,' in E.G. Firth, ed., *Profiles of a Province*; Audrey Saunders Miller, 'Yonge Street Politics, 1828 to 1832,' *OH* 62/2 (June 1970): 101–18; M.S. Cross, 'Stony Monday, 1849: The Rebellion Losses Riots in Bytown,' *OH* 63/3 (Sept. 1971): 177–90; and Graeme H. Patterson, 'Whiggery, Nationality, and the Upper Canadian Reform Tradition,' *CHR* 56/1 (Mar. 1975): 25–44. For the imperial context see D.W.L. Earl, 'British Views of Colonial Upper Canada, 1791–1841,' *OH* 53/2 (June 1961): 117–36; P. Burroughs, ed., *The Colonial Reformers and Canada, 1830–1849* (T: M&S 1969); Burroughs, *The Canadian Crisis and British Colonial Policy, 1828–1841* (T: MAC 1972); and Phillip A. Buckner, *The Transition to Responsible Government: British Policy in British North America, 1815–1850* (Westport, CT: Greenwood Press 1985). Representation and imagery of colonial authority receive consideration in Mark Francis, *Governors and Settlers: Images of Authority in the British Colonies, 1820–60* (L: MAC 1992). On conservatism, much of the literature previously cited with respect to elite formation and Loyalism is relevant, but George Metcalf, 'Draper Conservatism and Responsible Government in the Canadas, 1836–1847,' *CHR* 42/4 (Dec. 1961): 300–24, and T. Cook, 'John Beverley Robinson and the Conservative Blueprint,' *OH* (1972), deserve special mention. Note, as well, Irving Martin Abella, 'The "Sydenham Election" of 1841,' *CHR* 47/4 (Dec. 1966): 326–43, and I. Radforth, 'Sydenham and Utilitarian Reform,' in A. Greer and Radforth, eds., *Colonial Leviathan*.

As the focal point of reform and conservative divergence and political opposition, William Lyon Mackenzie has been a figure of central importance. There is a large and conflicting literature on Mackenzie. Margaret

Fairley, ed., *The Selected Writings of William Lyon Mackenzie, 1824–1837* (T: OUP 1960), is useful as a sampling of Mackenzie's reform journalism, while William Kilbourn, *The Firebrand: William Lyon Mackenzie and the Rebellion in Upper Canada* (T: Clarke, Irwin 1956), is a popular treatment of the leader of the failed uprising of 1837. L.F. Gates, *After the Rebellion: The Later Years of William Lyon Mackenzie* (T: Dundurn 1988), is a recent study on Mackenzie and the aftermath of insurrection. Among the many useful articles on Mackenzie are L.F. Gates, 'The Decided Policy of William Lyon Mackenzie,' *CHR* 40/3 (Sept. 1959): 185–208; Gates, '*Mackenzie's Gazette*: An Aspect of W.L. Mackenzie's American Years,' *CHR* 46/4 (Dec. 1965): 323–45; F.H. Armstrong, 'William Lyon Mackenzie, First Mayor of Toronto: A Study of a Critic in Power,' *CHR* 48/4 (Dec. 1967): 309–31; J.E. Rea, 'William Lyon Mackenzie – Jacksonian?' *Mid-American: An Historical Quarterly* (Chicago) 50 (1968): 223–35; Armstrong, 'William Lyon Mackenzie: A Persistent Hero,' *JCS* 6/3 (Aug. 1971): 21–36; P. Romney, 'William Lyon Mackenzie as Mayor of Toronto,' *CHR* 56/4 (Dec. 1975): 416–36; and F.K. Donnelly, 'The British Background of William Lyon Mackenzie,' *British Journal of Canadian Studies* 2/1 (June 1987): 61–73. Finally, Armstrong and Ronald J. Stagg provide the Mackenzie entry in the *DCB*, vol. 9.

The Rebellion of 1837 is the pivotal event in this history of reform/conservative political opposition in which Mackenzie figures centrally. The starting-point for an assessment of the rebellion is the lengthy introduction and voluminous documentation found in C. Read and R.J. Stagg, eds., *The Rebellion of 1837 in Upper Canada: A Collection of Documents* (O: CS/CUP 1985), and the brief summary provided in Read, *The Rebellion of 1837 in Upper Canada*, CHA Historical Booklet no. 46 (O: 1988). Read, *The Rising in Western Upper Canada, 1837–8: The Duncombe Revolt and After* (T: UTP 1982), supplants F. Landon, *Western Ontario and the American Frontier*, although Landon's articles 'The Duncombe Uprising of 1837 and Some of Its Consequences,' *TRSC* ser. 3, 25 (1931), sec. ii, 83–98, and 'The Common Man in the Era of the Rebellion in Upper Canada,' CHA *AR* (1937): 76–91, remain insightful. Among older works still worth consulting are E.C. Guillet, *The Lives and Times of the Patriots: An Account of the Rebellion in Upper Canada, 1837–1838, and of the Patriot Agitation in the United States, 1837–1842* (1938; repr. T: UTP 1968); Albert B. Corey, *The Crisis of 1830–1842 in Canadian-American Relations* (T: RP 1941); Oscar A. Kinchen, *The Rise and Fall of the Patriot Hunters* (NY: Bookman Associates 1956); and S.B. Ryerson, *Unequal Union*. D.G. Creighton, 'The Economic Background of the Rebellions of Eighteen Thirty-Seven,' *CJEPS* 3/3 (Aug. 1937): 322–34, reprinted in W.T. Easterbrook and M.H. Watkins, eds., *Approaches to Canadian Economic History*, remains valuable.

Supplementing these overviews and recent monographs are John Muggeridge, 'John Rolph: A Reluctant Rebel,' *OH* 51/4 (Autumn 1959): 217–29; J.P. Martyn, 'The Patriot Invasion of Pelee Island,' *OH* 56/3 (Sept. 1964): 153–66; Ronald J. Eady, 'Anti-American Sentient in Essex County in the Wake of the Rebellions of 1837,' *OH* 61/1 (Mar. 1969): 1–18; J.K. Johnson, 'The Social Composition of the Toronto Bank Guards, 1837–1838,' *OH* 64/2 (June 1972): 95–104; C. Read, 'The Duncombe Rising, Its Aftermath, Anti-Americanism, and Sectarianism,' *HS/SH* 9/17 (May 1976): 47–69; Read, 'The Short Hills Raid of June, 1838, and Its Aftermath,' *OH* 68/2 (June 1976): 93–115; M.S. Cross, '1837: The Necessary Failure,' in Cross and G.S. Kealey, eds., *Readings in Canadian Social History*, vol. 2, *Pre-Industrial Canada, 1760–1849* (T: M&S 1982); Betsy Boyce, *The Rebellion in Hastings: A New Look at the 1837–38 Rebellion in Hastings County, Based on the Rebellion Losses Claims of 1845* (Belleville, Ont.: Mika 1982); and Boyce, *The Rebels of Hastings* (T: UTP 1992).

The most significant, and widely reproduced, historical document of these years of political change was the *Report* of John George Lambton, 1st Earl of Durham, issued in 1839 in the administrative wake of the repression of rebellion. The most accessible current abridged version is G.M. Craig, ed., *Lord Durham's Report: An Abridgement of 'Report on the Affairs of British North America' by Lord Durham* (T: M&S 1963), the full text being available in Sir Charles Lucas, ed., *Lord Durham's Report on the Affairs of British North America*, 3 vols. (Oxford: Clarendon Press 1912; repr. NY: A.M. Kelley 1970). For commentary and background see Chester W. New, *Lord Durham: A Biography of John George Lambton, First Earl of Durham* (Oxford: Clarendon Press 1929), abridged by H.W. McCready as *Lord Durham's Mission to Canada* (T: M&S 1963); William G. Ormsby, *The Emergence of the Federal Concept in Canada, 1839–1845* (T: UTP 1969); G. Martin, *The Durham Report and British Policy: A Critical Essay* (Cambridge, Eng.: Cambridge University Press 1972); and Janet Ajzenstat, *The Political Thought of Lord Durham* (K&M: MQUP 1988).

Of those contemporary scholars writing on this period of political turmoil and rebellion perhaps the most stimulating is P. Romney. He treats political culture broadly and sensitively, integrating law and economy, class and personality, in a revisionist recasting of Upper Canadian history sympathetic to the reform cause. Key among his works are 'The Ordeal of William Higgins,' *OH* 67/2 (June 1975): 69–89; 'A Struggle for Authority: Toronto Society and Politics in 1834,' in V.L. Russell, ed., *Forging a Con-*

sensus; 'A Conservative Reformer in Upper Canada: Charles Fothergill, Responsible Government and the "British Party," 1824–1840,' CHA *HP* (1984): 42–62; *Mr. Attorney*; 'From the Types Riot to the Rebellion: Elite Ideology, Anti-Legal Sentiment, Political Violence, and the Rule of Law in Upper Canada,' *OH* 79/2 (June 1987): 113–44; 'From the Rule of Law to Responsible Government,' CHA *HP* (1988); 'Re-Inventing Upper Canada: American Immigrants, Upper Canadian History, English Law, and the Alien Question,' in R. Hall et al., eds., *Patterns of the Past*; 'Very Late Loyalist Fantasies: Nostalgic Tory "History" and the Rule of Law in Upper Canada,' in W. Wesley Pue and B. Wright, eds., *Canadian Perspectives on Law and Society: Issues in Legal History* (O: CUP 1988); and 'On the Eve of the Rebellion: Nationality, Religion and Class in the Toronto Election of 1836,' in D. Keane and C. Read, eds., *Old Ontario*. Note, as well, C. Wilton, 'Administrative Reform: A Conservative Alternative to Responsible Government,' *OH* 78/2 (June 1986): 105–25; Kenneth C. Dewar, 'Charles Clarke's "Reformator": Early Victorian Radicalism in Upper Canada,' *OH* 78/3 (Sept. 1986): 233–52; and Wilton, 'British to the Core: Responsible Government in Canada West,' in Wilton, ed., *Change and Continuity: A Reader on Pre-Confederation Canada* (T: MHR 1992).

The Rebellion of 1837, while situated chronologically almost midway between the beginnings and end of Upper Canadian society, signalled the passing of an old way of life. Charley Corncobb, 'poet laureate' of reform, put the message to lines of verse:

Toryism's sun is set
'Tis down, 'tis gone forever
Some say that it will start up yet,
But will it? Nonsense, never.

More was at stake than a simplistic notion of Toryism, however. Over the course of the 1840s, 1850s, and 1860s Upper Canada experienced a revolutionary transformation of its political, economic, cultural, and institutional life.

Much of this story of transformation is told in the political history of the Union of the Canadas, depicted in contrasting historiographic statements as a period of accomplishment laying the basis for the establishment of a transcontinental dominion in 1867, or, as another moment in the making of a hierarchically ordered society in which inequality was yet again deeply entrenched. The more favourable liberal assessment is developed in J.M.S. Careless, *The Union of the Canadas*, while S.B. Ryerson, *Unequal Union*, represents more of a condemnation. Older biographical treatments of the leading political figures of the age by J.M.S. Careless and D.G. Creighton, cited earlier, are still invaluable. P.G. Cornell, *The Alignment of Political Groups*, presents the essential contours of the formation of political groups that would eventually, decades later, develop into something approximating modern parties. S.J.R. Noel, *Patrons, Clients, Brokers*, is a more recent statement.

The institutional, social, and economic developments of the 1841–67 years were part and parcel of the politics of union. These were the years that seemed, for contemporaries, to be stamped with the marks of success. Previously cited writings on education, welfare, municipal legislation, tariffs and reciprocity, and railways are thus all relevant to an understanding of how this period of change ushered into being the beginnings of modern society, moving the history of Upper Canada toward the history of Ontario. In the process the history of the region became pivotal to the history of westward expansion, as indicated demographically in D. Gagan, 'Land, Population, and Social Change,' *CHR* (1978), and ideologically in D. Owram, *Promise of Eden: The Canadian Expansionist Movement and the Idea of the West, 1856–1900* (T: UTP 1980).

By the 1850s Upper Canada seemed perched on the edge of new breakthroughs as the worldwide economic recession of the 1840s lifted, and new adjustments to the dismantling of the British mercantile order appeared in the making. New politics of reform surfaced with the rise of the democratically inclined 'Clear Grits.' The so-called move to implement representation by population took on added potency in the 1850s as the residents of Upper Canada surpassed in numbers those of Lower Canada, and George Brown and others saw the potential to combat the entrenched political power of French Canada, a factor of importance as well in the increasing push for westward expansion. In the aftermath of Confederation and the British North America Act, Ontario boasted a population of 1,620,000; Quebec, 1,191,500. Confederation represented in part a political and cultural triumph of 'little Ontarioism' in which the threatening duality of francophone nationality was submerged in the demographic predominance of Ontario. As old Upper Canada gained the allegiance of 'white' English-speaking support to the west, the challenge to order posed by the 'dangerous classes' of the industrial-capitalist city was also diluted. In turn, the western interior, settled by people and perspectives born and bred in Upper Canada, moved slowly toward the achievement of a desired sociocultural (especially racial) hegemony. A valuable survey of all these themes appears in the closing chapters of Margaret Conrad et al., *History of the Canadian*

Peoples, vol. 1, *Beginnings to 1867* (T: CCP 1993), but an older statement, J.M.S. Careless, 'The 1850s,' in Careless, ed., *Colonists & Canadiens, 1760–1867* (T: MAC 1971), is also useful.

Central to the political development of these pre-Confederation years was the attainment of what has come to be known as responsible government, which conveniently masked a host of class, racial, gender, and regional divisions. Once regarded as the democratic expansion of government and the end of oligarchic rule, responsible government has recently been cast as something other than an administrative set of changes that brought the people into more direct forms of political involvement and representation. Instead, a new set of writings suggests that new boards of expert authority, as well as the additional responsibilities of local government and municipal administration, tended to lower a limiting facade of representative government over popular initiatives, functioning as a constraint on popular power while the actual authority of government was concentrated in executive and appointed posts. Representative government was thus more a 'representation' than it was an effective politics of democracy. This argument appears in a number of essays in A. Greer and I. Radforth, eds., *Colonial Leviathan*, and is especially associated with the educational scholarship of B. Curtis, cited earlier. As Upper Canada became Ontario, and as Ontario increasingly assumed centrality in the emerging Canadian state, various internal and external constituencies thus aligned and realigned along new axes of broader Canadian power. This was what much of the Union/Confederation periods were all about.

When, in the 1860s, the political remaking of British North America produced Confederation, with Ontario as its architectural cornerstone, these linked developments in the economic, social, and political history of Upper Canada were all at work as the final move toward political union was pushed and pulled by sectionalism, railways, and the administration of power. Peter B. Waite, *The Life and Times of Confederation, 1864–1867: Politics, Newspapers, and the Union of British North America* (T: UTP 1962), offers a statement on the issues of Confederation as they affected Upper Canada/Canada West in the 1860s, as does W.L. Morton, *The Critical Years*.

Ontario would, of course, eventually dominate the new Dominion and, in the process, convey to the rest of the country a sense of Upper Canada's all-pervasive power. Yet this mythological 'centre,' long designated *Upper Canada* in an allusion not only to its geographical location relative to Atlantic Canada but also, perhaps, to its haughty superiority and designs on leadership, was fragmented by regions and internal conflicts associated with long-standing divisions of class, race and ethnicity, and gender. Some of this can be gleaned by reading C. Berger, *The Sense of Power: Studies in the Ideas of Canadian Imperialism, 1867–1914* (T: UTP 1970), against the grain of much recent social history. As the reality of Ontario's powerful, but narrow, interests hardened in the pact that was Confederation, the mythology of *Upper* Canada consolidated, obscuring relations of authority and subordination within Ontario, a historical construction as useful to some Canadians as it has been costly to others.

IAN ROSS ROBERTSON

The Maritime Colonies,
1784 to Confederation

The two major concerns for historians interested in the Maritimes have
been the production of historical literature on the region and its integration
into 'national' histories. For a lengthy period there was a lack of material on
the Maritimes. In a convocation address delivered in Fredericton at the
University of New Brunswick in 1943, Daniel Cobb Harvey, the most distinguished Maritime historian of his generation, said:

Hardly a day goes by without some complaint that our histories of Canada ignore
the Maritime Provinces, or give inaccurate accounts of them, or treat them as a
mere appendix to the history of Central Canada; and, when the authors of these histories are reproached for their sins of omission, they naturally reply that they were
unable to find an adequate history of any of these provinces from which to get their
information. Unfortunately, that reply is unanswerable ... ('Archives and Historical
Research in the Maritimes,' *DR* 23 [1943–4]: 193–206)

Half a century later that reply is answerable. There exists a rich body of
historical literature readily available to anyone who visits a library with significant holdings in Canadian history. Much of this development can be
traced to the work of the journal *Acadiensis*, founded in 1971. The first editor, Phillip A. Buckner, declared the intention of encouraging scholarship
in an area 'badly neglected by historians and only infrequently dealt with in
established journals' ('Acadiensis II,' *Acadiensis* 1/1 [Autumn 1971]: 3–9).
This chapter explores the body of writing that has emerged concerning the
Maritimes from 1784 to Confederation.

BIBLIOGRAPHIES AND REFERENCE WORKS

There is no comprehensive modern one-volume bibliography on the history of the region to which students may refer. Indeed, all the published bibliographies for more limited areas, such as Cape Breton Island, appeared in print so long ago as to be outdated by the progress of scholarship.

The most useful single reference work is the multivolume *Dictionary of Canadian Biography* (T: UTP 1966–); in fact, the series is of incalculable value. Much pioneering work appeared in the *DCB*, and frequently it provides the student or teacher of Maritime history with concrete examples of general trends or developments simply not available elsewhere. The standard of editing is such that the reader can be assured in virtually all cases that any statement of fact represented state-of-the-art published knowledge when the volume in which it appeared went to press. Since all volumes covering notable persons who died by 1900 have been published, the vast majority of those who flourished in the pre-Confederation period have been dealt with already. But the project continues, and those notables from the British colonial era who lived past 1900 have yet to receive their due. For an early estimate of the importance of the project for Maritime historical writing see William G. Godfrey, 'Some Thoughts on the D.C.B. and Maritime Historiography,' *Acadiensis* 7/2 (Spring 1978): 107–15.

The relevant volumes for 1784–1867 are four through twelve. Examined in sequence of publication, they provide a fascinating perspective on the evolution of Canadian history as a specialized field of study over the past two decades. Emphasis has changed from the inclusion of predominantly political figures to a quite laboured attempt to find examples of trade union leaders, members of minority groups, women, and others whose lives can be documented. The *Dictionary of Canadian Biography Index, Volumes I to XII* (T: UTP 1991) contains a cumulative nominal index as well as an alphabetized list of subjects of biographies.

PERIODICALS

For various reasons, including the small population of the Maritime provinces, and consequently the tiny and uneconomic potential markets for books, a high proportion of historical literature of value will be found in periodicals. The most useful journal and one which has maintained exceptionally high standards is the semi-annual *Acadiensis* (1971–). It invariably includes review articles in which authors evaluate recent historical literature relevant to particular themes or subjects in Maritime history – for example, Lewis J. Poteet, 'Recent Work in Maritime Linguistics,' *Acadiensis* 16/2 (Spring 1987): 122–9; some of these critical essays are twenty or more pages in length. Valuable bibliographical updates have also appeared in *Acadiensis*:

commencing in 1975, they were a feature of every issue until the autumn 1990 number; since then, their appearance has been irregular. Most issues contain published documents which lend immediacy to the understanding of a situation or problem. An index to the first twenty volumes, *The Acadiensis Index, 1971–1991* (F: AP 1992), is available. Two collections of pre-Confederation articles drawn from the journal have been published: P.A. Buckner and David Frank, eds., *The Acadiensis Reader*, vol. 1, *Atlantic Canada before Confederation* (F: AP 1985; 2nd ed., 1990). The second edition contains two articles originally published elsewhere than the journal.

The following more specialized provincial or Acadian periodicals have also published valuable articles from time to time: *Cahiers*, published by La Société historique acadienne (1961–); *The Island Magazine* (1976–); *Collections*, published by the Nova Scotia Historical Society (1878–); *Nova Scotia Historical Quarterly* (1971–80); and *Nova Scotia Historical Review* (1981–). One weakness of *IM* is the lack of footnotes or endnotes documenting the text, but each article does include a note on sources at the end; and researchers should be warned that NSHS, *Collections*, has appeared irregularly, especially in recent decades. Any serious research endeavour on the Acadians, New Brunswick, Nova Scotia, or Prince Edward Island should include searches of these journals.

GENERAL TEXTS

The closest thing to a general text covering the history of the region for the relevant period is W.S. MacNutt, *The Atlantic Provinces: The Emergence of Colonial Society, 1712–1857* (T: M&S 1965). Although it is a notable effort, the organization by chronological chapters means a grouping of disparate themes and narratives, which makes for difficult reading. A collection of scholarly articles that brought together several older studies by a number of authors, George A. Rawlyk, ed., *Historical Essays on the Atlantic Provinces* (T: M&S 1967), may be regarded as a supplement to the two editions of *The Acadiensis Reader* cited previously.

Much of the historical writing on the region has dealt with particular provinces, and consequently it is reasonable to group a large portion of the historical literature by individual colony. The focus of the writing has reflected the reality of the particularisms within the region. The land question in Prince Edward Island ensured that the political and social history of that colony, whose resource endowment had already dictated that its economy would be primarily agricultural, would be unique. After 1815 the economies of Nova Scotia and New Brunswick diverged greatly. In fact, the concept of the three colonies as constituting a coherent region took shape only after Confederation, and to insist on understanding them as a region when they did not function as such would be anachronistic.

But there are also topics for which provincial categorization would make little sense. The most obvious concern works on the Micmacs, immigration and ethnic groups, women, and aspects of the economic history of the region. The trends in these areas often cut across provincial boundaries, and it is with them that we will begin.

ABORIGINAL PEOPLES

The Micmac lived in all three Maritime colonies, and the only other indigenous groups were the Malecite and the Passamaquoddy, who lived in the Saint John River Valley and Passamaquoddy Bay respectively. English spelling varies for the names of these peoples.

The Micmac were by far the most numerous. The pre-eminent work on the Micmac for this period is Leslie F.S. Upton, *Micmacs and Colonists: Indian-White Relations in the Maritimes, 1713–1867* (V: UBCP 1979). This book represents the culmination of years of research by the author, and incorporates several of his articles that appeared initially in *Acadiensis*. Upton explains the way in which the Micmac were dispossessed of their ancestral lands, relegated to the margins of colonial society, and treated in blatantly unequal and unfair ways. But there were limits imposed on the interaction between settlers and indigenous peoples. In the entry 'Pierre Benoît,' *DCB*, vol. 4 (1979), Upton tells the story of a Malecite shot in 1786 by a disbanded Loyalist soldier who was hanged for murder as a result. His *DCB* entries 'Joseph Malie' and 'Andrew James Meuse,' both in vol. 7 (1988), focus on strong Micmac chiefs who emerged in the middle decades of the nineteenth century. 'Charles Glode,' *DCB*, vol. 8 (1985), is an account of a Micmac who made the successful transition to farming – and appears to have been regarded with some disapproval by other Micmacs.

Quite different in approach, and emphasizing continuities in Micmac culture, are the works of Ruth Holmes Whitehead, which have greatly deepened and enriched our understanding of Micmac history. *Elitekey: Micmac Material Culture from 1600 A.D. to the Present* (H: Nova Scotia Museum 1980) is a concise, well-illustrated introduction to the subject. *Micmac Quillwork: Micmac Indian Techniques of Porcupine Quill Decoration, 1600–1950* (H: Nova Scotia Museum 1982), is a major work of scholarship on a distinctively Micmac form of decorative art, namely, porcupine quillwork on birch-bark, and deserves the term 'definitive.' Whitehead's article 'I Have

Lived Here Since the World Began: Atlantic Coast Artistic Traditions,' in Julia D. Harrison et al., *The Spirit Sings: Artistic Traditions of Canada's First Peoples* (T: M&S/Glenbow Museum 1987), explores parallels and contrasts between the material cultures of the Micmac, the Malecite, and the Beothuk. 'Mary Christianne Paul,' *DCB*, vol. 11 (1982), is a brief study of a successful Micmac artist, and 'Jacques-Pierre Peminuit Paul,' *DCB*, vol. 12 (1990), is an account of a Micmac with an exceptional reputation among his own people as a shaman. More recently, Whitehead edited *The Old Man Told Us: Excerpts from Micmac History, 1500–1950* (H: Nimbus 1991), a collection, arranged chronologically, of firsthand accounts of Micmacs, some presented in the Natives' own reported words.

The person who did the most in the nineteenth century to document Micmac ways of life was the missionary Silas Tertius Rand, and there is a biographical sketch of him in *DCB*, vol. 11. Much of our information on Native peoples comes from records of attempts by churches or charitable organizations or individuals to assist or to mould the Natives. Judith Fingard published an account of a venture that did not have a happy history: 'The New England Company and the New Brunswick Indians, 1786–1826: A Comment on the Colonial Perversion of British Benevolence,' *Acadiensis* 1/2 (Spring 1972): 29–42. Two *DCB* entries relevant to the experience of the New England Company are 'Molly Ann Gell' and 'Oliver Arnold,' both in vol. 6 (1987). A prominent New Brunswicker who took an interest in the situation of the Indians was Moses Henry Perley, and a biographical sketch of him will be found in *DCB*, vol. 9 (1976). A Malecite on whose behalf Perley attempted to intercede is limned in the entry 'Pierre Denis,' *DCB*, vol. 7; it emphasizes the no-win situation often faced by the Native peoples.

William D. Hamilton and William A. Spray, eds., *Source Materials Relating to the New Brunswick Indian* (F: Hamray Books 1976), parts 4 and 5 – more than half the book, in fact – focus on the years 1784–1867. Hamilton, 'Indian Lands in New Brunswick: The Case of the Little South West Reserve,' *Acadiensis* 13/2 (Spring 1984): 3–28, traces the history of a specific case of dispossession from 1763 to the present era. The entry 'John Julien,' *DCB*, vol. 5 (1983), on a Micmac chief in the Miramichi region, is relevant to the story.

For those wishing to do further reading, the following two review articles are invaluable guides, since they detail some relevant material in highly specialized publications: Harold Franklin McGee, Jr, 'No Longer Neglected: A Decade of Writing concerning the Native Peoples of the Maritimes,' *Acadiensis* 10/1 (Autumn 1980): 135–42; and Ralph T. Pastore, 'Native History in the Atlantic Region during the Colonial Period,' *Acadiensis* 20/1 (Autumn 1990): 200–25.

LOYALISTS

The arrival of the American Loyalists decisively displaced the Native peoples from the mainstream of life in the Maritime region, and pushed them into ever-shrinking geographical areas. The newcomers, many of them veteran soldiers on the losing side in a bitter civil war, arrived in such numbers – approximately 32,000 – that in one year the European-descended population in the region increased by about 160 per cent. In fact, virtually everyone already residing in Nova Scotia and New Brunswick felt threatened to some degree; Prince Edward Island, then known as the Island of St John, was a separate case that defies easy summary. Part of plate 32, 'Maritime Canada, Late 18th Century,' in *Historical Atlas of Canada*, vol. 1, *From the Beginning to 1800*, ed. R. Cole Harris (T: UTP [1987]), deals with the distribution of the Loyalist settlers within the region. The Loyalist influx led directly to the creation of New Brunswick as a colony the Loyalists could call their own, and also to the establishment of Cape Breton Island as a separate colony. On the creation of the new colonies see Marion Gilroy, 'The Partition of Nova Scotia, 1784,' *CHR* 14/4 (Dec. 1933): 375–91.

First, who was a Loyalist? J.M. Bumsted has written a thought-provoking article on this matter, 'Loyalists and Nationalists: An Essay on the Problem of Definition,' originally published in 1979 and reprinted in Bumsted, ed., *Interpreting Canada's Past*, vol. 1, *Before Confederation* ([1st ed.], T: OUP 1986). A useful starting-point for any discussion or real understanding of the subject, it should be supplemented by the riveting account of how someone might become a Loyalist in 'The Narrative of Lieutenant James Moody,' *Acadiensis* 1/2 (Spring 1972): 72–90. There is a brief introduction by W.S. MacNutt, author of 'The Loyalists: A Sympathetic View,' *Acadiensis* 6/1 (Autumn 1976): 3–20. For a biographical sketch of Moody see *DCB*, vol. 5. The trauma experienced by Loyalist women in particular is the focus of Beatrice Ross Buszek, '"By Fortune Wounded": Loyalist Women in Nova Scotia,' *NSHR* 7/2 (Dec. 1987): 45–62.

The best survey of the Loyalist migration as a whole is Wallace Brown and Hereward Senior, *Victorious in Defeat: The Loyalists in Canada* (T: Methuen 1984). A general treatment of the Loyalists' impact on the Maritimes is the chapter concerning the 1780s in John G. Reid, *Six Crucial Decades: Times of Change in the History of the Maritimes* (H: Nimbus 1987); he concludes with a useful three-page list of suggestions for 'Further Reading.' Concerning the effects of the Loyalist migration on cultural development see Gwendolyn Davies, 'Consolation to Distress: Loyalist Literary Activity in the Maritimes,' *Acadiensis* 16/2 (Spring 1987): 51–68.

The arrival of the Loyalists had a different significance in each Maritime colony, and the historical literature on the subject is rich. New Brunswick has long been referred to as the Loyalist province because the 14,000 Loyalists who were directed there far outnumbered all other inhabitants, who were divided into the culturally discrete groups of Micmacs, Malecites, Acadians, and Planters of New England origin. In such circumstances, the Loyalists placed their imprint on the new colony at once. But who were they and where did they come from? Esther Clark Wright demolished some old myths with her book *The Loyalists of New Brunswick* (Moncton, NB: Moncton Publishing 1955). A commonly held belief was that New Brunswick Loyalists came predominantly from Massachusetts, where they were part of the social elite. At a popular level that view has never entirely disappeared, but Wright's painstaking research led her to conclude that only a tiny minority – perhaps 6 per cent – actually came from Massachusetts, with much larger numbers originating in New York and New Jersey. Through study of the claims Loyalists made for compensation for losses suffered at the hands of the rebels, she established that few were from the elite and that in fact the Loyalists as a whole represented a cross-section of society in the old colonies to the south.

Neil MacKinnon has written about the difficult early years of the Loyalists who settled on the peninsula of Nova Scotia in *This Unfriendly Soil: The Loyalist Experience in Nova Scotia, 1783–1791* (K&M: MQUP 1986). His findings on the origins of Nova Scotia Loyalists are consistent with those of Wright for New Brunswick; and an earlier article of his, 'The Changing Attitudes of the Nova Scotian Loyalists towards the United States, 1783–1791,' *Acadiensis* 2/2 (Spring 1973): 43–54, reveals the disillusion which could lead to return to the United States. For a fresh examination of Shelburne, which experienced a large influx of Loyalist settlers, followed by rapid out-migration, see Charles Wetherell and Robert W. Roetger, 'Another Look at the Loyalists of Shelburne, N.S., 1783–95,' *CHR* 70/1 (Mar. 1989): 76–91; the authors suggest that much of the explanation for the decline in population can be explained by demographic analysis. Students of Shelburne should also consult Marion Robertson, *King's Bounty: A History of Early Shelburne, Nova Scotia* (H: Nova Scotia Museum 1983).

Another important and detailed study of the earliest years after arrival is David G. Bell, *Early Loyalist Saint John: The Origin of New Brunswick Politics, 1783–1786* (F: New Ireland Press 1983), which emphasizes the intense political conflict among Loyalists after settlement in their new home. Ann Gorman Condon, *The Envy of the American States: The Loyalist Dream for New Brunswick* (F: New Ireland Press 1984), focuses on twenty prominent

New Brunswick Loyalists, their hopes for the colony, and their disappointments. For a sample of notable New Brunswick Loyalists see the *DCB* entries 'Elias Hardy,' 'Abijah Willard,' 'William Lewis,' 'Benjamin Marston,' 'Abraham De Peyster,' and 'Christopher Sower,' vol. 4; 'Edward Winslow,' 'Gabriel George Ludlow,' 'George Duncan Ludlow,' 'Jonathan Odell,' and 'Amos Botsford,' vol. 5; and 'Jonathan Bliss,' 'Ward Chipman [Sr],' 'George Leonard,' 'John Robinson,' 'John Saunders,' and 'William Paine,' vol. 6. A study of these people gives some idea of the diversity within the Loyalist elite in terms of origin, personal history, political opinion, and ultimate fate. As an indication of the political sophistication of New Brunswick during its settlement phase, Condon published, with an introduction, '"The Young Robin Hood Society": A Political Satire by Edward Winslow,' *Acadiensis* 15/2 (Spring 1986): 120–43. T.W. Acheson has written about the fortunes of the Loyalists who settled in Charlotte County in 'A Study in the Historical Demography of a Loyalist County,' *HS/SH* 1/1 (Apr. 1968): 53–65. On the changing image of the New Brunswick Loyalists over time see Murray Barkley, 'The Loyalist Tradition in New Brunswick: The Growth and Evolution of an Historical Myth, 1825–1914,' *Acadiensis* 4/2 (Spring 1975): 3–45.

An estimated 3500 of the Loyalists who migrated to the Maritimes were Black, and they have been the subject of an exceptionally valuable book by James W.StG. Walker, *The Black Loyalists: The Search for a Promised Land in Nova Scotia and Sierra Leone, 1783–1870* (NY: Africana 1976; repr. T: UTP 1992). Also see Walker, 'The Establishment of a Free Black Community in Nova Scotia, 1783–1840,' in Martin L. Kilson and Robert I. Rotberg, eds., *The African Diaspora: Interpretive Essays* (Cambridge, MA: Harvard University Press 1976); and his *DCB* entries for Black Loyalists 'Thomas Peters,' vol. 4; and 'Boston King' and 'David George,' vol. 5. All three left the Maritimes as part of a migration of 1200 Black Loyalists to Sierra Leone in 1792, which appears to have stripped the Black population of the Maritimes of much of its leadership.

Two important articles by Margaret Ells on the Loyalists of Nova Scotia appear in G.A. Rawlyk, ed., *Historical Essays on the Atlantic Provinces*, 'Loyalist Attitudes' and 'Governor Wentworth's Patronage,' initially published in 1935 and 1942 respectively. Concerning the controversial Wentworth, who was lieutenant-governor of Nova Scotia from 1792 to 1808 and who had been the last royal governor of New Hampshire, also see the entry in *DCB*, vol. 5, and Brian C.U. Cuthbertson, *The Loyalist Governor: Biography of Sir John Wentworth* (H: Petheric 1983). Cuthbertson published two other biographies relevant to understanding the Loyalist impact on Nova Scotia: *The*

Old Attorney General: A Biography of Richard John Uniacke (H: Nimbus [1980]), a work on one of the most prominent political opponents of the Loyalists in Nova Scotia; and *The First Bishop: A Biography of Charles Inglis* (H: Waegwoltic 1987), a study of an Irish-born Loyalist clergyman who became the first Church of England (Anglican) bishop of Nova Scotia and also, coincidentally, the first overseas bishop of that denomination. For a biographical sketch of Wentworth's predecessor as governor of Nova Scotia, a beleaguered military man with few political skills, who never established a positive relationship with the Loyalists, see 'John Parr,' *DCB*, vol. 4.

The Loyalist migration also led to the establishment of Cape Breton as a separate colony, an experiment that was not a success. Although on paper the colonists possessed the right to an elected assembly, none was ever called, and in 1820 the island was reannexed to Nova Scotia. The most useful published sources on Cape Breton Loyalists are Robert J. Morgan, 'The Loyalists of Cape Breton,' in Don Macgillivray and Brian Tennyson, eds., *Cape Breton Historical Essays* (Sydney, NS: College of Cape Breton Press 1980), originally published in 1975, and Morgan's *DCB* entries for the following individuals, who had been, respectively, mayors of New York and Albany: 'David Mathews,' vol. 4; and 'Abraham Cornelius Cuyler,' vol. 5.

Prince Edward Island Loyalism had an entirely distinct flavour, and an authoritative account will be found in J.M. Bumsted, *Land, Settlement, and Politics on Eighteenth-Century Prince Edward Island* (K&M: MQUP 1987).

One may pursue the Loyalist migration further, and also find critical assessments of the changing state of scholarship on the subject, through reading a series of review articles in *Acadiensis*: W. Brown, 'Loyalist Historiography,' 4/1 (Autumn 1974): 133–8; David A. Wilson, 'The Ambivalent Loyalists,' 14/1 (Autumn 1984): 122–37; W.H. Nelson, 'The Loyalist Legacy,' 15/1 (Autumn 1985): 141–5; and W.G. Godfrey, 'Volume VI of the D.C.B.: The "Last Survivor(s)" Revisited,' 17/1 (Autumn 1987): 137–43. As the title of Godfrey's article indicates, he focuses on *DCB*, vol. 6; in the course of it, he examines the extent to which Loyalist entries in that volume reinforce or bring into question other scholarly writing on the Loyalist phenomenon in the Maritime colonies.

IMMIGRANTS FROM THE UNITED KINGDOM

Between the 1780s and Confederation the three major immigrant groups aside from the Loyalists were the English, Irish, and Scots. Of the three, the English have been the least studied. Perhaps because of the assumption that they constituted a national, cultural, or racial norm from which others deviated, it has been difficult to gain acceptance for the notion that the English are 'ethnic' in the sense that the Irish, the Scots, and innumerable other groups are. For example, the series Canada's Ethnic Groups, published by the Canadian Historical Association, has not – at least not yet – devoted a booklet to the English as such. Among Maritimers of ultimately English origin, many had American Loyalist roots, but many also came direct from England, and there should be analysis of their points of origin, their reasons for leaving, the skills they brought, their patterns of clustering, and the general significance of their migration. In *The Canadian Encyclopedia*, vol. 2 (2nd ed., E: Hurtig 1988), the reader will find an essay on the English, but such inclusion is unusual, and the author in this instance, George Woodcock, includes no bibliography and little material on English migration to the Maritime colonies. The *DCB* is of assistance, for it includes entries on some individuals; see, for example, 'William Black,' vol. 6, an immigrant from Yorkshire whose family settled on the Isthmus of Chignecto, Nova Scotia, and who became a prominent Wesleyan Methodist clergyman. J.M. Bumsted has written about the appeal of ethnic studies in general terms and has also commented perceptively on the anomaly of overlooking the English as an ethnic group in 'Ethnicity and Culture in Maritime Canada,' in P.A. Buckner, ed., *Teaching Maritime Studies* (F: AP 1986).

The Irish have received much more attention than the English, and a good place to begin is D.A. Wilson, *The Irish in Canada*, CHA Canada's Ethnic Groups Booklet no. 12 (O: 1989). Like all contributions to the series, it contains 'Suggestions for Further Reading.' In recent years several collections of essays devoted in whole or in part to Irish immigration and ethnicity in the Maritimes have appeared in print: Cyril J. Byrne and Margaret Harry, eds., *Talamh An Eisc: Canadian and Irish Essays* (H: Nimbus 1986); Peter M. Toner, ed., *New Ireland Remembered: Historical Essays on the Irish in New Brunswick* (F: New Ireland Press 1988); and Thomas P. Power, ed., *The Irish in Atlantic Canada, 1780–1900* (F: New Ireland Press 1991). Concerning New Brunswick, where the Irish constituted one-third of the population at the end of the British colonial era, see John J. Mannion, *Irish Settlements in Eastern Canada: A Study of Cultural Transfer and Adaptation* (T: UTP 1974), which includes material on the Irish of the Miramichi region; and P.M. Toner, 'The Origins of the New Brunswick Irish, 1851,' *JCS* 23/1–2 (Spring–Summer 1988): 104–19. In the 1980s *The Abegweit Review* published three special issues on the Irish role in Prince Edward Island, with the most rigorously researched and valuable articles being two local studies by Peter McGuigan: 'From Wexford and Monaghan: The Lot 22 Irish,' 5/1

(Winter 1985): 61–96; and 'The Lot 61 Irish: Settlement and Stabilization,' 6/1 (Spring 1988): 33–63. For Cape Breton see A.A. MacKenzie, *The Irish in Cape Breton* (Antigonish, NS: Formac 1979).

The Scots have also generated a significant body of historical literature relevant to the Maritime colonies. J.M. Bumsted, author of *The Scots in Canada*, CHA Canada's Ethnic Groups Booklet no. 1 (O: 1982), has written an article specifically focused on their migration to the region, 'Scottish Emigration to the Maritimes, 1770–1815: A New Look at an Old Theme,' *Acadiensis* 10/2 (Spring 1981): 65–85. In addition, he published an authoritative reassessment of the first wave of Highland emigration to British North America in general, *The People's Clearance: Highland Emigration to British North America, 1770–1815* (Edinburgh/W: Edinburgh University Press/UMP 1982). Bumsted also contributed a paper to Terrence Murphy and C.J. Byrne, eds., *Religion and Identity: The Experience of Irish and Scottish Catholics in Atlantic Canada* (SJ: Jesperson Press 1987). A substantial study by Douglas Campbell and R.A. MacLean, *Beyond the Atlantic Roar: A Study of the Nova Scotia Scots* (T: M&S 1974), combines the approaches of sociology and history. On cultural retention among the Scots of Nova Scotia see Charles W. Dunn, *Highland Settler: A Portrait of the Scottish Gael in Nova Scotia* (T: UTP 1953). Margaret MacDonell, *The Emigrant Experience: Songs of Highland Emigrants in North America* (T: UTP 1982), deals with one aspect of cultural transfer, and contains much material on both Nova Scotia and Prince Edward Island. She published a biographical sketch of one bard from the Isle of Skye who settled in Prince Edward Island: 'Calum Bàn MacMhannain,' *DCB*, vol. 5.

Cape Breton Island has long been famed for the importance of its Scottish presence. D.C. Harvey, 'Scottish Immigration to Cape Breton,' in D. Macgillivray and B. Tennyson, eds., *Cape Breton Historical Essays*, is an early scholarly study, originally published in 1941. More recently, the historical geographer Stephen J. Hornsby addressed the subject in 'Migration and Settlement: The Scots of Cape Breton,' in Douglas Day, ed., *Geographical Perspectives on the Maritime Provinces* (H: Saint Mary's University 1988), and 'Scottish Emigration and Settlement in Early Nineteenth-Century Cape Breton,' in Kenneth Donovan, ed., *The Island: New Perspectives on Cape Breton's History, 1713–1990* (F/Sydney, NS: AP/University College of Cape Breton Press 1990). These articles were a prelude to Hornsby's fine study *Nineteenth-Century Cape Breton: A Historical Geography* (K&M: MQUP 1992).

Useful review articles on the Scots and the Irish of the Maritimes and the historical contexts in which they should be understood appear frequently in

Acadiensis. On the Irish see P.M. Toner, 'The Unstrung Harp: Canada's Irish,' 7/2 (Spring 1978): 156–9; William M. Baker, 'The Irish Connection,' 12/2 (Spring 1983): 124-31; and D.A. Wilson, 'The Irish in North America: New Perspectives,' 18/1 (Autumn 1988): 199–215. Toner discusses recent literature on both groups in 'Lifting the Mist: Recent Studies on the Scots and Irish,' 18/1 (Autumn 1988): 215–26, and Marianne McLean examines one category of sources concerning the immigrant experience in 'Emigrant History and Letters Home,' 14/2 (Spring 1985): 126–33.

BLACKS

The most visible minority group within the Maritimes in the pre-Confederation era was the Black population. In addition to the Loyalist Blacks who remained in the region when others migrated to West Africa in 1792, Black refugees came from the United States during the War of 1812, and of course individuals or smaller groups entered the region for various reasons. A good example would be John Marrant, an important early Black clergyman in Nova Scotia, a freeborn native of New York who arrived by way of London after receiving a letter from his brother, a Loyalist, indicating a need for Black clergy; students will find an entry for him in *DCB*, vol. 4. For a biographical sketch of a leading Black Nova Scotian refugee from the War of 1812 period see 'Septimus D. Clarke,' *DCB*, vol. 8. In later years modest numbers of escaped slaves moved to the region from the United States.

J.W.StG. Walker published 'Black History in the Maritimes: Major Themes and Teaching Strategies,' in P.A. Buckner, ed., *Teaching Maritime Studies*, with a useful bibliography appended. Walker is also the author of two general treatments of Canadian Blacks, which include significant material on the Maritimes: *A History of Blacks in Canada: A Study Guide for Teachers and Students* (Hull, Que.: Government of Canada 1980) and *Racial Discrimination in Canada: The Black Experience*, CHA Historical Booklet no. 41 (O: 1985). Other general studies include Robin W. Winks, *The Blacks in Canada* (M/New Haven, CT: MQUP/Yale University Press 1971). D. Murray Young published a thought-provoking review essay on Winks's book in *Acadiensis* 2/1 (Autumn 1972): 105–12.

The largest Black population in the region was in Nova Scotia, but Blacks still formed only a tiny minority – between 1 and 2 per cent – of the total population in the colony, which meant that they had little possibility of exerting significant influence. Yet over the course of the nineteenth century there was increasing institutional autonomy among Black Nova

Scotians, a trend most evident in religion. See the *DCB* entry 'Richard Preston,' vol. 8, appendix; and Savanah E. Williams, 'The Role of the African United Baptist Association in the Development of Indigenous Afro-Canadians in Nova Scotia, 1782–1978,' in Barry Moody, ed., *Repent and Believe: The Baptist Experience in Maritime Canada* (Hantsport, NS: Lancelot 1980). Bridglal Pachai published two volumes on the history of Nova Scotia Blacks, *Beneath the Clouds of the Promised Land: The Survival of Nova Scotia's Blacks*, vol. 1, *1600–1800*; vol. 2, *1800–1989* (H: Black Educators Association of Nova Scotia 1987–90). For a brief general history of race relations between Black Nova Scotians and the majority society see Donald Clairmont and Fred Wien, 'Blacks and Whites: The Nova Scotia Race Relations Experience,' in D. Campbell, ed., *Banked Fires: The Ethnics of Nova Scotia* (Port Credit, Ont.: Scribblers' Press 1978). For a study of Blacks in one area of Nova Scotia, covering the entire period of this chapter, see G.A. Rawlyk, 'The Guysborough Negroes: A Study in Isolation,' *DR* 48/1 (Spring 1968): 24–36.

Black New Brunswickers formed less than 1 per cent of the population during the British colonial era. W.A. Spray, the author of a small volume entitled *The Blacks in New Brunswick* (F: Brunswick Press 1972), has also written 'The Settlement of the Black Refugees in New Brunswick, 1815–1836,' *Acadiensis* 6/2 (Spring 1977): 64–79. See too Spray's entry 'Robert J. Patterson,' *DCB*, vol. 11, a Black who arrived in Saint John in 1852, participated in antislavery demonstrations, and in 1859 opened a dining establishment which became the most popular in the city. Black Prince Edward Islanders probably never exceeded 200 in number, and the largest concentration was in a racially mixed part of Charlottetown known as the Bog. Folklorist and legal historian Jim Hornby published a study entitled *Black Islanders: Prince Edward Island's Historical Black Community* (CH: Institute of Island Studies 1991).

ACADIANS

The Acadians, French-speaking Roman Catholics, were the most important minority group in the region defining itself in terms of language as well as a shared past. Dispersed by exile during the Seven Years' War, the Acadians slowly re-established themselves in the region over the ensuing century. Typically, they lived in homogeneous communities remote from centres of provincial influence, and steadfastly maintained their identity. Brief introductions to Acadian history between the arrival of the Loyalists and Confederation will be found in Naomi E.S. Griffiths, *The Acadians: Creation of a*

People (T: MHR 1973), and Daniel MacInnes, 'The Acadians: Race Memories Isolated in Small Space,' in D. Campbell, ed., *Banked Fires*. Jean Daigle, ed., *The Acadians of the Maritimes: Thematic Studies* (Moncton, NB: Centre d'études acadiennes 1982), originally published in French in 1980, is a comprehensive collection of articles touching on many aspects of Acadian history. As a group, Acadians became widely known throughout the literate world after the publication in 1847 of an epic poem on the expulsion of 1755 by the American Henry Wadsworth Longfellow. See N.E.S. Griffiths, 'Longfellow's *Evangeline*: The Birth and Acceptance of a Legend,' *Acadiensis* 11/2 (Spring 1982): 28–41; M. Brook Taylor, 'The Poetry and Prose of History: *Evangeline* and the Historians of Nova Scotia,' *JCS* 23/1–2 (Spring–Summer 1988): 46–67; and Carl A. Brasseaux, *In Search of Evangeline: Birth and Evolution of the Evangeline Myth* (Thibodaux, LA: Blue Heron Press 1988).

Like the Blacks, the Acadians had to struggle for influence within institutions affecting their lives. One of the most important for Acadians was the Roman Catholic Church, and in the pre-Confederation period their priests were often non-Acadians. Some were self-exiles from revolutionary France, like the remarkably strong-willed and important Jean-Mandé Sigogne, for whom there is a substantial entry in *DCB*, vol. 7. For additional sketches of French priests see 'Jean-Baptiste Allain,' 'Gabriel Champion,' and 'Amable Pichard,' vol. 5; and 'François Lejamtel,' vol. 6. Other clergy might be Quebeckers like 'François-Xavier-Stanislas Lafrance' or 'Camille Lefebvre,' on whom N.E.S. Griffiths has written in volumes 9 and 12, respectively. For Acadian priests see 'Hubert Girroir,' 'Sylvain-Ephrem Perrey,' and 'François-Xavier Babineau,' vol. 11. Unlike Blacks, Acadians were present in sufficient numbers that they began to elect some of their own to legislative assemblies in the pre-Confederation period. See 'Amand Landry,' vol. 10 (1972); 'Simon d'Entremont,' vol. 11; and 'Stanislaus Francis Perry,' vol. 12. A prominent Acadian lay teacher and community leader is limned in 'Juste Haché,' vol. 12, and a notable Acadian merchant in 'Tranquille Blanchard,' vol. 7. For a fascinating account of an Acadian woman who, after being exiled as an infant in 1755, became a businesswoman in Quebec, see 'Vénérande Robichaux,' vol. 7.

The unrivalled authority on the Acadians of Prince Edward Island is Georges Arsenault. He synthesized much of his research in *The Island Acadians, 1720–1980* (CH: Ragweed 1989), initially published in French in 1987, but also see his *Complaintes acadiennes de l'Ile-du-Prince-Edouard* (M: Leméac 1980) and 'Le dilemme des Acadiens de l'Ile-du-Prince-Edouard au 19e siècle,' *Acadiensis* 14/2 (Spring 1985): 29–45.

For surveys of historical literature on Acadia see Martin S. Spigelman, 'Survival: New Views on Francophone Minorities in Canada,' *Acadiensis* 7/2 (Spring 1978): 141–50; Pierre Trépanier, 'Clio en Acadie,' *Acadiensis* 11/2 (Spring 1982): 95–103; and Jacques Paul Couturier, 'Tendances actuelles de l'historiographie acadienne (1970–1985),' CHA *HP* (1987): 230–50. N.E.S. Griffiths deals with a question in relation to Acadian history which has much broader application and which is especially relevant in an anti-intellectual era of political correctness: 'Comment une étrangère peut-elle écrire l'histoire de l'Acadie?' *Cahiers* 8/1 (mars 1977): 23–9.

WOMEN

Women constitute a special category in terms of historical literature – approximately half the population, but often entirely absent from historical accounts that purport to be general histories. The history of Maritime women is only beginning to be written, and this process will necessarily be lengthy, since recovery of the past of so much of the population is at stake. The work by Alison Prentice et al., *Canadian Women: A History* (T: HBJ 1988), includes material on the Maritime region, as does Constance Backhouse, *Petticoats and Prejudice: Women and Law in Nineteenth-Century Canada* (T: OS/Women's Press 1991).

A second reason that the writing of women's history for the period under study will require much time and effort is that women lived their existence largely within patriarchal confines, in effect restricted to the private, domestic realm. This means that their history is not as easy to retrieve as that of men, who had the public sphere to themselves, ran the newspapers, contested elections, made the laws, staffed the professions, operated almost all the businesses, and so on – in the process dominating the conventional public records that historians use. Women were of course denied the right to vote in all but exceptional cases. The exceptions constituted loopholes which were plugged by the end of the colonial period. Yet the lines between men's and women's spheres were not so rigid as the conventional dichotomy might suggest. For example, M.G. Parks, ed., *My Dear Susan Ann: Letters of Joseph Howe to His Wife, 1829–1836* (SJ: Jesperson Press 1985), reveals how dependent Howe was on his wife for management of his newspaper when he was absent, as he frequently was, from Halifax; and Gail G. Campbell, 'Disfranchised but Not Quiescent: Women Petitioners in New Brunswick in the Mid-19th Century,' *Acadiensis* 18/2 (Spring 1989): 22–54, provides interesting evidence on women's use of an avenue of political expression other than the vote, namely, the petition.

The private, domestic sphere that women occupied is now receiving study. For an examination of an upper-class Victorian family unit, with sensitive attention to the role of women, see J.M. Bumsted, 'The Household and Family of Edward Jarvis, 1828–1852,' *IM* 14 (Fall–Winter 1983): 22–8; Bumsted and Wendy Owen place the same family in a comparative perspective, emphasizing participation in a common culture transcending location and race, in 'The Victorian Family in Canada in Historical Perspective: The Ross Family of Red River and the Jarvis Family of Prince Edward Island,' *Manitoba History* 13 (Spring 1987): 12–18, reprinted in Angus D. Gilbert et al., eds., *Reappraisals in Canadian History*, vol. 1, *Pre-Confederation* (Scarborough, Ont.: PH 1993). The volume by Margaret Conrad, Toni Laidlaw, and Donna Smyth, eds., *No Place Like Home: Diaries and Letters of Nova Scotia Women, 1771–1938* (H: Formac 1988), provides a valuable documentary introduction to the private writings of women. A biographical sketch of one featured diarist, Eliza Ann Chipman, will be found in *DCB*, vol. 8. Also see two related articles Conrad has written, originally published in 1983 and 1984, respectively: 'Recording Angels: The Private Chronicles of Women from the Maritime Provinces of Canada, 1750–1950,' in A. Prentice and Susan Mann Trofimenkoff, eds., *The Neglected Majority: Essays in Canadian Women's History*, vol. 2 (T: M&S 1985), and '"Sundays Always Make Me Think of Home": Time and Place in Canadian Women's History,' in Veronica Strong-Boag and Anita Clair Fellman, eds., *Rethinking Canada: The Promise of Women's History* (T: CCP 1986; 2nd ed., 1991).

The emphasis on diaries and private writings of women should not obscure the fact that women did occasionally break into print during the British colonial period. For example, turning again to the *DCB*, one can cite the published writings of the half-sisters 'Sarah Herbert' and 'Mary Eliza Herbert,' portrayed in vols. 7 and 10, respectively; 'Emily Elizabeth Shaw (Beaven),' vol. 7; 'Grizelda Elizabeth Cottnam Tonge,' vol. 6; 'Julia Catherine Beckwith (Hart),' vol. 9, a native of Fredericton and the first person to write and publish a novel in British North America; 'Elizabeth Newell Lockerby,' vol. 11, a Cavendish, Prince Edward Island, native who apparently sold her poetry door-to-door in Charlottetown in the 1860s. G. Davies has set in context the careers of such women with '"Dearer Than His Dog": Literary Women in Pre-Confederation Nova Scotia,' initially published in 1987 but most accessible in her *Studies in Maritime Literary History, 1760–1930* (F: AP 1991).

Education was one possible route out into the world beyond domesticity. On the broadening of educational and employment opportunities for Maritime women in the nineteenth century, and also the 'gender ideology' inhibiting further movement, see J.G. Reid, 'The Education of Women at Mount Allison, 1854–1914,' *Acadiensis* 12/2 (Spring 1983): 3–33, and his entry for the first chief preceptress of the 'female branch' of the institution, 'Mary Electa Adams,' *DCB*, vol. 12; James D. Davison, 'Alice Shaw and Her Grand Pre Seminary: A Story of Female Education,' in B. Moody, ed., *Repent and Believe*; and Janet Guildford, '"Separate Spheres": The Feminization of Public School Teaching in Nova Scotia, 1838–1880,' *Acadiensis* 22/1 (Autumn 1992): 44–64. One young woman who entered Mount Allison in 1866 would become the first female to practise medicine in Nova Scotia: see 'Maria Louisa Angwin,' *DCB*, vol. 12.

Atlantis, an academic periodical specializing in women's topics and published in the Maritimes, includes some articles of historical interest, although it has not demonstrated a specific commitment to the history of Maritime women. See A. Prentice, 'Writing Women into History: The History of Women's Work in Canada,' 3/2, part 2 (Spring 1978): 72–83; Mary Sparling, '"The Lighter Auxiliaries": Women Artists in Nova Scotia in the Early Nineteenth Century,' 5/1 (Fall 1979): 83–106; and Sheva Medjuck, 'Women's Response to Economic and Social Change in the Nineteenth Century: Moncton Parish, 1851–1871,' 11/1 (Fall 1985): 7–21.

The *DCB* contains articles on women with documented accomplishments, some of whom apparently received little recognition in their own time. Two examples are Charlottetown painter 'Fanny Amelia Wright (Bayfield)' and 'Martha Hamm Lewis,' the first woman to train in the normal schools of New Brunswick, both in vol. 12. Other entries for Maritime women include a Nova Scotian midwife, 'Elizabeth Osborn,' vol. 4; early Maritime schoolmistress 'Deborah How (Cottnam),' vol. 5; Nova Scotian estate manager 'Mary (Polly) Cannon' and Halifax merchant 'Sarah Deblois,' vol. 6; and ceramics collector 'Susanna Lucy Anne Haliburton (Weldon)' and 'Honoria Conway,' a Saint John woman who chose a religious vocation and was known as Mother Mary Vincent, vol. 12. Cannon has also been the subject of one of the relatively few research articles in *Acadiensis* focusing on women during the colonial period: Lois D. Kernaghan, 'A Man and His Mistress: J.F.W. DesBarres and Mary Cannon,' 11/1 (Autumn 1981): 23–42.

For review articles on the development of women's history in the Maritime region see the following in *Acadiensis*: Ruth Pierson, 'Women's History: The State of the Art in Atlantic Canada,' 7/1 (Autumn 1977): 121–31; M. Conrad, 'The Re-Birth of Canada's Past: A Decade of Women's History,' 12/2 (Spring 1983): 140–62; and G.G. Campbell, 'Canadian Women's History: A View from Atlantic Canada,' 20/1 (Autumn 1990): 184–99.

Conrad deals with the integration of research on women into teaching in 'Out of the Kitchen and into the Curriculum: Women's Studies in Maritime Canada,' in P.A. Buckner, ed., *Teaching Maritime Studies*. There are a multitude of possibilities for research in women's history, including the role of women in migration and within ethnic groups.

ECONOMIC HISTORY

The student should begin with general histories of Canadian economic development, and also British colonial policy, which defined the political and regulatory framework within which economic agents operated. A recent synthesis by Kenneth Norrie and Douglas Owram, *A History of the Canadian Economy* (T: HBJ 1991), combines a sophisticated grasp of economics as an academic discipline with knowledge of modern historical scholarship; sections of chapters deal with the Maritimes and assist in placing the economic history of the region within a broad context. Other general studies include Ben Forster, *A Conjunction of Interests: Business, Politics, and Tariffs, 1825–1879* (T: UTP 1986), and Michael Bliss, *Northern Enterprise: Five Centuries of Canadian Business* (T: M&S 1987). Two much older books, one focusing on British policy and the other a survey based on the staples approach, remain useful: Gerald S. Graham, *Sea Power and British North America, 1783–1820: A Study in British Colonial Policy* (1941; NY: Greenwood 1968), and W.T. Easterbrook and Hugh G.J. Aitken, *Canadian Economic History* (T: MAC 1956), often reprinted.

Despite its age, S.A. Saunders's *The Economic History of the Maritime Provinces* (1939; repr., intro. T.W. Acheson, F: AP 1984) still provides a good introduction to the economic history of the Maritimes, written by a scholar with a primary interest in the region. Michael Clow has published an extended review essay on the significance of this book: 'Situating a Classic: Saunders Revisited,' *Acadiensis* 15/1 (Autumn 1985): 145–52. Saunders also wrote two articles on a trading agreement with the United States around which there is occasional confusion because of temporal overlap with the positive economic impact of the American Civil War in the years immediately before Confederation. See 'The Maritime Provinces and the Reciprocity Treaty,' in G.A. Rawlyk, ed., *Historical Essays on the Atlantic Provinces*, originally published in 1934; and 'The Reciprocity Treaty of 1854: A Regional Study,' *CJEPS* 2/1 (Feb. 1936): 41–53. Historical geographers have provided some of the most-helpful background reading on the economy of the pre-Confederation region. See R.C. Harris and John Warkentin, *Canada before Confederation: A Study in Historical Geography* (T:

OUP 1974), ch. 5, which is particularly strong on settlement patterns; and a provocative overview by Andrew Hill Clark, 'Contributions of Its Southern Neighbors to the Underdevelopment of the Maritime Provinces Area, 1710–1867,' in Richard A. Preston, ed., *The Influence of the United States on Canadian Development: Eleven Case Studies* (Durham, NC: Duke University Press 1972).

A mistake outsiders make frequently when looking at the Maritimes is to assume that the region can be understood as an homogeneous entity. In fact, each colony was distinct in character, that distinctiveness revolving around the ways in which its people made their living. In New Brunswick, the timber colony, many inhabitants depended on forest industries for most or at least a significant part of their livelihood. Prince Edward Island was overwhelmingly agricultural. Nova Scotia had a more balanced economy, with several significant sectors. Because of the diverse circumstances, most of the material on the economy of the pre-Confederation region will be presented in the sections of this chapter dealing with individual colonies.

Yet, despite the divergences, to a certain extent the people of the Maritime region had a common economic history, mostly centred around the sea. Two of the most important components of the sea-based economy were shipbuilding – that is, the manufacture of vessels – and shipping services. A classic account is Frederick William Wallace, *Wooden Ships and Iron Men: The Story of the Square-Rigged Merchant Marine of British North America, the Ships, Their Builders and Owners, and the Men Who Sailed Them* (L: Hodder & Stoughton 1924). Eric W. Sager and Lewis R. Fischer have provided a concise treatment of these subjects in *Shipping and Shipbuilding in Atlantic Canada, 1820–1914*, CHA Historical Booklet no. 42 (O: 1986). Their 'Atlantic Canada and the Age of Sail Revisited,' *CHR* 63/2 (June 1982), 125–50, focuses on shipping services, as does E.W. Sager with Gerald E. Panting, *Maritime Capital: The Shipping Industry in Atlantic Canada, 1820–1914* (K&M: MQUP 1990), an exceptionally important recent contribution to Maritime economic history. Built around a strong base of statistical analysis, this rich study distils the results of a series of six books published in the 1970s and 1980s following conferences sponsored by the Atlantic Canada Shipping Project, a major research undertaking based at Memorial University of Newfoundland. Complete bibliographic references to the six will be found in *Maritime Capital*, p. 224, n. 5, para. 2, and in fact reading *Maritime Capital* beforehand provides an intelligible framework within which to place the papers and commentaries published in the conference volumes. Also see Sager and Fischer, 'Patterns of Investment in the Shipping Industries of Atlantic Canada, 1820–1900,' *Acadiensis* 9/1

(Autumn 1979): 19–43, and two noteworthy articles that illuminate particular aspects of the commercial history of the region in the early part of the period under consideration: David S. Macmillan, 'The "New Men" in Action: Scottish Mercantile and Shipping Operations in the North American Colonies, 1760–1825,' in Macmillan, ed., *Canadian Business History: Selected Studies, 1497–1971* (T: M&S 1972); and S. Basdeo and H. Robertson, 'The Nova Scotia – British West Indies Commercial Experiment in the Aftermath of the American Revolution, 1783–1802,' *DR* 61/1 (Spring 1981): 53–69.

The labourers involved in the sailing industry have been the subject of several scholarly works. See, in particular, J. Fingard, *Jack in Port: Sailortowns of Eastern Canada* (T: UTP 1982), and E.W. Sager, *Seafaring Labour: The Merchant Marine of Atlantic Canada, 1820–1914* (K&M: MQUP 1989). For an extended review essay on the Fingard book see Richard Rice, 'Sailortown: Theory and Method in Ordinary People's History,' *Acadiensis* 13/1 (Autumn 1983): 154–68. James Naylor places the two books in a broader context in his review article 'Working-Class History in English Canada in the 1980s: An Assessment,' *Acadiensis* 19/1 (Fall 1989): 157–69.

NOVA SCOTIA

Although we lack a good general history of Nova Scotia from the 1780s to the 1860s, there are some suggestive overviews. B. Moody, for example, gives a sense of the difficult situation of Nova Scotians after the American Revolution in 'Out of Chaos,' *Horizon Canada* 3/6 (Sept. 1985): 697–703, while W.R. Copp's 1937 article 'Nova Scotian Trade during the War of 1812,' reprinted in G.A. Rawlyk, ed., *Historical Essays on the Atlantic Provinces*, suggests the subsequent period of the War of 1812 represented a very different historical experience for Nova Scotia than it was for Upper Canada. For Nova Scotia it was an era of expanding and increasing economic opportunities as the British navy drove American competitors off the high seas and protected the colony from military threats. But the most pervasive assumptions regarding Nova Scotia relate to the era after 1815 and especially after 1830, which is often referred to as the golden age, a time when the colony had it better than ever before, and when its relative standing in British North America as a whole peaked. See Lawrence J. Burpee, 'The Golden Age of Nova Scotia,' *QQ* 36/3 (Summer 1929): 380–94, and D.C. Harvey, 'The Spacious Days of Nova Scotia,' *DR* 19/2 (July 1939): 133–42.

The golden age hypothesis usually relies on evidence drawn from three areas of Nova Scotia history: the economy, politics, and culture. Each sphere is considered here in sequence.

The economy of Nova Scotia was diversified and featured several significant sectors: shipbuilding, shipping services, fishing, agriculture, and coal mining. Shipping services and shipbuilding have already been dealt with in the treatment of common elements in the regional economy, but also note David Alexander and G.E. Panting, 'The Mercantile Fleet and Its Owners: Yarmouth, Nova Scotia, 1840–1889,' *Acadiensis* 7/2 (Spring 1978): 3–28; Rosemary E. Ommer, 'Anticipating the Trend: The Pictou Ship Register, 1840–1889,' *Acadiensis* 10/1 (Autumn 1980): 67–89; and from the *DCB*, 'Thomas Killam,' vol. 9, and 'William Dawson Lawrence,' vol. 11. Unfortunately there is not much historical literature on fishing or fishermen in Nova Scotia, apart from B.A. Balcom's brief *History of the Lunenburg Fishing Industry* (Lunenburg, NS: Lunenburg Marine Museum Society 1977) and a useful discussion in S.J. Hornsby, *Nineteenth-Century Cape Breton*. Hornsby's monograph also provides a good place to start an examination of mining in Nova Scotia. See too J.S. Martell's 1945 article 'Early Coal Mining in Nova Scotia,' reprinted in D. Macgillivray and B. Tennyson, eds., *Cape Breton Historical Essays*; and Marilyn Gerriets, 'The Impact of the General Mining Association on the Nova Scotia Coal Industry, 1826–1850,' *Acadiensis* 21/1 (Autumn 1991): 54–84. Gerriets assesses the record of monopoly property rights in the development of Nova Scotia coal resources, and sober reflection on her findings is certain to raise concerns as to the consequences of monopoly, whatever the identity of the monopolist.

One notable feature of Nova Scotian economic history was the commercial orientation of the Halifax elite, as David A. Sutherland makes clear in 'Halifax Merchants and the Pursuit of Development, 1783–1850,' *CHR* 59/ 1 (Mar. 1978): 1–17. Julian Gwyn deals with an important element in the traditional strategy of Nova Scotian merchants in '"The End of an Era": Rum, Sugar and Molasses in the Economy of Nova Scotia, 1770–1854,' in James H. Morrison and James Moreira, eds., *Tempered by Rum: Rum in the History of the Maritime Provinces* (Porters Lake, NS: Pottersfield Press 1988), 111–33. The *DCB* contains sketches of notable Halifax merchants, who included major figures in international commerce: 'William Forsyth,' vol. 5; 'Sir Samuel Cunard,' vol. 9; 'Enos Collins,' vol. 10; and 'Sir Edward Kenny,' vol. 12. In a number of articles J. Gwyn has argued that there were significant signs of weakness in the economy: '"A Little Province Like This": The Economy of Nova Scotia under Stress, 1812–1853,' *CPRH*, vol. 6 (1988); 'Imports and the Changing Standard of Living in Nova Scotia, 1832–1872,' *NSHR* 11/2 (Dec. 1991): 43–64; 'Golden Age or Bronze

Moment? Wealth and Poverty in Nova Scotia: The 1850s and 1860s,' *CPRH*, vol. 8 (1992); and, with Fazley Siddiq, 'Wealth Distribution in Nova Scotia during the Confederation Era, 1851 and 1871,' *CHR* 73/4 (Dec. 1992): 435–52. Indeed, his central argument is that historians should dispense with the notion of a golden age in the realm of the economy, and that insofar as there were expanded economic opportunities in the final decades of the colonial era, they accrued largely to the elite, especially in the area of Halifax, with farmers, aside from the Fundy region, suffering economic decline.

Agriculture is often portrayed as the weak link in the Nova Scotian economy, and various explanations have been given. For an overview see Robert A. MacKinnon and Graeme Wynn, 'Nova Scotian Agriculture in the "Golden Age": A New Look,' in D. Day, ed., *Geographical Perspectives on the Maritimes*. Concerning more specific themes see the following by Wynn: 'Late Eighteenth-Century Agriculture on the Bay of Fundy Marshlands,' *Acadiensis* 8/2 (Spring 1979): 80–9, and 'Exciting a Spirit of Emulation among the "Plodholes": Agricultural Reform in Pre-Confederation Nova Scotia,' *Acadiensis* 20/1 (Autumn 1990): 5–51. Wynn has also written an article drawing on material generated by two co-authors, R.A. MacKinnon and Rusty Bittermann, as well as his own research, entitled 'Of Inequality and Interdependence in the Nova Scotian Countryside, 1850–70,' *CHR* 74/1 (Mar. 1993): 1–43. The data, which come from two communities in eastern Nova Scotia, reinforce the image of pervasive rural poverty that J. Gwyn and F. Siddiq had presented, and indicate coping strategies families used to counteract the insufficient productivity of their farms. Bittermann has published an article on one of these strategies, namely, selling their labour power, primarily but not exclusively in agriculture, the timber trade, and shipyards: 'Farm Households and Wage Labour in the Northeastern Maritimes in the Early 19th Century,' *L/LT* 31 (Spring 1993): 13–45; his evidence is drawn from Prince Edward Island as well as Nova Scotia. A vocal advocate of improvement in agricultural technique was the Scottish merchant John Young, and a biographical sketch of him will be found in *DCB*, vol. 7. Also see Alan R. MacNeil, 'Cultural Stereotypes and Highland Farming in Eastern Nova Scotia, 1827–1861,' *HS/SH* 19/37 (May 1986): 39–56, and S.J. Hornsby, *Nineteenth-Century Cape Breton*.

Nova Scotia's claim to a golden age in the political realm was firmly based on the fact that it was the first British colony to gain responsible government, and on the person of Joseph Howe, a legendary political hero, a first-rate journalist, and perhaps the most renowned public speaker in the colonies during a century that greatly prized the art of oratory. A generation ago political scientist J. Murray Beck published *The Government of Nova Scotia* (T: UTP 1957), much of which concerns the colonial era, and since then he has made many further contributions to the understanding of Nova Scotian political history. See, for example, 'Ups and Downs of Halifax Influence in Nova Scotia Government, 1749–1981,' *TRSC* ser. 4, 19 (1981), sec. iii, 69–80; and the *DCB* entries 'William Hersey Otis Haliburton,' vol. 6; 'Jotham Blanchard,' vol. 7; 'James Boyle Uniacke,' vol. 8; 'Alexander Stewart,' vol. 9; and 'Sir William Young,' vol. 11. Beck's *Politics of Nova Scotia*, vol. 1, *1710–1896* (Tantallon, NS: Four East Publications 1985), does not make an original contribution, and its value to university-level students is much less than that of his other books.

Beck is best known for his work on Howe, most notably the biography *Joseph Howe*, vol. 1, *Conservative Reformer, 1804–1848*; vol. 2, *The Briton Becomes Canadian, 1848–1873* (K&M: MQUP 1982–3); and *Joseph Howe: Voice of Nova Scotia* (T: M&S 1964), a selection of Howe's writings and speeches. For commentary on Beck's portrayal of Howe see P.A. Buckner, 'Canadian Biography and the Search for Joseph Howe,' *Acadiensis* 14/1 (Autumn 1984): 105–16; and D.A. Sutherland's review of the first volume of the Howe biography, *CHR* 64/1 (Mar. 1983): 47–50. Two collections of Howe's writings, with introductions by M.G. Parks, were published on the centenary of his death: *Western and Eastern Rambles: Travel Sketches of Nova Scotia* (T: UTP 1973) and *Poems and Essays* (T: UTP 1973). For a wider range of assessments of Howe's career, students should turn to G.A. Rawlyk, ed., *Joseph Howe: Opportunist? Man of Vision? Frustrated Politician?* (T: CC 1967), or the more recent papers from an excellent conference, Wayne A. Hunt, ed., *The Proceedings of the Joseph Howe Symposium, Mount Allison University* (Sackville, NB/H: Centre for Canadian Studies, Mount Allison University/Nimbus 1984).

For biographical sketches of significant individuals in Nova Scotia politics written by authors other than Beck see the *DCB* entries 'William Wilkie,' vol. 5; 'William Cottnam Tonge,' vol. 6; 'Herbert Huntington,' vol. 8; 'James William Johnston,' vol. 10; and 'Sir Adams George Archibald,' vol. 12. One can also turn to Rosemarie Langhout, 'Developing Nova Scotia: Railways and Public Accounts, 1848–1867,' *Acadiensis* 14/2 (Spring 1985): 3–28, which indicates that the public accounts of Nova Scotia after 1848 reveal 'a radical policy of government intervention' in the economy.

Claims for a Nova Scotian golden age probably carry most weight in the realm of literary culture. D.C. Harvey's 1933 article 'The Intellectual Awakening of Nova Scotia,' reprinted in G.A. Rawlyk, ed., *Historical Essays on the Atlantic Provinces*, long ago labelled this period. The substance of the claim rests primarily on the careers of two important figures in the early development of Canadian literature, both satirists: Thomas McCulloch, a Scottish immigrant Calvinist clergyman, and Thomas Chandler Haliburton, a native of the colony who was first a lawyer and then a judge. Both writers await definitive biographies, although an entry will be found for McCulloch in *DCB*, vol. 7, and for Haliburton in vol. 9. Brief assessments of their roles in Canadian literature are in William Toye, gen. ed., *The Oxford Companion to Canadian Literature* (T: OUP 1983), while Janice Kulyk Keefer places them in regional context in *Under Eastern Eyes: A Critical Reading of Maritime Fiction* (T: UTP 1987). On McCulloch see D.C. Harvey, 'Dr. Thomas McCulloch and Liberal Education,' *DR* 23/3 (Oct. 1943): 352–62; and B. Anne Wood, 'Thomas McCulloch's Use of Science in Promoting a Liberal Education,' *Acadiensis* 17/1 (Autumn 1987): 56–73. For Haliburton see Richard A. Davies, ed., *On Thomas Chandler Haliburton: Selected Criticism* (O: Tecumseh 1979); and Frank M. Tierney, ed., *The Thomas Chandler Haliburton Symposium* (O: University of Ottawa Press 1985), which includes M.B. Taylor's 'Thomas Chandler Haliburton as a Historian,' a revision of a paper that first appeared in *Acadiensis* 13/2 (Spring 1984): 50–68. Accessible examples of their satiric writings are T. McCulloch, *The Mephibosheth Stepsure Letters*, ed. G. Davies (O: CUP 1990); T.C. Haliburton, *Recollections of Nova Scotia: The Clockmaker*, ed. Bruce Nesbitt (O: Tecumseh 1984), and his *The Old Judge: or, Life in a Colony*, ed. M.G. Parks (O: Tecumseh 1978).

Concerning the milieu in which the two wrote see Carrie MacMillan, 'Colonial Gleanings: "The Club" Papers (1828–31),' *Essays on Canadian Writing* 31 (Summer 1985): 51–64, and Paul A. Bogaard, ed., *Profiles of Science and Society in the Maritimes Prior to 1914* (F: AP 1990). G. Davies's collection of articles, *Studies in Maritime Literary History*, includes examinations of McCulloch and Haliburton. Fred Cogswell provided surveys of early Maritime literature in 'The Maritime Provinces, 1720–1815' and 'Literary Activity in the Maritime Provinces, 1815–1880,' both in Carl F. Klinck, gen. ed., *Literary History of Canada: Canadian Literature in English* (T: UTP 1965); and M.B. Taylor has written a comprehensive and authoritative scholarly account of early historical writing on the Maritimes in *Promoters, Patriots, and Partisans: Historiography in Nineteenth-Century English Canada* (T: UTP 1989). Also see Thomas B. Vincent, ed., *Narrative Verse Satire in Maritime Canada, 1779–1814* (O: Tecumseh 1978), and K. Donovan, '"May Learning Flourish": The Beginnings of a Cultural Awakening in Cape Breton during the 1840s,' in Donovan, ed., *The Island*.

For biographical sketches of other notable contributors to the intellectual flowering of the colony see the *DCB* entries 'Abraham Gesner' and 'Alexander Forrester,' vol. 9; 'Andrew Shiels,' vol. 10; 'John Mockett Cramp' and 'David Honeyman,' vol. 11; and 'Thomas Beamish Akins,' 'Sir John William Dawson,' and 'Theodore Harding Rand,' vol. 12. Some, such as Dawson, Gesner, and Haliburton, had major international reputations. Despite the relative wealth and refinement in this period, there were limits: for example, William Valentine (vol. 7), the most prominent portrait painter in Halifax during the 1815–50 period, had to revert to painting houses and signs from time to time in order to make ends meet. And Robert Field (vol. 5), his predecessor as the leading portraitist in the town, exhausted the market in eight years, 1808–16, and left for Jamaica, where he apparently died of yellow fever. Nova Scotia was not a society in which it was easy for the artistically inclined to make a living.

It is certain that for some Nova Scotians, at least, there was no golden age. J. Fingard dealt with this issue in *The Dark Side of Life in Victorian Halifax* (Porters Lake, NS: Pottersfield Press 1989). Earlier studies on related topics include George E. Hart, 'The Halifax Poor Man's Friend Society, 1820–27: An Early Social Experiment,' *CHR* 34/2 (June 1953): 109–23; Mary Ellen Wright, 'Unnatural Mothers: Infanticide in Halifax, 1850–1875,' *NSHR* 7/2 (Dec. 1987): 13–29; and three articles by Fingard: 'Attitudes towards the Education of the Poor in Colonial Halifax,' *Acadiensis* 2/2 (Spring 1973): 15–42; 'English Humanitarianism and the Colonial Mind: Walter Bromley in Nova Scotia, 1813–25,' *CHR* 54/2 (June 1973): 123–51; and 'The Relief of the Unemployed Poor in Saint John, Halifax, and St. John's, 1815–1860,' *Acadiensis* 5/1 (Autumn 1975): 32–53. On the roots of the out-migration that was to plague post-Confederation Nova Scotia – and indeed all the Maritimes – see Alan A. Brookes, 'The Golden Age and the Exodus: The Case of Canning, Kings County,' *Acadiensis* 11/1 (Autumn 1981): 57–82.

The world of religion has developed a considerable body of historical literature. On the Church of England in Nova Scotia see J. Fingard, *The Anglican Design in Loyalist Nova Scotia, 1783–1816* (L: SPCK 1972); B.C.U. Cuthbertson, *The First Bishop*; Allen B. Robertson, 'Charles Inglis and John Wesley: Church of England and Methodist Relations in Nova Scotia in the Late Eighteenth Century,' *NSHR* 7/1 (June 1987): 48–63; and 'John Inglis,' *DCB*, vol. 7. The first Church of England bishop of Fredericton, who served forty-seven years (1845–92) and therefore is a major figure in the history of that denomination in New Brunswick, is portrayed in 'John Medley,' *DCB*, vol. 12. Methodism in the eastern colonies has recently been the subject of a major collaborative work by Charles H.H. Scobie and John Webster Grant, eds., *The Contribution of Methodism to Atlantic Canada* (K&M: MQUP 1992), while Presbyterians must make do for the present with a more narrowly focused work, Laurie Stanley, *The Well-Watered Garden: The Presbyterian Church in Cape Breton, 1798–1860* (Sydney, NS: University College of Cape Breton Press 1983).

Of course the *DCB* is a fund of information on significant clergy and laity from several denominations. Aside from those mentioned elsewhere in this article, the following is only a sampling: among Baptists, 'John Burton' and 'Joseph Dimock,' vol. 7; 'Edmund Albern Crawley,' vol. 11; and 'John Pryor,' vol. 12; and among those who can be summarized under the term 'Presbyterian,' 'Andrew Brown,' 'James Drummond MacGregor,' and 'Duncan Ross,' vol. 6; 'Donald Allan Fraser,' vol. 7; and 'Thomas Trotter,' vol. 8.

On Roman Catholicism see Mason Wade, 'Relations between the French, Irish and Scottish Clergy in the Maritime Provinces, 1774–1836,' CCHA, *Study Sessions* 39 (1972): 9–33; T. Murphy, 'The Emergence of Maritime Catholicism, 1781–1830,' *Acadiensis* 13/2 (Spring 1984): 29–49; 'William Fraser' and 'William Walsh,' *DCB*, vol. 8; 'Thomas Louis Connolly,' *DCB*, vol. 10; and A.J.B. Johnston, 'Popery and Progress: Anti-Catholicism in Mid-Nineteenth-Century Nova Scotia,' *DR* 64/1 (Spring 1984): 146–63. Murphy has also published a comprehensive review article, 'The Religious History of Atlantic Canada: The State of the Art,' *Acadiensis* 15/1 (Autumn 1985): 152–74.

The growth of Halifax in the late colonial period led to a construction boom, which has been described in Susan Buggey, 'Building Halifax, 1841–1871,' *Acadiensis* 10/1 (Autumn 1980): 90–112. More generally, on historical trends in Maritime building styles see Peter Ennals and Deryck Holdsworth, 'Vernacular Architecture and the Cultural Landscape of the Maritime Provinces – A Reconnaissance,' *Acadiensis* 10/2 (Spring 1981): 86–106. For a relevant review article see Shane O'Dea, 'Architecture and Building History in Atlantic Canada,' *Acadiensis* 10/1 (Autumn 1980): 158–63.

CAPE BRETON ISLAND

The most important scholarly book on Cape Breton for this period is S.J. Hornsby, *Nineteenth-Century Cape Breton*. R. Bittermann has published two studies of one rural community: 'The Hierarchy of the Soil: Land and Labour in a 19th Century Cape Breton Community,' *Acadiensis* 18/1

(Autumn 1988): 33–55; and 'Economic Stratification and Agrarian Settlement: Middle River in the Early Nineteenth Century,' in K. Donovan, ed., *The Island*. On Cape Breton as an autonomous colony, and on the movement to reassert that autonomy, see R.J. Morgan, 'Cape Breton by Itself,' *Horizon Canada* 9/4 (Mar. 1987): 2390–5, and 'Separatism in Cape Breton, 1820–1845,' in K. Donovan, ed., *Cape Breton at 200: Historical Essays in Honour of the Island's Bicentennial, 1785–1985* (Sydney, NS: University College of Cape Breton Press 1985). Morgan also published a study of Cape Breton under stress at mid-century, '"Poverty, Wretchedness, and Misery": The Great Famine in Cape Breton, 1845–1851,' *NSHR* 6/1 (June 1986): 88–104.

As with many parts of the Maritimes which have been insufficiently studied, the *DCB* is one of the best sources on colonial Cape Breton. See, for example, 'Richard Gibbons [Sr],' vol. 4; 'William Macarmick,' 'William McKinnon,' and 'Richard Stout,' vol. 5; 'John Despard,' 'Archibald Charles Dodd,' 'John Janvrin,' 'Laurence Kavanagh,' and 'John Murray,' vol. 6; 'George Robert Ainslie,' vol. 7; 'Iain *MacDhòmhnaill'ic Iain*,' vol. 8; 'Richard Smith,' vol. 9; and 'Thomas Dickson Archibald' and 'John Bourinot,' vol. 11.

Kenneth G. Pryke provides a thoughtful and critical examination of recent writing on historical themes in his review article 'Cape Breton: Identity and Nostalgia,' *Acadiensis* 22/1 (Autumn 1992): 169–84.

NEW BRUNSWICK

New Brunswick is uniquely fortunate among the Maritime provinces in that a major regional scholar published a comprehensive history of the colonial period: W.S. MacNutt, *New Brunswick: A History, 1784–1867* (T: MAC 1963). Although the reliable narrative and clear interpretations of this volume are blessings for anyone seeking to establish a footing in New Brunswick history, there has been much scholarly research and publication on the colony since it appeared in 1963.

It is a commonplace observation that the timber trade and the lumber business (lumber being timber made into planks, boards, deals, or other products) dominated the economy of New Brunswick, and for many people it defined the character of the colony. Accordingly, the historical geographer G. Wynn has published a splendid book entitled *Timber Colony: A Historical Geography of Early Nineteenth Century New Brunswick* (T: UTP 1981). Wynn has become recognized as the prime authority on the forest industries of New Brunswick and their ramifications. Students should also consult the following articles: 'Administration in Adversity: The Deputy Surveyors and Control of the New Brunswick Crown Forest before 1844,' *Acadiensis* 7/1 (Autumn 1977): 49–65; and '"Deplorably Dark and Demoralized Lumberers"? Rhetoric and Reality in Early Nineteenth-Century New Brunswick,' *Journal of Forest History* 24/4 (Oct. 1980): 168–87, which examines contemporary conventional wisdom about the supposedly negative impact of the timber trade on agriculture. Wynn's 'Hail the Pine!' *Horizon Canada* 4/1 (Nov. 1985): 872–7, provides an admirably concise summary of the significance of the timber trade for New Brunswick, with helpful illustrations and a glossary of relevant terms. D.M. Young published an extended review of Wynn's *Timber Colony* in *Acadiensis* 11/2 (Spring 1982): 103–9. Also see Gilbert Allardyce, '"The Vexed Question of Sawdust": River Pollution in Nineteenth Century New Brunswick,' *DR* 52/2 (Summer 1972): 177–90; and Béatrice Craig, 'Agriculture and the Lumberman's Frontier in the Upper St. John Valley, 1800–1870,' *Journal of Forest History* 32/3 (July 1988): 125–37, reprinted in J.M. Bumsted, ed., *Interpreting Canada's Past*, vol. 1, *Pre-Confederation* (2nd ed., T: OUP 1993).

The *DCB* contains many fine sketches illuminating the firms and personalities that dominated the timber trade in colonial New Brunswick. See, for example, 'William Davidson,' vol. 4; 'William Pagan,' vol. 5; 'John Black,' 'James Fraser,' 'Robert Pagan,' and 'Christopher Scott,' vol. 6; 'Allan Gilmour (1775–1849),' vol. 7; 'Alexander Rankin,' vol. 8; 'Joseph Cunard' and 'Robert Rankin,' vol. 9; and 'Allan Gilmour (1805–84),' vol. 11. Several of these entries are useful in understanding the history of the Miramichi region, where the timber trade played an overwhelmingly important role. Scott W. See explains how rivalries between Miramichi timber entrepreneurs could lead to electoral violence in his superb article 'Polling Crowds and Patronage: New Brunswick's "Fighting Elections" of 1842–3,' *CHR* 72/2 (June 1991): 127–56. This study is a sophisticated example of how meticulous research into the history of a colony like New Brunswick can be enriched by critical awareness of international historiography concerning such matters as the behaviour of crowds. For a graphic documentary account see W.A. Spray, ed., 'The 1842 Election in Northumberland County,' *Acadiensis* 8/1 (Autumn 1978): 97–100. Together, the research article and the document offer fascinating insights into the electoral mores of New Brunswick in the 1840s.

Until recently, New Brunswick agriculture has rarely received scholarly attention for its own sake, as opposed to its relationship to the timber trade. But three studies indicate a new direction in historical writing on the colony, for although they take care to relate the farm to forest industries, the principal focus is agriculture. See B. Craig, 'Le développement agricole dans la haute vallée de la rivière Saint-Jean en 1860,' *JCHA* 3 (1992): 13–26; Craig, 'Agriculture in a Pioneer Region: The Upper St. John River Valley in the First Half of the 19th Century,' and T.W. Acheson, 'New Brunswick Agriculture at the End of the Colonial Era: A Reassessment,' both in Kris Inwood, ed., *Farm, Factory and Fortune: New Studies in the Economic History of the Maritime Provinces* (F: AP 1993).

Saint John was by far the largest city in the colonial Maritimes, and T.W. Acheson has published an excellent scholarly history of its development, *Saint John: The Making of a Colonial Urban Community* (T: UTP 1985). J. Fingard has written an extended review essay on Acheson's book, 'The Emergence of the Saint John Middle Class in the 1840s,' *Acadiensis* 17/1 (Autumn 1987): 163–9. Also see Acheson, 'The Great Merchant and Economic Development in St. John, 1820–1850,' *Acadiensis* 8/2 (Spring 1979): 3–27; Carl M. Wallace, 'Saint John Boosters and the Railroads in Mid-Nineteenth Century,' *Acadiensis* 6/1 (Autumn 1976): 71–91; Robert H. Babcock, 'Economic Development in Portland (Me.) and Saint John (N.B.) during the Age of Iron and Steam, 1850–1914,' *American Review of Canadian Studies* 9/1 (Spring 1979): 3–37; and Geoffrey Bilson, 'The Cholera Epidemic in Saint John, N.B., 1854,' *Acadiensis* 4/1 (Autumn 1974): 85–99. S.W. See has written about sectarian violence in the city in 'The Orange Order and Social Violence in Mid-Nineteenth Century Saint John,' *Acadiensis* 13/1 (Autumn 1983): 68–92; and more recently he has dealt with the same subject in relation to the town of Woodstock in '"Mickeys and Demons" vs. "Bigots and Boobies": The Woodstock Riot of 1847,' *Acadiensis* 21/1 (Autumn 1991): 110–31. Both articles indicate that the New Brunswick justice system treated the Irish Roman Catholic element unfairly in the aftermath of communal rioting – in effect, that it took sides with Protestants.

On the settlement of New Brunswick see G. Wynn, 'Population Patterns in Pre-Confederation New Brunswick,' *Acadiensis* 10/2 (Spring 1981): 124–38. Concerning the fate of those who became unable to support themselves see Brereton Greenhous, 'Paupers and Poorhouses: The Development of Poor Relief in Early New Brunswick,' *HS/SH* 1/1 (Apr. 1968): 103–26; James M. Whalen, 'The Nineteenth-Century Almshouse System in Saint John County,' *HS/SH* 4/7 (Apr. 1971): 5–27; and Whalen, 'Social Welfare in New Brunswick, 1784–1900,' *Acadiensis* 2/1 (Autumn 1972): 54–64.

New Brunswick politics featured intense confrontation in the last decade of the eighteenth century, and much of it revolved around the relationship between the lieutenant-governor, Thomas Carleton, and James Glenie, a Scottish timber entrepreneur and politician who had clashed with him when both served in the British army during the American Revolution. George F.G. Stanley, a future New Brunswick lieutenant-governor himself, published a fascinating paper, 'James Glenie: A Study in Early Colonial Radicalism,' NSHS, *Collections* 25 (1942): 145–73. But the writings of W.G. Godfrey have changed our perceptions of this conflict considerably: 'James Glenie and the Politics of Sunbury County,' in L.D. McCann, ed., *People and Place: Studies of Small Town Life in the Maritimes* (F: AP 1987); and 'Thomas Carleton' and 'James Glenie,' *DCB*, vol. 5.

Eventually Carleton and Glenie left New Brunswick, and with the timber boom, which resulted from the sudden rise in British economic protection for colonial timber, politics seemed to be a secondary concern for decades. In part this situation may be explained by the fact that revenues from timber harvested on Crown lands went directly into the colonial treasury, making the lieutenant-governors independent of taxation measures requiring approval by the assembly. Thus the importance of the timber trade went beyond economic considerations. W.S. MacNutt published a sterling article on the issue: 'The Politics of the Timber Trade in Colonial New Brunswick, 1825–1840,' *CHR* 30/1 (Mar. 1949): 47–65, reprinted in G.A. Rawlyk, ed., *Historical Essays on the Atlantic Provinces*. For biographical sketches of the most important lieutenant-governors in the story of the timber revenues see the *DCB* entries 'George Stracey Smyth,' vol. 6; 'Sir Archibald Campbell,' vol. 7; and 'Sir Howard Douglas,' vol. 9.

By the late 1830s the assembly gained control of the timber revenues and so had more leverage with the provincial administration. Still, conventional party divisions were slow to develop, partly because the colony, although relatively small in population, was highly regionalized. It was only in 1854 that a government identifying itself as 'Reform' came to office; for a study of the development of political parties in one county see G.G. Campbell, '"Smashers" and "Rummies": Voters and the Rise of Parties in Charlotte County, New Brunswick, 1846–1857,' CHA *HP* (1986): 86–116. J.K. Chapman has argued that the temperance movement, that is, the organized attempt to restrict the sale and consumption of beverage alcohol, was the first mass movement in New Brunswick to cut across conventional lines of ethnicity, class, and religion; see 'The Mid-19th Century Temperance Movements in New Brunswick and Maine,' *CHR* 35/1 (Mar. 1954): 43–60.

The public figures dominating the colonial period have been subjects of biographical sketches in the *DCB*. Among those who could be described more aptly as office-holders or 'placemen' than as politicians see 'John Murray Bliss,' vol. 6; 'William Franklin Odell' and 'Charles Jeffery Peters,' vol. 7; 'Ward Chipman [Jr]' and 'George Frederick Street,' vol. 8; 'William Black' and especially 'Thomas Baillie,' vol. 9. A study of an important early politician who favoured expanding the rights of the assembly is 'Samuel Denny Street,' vol. 6. Street also had a talent for satiric verse; for a sample see T.B. Vincent, ed., 'Creon: A Satire on New Brunswick Politics in 1802,' *Acadiensis* 3/2 (Spring 1974): 80–98. Entries for significant politicians include 'Charles Simonds,' vol. 8; 'John Richard Partelow' and 'John Ambrose Street,' vol. 9; 'Lemuel Allan Wilmot,' vol. 10; 'John Hamilton Gray (1814–1889),' vol. 11; and 'Robert Duncan Wilmot,' vol. 12. The lieutenant-governors during the 1840s and through 1854 are found in the entries 'Sir John Harvey,' vol. 8; and 'Sir William MacBean George Colebrooke' and 'Sir Edmund Walker Head,' vol. 9. Concerning the franchise and who exercised it – by legal right or by 'custom' – in one New Brunswick county in the 1840s and 1850s see G.G. Campbell, 'The Most Restrictive Franchise in British North America? A Case Study,' *CHR* 71/2 (June 1990): 159–88. A book-length study of a prominent politician, which contains much information on religious and ethnic controversies, is W.M. Baker, *Timothy Warren Anglin, 1822–96: Irish Catholic Canadian* (T: UTP 1977).

New Brunswick could not claim to have the same degree of intellectual development as Nova Scotia in the colonial period. But by 1859 the old Anglican King's College, established in 1829, had been turned into the non-denominational University of New Brunswick, and the foundations of higher education were being securely laid. Concerning one scholarly Scottish scientist appointed to King's in 1837 see 'James Robb,' *DCB*, vol. 9; and Alfred Goldsworthy Bailey, ed., *The Letters of James and Ellen Robb: Portrait of a Fredericton Family in Early Victorian Times* (F: AP 1983). Robb's fellow-Scot, William Brydone Jack, who accepted appointment to King's in 1840 and became president of the University of New Brunswick twenty years later, is the subject of an entry in *DCB*, vol. 11. For a sketch of the Anglican professor of theology who embodied the reasons for the unpopularity of King's and who was pensioned off in 1861 see 'Edwin Jacob,' *DCB*, vol. 9. Martin Hewitt deals with the dissemination of knowledge at a popular level in 'Science as Spectacle: Popular Scientific Culture in Saint John, New Brunswick, 1830–1850,' *Acadiensis* 18/1 (Autumn 1988): 91–119. The first historian of New Brunswick, also a merchant, is limned in 'Peter Fisher,' *DCB*, vol. 7. Reavley Gair, ed., *A Literary and Linguistic History of New Brunswick* (F: Fiddlehead 1985), includes articles dealing with the colonial period and the languages of Native peoples.

PRINCE EDWARD ISLAND

There is no satisfactory general history of Prince Edward Island in the British colonial period that incorporates the results of modern scholarship. But the centenary of the island's entry into Confederation provoked the publication of two volumes attempting general coverage, which are worth noting. David Weale and Harry Baglole, *The Island and Confederation: The End of an Era* (Summerside, PEI: Williams & Crue 1973), is a brief treatment with a distinctive thesis. Francis W.P. Bolger, ed., *Canada's Smallest Province: A History of P.E.I.* (CH: Prince Edward Island 1973 Centennial Commission 1973), is a pot-pourri of articles ranging in quality from poor to adequate, and it should be not be relied upon in the absence of alternative sources. In the same year a special issue of *Canadian Antiques Collector* 8/1 (Jan.–Feb. 1973) included many brief articles of historical interest.

Other books whose titles suggest comprehensiveness have been published since 1973. Errol Sharpe, *A People's History of Prince Edward Island* (T: Steel Rail 1976), contains so many factual errors and contrived interpretations that students should use it only with great caution. Douglas Baldwin, *Land of the Red Soil: A Popular History of Prince Edward Island* (CH: Ragweed 1990), does not cite sources and makes no distinctive contribution. It is based on Baldwin's earlier book, *Abegweit: Land of the Red Soil* (CH: Ragweed 1985), a text for grade six students.

In the 1950s two superb volumes appeared which provide general historical treatments of broad themes. Frank MacKinnon, *The Government of Prince Edward Island* (T: UTP 1951), is a work by a political scientist and it contains a great deal of accurate historical information; part 1 is specifically devoted to the colonial period. A.H. Clark, *Three Centuries and the Island: A Historical Geography of Settlement and Agriculture in Prince Edward Island, Canada* (T: UTP 1959), is a pioneering study in the discipline of historical geography and contains a multitude of useful maps; chapters 4–6 focus on the British colonial era. Both books can still be used with great profit, for nothing has superseded them. Unfortunately, they were the only works of scholarly rigour concerning the island published during the 1950s and 1960s. G. Wynn has outlined the importance of Clark's work for his discipline in 'W.F. Ganong, A.H. Clark and the Historical Geography of Maritime Canada,' *Acadiensis* 10/2 (Spring 1981): 5–28.

H. Baglole, ed., *Exploring Island History: A Guide to the Historical Resources of Prince Edward Island* (Belfast, PEI: Ragweed 1977), includes many helpful and stimulating articles, which introduce students to important themes. The following deserve special mention: Baglole, 'The Land Question';

Louis Pellissier, 'The Native People of Prince Edward Island'; D. Weale, 'Island Social History'; Wayne E. MacKinnon, 'Island Politics and Government'; John Cousins, 'Prince Edward Island Shipbuilding' and 'Studying Prince Edward Island Folk Songs'; and Allan Graham, 'Island Literature.' T.K. Pratt's *Dictionary of Prince Edward Island English* (T: UTP 1988) can be read for pleasure and occasional insights into aspects of island history. Also see two articles by the same author: 'The Proverbial Islander,' *IM* 10 (Fall–Winter 1981): 8–11; and 'Island English: The Case of the Disappearing Dialect,' in Verner Smitheram et al., eds., *The Garden Transformed: Prince Edward Island, 1945–1980* (CH: Ragweed 1982).

The predominance of leasehold tenure as a means of landholding made Prince Edward Island unique within English-speaking British North America throughout the British colonial period. In 1767 the imperial government imposed this system on the island by means of a lottery held in London. It allocated townships of approximately 20,000 acres to favourites or groups of favourites of the Crown, some of whom treated their estates as speculative assets. J.M. Bumsted has examined the factors that determined this policy in 'British Colonial Policy and the Island of St. John, 1763–1767,' *Acadiensis* 9/1 (Autumn 1979): 3–18. Although the landholding system was the focus of controversy, it was not finally abolished by legislation until 1875, after the island entered Confederation. Because of the importance of agriculture, the land question, as it became known, dominated historical development on the island during the colonial period. Given the significance of the land question and the fact that the leasehold system was established in 1767, the lack of any treatment of the subject in *HAC*, vol. 1, or vol. 2, *The Land Transformed, 1800–1891*, ed. R. Louis Gentilcore (T: UTP 1993), ranks as one of the most flagrant oversights of the project.

For a brief historical overview of the land question from establishment to legislated abolition see Ian Ross Robertson's introduction to his edition of *The Prince Edward Island Land Commission of 1860* (F: AP 1988), partially reprinted in R. Douglas Francis and Donald B. Smith, eds., *Readings in Canadian History*, vol. 1, *Pre-Confederation* (3rd ed., T: HRW 1990). The main body of this book is an abridged version of the proceedings and report of a royal commission. The testimony before the commission produced the most important single document for understanding the leasehold system as it had evolved to 1860. Another relevant general article, focusing on the importance of ethnicity, is I.R. Robertson's 1977 article 'Highlanders, Irishmen, and the Land Question in Nineteenth-Century Prince Edward Island,' most accessible in J.M. Bumsted, ed., *Interpreting Canada's Past*, vol. 1 (1st and 2nd eds.). H. Baglole, comp., *The Land Question: A Study Kit of*

Primary Documents (CH: Department of Education 1975), is an excellent introduction to the land question, but it is out of print and not widely available; those who are in a position to use it can profit greatly.

J.M. Bumsted covered the first generation in the history of the land question in his excellent synthesis *Land, Settlement, and Politics on Eighteenth-Century Prince Edward Island.* This book, essential reading for anyone interested in eighteenth-century British North America, will stand as the definitive account of its subject for many years to come. Bumsted's article 'The Origins of the Land Question on Prince Edward Island, 1767–1805,' *Acadiensis* 11/1 (Autumn 1981): 43–56, was a brilliant precursor to the monograph. In addition, Bumsted published thought-provoking articles on absentee and resident proprietors who made reasonable attempts to fulfil the conditions under which the land had been granted: 'Sir James Montgomery and Prince Edward Island, 1767–1803,' *Acadiensis* 7/2 (Spring 1978): 76–102; 'Lord Selkirk of Prince Edward Island,' *IM* 5 (Fall–Winter 1978): 3–8; and 'Captain John MacDonald and the Island,' *IM* 6 (Spring–Summer 1979): 15–20. His article 'Settlement by Chance: Lord Selkirk and Prince Edward Island,' *CHR* 59/2 (June 1978): 170–88, explains why the earl chose the island. Bumsted also published a *DCB* entry for a woman who managed the family estate while her brother was absent on military service during the American Revolutionary War: 'Helen MacDonald of Glenaladale,' vol. 5.

Among contemporary accounts of this period worth consulting, both Patrick C.T. White, ed., *Lord Selkirk's Diary, 1803–1804: A Journal of His Travels to British North America and the Northeastern United States* (T: CS 1958), and J.M. Bumsted, ed., *The Collected Writings of Lord Selkirk, 1799–1809* (W: Manitoba Record Society 1984), provide a proprietor's view of events and conditions on the island. More noteworthy still is the writing of John Stewart, one of the king-makers of the early period, whose *An Account of Prince Edward Island, in the Gulf of St. Lawrence, North America* (1806; repr. NY: Johnson Reprint 1967) was the first book-length history of the island. M.B. Taylor placed Stewart's book in context as the work of a participant-historian in *Promoters, Patriots, and Partisans.* Students should also consult 'John Stewart,' *DCB*, vol. 6.

The land question ensnared the early governors of Prince Edward Island, and destroyed the careers of several. F. MacKinnon, *The Government of Prince Edward Island*, ch. 5, provides a brief general account of political aspects of the land question. The *DCB* published excellent entries on the two governors in charge of administering the island from 1769, when it gained separate status from Nova Scotia, until 1805; 'Walter Patterson,' vol. 4, is a critical sketch of the first, and 'Edmund Fanning,' vol. 5, gives a fascinating portrait of the only governor in the island's first fifty-five years as an autonomous colony who was not removed from office involuntarily because of involvement in quarrels surrounding the land question. As an American Loyalist, Fanning had learned well his lessons on the dangers of finding oneself on the wrong side in politics. W.S. MacNutt offered a more traditional account in 'Fanning's Regime on Prince Edward Island,' *Acadiensis* 1/1 (Autumn 1971): 37–53.

Even the early Supreme Court judges were deeply involved in the politics of the land question. The *DCB* is the essential source here, as it is on many topics concerning colonial Prince Edward Island. Entries that touch upon the evolution of the island judiciary from the late eighteenth century to the middle decades of the nineteenth are 'Peter Stewart,' vol. 5; 'Caesar Colclough' and 'Thomas Tremlett,' vol. 6; and 'Edward James Jarvis,' vol. 8.

For more than a generation the land question involved intra-elite conflict over the ownership of large blocks of land, which were largely uninhabited. The stakes for the future of family fortunes were high, in speculative terms, and the politics of this period could be brutally visceral. Two entries in the *DCB* that bring out the ferocity of island public life in the opening decades of the nineteenth century are 'William Johnston' and 'James Bardin Palmer,' vol. 6. Early in his career on the island Palmer had been the central figure in a controversial group that has been described as Canada's first political party, the Society of Loyal Electors. The first professional historian to study the organization was D.C. Harvey, 'The Loyal Electors,' *TRSC* ser. 3, 24 (1930), sec. ii, 101–10; more recently, J.M. Bumsted has published 'The Loyal Electors of Prince Edward Island,' *IM* 8 (1980): 8–14. The Loyal Electors had enjoyed the patronage of the lieutenant-governor of the day, who has been the subject of a biography by G.N.D. Evans, *Uncommon Obdurate: The Several Public Careers of J.F.W. DesBarres* (T: UTP 1969).

By 1830 the island had a respectable number of settlers who were beginning to question the legitimacy of the leasehold system. The first radical thrust with mass support was the Escheat movement of the 1830s and early 1840s, which argued for reversion of the estates to the Crown on the grounds that proprietors had not fulfilled the granting conditions. Then, according to the Escheators, the Crown could regrant the occupied land to the farmers who were working it. The pioneering scholarly authority on Escheat and particularly its leadership is H. Baglole, whose work has displayed meticulous research and sound judgment. See his 'William Cooper,'

DCB, vol. 9, and 'William Cooper of Sailor's Hope,' *IM* 7 (Fall–Winter 1979): 3–11. Additional entries by other authors in the *DCB* which assist in understanding the history of the Escheat movement are 'George R. Dalrymple' and 'Sir Charles Augustus FitzRoy,' vol. 8; '[Rev.] John McDonald,' vol. 10; and 'John MacKintosh,' vol. 11. R. Bittermann, 'Agrarian Protest and Cultural Transfer: Irish Immigrants and the Escheat Movement on Prince Edward Island,' in T.P. Power, ed., *The Irish in Atlantic Canada*, deals with a peripheral question and reports negative findings.

The Escheators failed to abolish leasehold tenure, and a more moderate reform movement supplanted them. The *DCB* published articles on the two leading reformers in the period from the mid-1840s to the late 1860s, 'George Coles,' vol. 10, a manufacturer; and 'Edward Whelan,' vol. 9, a journalist. Island politics in the reform period was especially complex, and I.R. Robertson, 'Reform, Literacy, and the Lease: The Prince Edward Island Free Education Act of 1852,' *Acadiensis* 20/1 (Autumn 1990): 52–71, argues that the land question is important even for understanding educational reform. On responsible government see F. MacKinnon, *The Government of Prince Edward Island*, ch. 3, for a reliable narrative. W.S. MacNutt, 'Political Advance and Social Reform, 1842–1861,' in F.W.P. Bolger, ed., *Canada's Smallest Province*, is weakest on political matters and repeats previously published mistakes. Some confusion was dispelled in 'Sir Henry Vere Huntley,' *DCB*, vol. 9; yet it was the studies 'Francis Longworth [Jr]' and 'John Longworth,' vol. 11, in particular, which corrected gross errors.

The actual working of the leasehold system requires much more research. Marilyn Bell has edited and introduced diary excerpts which convey the perspective of a non-resident proprietor visiting his estate: mixing with the colonial elite, soaking up local customs, eating and drinking heartily, and interviewing tenants in arrears with their rent dominate the account in 'Mr. Mann's Island: The Journal of an Absentee Proprietor, 1840,' *IM* 33 (Spring–Summer 1993): 17–24. Brief but excellent studies of resident landlords in the nineteenth century are 'Charles Worrell,' *DCB*, vol. 8, and Deborah Stewart, 'Robert Bruce Stewart and the Land Question,' *IM* 21 (Spring–Summer 1987): 3–11. Worrell, a somewhat sympathetic character, left for England after more than four decades of futile attempts to make his estate work; the land agent who in effect defrauded him after he departed was William Henry Pope, and there is an entry for him in *DCB*, vol. 10. A major figure behind the scenes in Conservative circles, W.H. Pope would later become known as the most determined of all 'Fathers of Confederation' from Prince Edward Island, and the fact that he was one of the most unpopular and distrusted political figures of his age gives some insight into the bad odour associated with the Confederation movement on the island. For a study of the only landlord against whom there was an assassination attempt see 'Donald McDonald,' *DCB*, vol. 8. The *DCB* has also published an entry for the most important land agent in the history of the land question, 'James Horsfield Peters,' vol. 12. An exceptionally able individual, Peters was also a leader in attempts to improve agricultural techniques in the colony. Concerning organized efforts to promote better farming methods see Elinor Vass, 'The Agricultural Societies of Prince Edward Island,' *IM* 7 (Fall–Winter 1979): 31–7, and for an excellent account of a method of renewing soil fertility which emerged late in the colonial period see D. Weale, 'The Mud Diggers,' *IM* 5 (Fall–Winter 1978): 22–30.

The organization that brought the leasehold system into crisis by the middle years of the 1860s was the Tenant Union, formed in 1864, and usually known as the Tenant League. *IM* has published two articles dealing with aspects of its dramatic history: I.R. Robertson, 'The *Posse Comitatus* Incident of 1865,' 24 (Fall–Winter 1988): 3–10, and P. McGuigan, 'Tenants and Troopers: The Hazel Grove Road, 1865–68,' 32 (Fall–Winter 1992): 22–8. Robertson outlines some of the political impact the league had in 'Political Realignment in Pre-Confederation Prince Edward Island, 1863–1870,' *Acadiensis* 15/1 (Autumn 1985): 35–58.

Landlords and agents occasionally combined their proprietory activities with such other enterprises as shipbuilding and shipping. Two examples are 'John Cambridge,' about whom one may read in *DCB*, vol. 6, and James Yeo, Sr, the central figure in Basil Greenhill and Ann Giffard, *Westcountrymen in Prince Edward's Isle: A Fragment of the Great Migration* (T: UTP 1967). Unfortunately, the island timber trade, intimately linked to shipbuilding and the land question, and highly lucrative and therefore important in explaining the growth of some fortunes, has received almost no attention. When historians do approach the subject, they will find it difficult to be precise because so much island timber was taken surreptitiously by shipbuilders or others who did not have permission from the legal owners. In other words, timber 'entrepreneurs' on Prince Edward Island were often thieves, and although they could be brazen in carrying out their thefts, they had as little interest as smugglers in leaving behind incriminating documentation. Hence the difficulty for researchers.

Any account of the history of colonial Prince Edward Island that suggested it centred exclusively on the land question would be inaccurate. Religion, for example, played a major role in the lives of islanders, and they created a unique evangelical offshoot of the Church of Scotland, known as the McDonaldites, followers of the Rev. Donald McDonald. D. Weale has written about the movement in 'The Time Is Come! Millenarianism in Colonial Prince Edward Island,' *Acadiensis* 7/1 (Autumn 1977): 35–48, and has provided a biographical sketch of McDonald in *DCB*, vol. 9. Many islanders had strong views of the proper relationship of church and state with respect to education, and these were sometimes expressed in politics. On this subject see I.R. Robertson, 'The Bible Question in Prince Edward Island from 1856 to 1860,' *Acadiensis* 5/2 (Spring 1976): 3–25, and his 'Party Politics and Religious Controversialism in Prince Edward Island from 1860 to 1863,' *Acadiensis* 7/2 (Spring 1978): 29–59. Much debate surrounded proposals to provide public funds for St Dunstan's College, a central purpose of which was to provide candidates for the Roman Catholic priesthood with preliminary training. For a thorough, scholarly, and well-written account of the college see G. Edward MacDonald, *The History of St. Dunstan's University, 1855–1956* (CH: Board of Governors of St Dunstan's University/ Prince Edward Island Museum and Heritage Foundation 1989). The same author has provided *DCB* entries on the first three Catholic bishops of Charlottetown: 'Angus Bernard MacEachern,' vol. 6; 'Bernard Donald Macdonald,' vol. 8; and 'Peter McIntyre,' vol. 12. Since there was no Church of England bishop on the island, these Roman Catholic clerics were in a unique position to exert political weight and claim social precedence. Harry Holman has published a succinct account of the island's bloodiest civil disorder, based on a witches' brew of ethnic, religious, class, and political conflict, in 'The Belfast Riot,' *IM* 14 (Fall–Winter 1983): 3–7; until this affray on 1 March 1847 there appears to have been a casual attitude toward intimidation and violence at elections, but the riot changed that and there was no repetition.

'Maritime' aspects of the island economy have not received sufficient attention in the historical literature. The work by Greenhill and Giffard, *Westcountrymen in Prince Edward's Isle*, has scratched the surface by focusing on one powerful magnate. Two articles by L.R. Fischer are helpful on shipping: 'The Port of Prince Edward Island, 1840–1889: A Preliminary Analysis,' in Keith Matthews and G.E. Panting, eds., *Ships and Shipbuilding in the North Atlantic Region* (SJ: Maritime History Group, Memorial University of Newfoundland 1978); and 'The Shipping Industry of Nineteenth Century Prince Edward Island: A Brief History,' *IM* 4 (Spring–Summer 1978): 15– 21. Kennedy Wells, *The Fishery of Prince Edward Island* (CH: Ragweed 1986), includes historical material.

Although predominantly a rural society, colonial Prince Edward Island had urban concentrations of population. Irene L. Rogers, *Charlottetown: The Life in Its Buildings* (CH: Prince Edward Island Museum and Heritage

Foundation 1983), contains a wealth of architectural detail but disappoints as urban history, for, despite its subtitle, there is little life in this book. Yet her biographical sketch 'Mark Butcher,' *DCB*, vol. 11, provides a case study of the success of a Charlottetown artisan in the middle decades of the nineteenth century, and Robert C. Tuck, 'The Charlottetown Boyhood of Robert Harris,' *IM* 3 (Fall–Winter 1977): 7–12, gives an interesting perspective on life in the capital in the 1850s and 1860s. M. Hewitt, 'The Mechanics' Institutes of Prince Edward Island,' *IM* 21 (Spring–Summer 1987): 27–32, sheds some light on social and intellectual life in Charlottetown and other parts of the island in the late colonial period. The volume by D. Baldwin and Thomas Spira, eds., *Gaslights, Epidemics and Vagabond Cows: Charlottetown in the Victorian Era* (CH: Ragweed 1988), is of slight value and does virtually nothing to illuminate the relationship of Charlottetown to the rest of the island – a weakness it shares with Rogers's work. In short, the story of Charlottetown as the metropolitan centre of the island, and how it exerted its hegemony, has yet to be told. D. Baldwin, 'The Growth and Decline of the Charlottetown Banks, 1854–1906,' *Acadiensis* 15/2 (Spring 1986): 28–52, is a useful beginning on one aspect. The historian of Summerside, Robert Allan Rankin, has done a competent job of explaining the growth and development of that town, and conveying the texture of life in it, with his *Down at the Shore: A History of Summerside, Prince Edward Island (1752–1945)* (CH: Prince Edward Island Heritage Foundation 1980).

Social history aside from issues centred on the land question is in its infancy in island historiography. There are many subjects on which no studies exist: the urban poor and attitudes toward them, treatment of those with mental afflictions, and institutions devoted to charity and to housing indigents. For a critique of Prince Edward Island historical writing as of 1982 see J.M. Bumsted, '"The Only Island There Is": The Writing of Prince Edward Island History,' in V. Smitheram et al., eds., *The Garden Transformed*. Bumsted drew attention to neglected topics, such as economic history and social conflict, and more than a decade later there is still a great deal to be done in these areas.

Island historians have not been the only ones at fault. Some who purport to write on such themes in Maritime history as a whole simply ignore the island. One article by Daniel Francis, titled 'The Development of the Lunatic Asylum in the Maritime Provinces,' *Acadiensis* 6/2 (Spring 1977): 23–38, dismissed the island in the opening footnote, although ample primary sources were available to carry out the sort of research the author did for Nova Scotia and New Brunswick. It is difficult to explain such negligence, although in fairness to Francis, the same mental block (a refusal to accept island history as part of Maritime history or a willingness to accept a vision of the Maritimes that excludes Prince Edward Island) shows up in other works as well. In a thirty-three-page review article on Maritime historiography published in 1984, entitled '"A New Golden Age": Recent Historical Writing on the Maritimes,' *QQ* 91/2 (Summer 1984): 350–82, W.G. Godfrey mentioned scarcely any works concerning the island dated after 1973. Furthermore, this blindness to the island experience is not solely an English-language phenomenon among writers on the Maritimes; J.P. Couturier's previously cited 'Tendances actuelles de l'historiographie acadienne,' CHA *HP* (1987), does not refer to the work of G. Arsenault once. Thus, just as integration of Maritime experience into the broader British North American story has sometimes been lacking, consideration of island developments has often been absent from general treatments of Maritime subjects.

Since the early 1970s a great deal of valuable historical writing on Prince Edward Island has been published. But knowledge has grown in an incremental way, and the only scholarly works of synthesis to emerge have been Bumsted's book on the land question in the eighteenth century and Arsenault's general history of island Acadians. I.R. Robertson has written two review articles surveying island historical literature published between 1973 and 1988: 'Recent Island History,' *Acadiensis* 4/2 (Spring 1975): 111–18; and 'Historical Writing on Prince Edward Island since 1975,' *Acadiensis* 18/1 (Autumn 1988): 157–83.

CONFEDERATION

Confederation is a controversial subject in Maritime historiography, and not surprisingly, in light of the process. Aside from general studies of the Confederation movement, a good place to begin is J.G. Reid, 'The 1860s: Decade of Confederation,' in his *Six Crucial Decades*. A classic treatment still worth reading is William Menzies Whitelaw, *The Maritimes and Canada before Confederation* (1934; repr., ed. Peter B. Waite, T: OUP 1966). For a recent reinterpretation see P.A. Buckner, 'The Maritimes and Confederation: A Reassessment,' *CHR* 71/1 (Mar. 1990): 1–45, reprinted in Ged Martin, ed., *The Causes of Canadian Confederation* (F: AP 1990). One primary source on the Charlottetown Conference of September 1864, which only came to light a century later, demonstrates that, at least among the political class, there was more interest in Maritime union than traditional accounts have assumed: see W.I. Smith, ed., 'Charles Tupper's Minutes of the Charlottetown Conference,' *CHR* 48/2 (June 1967): 101–12.

The literature on the subject is almost endless, and the following is highly selective. It must be arranged colony by colony because the course of the movement was so different in each. First there is New Brunswick, the only colony which held an election on Confederation before implementation; in fact, New Brunswick held two elections, partly because, in the view of the British government, New Brunswickers made the wrong decision (against) the first time. The nature of the intervention by the lieutenant-governor, the British government's agent in Fredericton, raised fundamental questions of constitutional propriety, a fact which made the struggle all the more bitter. A.G. Bailey wrote two important articles on the subject: 'Railways and the Confederation Issue in New Brunswick, 1863–1865,' *CHR* 21/4 (Dec. 1940): 367–83, reprinted in Bailey, *Culture and Nationality* (T: M&S 1972); and 'The Basis and Persistence of Opposition to Confederation in New Brunswick,' *CHR* 23/4 (Dec. 1942): 374–97, reprinted in Ramsay Cook, ed., *Confederation* (T: UTP 1967), and in Bailey, *Culture and Nationality*. J.K. Chapman published 'Arthur Gordon and Confederation,' *CHR* 37/2 (June 1956): 141–57, concerning the lieutenant-governor, whose role became highly controversial; and C.M. Wallace dealt with the leading New Brunswick anti-Confederate in 'Albert Smith, Confederation, and Reaction in New Brunswick, 1852–1882,' *CHR* 44/4 (Dec. 1963): 285–312.

Among entries on leading New Brunswick figures in the *DCB* (excluding those entries already mentioned elsewhere in this chapter) see 'Edward Barron Chandler' and 'Charles Fisher,' vol. 10; 'John McMillan,' 'John Pickard,' and 'Sir Albert James Smith,' vol. 11; and 'Timothy Warren Anglin' and 'Sir Samuel Leonard Tilley,' vol. 12.

In Nova Scotia, no election was held before 1 July 1867 because the pro-Confederate politicians in office in Halifax knew how firmly opposed most voters were. The colony, which had been the first to win responsible government, was brought into Confederation regardless, and Nova Scotians reacted with an angry rejection of pro-Confederates at the first Dominion and provincial elections after 1 July. A scholarly account of the issue in Nova Scotia is K.G. Pryke, *Nova Scotia and Confederation, 1864–74* (T: UTP 1979). The leader of the opposition was Joseph Howe, and J.M. Beck has written a masterful defence of Howe's consistency in this matter in *Joseph Howe: Anti-Confederate*, CHA Historical Booklet no. 17 (O: 1965). Trenchant portraits of two other leading Nova Scotian anti-Confederates, 'William Annand' and 'Martin Isaac Wilkins,' will be found in *DCB*, vol. 11. For an analysis of the voting results in Nova Scotia at the first Dominion election see D.A. Muise, 'The Federal Election of 1867 in Nova Scotia: An Economic Interpretation,' NSHS, *Collections* 36 (1968): 327–51. The royal representatives in Nova Scotia were in a delicate position, acting on behalf of the imperial policy of favouring Confederation against the well-understood wishes of the population. All three relevant royal representatives have entries in the *DCB*, vol. 11: 'Sir Richard Graves MacDonnell,' 'Sir Charles Hastings Doyle,' and 'Sir William Fenwick Williams.' Donald F. Warner, 'The Post-Confederation Annexation Movement in Nova Scotia,' *CHR* 28/2 (June 1947): 156–65, is reprinted in R.D. Francis and D.B. Smith, eds., *Readings in Canadian History*, vol. 2, *Post-Confederation* (3rd ed., T: HRW 1990). Regarding Cape Breton's perspective see B. Tennyson, 'Economic Nationalism and Confederation: A Case Study in Cape Breton,' *Acadiensis* 2/1 (Autumn 1972): 39–53.

In Prince Edward Island, where an overwhelming majority of the population opposed Confederation, an election was held on 26 February 1867, with the result that the island did not enter the Dominion of Canada until 1873. D.C. Harvey, 'Confederation in Prince Edward Island,' *CHR* 14/2 (June 1933): 143–60, and F. MacKinnon, *The Government of Prince Edward Island*, ch. 6, established the basic narrative. F.W.P. Bolger, *Prince Edward Island and Confederation, 1863–1873* (CH: St Dunstan's University Press 1964), adds little of value. I.R. Robertson has related the political process which led the island into Confederation to both the land question and struggles over denominational education in the previously cited article 'Political Realignment,' *Acadiensis* (1985). For portraits of the leading anti-Confederate on the island, and the premier who brought the colony in, see 'Edward Palmer' and 'James Colledge Pope,' *DCB*, vol. 11.

CONCLUSION

This chapter began with the observation that production of historical literature on the Maritime region and the integration of this literature into 'national' histories have been the two major concerns for historians interested in the Maritimes. Over the past two decades, there has been a proliferation of works of high quality on the region, negating the excuse of earlier writers that there was a lack of useful material. But neglect of the region in general histories has provided a continuing theme for commentators with an interest in Maritime history. In 'Canadian History Textbooks and the Maritimes,' *Acadiensis* 10/1 (Autumn 1980): 131–5, W.G. Godfrey wrote: 'The tendency to pass over quickly to the real or aspiring heartland is all too apparent, even in an earlier time period when the Atlantic colonies were considerably more important.' Seven years later J.G. Reid noted a similar disposition on the part of authors of a popular textbook to read the post-

Confederation dominance of the centre over the Maritimes back into the early period: 'Towards the Elusive Synthesis: The Atlantic Provinces in Recent General Treatments of Canadian History,' *Acadiensis* 16/2 (Spring 1987): 107–21. In the still more recent '"Limited Identities" and Canadian Historical Scholarship: An Atlantic Provinces Perspective,' *JCS* 23/1–2 (Spring–Summer 1988): 177–98, P.A. Buckner stated: 'It should no longer be acceptable to write or publish a history of Canada that ignores or marginalizes the Atlantic region.' But he provided examples of exactly that problem, drawn from recent works. If this is so, then why is it so?

Part of the explanation may lie in the lack of synthesis within the historical literature on individual provinces and on the region as a whole. As already noted, among the three provinces the only one for which there exists a comprehensive scholarly study of the British colonial period is New Brunswick, and, given that the date of its publication is 1963, no one would argue that it has been informed by current scholarship. Synthesis of the history of the region has remained elusive. Diversity or fragmentation – the choice of a word is up to the beholder – was a fundamental characteristic, and understanding the complexity of the region is not easy. G. Wynn makes this point with some force in 'Ideology, Society, and State in the Maritime Colonies of British North America, 1840–1860,' in Allan Greer and Ian Radforth, eds., *Colonial Leviathan: State Formation in Mid-Nineteenth-Century Canada* (T: UTP 1992). For many historians not specializing in the Maritimes, the effort at comprehension apparently has not seemed worthwhile. This being the case, integration of Maritime history with the rest of British North American history will probably occur only when there is more synthesis in the work of Maritime historians themselves; and if the past is any guide, this integration may have to be done by Maritime specialists.

OLAF UWE JANZEN

Newfoundland and the International Fishery

Newfoundland has long prided itself on being the first colony of the British Empire, a claim based only in part on John Cabot's voyage of discovery in 1497. By the time Acadia and Quebec were established early in the seventeenth century, Newfoundland had been the annual destination for thousands of European fishermen for nearly a century. In a strictly Eurocentric sense, Newfoundland has an older history than any other part of Canada, a point reinforced by the recent confirmation that the Norse preceded Cabot to Newfoundland by five centuries. Clearly, history has been important in defining and shaping Newfoundland, and it was therefore appropriate that efforts began as early as the eighteenth century to explain that history.

Those efforts were long dominated by a tendency to explain the origins and character of Newfoundland society in terms of the fishery and trade, which gave the island both economic and strategic value to Europeans. Prominent subthemes, such as the appearance and growth of a resident European population, Newfoundland's constitutional development, and Newfoundland's place within the context of the competition between the North Atlantic powers, were invariably explained in terms of efforts to nurture and protect that fishery and trade. The formative role played by scholarly inquiry into the fishery and trade in the development of staple economic theory reinforced this tendency. Thus, the slow rate of population growth was attributed to the fishing industry's antipathy to settlement, wars were expressions of the competition to control the fishery, and the administrative structure that emerged in Newfoundland was linked to the system of regulation within and over the fishery and trade.

There is considerable validity to this approach, and research continues on the intricate structure of the fishing industry and trade. Where did the capital come from to invest in the fishery in the first place? How did the fishing industry and trade function? Why did they favour some European ports and not others? What determined the preference that a port or region would have for a particular method of curing fish? Yet as we discover more about the industry, we discover more about the people who were employed by it – how they were recruited, where they were recruited, why they were recruited. This in turn has contributed to an improved understanding of the origins of Newfoundland's resident population. We now realize that the fishery did not resist settlement but rather was responsible for generating settlement; a symbiosis, sometimes inadvertent, sometimes deliberate, always uneasy, enabled both the fishery and the permanent population to grow in the eighteenth century, and contributed to Britain's success in Newfoundland over France. A variety of disciplines – anthropology, sociology, geography, economics, legal history, religious studies, archaeology, and others – have contributed to a more discerning perception of the origins and growth of early Newfoundland society. In short, there is now a much livelier interest in the people of Newfoundland, not just in their economic mainstay, and one of the striking features of this interest is its interdisciplinary character.

BIBLIOGRAPHIES AND REFERENCE WORKS

Normally the newcomer to any history topic would begin by consulting a published bibliography. However, the only bibliography of quality in Newfoundland studies is not yet complete. The *Bibliography of Newfoundland*, comp. Agnes C. O'Dea, ed. Anne Alexander, 2 vols. (T: UTP 1986), is a handy guide to monograph literature, but it does not include journal articles. This severely limits its value, for some of the more innovative recent research has appeared only in that form. Several other reference works are also incomplete, though invaluable for those volumes that have been published. The *Historical Atlas of Canada*, vol. 1, *From the Beginning to 1800*, ed. R. Cole Harris (T: UTP [1987]), offers superb visual and graphic displays of key themes in Newfoundland history, but the volume describing the nineteenth century is still in progress at the time this essay is being written. Some contributions to the recent *Atlas of Newfoundland and Labrador* (SJ: BKW 1991), designed by Gary McManus and Clifford Wood, are useful but cannot compare with the much more substantial and intricate details of the numerous plates in the *HAC*. The *Dictionary of Canadian Biography* (T: UTP 1966–), with twelve volumes published to date, is indispensable in the study of Newfoundland history. The present volumes cover individuals who died prior to the close of 1900, so that, with very few exceptions, there are essays on almost all individuals who played prominent or significant roles in Newfoundland history before 1870. Still another reference work is the *Encyclopedia of Newfoundland and Labrador*, vols. 1–2 (SJ: Newfoundland Book Publishers); vols. 3–4 (SJ: Harry Cuff 1981–). Four volumes of a projected five have been published to date. The quality of its entries can be very uneven, and readers should take care in its use; however, several superb entries make up for the weaker ones.

PUBLISHED DOCUMENTS

Ideally, historians try to base research on original manuscript and documentary sources. Since these are rarely available except at specialized research libraries and archives, it is mainly through published compilations of documents that most readers can experience history as it was recorded. There are several continuing series of published documents in which individual volumes, or portions of volumes, touch upon Newfoundland history. For the better part of a century the Hakluyt Society has published nearly two hundred volumes on voyages of exploration and discovery with Cambridge University Press, while the Navy Records Society has published nearly a hundred volumes of documents relating to the history of the Royal Navy. In Canada the Champlain Society has undertaken a similar role of compiling and publishing collections of documents. Many of the volumes produced by these societies include reference to events, people, and developments in Newfoundland. An extremely thorough collection of documents pertaining to the exploitation and promotion of sixteenth-century Newfoundland as a fishery and as a target for settlement is David Beers Quinn, ed., *New American World: A Documentary History of North America to 1612*, 5 vols. (NY: Arno Press 1979). Two collections that include several centuries' worth of British documents pertaining to policy and law at Newfoundland are William Lawson Grant and James Munro, eds., *Acts of the Privy Council of England: Colonial Series*, 6 vols. (L: His Majesty's Stationery Office 1908–12), and Great Britain, Judicial Committee of the Privy Council, *In the Matter of the Boundary between the Dominion of Canada and the Colony of Newfoundland in the Labrador Peninsula*, 12 vols. (L: W. Clowes 1926–7). With a similar focus, but more restricted chronologically, is a new ongoing collection, Peter Thomas and Richard Simmons, eds., *Proceedings and Debates of the British Parliaments Respecting North America, 1754–1783*, 5 vols. (Millwood, NY: Kraus International 1982–). Finally, *By Great Waters: A Newfoundland and Labrador Anthology* (T: UTP 1974) is an eclectic selection of documents, edited and introduced by Peter Neary and Patrick O'Flaherty, which describe the island, its fishery, and its people through the eyes of contemporary observers from the Norse era to the present. Many of these documents have since appeared in more complete forms in other collections, yet because a significant number of the selections have been published in no other source, it remains a volume that should be consulted.

PERIODICALS

The study of Newfoundland history crosses many disciplines and nationalities. The journals likely to carry essential readings in the field are therefore extremely diverse. Many journal articles have dealt with sixteenth- and seventeenth-century Newfoundland, but the journal literature becomes substantial only as topics concentrate more on the late seventeenth and into the eighteenth century because it is then that a resident European society begins to emerge in Newfoundland. The *Canadian Historical Review* (1920–) has recently carried a number of articles that examine aspects of that society. Another is *Acadiensis* (1971–); subtitled *The Journal of the History of the Atlantic Region*, it has published a steady stream of articles on Newfoundland history, some of which have been reprinted in Phillip A. Buckner and David Frank, eds., *The Acadiensis Reader*, vol. 1, *Atlantic Canada before Confederation* (F: AP 1985; 2nd ed., 1990). *The Acadiensis Index, 1971–1991* (F: AP 1992) is a valuable guide to the first twenty volumes. *The Newfoundland Quarterly* (1901–) and *Newfoundland Studies* (1985–) are local journals. Although the former is directed at a general readership, it regularly publishes papers that were first presented to the Newfoundland Historical Society. The latter, published by Memorial University of Newfoundland, has quickly established itself as an important medium for scholarly works on Newfoundland history, folklore, geography, and culture. Three of these journals – the *CHR*, *Acadiensis*, and *NS* – regularly carry bibliographies of recent publications, which draw attention to the latest research on Newfoundland history.

HISTORIOGRAPHY

The first significant study of Newfoundland history was by John Reeves, who articulated a strong bias against merchants in his *History of the Government of the Island of Newfoundland* (1793; repr. NY: Johnson Reprint 1967). Reeves blamed all the ills of the island's budding society on what he perceived as an inescapable conflict between the fishing interests and the island's residents. This view became entrenched in the first 'modern' analysis (modern in the sense that it was based on archival research), *A History of Newfoundland from the English Colonial and Foreign Records* by Daniel W. Prowse (L: MAC 1895; repr. Belleville, Ont.: Mika 1979), and persists in such relatively recent treatments of Newfoundland history as G.O. Rothney, *Newfoundland: A History*, CHA Historical Booklet no. 10 (O: 1964), W.S. MacNutt, *The Atlantic Provinces: The Emergence of Colonial Society, 1712–1857* (T: M&S 1965), and St John Chadwick, *Newfoundland: Island into Province* (Cambridge, Eng.: Cambridge University Press 1967).

A vigorous renewal of scholarly interest in Newfoundland history during the past two decades, however, has substantially revised our traditional views and even forced some of the standard interpretations to be abandoned. A fairly successful attempt to synthesize much of this revisionist research is Frederick W. Rowe, *A History of Newfoundland and Labrador* (T: MHR 1980). When used in conjunction with Keith Matthews, *Lectures on the History of Newfoundland, 1500–1800* (SJ: BKW 1988), Rowe's book provides a useful introduction to the current state of Newfoundland history. Rowe shows sensible awareness of the degree to which recent research has overturned the received wisdom of earlier studies, while Matthews, one of the pioneers of the revisionist process, brings the scholar's familiarity with the material to bear on the subject. Unfortunately, Rowe's book ignores those areas of Newfoundland history where little or no work had yet been done. Moreover, it was published in 1980, and is therefore no longer current. As for Matthews's *Lectures*, these are wide-ranging but relatively brief; they are outlines rather than lectures of substance, offering too little support for their sometimes provocative insights.

The reader would be correct to conclude from this discussion that a definitive survey of Newfoundland history still waits to be written. While older studies continue to deserve respect, they must be used with circumspection. Since the circulation and influence of these older studies remain more widespread than that of the more recent revisionist works, the need for caution is all the greater. Useful guides through the historiographical minefield include: K. Matthews, 'Historical Fence-Building: A Critique of the Historiography of Newfoundland,' *NQ* 74/1 (Spring 1978): 21–30; F.W. Rowe, 'Myths of Newfoundland,' *NQ* 74/4 (Winter 1979): 3–16; and P. Neary, 'The Writing of Newfoundland History: An Introductory Survey,' in James K. Hiller and Neary, eds., *Newfoundland in the Nineteenth and Twentieth Centuries: Essays in Interpretation* (T: UTP 1980). Also recommended is Eric W. Sager, 'Newfoundland's Historical Revival and the Legacy of David Alexander,' *Acadiensis* 11/1 (Autumn 1981): 104–15.

THE FISHERY IN THE SIXTEENTH CENTURY

To understand the speed with which European discovery of Newfoundland late in the fifteenth century was followed by the rapid exploitation of its fishing grounds by thousands of European fishermen, one must know something about the European economy at this time. A thorough though somewhat dated introduction appears in E.E. Rich and C.H. Wilson, eds., *The Cambridge Economic History of Europe*, vol. 5, *The Economic Organization of Early Modern Europe* (Cambridge, Eng.: Cambridge University Press 1977). A more sweeping but possibly clearer account is given in the opening chapters of Ralph Davis, *The Rise of the Atlantic Economies* (Ithaca, NY: Cornell University Press 1973). Together with plates 21, 'The Migratory Fisheries,' and 22, 'The 16th Century Fishery,' in the *HAC*, vol. 1, these studies will prepare the reader for more specialized works.

Of these, the most influential has perhaps been Harold Adams Innis, *The Cod Fisheries: The History of an International Economy* (1940; rev. ed., T: UTP 1954). Though dated and lacking the sophistication of analysis that is now essential, this pioneering work still impresses one with its massive detail and the international flavour of its sources. D.B. Quinn, 'The Newfoundland Trades: Cod-Fishing and Whaling, 1514–1613,' followed by a strong collection of documents, appears in the fourth volume of *New American World*. These works underscore the complexities and international character of the early fishing industry and trade. A useful overview of the early fishery is John Gilchrist, 'Exploration and Enterprise: The Newfoundland Fishery, c.1497–1677,' in David S. Macmillan, ed., *Canadian Business History: Selected Studies, 1497–1971* (T: M&S 1972). However, care should be exercised in accepting Gilchrist's explanation for the different cures of fish adopted by different nationalities. Insufficient emphasis is given to the role played by market preferences.

A survey of Portuguese participation from the early beginnings to the modern era is given in Sally C. Cole, 'Cod, God and Family: The Portuguese Newfoundland Cod Fishery,' *Mast: Maritime Anthropological Studies* 3/1 (1990): 30–47. The devastating attack on the Portuguese fishing fleet by the English is discussed in D.B. Quinn, 'Sir Bernard Drake,' *DCB*, vol. 1 (1966). The most significant sixteenth-century Iberian fishery, however, was that based in the Basque ports of northern Spain. H.A. Innis traces it in 'The Rise and Fall of the Spanish Fishery in Newfoundland,' *TRSC* ser. 3, 25 (1931), sec. ii, 51–70, reprinted in Mary Q. Innis, ed., *Essays in Canadian Economic History* (T: UTP 1956). Innis attributes the decline of the fishery to the policies of the central government in Madrid.

Interest in the Basque presence in Newfoundland of late has focused much more on their whale fishery in the Straits of Belle Isle between the 1540s and the end of that century. Selma Barkham's pioneering archival research in Spain, and the archaeological efforts at Red Bay of Robert Grenier and James A. Tuck, have revealed a whole new chapter in Newfoundland history. Two useful accounts are S. Barkham, 'The Documentary Evidence for Basque Whaling Ships in the Strait of Belle Isle,' and J.A. Tuck, 'A Sixteenth Century Whaling Station at Red Bay, Labrador,' both in G.M. Story, ed., *Early European Settlement and Exploitation in Atlantic Canada: Selected Papers* (SJ: Memorial University of Newfoundland 1982). A more recent update of Barkham's research is provided in her 'The Basque Whaling Establishments in Labrador, 1536–1632 – A Summary,' *Arctic* 37/4 (Dec. 1984): 515–19, while Tuck and Grenier describe their work in detail in 'A 16th-Century Basque Whaling Station in Labrador,' *Scientific American* 245/5 (Nov. 1981): 180–4, 186–8, 190. Jean-Pierre Proulx has used these and many other scattered references, together with his own research, to develop an extremely readable and perceptive survey, *Basque Whaling in Labrador in the 16th Century* (O: National Historic Sites 1993).

Spain became a negligible factor within the fishing industry after the sixteenth century, but its continued role as a principal market for Newfoundland cod is critical in understanding the persistent efforts by France and England through subsequent centuries to dominate the region. The first French fishermen to exploit the fishing grounds at Newfoundland were Bretons, Normans, and French Basques, whose pioneering role is explained in Joseph LeHuenen, 'The Role of the Basque, Breton and Norman Cod Fishermen in the Discovery of North America from the XVIth to the End of the XVIIIth Century,' *Arctic* 37/4 (Dec. 1984): 520–7. René Bélanger surveys the sixteenth-century French Basque presence in the Gulf of St Lawrence in *Les Basques dans l'estuaire du Saint-Laurent, 1535–1635* (M: PUQ 1971). The English presence became substantial only during the late 1500s. The most thorough study of the organization and prosecution of the early English fishing industry remains Gillian T. Cell, *English Enterprise in Newfoundland, 1577–1660* (T: UTP 1969), though Cell has since modified her interpretation of the competition between seasonal fishermen and early-seventeenth-century colonists.

THE FISHERY IN THE SEVENTEENTH AND EIGHTEENTH CENTURIES

A brief but reliable survey of the seventeenth-century Newfoundland fishery and trade appears in Kenneth Norrie and Douglas Owram, *A History of the Canadian Economy* (T: HBJ 1991). For those fortunate to have access to it, the essay by K. Matthews entitled 'Fisheries: 1500–1800,' in the *ENL*, vol. 2 (1984), is succinct and extremely instructive. Another highly recommended overview appears in the opening chapters of C. Grant Head, *Eighteenth Century Newfoundland: A Geographer's Perspective* (O: CUP 1976). Plates 23, 'The 17th Century Fishery'; 21, 'The Migratory Fisheries'; 25, 'The Newfoundland Fishery, 18th Century'; and 28, 'The Fishery in Atlantic Commerce,' of the *HAC*, vol. 1, are invaluable aids to the literature. None, however, manage to convey the full complexity and diversity of the fishery and its trade. For this, more specialized sources must be consulted.

The diversity of nations participating in the fish trade persisted into the seventeenth century. Dutch involvement in the trade during this century is discussed in Jan Kupp, 'Le développement de l'intérêt hollandais dans la pêcherie de la morue de Terre-Neuve: l'influence hollandaise sur les pêcheries de Terre-Neuve au dix-septième siècle,' *RHAF* 27/4 (mars 1974): 565–9. However, the Dutch left the Newfoundland fishing industry itself to the English and especially to the French, who dominated the seventeenth-century Newfoundland fishery and trade in every aspect: in quantities of men, ships, production, and in the area of exploitation. Unfortunately, there are few studies in English on the French fishery and trade. Apart from H.A. Innis, *The Cod Fisheries*, the most useful survey in English is the essay by Michael Bell within the entry 'France' in *ENL*, vol. 2. Most research on the French fishery is understandably in French. The touchstone for almost all these studies has been Charles de La Morandière, *Histoire de la pêche française de la morue dans l'Amérique septentrionale*, 3 vols. (P: Maisonneuve et Larose 1962–6). This work is massive and extremely thorough, but essentially descriptive. Analysis was left to those who followed this pioneering effort. A useful and more digestible overview of the French fishery is Laurier Turgeon, 'Le temps des pêches lointaines: permanences et transformations (vers 1500–vers 1850),' in Michel Mollat, ed., *Histoire des pêches maritimes en France* (Toulouse, Fr.: Privat 1987).

Such broad surveys rest on a solid foundation of research on the major French ports outfitting for the fishery and active in the trade. One example is L. Turgeon, 'Pour redécouvrir notre 16e siècle: les pêches à Terre-Neuve d'après les archives notariales de Bordeaux,' *RHAF* 39/4 (printemps 1986): 523–49. Unfortunately, such studies tend more usually to be published in obscure or uncommon journals. Collectively they focus attention not only on the inner dynamics of the fishing industry but also on the extremely decentralized character of the French industry. They also underscore the degree to which the choice of fishery was governed by market preferences, though there were determined efforts by an increasingly mercantilist French government to encourage the fishery and trade. These initiatives are discussed in L. Turgeon, 'Colbert et la pêche française à Terre-Neuve,' in Roland Mousnier, dir., *Un nouveau Colbert: actes du colloque pour le tricentenaire de la mort de Colbert* (P: Sedes 1985).

The English fishery during this same period exhibited very different characteristics. It was highly regionalized (in the so-called West Country of England), and concentrated almost exclusively on those foreign markets that desired a dry, lightly salted cure. For years the standard works on the English fishery have been Charles Burnet Judah, Jr, *The North American Fisheries and British Policy to 1713* (Urbana, IL: University of Illinois 1933), Ralph Lounsbury, *The British Fishery at Newfoundland, 1634–1763* (New Haven, CT: Yale University Press 1934; repr. NY: Archon 1969), and H.A. Innis, *The Cod Fisheries*. These pioneering works influenced more recent studies such as G.T. Cell, *English Enterprise in Newfoundland*. Nevertheless, while still useful in some ways (Innis's command of the sources remains impressive), these interpretations should be treated with great caution, as K. Matthews explains in his previously cited essay, 'Historical Fence-Building,' *NQ* (1978). There is also a growing literature on local centres of the British fishing industry and trade, though here, too, there is a tendency to publish in obscure journals. One exception is Rosemary E. Ommer, 'The Cod Trade in the New World,' in Alan Jamieson, ed., *A People of the Sea: The Maritime History of the Channel Islands* (L: Methuen 1987), which describes participation of the Channel Islands in the Newfoundland fishery and trade.

The eighteenth century witnessed a reversal of fortunes in the European fisheries. The French endured the wars that marked the transition from the seventeenth to the eighteenth centuries better than did the English, but a variety of factors in the marketing, production, and metropolitan apexes of the North Atlantic triangle enabled the English to overtake the French. One scholar who has written prolifically about this reversal of fortunes has been Jean-François Brière. He concentrates on St Malo and Granville, with particular attention to the reasons why these ports thrived while so many other French ports withdrew from the Newfoundland fishery; by the late eighteenth century, St Malo and Granville had engrossed about 80 per cent of the French fishing industry and trade. Brière first published his conclusions as articles in several sources, synthesizing them recently as *La pêche française en Amérique du Nord au XVIIIe siècle* (Saint-Laurent, Que.: Fides 1990). Brière's work should be compared with Raymonde Litalien's'-Granville et la pêche à la morue dans le golfe du Saint-Laurent au XVIIIe siècle, d'après les registres de l'Inscription maritime,' *Etudes canadiennes/ Canadian Studies* 13 (1982): 25–31. This article is useful both for its discussion of methodology and for its analysis of the Granvillais fishing industry.

By the eve of the French Revolution the French industry was in a state of extreme crisis caused in large measure by market conditions. This left it very vulnerable to the severe disruption of the wars that followed. However, very little research has been published on the French fishery and trade after the French Revolution. The one facet that has been covered concerns the role played by the islands of St Pierre and Miquelon, which were returned to France under the terms of the Peace of Paris in 1763. Olivier Guyotjeannin has written a survey history, *Saint-Pierre et Miquelon* (P: Editions L'Harmattan 1986), but his treatment is superficial. An extremely well researched essay by Jean-Yves Ribault, 'La population des Iles Saint-Pierre et Miquelon de 1763 à 1793,' *Revue française d'histoire d'outre-mer* 53 (1966): 5–66, gives a better sense of the islands' role as a service centre for the French metropolitan fishery and as a base for its own residential fishery. No research has yet been published on the close economic or social interaction between these French islands and the adjacent south coast of Newfoundland, though it is clear that the relationship was important for both parties.

Excellent research exists on the subject of the French trade in cod. An overall survey of the trade during the eighteenth century is provided by Christopher Moore, 'Cape Breton and the North Atlantic World in the Eighteenth Century,' in Kenneth Donovan, ed., *The Island: New Perspectives on Cape Breton's History, 1713–1990* (F/Sydney, NS: AP/University College of Cape Breton Press 1990). Despite its title Moore's analysis has great bearing on the state of the French fishing economy in Newfoundland. Government regulation within both the production and marketing of cod is examined in J.-F. Brière, 'L'état et le commerce de la morue de Terre-Neuve en France au XVIIIe siècle,' *RHAF* 36/3 (déc. 1982): 323–38. Brière shows that the cost of fish to consumers was determined more by charges added after its arrival in France than by the cost of production. The high cost of fish meant that it was less a dietary mainstay than a supplement, a point affirmed by L. Turgeon's investigation into market demands, 'Pour une histoire de la pêche: le marché de la morue à Marseille au XVIIIe siècle,' *HS/SH* 14/28 (Nov. 1981): 295–322. (A correction of table 3 on page 307 appears in *HS/SH* 15/29 [May 1982]: 296.) A superb discussion of the hectic schedule of a fishing and trading expedition is provided by Brière in 'Le commerce triangulaire entre les ports terre-neuviers français, les pêcheries d'Amérique du nord et Marseille au 18e siècle: nouvelles perspectives,' *RHAF* 40/2 (automne 1986): 193–214. This article could usefully be compared with Ian K. Steele's 'Instructing the Master of a Newfoundland Sack Ship,' *Mariner's Mirror* 63/2 (May 1977): 191–3, and with the fourth chapter, 'The Merchant Triangle in Action,' of R.E. Ommer, *From Outpost to Outport: A Structural Analysis of the Jersey-Gaspé Cod Fishery, 1767–1886* (K&M: MQUP 1991). All these analyses are enhanced when read in conjunction with *HAC*, vol. 1, plates 28, 'The Fishery in Atlantic Commerce,' and 48, 'Canadian North Atlantic Trade.'

The English fishery, like that of the French, fell into increasingly fewer hands as many West Country ports withdrew, either because they could not compete or because new or less risky opportunities appeared. The late seventeenth and early eighteenth centuries were difficult times for the English fishery, as they were for the French. Yet, as David J. Starkey demonstrates in 'Devonians and the Newfoundland Trade,' in Michael Duffy et al., *The New Maritime History of Devon*, vol. 1, *From Early Times to the Late Eighteenth Century* (L: Conway Maritime Press 1993), the English fishery survived the adversity to enter into a period of unparalleled growth and prosperity after 1730. The fishery expanded in part because Ireland and the American colonies gave English outfitters a diversity of sources from which to draw labour and supplies, and in part because the development of a resident population and fishery in Newfoundland made the British fishery in Newfoundland less vulnerable to the disruptions caused by the wars of that era. Though these developments were examined in R. Lounsbury, *The British Fishery at Newfoundland*, and H.A. Innis, *The Cod Fisheries*, a more reliable overview today is that provided in C.G. Head, *Eighteenth Century Newfoundland*.

Anglo-American involvement in Newfoundland's fishery and trade has attracted considerable attention because of the way in which it contributed to the ability of some American colonies, especially those of New England, to balance their trade deficit with England. In chapter 5 of their examination of *The Economy of British America, 1607–1789* (Chapel Hill, NC: University of North Carolina Press 1985), John J. McCusker and Russell R. Menard not only summarize Newfoundland's importance to the New England economy but insist as well that Newfoundland's transformation from a seasonal fishery into a colony of settled communities was made possible by its economic linkages with America. McCusker and Menard also provide an exceptionally lucid explanation of the concepts of staple trades and mercantilism. In the course of revealing how essential the fish trade was for the colonial New England economy, James G. Lydon also gives considerable detail on how the trade in fish actually worked in 'Fish and Flour for Gold: Southern Europe and the Colonial American Balance of Payments,' *Business History Review* 39/2 (Summer 1965): 171–83, as well as in 'Fish for

Gold: The Massachusetts Fish Trade with Iberia, 1700–1773,' *New England Quarterly* 54/4 (Dec. 1981): 539–82.

Irish involvement in Newfoundland began with the late-seventeenth-century practice of English fishing ships stopping at ports in southeastern Ireland for provisions and labour before proceeding to Newfoundland. A vigorous Irish commercial connection with Newfoundland subsequently emerged, which developed into an intricate social and cultural network of great significance to the emerging colonial society in Newfoundland. This subject has been the special preserve of John J. Mannion, whose extensive writings on the Irish-Newfoundland commercial connection include 'The Waterford Merchants and the Irish-Newfoundland Provisions Trade, 1770–1820,' *CPRH*, vol. 4 (1982); 'Patrick Morris and Newfoundland Irish Immigration,' in Cyril J. Byrne and Margaret Harry, eds., *Talamh an Eisc: Canadian and Irish Essays* (H: Nimbus 1986); 'Irish Merchants Abroad: The Newfoundland Experience, 1750–1850,' *NS* 2/2 (Fall 1986): 127–90; 'A Transatlantic Merchant Fishery: Richard Welsh of New Ross and the Sweetmans of Newbawn in Newfoundland, 1734–1862,' in Kevin Whelan and William Nolan, eds., *Wexford: History and Society. Interdisciplinary Essays on the History of an Irish County* (Dublin, Eire: Geography Publications 1987); and 'Migration and Upward Mobility: The Meagher Family in Ireland and Newfoundland, 1730–1830,' *Irish Economic and Social History* 15 (1988): 54–70. Mannion also contributed entries on Irish merchants to the *DCB*: 'Archibald Nevins,' vol. 5 (1983); 'Henry Shea,' vol. 6 (1987); 'Thomas Meagher,' 'Patrick Morris,' and 'Pierce Sweetman,' vol. 7 (1988).

Collectively, Mannion's publications provide useful points of comparisons within the Irish-Newfoundland commercial community, as well as with English merchants. To an extent, it is also possible to draw comparisons with the Scottish experience. D.S. Macmillan, 'The "New Men" in Action: Scottish Mercantile and Shipping Operations in the North American Colonies, 1760–1825,' in Macmillan, ed., *Canadian Business History*, shows that the Scots also responded to economic opportunities within the late-eighteenth-century British fishery.

Despite the importance of American, Irish, and even Scottish linkages, the British commercial presence in Newfoundland remained dominated by West Country English merchants. A detailed examination of these merchants, with particular attention to those of Poole, has been undertaken by W. Gordon Handcock. In his paper 'The Poole Mercantile Community and the Growth of Trinity, 1700–1839,' *NQ* 80/3 (Winter 1985): 19–30, and in a series of contributions to the *DCB*, including 'John Slade,' vol. 4 (1979); 'Charles Garland,' 'Thomas Slade,' 'Thomas Street,' and 'John Waldron,' vol. 5; and 'George Garland,' vol. 6, Handcock shows how profits from the fishery, together with the needs of a growing residential population, encouraged a withdrawal from the fishing industry itself and a shift into the business of supplying and trading with the residential population. This theme also permeates Handcock, *Soe Longe As There Comes Noe Women: Origins of English Settlement in Newfoundland* (SJ: BKW 1989).

Such diversification meant that the abrupt disappearance of the West Country merchants from the fishing industry during the era of the French Revolutionary and Napoleonic Wars did not signify the termination of an activity under the stress of war (as was the case with the French) so much as its transformation. Shannon Ryan examines this process in 'Fishery to Colony: A Newfoundland Watershed, 1793–1815,' *Acadiensis* 12/2 (Spring 1983): 34–52. He demonstrates how the economic strains of wartime accelerated the process by which the British fishing industry became resident in Newfoundland, with British merchants now concentrating almost exclusively on supplying the fishery and residents of Newfoundland with provisions, gear, and other necessities. These themes can also be traced through the biographical studies of specific individuals available in the *DCB*. In addition to those previously mentioned, see K. Matthews's entries 'Samuel Bulley,' 'Robert Newman,' 'Peter Ougier,' and 'Andrew Pinson,' vol. 5, as well as William H. Whiteley's 'Jeremiah Coghlan,' vol. 4.

THE EUROPEAN SETTLING OF NEWFOUNDLAND

Europeans were lured to Newfoundland by the fishery, yet their presence was required only for a few months of the year. The fishing population was a migratory or seasonal one, returning to European homelands at the end of each fishing season. Attempts to colonize the island early in the seventeenth century seemingly failed, and a resident population emerged only in the late seventeenth and early eighteenth centuries. Not until 1825 was Newfoundland granted official status as a colony, prior to which it remained officially a fishing post. Historians have long explained this slow rate of growth and development in terms of a fundamental hostility between the needs of a migratory fisherman for free access to beaches and shore resources and the needs of the settler for permanent occupation of property. This perception has recently given way to a recognition that the growth of a permanent population in Newfoundland was always most successful where merchants and traders had established themselves. The fragility of aboriginal populations, the seeming failure of colonization efforts as diverse as those of the Norse, the English, and the French, together with the difficulties experienced in the nineteenth and twentieth centuries in diversifying the economy, have fostered a stronger appreciation for other limiting factors, such as environmental ones.

The idea of establishing permanent settlements on the island was first encouraged late in the sixteenth century. Some of the promotional literature appears in the third volume of D.B. Quinn's collection *New American World*, although it is the fourth volume of this documentary compilation, subtitled *Newfoundland: From Fishery to Colony; Northwest Passage Searches*, that contains the richest sampling. Some of these documents relate to Humphrey Gilbert's voyage of 1583. A complete documentation is available in D.B. Quinn, ed., *The Voyages and Colonising Enterprises of Sir Humphrey Gilbert*, 2 vols. (L: Hakluyt 1940; repr. NY: Kraus 1967). Quinn also wrote the entry 'Sir Humphrey Gilbert,' *DCB*, vol. 1, and *Sir Humphrey Gilbert and Newfoundland* (SJ: Newfoundland Historical Society 1983), a superb booklet which places Gilbert firmly in his English and North Atlantic social context. The essay is reprinted in D.B. Quinn, *Explorers and Colonies: America, 1500–1625* (L/ Ronceverte, WV: Hambledon Press 1990). Gilbert is best remembered for having formally annexed Newfoundland to the Crown of England. The precise meaning of this act is explained in Patricia Seed, 'Taking Possession and Reading Texts: Establishing the Authority of Overseas Empires,' *WMQ* 3rd ser., 49/2 (Apr. 1992): 183–209. Though it had no immediate significance, Gilbert's action, together with Cabot's discovery, would add substance to subsequent British claims to sovereignty over Newfoundland.

The first attempt at colonization occurred at Cupids Cove in 1610 under the leadership of John Guy on behalf of the London and Bristol Company or, more commonly, the Newfoundland Company. The best work to date on this enterprise is G.T. Cell, ed., *Newfoundland Discovered: English Attempts at Colonization, 1610–1630* (L: Hakluyt 1982). Cell's 'Introduction' is thorough, and revises to some extent her conclusions in *English Enterprise in Newfoundland*. Also available is Cell, 'The Cupids Cove Settlement: A Case Study of the Problems of Early Colonization,' in G.M. Story, ed., *Early European Settlement*. Another Cell essay, 'The Newfoundland Company: A Study of Subscribers to a Colonizing Venture,' *WMQ* 3rd ser., 22/4 (Oct. 1965): 611–25, examines the English social and economic context for the colonization of Newfoundland at this time. It should be read in conjunction with Carole Shammas, 'English Commercial Development and American Colonization, 1560–1620,' in Kenneth R. Andrews et al., eds., *The Westward Enterprise: English Activities in Ireland, the Atlantic and America, 1480–1650* (Detroit, MI: Wayne State University Press 1979). The *DCB*, vol. 1, also contains detailed profiles of John Guy, the pirate Peter Easton, and several of the Cupids Cove colonists.

Other English colonization efforts have received uneven treatment. Sir William Vaughan's attempt to establish a colony at Renewse was not successful, though it remains of interest because of the appointment of Sir Richard Whitbourne to govern and reorganize it in 1618. Whitbourne's essay *A Discourse and Discovery of New-Found-Land*, published in 1620, revised in 1622, and reprinted in the two document collections edited by G.T. Cell and D.B. Quinn, is an invaluable source of information on Newfoundland's fishery and the settlement efforts at this time. Whitbourne's connection with the Renewse settlement continued after Lord Falkland took over the enterprise around 1620. A thorough discussion of the Renewse colony appears in Cell, ed., *Newfoundland Discovered*. Cell also wrote the entries 'Sir Francis Tanfield' and 'Sir Richard Whitbourne' in the *DCB*, vol. 1.

In contrast with the cursory treatment accorded the Renewse colony, there is a considerable literature on the efforts of George Calvert, Lord Baltimore, to establish a colony at Ferryland. Apart from G.T. Cell, ed., *Newfoundland Discovered*, and her earlier *English Enterprise in Newfoundland*, the most useful works on this colony so far are articles. In 'George Calvert and Newfoundland: "The Sad Face of Winter,"' *Maryland Historical Magazine* 71/1 (Spring 1976): 1–18, Thomas Coakley explains Calvert's decision to withdraw from the colony in terms of the difficult environmental challenge facing the colonists in Newfoundland.

Calvert is of particular interest because he was known to be sympathetic to Roman Catholicism at a time when Catholics in England faced discrimination and growing persecution; Calvert would eventually convert to Catholicism. This has long raised questions whether Calvert was motivated into sponsoring a colony in Newfoundland out of a desire to create a religious haven for Catholics. Coakley makes clear that this was not the case, a conclusion subsequently reinforced in two essays by Raymond J. Lahey: 'The Role of Religion in Lord Baltimore's Colonial Enterprise,' *Maryland Historical Magazine* 72/4 (Winter 1977): 492–511; and 'Avalon: Lord Baltimore's Colony in Newfoundland,' in G.M. Story, ed., *Early European Settlement*. More recently, Luca Codignola found no documentary evidence in the Papal Archives in the Vatican that would link the Ferryland colony and Catholicism; see *The Coldest Harbour of the Land: Simon Stock and Lord Baltimore's Colony in Newfoundland, 1621–1649* (M: MQUP 1988).

Allan M. Fraser's entry 'Sir George Calvert,' *DCB*, vol. 1, concludes that Calvert had no lasting influence on Newfoundland. Current research may eventually force us to revise this assessment, but as yet there is too little evidence to argue convincingly that Ferryland, in contrast with the other efforts, was 'successful' as a colonization venture. After Calvert's departure, Sir David Kirke took Ferryland over and quickly clashed with the seasonal fishermen. His tenure is discussed in John S. Moir's entry 'Sir David Kirk,' *DCB*, vol. 1. Eventually, Kirke was made to return to England to answer charges of interference with the fishery. This action has provided much ammunition for those who maintain that the growth of Newfoundland settlement was impaired by an unremitting hostility between the fishing interests and the settlers. It is therefore useful to compare the English experience at colonizing Newfoundland with that of the French.

The French colony of Plaisance (Placentia, as it was known to the English) was founded in 1660. John Humphreys provides an excellent account of the unhappy history of Plaisance in *Plaisance: Problems of Settlement at this Newfoundland Outpost of New France, 1660–1690* (O: National Museums of Canada 1970). While he does indicate that the colony's growth was impaired by friction between metropolitan fishermen and the residents, he makes clear that its lack of success was caused more by environmental limitations and the colony's inability to satisfy the role it was expected to play in the French mercantile empire of the North Atlantic. Unlike the English colonies, Plaisance was a creation of the French government, and yet, despite enormous expenditures on local defences and the garrison, the colony languished. Frederick J. Thorpe explores this paradox in 'Fish, Forts and Finance: The Politics of French Construction at Placentia, 1699–1710,' CHA *HP* (1971): 52–63. See also 'La Poippe' and 'Antoine Parat,' both of whom served as governors at Plaisance, in the *DCB*, vol. 1.

The seeming failure of colonization, whether by corporate, private, or government sponsors, did not preclude permanent settlement in Newfoundland. A resident population did develop on the island during the seventeenth century. While it remained extremely small (probably less than two thousand people) and was constantly changing, it persisted into the eighteenth century when finally it began to grow. Until the early nineteenth century, this process was largely dependent on migration from England and Ireland. Thereafter, population growth was derived almost exclusively from natural increase. A substantial literature, mostly by historical geographers, has developed to define and to explain the population growth of Newfoundland. The complementary relationship between the fishery and the resident population lies at the heart of C.G. Head, *Eighteenth Century Newfoundland*. Another seminal work is J.J. Mannion, ed., *The Peopling of Newfoundland: Essays in Historical Geography* (SJ: Institute of Social and Economic Research,

Memorial University of Newfoundland 1977), which includes essays by the editor, Patricia A. Thornton, Chesley W. Sanger, and Alan G. Macpherson that link permanent settlement to merchant activities in various parts of Newfoundland in several different eras.

In introducing these essays, Mannion makes an extremely useful distinction between seasonal, temporary, and permanent migration. Seasonal migrants came to Newfoundland to fish; they returned to the British Isles at the end of each season. Temporary migrants remained at Newfoundland for a few years before returning eventually to the British Isles. Permanent migrants came and stayed for the rest of their lives. These distinctions are necessary to avoid the trap of accepting contemporary population estimates, which were based on the simplistic distinction between migratory and resident fishermen. W.G. Handcock provides a realistic assessment of the permanent population in his publications. He also punctures the myth that the fishery was responsible for discouraging settlement growth by demonstrating that the resident population originated in the same southwestern region of England in which the British fishery was based. The relationship between commercial development in Newfoundland and the growth of settlement is demonstrated in Handcock's previously cited essay 'The Poole Mercantile Community and the Growth of Trinity, 1700–1839,' NQ (1985). A complete exposition of these and other themes is provided in Handcock, *Soe Longe As There Comes Noe Women*. This research is graphically presented in *HAC*, vol. 1, plate 26, 'Trinity, 18th Century.'

No similar monograph has yet been written on Irish migration to Newfoundland. Thomas Nemec prepared an essay, 'Irish Settlement in Newfoundland,' for the *ENL*, vol. 3 (1991). Nemec has also contributed an instructive case study of an Irish-Newfoundland community, 'Trepassey, 1505–1840 A.D.: An Ethnohistorical Reconstruction of Anglo-Irish Outport Society,' NQ 69/4 (Mar. 1973): 17–28. A companion essay, 'Trepassey, 1840–1900: An Ethnohistorical Reconstruction of Anglo-Irish Outport Society,' NQ 70/1 (June 1973): 15–24, extends the story into the nineteenth century. J.J. Mannion's previously cited significant essays linking the English fishing industry with southeast Ireland's role as an important provisioning and labour recruiting centre should also be consulted.

In demonstrating that the commercial network in eighteenth-century Newfoundland was essential to the development and growth of a permanent residential population, Handcock, Mannion, Head, Matthews, and others have overturned the traditional perception of merchants as unrelenting foes of settlement. They have also influenced subsequent research on settlement in Newfoundland. Thus, Olaf Uwe Janzen emphasizes the role played by St Malo merchants in establishing and maintaining Franco-Irish settlements in southwestern Newfoundland in '"Une Grande Liaison": French Fishermen from Ile Royale on the Coast of Southwestern Newfoundland, 1714–1766 – A Preliminary Survey,' *NS* 3/2 (Fall 1987): 183–200. Nevertheless, it is also apparent that year-round residency required innovative measures by the inhabitants themselves if they were to survive, especially through the long and difficult winter. One such strategy was the practice of 'winter-housing,' in which residents of coastal villages fragmented into family units and dispersed into the interior to subsist on hunting and trapping during the winter; see Philip E.L. Smith, 'In Winter Quarters,' *NS* 3/1 (Spring 1987): 1–36, and his 'Transhumant Europeans Overseas: The Newfoundland Case,' *Current Anthropology* 28/2 (Apr. 1987): 241–50. In 'The Evolution of Sealing and the Spread of Permanent Settlement in Northeastern Newfoundland,' in J.J. Mannion, ed., *The Peopling of Newfoundland*, C.W. Sanger shows that the commercial harvesting of new resources had an immediate effect on permanent demographic patterns. The origins of the seal fishery are explained in J.K. Hiller, 'The Newfoundland Seal Fishery: An Historical Introduction,' *Bulletin of Canadian Studies* 7/2 (Winter 1983–4): 49–72.

Other developments that broadened the resource basis on which population growth could rest are more prosaic. In *Eighteenth Century Newfoundland*, C.G. Head hints at a connection between the appearance of the potato in Newfoundland in the middle of the eighteenth century and the growth thereafter of a permanent population. Most crops, however, were grown as part of a household subsistence economy; commercial agriculture developed late and only under special circumstances, according to Robert MacKinnon, 'Farming the Rock: The Evolution of Commercial Agriculture around St. John's, Newfoundland, to 1945,' *Acadiensis* 20/2 (Spring 1991): 32–61. In 'The Staple Model Reconsidered: The Case of Agricultural Policy in Northeast Newfoundland, 1785–1855,' *Acadiensis* 21/2 (Spring 1992): 48–71, Sean Cadigan puts to rest the old myth that government and the merchant community were opposed to agricultural development, but he shows that the politicization of agricultural development by early-nineteenth-century reformers, together with the desire of colonial administrators to reduce public dependence on relief whenever the fishery failed, created unreasonable expectations about the island's agricultural potential. In his essay 'Patrick Morris and Newfoundland Irish Immigration,' in C.J. Byrne and M. Harry, eds., *Talamh an Eisc*, J.J. Mannion analyses the particular efforts, ultimately unsuccessful, of one merchant to promote agricultural development and settlement in the early nineteenth century. Mannion also describes the career of an Irish farmer in Newfoundland, 'John O'Brien,' *DCB*, vol. 8 (1985).

The proportion of permanent residents to temporary or seasonal ones grew steadily until finally, during the American Revolutionary War, the residential population permanently exceeded the non-residential one. There has been considerable interest in characterizing the society that emerged with this growth. In 'Newfoundland in the Period before the American Revolution,' *Pennsylvania Magazine of History and Biography* 65/1 (Jan. 1941): 56–78, Wilfred Brenton Kerr explains in terms of British nationalism the failure of the residential population to be moved by the passions aroused by the American Revolution. That explanation no longer stands the test of close scrutiny, for Newfoundland lacked the homogeneity and unity that would have made any kind of consensus by its residential population possible. Contemporary impressions of seventeenth- and eighteenth-century Newfoundland make it clear that the population lacked the means, let alone the sense, of cohesion or homogeneity of expression. For example, see the accounts in Jean Murray, ed., *The Newfoundland Journal of Aaron Thomas, 1794* (Don Mills, Ont.: Longmans 1968); A.M. Lysaght, ed., *Joseph Banks in Newfoundland and Labrador, 1766: His Diary, Manuscripts and Collections* (Berkeley and Los Angeles, CA: University of California Press 1971); Rene Wicks, 'Newfoundland Social Life, 1750–1850,' *NQ* 70/4 (Fall 1974): 17–23; and P. Neary and P. O'Flaherty, eds., *By Great Waters*. Only as the eighteenth century drew to a close did this begin to change, a process which S. Ryan examines in the previously cited essay 'Fishery to Colony,' *Acadiensis* (1983).

Nevertheless, within the communities themselves, certain social characteristics had by then become well established. In previously cited essays by T. Nemec, 'Trepassey, 1505–1840 A.D.' and 'Trepassey, 1840–1900,' *NQ* (1973), and W.G. Handcock, 'The Poole Mercantile Community and the Growth of Trinity, 1700–1839,' *NQ* (1985), the same conclusion is reached: class differences, not economic or religious ones, were the major bases of social divisions within each community.

Fundamental to any understanding of such differences within local societies is an understanding of the 'truck system,' through which merchants from the eighteenth century onward controlled labour through a system of wage payment in supplies. An excellent discussion of the truck system appears in various portions of R.E. Ommer, *From Outpost to Outport*. The system was exploitive and prone to abuse, and British officials became convinced it contributed to the transformation of the fishery from a seasonal to a residential activity; see John E. Crowley, 'Empire versus Truck: The Official Interpretation of Debt and Labour in the Eighteenth-Century New-foundland Fishery,' *CHR* 70/3 (Sept. 1989): 311–36. One abuse was the degree to which rum from the West Indies was used as a cheap substitute for the payment of wages, a problem that predated even the truck system; see Peter Pope, 'Historical Archaeology and the Demand for Alcohol in 17th Century Newfoundland,' *Acadiensis* 19/1 (Fall 1989): 72–90. Efforts to over-turn the truck system were made, though two recent essays by S. Cadigan maintain that the development of a wages and lien system in the early nine-teenth century had less to do with such efforts than with structural changes within the fishing society itself; see 'Seamen, Fishermen and the Law: The Role of the Wages and Lien System in the Decline of Wage Labour in the Newfoundland Fishery,' in Colin Howell and Richard J. Twomey, eds., *Jack Tar in History: Essays in the History of Maritime Life and Labour* (F: AP 1991), and 'Merchant Capital, the State, and Labour in a British Colony: Servant-Master Relations and Capital Accumulation in Newfoundland's Northeast-Coast Fishery, 1775–1799,' *JCHA* 2 (1991): 17–42. The current state of the debate on the truck system is provided in R.E. Ommer, ed., *Merchant Credit and Labour Strategies in Historical Perspective* (F: AP 1990); Newfoundland is treated in useful essays by J.K. Hiller and Robert M. Lewis. A third essay, one by David A. Macdonald, 'They Cannot Pay Us in Money: Newman and Company and the Supplying System in the Newfoundland Fishery, 1850–1884,' first appeared in *Acadiensis* 19/1 (Fall 1989): 142–55. Possibly the most useful article on the theme was a review of Ommer's collection by Stu-art Pierson in *NS* 8/1 (Spring 1992): 90–108. It is a thoughtful discourse on the ambivalency with which merchants, credit, and truck are now per-ceived. Clearly, there is no. longer any excuse for students to indulge in the stereotype of the grasping, greedy, and destructively exploitive robber bar-ons; this image has been firmly rejected. Yet the questions Pierson raises also indicate that a consensus has not yet been reached on how to replace that image.

The English and Irish origins of the resident population meant that Newfoundland was divided into equal proportions of Protestants and Roman Catholics. This representation, together with the role that religious organizations have played in alleviating the more extreme social conditions on the island, has resulted in considerable interest in the religious history of Newfoundland. In the seventeenth century, there were sporadic visits by clergymen and preachers. Another, frequently overlooked, source of reli-gious service was the Royal Navy, whose warships since roughly the middle of the seventeenth century patrolled and protected the fishery. Chaplains often served on these ships and attended to the needs of early residents; see

'The Navy as Moral Guardian: Newfoundland,' in Waldo E.L. Smith, *The Navy and Its Chaplains in the Days of Sail* (T: RP 1961). The activities of one such chaplain, who served at St John's early in the eighteenth century, are described in 'John Jackson,' *DCB*, vol. 2 (1969).

The first concerted effort to provide Newfoundland with religious service came in the eighteenth century with the Society for the Propagation of the Gospel in Foreign Parts, the missionary arm of the Church of England; see Ruth M. Christensen, 'The Establishment of S.P.G. Missions in Newfoundland, 1703–1783,' *Historical Magazine of the Protestant Episcopal Church* 20 (1951): 207–29. An excellent impression of the challenges that SPG missionaries faced in Newfoundland is provided by several biographical essays in the *DCB*: 'Henry Jones' and 'Robert Kilpatrick,' vol. 3 (1974); 'Edward Langman,' vol. 4; and 'James Balfour,' vol. 5.

Protestant dissenters also had a significant presence in eighteenth-century Newfoundland. The first Methodist preacher was Laurence Coughlan, whose life is the subject of an entry by P. O'Flaherty in *DCB*, vol. 4, and an article by Hans Rollmann, 'Laurence Coughlan and the Origins of Methodism in Newfoundland,' in Charles H.H. Scobie and John Webster Grant, eds., *The Contribution of Methodism to Atlantic Canada* (K&M: MQUP 1992). Rollmann has also published research on early Congregationalists and other dissenters; see, for instance, his 'John Jones, James O'Donel, and the Question of Religious Tolerance in Eighteenth-Century Newfoundland: A Correspondence,' *NQ* 80/1 (Summer 1984): 23–7. See, too, the entry 'John Jones' by Frederic F. Thompson in *DCB*, vol. 4.

The most comprehensive introduction to the study of Roman Catholicism in eighteenth- and nineteenth-century Newfoundland is R.J. Lahey, 'Catholicism and Colonial Policy in Newfoundland, 1779–1845,' in Terrence Murphy and Gerald Stortz, eds., *Creed and Culture: The Place of English-Speaking Catholics in Canadian Society, 1750–1930* (K&M: MQUP 1993). While the survey is somewhat traditional and should therefore be used with caution, it manages to cover the social, constitutional, and cultural themes both thoroughly and accurately. One of the most significant developments in the history of Roman Catholicism in Newfoundland is the granting of official religious tolerance in 1784, which opened the door to the subsequent establishment of an organized Catholic Church on the island. H. Rollmann has written several extremely useful essays on this process, including 'Richard Edwards, John Campbell, and the Proclamation of Religious Liberty in Eighteenth-Century Newfoundland,' *NQ* 80/2 (Fall 1984): 4–12, and 'Religious Enfranchisement and Roman Catholics in Eighteenth-Century Newfoundland,' in T. Murphy and C.J. Byrne, eds.,

Religion and Identity: The Experience of Irish and Scottish Catholics in Atlantic Canada (SJ: Jesperson Press 1987). The first priest to arrive in Newfoundland following the proclamation of official tolerance of Roman Catholicism was James Louis O'Donel. His life is described in Philip O'Connell, 'Dr. James Louis O'Donnell [*sic*] (1737–1811), First Bishop of Newfoundland,' *Irish Ecclesiastical Record* 103 (1965): 308–24; R.J. Lahey, *James Louis O'Donel in Newfoundland, 1784–1807: The Establishment of the Roman Catholic Church* (SJ: Newfoundland Historical Society 1984); and 'James Louis O'Donel,' *DCB*, vol. 5. C.J. Byrne edited a valuable collection of letters by early leaders of Newfoundland's Roman Catholic Church, *Gentlemen-Bishops and Faction Fighters: The Letters of Bishops O'Donel, Lambert, Scallan and Other Irish Missionaries* (SJ: Jesperson Press 1984), to which H. Rollmann has responded with 'Gentlemen-Bishops and Faction-Fighters: Additional Letters Pertaining to Newfoundland Catholicism, from the Franciscan Library at Killiney (Ireland),' *JCCHS* 30/1 (Apr. 1988): 3–19.

The development of a permanent and growing residential population in Newfoundland also necessitated the establishment of local institutions of law and government. This need contradicted government's preference for a seasonal fishery, whose legal matters could be handled when the fishermen returned to England, and whose minimal administrative requirements in Newfoundland could then be provided by the fishery itself. This need also contradicted the wishes of the merchants, who objected to all innovations that might lead to the imposition of regulations on what was otherwise a 'free fishery.' K. Matthews argues in his *Lectures on the History of Newfoundland* that this fear of government regulation was the real reason why merchants objected to settlement, even as they encouraged permanent settlement in Newfoundland through their activities there. Despite both government and commercial resistance to the introduction of local government, the burgeoning population made some administrative measures necessary. The result was the appearance of various ad hoc measures, coupled with the occasional act of Parliament, that over time gave Newfoundland a legal and administrative system and, eventually, local government. This process is chronicled in essays in the *ENL*, 'Government,' vol. 2, and 'Judicature,' vol. 3, though these accounts should be used with extreme caution because of their traditional interpretation. Christopher English provides a more analytical assessment in 'The Development of the Newfoundland Legal System to 1815,' *Acadiensis* 20/1 (Autumn 1990): 89–119. Many of the developments pertaining to British policy toward Newfoundland and to the growth of a Newfoundland legal and constitutional structure can be traced through W.L. Grant and J. Munro, eds., *Acts of the Privy Council of England,* as well as through Great Britain, Judicial Committee of the Privy Council, *In the Matter of the Boundary between the Dominion of Canada and the Colony of Newfoundland in the Labrador Peninsula.*

Most of the governors of Newfoundland, from the inception of the system of naval governors with Henry Osborne in 1729 through to the introduction of civilian administrations under Governor Thomas Cochrane in 1825, appear in the *DCB*, vols. 2–10. These entries are invaluable if only because few governors would otherwise receive scholarly attention. The exception is Governor Hugh Palliser (1764–8), whose name is associated with one of Parliament's infrequent attempts to address the need for administrative order in the fishery; he is often identified as a key figure in the definition of British policy toward Newfoundland. The best work on Palliser appeared in several essays by W.H. Whiteley, including 'Governor Hugh Palliser and the Newfoundland and Labrador Fishery, 1764–1768,' *CHR* 50/2 (June 1969): 141–63; 'James Cook, Hugh Palliser, and the Newfoundland Fisheries,' *NQ* 69/2 (Oct. 1972): 17–22; and 'Sir Hugh Palliser,' *DCB*, vol. 4. A useful corrective to the impression that Palliser dominated the process of defining British policy is given in J.E. Crowley's previously cited article 'Empire versus Truck,' *CHR* (1989).

This process of defining policy was particularly energetic after the American Revolution, and generated a body of testimony that was recently edited by Sheila Lambert and reprinted in an extremely important collection, *House of Commons Sessional Papers of the Eighteenth Century*, vol. 90, *George III (Newfoundland, 1792–93)* (Wilmington, DE: Scholarly Resources 1975). By then the growing complexity and permanence of Newfoundland society encouraged the view that a new approach was needed to administer Newfoundland, one more suited to a residential population than a trade. This process can be traced through such *DCB* entries as 'Aaron Graham,' 'Richard Hutchings,' and 'Mark Milbanke,' vol. 5; and 'John Reeves,' vol. 6. Gradually there emerged a sentiment for administrative and political change, one that is generally, though not always accurately, defined as a 'reform' sentiment. This is discussed at greater length later in the chapter.

BEOTHUK AND MICMAC

When Europeans came to Newfoundland, first to catch fish and later to settle, they found the island already inhabited by an indigenous people. The Beothuk, as they were known, have attracted a great deal of study, in part because of their tragic extinction early in the nineteenth century but even more so because of the sensational myths that sprang up to explain that extinction. The definitive source for information about the Beothuk remains James P. Howley, *The Beothucks, or Red Indians: The Aboriginal Inhabitants of Newfoundland* (Cambridge, Eng.: Cambridge University Press 1915; repr. T: Coles 1980). It is full of descriptive material and reprinted documents, an unsurpassed treasure trove of information. It has been supplemented but not replaced by works such as Ingeborg Marshall, 'An Unpublished Map Made by John Cartwright between 1768 and 1773 Showing Beothuk Indian Settlements and Artifacts and Allowing a New Population Estimate,' *Ethnohistory* 24/3 (Summer 1977): 223–49, and, more recently, *Reports and Letters by George Christopher Pulling Relating to the Beothuk Indians of Newfoundland*, ed. I. Marshall (SJ: BKW 1989).

The Beothuk avoided contact with the Europeans, withdrawing from those parts of the coast frequented by fishermen. John Guy's encounter with the Beothuk in 1612 was the last recorded contact until Europeans began to push into the Notre Dame Bay region in the mid-eighteenth century; see William Gilbert, '"Divers Places": The Beothuk Indians and John Guy's Voyage into Trinity Bay in 1612,' *NS* 6/2 (Fall 1990): 147–67. As fishermen, and more significantly over-winterers, encroached upon the salmon rivers and fur-trapping regions of the northeast coast of the island, contact was renewed and, more often than not, involved friction and violence. The brutality of these incidents was sufficiently deliberate on both sides that a tradition of unremitting hostility developed. The British authorities desired peaceful relations with the Beothuk, if only out of a conviction that the fishery thrived best under conditions of peace and harmony. Expeditions led by John Cartwright in 1768 and David Buchan in 1811–12 failed to establish peaceful contact with the Beothuk; see 'John Solomon Cartwright' and 'David Buchan,' *DCB*, vol. 7. Missionary efforts to promote peace and friendship between the European and Native cultures were equally unsuccessful; these are discussed in I. Marshall, 'Methodists and Beothuk: Research in Methodist Archives,' *NS* 2/1 (Spring 1986): 19–28, and P.E.L. Smith, 'Beothuks and Methodists,' *Acadiensis* 16/1 (Autumn 1986): 118–35. Such efforts had little chance for success because by then the population of the Beothuk had probably already declined below the threshold of viability. In 1829 Shawnadithit, the last known surviving Beothuk, died of tuberculosis; see her entry in *DCB*, vol. 6.

Predictably, perhaps, the extinction of the Beothuk has become shrouded in sensation and myth. The demonstrable hostility and violence between Natives and Europeans in the late eighteenth century provided the dubious basis for claims that the Beothuk were 'hunted for sport,' that white men massacred the Beothuk by the hundred and that their extinction was therefore an act of genocide. That their extinction was a tragedy is undeniable; perhaps it could even have been prevented. Yet sober inquiry has challenged the worst excesses of the standard mythology, and we are beginning to recognize that how we perceive the Beothuk often says more about us than it does about them. This point is eloquently made by Richard Budgel in 'The Beothuks and the Newfoundland Mind,' *NS* 8/1 (Spring 1992): 15–33. The more extreme myths about the Beothuk are dismissed by F.W. Rowe in *Extinction: The Beothucks of Newfoundland* (T: MHR 1977), while Leslie F.S. Upton methodically picks them apart in 'The Extermination of the Beothucks of Newfoundland,' *CHR* 58/2 (June 1977): 133–53, and 'The Beothucks: Questions and Answers,' *Acadiensis* 7/2 (Spring 1978): 150–5. Upton suggests that the Beothuk never numbered more than two thousand at best and that these low numbers, together with their hunter-gatherer subsistence economy, made them vulnerable to any disruption or interruption of a fragile food chain, such as was occasioned by their retreat from the coast to avoid European contact. Upton's thesis is reinforced by J.A. Tuck and Ralph T. Pastore in 'A Nice Place to Visit, but ... Prehistoric Human Extinctions on the Island of Newfoundland,' *Canadian Journal of Archaeology* 9/1 (1985): 69–80, which shows that the Beothuk extinction was not unprecedented. Pastore, 'Fishermen, Furriers, and Beothuks: The Economy of Extinction,' *Man in the Northeast* 33 (Spring 1987): 47–62, examines why the Beothuk did not establish an economic relationship with Europeans which might have cushioned them against the factors contributing to their demise. One of those factors may have been the reduced gene pool caused not only by their small numbers but also by lack of amicable contact with other aboriginal people, a point made in Pastore, 'The Collapse of the Beothuk World,' *Acadiensis* 19/1 (Fall 1989): 52–71. Disease also played its part according to I. Marshall, 'Disease as a Factor in the Demise of the Beothuk Indians,' *Culture* 1/1 (1981): 71–7; reprinted in Carol Wilton, ed., *Change and Continuity: A Reader on Pre-Confederation Canada* (T: MHR 1992).

One recurring – and controversial – explanation for the Beothuk extinction is that Micmacs from Nova Scotia were hostile to the Beothuk and contributed to their demise. According to Charles A. Martijn, 'An Eastern Micmac Domain of Islands,' in William Cowan, ed., *Actes du vingtième congrès des algonquinistes* (O: CUP 1989), the Micmac included Newfoundland as part of their hunting territory. These visits, and the technology that made it possible, are examined in several essays in C.A. Martijn, ed., *Les Micmacs et la mer* (M: Recherches amérindiennes au Québec 1986). Eventually some Micmac settled permanently at Conne River in the Bay d'Espoir on the south coast. Another group settled at Bay St George on the west coast in the middle of the eighteenth century according to Dennis A. Bartels and O.U. Janzen, 'Micmac Migration to Western Newfoundland,' *Canadian Journal of Native Studies* 10/1 (1990): 71–94. By the nineteenth century the Micmac were an established fixture of island society; see R.T. Pastore, *The Newfoundland Micmacs: A History of Their Traditional Life* (SJ: Newfoundland Historical Society 1978), and 'Indian Summer: Newfoundland Micmacs in the Nineteenth Century,' in Richard A. Preston, ed., *Canadian Ethnology Society: Papers from the Fourth Congress, 1977* (O: National Museum of Man 1978). The link between the arrival of the Micmac and the extinction of the Beothuk was made soon after the last Beothuk died. D.A. Bartels challenges this interpretation in 'Time Immemorial? A Research Note on Micmacs in Newfoundland,' *NQ* 75/3 (Christmas 1979): 6–9. However, I. Marshall continues to maintain that there were extensive and lasting hostilities between the two people, and that the Micmacs therefore contributed to the Beothuk decline; see 'Beothuk and Micmac: Re-examining Relationships,' *Acadiensis* 17/2 (Spring 1988): 52–82.

The history of aboriginal Newfoundland is not limited to the Beothuk and Micmac; Labrador has a substantial aboriginal population. Their history, however, is discussed elsewhere in this essay's treatment of Labrador as a distinct region.

THE ANGLO-FRENCH COMPETITION FOR NEWFOUNDLAND

One important theme in Newfoundland history during this period concerns the competition between England and France for access to, and control over, the fishery. This competition coloured British policy toward Newfoundland and has generated a substantial literature. Despite its age, Gerald S. Graham's *Empire of the North Atlantic: The Maritime Struggle for North America* (T: UTP 1950) is unsurpassed in its survey of the North Atlantic context for this competition. Both countries prized the fishery as a strategic asset by virtue of its reputation for transforming landsmen into experienced mariners who might then be able to serve in their respective national navies when needed; in the language of the day, the fishery was a 'nursery for seamen.' Graham wrote several assessments of the effect this perception had on British policy toward Newfoundland and of the steps taken to ensure its defence. Of these, the most succinct, and still an important starting-point, is 'Fisheries and Sea Power,' CHA *AR* (1941): 24–31, reprinted in George A. Rawlyk, ed., *Historical Essays on the Atlantic Provinces* (T: M&S 1967). See also Graham, 'Newfoundland in British Strategy from Cabot to Napoleon,' in R.A. MacKay, ed., *Newfoundland: Economic, Diplomatic, and Strategic Studies* (T: OUP 1946; repr. NY: AMS Press 1979).

How effectively the fishery actually fulfilled its role as a nursery for seamen is a matter of some question. Both G.S. Graham and, more recently, D.J. Starkey in 'The West Country–Newfoundland Fishery and the Manning of the Royal Navy,' in Robert Higham, ed., *Security and Defence in South-West England before 1800* (Exeter, Eng.: University of Exeter Press 1987), have argued that the fishery provided the navy with relatively few mariners. Instead, the image as a nursery for seamen was manipulated by the merchant community to discourage the introduction to the fishery of government and regulations that would ensue if a migratory fishery gave way to a residential one.

In the end, reality mattered less than perceptions; eighteenth-century French policy like its British counterpart was dedicated to the preservation of continued access by its fishermen to the fishery. Yet care should be taken in drawing conclusions about how that access was to be secured. There has been a regrettable tendency to assume that the efforts of fishing interests to secure protection for their investments in Newfoundland had the desired effect, and that wartime military planning was guided constantly by an acceptance of the fisheries' strategic significance. G.S. Graham and D.J. Starkey both cast doubt on this view, while James D. Alsop in 'The Age of the Projectors: British Imperial Strategy in the North Atlantic in the War of Spanish Succession,' *Acadiensis* 21/1 (Autumn 1991): 30–53, demonstrates that Newfoundland interests, whether commercial or military, could not move government to act in their behalf unless their appeal was carefully tuned to government priorities in Europe. It should therefore come as no surprise that the security of access by England's rivals to the fishery was established more through diplomatic efforts than military or naval ones.

This truth is best revealed in the history of the definition of what became known as the 'French' or 'Treaty Shore.' The origins and consequences of the decision to grant France the right to fish in Newfoundland after France had conceded British sovereignty over the island in 1713 was the focus of an authoritative study by F.F. Thompson, *The French Shore Problem in Newfoundland: An Imperial Study* (T: UTP 1961). More recently, French diplomatic manoeuvrings to define their treaty rights as advantageously as possible were explored in J.-F. Brière, 'Pêche et politique à Terre-Neuve au XVIIIe siècle: la France véritable gagnante du traité d'Utrecht?' *CHR* 64/2 (June 1983): 168–87, and in J.K. Hiller, 'Utrecht Revisited: The Origins of French Fishing Rights in Newfoundland Waters,' *NS* 7/1 (Spring 1991):

23–39. In 'The Comte de Vergennes, The Newfoundland Fisheries, and the Peace Negotiation of 1783: A Reconsideration,' *CHR* 46/1 (Mar. 1965): 32–46, Orville T. Murphy examines the particular way in which the fisheries figured in the diplomacy that concluded the American Revolution and, in the process, redefined the boundaries of the French Shore. Jonathan Dull provides Murphy's theme with a wider context in *The French Navy and American Independence: A Study of Arms and Diplomacy, 1774–1787* (Princeton, NJ: Princeton University Press 1975). Both Murphy and Dull supersede Dallas D. Irvine, 'The Newfoundland Fishery: A French Objective in the War of American Independence,' *CHR* 13/3 (Sept. 1932): 268–84, though Irvine and Murphy both are useful in reminding us that after 1775 the Americans joined France and England in their determination to preserve their shares of the fisheries. American efforts to secure access to the Newfoundland fisheries following the colonies' break with Great Britain were based more on the fisheries' economic value than any strategic benefits according to A.M. Fraser, 'The Treaty Basis of American Fishing Rights, 1783–1888,' in R.A. MacKay, ed., *Newfoundland*. And Spain was still a factor in the diplomacy of the fisheries according to Vera Lee Brown, 'Spanish Claims to a Share in the Newfoundland Fisheries in the Eighteenth Century,' CHA *AR* (1925): 64–82.

Neither British strategy nor the tendency for Newfoundland's fate to be decided at the negotiating table precluded hostilities on the island itself. In the seventeenth century, sudden descents on the fisheries at Newfoundland were carried out by hostile forces, sometimes with great destruction. For example, see Donald G. Shomette and Robert D. Haslach, *Raid on America: The Dutch Naval Campaign of 1672–1674* (Columbia, SC: University of South Carolina Press 1988). The French colony of Plaisance was therefore protected by fortifications and a garrison; their military history and social and economic impact are discussed in J.-P. Proulx, 'The Military History of Placentia: A Study of the French Fortifications,' in his *Placentia, Newfoundland* (O: Parks Canada 1979).

The British authorities resisted a similar approach. Protection of the fish trade in wartime was provided by escorted convoys and warships stationed in the approaches to the major markets in Europe; this strategy is discussed in R. Patrick Crowhurst, *The Defence of British Trade, 1689–1815* (Folkestone, Eng.: Dawson & Sons 1977), and Sari Hornstein, *The Restoration Navy and English Foreign Trade, 1674–1688* (Brookfield, VT: Scolar Press 1991). Yet the possibility of overland attacks on the English settlements by French forces stationed at Plaisance inspired the citizenry at St John's to build themselves a fort as early as 1693; see O.U. Janzen, 'New Light on the

Origins of Fort William at St. John's, Newfoundland, 1693–1696,' *NQ* 83/2 (Fall 1987): 24–31. Those fears were well founded; during the winter of 1696–7, Pierre Le Moyne d'Iberville led a campaign that wiped out practically every English settlement in Newfoundland. This raid is described in extremely thorough detail in Alan F. Williams, *Father Baudoin's War: D'Iberville's Campaigns in Acadia and Newfoundland, 1696, 1697* (SJ: Department of Geography, Memorial University 1987), a book which also provides an excellent profile of Newfoundland at the end of the seventeenth century. D'Iberville's attack was repeated twice during the War of the Spanish Succession (1702–13); the best account of these attacks, apart from G.S. Graham, *Empire of the North Atlantic*, can be found in *DCB* entries 'Daniel d'Auger de Subercase,' 'Pierre Le Moyne d'Iberville et d'Ardillières,' and 'Philippe Pastour de Costebelle,' vol. 2; and 'Joseph de Monbeton de Brouillan, *dit* Saint-Ovide,' vol. 3.

D'Iberville's raid forced the British to fortify and garrison St John's, ushering in nearly two centuries of military presence there, which contributed immeasurably to the demographic and economic growth of St John's and its development into an administrative and political capital. This process is described in a valuable survey by James E. Candow, 'The British Army in Newfoundland, 1697–1824,' *NQ* 79/4 (Spring 1984): 21–8, as well as in an essay, 'Military Garrisons,' by O.U. Janzen in the *ENL*, vol. 3. Colonel G.W.L. Nicholson's military history of Newfoundland, *The Fighting Newfoundlander: A History of the Royal Newfoundland Regiment* (SJ: Government of Newfoundland 1964), is well researched but is not as strong on the social and economic context of the Newfoundland garrisons. A useful examination of civil-military relations at St John's and Placentia during the early years of the garrison is provided in Glanville Davies, 'Military Leadership at Newfoundland before 1729,' *Journal of the Society for Army Historical Research* 59 (Winter 1981): 194–200. Davies's interpretation should be supplemented – and in some instances balanced – by the several insightful entries in the *DCB* on the early military commanders at St John's and Placentia. See 'Sir John Gibsone,' 'Samuel Gledhill,' 'Thomas Lloyd,' 'John Moody,' and 'Michael Richards,' vol. 2. Paul O'Neill's chapter, 'A Military Animal,' in his *The Story of St. John's, Newfoundland*, vol. 1, *The Oldest City* (Erin, Ont.: Press Porcepic 1975), is an episodic chronicle at best. Placentia is better served by the section entitled 'Placentia: 1713–1811,' in J.-P. Proulx, *Placentia, Newfoundland*.

In the literature on Newfoundland's military history during the eighteenth century most attention has been given either to specific campaigns or to particular military or strategic problems. Thus, the French raid on the fisheries in 1762 has received considerable treatment. Major Evan Fyers's article 'The Loss and Recapture of St. John's, Newfoundland, in 1762,' *Journal of the Society for Army Historical Research* 11 (1932): 179–215, is excellent for its detail but offers little strategic analysis. Georges Cerbelaud Salagnac, 'La reprise de Terre-Neuve par les Français en 1762,' *Revue française d'histoire d'outre-mer* 63/2 (1976): 211–22, is extremely good and avoids the conclusion, favoured by most English-speaking historians, that the object of the French attack was to hold St John's as a bargaining chip at the peace table. The attack was conceived as a hit-and-run raid, a point that is supported in O.U. Janzen, 'The French Raid upon the Newfoundland Fishery in 1762: A Study in the Nature and Limits of Eighteenth-Century Sea Power,' in William B. Cogar, gen. ed., *Naval History: The Seventh Symposium of the U.S. Naval Academy* (Wilmington, DE: Scholarly Resources 1988).

One serendipitous result of the raid was that the French made detailed charts of Trinity during their brief occupation, thereby adding substantially to our knowledge of what was already one of the best-documented communities in eighteenth-century Newfoundland. W.G. Handcock describes both the raid and the charts in 'State-of-the-Art French Cartography in Eighteenth Century Newfoundland: The Work of Marc Antoine Sicre de Cinq-Mars,' *NS* 4/2 (Fall 1988): 145–62. It is James Cook, however, who is invariably associated with cartographic surveys of eighteenth-century Newfoundland, and with good reason. His work with the British relief expedition to St John's in 1762 was of such quality that he was immediately commissioned to chart the south, north, and west coasts of the island. This work, between 1763 and 1767, affirmed British sovereignty over areas of Newfoundland where British control was tenuous or relatively new. Cook's achievements in Newfoundland are examined in W.H. Whiteley's previously cited 'James Cook, Hugh Palliser, and the Newfoundland Fisheries,' *NQ* (1972), as well as in *James Cook in Newfoundland, 1762–1767* (SJ: Newfoundland Historical Society 1975). Yet no study would be complete without reference to Glyndwr Williams's entry 'James Cook,' *DCB*, vol. 4, or J.C. Beaglehole's exceptional *The Life of Captain James Cook* (Stanford, CA: Stanford University Press 1974).

The defence of the fisheries during the war of the American Revolution is the focus of O.U. Janzen, 'The Royal Navy and the Defence of Newfoundland during the American Revolution,' *Acadiensis* 14/1 (Autumn 1984): 28–48. In 'The American Threat to the Newfoundland Fisheries, 1776–1777,' *American Neptune* 48/3 (Summer 1988): 154–64, Janzen develops his analysis further by arguing that American privateers operating in Newfoundland waters were primarily interested in intercepting transatlantic commercial shipping. Fishing vessels were little more than targets of convenience; plundering them of their men, provisions, rigging, and sails enabled privateers to extend their cruising time and improve their chances of capturing a rich prize. An important source for this research is William Bell Clark and W.J. Morgan, eds., *Naval Documents of the American Revolution* (Washington, DC: Government Printing Office 1964–), which to date has published nine volumes of operational documents from primarily American and British sources.

At the beginning of the French Revolutionary and Napoleonic Wars Newfoundland was briefly threatened by a French expedition, which, however, was an exceptional event. For the most part the British controlled military actions in the region, beginning with the seizure of the French islands of St Pierre and Miquelon, described in J. Mackay Hitsman, 'The Capture of St Pierre-et-Miquelon, 1793,' *Canadian Army Journal* 13/3 (July 1959): 77–81. The greatest threat to the security of the fishery came not from the French but from disaffected Irish soldiers who planned an uprising in 1797; this event has been examined in several general sources, but receives particular attention in A. Fisk, 'Mutiny in Newfoundland, August 1797,' *Canadian Defence Quarterly* 16/1 (Summer 1986): 58–62.

Of greater significance than the tactical or strategic problems that they present, the late-eighteenth-century wars had a profound effect on the development of Newfoundland society. This point is stressed in S. Ryan's previously cited article 'Fishery to Colony,' *Acadiensis* (1983). By the time those wars finally drew to a close in 1815 the fishery was almost entirely residential, and the migration of English and Irish labourers to Newfoundland decreased dramatically. The traumatic shift from artificial wartime prosperity to peacetime competition is described in James G. Flynn, 'The Effects of the War of 1812 on the Newfoundland Economy, with an Additional Comment on Post-War Depression,' *NQ* 77/2–3 (Summer–Fall 1981): 67–72, as well as in Ryan's article. The seeming recovery of the fishing economy in the decades that followed would not last; profound structural changes occurred in both the fishing industry and the trade which Newfoundland's infant political system was ill-equipped to handle, despite the decision in 1824 to grant Newfoundland colonial status and, eight years later, to grant it representative government.

THE FISHERY IN THE NINETEENTH CENTURY

Several readings provide invaluable surveys of the nineteenth-century fishing economy, though few have had as great an impact as David Alexander,

'Newfoundland's Traditional Economy and Development to 1934,' *Acadiensis* 5/2 (Spring 1976): 56–78, reprinted in J.K. Hiller and P. Neary, eds., *Newfoundland in the Nineteenth and Twentieth Centuries*. Over the years S. Ryan has contributed several detailed examinations of specific aspects of that saltfish economy. His entry 'Fisheries: 1800–1900' in the *ENL*, vol. 2, together with his superb analysis 'The Newfoundland Salt Cod Trade in the Nineteenth Century,' in Hiller and Neary, eds., *Newfoundland in the Nineteenth and Twentieth Centuries*, provides as instructive an introduction to the complex interactions among productivity, demographic growth, and market conditions as one can find. Ryan provides a more detailed assessment of the fish trade in two recent works: the whole trade is analysed in *Fish Out of Water: The Newfoundland Saltfish Trade, 1814–1914* (SJ: BKW 1986), while the trade with Spain is the focus of *Newfoundland-Spanish Saltfish Trade, 1814-1914* (SJ: Harry Cuff 1983). The withdrawal of British merchants from the fishing industry and trade is addressed in Peter Perry, 'The Newfoundland Trade: The Decline and Demise of the Port of Poole,' *American Neptune* 28/4 (Fall 1968): 275–83; H.J. Trump, 'Newfoundland Trade from the Port of Teignmouth in the 19th Century,' *Transport History* 9 (Winter 1978): 260–8; and R.E. Ommer, *From Outpost to Outport*.

The commercial seal fishery developed as an important ancillary to the cod-fishing industry late in the eighteenth century. Useful introductions to this topic are provided in J.K. Hiller's previously cited article 'The Newfoundland Seal Fishery,' *Bulletin of Canadian Studies* (1983–4); Government of Canada, *Seals and Sealing in Canada: Report of the Royal Commission on Seals and the Sealing Industry in Canada*, 3 vols. (O: Supply and Services Canada 1986); and J.E. Candow, *Of Men and Seals: A History of the Newfoundland Seal Hunt* (O: Canadian Parks Services, Environment Canada 1989). C.W. Sanger examines the introduction of steam technology to the seal fishery shortly after the middle of the nineteenth century in 'The 19th Century Newfoundland Seal Fishery and the Influence of Scottish Whalemen,' *Polar Record* 20/126 (Sept. 1980): 231–51; see also his article 'The Dundee-St. John's Connection: 19th Century Interlinkages between Scottish Arctic Whaling and the Newfoundland Seal Fishery,' *NS* 4/1 (Spring 1988): 1–26. Sanger links the expansion of the demographic frontier to the seal fishery in his previously cited article 'The Evolution of Sealing,' in J.J. Mannion, ed., *The Peopling of Newfoundland*.

The seeming failure of the traditional fishing economy to support economic development has intrigued many scholars. Because the merchants who controlled the fishing industry before the turn of the nineteenth century were not residents of Newfoundland, profits generated by the fishery never remained in Newfoundland but flowed instead to the British Isles where the wealth was used to support an ostentatious way of life and political ambitions, a point made in Derek Beamish, John Hillier, and H.F.V. Johnstone, *Mansions & Merchants of Poole & Dorset*, vol. 1 (Poole, Eng.: Poole Historical Trust 1976). The consequences to the economic development, or underdevelopment, of Newfoundland are explained in James F. Shepherd, 'Staples and Eighteenth-Century Canadian Development: The Case of Newfoundland,' in Roger L. Ransom, Richard Sutch, and Gary M. Walton, eds., *Explorations in the New Economic History: Essays in Honor of Douglass C. North* (NY: Academic Press 1982). The story is carried into the next century in Steven Antler, 'The Capitalist Underdevelopment of Nineteenth-Century Newfoundland,' in Robert J. Brym and R. James Sacouman, eds., *Underdevelopment and Social Movements in Atlantic Canada* (T: New Hogtown Press 1979).

Yet it is also clear from J.J. Mannion, 'Patrick Morris and Newfoundland Irish Immigration,' in C.J. Byrne and M. Harry, eds., *Talamh an Eisc*, that merchants did support some efforts at economic diversification, if only to complement the fishing economy. The particular example of the relationship between the traditional fishing economy and investment in the shipping industry is examined in several publications by scholars involved with the Atlantic Canada Shipping Project in the 1970s. See E.W. Sager, 'The Port of St. John's, Newfoundland, 1840–1889: A Preliminary Analysis,' in K. Matthews and Gerald E. Panting, eds., *Ships and Shipbuilding in the North Atlantic Region* (SJ: Maritime History Group, Memorial University of Newfoundland 1978); Sager, 'The Merchants of Water Street and Capital Investment in Newfoundland's Traditional Economy,' in Lewis R. Fischer and Sager, eds., *The Enterprising Canadians: Entrepreneurs and Economic Development in Eastern Canada, 1820–1914* (SJ: Maritime History Group, Memorial University of Newfoundland 1979); Sager and Panting, 'Staple Economies and the Rise and Decline of the Shipping Industry in Atlantic Canada, 1820–1914,' in Fischer and Panting, eds., *Change and Adaptation in Maritime History: The North Atlantic Fleets in the Nineteenth Century* (SJ: Maritime History Group, Memorial University of Newfoundland 1985); and Sager, with Panting, *Maritime Capital: The Shipping Industry in Atlantic Canada, 1820–1914* (K&M: MQUP 1990).

NEWFOUNDLAND POLITICS TO 1869

The unpredictability of the Newfoundland fishing economy contributed to the volatility of nineteenth-century Newfoundland politics. Traditionally political history began with representative government in 1832, a view captured in the title of the standard work on early-nineteenth-century Newfoundland politics, Gertrude E. Gunn, *The Political History of Newfoundland, 1832–1864* (T: UTP 1966). This view has been modified by recent efforts to analyse the sources of the Newfoundland reform impulse between 1800 and 1832. K. Matthews wrote an influential essay on the men who were eventually credited with achieving representative government for Newfoundland, 'The Class of '32: St. John's Reformers on the Eve of Representative Government,' *Acadiensis* 6/2 (Spring 1977): 80–94. Matthews argues that the reformers tended to be newcomers to the island, who brought the reform impulse with them from the British Isles, and that, prior to their appearance, reform initiative tended to come from 'above,' from colonial administrators, rather than from 'below.' P. O'Flaherty takes issue with this interpretation in 'The Seeds of Reform: Newfoundland, 1800–18,' *JCS* 23/3 (Fall 1988): 39–59, maintaining that local conditions and factors played a significant part in the emergence of the reform impulse. O'Flaherty pursues this argument further in 'Government in Newfoundland before 1832: The Context of Reform,' *NQ* 84/2 (Fall 1988): 26–30. Key individuals in this so-called reform process make their appearance in several volumes of the *DCB*: 'William Carson,' 'Sir Francis Forbes,' 'Newman Wright Hoyles,' 'Patrick Morris,' and 'John Ryan,' vol. 7; and 'Thomas Holdsworth Brooking,' vol. 9 (1976). The *DCB* should also be consulted for essays on the governors whose reports contributed to Great Britain's decision to abandon the fiction that Newfoundland was little more than an oversized fishing station: see 'Sir John Thomas Duckworth' and 'Sir Erasmus Gower,' vol. 5; 'James Gambier' and 'Sir Richard Goodwin Keats,' vol. 6; 'Sir Charles Hamilton,' vol. 7; and 'Sir Thomas John Cochrane,' vol. 10 (1972).

The political affairs of Newfoundland after 1832 are given general treatment in W.S. MacNutt, *The Atlantic Provinces*, chs. 8–10; S.J.R. Noel, *Politics in Newfoundland* (T: UTP 1971), chs. 1–2; and F.W. Rowe, *A History of Newfoundland and Labrador*, ch. 14. To add to or revise these interpretations, students should make extensive use of the numerous entries found in the *DCB*. For instance, the 1832 election gave control of both the Council and Assembly to the predominantly Protestant merchants of St John's or their agents, like John Wills Martin (vol. 7). Satisfied with the degree of political influence that representative government gave them, they lost their enthusiasm for further change. They were supported in their conservatism by individuals like Chief Justice Henry John Boulton (vol. 9), newspaper editor Henry David Winton (vol. 8), George Lilly (vol. 7), and others. At the same time the Assembly came increasingly under the control of a more radical point of view. William Carson (vol. 7) remained an important reformer, but, more and more, the typical reformer was Irish and Catholic, like Patrick Morris (vol. 7), John Valentine Nugent (vol. 10), Peter Brown (vol. 7), and John Kent (vol. 10). Their power base among poorer fishermen encouraged a populist political agenda, with the result that the sectarian character of political polarization was often class based. Nevertheless, disputes such as that between Kent and Edward Kielley (vol. 8), which exposed the intensity of animosity, were often highly personal in nature. By the early 1840s the radicals controlled the Assembly and the conservatives, the Council. The ensuing stalemate so exasperated Governor Sir Henry Prescott (vol. 10) that he tried to resign in 1838, eventually succeeding in 1841. Replacing him was Sir John Harvey (vol. 8), under whom the constitutional arrangement of 1832 was suspended and the two legislative chambers amalgamated.

Harvey attempted to overcome the divisive tensions of the 1830s and 1840s by promoting social harmony and a sense of colonial patriotism. In 'Culture, State Formation and the Invention of Tradition: Newfoundland, 1832–1855,' *JCS* 23/1–2 (Spring–Summer 1988): 86–103, reprinted in J.M. Bumsted, ed., *Interpreting Canada's Past*, vol. 1, *Pre-Confederation* (2nd ed., T: OUP 1993), Phillip McCann examines the social rituals and festivities expressive of nativism, patriotism, and local culture that were invented as a result. These activities quickly came to be seen as 'traditional' and were to enter the incipient national and social consciousness of mid-nineteenth-century Newfoundland.

The so-called struggle for responsible government dominates the political history of other British North American colonies in the 1840s, and students would be well advised to familiarize themselves with those sources that examine the larger context. P.A. Buckner has little to say about Newfoundland in *The Transition to Responsible Government: British Policy in British North America, 1815–1850* (Westport, CT: Greenwood Press 1985), yet he provides an invaluable analysis of the way in which British administration and political policy in British North America was shaped. In Newfoundland the experiment with the amalgamated assembly caused the debate over responsible government to be delayed. When John Gaspard LeMarchant (*DCB*, vol. 10) replaced John Harvey as governor in 1847, and quickly expressed his disapproval at the power exercised by the merchant class, the decision was made to restore representative government in the colony. Almost immediately, the debate over the principle of responsibility began. Prominent in that debate would be newspaper editor Robert John Parsons (vol. 11 [1982]), Philip Francis Little (vol. 12 [1990]), and John Kent. Their efforts to secure what neighbouring colonies already enjoyed were resisted, both by the merchant class and by some British officials, like the governor from 1852 until 1855, Ker Baillie Hamilton (vol. 11), who was convinced that Newfoundland's political polarization made the colony unfit for self-government. Acting solicitor-general, Hugh William Hoyles (vol. 11), unsuccessfully represented Newfoundland in a petition to London against responsible government. By 1854, however, the British government generally, and the colonial secretary, the Duke of Newcastle, in particular, were unreceptive to such arguments, and instructed the governor to accept the principle.

Clearly the role of the British government in bringing responsible government to Newfoundland is crucial; this is all the more reason for students to consult Buckner's study. Nevertheless, an important element that added complexity to the debate was political sectarianism. The sectarian character of political polarization in Newfoundland was such that church and state had long been hopelessly entangled. It was partly because of this fact that the British government had granted representative government with such misgivings in 1832, believing that the island was not yet ready for it. It also contributed to the decision to suspend representative government in 1842. The unusual direction in which Newfoundland politics seemed to go led John Manning Ward to give some attention to the island in a chapter entitled 'Anomalous Societies: Newfoundland and New South Wales,' in his *Colonial Self-Government: The British Experience, 1759–1856* (T: UTP 1976).

Of the clergymen who figured prominently in the political affairs of the colony, Anglican bishop Edward Feild has received the most attention; for instance, see Frederick Jones, *Edward Feild, Bishop of Newfoundland, 1844–1876* (SJ: Newfoundland Historical Society 1976). Jones also examines the bishop's career in 'The Making of a Colonial Bishop: Feild of Newfoundland' and 'The Early Opposition to Bishop Feild of Newfoundland,' *JCCHS* 15/1 (Mar. 1973): 2–13; 16/2 (June 1974): 30–4, as well as in 'The Great Fire of 1846 and the Coming of Responsible Government in Newfoundland,' *Bulletin of Canadian Studies* 6/2–7/1 (Autumn 1983): 61–9. Fortunately the *DCB* is available with several excellent essays that compensate for the lack of attention given the other religious figures; see entries on Roman Catholic bishops Michael Anthony Fleming (vol. 7) and John Thomas Mullock (vol. 9), and Church of England bishop Aubrey George Spencer (vol. 10) in addition to that on Feild (vol. 10). Edward Troy (vol. 10) was another Catholic clergyman who figured prominently in the turbulent politics of the 1830s. P. McCann examines one side of the sectarian question in 'Bishop Fleming and the Politicization of the Irish Roman Catholics in

Newfoundland, 1830–1850,' in T. Murphy and C.J. Byrne, eds., *Religion and Identity*. The theme of religion in politics persists into the 1850s and 1860s. J.K. Hiller introduces a document reflecting a Protestant view of the 1855 election in Bonavista Bay, the election that ushered in responsible government to Newfoundland, in 'The 1855 Election in Bonavista Bay: An Anglican Perspective,' *NS* 5/1 (Spring 1989): 69–76. F. Jones explores both sides of the sectarian question in 'Bishops in Politics: Roman Catholic v Protestant in Newfoundland, 1860–2,' *CHR* 55/4 (Dec. 1974): 408–21, while E.C. Moulton focuses on the climax to Newfoundland's era of sectarian strife in 'Constitutional Crisis and Civil Strife in Newfoundland, February to November, 1861,' *CHR* 48/3 (Sept. 1967): 251–67.

The polarization of Newfoundland politics along ethnic, religious, and economic lines was exacerbated by a deteriorating fishing economy by the early 1860s. This situation encouraged some Newfoundlanders to support the idea of a federal union with the rest of British North America. Newfoundland's flirtation with Confederation has received considerable attention, despite (or perhaps because of) the rejection of the idea by island voters in 1869. A brief flurry of publications on the subject was generated by Newfoundland's admission to the Canadian federation in 1949. H.B. Mayo looked at the earlier century in 'Newfoundland and Confederation in the Eighteen-Sixties,' *CHR* 29/2 (June 1948): 125–42. A.M. Fraser examined not only the 1860s but later decades as well in 'The Nineteenth-Century Negotiations for Confederation of Newfoundland with Canada,' CHA *AR* (1949): 14–21. More recently, Peter B. Waite devoted a chapter to Newfoundland in his study *The Life and Times of Confederation, 1864–1867: Politics, Newspapers, and the Union of British North America* (T: UTP 1962). However, the best work in recent years is J.K. Hiller's 'Confederation Defeated: The Newfoundland Election of 1869,' in Hiller and P. Neary, eds., *Newfoundland in the Nineteenth and Twentieth Centuries*. Hiller carefully sets out the religious, social, and economic context for the 1869 campaign which saw heated emotions lead to a rejection of Confederation by Newfoundland voters. F. Jones offers both a historiographical survey of the theme and a mild revision of Hiller's essay in '"The Antis Gain the Day": Newfoundland and Confederation in 1869,' in Ged Martin, ed., *The Causes of Canadian Confederation* (F: AP 1990). Jones maintains that union with Canada was genuinely not in Newfoundland's best interests in 1869. The *DCB* provides several excellent biographies of key figures in the Confederation debate, including 'Charles James Fox Bennett' and 'Sir Anthony Musgrave,' vol. 11; and 'Sir Frederic Bowker Terrington Carter' and 'Stephen John Hill,' vol. 12. There are also instructive entries on such lesser known figures as 'John Bemister' and 'Sir Robert John Pinsent,' vol. 12. Readers wishing to place the Confederation question of the 1860s into a broader context of Newfoundland's several responses to the idea in both the nineteenth and twentieth centuries should consult Terry Campbell and G.A. Rawlyk, 'The Historical Framework of Newfoundland and Confederation,' in Rawlyk, ed., *The Atlantic Provinces and the Problems of Confederation* (SJ: BKW 1979).

SOCIAL HISTORY

Newfoundland social history, like its political history, was dominated by the denominational polarization of island society. A useful starting-point in understanding the social and political character of nineteenth-century Newfoundland is therefore F. Jones, 'The Church in Nineteenth Century Newfoundland,' *Bulletin of Canadian Studies* 5/1 (Apr. 1981): 25–40. One consequence of the powerful sectarian factor is the system of education which, to this day, is denominational. Accordingly, the history of education is inseparable from that of religious institutions.

Church involvement in early education is traced in F.W. Rowe, *Education and Culture in Newfoundland* (T: MHR 1976), and in more particular detail in Sister Mary Nolasco Mulcahy, 'The St. John's Schools of Industry,' *NQ* 78/4 (Spring 1983): 17–22, and Bonita Power and H. Rollmann, 'Bonavista's "Hewers of Wood and Drawers of Water": The First School in Newfoundland,' Humanities Association of Canada, *Bulletin* 17/1 (Apr. 1989): 27–33. A useful but uncritical summary of the development of education is contained in William B. Hamilton, 'Society and Schools in Newfoundland,' in J. Donald Wilson, Robert M. Stamp, and Louis-Philippe Audet, eds., *Canadian Education: A History* (Scarborough, Ont.: PH 1970). For a more analytical look at the origins of education in Newfoundland see John W. Netten, 'Aims of Education in Newfoundland: A Historical Overview,' and P. McCann, 'The History of Education in Newfoundland: An Essay in Exploration,' both in Ishmael Baksh and Romulo Magsino, eds., *Schools and Society Readings* (SJ: Department of Educational Foundations, Memorial University of Newfoundland 1980). P. McCann also provides an excellent analysis of the relationship between church and education in 'The Newfoundland School Society, 1823–1836: Missionary Influence or Cultural Imperialism?' in J.A. Mangan, ed., *Benefits Bestowed? Education and British Imperialism* (Manchester, Eng.: Manchester University Press 1988).

W.G. Handcock's entry 'Samuel Codner,' *DCB*, vol. 8, demonstrates that the origins of education in Newfoundland owed something to local merchant/philanthropists. Nevertheless, the denominational character of education was overwhelming and impinged heavily upon political debate in nineteenth-century Newfoundland; see F. Jones, 'Religion, Education and Politics in Newfoundland, 1836–1875,' *JCCHS* 12/4 (Dec. 1970): 64–76, as well as P. McCann, 'The Politics of Denominational Education in the Nineteenth Century in Newfoundland,' in William McKim, ed., *The Vexed Question: Denominational Education in a Secular Age* (SJ: BKW 1988). The role of Edward Feild, the Church of England bishop in Newfoundland at mid-century, in establishing the denominational system of education is examined in J.W. Netten, 'Edward Feild, Protagonist of Denominational Education,' in Robert S. Patterson, John Chalmers, and John Friesen, eds., *Profiles of Canadian Educators* (T: D.C. Heath Canada 1974). The relationship between education and economic development is addressed superbly in D. Alexander, 'Literacy and Economic Development in Nineteenth Century Newfoundland,' *Acadiensis* 10/1 (Autumn 1980): 3–34, subsequently reprinted in Alexander, *Atlantic Canada and Confederation: Essays in Canadian Political Economy* (T: UTP 1983). P. McCann explores various relationships in 'Class, Gender and Religion in Newfoundland Education, 1836–1901,' *Historical Studies in Education/Revue d'histoire de l'éducation* 1/2 (Fall 1989): 179–200.

Religious institutions also played an influential role in the provision of public health and welfare services. The social problems associated with underdevelopment and widespread poverty were pervasive in nineteenth-century Newfoundland yet difficult to relieve. Judith Fingard places the problem in a British North American context in 'The Winter's Tale: Contours of Pre-Industrial Poverty in British America, 1815–1860,' CHA *HP* (1974): 65–94. Fingard focuses on the urban setting in the widely reprinted essay 'The Relief of the Unemployed Poor in Saint John, Halifax, and St. John's, 1815–1860,' *Acadiensis* 5/1 (Autumn 1975): 32–53. Sister M.N. Mulcahy's previously cited 'The St. John's Schools of Industry,' *NQ* (1983), looks at one approach to the challenge of poverty and public welfare. Stuart R. Godfrey introduces his *Human Rights and Social Policy in Newfoundland, 1832–1982: Search for a Just Society* (SJ: Harry Cuff 1985) with an examination of public welfare in early-nineteenth-century Newfoundland, while the particular experience of St John's is the focus of Melvin Baker, 'The Politics of Poverty: Providing Public Poor Relief in Nineteenth Century St. John's,' in his *Aspects of Nineteenth Century St. John's Municipal History* (SJ: Creative Printers and Publishers 1982).

The larger question of maintaining public order has not been given the attention it is due. M. Baker discusses the origins of police services in 'Policing in St. John's, 1806–1871,' in his *Aspects of Nineteenth Century St. John's*. However, nineteenth-century authorities relied considerably on military aid to the civil power; see O.U. Janzen, 'Military Garrisons,' *ENL*, vol. 3. The military establishment in St John's was also a significant source of relief services in certain emergencies. Fires were one such kind of emergency. Built almost entirely of wood and with little effective attention to planning, St John's was vulnerable to fire. John C. Weaver and Peter De Lottinville use St John's as one of their examples in 'The Conflagration and the City: Disaster and Progress in British North America during the Nineteenth Century,' *HS/SH* 13/26 (Nov. 1980): 417–49. M. Baker examines the most catastrophic fire of the early nineteenth century in his article 'The Great St. John's Fire of 1846,' *NQ* 79/1 (Summer 1983): 31–4, and analyses attempts to address this threat in 'Voluntarism and the Fire Service in Nineteenth Century St. John's,' in his *Aspects of Nineteenth Century St. John's*. P. O'Neill examines many of these themes in his detailed but essentially descriptive work, *The Story of St. John's, Newfoundland*, vol. 1; vol. 2, *A Seaport Legacy* (1976). Baker covers public health in 'Disease and Public Health Measures in St. John's, Newfoundland, 1832–1855,' *NQ* 78/4 (Spring 1983): 26–9. Baker was also one of the first to look at the treatment of mental illness in 'Insanity and Politics: The Establishment of a Lunatic Asylum in St. John's, Newfoundland, 1836–1855,' *NQ* 77/2–3 (Summer–Fall 1981): 27–31, though it has since been superseded and expanded by Patricia O'Brien, *Out of Mind, Out of Sight: A History of the Waterford Hospital* (SJ: BKW 1989).

Newfoundland labour history has tended to focus on the emergence of organized labour in the late nineteenth and twentieth centuries. Relatively little work has been done on the earlier period. One exception is the attention given to maritime labour by the Atlantic Canada Shipping Project and subsequently by the Maritime History Group at Memorial University of Newfoundland. E.W. Sager provides an overview of this work in 'The Maritime History Group and the History of Seafaring Labour,' *L/LT* 15 (Spring 1985): 165–72. Sager's conclusions about the condition of seafaring labour in Newfoundland appear in *Seafaring Labour: The Merchant Marine of Atlantic Canada, 1820–1914* (K&M: MQUP 1989). Sager makes it clear that the condition of labour in the cod-fishing fleets did not follow precisely the same pattern as elsewhere in Atlantic Canada, in part because the fishing fleet was slower than other fleets to respond to the forces of industrialization. See also E.W. Sager, with G.E. Panting, *Maritime Capital*. Linda Little published her research into some early-nineteenth-century labour protests in 'Collective Action in Outport Newfoundland: A Case Study from the 1830s,' *L/LT* 26 (Fall 1990): 7–35.

One field in which very little scholarly work has been done is that of the history of science and technology. Essays such as James S. Pringle's 'Jewell David Sornborger (1869–1929): An Early Biological Explorer in Newfoundland and Labrador,' *Canadian Horticultural History* 1/4 (1988): 210–21, is an exception that helps prove the rule. Fortunately, the *DCB* offers some studies that help to correct this deficiency. Frederic Newton Gisborne, who was instrumental in developing the island's telegraph systems in the 1850s and 1860s, receives solid treatment in volume 12. The geological reconnaissances in the interior of Newfoundland, by William Eppes Cormack (vol. 9) in the 1820s and Joseph Beete Jukes (vol. 9) in the 1840s, laid some of the groundwork for the geological surveys of Alexander Murray (vol. 11) in the 1860s. Apart from these entries in the *DCB*, the only scholarly treatment on the important work of these men is J. Malpas and A.F. King, 'Pioneers of Geological Exploration, Mapping and Mining in Newfoundland,' in Donald Steele, ed., *Early Science in Newfoundland and Labrador* (SJ: Avalon Chapter of Sigma Chi 1987). Another essay with an entirely different scientific focus in this intriguing collection is A.G. Macpherson, 'Early Moravian Interest in Northern Labrador Weather and Climate: The Beginning of Instrument Recording in Newfoundland.'

LABRADOR

Labrador is often overlooked when the history of Newfoundland is considered, even though it was part of the experience of the Norse, later the Basques, and more recently the British migratory and Newfoundland residential fishermen. F.W. Rowe devotes a chapter of *A History of Newfoundland and Labrador* to Labrador. An extremely useful cultural survey is David Zimmerly, *Cain's Land Revisited: Cultural Change in Central Labrador, 1775–1972* (SJ: Institute of Social and Economic Research, Memorial University of Newfoundland 1975). However, Zimmerly's chronology excludes several important early themes of Labrador history. Until the Conquest Labrador was part of the French domain in North America. Then, in 1763, it was formally transferred over from French to British control. This transfer is examined in G.O. Rothney, 'L'annexation de la côte du Labrador à Terre-Neuve en 1763,' *RHAF* 17/2 (sept. 1963): 213–43. Together with subsequent territorial changes, this transfer is also given graphic treatment in plate 7.5 of G. McManus and C. Wood, *Atlas of Newfoundland and Labrador*. British efforts to extend their fishing industry into the region are examined in G.O. Rothney, 'The Case of Bayne and Brymer: An Incident in the Early History of Labrador,' *CHR* 15/3 (Sept. 1934): 264–75, and R.P. Crowhurst,

'The Labrador Question and the Society of Merchant Venturers, Bristol, 1763,' *CHR* 50/4 (Dec. 1969): 394–405.

Several contemporary descriptions of Labrador during this period are available, including A.M. Lysaght, ed., *Joseph Banks in Newfoundland and Labrador*; Sidney C. Richardson, ed., 'Journal of William Richardson Who Visited Labrador in 1771,' *CHR* 16/1 (Mar. 1935): 54–61; and, what is arguably the most detailed and fascinating memoir of all, George Cartwright, *A Journal of Transactions and Events, during a Residence of Nearly Sixteen Years on the Coast of Labrador*, 3 vols. (Newark, Eng.: Allin and Ridge 1792; facsimile repr., Ann Arbor, MI: University Microfilms 1980). For more on Cartwright's life see the *DCB*, vol. 5. Cartwright went bankrupt three times in his effort to make a success of his investment in Labrador.

The challenges faced by Cartwright and others were enormous, and the British authorities struggled to work out the most efficacious means of administering the region. These efforts were examined in a series of articles by W.H. Whiteley: the previously cited 'Governor Hugh Palliser and the Newfoundland and Labrador Fishery,' *CHR* (1969); 'Newfoundland, Quebec and the Administration of the Coast of Labrador, 1774–1783,' *Acadiensis* 6/1 (Autumn 1976): 92–112; and 'Newfoundland, Quebec and the Labrador Merchants, 1783–1809,' *NQ* 73/4 (Dec. 1977): 18–26.

One concern of the British authorities was friction between Natives and European fishermen. Local Indians had a fairly cooperative relationship with Europeans dating back to the French period. L. Turgeon examines sixteenth-century contact between Indians and Basques in 'Pêcheurs basques et indiens des côtes du Saint-Laurent au XVIe siècle: perspectives de recherches,' *Etudes canadiennes/Canadian Studies* 13 (1982): 9–14; see also S. Barkham, 'A Note on the Strait of Belle Isle during the Period of Basque Contact with Indians and Inuit,' *Etudes inuit/Inuit Studies* 4/1–2 (1980): 51–8, and L. Turgeon and Evelyne Picot-Bermond, 'Pêcheurs basques et la traite de la fourrure dans le Saint-Laurent au XVIe siècle,' in Bruce G. Trigger, Toby Morantz, and Louise Dechêne, eds., *'Le Castor Fait Tout': Selected Papers of the Fifth North American Fur Trade Conference, 1985* (M: Lake St Louis Historical Society 1987). Contact between Inuit and Europeans, however, was characterized largely by friction during both the French and early British period. François Trudel analyses the impact of the Inuit on French sedentary fisheries in 'The Inuit of Southern Labrador and the Development of French Sedentary Fisheries (1700–1760),' in R.A. Preston, ed., *Canadian Ethnology Society: Papers from the Fourth Congress*.

The British responded to Inuit friction after 1763 by encouraging the Moravians to establish a mission far to the north of the areas frequented by

European fishermen, according to W.H. Whiteley, 'The Establishment of the Moravian Mission in Labrador and British Policy, 1763–83,' *CHR* 45/1 (Mar. 1964): 29–50. The Moravian Brethren had already demonstrated their success at establishing good relations with the Inuit in Greenland, though their first attempt to extend their activities to Labrador in 1752 was unsuccessful; see J.K. Hiller, 'The Moravian Expedition to Labrador, 1752,' *NQ* 65/2 (Nov. 1966): 19–22. The early years of the Moravian mission to Labrador are given comprehensive treatment in two essays by Hiller: 'The Moravians in Labrador, 1771–1805,' *Polar Record* 15/99 (Sept. 1971): 839–54; and 'Early Patrons of the Labrador Eskimos: The Moravian Mission in Labrador, 1764–1805,' in Robert Paine, ed., *Patrons and Brokers in the East Arctic* (SJ: Institute of Social and Economic Research, Memorial University of Newfoundland 1971). Hiller also contributed entries on Christian Larsen Drachart and Jens Haven, two Moravian missionaries, to the *DCB*, vol. 4.

The Moravian impact on the Inuit is examined in several publications. H. Anthony Williamson develops a general approach in 'The Moravian Mission and Its Impact on the Labrador Eskimo,' *Arctic Anthropology* 2/2 (1964): 32–6. A focused study is J. Garth Taylor, 'Moravian Mission Influence on Labrador Inuit Subsistence: 1776–1830,' in D.A. Muise, ed., *Approaches to Native History: Papers of a Conference Held at the National Museum of Man, October 1975* (O: National Museums of Canada 1977). Our best opportunity to examine the Inuit encounter with the Moravians in particular and Europeans in general is through the life of the Inuit woman Mikak; see the entry by W.H. Whiteley in the *DCB*, vol. 4, and the two-part essay by J.G. Taylor, 'The Two Worlds of Mikak,' parts 1 and 2, *The Beaver* 314/3 (Winter 1983): 4–13; 314/4 (Spring 1984): 18–25. The Moravian fur trade with the Inuit is assessed in Barnett Richling, 'Not by Seals Alone: The Moravians in the Fur Trade – Souls and Skins,' *The Beaver* 68/1 (Feb.–Mar. 1988): 29–35. Elsewhere, Richling argues that Moravian involvement in the fur trade caused their relationship with the Hudson's Bay Company to be one of competition, not of cooperation, as was usually the case elsewhere between the company and missionaries; see Richling, 'Without Compromise: Hudson's Bay Company and Moravian Mission Trade Rivalry in Nineteenth Century Labrador,' in B.G. Trigger, T. Morantz, and L. Dechêne, eds., '*Le Castor Fait Tout*.' Carol Brice-Bennett examines not only the ethical dilemma faced by the Moravians because of the way they combined evangelism and trade but also the way in which Moravian merchant credit greatly contributed to the erosion of the Inuit way of life; see 'Missionaries as Traders: Moravians and the Inuit, 1771–

1860,' in R.E. Ommer, ed., *Merchant Credit and Labour Strategies*. Finally, in '"Very Serious Reflections": Inuit Dreams about Salvation and Loss in Eighteenth-Century Labrador,' *Ethnohistory* 36/2 (Spring 1989): 148–69, B. Richling uses missionary accounts of Inuit dreams to interpret Inuit responses to their circumstances in the late eighteenth century and to the missionaries' efforts to convert them to Christianity.

Significant European settlement in Labrador did not develop until the early nineteenth century, long after the resident population in Newfoundland began to show sustained growth. Yet the two experiences were similar, both in terms of the limiting factors and in terms of the role of merchants. The settlement history of Labrador is therefore of interest both in its own right and as the basis for comparisons with Newfoundland. P.A. Thornton shows that Labrador settlement grew out of, not despite, the commercial fisheries there; see her contribution to J.J. Mannion, ed., *The Peopling of Newfoundland*, as well as 'Newfoundland's Frontier Demographic Experience: The World We Have Not Lost,' *NS* 1/2 (Fall 1985): 141–62, and 'The Transition from the Migratory to the Resident Fishery in the Strait of Belle Isle,' *Acadiensis* 19/2 (Spring 1990): 92–120, reprinted with commentary and discussion in R.E. Ommer, ed., *Merchant Credit and Labour Strategies*. David Anderson examines Labrador settlement through a study of one community, from its eighteenth-century origins to the twentieth century, in 'The Development of Settlement in Southern Labrador with Particular Reference to Sandwich Bay,' *Bulletin of Canadian Studies* 8/1 (Spring 1984): 23–49. John C. Kennedy looks at changing gender balances in 'The Changing Significance of Labrador Settler Ethnicity,' *Canadian Ethnic Studies* 20/3 (1988): 42–62.

CONCLUSION

The field of Newfoundland history is in a healthy state of vigorous activity. What makes the field so exciting is the degree to which the substantial body of recent scholarly activity has generated as many questions as it has perhaps resolved. The era of the sixteenth-century international fishery is a case in point. The basic details have been reasonably well understood for quite some time, yet many particular aspects still require research, such as Portuguese participation in the fishery of that era, the reasons why France was able to move so quickly to a position of dominance in the fishery, or the reasons why the English were so slow to participate in the fishery that they ostensibly discovered – was it a lack of markets, a lack of capital, a lack of skills or experience?

Furthermore, though our understanding of Newfoundland society can no longer be said to be in its infant stage, there is good reason to conclude that it has not yet matured. More local studies are needed (there is none, for instance, on Harbour Grace, one of the most significant communities in early-nineteenth-century Newfoundland), if only to overcome the tendency to divide island society into two homogeneous halves, one of West Country English extraction, the other of Irish extraction. Community studies undertaken on Trinity, Placentia, Trepassey, and St John's suggest that Newfoundland was fragmented into a large number of particularistic communities by the nature of external economic linkages, by the precise source region for the local population, and by the nature and availability or scarcity of local resources and opportunities. This fragmentation mitigated against the emergence of a 'Newfoundland identity' before the nineteenth century, and it is still anyone's guess when such an identity did emerge. The degree to which such fragmentation contributed to the ability of St John's to develop its role as the political, economic, and cultural capital of Newfoundland also needs to be explored. Similarly, while the presence of the military and that of the navy in Newfoundland have never been ignored because of their significance to the administrative history of the colony, there has not been very much work done on their social and economic impact.

Finally, the field of early Newfoundland history requires more effort at synthesis of existing and recent research. None of the recent outpouring of scholarly publications have been incorporated into a new survey study. This is especially true of the substantial literature on the French fishery, of which too little has been published in English. The Anglocentrism of Newfoundland history is understandable, even expected. Yet the imperial, social, economic, and cultural themes of Newfoundland history cannot always be fully understood without reference to British perceptions of, and responses to, the French presence within the fishery. Moreover, there are striking differences and equally striking similarities between the French and English experiences which invite comparison. Finally, there have been important methodological developments within the French scholarly community that merit attention by its English counterpart.

In short, the vigorous level of recent scholarly activity in Newfoundland history suggests that this field continues to provide a broad range of research opportunities.

KERRY ABEL

The Northwest and the North

While most people probably think of the history of the western interior of Canada in terms of the period of immigration and agricultural settlement at the end of the nineteenth century, the history of the region before it became a part of Canada is complex and fascinating. The exploits of northern adventurer-explorers and fur traders have attracted the attention of writers and their audiences for many years; the Northwest has been romanticized in the best nineteenth-century traditions. While elements of that mystical fascination remain, contemporary historians are more interested in explaining the processes of interaction between the First Nations and European newcomers or examining the development of settler societies.

Within the broad region referred to as the Northwest, there are, of course, many subregions with distinct peoples, economies, and histories. Not all these regions have received equal attention from historians. The Prairie West has been perhaps the most fortunate. The North, on the other hand, is generally ignored by historians in our generation, relegated to the peripheries of historical development as it is relegated to the peripheries of maps. Much of what we know about pre-Confederation northern history comes, in fact, through anthropological studies of cultural change among aboriginal peoples exposed to European contacts. Another important gap is the history of these regions from the perspective of the original inhabitants. Nevertheless, in the past twenty years a publishing boom has provided us with a number of new insights into the pre-Confederation history of the Northwest. This chapter will address the wide range of topics and approaches to those topics that are now available to the reader.

BIBLIOGRAPHIES AND GENERAL WORKS

No single bibliography covers the vast geographical area considered in this chapter, and, indeed, there are no bibliographies available for some parts of the region. Readers interested in Prairie history are best served. The standard reference is Bruce Braden Peel, *A Bibliography of the Prairie Provinces to 1953* (2nd ed., T: UTP 1973). Although it is now twenty years since it was last issued, the Peel bibliography was a massive undertaking that contains much useful material on the period prior to 1867. Several years ago books and pamphlets referred to in this bibliography were microfilmed and made available for purchase as a set; as a result many university libraries in Canada have copies of what would otherwise be difficult to locate for the average reader. Other bibliographies on select topics include Ved Arora, ed., *The Saskatchewan Bibliography* (Saskatoon, Sask.: Saskatchewan Provincial Library 1980), and Gloria M. Strathern, *Alberta, 1954–1979: A Provincial Bibliography* (E: UAP 1982).

For the North there are no bibliographies of specifically historical references, but readers should be familiar with the sixteen-volume *Arctic Bibliography*, produced by the Arctic Institute of North America (Washington, DC: Department of Defense 1953–75). In 1964 Jim Lotz compiled the first *Yukon Bibliography* for the Northern Co-ordination and Research Centre, Department of Northern Affairs and Natural Resources, in Ottawa, which has subsequently been updated by the Boreal Institute in Edmonton in 1973, 1975, and 1977–84.

Readers who are new to the subject of the history of the Northwest may want to consult a general textbook. One of the most thorough and interesting surveys of the southern regions is Gerald Friesen, *The Canadian Prairies: A History* (T: UTP 1984). Kenneth S. Coates and William R. Morrison provide a breezy survey of Yukon history in *Land of the Midnight Sun* (E: Hurtig 1988). There is as yet no general history of the Northwest Territories, and general histories of the provinces usually neglect their northern regions. One exception is W.L. Morton's classic *Manitoba: A History* (1957; 2nd ed., T: UTP 1967), which does include sections on the North, particularly about the first European forays into Hudson Bay.

A great deal of historical research is undertaken each year by government agencies, including provincial heritage and historical sites services and Environment Canada (Parks). Often these studies are overlooked by the general reader, but many have useful information unavailable elsewhere. For a guide to the types of materials produced by government agencies, see Frits Pannekoek, 'A Selected Western Canada Historical Resources Bibliography,' *Prairie Forum* 15/2 (Fall 1990): 329–74.

Finally, the *Dictionary of Canadian Biography* (T: UTP 1966–), with twelve volumes published to date, is indispensable in the study of the Northwest and North. The present volumes cover individuals who died prior to the close of 1900, so that, with very few exceptions, there are essays on almost all who played a prominent role in the area before Confederation. Perhaps more valuable still are the many entries on those who were not prominent in the usual meaning of the term, but rather representative of broader categories of individuals.

PUBLISHED DOCUMENTS

Readers have always been fascinated by the stories of the European adventurers, explorers, and traders who first brought the Northwest to the attention of the outside world. Publishers have responded to that demand with dozens of published reprints of diaries, letters, and other records pertaining to this period of northwestern history. Several societies have been formed over the years for the purpose of selecting and publishing these materials. Since 1905 the Toronto-based Champlain Society has published over eighty volumes, and although the emphasis has been on New France and Ontario, a number pertain to the Northwest. These are listed separately in the appropriate sections later in the chapter.

In 1938 the Hudson's Bay Record Society was founded in London to arrange the publication of materials from the rich Hudson's Bay Company archives. For the first decade the HBRS co-published its volumes with the CS, but thereafter they appeared under the Record Society's own name. The HBRS headquarters was transferred to Winnipeg in 1974, and the following year Hartwell Bowsfield of York University, Toronto, became the first Canadian general editor. When the Record Society disbanded in 1983, the Rupert's Land Research Centre in Winnipeg took on the task of publishing fur trade materials and in 1989 initiated its own series in co-production with McGill-Queen's University Press. Another organization that had its origins in London is the Hakluyt Society. Founded in 1846, it specializes in the publication of rare materials on voyages, travels, and exploration. It has produced over two hundred volumes to date, including many on arctic expeditions, as will be noted later.

Finally, in 1965 the Manitoba Record Society began publishing documents relating to the history of that province. Among its more ambitious undertakings is a project to publish all the writings of Lord Selkirk, founder of the first immigrant agricultural settlement in western Canada. Two volumes of Selkirk's writings have been published to date; the entire series of the Manitoba Record Society now consists of ten volumes.

PERIODICALS

The region is very well served by a variety of journals and periodicals representing scholarly work in many disciplines that will be of interest to students of history. Each province has a journal that emphasizes its own provincial history. *Alberta History* (1975–) is published quarterly by the Alberta Historical Society; its predecessor was the *Alberta Historical Review* (1953–75). *Saskatchewan History* (1948–) is produced in Regina by the Saskatchewan Archives Board and appears three times a year. The Manitoba Historical Society publishes *Manitoba History* (1980–), which replaced the earlier series, *Transactions of the Historical and Scientific Society of Manitoba*.

The *Canadian Historical Review* has been publishing occasional articles on the Northwest since the founding of that journal in 1920. One useful feature of this journal is its quarterly listing of recently published books, articles, and graduate theses pertaining to Canada, arranged according to region, time period, and theme. These lists are an effective way to keep up with new publications. Readers should also be aware of *Prairie Forum* (1976–), a scholarly journal published by the Canadian Plains Research Centre in Regina. It appears twice a year with interdisciplinary articles and book reviews pertaining to Prairie history. An interesting new experiment for readers of northern history is *The Northern Review* (1988–), published at Yukon College. This journal combines interdisciplinary scholarly work with articles, stories, and poetry from contributors outside the universities for a blend of perspectives on the North.

Since 1920 the Hudson's Bay Company has published *The Beaver*, a journal that has evolved from a company bulletin for employees to a journal of northern history to a journal of popular Canadian history. It continues to include articles on the North and West, and its illustrations are always of interest. Other periodicals dealing with northern topics occasionally present historical essays. These are *Arctic* (1948–) from the Arctic Institute of North America; *North/Nord* (1954–) from the Department of Indian Affairs and Northern Development; and *Musk-Ox* (1967–) from the University of Saskatchewan. While the focus of these journals is not primarily historical, they are useful references for a range of northern topics.

The history of Native peoples in the Northwest is addressed from time to time in a variety of journals. The *Western Canadian Journal of Anthropology* (1969–) and *Arctic Anthropology* are particularly useful, although journals like *Anthropologica* also have an interest in the Native peoples of the region. The *Canadian Journal of Native Studies* (1981–) produced at Brandon University and the *Native Studies Review* (1984–) from the University of Saskatchewan also occasionally include articles of interest to historians.

HISTORIOGRAPHY

The primary preoccupation of historians of the West and Northwest has been the problem of the relation between region and nation. Sometimes that relationship has been characterized as one between centre and periphery or between metropolis and hinterland. At other times the concept of the frontier has been adapted from the ideas of American historian Frederick Jackson Turner, and attempts have been made to evaluate the development of the Canadian Northwest in those terms. While few Canadian historians have been convinced that the American frontier model was relevant to Canada, debates about its applicability have generated some interesting studies about distinctions between the development of the Canadian and American Wests. Much of the earlier historical writing about the Northwest, then, was not so much interested in the internal dynamics of the region but rather focused on the relationship between the development of the region and that of Canada as a whole.

Perhaps the most influential historian in this context was Harold Adams Innis. This economic historian was interested in explaining the forces that had shaped Canada, and beginning in 1930 he published a series of studies that examined natural resource extraction and export. He argued that the nature of fish, fur, timber, minerals, and wheat as commodities determined the patterns of Canadian geographical growth as well as those of the political and economic systems. It was not the presence of a frontier that distinguished Canada from Europe, according to Innis. Instead, Canadian history was shaped by the staple commodities as well as Canada's dependence on European markets for these products. These ideas are commonly referred to as the staples thesis.

Obviously the resources of the West and North played a crucial part in Innis's theories. *The Fur Trade in Canada: An Introduction to Canadian Economic History* (1930; rev. ed., T: UTP 1970) provided one of the first detailed reconstructions of fur trade history as well as an extended discussion of staples development. The dynamics of the fur trade gave Innis evidence for his argument that Canada's east-west development was a natural outcome of economic forces, not an imposed structure created artificially by nineteenth-century politicians. Innis explored these ideas further in *Settlement and the Mining Frontier* (T: MAC 1936).

Innis's thesis about staples and their impact on Canadian history has been widely influential. Economists, political scientists, historians, and a new generation of political economists have expanded on Innis's theories or reacted against them in a wide range of studies. Among the historians, Donald Grant Creighton joined Innis's ideas about east-west economies to an interest in political culture in *The Commercial Empire of the St. Lawrence, 1760–1850* (T: RP 1937), reprinted as *The Empire of the St. Lawrence* (T: MAC 1956). The result was the so-called Laurentian thesis in which Creighton proposed that the Great Lakes–St Lawrence water system provided access to the interior of the continent and laid the basis for a 'dream of western commercial empire' that has been pursued throughout Canadian history.

W.L. Morton, who was born in Manitoba, objected to the way in which the ideas of Innis and Creighton relegated regional development to a secondary place in 'national' history. Morton argued that there was more give-and-take between the Northwest and central Canada than the staples or Laurentian thesis would acknowledge. The West, according to Morton, had undoubtedly been affected by the designs of central Canada, but there were also local factors at work that helped to create the region as we know it. Morton directly challenged the Laurentian thesis in 'Clio in Canada: The Interpretation of Canadian History,' *University of Toronto Quarterly* 15/3 (Apr. 1946): 227–34, reprinted in A.B. McKillop, ed., *Contexts of Canada's Past: Selected Essays of W.L. Morton* (T: MAC 1980), and in 1957 he explored these themes in *Manitoba: A History*. J.M.S. Careless took this examination of the relation between centre and periphery even further, developing his own hybrid metropolitan thesis in such works as *Frontier and Metropolis: Regions, Cities and Identities in Canada before 1914* (T: UTP 1989).

Later in his life W.L. Morton shifted his regional focus to the North and developed a similar argument about the North both as a region and as an experience that made Canada unique. In 'The "North" in Canadian Historiography,' *TRSC* ser. 4, 8 (1970), sec. ii, 31–40, reprinted in A.B. McKillop, ed., *Contexts of Canada's Past*, Morton attempted to argue that the sense of what it means to be Canadian has been shaped by the fact that Canada is fundamentally a northern nation. This approach has intrigued other historians. For example, Carl Berger, 'The True North Strong and Free,' in Peter Russell, ed., *Nationalism in Canada* (T: MHR 1966), further explores the ideas of northernness that have crept into the Canadian consciousness, particularly in terms of Canadian nationalism.

Those who are interested in pursuing these questions of the changing interpretations of Canadian history are well advised to consult C. Berger, *The Writing of Canadian History: Aspects of English-Canadian Historical Writing since 1900* (1976; 2nd ed., T: UTP 1986), which includes chapters on

Innis, Creighton, and Morton, among others. See also Berger, 'William Morton: The Delicate Balance of Region and Nation,' in Berger and Ramsay Cook, eds., *The West and the Nation: Essays in Honour of W.L. Morton* (T: M&S 1976).

While W.L. Morton led the way in reacting to Innis and the national approach to Canadian history, historians of the fur trade have, in a sense, also been reacting to Innis by exploring the internal dynamics of that trade rather than its place in the international setting. One of the major issues being debated today is the question of the impact of the fur trade on Native peoples. To what extent did participation in a new economic system lead to social and cultural changes in the First Nations' societies? For a discussion of one important aspect of that literature see Sylvia Van Kirk, 'Fur Trade Social History: Some Recent Trends,' in Carol M. Judd and Arthur J. Ray, eds., *Old Trails and New Directions: Papers of the Third North American Fur Trade Conference* (T: UTP 1980). Other useful overviews are A.J. Ray, 'Reflections on Fur Trade Social History and Metis History in Canada,' *American Indian Culture and Research Journal* 6/1 (Summer 1982): 91–107, and Jacqueline Peterson and John Anfinson, 'The Indian and the Fur Trade: A Review of Recent Literature,' *Manitoba History* 10 (Autumn 1985): 10–18.

As the first extensive European agricultural experiment in the Northwest, the Red River Settlement has also received a great deal of consideration by historians, although much of it has focused on the events of 1869–70 when members of the settlement organized to resist the government of Canada in its attempt to take over their lands. These studies tended to consider the settlement in terms of larger national issues, leading F. Pannekoek to call for more examination of the internal dynamics of the society itself in his article 'The Historiography of the Red River Settlement, 1830–1868,' *Prairie Forum* 6/1 (Spring 1981): 75–85. Following that line of thinking, Pannekoek has also argued that historians have not taken into account the role of the churches in early northwestern history and suggested that a failure to make use of church records as sources has distorted our understanding of western history. See his '"Insidious" Sources and the Historical Interpretation of the Pre-1870 West,' in Barry Ferguson, ed., *The Anglican Church and the World of Western Canada, 1820–1870* (R: CPRC 1991). In the introduction to that same volume, Ferguson provides an effective discussion of the writing of church history in Canada, particularly relating to the issue of the role of churches in the social development of the West.

The writing of history pertaining to northern Canada for the pre-Confederation period has not developed sufficiently to permit much in the way of historiographical analysis. Only the fur trade has received much attention; most other work deals with the post-Confederation extension of government plans and programs to the North. This point is reinforced in K.S. Coates and W.R. Morrison, 'Northern Visions: Recent Writing in Northern Canadian History,' *Manitoba History* 10 (Autumn 1985): 2–9.

ANCIENT HISTORY

Not many years ago most historians ignored the history of North America before the arrival of Europeans. In some places that precontact period is still referred to as 'prehistory,' implying somehow that before Europeans arrived, there was no history to consider. Of course that idea is false, but writing the history of the Northwest before contact is a difficult proposition. There are no written records and devastating epidemics in the eighteenth and nineteenth centuries led to a loss of many oral traditions. Historians are only recently learning to cope with these challenges and are now attempting to reconstruct this past. There is not much available yet to the reader, but some sources are worth consulting.

Brian Fagan, *The Great Journey: The Peopling of Ancient America* (NY: Thames and Hudson 1987), provides a readable survey of current theories on early populations in the continent as a whole. Several chapters in Robert McGhee, *Ancient Canada* (O: Canadian Museum of Civilization 1989), pertain specifically to the West and the North. Graham A. MacDonald presents an interesting glimpse of a debate about one particular aspect of ancient arctic history in 'Tryggvi J. Oleson and the Origins of Thule Culture: A Controversy Revisited,' *Manitoba History* 15 (Spring 1988): 45–58. In so doing, MacDonald not only tells us something about that history, but also provides us with a sense of how archaeologists develop their theories.

Perhaps the best source for the latest scholarship on ancient history is to be found in the *Historical Atlas of Canada*, vol. 1, *From the Beginning to 1800*, ed. R. Cole Harris (T: UTP [1987]). Plates 1 and 4 map the massive environmental changes in Canada from 18,000 BC to AD 1000. Plate 2 illustrates what is known about the people of the Northwest circa 9500 to 8200 BC, while plates 5 through 9 follow the changing cultural distributions of aboriginal peoples to the point of European contact. Of particular interest to readers of the history of the Northwest are plates 10, 'Bison Hunters of the Plains'; 11, 'Peopling the Arctic'; 14, 'Prehistoric Trade'; and 15, 'Cosmology.'

While nearly all the work on the ancient history of the Northwest has been written by archaeologists, historian Olive Patricia Dickason attempts to synthesize their findings and sketch a possible history of the Northwest from 17,000 years ago to the year 1750 in 'A Historical Reconstruction for the Northwestern Plains,' *Prairie Forum* 5/1 (Spring 1980): 19–37, reprinted in R. Douglas Francis and Howard Palmer, eds., *The Prairie West: Historical Readings* (E: Pica Pica Press 1985).

Native perspectives on ancient history lie scattered in published versions of oral traditions, which obviously deal with much more than ancient times. Oblate missionary and early ethnographer Emile Petitot published *Traditions indiennes du Canada nord-ouest* (P: Maisonneuve Frères et C. Leclerc 1886) primarily from the stories of the people of the Mackenzie River basin, a people known today as the Dene. An interesting comparison is George Blondin, *When the World Was New: Stories of the Sahtú-Dene* (Yellowknife: Outcrop Books 1990). Some of the stories recorded in Julie Cruikshank, *Life Lived like a Story: Life Stories of Three Yukon Native Elders* (V: UBCP 1990), deal with ancient times. See also the section 'First Nations' later in the chapter.

EUROPEAN EXPLORATION

Obviously Europeans did not 'discover' the Northwest, but the stories of their exploration of these lands continue to fascinate readers. For a basic chronology and listing of names, the standard reference remains Alan Cooke and Clive Holland, *The Exploration of Northern Canada, 500 to 1920: A Chronology* (T: Arctic History Press 1978). Daniel Francis's survey, *Discovery of the North: The Exploration of Canada's Arctic* (E: Hurtig 1986), is an introduction to the topic intended for the non-specialist reader. A number of general studies examine the details of different periods of this exploration. Tryggvi J. Oleson's contribution to the Canadian Centenary Series, *Early Voyages and Northern Approaches, 1000–1632* (T: M&S 1963), was highly controversial because of some of the author's conclusions about early Norse contacts in the Northeast (see the reference to G.A. MacDonald's discussion of that controversy in the preceding section 'Ancient History'). The chapters of the book dealing with British approaches into the North are more straightforward. Similar ground is covered in 'The Northern Approaches to Canada,' an essay written by Oleson in collaboration with W.L. Morton, which appears in the first volume of the *DCB* (1966). The early expeditions were motivated by interest in discovering a northwest passage to the riches of the Oriental trade. Leslie H. Neatby, *In Quest of the North West Passage* (L: Longmans, Green 1958), provides a more detailed history of that search. The opening chapters of Arthur S. Morton's extensive study, *A History of the Canadian West to 1870–71* (1939; 2nd ed., ed. Lewis G. Thomas, T: UTP 1973), are a useful initiation to the subject of inland exploration. Theodore J. Karamanski, *Fur Trade and Exploration: Opening the Far Northwest, 1821–1852* (V: UBCP 1983), may not provide exciting reading but does serve as an introduction to European expansion into the regions of what is now northern British Columbia and the Yukon. An interesting examination of several aspects of the nineteenth-century exploration of the Arctic may be found in Hugh N. Wallace, *The Navy, the Company, and Richard King: British Exploration in the Canadian Arctic, 1829–1860* (M: MQUP 1980).

The first volume of the *HAC* includes several useful maps and lists of explorers: plate 36, 'French Exploration,' and plate 37, 'Re-establishment of Trade, 1654–1666,' illustrate the first French explorations beyond the Great Lakes; plate 58, 'Exploration from Hudson Bay,' details eighteenth-century travels; and plate 67, 'Exploration in the Far Northwest,' depicts the journeys of those primarily engaged in the fur trade.

Perhaps the best of recent scholarship on the European explorers is to be found in the biographies in the *DCB*. Each entry is a fascinating blend of biographical detail and historical context. See, for example, 'Sir Martin Frobisher,' 'Henry Hudson,' and 'Jens Eriksen Munk,' vol. 1; 'Nicolas Jérémie,' 'Henry Kelsey,' and 'Pierre-Esprit Radisson,' vol. 2 (1969); 'Pierre Gaultier de Varennes et de La Vérendrye,' vol. 3 (1974); 'Samuel Hearne,' vol. 4 (1979); 'Sir Alexander Mackenzie' and 'Peter Pond,' vol. 5 (1983); 'Sir John Franklin,' vol. 7 (1988); and 'David Thompson,' vol. 8 (1985).

Of course many of these explorers have provided us with records of their own perceptions of their travels. Some contain interesting details about the lands through which they voyaged, while others contain ethnographic details about the people they met. Excerpts from a number of these narratives can be found in John Warkentin, ed., *The Western Interior of Canada: A Record of Geographical Discovery, 1612–1917* (T: M&S 1964).

Those who prefer the complete editions may consult such volumes as Arthur George Doughty and Chester Martin, eds., *The Kelsey Papers* (O: National Archives of Canada 1929); Joseph Burr Tyrrell, ed., *David Thompson's Narrative of His Explorations in Western America, 1784–1812* (T: CS 1916); George Back, *Narrative of the Arctic Land Expedition to the Mouth of the Great Fish River, and along the Shores of the Arctic Ocean, in the Years 1833, 1834, and 1835* (1836; repr. E: Hurtig 1970); John Henry Lefroy, *In Search of the Magnetic North: A Soldier-Surveyor's Letters from the North-West, 1843–44*, ed. George F.G. Stanley (T: MAC 1955); and E.E. Rich and A.M. Johnson, eds., *A Journal of a Voyage from Rocky Mountain Portage in Peace*

River to the Sources of Finlays Branch and North West Ward in Summer 1824 [by Samuel Black] (L: HBRS 1955). Perhaps the best known of the northwestern explorers are Samuel Hearne and Alexander Mackenzie. Samuel Hearne's records of his expeditions have been published in several forms, including Richard Glover, ed., *A Journey from Prince of Wales's Fort in Hudson's Bay to the Northern Ocean, 1769, 1770, 1771, 1772* (T: MAC 1958), as have Alexander Mackenzie's travels, such as W. Kaye Lamb, ed., *The Journals and Letters of Sir Alexander Mackenzie* (Cambridge, Eng.: Hakluyt 1970).

Sir John Franklin's career has produced something of a publishing dynasty. His own records of his first and second arctic expeditions are provided in *Narrative of a Journey to the Shores of the Polar Sea, in the Years 1819, 20, 21 and 22* (1823; repr. E: Hurtig 1970) and *Narrative of a Second Expedition to the Shores of the Polar Sea, in the Years 1825, 1826, and 1827* (1828; repr. E: Hurtig 1971). Some of his crew members left their own accounts for posterity. C. Stuart Houston has edited and published two of them: *To the Arctic by Canoe, 1819–1821: The Journal and Paintings of Robert Hood, Midshipman with Franklin* (M&L: Arctic Institute of North America/MQUP 1974) and *Arctic Ordeal: The Journal of John Richardson, Surgeon-Naturalist with Franklin, 1820–1822* (K&M: MQUP 1984).

Franklin did not return from his expedition of 1845, prompting a number of searches which themselves became well-known arctic expeditions. L.H. Neatby produced a study of those rescue attempts in *The Search for Franklin* (E: Hurtig 1970). Biographies of the participants may be found in the *DCB*, including 'Peter Warren Dease' and 'Sir James Clark Ross,' vol. 9 (1976); 'Sir Edward Belcher' and 'Sir Robert John Le Mesurier McClure,' vol. 10 (1972); 'Sir Richard Collinson,' vol. 11 (1982); and 'John Rae,' vol. 12 (1990). One of the most original studies of what might have ultimately happened to the lost Franklin expedition is David C. Woodman, *Unravelling the Franklin Mystery: Inuit Testimony* (K&M: MQUP 1991). A somewhat sensationalized look at the mystery, intended for a general audience, is Owen Beattie and John Greiger, *Frozen in Time: Unlocking the Secrets of the Franklin Expedition* (Saskatoon, Sask.: WPPB 1987).

Although by the mid-nineteenth century most attention in exploration had shifted north, new interest in the agricultural potential of the prairie-plains region was developing in the south. The reports of a succession of scientific expeditions and individual travellers stimulated outside interest in the fertility of the plains. Of the former, John Palliser led the first and most important, and Irene Spry edited the expedition's records, *The Papers of the Palliser Expedition, 1857–1860* (T: CS 1968). Among the latter, perhaps the most influential was the author, artist, and explorer Paul Kane. J. Russell

Harper prepared a catalogue of Kane's sketches and paintings, which also incorporates one of the artist's major writings: *Paul Kane's Frontier: Including 'Wanderings of an Artist among the Indians of North America' by Paul Kane* (T: UTP 1971). Another visual interpretation of the West is found in Richard J. Huyda, comp., *Camera in the Interior, 1858: H.L. Hime, Photographer* (T: Coach House Press 1975). Douglas Owram, *Promise of Eden: The Canadian Expansionist Movement and the Idea of the West, 1856–1900* (T: UTP 1980), traces changing Canadian perceptions of the West in the mid-nineteenth century and demonstrates how the reports of the expeditions of Palliser and John Macoun were used by Ontario promoters of western expansion. Owram concludes his study with a fascinating chapter on how westerners in turn rejected these images as they struggled to define themselves as a distinct society and not merely as a branch of 'empire Ontario.'

Another genre that may be of interest to readers for the glimpses it provides of both the visitor and the lands visited is sometimes referred to as travel literature. Among the more interesting of such accounts are: William F. Butler, *The Great Lone Land* (L: Sampson Low 1872) and *The Wild North Land* (1873; repr. E: Hurtig 1968); W.H. Dall, 'Travels on the Yukon and in the Yukon Territory in 1866–1868,' in F. Mortimer Trimmer, ed., *The Yukon Territory: The Narrative of W.H. Dall* (L: Downey 1898); Warburton Pike, *The Barren Ground of Northern Canada* (L: MAC 1892); Thomas McMicking, *Overland from Canada to British Columbia*, ed. Joanne Leduc (V: UBCP 1981); and Caspar Whitney, *On Snowshoes to the Barren Grounds* (NY: Harper 1896). Eric Ross, in *Beyond the River and the Bay* (T: UTP 1970), invented a travelogue account of a European's impressions of the Northwest in a unique and highly imaginative approach. This fictionalized reconstruction is useful for an understanding of geography and the fur trade, but is now out of date in its depictions of Native peoples, their role in the fur trade, and the nature of their societies.

Finally, it must be noted that European geographical knowledge of the Northwest was developed through a variety of sources other than exploration. Native people provided much useful information as is noted in the accounts of individual explorers; see also *HAC*, vol. 1, plate 59, 'Indian Maps.' The role of the Hudson's Bay Company is examined by Richard I. Ruggles in *A Country So Interesting: The Hudson's Bay Company and Two Centuries of Mapping, 1670–1870* (K&M: MQUP 1990).

THE FUR TRADE

The fur resources of the Northwest prompted the first European incursions into the region and continue to prompt historical inquiry. Perhaps the largest body of literature on the Northwest in recent years has been produced by historians, anthropologists, and ethnohistorians attempting to explain the dynamics of that trade and to evaluate its impact on the First Nations who participated in it. The first detailed examinations of that trade were made for rather different reasons. H.A. Innis was drawn to the trade to illustrate the exploitation of natural resource products that he believed had shaped the contours of modern Canada, an example that substantiated his staples thesis. His classic study *The Fur Trade in Canada* remains a basic reference, although most historians are now interested in other aspects of the issue and some have questioned the validity of many of Innis's interpretations; see W.J. Eccles, 'A Belated Review of Harold Adams Innis, *The Fur Trade in Canada*,' *CHR* 60/4 (Dec. 1979): 419–41.

Other early students of the trade, less committed to validating a specific thesis, fit it into an international business or political context. The results were often massive in scale if less striking in analysis. A.S. Morton, *History of the Canadian West*, for example, is a compilation of information on the expansion of European interests into the Northwest. An even larger work, E.E. Rich's *History of the Hudson's Bay Company, 1670–1870*, 2 vols. (L: HBRS 1958–9; repr. 3 vols., T: M&S 1960), while primarily an institutional history, does provide the reader with considerable detail on the politics and economics of the overall trade. Of this vintage, too, is John S. Galbraith, *The Hudson's Bay Company as an Imperial Factor, 1821–1869* (T: UTP 1957). Galbraith went on to publish a biography of one of its governors, Sir George Simpson, *The Little Emperor: Governor Simpson of the Hudson's Bay Company* (T: MAC 1976), which is representative of another common strand in early writing on the fur trade – a fascination with the colourful personalities it engaged. Although these studies had different points of emphasis, all share a lack of interest in the Native role in the trade. Their real concern was what the trade might have meant to its European and Canadian participants.

More recently, however, historians have turned to rather different questions about the trade, wondering instead what role Native peoples might have played in it. In 1974 anthropologist Charles A. Bishop produced *The Northern Ojibwa and the Fur Trade: An Historical and Ecological Study* (T: HRW 1974) using a model of what anthropologists were then calling cultural ecology to explain patterns of Ojibwa involvement in the trade. The same year, A.J. Ray also produced a detailed examination of the impact of a trade economy on the Cree and their neighbours. His *Indians in the Fur Trade: Their Role as Trappers, Hunters, and Middlemen in the Lands Southwest of Hudson Bay, 1660–1870* (T: UTP 1974) remains an important source for the history of the fur trade south of Hudson Bay as well as a thought-provoking interpretation of Native economic behaviour. In collaboration with Donald B. Freeman, Ray developed that interpretation further in *'Give Us Good Measure': An Economic Analysis of Relations between the Indians and the Hudson's Bay Company before 1763* (T: UTP 1978). Ray sees the northern Indians as skilled traders who were by no means the naive dupes of European businessmen, an idea he presents concisely in 'Indians as Consumers in the Eighteenth Century,' in C.M. Judd and Ray, eds., *Old Trails and New Directions*. Abraham Rotstein preferred to emphasize the political importance of the fur trade to First Nations in 'Trade and Politics: An Institutional Approach,' *Western Canadian Journal of Anthropology* 3/1 (1972): 1–28. He argued that early trade relations were modelled on Native expectations for political or diplomatic ceremonies and that fur traders were forced to accommodate themselves to those patterns. Indeed, Rotstein goes so far as to maintain that the political aspects of the trade were more important to some Native groups than the potential for economic gain.

Calvin Martin touched off a major discussion about Native participation in the trade with the publication of *Keepers of the Game: Indian-Animal Relationships and the Fur Trade* (Berkeley and Los Angeles, CA: University of California Press 1978). His examination of the northeastern woodland trade led him to ask why people who apparently shared a strong conservationist ethic would have been willing to participate in the fur trade to the extent that some animal species were hunted to near-extinction. He argued that it was necessary to look at spiritual beliefs for an answer, and the book is an extended development of the thesis that the people of the eastern woodlands blamed the animal spirits for the epidemics that were decimating their populations and declared a 'holy war of extermination' on those animals. Martin's theory may have failed to convince many, but it did generate a flurry of responses that have provided us with glimpses of aspects of the fur trade throughout the North and West. For example, see the collection of essays edited by ethnohistorian Shepard Krech III, *Indians, Animals and the Fur Trade: A Critique of 'Keepers of the Game'* (Athens, GA: University of Georgia Press 1981). Adrian Tanner, *Bringing Home Animals: Religious Ideology and Mode of Production of the Mistassini Cree Hunters* (NY: St Martin's Press 1979), argues that the Cree managed their game resources well in the fur trade and that their religious systems did not give way even through this period of tremendous change.

That question of the extent to which Native societies changed through participation in the fur trade is the subject of another body of literature.

When E.E. Rich prepared a volume for the Canadian Centenary Series entitled *The Fur Trade and the Northwest to 1857* (T: M&S 1967), he summarized his contemporaries' limited understanding of the role of Native peoples in the trade, the conventional theory being that Native peoples had quickly been drawn into the trade in a desire to obtain items of 'superior' European technology. Wherever the trade was introduced, Rich suggested, within a matter of only a decade Natives had become dependent on that imported technology to the extent that they lost the ability to support themselves and had come to rely entirely on the presence of foreign traders. That interpretation has become a central issue in much writing about the fur trade today. Just what was the impact of the trade on Natives? Did they all choose to participate? Why? Did the adoption of a foreign technology also mean the adoption of foreign value systems and religious ideas? No one would deny that participation in the trade brought changes to Native societies, but the discussion is revolving around the nature and extent of those changes. D. Francis and Toby Morantz argue persuasively in *Partners in Furs: A History of the Fur Trade in Eastern James Bay, 1600–1870* (K&M: MQUP 1983) that the Native traders themselves made choices about what changes they wished to make in their lives. In other words, they were not the passive victims of structural forces beyond their control. Paul Thistle develops a similar argument in *Indian-European Trade Relations in the Lower Saskatchewan River Region to 1840* (W: UMP 1986). On the other hand, Glen Makahonuk, 'Wage-Labour in the Northwest Fur Trade Economy, 1760–1849,' *Saskatchewan History* 41/1 (Winter 1988): 1–18, reprinted in Angus D. Gilbert et al., eds., *Reappraisals in Canadian History*, vol. 1, *Pre-Confederation* (Scarborough, Ont.: PH 1993), argues that wage labour in the fur trade was part of a newly developing capitalist system and that both Native and non-Native workers participated in these important structural changes. The idea that Native peoples were automatically enveloped by capitalism is bound to remain controversial.

Aspects of the social history of the trade have also received attention. For a quick overview see F. Pannekoek, *The Fur Trade and Western Canadian Society, 1670–1870*, CHA Historical Booklet no. 43 (O: 1987). S. Van Kirk's ground-breaking study *'Many Tender Ties': Women in Fur-Trade Society in Western Canada, 1670–1870* (W: Watson and Dwyer 1980) stressed the importance of Native and, later, Métis women as diplomats, interpreters, and cultural go-betweens in the western trade. Jennifer S.H. Brown looked at another aspect of fur trade social structure in *Strangers in Blood: Fur Trade Company Families in Indian Country* (V: UBCP 1980). Michael Payne reconstructs the social life of one major trade centre in *The*

Most Respectable Place in the Territory: Everyday Life in Hudson's Bay Company Service, York Factory, 1788–1870 (O: National Historic Parks and Sites 1989). A rather different view of fur trade social relations is provided by W.A. Sloan in 'The Native Response to the Extension of the European Traders into the Athabasca and Mackenzie Basin, 1770–1814,' *CHR* 60/3 (Sept. 1979): 281–99, in which he examines the period of intense competition between the Hudson's Bay and North West companies in the Far Northwest to paint an unsavoury picture of violence, rape, and kidnapping, all in the name of economic advantage. J.M. Bumsted and Wendy Owen, 'The Victorian Family in Canada in Historical Perspective: The Ross Family of Red River and the Jarvis Family of Prince Edward Island,' *Manitoba History* 13 (Spring 1987): 12–18, reprinted in A.D. Gilbert et al., eds., *Reappraisals in Canadian History*, vol. 1, provides an interesting glimpse into the life of one fur trade family. The authors argue that in spite of differences of location, race, and culture, the structures that shaped these families were very much alike. In other words, they claim that a common middle-class culture existed in British North America.

Aficionados of fur trade history meet regularly at the North American Fur Trade Conference to exchange ideas and the results of research on many fur trade topics, ranging from the interpretative issues of dependence and autonomy to the details of post construction or location. Readers may follow the presentations of some of these conferences in publications of selected papers. These include Malvina Bolus, ed., *People and Pelts: Selected Papers of the Second North American Fur Trade Conference, 1970* (W: Peguis 1972); C.M. Judd and A.J. Ray, eds., *Old Trails and New Directions*; Thomas C. Buckley, ed., *Rendezvous: Selected Papers of the Fourth North American Fur Trade Conference, 1981* (St Paul, MN: North American Fur Trade Conference 1984); and Bruce G. Trigger, T. Morantz, and Louise Dechêne, eds., *'Le Castor Fait Tout': Selected Papers of the Fifth North American Fur Trade Conference, 1985* (M: Lake St Louis Historical Society 1987).

Finally, for those interested in reading the original journals and accounts of the fur traders themselves, there are many published editions available. For the early fur trade the most interesting include Lawrence J. Burpee, ed., *Journals and Letters of Pierre Gaultier de Varennes de La Vérendrye and His Sons* (T: CS 1927); J.B. Tyrrell, ed., *Documents Relating to the Early History of Hudson Bay* (T: CS 1931); Robert Douglas and J.N. Wallace, eds., *Twenty Years of York Factory, 1694–1714: Jérémie's Account of Hudson Strait and Bay* (O: Thorburn and Abbott 1926); J.F. Kenny, ed., *The Founding of Churchill: Being the Journal of Captain James Knight, Governor-in-Chief in Hudson Bay, from the 14th of July to the 13th of September, 1717* (T: J.M. Dent & Sons

1932); and E.E. Rich and A.M. Johnson, eds., *James Isham's Observations on Hudsons Bay, 1743* (T: CS/HBRS 1949).

For documents produced by members of the North West Company see Louis-Rodrigue Masson, ed., *Les bourgeois de la Compagnie du Nord-Ouest*, 2 vols. (1889–90; NY: Antiquarian Press 1960), and W. Stewart Wallace, ed., *Documents Relating to the North West Company* (T: CS 1934). Few entire journals of North West Company traders have survived, but some interesting exceptions are Harry Duckworth's edition of *The English River Book: A North West Company Journal and Account Book of 1786* (K&M: MQUP 1989) and A.S. Morton, ed., *The Journal of Duncan M'Gillivray of the North West Company at Fort George on the Saskatchewan, 1794–5* (T: MAC 1929). The period of crisis immediately preceding the merger of the North West and Hudson's Bay companies is covered in Jean Morrison, ed., *The North West Company in Rebellion: Simon McGillivray's Fort William Notebook, 1815* (Thunder Bay, Ont.: Thunder Bay Historical Museum Society 1988).

Documents pertaining to the later history of the Hudson's Bay Company are also extensive. The crucial period during which the two companies merged is covered in E.E. Rich, ed., *Journal of Occurrences in the Athabasca Department by George Simpson, 1820 and 1821, and Report* (T: CS/HBRS 1938). A disgruntled employee's memoirs can be found in W.S. Wallace, ed., *John McLean's Notes of a Twenty-Five Year's Service in the Hudson's Bay Territory* (T: CS 1932). See also Alexander Hunter Murray, *Journal of the Yukon, 1847–48*, ed. L.J. Burpee (O: National Archives of Canada 1910). A fascinating glimpse of fur trade life from the perspective of a prominent trader's wife is Margaret Arnett MacLeod, ed., *The Letters of Letitia Hargrave* (T: CS 1947).

MISSION HISTORY

Until relatively recently few academic historians had devoted much attention to the history of Christian mission work in Canada. Many books were produced for the public by church presses and mission societies, but these volumes were intended to glorify, and encourage support for, the work of the missionaries. More recently the subject has become emotionally highly charged because of allegations of cultural genocide from Native groups. Nevertheless, there is a growing body of literature attempting to analyse the intentions of missionaries in the Northwest, the response of Native peoples to their work, and the long-term impact of mission presence.

Overviews of mission work produced by authors sympathetic to the goals of their subjects include Adrien-Gabriel Morice, *History of the Catholic*

Church in Western Canada, 2 vols. (T: Musson 1910); Pierre Duchaussois, *The Grey Nuns in the Far North, 1867–1917* (T: M&S 1919); Duchaussois, *Mid Snow and Ice: The Apostles of the Northwest* (L: Burns, Oates and Washbourne 1923); John Henry Riddell, *Methodism in the Middle West* (T: RP 1946); Joseph-Etienne Champagne, *Les missions catholiques dans l'Ouest canadien, 1818–1875* (O: Editions des études Oblats 1949); Thomas C.B. Boon, *The Anglican Church from the Bay to the Rockies* (T: RP 1962); and Gaston Carrière, 'Fondation et développement des missions catholiques dans la Terre de Rupert et les T.N.O., 1845–1861,' *Revue de l'Université d'Ottawa* 41 (1971): 253–82, 397–427. Readers should be cautioned that these studies are problematic to most of today's audience in that they tend to view the missionaries as heroes bringing the light of the Gospel to the poor unfortunate Natives; nevertheless, they contain useful information on the personnel and attitudes of the northwestern missions.

John Webster Grant, possessed of a more critical eye, produced an interesting analysis of missions in *Moon of Wintertime: Missionaries and the Indians of Canada in Encounter since 1534* (T: UTP 1984). Grant provides histories of mission work in the various regions and then develops his thesis that First Nations turned to Christianity as an alternative during times when their old world systems seemed to be breaking down under the pressure of contact with Europeans. Yet Kerry Abel has raised questions about the universal applicability of that thesis. In 'Prophets, Priests and Preachers: Dene Shamans and Christian Missions in the Nineteenth Century,' CHA *HP* (1986): 211–24, she argues that a number of religious movements in the Mackenzie Valley may have been manifestations of older religious beliefs rather than the result of adaptation of Christian beliefs. Another historian who has questioned the apparent 'success' of missionaries in obtaining converts is Ian A.L. Getty, who suggests that at least one mission society was not as successful as it claimed. His article 'The Failure of the Native Church Policy of the Church Missionary Society in the North-West,' in Richard Allen, ed., *Religion and Society in the Prairie West* (R: CPRC 1974), examines the possible reasons for the failure of one aspect of that program.

Another perspective is taken in a variety of studies that emphasize the missionary as an agent of colonization and assimilation. Robert Coutts makes this point in 'Anglican Missionaries as Agents of Acculturation: The Church Missionary Society at St. Andrew's Red River, 1830–1870,' in B. Ferguson, ed., *The Anglican Church and the World of Western Canada*, as does Winona Stevenson in 'The Red River Indian Mission School and John West's "Little Charges," 1820–1833,' *Native Studies Review* 4/1–2 (1988): 129–66. David Mulhall provides a fascinating glimpse into the mind of one of the best-known northern missionaries in *Will to Power: The Missionary Career of Father Morice* (V: UBCP 1986).

Relations among missionaries and between missionaries and the Hudson's Bay Company have also interested historians. Frank A. Peake, for instance, in 'Fur Traders and Missionaries: Some Reflections on the Attitudes of the H.B.C. towards Mission Work amongst the Indians,' *Western Canadian Journal of Anthropology* 3/1 (1972): 72–93, provides an introduction to that complex relationship, while G. Carrière considers the question with an emphasis on the Roman Catholic missions in 'L'Honorable Compagnie de la Baie d'Hudson et les missions dans l'Ouest canadien,' *Revue de l'Université d'Ottawa* 36 (1966): 15–39, 232–57. In the Far North, competition between Roman Catholic and Anglican was legendary. Craig Mishler reconstructs one episode in that conflict in 'Missionaries in Collison: Anglicans and Oblates among the Gwich'in, 1861–65,' *Arctic* 43/2 (June 1990): 121–6.

Readers should also consult the many entries in the *DCB* for a sampling of the history of the northwestern missions. Some examples are 'James Evans' and 'John West,' vol. 7; 'Pierre-Henri Grollier,' vol. 9; 'Henry Budd,' vol. 10; 'David Anderson,' 'John Black,' 'James Hunter,' and 'John McLean,' vol. 11; 'Alexandre-Antonin Taché,' vol. 12; and 'William Carpenter Bompas,' vol. 13 (in press).

For those who are interested in reading the original journals of mission workers, the choices are somewhat limited; see Hugh Dempsey, ed., *The Rundle Journals, 1840–1848*, intro. G.M. Hutchinson (Calgary, Alta.: Alberta Historical Society 1977), and Katherine Pettipas, ed., *The Diary of the Reverend Henry Budd, 1870–1875* (W: Manitoba Record Society 1974). There are also dozens of missionary memoirs that are not strictly speaking published documents but that certainly give readers a taste of the ideas missionaries had about their work, including their attitudes to Native peoples to whom their work was directed. See, for example, Alexandre-Antonin Taché, *Vingt années de missions dans le nord-ouest de l'Amérique* (M: T.A. Bernier 1888); E.-J.-B.-M. Grouard, *Souvenirs de mes soixante ans d'apostolat dans l'Athabaska-Mackenzie* (W: La Liberté 1922); Egerton Ryerson Young, *By Canoe and Dog-Train among the Cree and Saulteaux Indians* (T: William Briggs 1890); and Hiram A. Cody, *An Apostle of the North: Memoirs of the Right Reverend William Carpenter Bompas* (L: Seeley 1908). An entertaining pair of memoirs is John McDougall, *Saddle, Sled and Snowshoe* (T: William Briggs 1896), and its sequel, *Pathfinding on Plain and Prairie* (T: William Briggs 1898; repr. T: Coles 1971). One of the few memoirs by a woman serving in the mission field was compiled by S.A. Archer, *A Heroine of the*

North: Memoirs of Charlotte Selina Bompas, 1830–1917 (L: Society for Promoting Christian Knowledge 1929).

FIRST NATIONS

There has been a flurry of interest in the past fifteen years in the history of First Nations throughout the Northwest. Essentially these works fall into two categories: first, histories of Native/non-Native relations; and, second, what might be called 'national' histories of various Native groups. Unfortunately, there are as yet no effective general surveys of the history of First Nations in the Northwest. For the North, readers should begin with the updated edition of Keith Crowe, *A History of the Original Peoples of Northern Canada* (rev. ed., K&M: MQUP 1991).

Most work to date on Native history pertains specifically to that period of interaction between aboriginal peoples and European newcomers and so more properly should be called the history of Native/non-Native relations rather than Native history as a whole. And of that literature, relatively little analysis has been done of Inuit-European contact in spite of the fact that intensive interaction between Inuit and outsider has been relatively recent. Dorothy Harley Eber looks at one aspect of that history in *When the Whalers Were Up North: Inuit Memories from the Eastern Arctic* (K&M: MQUP 1989). Philip Goldring has also studied the eastern Arctic and published his results in such essays as 'Inuit Economic Responses to Euro-American Contacts: Southeast Baffin Island, 1824–1940,' in CHA *HP* (1986): 146–72.

Although they are steeped in late-nineteenth-century assumptions about race and culture, observations by anthropologists who lived among the Inuit continue to be interesting reading and provide glimpses of Inuit life before there had been much interaction with newcomers. Classic accounts include Franz Boas, 'The Central Eskimo,' in the *Sixth Annual Report of the Bureau of American Ethnology for the Years 1884–1885* (Washington, DC: Smithsonian Institution 1888): 399–669, and Vihjalmur Stefansson, *My Life with the Eskimo* (NY: MAC 1913).

The literature on Indian-European relations is more extensive. Good general introductions to the topic are J.R. Miller, *Skyscrapers Hide the Heavens: A History of Indian-White Relations in Canada* (1989; rev. ed., T: UTP 1991), and O.P. Dickason, *Canada's First Nations: A History of Founding Peoples from Earliest Times* (T: M&S 1992), although they deal with a much broader spatial and chronological sweep than is covered in this chapter. K.S. Coates has developed an interesting survey of interaction in the Yukon in *Best Left as Indians: Native-White Relations in the Yukon Territory, 1840–*

1973 (K&M: MQUP 1991). For an anthropological interpretation of inter- action on the plains see Oscar Lewis, *The Effects of White Contact upon Black- foot Culture with Special Reference to the Role of the Fur Trade* (Seattle, WA: University of Washington Press 1966).

Recently some historians have been attempting to go beyond the topic of Native/non-Native relations and write what might be called 'national' his- tories of particular groups. Among the national histories are works by both historians and anthropologists. David Mandelbaum, *The Plains Cree: An Ethnographic, Historical and Comparative Study* (R: CPRC 1979), was origi- nally published in 1949 but remains a pioneering work in the field, although it lacks a strong historical sense. Mandelbaum argues that the people who became the Plains Cree were indigenous to more eastern wooded areas. They invaded the plains and were able to displace the original populations because of their access to guns through the establishment of the fur trade in their homelands. Dale Russell takes issue with that interpretation in *Eigh- teenth-Century Western Cree and Their Neighbours* (O: Canadian Museum of Civilization 1991), but it receives support in John S. Milloy, *The Plains Cree: Trade, Diplomacy and War, 1790–1870* (W: UMP 1988). Milloy provides a political and military history that focuses on the strategies used by the Cree during a period of territorial expansion and intensive contact with Europe- ans. Peter Douglas Elias deals with the experiences of another plains group in *The Dakota of the Canadian Northwest: Lessons for Survival* (W: UMP 1988), the first three chapters covering the pre-Confederation period. The history of the Native people of the subarctic Northwest Territories and northern Prairie provinces is covered in K. Abel, *Drum Songs: Glimpses of Dene History* (K&M: MQUP 1993). Finally, one interesting experiment is Catharine McClellan et al., *Part of the Land, Part of the Water: A History of the Yukon Indians* (V: Douglas & McIntyre 1987). In this beautifully illus- trated book, the authors attempt to incorporate academic and Native con- cepts of history as well as to address a wide variety of audiences from the specialist to the novice. It deserves to be read not only as a history of Yukon Natives, but as an innovative experiment in both research and presentation.

For those interested in an anthropological approach to an understanding of Native cultures and languages, the basic reference is the multivolume series *Handbook of North American Indians* (Washington, DC: Smithsonian Institution 1978–), under the general editorship of William C. Sturtevant. Although the volume covering the prairie-parkland region is yet to be pub- lished, we do have volume 5, *Arctic*, ed. David Damas (1984), and volume 6, *Subarctic*, ed. June Helm (1981). Each contains essays by prominent anthro- pologists on such subjects as language, culture, archaeology, and contact history; there are numerous illustrations and extensive bibliographies. Historians, however, will be frustrated to discover that although 'history' plays a role in some of the contributions, the approach is fundamentally ahistorical in the sense that cultural change since the arrival of Europeans is measured against a seemingly unchanging 'traditional' past and little use is made of historical source materials to enrich an understanding of Native history before the visits of twentieth-century anthropologists.

The religious beliefs and practices of First Nations have long been a subject of fascination. Basil Johnston provides an introduction to one northern group in *Ojibway Heritage: The Ceremonies, Rituals, Songs, Dances, Prayers, and Legends of the Ojibway* (1976; repr. T: M&S 1988). An interesting approach is taken in J.S.H. Brown and Robert Brightman, eds., *The Orders of the Dreamed: George Nelson on the Cree and Northern Ojibwa Religion and Myth, 1823* (W: UMP 1988). The editors provide a transcript of one fur trader's observations, with a commentary and a concluding essay by Emma LaRocque, 'On the Ethics of Publishing Historical Documents,' in which she discusses the issue of whether such materials do anything more than perpetuate racism.

In search of a Native perspective on their own history, scholars have recently sought out oral traditions. While such traditions present problems for historians trained in the European academic manner, they can potentially provide substantial rewards. Fortunately, too, more and more stories are being published and are now available to students who wish to delve into Native oral traditions for themselves. Oblate missionary E. Petitot's *Traditions indiennes du Canada nord-ouest* and G. Blondin's *When the World Was New* have already been noted in the section on ancient history. J. Cruikshank has organized a number of projects to record the oral traditions of Yukon Native peoples, including *Athapaskan Women: Lives and Legends* (O: Canadian Museum of Civilization 1979). In her collection *Life Lived like a Story*, three Yukon women elders tell the story of their own lives and of their people's history in a fascinating experiment in oral history, although most of the stories take place in the twentieth century. She also explores the idea of using oral traditions as a source for early history in a thought-provoking article, 'Legend and Landscape: Convergence of Oral and Scientific Traditions in the Yukon Territory,' *Arctic Anthropology* 18/2 (1981): 67–94. The Dene Wodih Society compiled *Wolverine Myths and Visions: Dene Traditions from Northern Alberta* (E: UAP 1990). The editors of this volume, Pat Moore and Angela Wheelock, offer introductions that are primarily of interest to anthropologists and linguists, but the stories, many of which are followed by a 'Storyteller's Commentary,' will appeal to a wider audience.

Of particular note is the fact that an attempt was made to reproduce the rhythms of Native speech in English. Other collections include Carl Ray and James Stevens, *Sacred Legends of the Sandy Lake Cree* (T: M&S 1971), and B. Johnston, *Tales the Elders Told: Ojibwa Legends* (T: Royal Ontario Museum 1981).

Stories from the plains may be found in L. Bloomfield, *Sacred Stories of the Sweet Grass Cree* (1930; repr. NY: AMS Press 1976); part 2 of Marius Barbeau, *Indian Days on the Western Prairies* (1957; repr. O: National Museums of Canada 1965), which includes tales of both the Stoney and Western Cree people of southern Alberta; and Eleanor Brass, *Medicine Boy and Other Cree Tales* (Calgary, Alta.: Glenbow 1978). Knud Rasmussen recorded a number of traditions of the Inuit of the central Arctic (a people once known as the Copper Eskimo); these were published in volume 9 of the *Fifth Thule Expedition, 1921–1924* (Copenhagen: Gyldendal 1929). Volume 10, part 2, of the same series (1942) includes traditions of the Inuvialuit, known to Rasmussen as the Mackenzie Eskimo. Inuit stories were more recently published in Herbert T. Schwarz, *Elik, and Other Stories of the Mackenzie Eskimos* (T: M&S 1970), and Maurice Métayer, ed., *Tales from the Igloo* (E: Hurtig 1972).

The *DCB* has solicited many entries on Native people, providing one of the most useful sources on individuals who are rarely noted in more general historical studies. Although many of the biographies are necessarily short and often vague on some aspects of the individual's life, the entries do provide important glimpses into the experiences of these people and their communities. See, for example, 'Thanadelthur,' vol. 2; 'Matonabbee,' vol. 4; 'Aw-gee-nah,' vol. 6 (1987); 'Abishabis' and 'Eenoolooapik,' vol. 7; 'Isapo-Muxika [Crowfoot],' vol. 11; and 'Natawista [Medicine Snake Woman]' and 'Sahneuti,' vol. 12.

METIS

The meaning and appropriateness of the terms 'Métis,' 'métis,' 'mixed-blood,' 'country-born,' and 'half-breed' are still subjects of considerable discussion. Obviously interaction between aboriginal peoples and their European trade partners gave rise to marriages and families; the children of these unions came to play a vital role in the history of the Northwest. John E. Foster, 'The Metis: The People and the Term,' *Prairie Forum* 3/1 (Spring 1978): 79–90, discusses the problems of terminology, and the introductory essay in J. Peterson and J.S.H. Brown, eds., *The New Peoples: Being and Becoming Métis in North America* (W: UMP 1985), is also helpful. For a brief overview of Métis history see J.S.H. Brown, 'The Métis: Genesis and Rebirth,' in Bruce Cox, ed., *Native People, Native Lands: Canadian Indians, Inuit and Metis* (O: CUP 1987).

While much attention has been given to the role of the Métis in the Red River Uprising of 1869–70 and the Saskatchewan Rebellion of 1885, relatively little has been written about Métis history before 1869. For many years, historians treated the Métis of Red River as an interesting and unique group that originated in the fur trade contacts of that region. More recently, however, J. Peterson has suggested that at least some of the Métis at Red River had actually originated in the French-Indian communities of the Great Lakes region, what the Americans refer to as the Old North West. Her summary of the research that led to this conclusion is in 'Many Roads to Red River: Métis Genesis in the Great Lakes Region, 1680–1815,' in Peterson and J.S.H. Brown, eds., *The New Peoples*. For more on the French-Indian communities from which these people migrated see Helen Hornbeck Tanner, ed., *Atlas of Great Lakes Indian History* (Norman, OK: University of Oklahoma Press 1987). Other aspects of the emergence of the Métis are discussed in O.P. Dickason, 'From "One Nation" in the Northeast to "New Nation" in the Northwest: A Look at the Emergence of the Métis,' and J.E. Foster, 'Some Questions and Perspectives on the Problem of Métis Roots,' both in J. Peterson and J.S.H. Brown, eds., *The New Peoples*.

For the most part, however, the history of the Métis before Confederation has tended to emphasize the economic role of the Métis in the fur trade. Perhaps best known is their participation in the vitally important pemmican industry. One introduction to that topic is A.J. Ray, 'The Northern Great Plains: Pantry of the Northeastern Fur Trade, 1774–1885,' *Prairie Forum* 9/2 (Fall 1984): 263–80. W.L. Morton's 1961 essay 'The Battle at the Grand Coteau, July 13 and 14, 1851,' reprinted in Donald Swainson, ed., *Historical Essays on the Prairie Provinces* (T: M&S 1970), recounts the events of the final military confrontation between the Métis and a group of Plains Indians in their struggle over access to the buffalo resources. The battle is a little-known episode but nonetheless one of crucial significance in the shifting balance of power on the plains in the period prior to widespread European settlement.

The Red River Métis were also known for their ongoing opposition to Hudson's Bay Company claims that it had monopoly trading rights in Rupert's Land. When Lord Selkirk was permitted to establish an agricultural settlement at a key point in the North West Company's transportation network and in the midst of Métis buffalo-hunting country, the Métis were concerned. Aspects of this situation are explored in M.A. MacLeod and W.L. Morton's biography *Cuthbert Grant of Grantown* (T: M&S 1974), a life-and-times study of a prominent Red River Métis leader, which takes the reader through the period of intense competition between the North West and Hudson's Bay companies.

After the merger of the two companies in 1821, many Métis took it upon themselves to challenge the new Hudson's Bay Company's claim to monopoly trade rights by establishing themselves as independent traders. The company attempted initially to eliminate the competition through trade strategies, but eventually resorted to legal arguments. In 1849 several Métis traders were brought to trial at Red River; the outcome was a moral victory for the Métis 'free traders.' This episode, often referred to as the Sayer Trial (after one of the defendants), is covered in such general histories as W.L. Morton, *Manitoba*, and G. Friesen, *The Canadian Prairies*, but also see Kathryn M. Bindon, 'Hudson's Bay Company Law: Adam Thom and the Institution of Order in Rupert's Land, 1839–54,' in David H. Flaherty, ed., *Essays in the History of Canadian Law*, vol. 1 (T: OS 1981), and *DCB* entries 'Pierre-Guillaume Sayer,' vol. 7, and 'Adam Thom,' vol. 11.

Métis opposition to the Hudson's Bay Company monopoly took many other forms as well. Perhaps one of the most interesting opponents was Alexander K. Isbister, an unusual Métis who received a university education in Scotland and apparently moved successfully among British society, but also devoted his energies to promoting the cause of his homeland in the Northwest. Isbister is the subject of a full-length biography by Barry Cooper, *Alexander Kennedy Isbister: A Respectable Critic of the Honourable Company* (O: CUP 1988). Cooper's biography will make many historians uneasy because it does not include a strong sense of the historical context of Isbister's life and the author does not attempt to explain where he thinks the analysis fits into current fur trade historiography. As a political scientist, Cooper is more interested in questions of political strategy and political consciousness in the setting of Red River and other parts of the Northwest than he is in the historical analysis of Isbister's life. The *DCB* entry 'Alexander Kennedy Isbister,' vol. 11, is helpful here.

There is a growing debate about the history of the Métis from the middle to the late nineteenth century. On the one hand are those who argue that the Métis were gradually displaced from their homes in the Red River Valley as the lands became increasingly desirable to outsiders for the purpose of agricultural settlement. The Red River Uprising and the Saskatchewan Rebellion are sometimes seen as the culmination of that process. G.F.G. Stanley's examination of the rebellions, *The Birth of Western Canada:*

A History of the Riel Rebellions (1936; repr. T: UTP 1961), presented an image of a 'primitive' society being forced to retreat in the face of the pressures of an expanding 'civilized' society. While more recent studies reject the racist overtones of the language, some have accepted Stanley's premise of a retreat in the face of pressure. Douglas N. Sprague has taken the interpretation a step further and argued that the Métis were deliberately cheated out of what was rightfully theirs. While most of his work has examined the post-1870 West, he and R.P. Frye pushed back in time to compile *The Genealogy of the First Métis Nation: The Development and Dispersal of the Red River Settlement, 1820–1900* (W: Pemmican 1983). Although it is primarily a reconstruction of families, this volume does include an introductory essay that summarizes Sprague's interpretation of Métis history. That essay is conveniently reprinted in R.D. Francis and Donald B. Smith, eds., *Readings in Canadian History*, vol. 1, *Pre-Confederation* (3rd ed., T: HRW 1990). On the other hand, not all historians have agreed that the Métis were forced into retreat. Gerhard Ens challenges that interpretation in 'Dispossession or Adaptation? Migration and Persistence of the Red River Metis, 1835–1890,' CHA *HP* (1988): 120–44. He argues that the Métis movement out of Red River was a response to 'new economic opportunities': a pull rather than a push. The distinction is not a minor one. The image of the Métis generated by Ens is one of men and women taking control of their own lives and circumstances, while Stanley's and Sprague's works present the Métis as a relatively passive people being victimized by their circumstances.

Biographies can reveal something of Métis history. Until the *DCB* project, readers could turn to A.-G. Morice, *Dictionnaire historique des Canadiens et des Métis français de l'Ouest* (Q: J.P. Garneau 1908). While it would require painstaking research to verify the details of the entries of some of the lesser known figures in this dictionary, the work will probably remain as the only source of information on some of the Métis. More useful to the modern reader, though, are entries in the *DCB*. A survey of these entries makes it graphically clear that the experiences of the Métis in the Northwest were extraordinarily diverse. Some became leaders among their Native relatives, like François Beaulieu, patriarch of the Athabasca District (vol. 10). Others, like brothers Richard Charles and William Lucas Hardisty (vol. 11) or William Sinclair (vol. 9), became senior officers of the Hudson's Bay Company. Still others, like Pierre-Guillaume Sayer (vol. 7), preferred to work in opposition to the company as independent traders. William Kennedy (vol. 11) began as a servant of the Hudson's Bay Company but became better known as the leader of two expeditions in search of Sir John

Franklin. When he retired to Red River, he played an active role in the community as part of its social elite. John Bunn (vol. 9), whose mother was Métis, served Red River as a medical doctor as well as coroner, magistrate, and numerous other important positions, while celebrating his mixed ancestry. Other interesting biographies include 'Joseph Cadotte,' vol. 6; 'Pierre-Chrysologue Pambrun,' vol. 7; 'Cuthbert Grant' and 'Louis Guiboche,' vol. 8; and 'John Norquay,' vol. 11.

By mid-nineteenth century, however, racial attitudes at Red River were beginning to harden, and people of mixed ancestry began to find themselves marginalized. Women were at the centre of these changes. White wives became more desirable than Métis wives, and the newly arrived women brought with them attitudes toward race and class that made it increasingly difficult for Native and Métis women to play a continuing role as social leaders. For specific examples see the *DCB* entries 'Nancy McKenzie' and 'Sarah McLeod (Ballenden),' vol. 8; and 'Sally Ross,' vol. 11. There is extensive discussion of these changing attitudes in S. Van Kirk, *'Many Tender Ties.'*

Aspects of Métis cultural history are explored in J.S.H. Brown, *Strangers in Blood*, and S. Van Kirk, *'Many Tender Ties.'* More detailed studies of specific topics in Métis cultural history may be found in the essays in J. Peterson and J.S.H. Brown, eds., *The New Peoples*. Among them, Ted J. Brasser suggests that a distinctive Métis artistic tradition may have developed, and John C. Crawford argues that the language spoken by many western Métis constitutes a distinct language known as Michif. S. Van Kirk explores Métis identity in '"What If Mama Is an Indian?" The Cultural Ambivalence of the Alexander Ross Family.' The papers in this volume were presented at a conference held to honour the grandfather of Métis cultural studies, Marcel Girard, an anthropologist whose two-volume study *Le métis canadien: son rôle dans l'histoire des provinces de l'Ouest* (P: Institut d'ethnologie 1945) is now available in English translation as *The Metis in the Canadian West* (E: UAP 1986), with an introduction by George Woodcock. Another collection of essays that covers the Métis cultural and economic life was put together by Antoine S. Lussier and D. Bruce Sealey, *The Other Natives: The/ les Métis*, vol. 1, *1700–1885* (W: Manitoba Métis Federation Press/Editions Bois-Brûlés 1978).

There have been a number of studies published that are interesting not so much as historical analysis but as a source of encouragement of Métis pride and even nationalism. The first of this genre was Auguste-Henri de Trémaudan, *Histoire de la nation métisse dans l'Ouest canadien* (1936; repr. St Boniface, Man.: Editions des Plaines 1979), reprinted in English as *Hold*

High Your Heads: History of the Metis Nation in Western Canada (W: Pemmican 1982). More recently A.S. Lussier and D.B. Sealey collaborated on *The
Métis: Canada's Forgotten People* (W: Manitoba Métis Federation Press 1975)
with a similar goal in mind. Another booster of Métis national pride is Don
McLean, *Home from the Hill: A History of the Metis in Western Canada* (2nd
ed., R: Gabriel Dumont Institute 1987).

RED RIVER SETTLEMENT

Not entirely a product of the fur trade and yet an integral part of it, the settlement that developed at the forks of the Red and Assiniboine rivers has
been the focus of much historical controversy over the years. That debate
begins with questions surrounding the founding of the settlement. There
has never been a fully satisfactory biography of Thomas Douglas, 5th Earl
of Selkirk, who sponsored and organized the original immigration project.
The entry in volume 5 of the *DCB* provides an introduction, and the most
commonly used full-length biography is John Morgan Gray, *Lord Selkirk of
Red River* (T: MAC 1963). More often, Selkirk appears as a character in
other histories. J.M.Bumsted has discussed the different images of Selkirk
that have been developed by several generations of historians in 'Lord Selkirk and Manitoba Historians: A New View,' *Manitoba History* 2 (1981): 2–
7. These interpretations range from the conclusion that Selkirk was an
enemy of fur trade interests to the conclusion that he was a visionary leader
who founded a new and unique society.

The Scottish families who participated in Selkirk's experiments have
often been portrayed as the victims of the Highland Clearances in Scotland:
poor crofters driven from their lands to a life of hardship and suffering in
remote parts of North America. J.M. Bumsted objected to that interpretation in his study of the broader context of Scottish resettlement, *The People's
Clearance: Highland Emigration to British North America, 1770–1815* (Edin-
burgh/W: Edinburgh University Press/UMP 1982). Bumsted argues that
this older interpretation can be challenged on two points. First, he suggests
that the Highlanders were not victims pushed off their lands, but ambitious
people who chose to leave in anticipation of finding better lives for themselves in North America. Second, he suggests that Selkirk was no modern
visionary, but an inherently conservative man who hoped that his settlements would become places for the preservation of Highland culture,
which, Selkirk believed, was succumbing to the onslaught of modernization
in Scotland.

For readers who would like to consult the kinds of material that Bumsted is reacting against, there are a number of possibilities. In 1856 Red River resident Alexander Ross put together one of the earliest histories of the community, *The Red River Settlement: Its Rise, Progress, and Present State* (1856; repr. E: Hurtig 1972). W.L. Morton improved considerably upon Ross with a general overview of the settlement in his provincial history, *Manitoba*. Others, like Alexander Begg's *History of the North-West*, 3 vols. (T: Hunter Rose 1894–5), depicted the settlement as a harmonious community floating in a sort of northwest golden age. F. Pannekoek challenged that perspective and argued that the settlement seethed with religious conflict, which led eventually to the uprising of 1869–70. He explores this thesis in a number of essays, including 'The Anglican Church and the Disintegration of Red River Society, 1818–1870,' in C. Berger and R. Cook, eds., *The West and the Nation*, reprinted in R.D. Francis and H. Palmer, eds., *The Prairie West*. Recently he has written a more detailed study on the subject, *A Snug Little Flock: The Social Origins of the Riel Resistance of 1869–70* (W: Watson and Dwyer 1991).

While Selkirk intended his settlement at Red River to be a haven for the preservation of Scottish Highland culture, it quickly became a very cosmopolitan community, attracting retired fur traders and their families, French Canadians, Americans, Native peoples, and others. A quick perusal of the *DCB* provides an excellent sense of the variety of people and their experiences that might be found at Red River before Confederation. Roman Catholic clergy included Bishop Joseph-Norbert Provencher (vol. 8) and missionaries George-Antoine Bellecourt (vol. 10) and Sévère Dumoulin (vol. 8). Marie-Louise Valade (vol. 9) established the presence of the Grey Nuns at the settlement, with their crucial education and health care work. Anglican clergy included Bishop David Anderson (vol. 11) and missionaries David Thomas Jones (vol. 7) and William Cockran (vol. 9). The first Presbyterian minister to the settlement was John Black (vol. 11). Men of business and commerce included Robert Logan (vol. 9) and Andrew Graham Ballenden Bannatyne (vol. 11). Retired fur traders like Alexander Ross (vol. 8) and Joseph James Hargrave (vol. 12) took an active part in the social and political life of the community. Adam Thom (vol. 11) was the controversial first lawyer. Military man Andrew H. Bulger (vol. 8) served as one of the colony's governors. Louis Riel (vol. 9), father of the more famous Riel, was a Métis leader in his own right. The emphasis on Scottish settlement often obscures the fact that Selkirk was not the first to bring white women to the West. Marie-Anne Gaboury (vol. 10) arrived at an earlier date as part of the fur trade connection with Quebec.

As for Native peoples at Red River, one can turn to the entry on the prominent Saulteaux chief Peguis in *DCB*, vol. 9. Another fascinating glimpse into the lives of Native people at Red River can be obtained through the work of John Tanner, the subject of an entry in *DCB*, vol. 7. Tanner was an American captured by the Shawnee and eventually brought to Red River as the adopted son of a Saulteaux. He recorded his experiences in *A Narrative of the Captivity and Adventures of John Tanner (U.S. Interpreter at Saut de Ste Marie) during Thirty Years Residence among the Indians in the Interior of North America*, ed. Edwin James (1830; repr. Minneapolis, MN: Ross and Haines 1956). This memoir includes much valuable information about the life of the Saulteaux people, a branch of the Ojibwa who had established themselves on the edges of the plains.

Other aspects of Red River history are discussed in a number of specialized studies. Alvin C. Gluek, Jr, explored the relations between Red River and St Paul, Minnesota, from 1821 to 1870 in *Minnesota and the Manifest Destiny of the Canadian Northwest* (T: UTP 1965). W.L. Morton's lengthy introduction to *London Correspondence Inward from Eden Colvile, 1849 to 1852*, ed. E.E. Rich (L: HBRS 1956), provides an excellent perspective on the society that had developed at Red River by the mid-nineteenth century. G.F.G. Stanley, *Toil & Trouble: Military Expeditions to Red River* (T: Dundurn 1989), includes three chapters on the period before the Red River Uprising. An often-read source is W.J. Healy, *Women of Red River* (W: Russell, Lang 1923). It is a light and breezy collection of impressions compiled from women's recollections of life in the region to the 1870s, and although it does not include any real historical analysis, it does provide the reader with a vivid sense of how some women perceived their lives and their place in Red River society.

CONCLUSION

While the writing of the history of the Northwest has emphasized European exploration and aspects of the fur trade, there is a rich and growing body of literature dealing with many other topics. Among these are interaction between Natives and missionaries, the role of churches in the formation of western society, the impact of the environment on human history, and the role of cultural expectations in dealing with the experiences of settlement in a new land.

In many ways historical examination of the fur trade and the Prairie West has followed the trends observable in other fields of history. There is an interest in social history and the patterns of everyday life instead of the older concern with imperial politics and international events. There is also much more interest in the history of groups once ignored by historians, particularly women and First Nations. Unfortunately, northern history is only beginning to develop in the same direction and much work remains to be done. As well, local and regional studies have become a vital part of the post-Confederation history of the West but have not yet really influenced the writing of pre-Confederation history. Perhaps some of the insights of that work will someday be applied to the earlier history of the Northwest.

One of the most interesting new directions in northwestern history has been the development of an awareness of Native history. For too long, Canadian historians assumed that 'real' history began only with the arrival of Europeans and that only the actions of European traders and settlers mattered. But in the last decade or so, innovative methods in reconstructing histories that many thought were lost have brought a new sensitivity to historical writing. Sources and methods adapted from archaeology, linguistics, anthropology, ethnology, and ethnohistory have broadened not only our understanding of the events of history, but also have given us new tools for approaching more traditional historical topics. Some of the work on the fur trade and Native peoples described in this chapter has been in the forefront of this movement.

TINA LOO

The Pacific Coast

'The History of British Columbia is brief,' observed British traveller and author William Adolph Baillie-Grohmann at the turn of the century. 'Gold made it and gold unmade it.'[1] Despite the fact he overlooked the millennia-old presence of Native peoples, this visitor's pithy comment does capture two fundamental realities of life in the area that became British Columbia. The first is the centrality of primary resource extraction in shaping the region's economy, society, and politics. Whether we consider the Native peoples of the Northwest Coast, whose complex cultures were built on the twin staples of cedar and salmon, or the European fur traders and gold-seekers who came for adventure and profit, British Columbia's history is inextricably intertwined with the exploitation of resources. Their location determined settlement patterns and social relations, juxtaposing alien cultures in equally alien environments, while the vagaries and vicissitudes of the marketplace influenced the region's economic fortunes and political organization.

British Columbia's dependence on staples like gold also accentuated the dual character of colonial existence in North America and accounts for the second reality of life for both Natives and non-Natives: the fact that it was lived on two scales, the international and the local. Though sheer distance from the imperial centre and a rugged geography made colonial life in both Vancouver Island and British Columbia (the two were separate colonies until 1866) intensely local, neither colony was immune from external influ-

I would like to thank Robert L. Fraser of the *Dictionary of Canadian Biography* for his help in compiling the British Columbia entries, and Jean Barman for her advice.

1 W.A. Baillie-Grohmann, *Fifteen Years' Sport and Life in the Hunting Grounds of Western America and British Columbia* (L: Horace Cox 1900) 316.

ences. Developments in the international economy or the world market for furs, gold, and lumber, changes in British Colonial Office policy or the geopolitics of Anglo-American, Russian, or Spanish relations, all sent reverberations through the North American colonial world which helped 'make' and 'unmake' the communities that comprised the distant 'imperial stump field' of British Columbia. In short, though this bibliographic essay is arranged thematically and chronologically, both the importance of economic activity and the duality of colonial life should be seen as continuities in British Columbia's history to Confederation.

GENERAL WORKS

British Columbia's history is reasonably well represented in a number of general texts, the most recent of which are Jean Barman, *The West beyond the West: A History of British Columbia* (T: UTP 1991), and George Woodcock, *British Columbia: A History of the Province* (V: Douglas & McIntyre 1990). Though both are good starting-points, neither is particularly strong on the region's political and economic past, opting instead for a more social history perspective. Margaret A. Ormsby, *British Columbia: A History* (T: MAC 1958), complements Barman and Woodcock and will go some distance in providing a political history perspective; however, this work tends to be somewhat discursive and less analytical than the other two. Those wishing to learn more about the region's economy and politics would do better to supplement their reading of these texts with the more narrowly focused articles listed in the following thematic sections. Those wishing to learn more about earlier societal formation would do well to consult geographers R. Cole Harris and John Warkentin's overview in chapter 7 of their *Canada before Confederation: A Study in Historical Geography* (T: OUP 1974).

Students interested in the region prior to 1846, when the international boundary was set at the forty-ninth parallel, should not overlook histories of Oregon and Washington. The early chapters of Carlos A. Schwantes, *The Pacific Northwest: An Interpretive History* (Lincoln, NE: University of Nebraska Press 1989), which discuss the European exploration of the area, the maritime and land-based fur trades, Native and non-Native relationships, and American immigration into the region via the Oregon trail, are of interest to historians of British Columbia. Though Schwantes's treatment is the most recent, the text by Dorothy O. Johansen and Charles M. Gates, *Empire of the Columbia: A History of the Pacific Northwest* (NY: Harper and Brothers 1957), is still very helpful and widely used.

Also useful as a starting-place are a number of anthologies, including

Jean Friesen and H. Keith Ralston, eds., *Historical Essays on British Columbia* (T: M&S 1976); W. Peter Ward and Robert A.J. McDonald, eds., *British Columbia: Historical Readings* (V: Douglas & McIntyre 1981); Patricia E. Roy, ed., *A History of British Columbia: Selected Readings* (T: CCP 1989); Thomas Thorner, ed., *Sa ts'e: Historical Perspectives on Northern British Columbia* (Prince George, BC: College of New Caledonia Press 1989); and J. Barman and R.A.J. McDonald, eds., *Readings in the History of British Columbia* (Richmond, BC: Open Learning Agency 1990).

BIBLIOGRAPHIES AND REFERENCE WORKS

Two bibliographies deal specifically with the period prior to Confederation: Gloria M. Strathern, *Navigations, Traffiques and Discoveries, 1774–1848: A Guide to Publications Relating to the Area Now British Columbia* (VI: Social Sciences Research Centre, University of Victoria 1970), and its companion, Barbara J. Lowther, *A Bibliography of British Columbia: Laying the Foundations, 1849–1889* (VI: Social Sciences Research Centre, University of Victoria 1968). More specialized are James Bowman, *Big Country: A Bibliography of the History of Kamloops Region and Southern Cariboo* (Burnaby, BC: Department of Sociology and Anthropology, Simon Fraser University 1977); Linda Hale, *Vancouver Centennial Bibliography: A Project of the Vancouver Historical Society*, 4 vols. (V: Vancouver Historical Society 1986); Anne McIntyre Knowlan, *The Fraser Valley: A Bibliography* (Abbotsford, BC: Fraser Valley College 1988); and Hale and J. Barman, eds., *British Columbia Local Histories: A Bibliography* (VI: Heritage Trust 1991).

An excellent but often overlooked general index and collection of material relating to Canada (including much on British Columbia) published before 1900 is provided by the Canadian Institute for Historical Microreproductions, which has both indexed its material by author, title, and subject and reproduced it on microfiche. *America: History and Life* is the most comprehensive index to journal articles, book reviews, and theses in both American and Canadian history. It is indexed by author and subject annually. As well, there are five-year cumulative indices.

Two good sources for the political history of British Columbia are worth noting. The first is James E. Hendrickson, ed., *Journals of the Colonial Legislatures of Vancouver Island and British Columbia, 1851–1871*, 5 vols. (VI: Provincial Archives of British Columbia 1980), which has a useful introductory essay in volume 1. The second is the Irish University Press Series of British Parliamentary Papers. There are one thousand volumes of extracts from British parliamentary papers, thirty-three of which relate to Canada and cover the period 1801–1900. Each volume has a table of contents, but it is more helpful to use the general index entitled *Checklist of British Parliamentary Papers in the Irish University Press 1000 Volume Series, 1801–1899* (Dublin, Eire: The Press 1977). The volumes relating to British Columbia and Vancouver Island contain many of the more important dispatches between the colonial governor and the Colonial Office relating to a wide variety of matters, including the fur trade, land settlement, and the gold rush.

The enormous literature on Native peoples is dealt with throughout most of this volume, but the following bibliographies are good places to begin: Wilson Duff and Michael Kew, *A Selected Bibliography of Anthropology of British Columbia* (V: University of British Columbia Library 1973); Robert Steven Grumet, *Native Americans of the Northwest Coast: A Critical Bibliography* (Bloomington, IN: Indiana University Press for the Newberry Library 1979); and Alan L. Hoover, *A Selection of Publications on the Indians of British Columbia* (VI: British Columbia Provincial Museum 1982).

Biographical information on many fur trade and colonial figures is contained in J.B. Kerr, *Biographical Dictionary of Well-Known British Columbians* (V: Kerr and Begg 1890); *British Columbia: Pictorial and Biographical* (W: S.J. Clarke 1914); and Jean Gould, *Women of British Columbia* (Saanichton, BC: Hancock House 1975). The first two works reflect the social attitudes of the time, but are nevertheless useful as a supplement to the multivolume *Dictionary of Canadian Biography* (T: UTP 1966–). The *DCB* is an ongoing project of the University of Toronto Press which is aimed at compiling biographies of eminent and representative Canadians. Currently there are twelve volumes, each covering a particular time period. Inclusion is by the subject's date of death. Gould's book provides a much-needed look at the social and domestic world of British Columbia, something that remains largely invisible given the heroic and masculine focus of much of its history.

These biographies of British Columbia's inhabitants are complemented by two biographies of the region itself. G.P.V. Akrigg and Helen B. Akrigg, in *British Columbia Place Names* (VI: Sono Nis Press 1986), examine the province's place-names, many of which have their origins in the pre-Confederation period. Less comprehensive in scope but more informative and pleasantly quirky, however, is Captain John T. Walbran, *British Columbia Coast Names* (1909; repr. V: Library's Press 1971). Innocuous though its title appears, Walbran's book takes the reader through much of the history of the Spanish, Russian, American, and British presence on the coast, the maritime fur trade, Native and non-Native relations, and colonial politics, all under the pretence of describing the origins of coastal place-names. Also regional in its focus and useful to historians of colonial British Columbia is the *Historical Atlas of Canada*, vol. 1, *From the Beginning to 1800*, ed. R.C. Harris (T: UTP [1987]). The *HAC* explicates the social, political, and economic aspects of Canada's past in a series of detailed maps.

PERIODICALS

British Columbia's history is presented in *BC Studies* (1968–), an interdisciplinary journal published by the University of British Columbia. The *British Columbia Historical Quarterly*, published between 1937 and 1958, and now outdated and antiquarian in its approach, contains many useful articles. As well, both *BCS* and the *Canadian Historical Review* (1920–) list recent publications relating to British Columbia at the end of each issue. *The Beaver*, published since 1920 by the Hudson's Bay Company, regularly contains pieces on the fur trade and other aspects of British Columbia history. Though aimed at a more popular audience, many of *The Beaver*'s articles are written by professional historians.

Equally useful, particularly for those interested in the period prior to 1846 and the establishment of the international boundary at the forty-ninth parallel, are a number of American journals. These include the *Oregon Historical Quarterly* (1900–) and the *Pacific Historical Quarterly* (1936– ; formerly the *Washington Historical Quarterly*, 1906–36), both of which contain articles relating to the period when the territory was jointly occupied by the British Hudson's Bay Company and America fur traders and settlers.

HISTORIOGRAPHY

Two good places to start an examination of British Columbia historiography are Allan Smith, 'The Writing of British Columbia History,' *BCS* 45 (Spring 1980): 73–102, reprinted in W.P. Ward and R.A.J. McDonald, eds., *British Columbia: Historical Readings*; and H.K. Ralston, 'Time and Pattern in British Columbia,' in Dickson M. Falconer, ed., *British Columbia: Patterns in Economic, Political and Cultural Development – Selected Readings* (VI: Camosun College 1982). Smith and Ralston both point out that though British Columbia's historians have situated the colony in the larger frameworks of nation, continent, and empire, the region is generally overlooked in national histories. The gold rushes are, however, an exception to the general pattern of oversight because they have provided scholars with an opportunity to test the applicability of Frederick Jackson Turner's frontier thesis in the Canadian context, and thus link British Columbia to developments in other regions. Though S.D. Clark, 'Mining Society in British

Columbia and the Yukon,' first published in 1942 and now reprinted in Ward and McDonald, eds., *British Columbia: Historical Readings*, argues that British Columbia does fit the Turnerian model, other historians disagree, contending that the colony is more accurately described as an extension of British imperial authority. On this question see Barry M. Gough, 'The Character of the British Columbia Frontier,' *BCS* 32 (Winter 1976–7): 28–40, also reprinted in the Ward and McDonald collection.

The absence of British Columbia is not simply due to the centralist bias of the country's historians, however. In many ways British Columbia defies integration into existing frameworks for understanding Canada's colonial past. Though the area that became British Columbia was the site of North West Company activity, the pedlars' presence there was so transient and fleeting that the region never became wholly integrated into the commercial realm of the Montreal merchants, and hence does not fit into Donald Grant Creighton's Laurentian thesis – for a description of which see Carl Berger, *The Writing of Canadian History: Aspects of English-Canadian Historical Writing since 1900* (1976; 2nd ed., T: UTP 1986). Nor does British Columbia's colonial past share many similarities with that of the other western provinces. Though Prairie history has an integrity of its own, that region's settlement was more closely tied to developments in central Canada, and hence it is more easily integrated into national histories. British Columbia entered the ambit of the European world relatively late, for unlike the other British North American colonies, it was not 'discovered' by Europeans until the late eighteenth century, and significant non-Native settlement did not begin until the mid-nineteenth century. Even with European settlement, the colony's geography created obstacles to its integration with the region beyond the mountains. As H.K. Ralston notes in 'Patterns of Trade and Investment on the Pacific Coast, 1867–1892: The Case of the British Columbia Salmon Canning Industry,' *BCS* 1 (Winter 1968–9): 37–45, and J.M.S. Careless argues in 'The Lowe Brothers, 1852–70: A Study in Business Relations on the North Pacific Coast,' *BCS* 2 (Summer 1969): 1–18 (both reprinted in W.P. Ward and R.A.J. McDonald, eds., *British Columbia: Historical Readings*), British Columbia's economic linkages, as well as its social and political ones, were forged with the Pacific rim and along north-south lines or with London directly. Ties with central and eastern Canada were neither missed nor sought. Thus, as the title of J. Barman's text indicates, the Pacific Coast was truly 'the west beyond the west.'

Despite British Columbia's exceptionalism, the colony does share some similarities with the rest of Canada. Like other British North American colonies, British Columbia's European origins can be explained by Harold

Adams Innis's staples theory. In *The Fur Trade in Canada: An Introduction to Canadian Economic History* (1930; rev. ed., T: UTP 1970), Innis argued that Canada's history and development is really the history of the serial exploitation of primary resources: beginning in the sixteenth century with cod, and the seventeenth century with furs, followed by timber, wheat, and minerals. European interest in these staples initiated Canada's settlement and guided its social and political development. British Columbia was no exception to this pattern, for, as we will see, resource exploitation was the *raison d'être* of the non-Native presence on the Pacific Coast.

There are also two other commonalities in the histories of British Columbia and the rest of Canada. The first is that provided by the imperial tie. Though by the time British Columbia entered the colonial world Britain was losing interest in its possessions, these colonists, like their British North American counterparts, and particularly the administrative elite, still looked to London for guidance in matters political and social. Colonial political culture was characterized, as will be discussed, by a desire for centralized authority and a fear of strong local governments, and the tone and texture of social life and institutions was coloured by British notions of class and respectability. The second similarity stems from the first: though British Columbians' affinity for things English was not diminished by their geographic distance from the imperial centre, they also defined themselves against the more palpable and immediate American presence. A distaste for and, indeed, a very real fear of the Americans animated colonial politics in British Columbia as it did in other parts of British North America.

NATIVE PEOPLES PRECONTACT

British Columbia's economic potential may have attracted many immigrants during the late eighteenth and nineteenth centuries, but the region did not have to wait until they arrived for this potential to be realized. The material abundance of the Northwest Coast gave rise to one of the richest Native cultures in North America – the richest, in fact, north of the incredible aboriginal civilizations of Central and South America. Though gauging the precontact Native population and its distribution is problematic, it is estimated that almost half of Canada's aboriginal peoples lived in the area that became British Columbia. Two-thirds of them lived along the coast, harvesting salmon and cedar, the twin staples of both precontact and postcontact cultures, as well as other kinds of food. Cultural diversity characterized the Natives of British Columbia. Thirty-four distinct languages were spoken by peoples who possessed a variety of forms of social and political organization, ranging from the highly structured and hierarchical coastal Kwakiutl and Haida to the more egalitarian tribal groups of the region's interior. Whatever their social and political organization, the tribal groups that called British Columbia home did not exist in isolation, nor did they all lead lives of economic subsistence. It has been estimated that fifty different kinds of trade goods, including sea-lion teeth, cedar canoes, jade adze blades, mountain-goat skins, dried salmon, and dried seaweed were exchanged along well-established trade routes well before the arrival of the first Europeans. Thus the encounter between British Columbia's aboriginal peoples and the Spanish, the Russians, the 'Boston men' (the Americans), and the British 'King George men' in the late eighteenth century was not the meeting of new and old worlds, but of two equally old and rich ones.

As noted, Native peoples are dealt with throughout most of this volume, but the following are good introductions to an enormous and well-developed literature. General overviews, which deal with the precontact population and its distribution as well as untangling the cultural characteristics of the diverse number of tribal groups in the region, are found in W. Duff, *The Indian History of British Columbia*, vol. 1, *The Impact of the White Man* (VI: Provincial Museum 1965), and Knut R. Fladmark, *British Columbia Prehistory* (O: National Museums of Canada 1986). Particularly useful introductions to the tribal groups of the Northwest Coast and the northern interior, as well as to the more specialized ethnographic literature that is not listed here, is the multivolume *Handbook of North American Indians*, gen. ed. William C. Sturtevant (Washington, DC: Smithsonian Institution 1978–). Volume 6, *Subarctic*, ed. June Helm (1981), and volume 7, *Northwest Coast*, ed. Wayne Suttles (1990), cover the area that is now British Columbia. Students will find the essay by Douglas Cole and David Darling, 'History of the Early Period,' in the latter volume especially helpful. Hilary Stewart's books, though aimed at a more popular audience, are excellent introductions to the coastal Native material culture and economy: *Indian Fishing: Early Methods on the Northwest Coast* (V: J.J. Douglas 1977), *Artifacts of the Northwest Coast Indians* (rev. ed., North Vancouver, BC: Hancock House 1981), and *Cedar: Tree of Life to the Northwest Coast Indians* (V: Douglas & McIntyre 1988).

Unfortunately the volume of the *Handbook of North American Indians* dealing with the tribal groups of the central and southern interior of British Columbia has not yet been published. Students wishing information on the Natives of these regions should consult the specialized treatments available in the Anthropology in British Columbia Memoir series published by the British Columbia Provincial Museum at Victoria; see W. Duff, *The Upper*

Stalo Indians of the Fraser Valley, British Columbia, Memoir 1 (1952); Diamond Jenness, *The Faith of a Coast Salish Indian,* Memoir 3 (1955); W. Suttles, *Katzie Ethnographic Notes,* Memoir 3 (1955); and Duff, *Histories, Territories and Laws of the Kitwancool,* Memoir 4 (1959; repr. 1989). In a similar series of memoirs published by the American Museum of Natural History at New York, Franz Boas edited several relevant works by James Teit: *The Thompson Indians of British Columbia* (1900); *The Lilooet Indians* (1906); and *The Shuswap* (1909). Other works worth consulting are J. Teit, *Traditions of the Thompson River Indians of British Columbia* (1898; repr. NY: Kraus 1969); Ralph Maud, ed., *The Salish People: The Local Contributions of Charles Hill-Tout,* 4 vols. (V: Talonbooks 1978); and W. Suttles, *Coast Salish Essays,* ed. R. Maud (V: Talonbooks 1987).

On precontact trade see *HAC,* vol. 1, plates 13, 'The Coast Tsimshian'; and 14, 'Prehistoric Trade.'

EUROPEAN EXPLORATION AND THE MARITIME FUR TRADE

The diverse Native nations of British Columbia were joined by a diverse number of European nations in the late eighteenth century. European interest in the Northwest Coast was fuelled by economic considerations as well as those of empire and expressed in the mercantilist policies of Spain, Britain, and Russia. For a general introduction to European exploration see Glyndwr Williams, *The Expansion of Europe in the Eighteenth Century: Overseas Rivalry, Discovery and Exploration* (NY: Walker 1966), Derek Pethick, *First Approaches to the Northwest Coast* (V: J.J. Douglas 1976), and Arthur J. Lower, *Ocean of Destiny: A Concise History of the North Pacific, 1500–1978* (V: UBCP 1978). Erna Gunther, *Indian Life on the Northwest Coast of North American As Seen by the Early Explorers and Traders during the Last Decades of the Eighteenth Century* (Chicago, IL: University of Chicago Press 1972), and John Frazier Henry, *Early Maritime Artists of the Pacific Northwest Coast, 1741–1841* (Seattle, WA: University of Washington Press 1984), provide overviews of how these European visitors perceived the landscape.

Though the Spanish had explored the west coast of North America as far north as San Francisco in the late sixteenth century and the British had begun their reconnaissance of the area around Hudson Bay a century later, in 1670, the first Europeans to set eyes on what was to become British Columbia were likely the Russians. Under the command of Vitus Bering, two expeditions were launched in 1728 and 1740 from the Russian Pacific port of Okhotsk. In addition to discovering much about the geography of coastal America, Bering discovered the sea otter, whose pelt was highly valued in China. A number of Russian merchants began trading with Aleut hunters, and a lucrative and highly secretive exchange was initiated. Students can best approach the Russian fur trade through Raisa V. Makarova, *Russians on the Pacific, 1743–1799* (K: Limestone Press 1975), and P.A. Tikhmenev, *A History of the Russian-American Company* (Seattle, WA: University of Washington Press 1978), both translated and edited by Richard A. Pierce and Alton S. Donnelly, as well as James R. Gibson's two monographs, *Feeding the Russian Fur Trade: Provisionment of the Okhotsk Seaboard and the Kamchatka Peninsula, 1639–1856* (Madison, WI: University of Wisconsin Press 1969) and *Imperial Russia in Frontier America: The Changing Geography of Supply of Russian America* (NY: OUP 1976). While more narrowly focused, Raymond H. Fisher's *Bering's Voyages: Wither and Why* (Seattle, WA: University of Washington Press 1977) and Glynn Barratt's *Russia in Pacific Waters, 1715–1825: A Survey of the Origins of Russia's Naval Presence in the North and South Pacific* (V: UBCP 1981) are worth consulting. Dated but useful are Clarence L. Andrews, 'Russian Plans for American Domination,' *Washington Historical Quarterly* 18 (Apr. 1927): 83–92; S.R. Tompkins and M.L. Moorhead, 'Russia's Approach to America. Part I: From Russian Sources, 1741–1761,' *BCHQ* 8 (Apr. 1949): 55–66; and 'Russia's Approach to America. Part II: From Spanish Sources, 1761–1775,' *BCHQ* 18 (July–Oct. 1949): 231–55. A similarly helpful collection of articles is S. Frederick Starr, ed., *Russia's American Colony* (Durham, NC: Duke University Press 1987).

The Spanish soon joined the Russians in the Northwest. Following the ascension of Carlos III in 1759, Spain launched a series of expeditions from San Blas on Mexico's west coast. In 1774 the Spanish dropped anchor at the Queen Charlotte Islands and Nootka Sound. At both places they exchanged goods with the Haida and the Nootka peoples, but did little else. In two subsequent voyages, launched in 1775 and 1779, the Spanish explored parts of the Alaska panhandle and claimed them for Carlos. They were not, like the Russians, impressed by the region's economic potential. Warren L. Cook, *Flood Tide of Empire: Spain and the Pacific Northwest, 1543–1819* (New Haven, CT: Yale University Press 1973), is the best introduction to the Spanish presence in the Northwest. However, readers might also wish to consult John Kendrick, *Men with Wooden Feet: The Spanish Exploration of the Pacific Northwest* (T: NC Press 1985), and Christon I. Archer's two articles, 'The Transient Presence: A Re-Appraisal of Spanish Attitudes toward the Northwest Coast in the Eighteenth Century,' *BCS* 18 (Summer 1973): 3–32, reprinted in W.P. Ward and R.A.J. McDonald, eds., *British Columbia: Historical Readings*, and 'Spain and the Defence of the Pacific Ocean

Empire, 1750–1810,' *Canadian Journal of Latin American and Caribbean Studies* 11/2 (1986): 15–41. Somewhat more specialized is Iris Higbie Wilson Engstrand, *Spanish Scientists in the New World: The Eighteenth Century Expeditions* (Seattle, WA: University of Washington Press 1981). Many of the Spanish explorers have entries in the *DCB*, including 'Juan Francisco de la Bodega y Quadra,' 'Esteban José Martínez Fernández y Martínez de la Sierra,' and 'Juan Josef Pérez Hernández,' vol. 4 (1979).

Like the Russian and the Spanish, British interest in the Northwest Coast was driven by a combination of imperialism and materialism. Through the Hudson's Bay Company's land-based fur trade, the British had made inroads into the western interior of North America, but they were still preoccupied with the search for the mythical northwest passage, a sea that was thought to connect Hudson Bay with the riches of the Orient. They hoped that Captain James Cook, fresh from his voyages to New Zealand, Australia, and the Sandwich Islands, would succeed where others had not. In 1776, the *Resolution* and *Discovery* set out under Cook's command once again. Though northwest passage eluded them, Cook's party learned of the earlier Spanish arrival at Nootka and, by this time, the well-established Russian fur trade. Much to the surprise of Cook's men, the sea otter pelts they acquired for a few pieces of pewter or some green beads sold for $120 in Macao, a port of call on their return journey. The best overview of these British efforts is B.M. Gough, *Distant Dominion: Britain and the Northwest Coast of North America, 1579–1809* (V: UBCP 1980). Robin Fisher and Hugh J.M. Johnston's anthology, *Captain James Cook and His Times* (Seattle, WA: University of Washington Press 1979), is a good place to begin for those interested in Cook's exploration. In particular see David McKay's essay 'A Presiding Genius of Exploration: Banks, Cook and Empire, 1767–1805,' which places Northwest Coast exploration in its intellectual context. Also consult G. Williams, *The British Search for the Northwest Passage in the Eighteenth Century* (L: Longmans 1962); John Norris, 'The Strait of Anian and British North West America: Cook's Third Voyage in Perspective,' *BCS* 36 (Winter 1977–8): 3–22; and Lynne Withey, *Voyages of Discovery: Captain Cook and the Exploration of the Pacific* (NY: William Morrow 1987). J.C. Beaglehole edited *The Journals of Captain James Cook on His Voyages of Discovery: The Voyage of the 'Resolution' and 'Discovery,' 1776–1780*, parts 1 and 2 (L: Hakluyt 1967), which themselves provide a useful source, revealing attitudes toward the Native peoples and the alien landscape. Beaglehole is also the author of the biography *The Life of Captain James Cook* (Stanford, CA: Stanford University Press 1974). Finally, the *DCB* once again should be consulted for the background of many individuals who participated in Cook's third voyage, including, in addition to James Cook himself, 'Charles Clerke,' 'George Dixon,' 'Charles Duncan,' and 'James King,' vol. 4.

Cook's discovery of the trade in sea otter pelts marked the end of the Russian monopoly and sparked a rush for furs. The British and Russians were joined in quick succession by the French (though only half-heartedly) and the Americans. For forty years between 1785 and 1825 the maritime fur trade boomed, nearly wiping out the sea otter population. The most recent and comprehensive treatment of the maritime fur trade is J.R. Gibson, *Otter Skins, Boston Ships and China Goods: The Maritime Fur Trade on the Northwest Coast, 1785–1841* (K&M: MQUP 1992). Students may also wish to consult the article on which Gibson based his monograph: 'The Maritime Trade of the North Pacific Coast,' in *Handbook of North American Indians*, vol. 4, *History of Indian-White Relations*, ed. Wilcomb E. Washburn (1988). The first volume of the *HAC*, plate 66, 'New Caledonia and Columbia,' illustrates this maritime fur trade, but one should not overlook two articles by Frederic William Howay, which, while old, are still very good places to start: 'Early Days of the Maritime Fur-Trade on the Northwest Coast,' *CHR* 4/1 (Mar. 1923): 26–44, and 'An Outline Sketch of the Maritime Fur Trade,' CHA *AR* (1932): 5–14. J.R. Gibson discusses the Russian and American presence on the Northwest Coast in his 1975 article 'Bostonians and Muscovites on the Northwest Coast, 1788–1841,' reprinted in W.P. Ward and R.A.J. McDonald, eds., *British Columbia: Historical Readings*, and in 'The Russian Fur Trade,' in Carol M. Judd and Arthur J. Ray, eds., *Old Trails and New Directions: Papers of the Third North American Fur Trade Conference* (T: UTP 1980). Finally, French efforts are outlined in G.V. Blue, 'French Interest in Pacific America in the Eighteenth Century,' *Pacific Historical Review* 4/3 (1935): 246–66.

Many of those who travelled the waters of the Pacific Northwest Coast left journals of their voyages. Some of these accounts have been published and constitute one of the best sources for understanding the maritime fur trade on a human, rather than an economic or geopolitical, scale. One notable British visitor to the Northwest Coast was seventeen-year-old Frances H. Barkley, who accompanied her husband, Charles, to Nootka Sound in 1787. Her story can be found in F.H. Barkley, 'Extracts from the Diaries of Frances Hornby Barkley,' *BCHQ* 6 (Jan. 1942): 49–59, and Beth Hill, *The Remarkable World of Frances Barkley, 1769–1845* (Sidney, BC: Gray's 1978). William Sturgis, a successful British trader renowned for allegedly collecting six thousand pelts in one voyage, has his story told in F.W. Howay, 'William Sturgis: The Northwest Fur Trade,' *BCHQ* 8 (Jan. 1944): 11–45.

Other travel accounts worth consulting are W. Kaye Lamb and Tomas Bartoli, 'John Hanna and John Henry Cox: The First Maritime Fur Trader and His Sponsor,' *BCS* 84 (Winter 1989–90): 3–36; John Meares, *Voyages Made in the Years 1788 and 1789, from China to the North West Coast of North America* [comp. William Combe] (1790; repr. Amsterdam/NY: Johnson Reprint 1967); Nathaniel Portlock, *A Voyage round the World, but More Particularly to the North-West Coast of America: Performed in 1785, 1786, 1787, and 1788* (1789; repr. Amsterdam/NY: Johnson Reprint 1968); James Strange, *James Strange's Journal and Narrative of the Commercial Expedition from Bombay to the North-West Coast of America, Together with a Chart Showing the Tract of the Expedition*, intro. A.V. Venkatarama Ayyar (1928; repr. Fairfield, WA: Ye Galleon Press 1982); and Alexander Walker, *An Account of a Voyage to the North West Coast of America in 1785 & 1786*, ed. R. Fisher and J.M. Bumsted (V: Douglas & McIntyre [1982]). The 'Boston men' were particularly notable for their aggressive trading and adventurousness, as evidenced in two works edited by F.W. Howay, *The Journal of Captain James Colnett aboard the 'Argonaut' from April 26, 1789, to Nov. 3, 1791* (T: CS 1940) and *Voyages of the 'Columbia' to the Northwest Coast, 1787–1790, and 1790–1793* (1941; repr. Portland, OR: Oregon Historical Society Press in cooperation with the Massachusetts Historical Society 1990). See too Stephen Reynolds, *The Voyage of the 'New Hazard' to the North-West Coast, Hawaii and China, 1810–1813* (Salem, MA: Peabody Museum 1938). The biographies of a number of maritime fur traders also appear in the *DCB*, including 'James Hanna' and 'John Kendrick,' vol. 4; 'James Colnett,' 'Robert Gray,' 'Robert Haswell,' 'Alexander MacKay,' 'John Meares,' 'Nathaniel Portlock,' and 'Jonathan Thorn,' vol. 5 (1983); 'Charles William Barkley,' 'John Rodgers Jewitt,' and 'Alexander Walker,' vol. 6 (1987); and 'James Charles Stuart Strange,' vol. 7 (1988).

No matter which nations were involved, trade never occurred without incident. The traders' journals routinely reported petty thievery, aggression, and breaches of protocol by Natives and Europeans. Occasionally, however, it was accompanied by violence. F.W. Howay outlines these incidents in 'Indian Attacks upon Maritime Traders of the North-West Coast, 1705–1805,' *CHR* 6/3 (Sept. 1925): 287–309. Jean Braithwaite and W.J. Folan approach the same subject from a Native perspective in 'The Taking of the Ship "Boston": An Ethnohistoric Study of Nootkan-European Conflict,' *Syesis* (Victoria) 5 (1972): 259–66. Also see R. Fisher, 'Arms and Men on the Northwest Coast, 1774–1825,' *BCS* 29 (Spring 1976): 3–18, and his 'Cook and the Nootka,' in Fisher and H.J.M. Johnston, eds., *Captain James Cook and His Times*. Not all the subjects of these attacks were killed, however. Some, like American John Rodgers Jewitt and his shipmate John Thompson, were taken captive. H. Stewart has annotated and illustrated Jewitt's narrative, *The Adventures and Sufferings of John R. Jewitt, Captive of the Maquinna* (V: Douglas & McIntyre 1987). Maquinna's *DCB* entry is in vol. 5 (as 'Muquinna').

The British, Russian, and American trade in furs sparked a renewed interest among the Spanish in the Northwest Coast and precipitated an international crisis. Fearing that the Russians would make inroads at Nootka Sound, the Spanish, after an absence of fifteen years, decided to build and garrison a fort there in 1789 to solidify their claims to the coast. However, it was the British, not the Russians, who challenged Spain's hegemony. Though the two countries signed the Nootka Convention in 1790, the question of sovereignty remained unresolved until 1794, despite the diplomatic efforts of Juan Francisco de la Bodega y Quadra and Captain George Vancouver – see the entries of both in the *DCB*, vol. 4. On Vancouver consult Bern Anderson, *Surveyor of the Sea: The Life and Voyages of Captain George Vancouver* (T: UTP 1960); W.K. Lamb, ed., *George Vancouver: A Voyage of Discovery to the North Pacific Ocean and round the World, 1791–1795*, 4 vols. (L: Hakluyt 1984); R. Fisher, *Vancouver's Voyage: Charting the Northwest Coast, 1791–1795* (V&T: Douglas & McIntyre 1992); and C.F. Newcombe, *Menzies Journal of Vancouver's Voyage: April to October 1792*, Archives of British Columbia, Memoir 5 (VI: King's Printer 1923). The Nootka crisis is explored in W.L. Cook, *Flood Tide of Empire*; C.I. Archer, 'Retreat from the North: Spain's Withdrawal from Nootka Sound, 1793–1795,' *BCS* 37 (Spring 1978): 19–36; and D. Pethick, *The Nootka Connection: Europe and the Northwest Coast, 1790–1795* (V: Douglas & McIntyre 1980).

José Mariano Moziño and Jacinto Caamaño were among the Spanish who came to Nootka to help build a permanent fort, and their accounts are available in W.R. Wagner and W.A. Newcombe, eds., 'The Journal of Jacinto Caamaño,' parts 1 and 2, *BCHQ* 2 (July/Oct. 1938): 189–222, 265–301, and J.M. Moziño, *Noticias de Nutka: An Account of Nootka Sound in 1792*, trans. I.H.W. Engstrand (Seattle, WA/V: University of Washington Press/Douglas & McIntyre 1991). The Spanish also undertook a number of explorations of the coast in the 1790s, which may be followed in Donald C. Cutter, *Malaspina and Galiano: Spanish Voyages to the Northwest Coast, 1791 & 1792* (V&T: Douglas & McIntyre 1991), and J. Kendrick, ed. and trans., *The Voyage of the 'Sutil' and 'Mexicana,' 1792: The Last Spanish Exploration of the Northwest Coast of America* (Spokane, WA: Arthur H. Clark 1991). Many of those involved have entries in the *DCB*, including 'Pedro de Alberni,' 'Dionisio Alcalá-Galiano,' 'Manuel José Antonio Cardero,' 'Tadeo

Haenke,' 'Alejandro Malaspina,' and 'José Mariano Moziño Losada Suárez de Figueroa,' vol. 5; and 'Francisco de Eliza y Reventa' and 'Tomás de Suria,' vol. 6.

Historians of British Columbia's Native peoples agree that though the maritime fur trade was a joint enterprise involving both Natives and Europeans, it was not one of equals. With the exception of the Russians, who combined their economic interests with colonization, most Europeans preferred to remain on their ships or, at most, to set up camps along the shore and wait for the Natives to come to them. R. Fisher uses many of the journals of the maritime traders listed previously and demonstrates that when the Native traders did arrive, they proved to be shrewd traders and drove hard bargains. Indeed his *Contact and Conflict: Indian-European Relations in British Columbia, 1774–1890* (1977; 2nd ed., V: UBCP 1992) is now something of a classic. Students will find an abbreviated account in his 1977 article 'Indian Control of the Maritime Fur Trade and the Northwest Coast,' reprinted in W.P. Ward and R.A.J. McDonald, eds., *British Columbia: Historical Readings*. Also of interest is Thomas Vaughan, *Soft Gold: The Fur Trade and Cultural Exchange on the Northwest Coast of America* (Portland, OR: Oregon Historical Society 1982). It would be incorrect, however, to say that the Natives of the Northwest Coast were unscathed by their participation in the fur trade. As J.R. Gibson shows in 'Smallpox on the Northwest Coast,' *BCS* 56 (Winter 1982–3): 61–81, and Robert T. Boyd in 'Demographic History, 1774–1874,' in W. Suttles, ed., *Northwest Coast*, these initial contacts led to the spread of decimating diseases among the Natives in the region.

THE LAND-BASED FUR TRADE

Europeans approached British Columbia by land as well as sea in search of furs. At the end of the eighteenth century, the Montreal-based North West Company found itself at a disadvantage. The Hudson's Bay Company had abandoned its long-standing policy of waiting for Native middlemen to bring their furs to the Bay and ventured inland, establishing a series of posts along the way. As a result of the increased competition, the North-Westers embarked on a series of explorations to find better trade routes and new sources of furs. Three overland expeditions to British Columbia came out of this initiative. As a result of the first, Alexander Mackenzie became the first European to travel overland to the Pacific coast, arriving at Bella Coola in July 1793. Because the route Mackenzie followed proved too rugged to be useful as a brigade trail, the North-Westers were forced to try again.

The task fell to Simon Fraser, the man in charge of the North West Company's operations west of the Rockies. After establishing a number of posts in 'New Caledonia' (the central interior of what is now British Columbia), in 1808 Fraser and his party travelled down the perilous river that now bears his name, believing it was the Columbia. Such was not the case, however, and though the North-Westers had gained much knowledge of the territory, a useful brigade route eluded them, and they now had the added problem of provisioning a number of interior forts. For the North-Westers, however, it was third time lucky. In 1810 David Thompson's expedition managed to find the elusive Columbia and trace it to the Pacific. Upon arriving, they discovered American John Jacob Astor's Pacific Fur Company already building a fort at the river's mouth. The question of sovereignty was resolved following the War of 1812, with the two parties agreeing to joint occupation.

All three expedition leaders have entries in the *DCB*: 'Alexander Mackenzie,' vol. 5; 'David Thompson,' vol. 8 (1985); and 'Simon Fraser,' vol. 9 (1976). Furthermore, their journals are available and appear in a number of different forms. The preferred editions are W.K. Lamb, ed., *The Journals and Letters of Sir Alexander Mackenzie* (T: MAC 1970); Richard Glover, ed., *David Thompson's Narrative, 1784–1812* (T: CS 1962); and Lamb, ed., *The Letters and Journals of Simon Fraser, 1806–1808* (T: MAC 1960). Francis Hardwick et al. discuss the instrumental role Native peoples played in these early overland explorations of British Columbia in *The Helping Hand: The Debt of Alexander Mackenzie and Simon Fraser to Canadian Indians* (V: Tantalus 1973). Also of interest are Marion O'Neil, 'The Maritime Activities of the North West Company, 1813 to 1821,' *Washington Historical Quarterly* 21 (Oct. 1930): 243–67; Arthur S. Morton, 'The North West Company's Columbian Enterprise and David Thompson,' *CHR* 17/3 (Sept. 1936): 266–88; B.M. Gough, 'The North West Company's "Adventure to China,"' *Oregon Historical Quarterly* 76 (Dec. 1975): 309–31; and David V. Burley and Scott Hamilton, 'Rocky Mountain Fort: Archaeological Research and the Late Eighteenth-Century North West Company Expansion into British Columbia,' *BCS* 88 (Winter 1990–1): 3–20; as well as the memoirs of Ross Cox, an American fur trader, entitled *The Columbia River; or, Scenes and Adventures during a Residence of Six Years on the Western Side of the Rocky Mountains, among Various Tribes of Indians Hitherto Unknown* (1832; repr., ed. E.I. Stewart and J.R. Stewart, Norman, OK: University of Oklahoma Press [1957]). Daniel Williams Harmon provides insight into the drudgery and loneliness of daily life at Fort St James, a North West Company post, in his *Sixteen Years in Indian Country: The Journal of Daniel Wil-

liams Harmon, 1800–1816, ed. W.K. Lamb (T: MAC 1957). As for the Americans in general and the Astorians in particular, see Washington Irving, *Astoria; or, Anecdotes of an Enterprise beyond the Rocky Mountains*, ed. Richard Dilworth Rust (Boston, MA: Twayne Publishing 1976); LeRoy R. Hafen, ed., *Mountain Men and Fur Traders of the West* (Lincoln, NE: University of Nebraska Press 1982); and James P. Ronda, *Astoria and Empire* (Lincoln, NE: University of Nebraska Press 1990).

The North West Company's tenure in the Pacific Northwest was short-lived, however. In 1821 the Montrealers merged with their British rivals, an event which gave the Bay men dominion over the region from Hudson Bay to the Pacific. Present-day British Columbia fell into two fur trading districts, the Columbia (the area north of the Columbia River and including Vancouver Island) and New Caledonia (the mainland). The governor of the Hudson's Bay Company, George Simpson, took the opportunity provided by the merger to reorganize operations. Simpson was concerned with 'oeconomy,' and particularly with the lack of it in the Columbia District, where everything, he thought, was on too grand a scale except the trade. To rectify this, Simpson reduced the company's coastal operations by using the *Beaver*, a paddle-wheeled steamer, to collect furs. Equally importantly, Simpson encouraged company posts to become as self-sufficient as possible. Rather than simply acting as collection points for furs, many posts became farms, provisioning themselves and others with their own produce as well as dried salmon and potatoes procured from Natives. The Hudson's Bay Company set up an agricultural subsidiary, the Puget's Sound Agricultural Company, to coordinate its farming activities. In fact, in the Pacific Northwest, the Hudson's Bay Company is best described as a multi-resource company rather than strictly a fur trade concern.

The history of the Hudson's Bay Company has been the subject of numerous monographs, but the standard overview is provided by E.E. Rich, *History of the Hudson's Bay Company, 1670–1870*, 2 vols. (L: HBRS 1958–9; repr. 3 vols., T: M&S 1960), and, more recently, his *The Fur Trade and the Northwest to 1857* (T: M&S 1967). However, students might also find Theodore J. Karamanski, *Fur Trade and Exploration: Opening the Far Northwest, 1821–1852* (V: UBCP 1983), of value. Keith A. Murray discusses the role of the Hudson's Bay Company west of the Rockies in 'The Hudson's Bay Company in the Pacific Northwest,' in G. Thomas Edwards and C.A. Schwantes, eds., *Experiences in a Promised Land: Essays in Pacific Northwest History* (Seattle, WA: University of Washington Press 1986), while Donald C. Davidson explores the company's relationship with the Russians in 'Relations of the Hudson's Bay Company with the Russian

American Company on the Northwest Coast, 1829–1867,' *BCHQ* 5 (Jan. 1941): 33–51.

One Hudson's Bay Company governor, George Simpson, has received considerable attention: he was an odd and rather unpleasant character – the perfect subject for a biography. In addition to his entry in the *DCB*, vol. 8, see Frederick Merk, ed., *Fur Trade and Empire: George Simpson's Journal* (1931; rev. ed., Cambridge, MA: Harvard University Press 1968), and John S. Galbraith, *The Little Emperor: Governor Simpson of the Hudson's Bay Company* (T: MAC 1976). Portions of Simpson's own journals and letters are available in a number of forms: George Simpson, *Narrative of a Journey round the World, during the Years 1841 and 1842*, 2 vols. (L: Colburn 1847); Malcolm Mcleod, ed., *Peace River: A Canoe Voyage from Hudson's Bay to the Pacific by the Late Sir George Simpson* (O: J. Durie and Son 1872); and E.E. Rich, ed., *Part of Dispatch from George Simpson, Esqr., Governor of Ruperts Land, to the Governor & Committee of the Hudson's Bay Company, London, March 1, 1829; Continued and Completed March 24 and June 5, 1829* (L: CS/HBRS 1947).

W.K. Lamb tells the story of the company's paddle-wheeled steamer in, 'The Advent of the *Beaver*,' *BCHQ* 2 (July 1938): 163–84. On the agricultural operations of the Hudson's Bay Company in the Oregon territories see J.R. Gibson, *Farming the Frontier: The Agricultural Opening of the Oregon Country, 1786–1846* (V: UBCP 1985); as well as L.A. Wrinch, 'The Formation of the Puget's Sound Agricultural Company,' *Washington Historical Quarterly* 24 (Jan. 1933): 3–8; J.S. Galbraith, 'The Early History of the Puget's Sound Agricultural Company, 1838–1843,' *Oregon Historical Quarterly* 55 (Sept. 1954): 234–59; and B.M. Gough, 'Corporate Farming on Vancouver Island: The Puget's Sound Agricultural Company, 1846–1857,' *CPRH*, vol. 4 (1984).

There is also a considerable literature on the Hudson's Bay Company's forts and their operations in such works as John A. Hussey, *The History of Fort Vancouver and Its Physical Structure* (Tacoma, WA: Washington State Historical Society 1957); Donald A. Harris and George C. Ingram, 'New Caledonia and the Fur Trade: A Status Report,' *Western Canadian Journal of Anthropology* 3/1 (1972): 179–95; Hartwell Bowsfield, ed., *Fort Victoria Letters, 1843–1851*, intro. M.A. Ormsby (W: HBRS 1979); Mary Cullen, *The History of Fort Langley, 1827–1896* (O: National Historic Parks and Sites Branch, Parks Canada 1979); Morag MacLauchlan, 'The Founding of Fort Langley,' in E. Blanche Norcross, ed., *The Company on the Coast* (Nanaimo, BC: Nanaimo Historical Society 1983); and K.R. Fladmark, 'Early Fur Trade Posts of the Peace River Area of British Columbia,' *BCS* 65 (Spring 1985): 48–65. Many of the journals and letters of men working at such posts have been published. E.E. Rich alone has edited *The Letters of John McLoughlin, 1825–46*, 3 vols. (L: CS/HBRS 1941–4), *Peter Skene Ogden's Snake Country Journals, 1824–25 and 1825–26* (L: HBRS 1950), and *A Journal of a Voyage from Rocky Mountain Portage in Peace River to the Sources of Finlays Branch and North West Ward in Summer 1824 [by Samuel Black]* (L: HBRS 1955). In addition to these accounts see W. Stewart Wallace, ed., *John McLean's Notes of a Twenty-Five Year's Service in the Hudson's Bay Territory* (T: CS 1932).

Not surprisingly biographies of fur traders abound in the *DCB*. Among the most prominent are 'Samuel Black,' 'William Connolly,' 'John George McTavish,' 'Archibald Menzies,' and 'John Stuart,' vol. 7; 'Charles Dodd,' 'Archibald McDonald,' 'John McLoughlin,' 'James McMillan,' 'Peter Skene Ogden,' and 'Alexander Ross,' vol. 8; 'Duncan Finlayson,' 'Donald McLean,' and 'John Work,' vol. 9; 'Ovid Allard,' 'William Henry McNeill,' 'Dugald Mactavish,' 'Donald Manson,' and 'James Murray Yale,' vol. 10 (1972); 'Alexander Caulfield Anderson,' 'Alexander Grant Dallas,' 'John Tod,' and 'William Fraser Tolmie,' vol. 11 (1982); and 'Roderick Finlayson' and 'Joseph William McKay,' vol. 12 (1990). As well readers might consult H.D. Dee, 'An Irishman in the Fur Trade: The Life and Journals of John Work,' *BCHQ* 7 (Oct. 1943): 229–70, and T.R. McCloy, 'Fur Trade Biographies: An Index,' *BCHQ* 15 (July–Oct. 1951): 203–12.

In general, as R. Fisher argues in *Contact and Conflict*, aboriginal peoples – both men and women – dictated the terms of the land-based fur trade. Fisher's point is reinforced by the *DCB* entries for the Carrier chief Kwah (vol. 7) and the Okanagan chief Hwistesmetxe'quen (vol. 8), and still more by Charles A. Bishop, 'Kwah: A Carrier Chief,' in C.M. Judd and A.J. Ray, eds., *Old Trails and New Directions.* These items, together with Shepard Krech III, 'The Beaver Indians and the Hostilities at Fort St. John's,' *Arctic Anthropology* 20/2 (1983): 35–45, underscore the fact that, like those in the maritime trade, relations between Natives and Europeans in the land-based fur trade could often result in violence and bloodshed. Nevertheless, the fur trade was not without its dislocating cultural and ecological effects. For a discussion of them see Georgiana Ball, 'The Monopoly System of Wildlife Management of the Indians and the Hudson's Bay Company in the Early History of British Columbia,' *BCS* 66 (Summer 1985): 37–58, and Lorne Hammond, 'Marketing Wildlife: The Hudson's Bay Company and the Pacific Northwest, 1821–49,' *Forest and Conservation History* 37 (Jan. 1993): 14–25.

As well as outlining what might be called the administrative history of the Hudson's Bay Company and the working lives of some of its employees, historians have also turned their attention to its social history. Despite the fact that the fur trade extracted European men from their homes and placed them in distant and alien lands, they were never without society. As both Sylvia Van Kirk and Jennifer S.H. Brown demonstrate, European fur traders often married Native women for economic advantage and companionship. These women, as well as the children of these alliances, played a central role in fur trade operations and achieved a certain amount of status in fur trade society. Many of Van Kirk's examples in *'Many Tender Ties': Women in Fur-Trade Society in Western Canada, 1670–1870* (W: Watson and Dwyer 1980) are drawn from British Columbia, and a few are found in Brown, *Strangers in Blood: Fur Trade Company Families in Indian Country* (V: UBCP 1980).

Even though many traders had wives and families, fur trade life was still quite solitary, dangerous, and occasionally violent. According to John Tod, Hudson's Bay Company men considered a posting to New Caledonia the equivalent of being sent to Botany Bay, Australia. Privation – both social and material – were altogether too frequent occurrences for traders on the mainland. Conditions were little better in the Columbia District, where outbreaks of a mysterious fever (probably malaria) felled many. Violence, or the threat of violence, was also part of everyday life west of the Rockies. Though, as in the maritime trade, the threat of Native attacks kept traders on edge, Hudson's Bay Company men were more likely to feel the lash of a cat-o'-nine-tails or a blow from the flat side of a cutlass or a fist belonging to one of their own superiors. The Hudson's Bay Company had judicial powers, but discipline was usually maintained by a system of corporal punishment or 'club law,' as historian Adrien-Gabriel Morice called it, rather than the more costly and less expedient trial. Something of the flavour of violence and justice can be found in such works as A.-G. Morice, *The History of the Northern Interior of British Columbia* (1904; repr. Smithers, BC: Interior Stationery 1978); W.K. Lamb, 'Five Letters of Charles Ross,' *BCHQ* 7 (Apr. 1942): 103–18; and Madge Wolfenden, 'John Tod: Career of a Scotch Boy,' *BCHQ* 17 (July–Oct. 1954): 133–238. See also the work of Hamar Foster: 'Long-Distance Justice: The Criminal Jurisdiction of Canadian Courts West of the Canadas, 1763–1859,' *American Journal of Legal History* 34/1 (Jan. 1990): 1–48; 'Sins against the Great Spirit: The Law, the Hudson's Bay Company and the Mackenzie's River Murders, 1835–1839,' *Criminal Justice History* 11 (1990): 23–76; 'Mutiny on the *Beaver*: Law and Authority in the Fur Trade Navy, 1835–1840,' in Dale Gibson and W. Wesley Pue, eds., *Glimpses of Canadian Legal History* (W: Legal Research Institute 1991); and 'Killing Mr. John: Law and Jurisdiction at Fort Stikine,

1842–1846,' in John McLaren et al., eds., *Law for the Elephant, Law for the Beaver: Essays in the Legal History of the North American West* (R: CPRC 1992). Fort Vancouver's chaplain, the aptly named Herbert Beaver, also had many observations to make about fur trade life, including the form of discipline the company used, which can be found in *Reports and Letters of Herbert Beaver, 1836–1838, Chaplain to the Hudson's Bay Company and Missionary to the Indians at Fort Vancouver*, ed. Thomas E. Jessett (Portland, OR: Champoeg Press 1959).

VANCOUVER ISLAND

As it did a century earlier, a geopolitical jockeying for position ushered in a new era in the Pacific Northwest in the 1840s. Whereas Russian activity in the 1740s brought the first Europeans to the coast and precipitated the maritime fur trade, it was American activity that led to the creation of the colony of Vancouver Island in 1849 and the beginnings of European settlement in British Columbia.

Though both the British and the Americans had agreed to occupy the Oregon territories jointly following the War of 1812, the British presence in the region remained limited to the Hudson's Bay Company's posts. The Americans, on the other hand, began settling the area in the 1830s. It was only a matter of time before the interests of the fur trade company and those of the agricultural settlers clashed. Fearing American annexation, the Hudson's Bay Company moved its Columbia District headquarters from Fort Vancouver on the Columbia River to the newly constructed Fort Victoria on the southern tip of Vancouver Island in 1845. The decision proved to be a wise one, for despite British claims to sovereignty, in 1846 the Treaty of Washington granted the area north of the Columbia River to the forty-ninth parallel to the United States. The most comprehensive analysis of the Oregon question is F. Merk, *The Oregon Question: Essays in Anglo-American Diplomacy and Politics* (Cambridge, MA: Harvard University Press 1967). Various aspects of the crisis are also discussed in Frank E. Ross, 'The Retreat of the Hudson's Bay Company in the Pacific North-West,' *CHR* 18/3 (Sept. 1937): 262–80; Richard S. Cramer, 'British Magazines and the Oregon Question,' *Pacific Historical Review* 32/3 (1963): 369–82; B.M. Gough, 'The Royal Navy and the Oregon Crisis, 1844–1846,' *BCS* 9 (Spring 1971): 15–37; and J.R. Gibson, *Farming the Frontier*.

American settlement of the Oregon territories was viewed with some concern by the Hudson's Bay Company, which feared the new arrivals would interfere with its operations. Much to the company's chagrin, John

McLoughlin, Fort Vancouver's chief factor, aided many of the early settlers, allowing them to establish a foothold in the Columbia District. While he was chastised by his employer, McLoughlin is considered by many Americans to be the 'Father of Oregon.' On American migration into the Oregon territories see William A. Bowen, *The Willamette Valley: Migration and Settlement on the Oregon Frontier* (Seattle, WA: University of Washington Press 1978); Samuel N. Dicken and Emily F. Dicken, *The Making of Oregon: A Study in Historical Geography* (Portland, OR: Oregon Historical Society 1979); John Mack Faragher, *Women and Men on the Overland Trail* (New Haven, CT: Yale University Press 1979); Malcolm Clark, Jr, *Eden Seekers: The Settlement of Oregon, 1818–1862* (Boston, MA: Houghton Mifflin 1981); and D.O. Johansen, 'A Working Hypothesis for the Study of Migration,' in G.T. Edwards and C.A. Schwantes, eds., *Experiences in a Promised Land*.

The Treaty of Washington and the annexation of California at the end of the Mexican-American War in 1848 merely accentuated British fears of American manifest destiny and the need to reinforce their hold in the Pacific Northwest. The Hudson's Bay Company forts, though outposts of the British imperial realm, had not helped keep Oregon, but a colony might. In 1849 Vancouver Island became a British colony, and Fort Victoria, just six years old, was its administrative centre. The island was not a Crown Colony, but a proprietary one, and the Hudson's Bay Company was the proprietor. In return for the proprietorship and an extension of its monopoly on trade, the company agreed to colonize the island and install the usual institutions of representative government. J.S. Galbraith discusses this uneasy relationship between company and colony in *The Hudson's Bay Company as an Imperial Factor, 1821–1869* (T: UTP 1957). M.A. Ormsby's introduction to H. Bowsfield's collection *Fort Victoria Letters, 1843–1851*, and the letters themselves, are a good initiation to both the operations of the Hudson's Bay Company and fur trade life on the island. So too is W.K. Lamb, 'The Founding of Fort Victoria,' *BCHQ* 7 (Apr. 1943): 71–92. J.E. Hendrickson discusses the political developments that led to Vancouver Island becoming a colony in 'The Constitutional Development of Colonial Vancouver Island and British Columbia,' in W.P. Ward and R.A.J. McDonald, eds., *British Columbia: Historical Readings*. Two diaries provide a glimpse of island life under company proprietorship: 'The Diary of Martha Cheney Ella, 1853–1856,' edited in two parts by J.K. Nesbitt, *BCHQ* 13 (Apr./July–Oct. 1949): 91–112, 257–70; and, covering the years 1852–7, 'The Diary of Robert Melrose,' edited in three parts by W.K. Lamb, *BCHQ* 7 (Apr./July/Oct. 1943): 119–34, 199–218, 283–95.

The granting of the proprietorship of Vancouver Island to the Hudson's Bay Company was not without controversy. James Edward Fitzgerald was chief among those opposed to the company. He had his own scheme for settlement and charged that as a monopolistic business enterprise the Hudson's Bay Company could not discharge its colonization duties properly nor would it govern in the interests of all settlers. Fitzgerald published his critique as *An Examination of the Charter and Proceedings of the Hudson's Bay Company, with Reference to the Grant of Vancouver's Island* (L: T. Saunders 1849). It is thoroughly discussed in Paul Knaplund, 'James Stephen on Granting Vancouver Island to the Hudson's Bay Company, 1846–1848,' *BCHQ* 9 (Oct. 1945): 259–71; Knaplund, 'Letters from James Edward Fitzgerald to W.E. Gladstone concerning Vancouver Island and the Hudson's Bay Company, 1848–1850,' *BCHQ* 13 (Oct. 1949): 1–21; and J.S. Galbraith, 'James Edward Fitzgerald versus the Hudson's Bay Company: The Founding of Vancouver Island,' *BCHQ* 16 (July–Oct. 1952): 191–207, reprinted in D.M. Falconer, ed., *British Columbia: Patterns in Economic, Political and Cultural Development.* For an overview of the debate over granting the proprietorship of Vancouver Island to the Hudson's Bay Company see Richard Mackie, 'The Colonization of Vancouver Island, 1849–1858,' *BCS* 96 (Winter 1992–3): 3–40.

Though the British Colonial Office did not listen to Fitzgerald, his predictions of a conflict of interest were soon borne out. Richard Blanshard, Vancouver Island's first governor, and a man independent of the company, arrived in early 1850 but found that he had very little to do. With company men making up the vast majority of the population, the de facto government of the island was the Hudson's Bay Company. Blanshard was not only superfluous, but he also soon found himself at odds with the authority of the company. Nowhere was the conflict between Crown and company more clearly drawn than in the 'miserable affair' at Fort Rupert. Learning of the deaths of a number of British seamen near Fort Rupert on northeastern Vancouver Island, Blanshard appointed John Sebastian Helmcken, the Hudson's Bay Company surgeon, a justice of the peace and sent him to investigate. Neither Helmcken nor Blanshard was successful in collecting information, however, because the company men at Fort Rupert refused to cooperate, claiming they recognized no authority except that of the Hudson's Bay Company. Faced with such obstacles, Blanshard resigned as governor in November 1850 and was replaced by James Douglas, Fort Victoria's chief factor.

Blanshard's short and inglorious career is detailed in William E. Ireland, 'The Appointment of Governor Blanshard,' *BCHQ* 8 (July 1944): 213–26, and W.K. Lamb, 'The Governorship of Richard Blanshard,' *BCHQ* 14 (Jan.–Apr. 1950): 1–40. Also see 'Richard Blanshard,' *DCB*, vol. 12. The more substantial career of James Douglas is the subject of greater attention: Walter N. Sage, *Sir James Douglas and British Columbia* (T: UTP 1930); D. Pethick, *James Douglas: Servant of Two Empires* (V: Mitchell Press 1969); and 'James Douglas,' *DCB*, vol. 10. B.M. Gough discusses the Fort Rupert affair in *Gunboat Frontier: British Maritime Authority and Northwest Coast Indians, 1846–1890* (V: UBCP 1984), while a firsthand account is available in *The Reminiscences of Doctor John Sebastian Helmcken*, ed. Dorothy Blakey Smith (V: UBCP 1975). Vancouver Island's slow growth under the Hudson's Bay Company proprietorship is outlined in W.K. Lamb, 'The Census of Vancouver Island, 1855,' *BCHQ* 4 (Jan. 1940): 51–8, and the scale of the effort the company did make is charted in A.N. Mouat's article on the passengers of the *Norman Morison*, 'Notes on the *Norman Morison*,' *BCHQ* 3 (July 1939): 203–14.

Blanshard's departure and Douglas's appointment signalled the beginning of a period of political agitation in the colony. Vancouver Island's independent settlers (independent of the Hudson's Bay Company) repeated Fitzgerald's and Blanshard's complaints, and charged that the company was attempting to turn its economic monopoly into a political one. The appointment of James Douglas's brother-in-law, David Cameron, as chief justice of the island's Supreme Court was one example. A general outline of this birth of 'party politics' on Vancouver Island is available in M.A. Ormsby, *British Columbia: A History*. Many members of the anti-company party are covered in the *DCB*, including 'Andrew Muir,' vol. 8; 'James Cooper' and 'Kenneth McKenzie,' vol. 10; and 'Edward Edwards Langford,' vol. 12. For more on Langford see Sydney G. Pettit, 'The Trials and Tribulations of Edward Edwards Langford,' *BCHQ* 17 (Jan.–Apr. 1953): 5–40. On the other side see 'David Cameron,' *DCB*, vol. 10, as well as David R. Verchere, *A Progression of Judges* (V: UBCP 1989). One of Cameron's most controversial cases, one that led to charges of Hudson's Bay Company favouritism and calls for his removal, is considered in G. Hollis Slater, 'Rev. Robert John Staines: Pioneer Priest, Pedagogue and Political Agitator,' *BCHQ* 14 (Oct. 1950): 187–240; also see 'Robert John Staines,' *DCB*, vol. 8.

The year 1858 marked a change in the political status and social life of the island. The British government decided not to renew the Hudson's Bay Company's proprietorship that year, and though Vancouver Island continued to be governed by James Douglas, it became a Crown Colony. That year also marked the beginning of the Fraser River gold rush, an event that transformed Victoria, the colony's capital. Though its political status had changed, the island's politics remained polarized. The influence of the old fur trade elite that governed the proprietary colony did not diminish with the end of the company's tenure as proprietor, but was instead simply reinforced by the addition of some British administrators and Royal Navy men. This caused much consternation from some of the colony's gold rush immigrants, many of whom resented the power of the Family-Company Compact, as the island's elite was dubbed. Among the more outspoken opponents of the Family-Company Compact was the man who gave the group its name, newspaper editor Amor De Cosmos. Through his newspaper *The British Colonist*, De Cosmos attacked government policy and individual members of the compact, whom he identified as James Douglas, David Cameron, J.S. Helmcken, J.D Pemberton, J.W. McKay, and W.A.G. Young. See Lionel H. Laing, 'The Family-Company Compact,' *Washington Historical Quarterly* 22 (Apr. 1931): 117–28. There are a number of biographies of De Cosmos, but the most recent, and the best place to start, is the one in the *DCB*, vol. 12. Compact members in the *DCB* include, in addition to Douglas and Cameron, 'Sir William Alexander George Young,' vol. 11; and 'Joseph William McKay' and 'Joseph Despard Pemberton,' vol. 12.

Victoria and Vancouver Island consisted of more than the compact and its opponents, however. As Matthew Macfie observed in his *Vancouver Island and British Columbia: Their History, Resources and Prospects* (L: Longman, Green 1865), the gold rush brought a diverse number of people to Victoria. The fur trade workforce was quite heterogeneous, composed of Iroquois, French Canadians, and Hawaiians or Kanakas. On the latter group see Janice K. Duncan, *Minority without a Champion: Kanakas on the Pacific Coast, 1788–1850* (Portland, OR: Oregon Historical Society 1972), and her 'Kanaka World Travellers and Fur Trade Employees, 1785–1860,' *Hawaiian Journal of History* 7 (1973): 93–111. Two of the more visible groups of immigrants both came from the United States: the Chinese and the Blacks. The reaction to Chinese immigration is analysed in W.P. Ward, *White Canada Forever: Popular Attitudes and Public Policy toward Orientals in British Columbia* (M&K: MQUP 1978), and his 'The Oriental Immigrant and Canada's Protestant Clergy, 1855–1925,' *BCS* 22 (Summer 1974): 40–55. On Black immigrants to Vancouver Island see F.W. Howay, 'Negro Immigration into Vancouver Island in 1858,' *BCHQ* 3 (Apr. 1939): 101–13; Philip S. Foner, 'The Colored Inhabitants of Vancouver Island,' *BCS* 8 (Winter 1970–1): 29–33; Crawford Kilian, *Go Do Some Great Thing: The Black Pioneers of British Columbia* (V: J.J. Douglas 1978); and S.H.D. Carey, 'The Church of England and the Colour Question in Victoria, 1860,' *JCCHS* 24/2 (Oct. 1982): 63–74. Cyril E. Leonoff discusses early Jewish immigrants in Victoria in *Pioneers, Pedlars and Prayer Shawls: The Jewish Communities in British Columbia and the Yukon* (VI: Sono Nis Press 1978). The history of women among the gold rush settlers is covered in Nancy de Bertrand Lugrin, *The Pioneer Women of Vancouver Island* (VI: Women's Canadian Club of Victoria 1928), and Jackie Lay, 'To Columbia on the Tynemouth: The Emigration of Women and Girls in 1862,' in Barbara K. Latham and Cathy Kess, eds., *In Her Own Right: Selected Essays on Women's History in British Columbia* (VI: Camosun College 1980).

The Native population of the island outnumbered the non-Native one and could not afford to be ignored. Douglas had negotiated a series of treaties covering the area around Fort Victoria but did not do so for the other parts of the island where non-Native settlement was occurring, citing lack of funds as the reason. As a consequence, clashes between Natives and newcomers became more frequent as agricultural settlement on the island progressed. The treaties and conflicts are covered in B.A. McKelvie, 'The Victoria Voltigeurs,' *BCHQ* 20 (July–Oct. 1956): 221–39; W. Duff, 'The Fort Victoria Treaties,' *BCS* 3 (Fall 1969): 3–57; R. Fisher, *Contact and Conflict*; B.M. Gough, *Gunboat Frontier*; and Paul Tennant, *Aboriginal Peoples and Politics: The Indian Land Question in British Columbia, 1849–1989* (V: UBCP 1990). Nevertheless, Fisher, 'Indian Warfare and Two Frontiers: A Comparison of British Columbia and Washington Territory during the Early Years of Settlement,' *Pacific Historical Review* 50/1 (1981): 31–51, argues that such conflict was much less violent than the kind that characterized Native/non-Native relations south of the forty-ninth parallel.

Though the island began its life in the non-Native world as a fur trade preserve, its economy was never based on a single resource. For example, B.M. Gough's previously cited 'Corporate Farming on Vancouver Island,' *CPRH*, vol. 4, details agricultural operations similar to those carried out in the Oregon territories. The Hudson's Bay Company itself pursued profit in several fields, among the most important of which were the coal mines at Nanaimo and Prince Rupert: John H. Kemble, 'Coal from the Northwest Coast, 1848–1850,' *BCHQ* 2 (Apr. 1938): 123–30; B.A. McKelvie, 'The Founding of Nanaimo,' *BCHQ* 8 (July 1944): 169–88; H.K. Ralston, 'Miners and Managers: The Organization of Coal Production on Vancouver's Island by the Hudson's Bay Company, 1848–1862,' in E.B. Norcross, ed., *The Company on the Coast*; John Douglas Belshaw, 'Mining Technique and Social Division on Vancouver Island, 1848–1900,' *British Journal of Canadian Studies* 1/1 (June 1986): 45–65; Lynne Bowen, *Three Dollar Dreams* (Lantzville, BC: Oolichan Books 1987); Eric Newsome, *The Coal Coast: The History of Coal Mining in British Columbia, 1835–1900* (VI: Orca Press 1989);

Belshaw, 'The Standard of Living of British Miners on Vancouver Island, 1848–1900,' *BCS* 84 (Winter 1989–90): 37–64; and Terry Reksten, *The Dunsmuir Saga* (V&T: Douglas & McIntyre 1991). For other business endeavours on the island see the previously cited articles by H.K. Ralston, 'Patterns of Trade and Investment on the Pacific Coast,' *BCS* (1968–9), and by J.M.S. Careless, 'The Lowe Brothers, 1852–70,' *BCS* (1969), as well as Robert Lloyd Webb, *On the Northwest Coast: Commercial Whaling in the Pacific Northwest, 1790–1967* (V: UBCP 1988). An interesting contemporary observation of both island economic activity and Native peoples is *Robert Brown and the Vancouver Island Exploring Expedition*, ed. John Hayman (V: UBCP 1989).

BRITISH COLUMBIA

It was the gold rush, however, that transformed Vancouver Island's economy. As in the maritime and land-based fur trades, British Columbia's Native peoples were deeply implicated in this economic transformation as well. Indeed, as T.A. Rickard indicates in his 'Indian Participation in the Gold Discoveries,' *BCHQ* 2 (Jan. 1938): 3–18, it was the Native peoples who discovered the precious metal – a point followed up in R. Fisher, *Contact and Conflict*. As news of the discovery spread, hundreds of businesses opened almost overnight in Victoria to provision the Fraser River fortune-seekers, who began arriving in April 1858. By August at least sixteen thousand people had passed through the colonial capital on their way to the mainland. Most were fresh from California's gold-fields, bringing with them a reputation for lawlessness. James Douglas considered the miners the 'dregs of society,' and both he and many Victorians breathed a sigh of relief when they left the colonial capital without incident. Their departure only transferred the problem to a different part of the British territory, however. Douglas and the Colonial Office remained convinced that the influx of Americans into what was a sparsely populated (in terms of European presence) fur trade preserve would result in unmanageable outbreaks of violence among miners and between miners and Native peoples, and perhaps culminate in annexation. As a result, as it had done with Vancouver Island some nine years earlier in response to American aggression, the British government created the mainland colony of British Columbia in November 1858 to buttress its claim to the region. W.E. Ireland, 'Gold Rush Days in Victoria, 1858–1859,' *BCHQ* 12 (July 1948): 231–46, paints a picture of the influx of miners in the capital, and David Ricardo Williams looks at events on the mainland in 'The Administration of Criminal and Civil Justice in the

Mining Camps and Frontier Communities of British Columbia,' in Louis A. Knafla, ed., *Law and Justice in a New Land: Essays in Western Canadian Legal History* (T: Carswell 1986), reprinted in J.M. Bumsted, ed., *Interpreting Canada's Past*, vol. 1, *Pre-Confederation* (2nd ed., T: OUP 1993). Robie L. Reid discusses Douglas and the miners in 'John Nugent: The Impertinent Envoy,' *BCHQ* 8 (Jan. 1944): 53–76; and an account of the disruption to Native peoples caused by the advance of the mining frontier is in Edward S. Hewlett, 'The Chilcotin Uprising of 1864,' *BCS* 19 (Fall 1973): 50–72, and R. Fisher, *Contact and Conflict*. R.C. Harris surveys the early contact period in 'The Fraser Canyon Encountered,' *BCS* 94 (Summer 1992): 5–28, and 'The Lower Mainland,' in Graeme Wynn and Timothy Oke, eds., *Vancouver: A Region* (V: UBCP 1992). As well see the first plate in Bruce Macdonald, ed., *Vancouver: A Visual History* (V: Talonbooks 1992).

The San Juan Island 'Pig War' only confirmed the fact that the United States had designs on British territory. When the Hudson's Bay Company attempted to get compensation from American authorities for one of its pigs, which was shot by some American miners on San Juan Island, the Americans responded by claiming the islands for themselves. The subsequent crisis is the subject of K.A. Murray, *The Pig War* (Tacoma, WA: Washington State Historical Society 1968), and David Richardson, *Pig War Islands* (Eastsound, WA: Orcas Publishing 1971). Though the dispute was eventually settled and sovereignty sorted out in 1872, as B.M. Gough explains in 'British Policy in the San Juan Boundary Dispute, 1854–72,' *Pacific Northwest Quarterly* 62 (Apr. 1971): 59–68, the incident merely reinforced British fears.

If it was too late to prevent the entry of Americans into British territory, the least it could do, the Colonial Office thought, was to try to prevent lawlessness by establishing government institutions in the new colony quickly. Matthew Baillie Begbie, a Lincoln's Inn-trained but relatively untried barrister, was appointed Supreme Court judge of British Columbia and dispatched to the colony in 1859 to help James Douglas, who, having resigned his position with the Hudson's Bay Company, was doubling as governor of British Columbia and Vancouver Island. Begbie drafted the legislation creating the office of Gold Commissioner and Gold Commissioner's Courts, institutions that licensed the colony's gold miners and adjudicated mining disputes. The Gold Commissioner and the court he presided over forestalled the establishment of informal Miners' Meetings and the tradition of local government that characterized the California gold-fields, and contributed to the establishment of centralized administrative control in the new Eldorado. Begbie has attracted the attention of many scholars, most notably D.R.

Williams, who published a full-length biography, '... *The Man for a New Country': Sir Matthew Baillie Begbie* (Sidney, BC: Gray's 1977) as well as the entry in the *DCB*, vol. 12. S.G. Pettit authored a number of articles on Begbie as well: '"Dear Sir Matthew": A Glimpse of Judge Begbie,' 'Judge Begbie in Action: The Establishment of Law and the Preservation of Order in British Columbia,' 'His Honour's Honour: Judge Begbie and the Cottonwood Scandal,' and 'Tyrant Judge: Judge Begbie in Court,' *BCHQ* 11 (Jan./ Apr./July/Oct. 1947): 1–14, 113–48, 187–210, 273–94. As for Douglas during the gold rush, see Clarence G. Karr, 'James Douglas: The Gold Governor in the Context of His Times,' in E.B. Norcross, ed., *The Company on the Coast*.

Other legal personnel and the Royal Engineers, or Sappers, also played an important role in bringing government and control to British Columbia as well as contributing to the British cast of mainland society. Among the magistrates treated in the *DCB* are 'Chartres Brew' and 'John Boles Gaggin,' vol. 9; and 'William George Cox,' vol. 10. Supreme Court Registrar Arthur Thomas Busby appears in the *DCB*, vol. 10; D.B. Smith edited and annotated the journal Bushby kept on his first trip with Begbie, 'The Diary of Arthur Thomas Bushby, 1858–1859,' *BCHQ* 21 (Jan.–Oct. 1957): 83– 198. As for the Royal Engineers, see F.W. Howay, *The Work of the Royal Engineers in British Columbia, 1858 to 1863* (VI: R. Wolfenden 1910); Frances Woodward, 'The Influence of the Royal Engineers on the Development of British Columbia,' *BCS* 24 (Winter 1974–5): 3–51; and B. Hill, *Sappers: The Royal Engineers in British Columbia* (Ganges, BC: Horsdal and Schubert 1987). B.M. Gough discusses the orderly character of the British Columbia frontier in the previously cited 'The Character of the British Columbia Frontier,' *BCS* (1976–7). He also explores another response of the colonial government to the gold rush in '"Turbulent Frontiers" and British Expansion: Governor Douglas, the Royal Navy and the British Columbia Gold Rushes,' *Pacific Historical Review* 41/1 (1972): 15–32. However, Tina Loo, '"A Delicate Game": The Meaning of Law on Grouse Creek,' *BCS* 96 (Winter 1992–3): 41–65, suggests control was never absolute and order was something that often was negotiated rather than imposed.

Though Douglas and Begbie referred frequently to the inhabitants of the mainland colony as 'Americans' or 'Californians,' the population was not as homogeneous as those labels might imply. While it was true that many of those who sought their fortunes along the banks of the Fraser River had come most immediately from the United States and, specifically, California, most had their origins elsewhere. Chinese, Italians, Blacks, Mexicans,

French, English, and Welsh adventurers made their way to the gold colony. When gold was discovered in the Cariboo in 1862, British Columbia's cultural diversity was further increased by the addition of a number of Canadian Overlanders (so named because they had travelled overland to British Columbia).

Most groups have found their historians. On the Chinese, for example, see W.P. Ward, *White Canada Forever*; Tamara Adilman, 'A Preliminary Sketch of Chinese Women and Work in British Columbia, 1858–1950,' in B.K. Latham and Roberta J. Pazdro, eds., *Not Just Pin Money: Selected Essays on the History of Women's Work in British Columbia* (VI: Camosun College 1984); Peter S. Li, *The Chinese in Canada* (T: OUP 1988); and P.E. Roy, *A White Man's Province: British Columbia Politicians and Chinese and Japanese Immigrants, 1858–1914* (V: UBCP 1989). Alan Conway is responsible for two articles on Welsh miners: 'Welsh Gold Miners in British Columbia during the 1860s,' *BCHQ* 21 (Jan.–Oct. 1957): 51–74, and 'Welsh Gold Miners in British Columbia during the 1860s,' in *Cylchgrawn Llyfrgell Genedlaethol Cymru: The National Library of Wales Journal* 10 (1958): 375–89. And on the Canadian Overlanders look to Thomas McMicking, *Overland from Canada to British Columbia*, ed. Joanne Leduc (V: UBCP 1981), and Richard Thomas Wright, *Overland: 1858 Gold* (Saskatoon, Sask.: WPPB 1985).

Common to many of these groups of people was a desire to, as George Bowering says, make 'home away' – to re-create a familiar social environment in an alien setting. This desire was manifested most clearly among British immigrants like Henry Crease and Susan Allison, who had come to the colonies to maintain their social standing and the aesthetics of everyday life that went along with it. Both the Creases and the Allisons took pains to alter their domestic environments by surrounding themselves with remembrances of English country life. On the world such English immigrants made see Edward Philip Johnson, 'The Early Years of Ashcroft Manor,' *BCS* 5 (Summer 1970): 3–23; M.A. Ormsby, ed., *A Pioneer Gentlewoman in British Columbia: The Recollections of Susan Allison* (V: UBCP 1976); Christina B. Johnson-Dean, *The Crease Family Archives: A Record of Settlement and Service in British Columbia* (VI: Provincial Archives of British Columbia 1982); and 'Henry Crease,' *DCB*, vol. 13 (forthcoming).

Despite this influx of immigrants and the clashes between them and the colony's far more numerous Native population, James Douglas did not negotiate treaties or otherwise attempt to settle the Native land question in British Columbia. Douglas's inaction on this issue has generated something of a controversy among scholars of the region. Initially Douglas was looked upon as a friend of the Native people. In R. Fisher, *Contact and Conflict*, for example, Douglas appears as someone who was genuinely sensitive to the Native position and predicament. The portrayal of Douglas's approach to Natives is more critical, however, in P. Tennant's recent *Aboriginal Peoples and Politics* and his 'Aboriginal Rights and the Canadian Legal System: The West Coast Anomaly,' in J. McLaren et al., eds., *Law for the Elephant, Law for the Beaver.* A more general approach to developing Native policy is available in Dennis Madill, *British Columbia Indian Treaties in Historical Perspective* (O: Indian and Northern Affairs Canada 1981). On Native and non-Native relations in the wake of the gold rush, see Rolf Knight, *Indians at Work: An Informal History of Native Indian Labour in British Columbia, 1858–1930* (V: New Star 1978), which argues that British Columbia's Native peoples remained active in the province's economy well after non-Native settlement was entrenched; as well as R. Fisher, 'The Impact of European Settlement on the Indigenous Peoples of Australia, New Zealand and British Columbia: Some Comparative Dimensions,' *Canadian Ethnic Studies* 12/1 (1980): 1–14; and B.M. Gough, 'The Indian Policies of Great Britain and the United States in the Pacific Northwest in the Mid-Nineteenth Century,' *Canadian Journal of Native Studies* 2/2 (1982): 321–37. A case study by Carol Cooper, 'Native Women of the Northern Pacific Coast: An Historical Perspective,' *JCS* 27/4 (Winter 1992–3): 44–75, argues that the fur trade experience of Nishga and Tsimshian women gave them a certain amount of economic power, which allowed them to resist missionaries' efforts to impose narrow domestic roles and notions of female submissiveness on them.

The appropriation of their lands was not the only kind of colonization the Native peoples of British Columbia were subjected to. Christian missionaries made their appearance in British Columbia during the colonial period and, as in many other parts of North America, attempted to save a group of people many felt destined to become extinct by teaching them the habits of civilization. John Webster Grant supplies a sympathetic portrayal and overview of missionary efforts in British Columbia in the sixth chapter of his *Moon of Wintertime: Missionaries and the Indians of Canada in Encounter since 1534* (T: UTP 1984). Two other general treatments are R. Fisher, 'Missions to the Indians of British Columbia,' in W.P. Ward and R.A.J. McDonald, eds., *British Columbia: Historical Readings*, and Charles Lillard, *Warriors of the North Pacific: Missionary Accounts of the Northwest Coast, the Skeena and Stikine Rivers and the Klondike, 1829–1900* (VI: Sono Nis Press 1984).

The most common approach to missionary activity among Native peoples is denominational, often based on contemporary accounts. The efforts of the Roman Catholic Church are chronicled, for example, in such works as *Life, Letters and Travels of Father Pierre-Jean De Smet, S.J., 1801–1873*, ed. Hiram Martin Chittenden and Alfred Talbot Richardson, 4 vols. (1905; repr. NY: Kraus 1969); A.-G. Morice, *History of the Catholic Church in Western Canada, from Lake Superior to the Pacific, 1659–1895*, 2 vols. (T: Musson 1910); John McGloin, 'John Nobili, S.J., Founder of California's Santa Clara College: The New Caledonia Years, 1845–1848,' *BCHQ* 17 (July–Oct. 1953): 215–22; Kay Cronin, *Cross in the Wilderness* (V: Mitchell 1960); and Margaret Whitehead, *The Cariboo Mission: A History of the Oblates* (VI: Sono Nis Press 1981). There are also several relevant entries in the *DCB*, among which see 'John Nobili,' vol. 8; 'Modeste Demers' and 'Pierre-Jean De Smet,' vol. 10; 'Augustin-Magloire Blanchet,' 'Louis-Joseph d'Herbomez,' and 'Charles John Seghers,' vol. 11; and 'Paul Durieu' and 'Charles Pandosy,' vol. 12.

Among the Protestants, the Methodist missionary Thomas Crosby left two accounts, *Among the An-ko-me-nums or Flathead Tribes of Indians of the Pacific Coast* (T: William Briggs 1907) and *Up and Down the North Pacific Coast by Canoe and Mission Ship* (T: Missionary Society of the Methodist Church 1914). His efforts among the Tsimshian are analysed in Clarence Bolt, *Thomas Crosby and the Tsimshian: Small Shoes for Feet Too Large* (V: UBCP 1992). Anglican William Duncan was one of the most prominent missionaries on the Northwest Coast, and he is the subject of many studies, the best of which are Jean Usher, *William Duncan of Metlakatla: A Victorian Missionary in British Columbia* (O: National Museum of Man 1974), and her 1968 article 'Duncan of Metlakatla: The Victorian Origins of a Model Indian Community,' reprinted in W.P. Ward and R.A.J. McDonald, eds., *British Columbia: Historical Readings*. The standard history of the Anglicans in British Columbia is Frank A. Peake, *The Anglican Church in British Columbia* (V: Mitchell Press 1959). On the Baptists, see John B. Richards, *Baptists in British Columbia: A Struggle to Maintain 'Sectarianism'* (V: Northwest Theological College and Seminary 1977). Native reaction to these missionary endeavours is assessed by E. Palmer Patterson II in several works: *Mission on the Nass: The Evangelization of the Nishga, 1860–1890* (Waterloo, Ont.: Eulachon Press 1982); 'Kincolith, B.C.: Leadership Continuity in a Native Christian Village, 1867–1887,' *Canadian Journal of Anthropology* 3/1 (Fall 1982): 45–55; 'Early Nishga-European Contact to 1860: A People for "Those Who Talk of the Efficiency of Moral Lectures to Subdue the Obduracy of the Heart,"' *Anthropologica* 25/2 (1983): 193–219; and 'George Kinzadah-Simoogit in His Times,' *BCS* 82 (Summer 1989): 16–38.

Though the vast majority of those who came to British Columbia to participate in the Fraser and Cariboo rushes were men, women were represented among those who sought their fortunes. Fanny Bendixen, though by no means typical, was certainly one of the women who took advantage of the economic opportunities offered by the gold rush. Bendixen and other women (and men) did not pan for gold or sink shafts deep into the Cariboo soil, but made their livings providing services to miners. They ran general stores, saloons, bakeries, restaurants, freight companies, or, like Fanny, operated hotels. Others provided legal or medical services, did laundry, general carpentry, or shoed horses. In all, these people added another dimension to a colonial society centred on resource extraction. They built churches, libraries, schools, hospitals, as well as organizing a number of fraternal and other voluntary associations. Fanny's story is told in *DCB*, vol. 12. On women in the gold rush more generally consult S. Van Kirk, 'A Vital Presence: Women in the Cariboo Gold Rush, 1862–1875,' in Gillian Creese and Veronica Strong-Boag, eds., *British Columbia Reconsidered: Essays on Women* (V: Press Gang 1992). Relevant studies of others involved in the gold rush are Isabel Bescoby, 'Society in the Cariboo during the Gold Rush,' *Washington Historical Quarterly* 24 (July 1933): 195–207; S.D. Clark, 'Mining Society in British Columbia and the Yukon,' in W.P. Ward and R.A.J. McDonald, eds., *British Columbia: Historical Readings*; and R.T. Wright, *Remember Barkerville: A Gold Rush Adventure* (V: Special Interest Publications 1984).

The subject of education is addressed in several excellent studies: D.L. Maclaurin, 'Education before the Gold Rush,' *BCHQ* 2 (Oct. 1938): 247–63; F. Henry Johnson, *A History of Public Education in British Columbia* (V: UBC Publications Centre 1964); Johnson, *John Jessop: Gold Seeker and Educator* (V: Mitchell 1971); Gordon Selmon, 'Adult Education in Barkerville, 1863 to 1875,' *BCS* 9 (Spring 1971): 38–54; J. Barman, *Growing Up British in British Columbia: Boys in Private School* (V: UBCP 1984); and Barman, 'Transfer, Imposition or Consensus? The Emergence of Educational Structures in Nineteenth-Century British Columbia,' in Nancy M. Sheehan, J. Donald Wilson, and David C. Jones, eds., *Schools in the West: Essays in Educational History* (Calgary, Alta.: Detselig 1986). On churches, many of which were educational institutions as well as religious ones, see J.C. Goodfellow, 'John Hall: Pioneer Presbyterian in British Columbia,' *BCHQ* 7 (Jan. 1943): 31–48; T.E. Jessett, 'The Church of England in the Old Oregon Country,' *BCHQ* 17 (July–Oct. 1953): 197–205; Sister Mary Margaret Down, *A Century of Service, 1858–1958: A History of the Sisters of Saint Ann* (VI: Sisters of Saint Ann 1966); and Edith E. Down, 'The History of Catholic Education in British Columbia, 1847–1900,' CCHA, *Study Sessions* 50/2 (1983): 569–90.

Given the uncertainties of gold mining, the small fortunes made by some of the people servicing the industry likely outstripped the returns of many a miner. Mining was an expensive enterprise, particularly when the easily accessible surface gold was panned out. Most miners did not have the capital to sink shafts, haul out rock, and build extensive flumes and were forced to work in partnership with others or as wage labourers on some of the larger claims. Despite the optimistic tone of many of the handbooks for prospective miners, for every fortune made by a Cariboo Cameron (see 'John Cameron,' *DCB*, vol. 11) or a Billy Barker (see 'William Barker,' *DCB*, vol. 12), there were many more failures. Paul Phillips makes this clear in 'The Underground Economy: The Mining Frontier to 1920,' in Rennie Warburton and David Coburn, eds., *Workers, Capital and the State: Selected Papers* (V: UBCP 1988). So too do F.W. Howay, *The Early History of the Fraser River Mines* (VI: Banfield 1926), and Allan S. Trueman, 'Placer Gold Mining in Northern British Columbia, 1860–1880,' in T. Thorner, ed., *Sa ts'e: Historical Perspectives on Northern British Columbia*.

The contrast between dreams and reality is easily discerned in the many contemporary accounts of life in the gold-fields, among the most useful of which are James Anderson, *Sawney's Letters and Cariboo Rhymes* (1895; repr. VI: Queen's Printer 1962); W. Champness, *To Cariboo and Back* (1862; repr. Fairfield, WA: Ye Galleon Press 1972); Kinahan Cornwallis, *The New El Dorado; or British Columbia* (L: T.C. Newby 1858); William Downie, *Hunting for Gold: Reminiscences [sic] of Personal Experience and Research in the Early Days of the Pacific Coast from Alaska to Panama* (San Francisco, CA: California Publishing 1893); William Carew Hazlitt, *The Great Gold Fields of Cariboo* (1862; repr. VI: Klanak Press 1984); R. Byron Johnson, *A Very Far West Indeed: A Few Rough Experiences on the North-West Pacific Coast* (L: Sampson, Low, Marston, Low & Searle 1872); R.L. Reid, 'Two Narratives of the Fraser River Gold Rush,' *BCHQ* 16 (July 1952): 221–31; Reid, 'To the Fraser River Mines in 1858,' *BCHQ* 1 (Oct. 1937): 243–53; D.B. Smith, 'Harry Guillod's Journal of a Trip to Cariboo, 1862,' *BCHQ* 19 (July–Oct. 1955): 187–232; Alfred Penderell Waddington, *The Fraser Mines Vindicated; or, the History of Four Months* (VI: P. De Garro 1858); and Mark Sweeten Wade, *The Cariboo Road* (VI: Haunted Bookshop 1979).

Despite their importance, gold mining and the businesses that provided services to the miners were not the only kinds of economic activity on the mainland. For a greater sense of variety see F.W. Howay, 'Early Shipping in Burrard Inlet, 1863–1870,' *BCHQ* 1 (Jan. 1937): 3–20; Howay, 'Coal-

Mining on Burrard Inlet,' *BCHQ* 4 (Jan. 1940): 1–20; and W.E. Ireland, 'Early Flour Mills in British Columbia,' parts 1 and 2, *BCHQ* 5 (Apr./July 1940): 89–109, 191–213. The roots of a future major staple are highlighted in James Morton, *The Enterprising Mr. Moody, the Bumptious Captain Stamp: The Lives and Times of Vancouver's Lumber Pioneers* (North Vancouver, BC: J.J. Douglas 1977). See also 'Sewell Prescott Moody' and 'Edward Stamp,' in *DCB*, vol. 10.

British Columbia's social diversity and economic uncertainty animated its politics. Though both the island and the mainland were characterized by cultural diversity, the former, because of the predominance of Hudson's Bay Company men and English administrators among its elite, was considered more 'British' and the latter, more 'Canadian,' perhaps because of the presence of the Overlanders as well as the Americans. These labels were more than simple descriptions of social life; they were a shorthand or a code for describing political divisions. What made Vancouver Island 'British' and British Columbia 'Canadian' was not just the national origins of its more prominent inhabitants but a particular attitude toward government. From the days of the Hudson's Bay Company's proprietorship there were always those on Vancouver Island who considered the company's rule to be arbitrary and counter to the interests of the colony, an impression that continued despite the establishment of a House of Assembly in 1856. After 1858 the handful of dissenters on the island were joined by many on the mainland, where government continued under executive writ. For late-nineteenth-century immigrants, many of whom had come from colonies or countries with a long tradition of representative and responsible government, politics in British Columbia seemed anachronistic and autocratic indeed. The 'Britishness' that was associated with Vancouver Island, then, represented an elitist, undemocratic, and perhaps paternal political perspective. 'Canadian,' on the other hand, signified a political stance that was more populist and egalitarian.

Though the Fraser and Cariboo rushes fuelled the colonial economies of British Columbia and Vancouver Island, by 1865 both were running out of gas. With the easily accessible surface gold gone, mining had become a much more capital-intensive enterprise, well beyond the means of many miners. The decline in mining activity caused by the higher costs, in combination with a decline in the international economy, plunged both colonies into financial difficulties and raised the question of union. While uniting the island and mainland seemed sensible from an economic standpoint, union proved to be controversial because of the political divisions between the two colonies. Locating the new capital of the united colonies was contentious, for there was more at stake than economic gain. As M.A. Ormsby explains in *British Columbia: A History*, locating the capital symbolized the struggle between the political ideals of mainland populism and island paternalism. To the 'Canadians,' the triumph of Victoria over New Westminster in 1868 only proved the correctness of their claims and the need to be even more vigilant and critical of those who governed them.

The politics of Confederation were animated by the same interplay of social diversity and economic uncertainty and illustrated the same geographical split as the debate over union. The union of the colonies in 1866 did not begin to solve the economic problems that plagued the two regions and, making things worse, American imperialism once again threatened British Columbia's existence. The day after the British North America Act was proclaimed, the United States purchased Alaska, effectively enclosing British Columbia. See J.R. Gibson, 'The Sale of Russian America to the United States,' in S.F. Starr, ed., *Russia's American Colony*. In the face of its mounting debt and the American juggernaut, as well as British disinterest in her distant possessions, British Columbia had three options: the first was to retain its status as a British colony and struggle along as best it could; the second was union with the four provinces of the newly formed Dominion of Canada; and the final option was American annexation.

The events leading up to the determination to select the Canadian path of Confederation are the subject, as one would expect, of many studies. The most noteworthy are W.N. Sage, 'From Colony to Province,' *BCHQ* 3 (Jan. 1939): 1–14; W.E. Ireland, 'The Annexation Petition of 1869,' *BCHQ* 4 (Oct. 1940): 267–87; K.A. Waites, 'Responsible Government and Confederation: The Popular Movement for Popular Government,' *BCHQ* 6 (Apr. 1942): 97–123; I. Bescoby, 'A Colonial Administration: An Analysis of Administration in British Columbia, 1869–1871,' *Canadian Public Administration* 10/1 (Mar. 1967): 49–104, partially reprinted in J. Friesen and H.K. Ralston, eds., *Historical Essays on British Columbia*; W. George Shelton, ed., *British Columbia and Confederation* (VI: University of Victoria 1967); Charles Hou and Marlena Morgan, *The Destiny of British Columbia: Confederation or Annexation?* (V: BC Teachers' Federation 1984); and Charles John Fedorak, 'The United States Consul in Victoria and the Political Destiny of British Columbia, 1862–1870,' *BCS* 79 (Autumn 1988): 3–23.

Prominent actors have also come in for their share of scrutiny. *The Reminiscences of Doctor John Sebastian Helmcken*, edited by D.B. Smith, records impressions of the debate left by one of the principal opponents of Confederation (though he was eventually won over). The same reminiscences are the subject of W.E. Ireland, 'Helmcken's Diary of the Confederation

Negotiations, 1870,' *BCHQ* 4 (Apr. 1940): 111–28. Another anti-Confederate is dealt with in Gordon R. Elliott, 'Henry P. Pellew Crease: Confederation or No Confederation,' *BCS* (Winter 1971–2): 63–74. On the other
hand, for a study of a prominent proponent see W.N. Sage, 'Amor De Cosmos: Journalist and Politician,' *BCHQ* 8 (July 1944): 189–212. Finally, there
are the many entries in the *DCB*: in addition to that on Amor De Cosmos
see 'Frederick Seymour,' vol. 9; 'Robert William Weir Carrall,' vol. 10; 'Sir
Anthony Musgrave,' vol. 11; 'John Robson,' vol. 12; and 'Clement Francis
Cornwall,' 'Sir Henry Pering Pellew Crease,' and 'Sir Joseph William
Trutch,' vol. 13.

CONCLUSION

After the British Columbia Act was proclaimed in 1871, J.S. Helmcken, a
long-time resident of the colony, noted that though the new province was in
Canada, it was not yet of it. Owing to its location on the edge of a continent,
with the Pacific to the west and the Rocky Mountains to the east, and with a
transcontinental railway more than a decade away, British Columbia's position in the Dominion was something of an abstraction. In a sense, despite the
rancorous debate that had filled the chambers of the Legislative Assembly,
Confederation changed very little for British Columbia. The region had
been in Spanish, Russian, British, and American spheres of influence but
British Columbia as a whole was not identifiably Spanish, Russian, British,
or American. Though each of these nations had left an imprint – some more
lasting than others – on the region, in the form of place-names in some cases
to political culture in others, British Columbia could not be described precisely as Spanish, Russian, American, or even a British place, much less a
Canadian one. In part, this was due to distance. British Columbia was simply
too far away from the imperial centres of all these powers for them to have
exerted a profound effect on the colony's identity even if they had wanted to.
And they really did not. These nations saw British Columbia, first and fore-
most, as a resource base to be exploited for imperial glory.

Geopolitics may have piqued interest in British Columbia, but international economics and the pursuit of individual gain also shaped social relations within the region. The resource-based economy extracted a variety of
peoples from their homes and deposited them in an alien environment,
placing them cheek by jowl with a number of alien cultures, leaving all of
them to work out some sort of accommodation with each other. Given their
motives for coming to British Columbia, many people centred their lives on
work. Whether it was a fur trade post, a stretch of creek-bed in the Cariboo

fields, a logging camp on Burrard Inlet, or one of the towns that had sprung up on the margins of such locations to service them, community was intensely local and focused on making a living. The same was true even in Victoria and New Westminster: community could be said to centre on work – the work of administering the colony. The social elite of both places consisted of government and military personnel. Equally importantly, however, community in both these administrative centres and the smaller interior towns also centred on ethnicity. British settlers, like Susan Allison, and the Chinese, who worked the banks of the Fraser or ran laundries and general stores in Barkerville, conducted their lives in British Columbia according to the norms and practices of the old world societies they had come from. Regardless of whether work or ethnicity was the focal point, however, communities in British Columbia were more closely tied to worlds beyond provincial boundaries than to one another. Not only did the vagaries and vicissitudes of the international staple economy 'make' and 'unmake' British Columbia, as W.A. Baillie-Grohmann observed, but many of its inhabitants looked beyond the region's borders to define themselves and their sense of place. The province was a political construction foisted on a handful of loosely connected Native and non-Native communities, which, though they had an integrity of their own, did not fit together into a cohesive whole. Life in the region prior to 1871 was lived on two scales, the local and the international, and while the two existed in a dialectical relationship, each was to a certain degree separate from the other. There was very little 'colonial' identity so that in a sense 'British Columbia' did not really exist yet. It would have to await the integrating effects of a larger population, state control, and generations of historians.

J.M. BUMSTED

British North America in Its Imperial and International Context

As all students of Canadian history should quickly learn to appreciate, history is as much subject to fashions and fads as any other cultural endeavour. Once upon a time in Canada, certainly within the lifetime of more than a few of its seniors, this dominion was an integral part of the 'British Empi-ah' and its citizens were British subjects, whether they liked it or not. The decline of this state of affairs is to a considerable extent inextricably interwoven within the story of Canada, and the process of Canadianization has been a slow, gradual, and relatively recent one. Canada's place within the British Empire was secure in much of the historical writings of French Canadians until after the turn of the century, and continued to be so until well into the twentieth century in the writing of history by English Canadians. Indeed, English-speaking Canadians traditionally were taught English (seldom British) history as though its development and Canada's were virtually interchangeable – as Paul T. Phillips points out in *Britain's Past in Canada: The Teaching and Writing of British History* (V: UBCP 1989). The process of disengagement can be followed in Carl Berger, *The Writing of Canadian History: Aspects of English-Canadian Historical Writing since 1900* (1976; 2nd ed., T: UTP 1986), and Serge Gagnon, *Quebec and Its Historians: The Twentieth Century* (M: Harvest House 1985).

The shift to a Canadian perspective has perhaps in recent years gone too far, since many Canadian historians working on topics with important imperial dimensions – particularly in the so-called colonial period before 1867 – have not appreciated some of the shifts in interpretation and new evidence advanced by recent international literature on imperial subjects. But imperial history relating to British North America has not stood still. Part of what has happened, as we shall see subsequently, is that most of the current practitioners of what used to be called 'Imperial History' no longer regard themselves in such a light, but view themselves instead as cultural, or legal, or immigration historians. 'Imperial History' has come to be associated with a particular constellation and combination of political, constitutional, and economic developments, partly because of the way it was (and still is, in some places) taught. As Phillip A. Buckner pointed out at the beginning of his contribution to this guide's predecessor, the history of Canada was once seen as 'the history of the extension and evolution of British institutions overseas.' Canadian history is no longer so simple, but the history of the extension and evolution of British peoples and institutions overseas – particularly in non-political terms – remains an important part of the whole.

At the same time that Canada became less interested in the imperial connection, the Empire became less interested in Canada. Traditional British history devoted a good deal of attention to the early British Empire, seeing the coming to maturity of the so-called settlement colonies (including Canada) as a matter of great importance. The best example of such work can be found in J. Holland Rose et al., eds., *The Cambridge History of the British Empire*, vol. 6, *Canada and Newfoundland* (Cambridge, Eng.: Cambridge University Press 1930). Since World War II, as Britain has given up much of its Empire and the Third World has risen to prominence internationally, British historians have devoted far more attention to Britain's role in Africa and Asia, especially since 1880. Probably the most influential work on British imperialism in recent years has been Ronald Robinson and John Gallagher, with Alice Denny, *Africa and the Victorians: The Official Mind of Imperialism* (1961; 2nd ed., L: MAC 1981), which sparked a major debate documented in William Roger Louis, ed., *Imperialism: The Robinson and Gallagher Controversy* (NY: New Viewpoints 1976). In this discussion over late-nineteenth-century imperialism, Canada and the other settlement colonies have been quite irrelevant, and they are given little attention in most of the recent surveys of imperialism, such as Bernard Porter, *The Lion's Share: A Short History of British Imperialism, 1850–1970* (L: Longman 1975), Ronald Hyam, *Britain's Imperial Century, 1815–1914: A Study of Empire and Expansion* (L: Batsford 1976), and C.C. Eldridge, *Victorian Imperialism* (L: Hodder & Stoughton 1978).

Even for the earlier periods of the British Empire, a global perspective has become fashionable. Recent examples include Angus Calder, *Revolutionary Empire: The Rise of the English-Speaking Empires from the Fifteenth Century to the 1780s* (NY: Dutton 1981); P.J. Marshall and Glyndwr Williams, *The Great Map of Mankind: British Perceptions of the World in the Age of Enlightenment* (L: Dent 1982); C.A. Bayly, *Imperial Meridian: The British*

Empire and the World, 1780–1830 (L: Longman 1989), which begins in the Muslim empires and ends with colonial society in the early nineteenth century; and Bernard Bailyn and Philip D. Morgan, eds., *Strangers within the Realm: Cultural Margins of the First British Empire* (Chapel Hill, NC: University of North Carolina Press 1991), which explores cultural developments in a variety of colonial situations spread around the globe.

For a recent discussion of imperial historiography, consult the articles in two works edited by C.C. Eldridge, *British Imperialism in the Nineteenth Century* (L: MAC 1984) and *From Rebellion to Patriation: Canada and Britain in the Nineteenth and Twentieth Centuries* (Aberystwyth, Wales: Canadian Studies Group in Wales 1989). An older but not entirely outdated introduction can be found in Robin W. Winks, ed., *The Historiography of the British Empire-Commonwealth: Trends, Interpretations and Resources* (Durham, NC: Duke University Press 1966). While the recent focus of imperial study has been on the African and Asian empire (and its devolution) after 1880, students should not be led to believe that imperial history relating to British North America was permanently frozen somewhere in the 1950s. There has been much good new work done, and there is plenty more to be done.

Some alternate ways to the traditional imperialist categories for examining and evaluating Canada's prenational role in the international scene do exist. One of these alternatives is to employ Marxist categories of analysis, as does Eric J. Hobsbawm in his *The Age of Capital, 1848–1875* (NY: Scribner 1975) and *The Age of Empire, 1875–1914* (NY: Pantheon Books 1987). A specific application of this approach to Canada may be found in R.T. Naylor, *Canada in the European Age, 1453–1919* (V: New Star 1987), which is a far better and more stimulating book than its lack of enthusiastic reception by the historical fraternity would suggest. Another alternative is to situate Canada within the multinational Atlantic World rather than within a particular empire. A good example here is Nicholas P. Canny and Anthony Pagden, eds., *Colonial Identity in the Atlantic World, 1500–1800* (Princeton, NJ: Princeton University Press 1987), which features a fascinating chapter 'Nouvelle-France/Quebec/Canada' (mainly after 1800) by Gilles Paquet and Jean-Pierre Wallot.

Still other international perspectives for Canada are possible. One is the North Atlantic Triangle, a term popularized by John Bartlet Brebner in his influential *North Atlantic Triangle: The Interplay of Canada, the United States and Great Britain* (T: RP 1945; repr., intro. Donald Grant Creighton, T: M&S 1966) and continued by John L. Finlay in *Canada in the North Atlantic Triangle: Two Centuries of Social Change* (T: OUP 1975). The transatlantic triangle is more frequently reduced to the continental duality and usually called 'Canadian-American relations.' See, for example, Reginald C. Stuart, *United States Expansionism and British North America, 1775–1871* (Chapel Hill, NC: University of North Carolina Press 1988), Edelgard E. Mahant and Graeme S. Mount, *An Introduction to Canadian-American Relations* (2nd ed., T: Nelson 1989), J.L. Granatstein and Norman Hillmer, *For Better or for Worse: Canada and the United States to the 1990s* (T: CCP 1991), and Gordon T. Stewart, *The American Response to Canada since 1776* (East Lansing, MI: Michigan State University Press 1992). By and large the field of Canadian-American relations has suffered from the same problems as Imperialism, chiefly a very political and diplomatic emphasis, although recent work has begun dealing with economic matters. A somewhat different perspective on the same relationship, demonstrating its broader analytical possibilities, is provided by S.F. Wise and Robert Craig Brown, *Canada Views the United States: Nineteenth-Century Political Attitudes* (T: MAC 1967).

REFERENCE WORKS AND DOCUMENTARY COLLECTIONS

The standard journal for imperial history remains the *Journal of Imperial and Commonwealth History* (L: F. Cass 1972–), although its focus tends to be on the more recent period in the Third World. Useful bibliographies, besides those mentioned earlier, include Stanley Pargellis and D.J. Medley, eds., *Bibliography of British History: The Eighteenth Century, 1749–1789* (Oxford: Clarendon Press 1951), Lucy M. Brown and Ian R. Christie, eds., *Bibliography of British History, 1789–1851* (Oxford: Clarendon Press 1977), and H.J. Hanham, ed., *Bibliography of British History, 1851–1914* (Oxford: Clarendon Press 1976). The Royal Historical Society of Britain sponsors an *Annual Bibliography of British and Irish History* (L: Harvest Press 1976–), which lists articles in periodicals; the annual 'List of Publications on the Economic and Social History of Great Britain and Ireland,' in the *Economic History Review* includes a valuable section, 'Overseas Trade and Overseas Relations'; and the *Canadian Historical Review* (1920–) produces in every issue a listing entitled 'Recent Publications Relating to Canada.' When the *CHR* or somebody else finally gets these listings on line in the computer, students may actually have access to a relatively complete database for periodical articles in Canadian history.

The best bibliography for the older works, particularly strong on obscure journal articles and edited versions of documents, is Claude Thibault, comp., *Bibliographia Canadiana* (Don Mills, Ont.: Longman 1973). Students have a tendency to neglect the older literature on the grounds that it must surely have been superseded by some trendy new work. But in many cases – especially in the nineteenth and early twentieth centuries – authors, editors, and compilers tended to include in their works large excerpts from unpublished papers in their hands, which sometimes have now disappeared, and to edit and publish them at length in the journals. Even if the documents are now in an archival depository, students can frequently best gain access to them through the older works and journals. Research on 'original documents' (not quite the same thing as 'unpublished manuscripts') can be done from any decent research library. And for factual content, older studies are often more detailed. Many works listed herein and published before 1900 will be available on microform through the publication program of the Canadian Institute for Historical Microreproductions, which is producing all Canadiana before 1900 on microfiche cards; not all libraries have integrated this substantial listing into their online or card catalogues, and students should consult with their librarians for checklists and availability.

The serious student who wishes to examine primary documents, many of which are available only in the United Kingdom, needs to know about *A Guide to Manuscripts Relating to America in Great Britain and Ireland: A Revision of the Guide Edited in 1961 by B.R. Crick and Miriam Alman*, edited by John W. Raimo under the general supervision of Dennis Welland (Westport, CT: Meckler Books for the British Association for American Studies 1979), and the various publications of the (British) Royal Commission on Historical Manuscripts, including *Guide to the Location of Collections Described in the Reports and Calendars Series, 1870–1980* (L: HMSO 1982). The commission, located in London, near Chancery Lane, maintains a consolidated listing of private manuscripts in British repositories. Most of the public papers relating to the various colonies of the British Empire and to British colonial policy and action (including the familiar Colonial Office series) are located at the Public Record Office in Kew Gardens. For a guide see Ralph Bernard Pugh, *The Records of the Colonial and Dominions Offices* (L: Her Majesty's Stationery Office 1964). See too Valerie Bloomfield, *Guide to Resources for Canadian Studies in Britain, with Some Reference to Relevant Collections in Europe* (2nd ed., L: British Association for Canadian Studies 1983).

Collections of primary documents on Canada and the British Empire include Arthur George Doughty et al., eds., *Documents Relating to the Constitutional History of Canada*, 3 vols. (O: Public Archives of Canada 1907–35), and W.P.M. Kennedy, ed., *Statutes, Treaties and Documents of the Canadian Constitution, 1713–1929* (2nd ed., T: OUP 1930). Both the Kennedy and the Doughty collections are much neglected by professors and students in introductory courses these days. Other collections of value are K.N. Bell and W.P. Morrell, eds., *Select Documents on British Colonial Policy, 1830–60* (Oxford: Clarendon Press 1928), and Vincent Todd Harlow and A. Frederick Madden, eds., *British Colonial Developments, 1774–1834* (Oxford: Clarendon Press 1953).

MILITARY HISTORY

Five general points need to be made about the military history of the period 1763–1867. First, although British North America had its own militia units and privateers, the overall direction of military activity was in the hands of the British army and navy, and Canadian military operations were merely a minor fragment of the larger British picture. Second, most of the warfare or threat of warfare involved the Americans, who have their own versions of the various military conflicts in which they have been involved. Third, Canadian, British, and American military activities invariably impinged upon and involved the various Native peoples of the St Lawrence and Great Lakes region. The consequence of the preceding statements is the fourth point, which is that there are really several quite separate historiographies of military events – Canadian, British, American, and, more recently, Native. Finally, apart from recent analyses of Native participation, military history is currently one of the least fashionable subjects in the historian's repertoire, and most of the standard literature is very old, unrevised, and unrepentant. Much of the newer research is summarized in the biographical sketches of the multivolume *Dictionary of Canadian Biography* (T: UTP 1966–).

One of Canada's leading military historians, Desmond Morton, has written in his *A Military History of Canada* (rev. ed., E: Hurtig 1990), 'Someday someone will write a comprehensive book about the British army in Canada or about the pre-Confederation Canadian militia.' More to the point, someday someone will write a book which fully encompasses the British army, the British navy, the militia, and the privateers – and does a decent job of the war on the domestic front as well. In the meantime, besides Morton's balanced but brief survey, there are a number of useful overviews of Canada's military past. J. Mackay Hitsman, *Safeguarding Canada, 1763–1871* (T: UTP 1968), adequately covers this period, although he is weaker on the militia and the home front; but see also George F.G. Stanley, *Canada's Soldiers: The Military History of an Unmilitary People* (3rd ed., T: MAC 1974), D. Morton, *Canada and War: A Military and Political History* (T: Butterworths 1981), and Gwynne Dyer and Tina Viljoen, *The Defence of Can-*

ada, vol. 1, *In the Arms of the Empire* (T: M&S 1990). Mary Beacock Fryer, *Battlefields of Canada* (T: Dundurn 1986), is an attractive popularized work, copiously illustrated. An overall picture of the British navy in defence of Canada – even an old one – is sorely lacking. Part of the problem is suggested by Commander Tony German, *The Sea Is at Our Gates: The History of the Canadian Navy* (T: M&S 1990), which devotes a full ten pages to Canadian naval history before the establishment of the Canadian navy in 1910.

The period of the American Rebellion, 1763–83, is well served by the useful bibliography complied by Richard L. Blanco, *The War of the American Revolution: A Selected Annotated Bibliography of Published Sources* (NY: Garland 1984), and by the maps in plate 44, 'Indian War and American Invasion,' in *Historical Atlas of Canada*, vol. 1, *From the Beginning to 1800*, ed. R. Cole Harris (T: UTP [1987]). For most of the period before the beginning of actual warfare, British military attention was directed at the Old Northwest, which the government hoped to maintain as an Indian reserve. A general picture of British policy may be followed in Alfred LeRoy Burt, *The Old Province of Quebec* (T: RP 1933; repr., intro. Hilda Neatby, 2 vols., T: M&S 1968), H. Neatby, *Quebec: The Revolutionary Age, 1760–1791* (T: M&S 1966), and Michel Brunet, *Les Canadiens après la Conquête, 1759–1775: de la révolution canadienne à la révolution américaine* (M: Fides 1969).

Native resistance in the Great Lakes area in the wake of the Conquest, variously styled the Pontiac Uprising or the Beaver War, is discussed in Howard Henry Peckham, *Pontiac and the Indian Uprising* (Princeton, NJ: Princeton University Press 1947; repr. Chicago, IL: University of Chicago Press 1961); Dorothy V. Jones, *License for Empire: Colonialism by Treaty in Early America* (Chicago, IL: University of Chicago Press 1982); Francis Jennings, *Empire of Fortune: Crowns, Colonies, and Tribes in the Seven Years War in America* (NY: Norton 1988); Peter S. Schmalz, *The Ojibwa of Southern Ontario* (T: UTP 1991); and 'Pontiac' and 'Wabbicommicot,' *DCB*, vol. 3 (1974). Also useful is Paul L. Stevens, *A King's Colonel at Niagara, 1774–1776: Lt. Col. John Caldwell and the Beginnings of the American Revolution on the New York Frontier* (Youngstown, NY: Old Fort Niagara Association 1987). Two new works worthy of attention are Richard White, *The Middle Ground: Indians, Empires, and Republics in the Great Lakes Region, 1650–1815* (Cambridge, Eng.: Cambridge University Press 1991), and Gregory Evans Dowd, *A Spirited Resistance: The North American Indian Struggle for Unity, 1745–1815* (Baltimore, MD: Johns Hopkins University Press 1992).

With the outbreak of actual rebellion in 1775 the Americans decided to invade 'Canada' (that is, Quebec). The invasion is given overall consideration in Justin Harvey Smith, *Our Struggle for the Fourteenth Colony: Canada and the American Revolution*, 2 vols. (1907; repr. NY: Da Capo 1974), the title of which tells it all; Gustave Lanctôt, *Canada and the American Revolution, 1774–1783* (T: Clarke, Irwin 1967); G.F.G. Stanley, *Canada Invaded, 1775–1776* (T: Hakkert 1973); and Robert McConnell Hatch, *Thrust for Canada: The American Attempt on Quebec in 1775–1776* (Boston, MA: Houghton Mifflin 1979). The *DCB* has entries for most of the military leaders, including, among the attackers, 'Richard Montgomery,' vol. 4 (1979), and 'Benedict Arnold,' vol. 5 (1983), and, among the defenders, 'Allan Maclean,' vol. 4, and 'Guy Carleton, 1st Baron Dorchester,' vol. 5. These may be supplemented by Paul R. Reynolds, *Guy Carleton: A Biography* (T: Gage 1980), and M.B. Fryer, *Allan Maclean, Jacobite General: The Life of an Eighteenth Century Career Soldier* (T: Dundurn 1987). The curious career of Moses Hazen, a resident of Quebec who supported the Americans and recruited *Canadiens* on their account, is told in Allan S. Everest, *Moses Hazen and the Canadian Refugees in the American Revolution* (Syracuse, NY: Syracuse University Press 1976).

The Americans were beaten back in 1776, and a year later General John Burgoyne returned the favour, invading the United States from Canada, only to surrender his army at the Battle of Saratoga. The Burgoyne expedition is discussed in William Leete Stone, *The Campaign of Lieut. Gen. John Burgoyne and the Expedition of Lieut. Col. Barry St. Leger* (Albany, NY: J. Munsell 1877), and its leader, in Richard J. Hargrove, *General John Burgoyne* (Newark, NJ: University of Delaware Press 1983). A useful study of Britain's general military problems in America, including an insightful look at the débâcle of Saratoga, is contained in R. Arthur Bowler, *Logistics and the Failure of the British Army in America, 1775–1783* (Princeton, NJ: Princeton University Press 1975).

After Saratoga the British turned to the Loyalists and to guerilla warfare, partly because France entered the war and kept Britain busy in Europe and elsewhere. A good overview of the new policy and its results is Paul H. Smith, *Loyalists and Redcoats: A Study in British Revolutionary Policy* (Chapel Hill, NC: University of North Carolina Press 1964), which is highly critical of British Loyalist policy for its lack of realism. Also consult Ernest A. Cruikshank, *The Story of Butler's Rangers and the Settlement of Niagara* (Welland, Ont.: Tribune Printing House 1893); Howard Swiggett, *War out of Niagara: Walter Butler and the Tory Rangers* (NY: Columbia University Press 1933; repr. Port Washington, NY: Kennikat 1963); North Callahan, *Royal Raiders: The Tories of the American Revolution* (Indianapolis, IL: Bobbs-Merrill 1963); Hazel C. Mathews, *The Mark of Honour* (T: UTP 1965), a fine and often neglected study of Highland Scots in New York and later in British North America; M.B. Fryer, *King's Men: The Soldier Founders of Ontario* (T: Dundurn 1980); Robert S. Allen, gen. ed., *The Loyal Americans: The Military Rôle of the Loyalist Provincial Corps and Their Settlement in British North America, 1775–1784* (O: National Museums of Canada 1983); Earle Thomas, *Sir John Johnson, Loyalist Baronet* (T: Dundurn 1986); and the *DCB* entries 'John Butler' and 'Walter Butler,' vol. 4; and 'Edward Jessup,' vol. 5. The role of Fort Niagara, a critical meeting point for Loyalists and Natives, is examined in Bruce G. Wilson, *The Enterprises of Robert Hamilton: A Study of Wealth and Influence in Early Upper Canada, 1776–1812* (O: CUP 1983).

The guerilla warfare in New York inevitably involved Native peoples, especially the Iroquois of New York State. Barbara Graymont, *The Iroquois in the American Revolution* (Syracuse, NY: Syracuse University Press 1972), is a magisterial overview. In addition students should consult W.L. Stone, *Life of Joseph Brant-Thayendanegea: Including the Border Wars of the American Revolution*, 2 vols. (NY: A.V. Blake 1838; repr. NY: Kraus 1969); Charles M. Johnston, ed., *Valley of the Six Nations: A Collection of Documents on the Indian Lands of the Grand River* (T: CS 1964); Donald A. Grindge, Jr, *The Iroquois and the Founding of the American Nation* ([San Francisco, CA]: Indian Historian Press 1977); *The Iroquois in the American Revolution: 1976 Conference Proceedings* (Rochester, NY: Rochester Museum and Science Center 1981); Isabel Thompson Kelsay, *Joseph Brant, 1743–1807: Man of Two Worlds* (Syracuse, NY: Syracuse University Press 1984); R.S. Allen, *His Majesty's Indian Allies: British Indian Policy in the Defence of Canada, 1774–1815* (T: Dundurn 1992); and the *DCB* entry 'Thayendanegea (Joseph Brant),' vol. 5.

The war in the Atlantic region was considerably less dramatic, consisting mainly of small-scale privateering and guerilla raids. The most influential overview of the situation in the Maritimes is J.B. Brebner, *The Neutral Yankees of Nova Scotia: A Marginal Colony during the Revolutionary Years* (1937; repr., intro. W.S. MacNutt, T: M&S 1969). Alternative or modified readings are Wilfred Brenton Kerr, *The Maritime Provinces of British North America and the American Revolution* (Sackville, NB: Busy East Press 1941; repr. NY: Russell and Russell 1970); G.T. Stewart and George A. Rawlyk, *A People Highly Favoured of God: The Nova Scotia Yankees and the American Revolution* (T: MAC 1972); Rawlyk, *Nova Scotia's Massachusetts: A Study of Massachusetts–Nova Scotia Relations, 1630 to 1784* (M: MQUP 1973); and Donald Desserud, 'Nova Scotia and the American Revolution: A Study of Neutrality and Moderation in the Eighteenth Century,' in Margaret Conrad, ed., *Making Adjustments: Change and Continuity in Planter Nova Scotia, 1759–1800* (F: AP 1991). All of the foregoing have been greatly influenced by Brebner's concept of Yankee neutrality, and there is really not an alternate interpretation, although I suggest the outlines of one – based on a Civil War model – in David J. Bercuson et al., *Colonies: Canada to 1867* (T: MHR 1992), ch. 4. The attitude of Native peoples in the region toward the struggle is outlined in Leslie F.S. Upton, *Micmacs and Colonists: Indian-White Relations in the Maritimes, 1713–1867* (V: UBCP 1979).

Turning to the actual events themselves, a useful source is Frederic Kidder, *Military Operations in Eastern Maine and Nova Scotia during the Revolution: Chiefly Compiled from the Journals and Letters of Colonel John Allan, with Notes and a Memoir of Col. John Allan* (Albany, NY: J. Munsell 1867). The one major military operation in the Maritimes was the 'invasion' of the Chignecto Peninsula and the attack on Fort Cumberland in 1776, which can be followed in J.W. Porter, *Memoir of Col. Jonathan Eddy of Eddington, Me.* (Augusta, ME: 1877); Daniel Cobb Harvey, 'Machias and the Invasion of Nova Scotia,' CHA *AR* (1932): 17–28; W.B. Kerr, 'The American Invasion of Nova Scotia, 1776–7,' *Canadian Defence Quarterly* 13 (1936): 433–45; Maxwell Vesey, 'When New Brunswick Suffered Invasion,' *DR* 19 (1939): 197–204; J.H. Ahlin, *Maine Rubicon: Downeast Settlers during the American Revolution* (Calais, ME: Calais Advertiser Press 1966); and Ernest A. Clarke, 'Cumberland Planters and the Aftermath of the Attack on Fort Cumberland,' in M. Conrad, ed., *They Planted Well: New England Planters in Maritime Canada* (F: AP 1988). There are also *DCB* entries for the major players in the sorry events of the invasion: 'Ambroise Saint-Aubin' and 'Pierre Tomah,' vol. 4; and 'John Allan,' 'Jonathan Eddy,' 'Seth Noble,' and 'Israel Perley,' vol. 5.

The British navy had a difficult job in defending the Atlantic provinces but generally succeeded. A useful bibliography of the war at sea is Myron J. Smith, Jr, *Navies in the American Revolution: A Bibliography* (Metuchen, NJ: Scarecrow Press 1973). For a documentary record, albeit an American one, consult the multivolume *Naval Documents of the American Revolution* (Washington, DC: US Government Printing Office 1964–) edited by William Bell Clark and W.J. Morgan. Overviews from the British perspective are W.J. James, *The British Navy in Adversity: A Study of the War of American Independence* (NY: Russell and Russell 1970), and Nicholas Tracy, *Navies, Deterrence, and American Independence: Britain and Seapower in the 1760s and 1770s* (V: UBCP 1988). The defence of the fisheries during the rebellion is the focus of Olaf Uwe Janzen, 'The Royal Navy and the Defence of Newfoundland during the American Revolution,' *Acadiensis* 14/1 (Autumn 1984): 28–48, and his 'The American Threat to the Newfoundland Fisheries, 1776–1777,' *American Neptune* 48/3 (Summer 1988): 154–64.

Privateering is discussed in general in John G. Leefe, *The Atlantic Privateers* (H: Petheric 1978), but see also George E.E. Nichols, 'Notes on Nova Scotian Privateers,' NSHS, *Collections* 13 (1908): 111–52; George Mullane, 'The Privateers of Nova Scotia,' NSHS, *Collections* 20 (1921): 17–42; J.E. Mullins, comp., *Liverpool Privateering, 1756–1815* (Liverpool, NS: n.p. 1936); and John Dewar Faibisy, 'Yankee Raiders and the Republican Excursion into Nova Scotia, 1776–1777,' *The Log of Mystic Seaport* 29 (1977): 82–91. The effects of privateering can be best illustrated in *The Diary of Simeon Perkins*, vol. 1, *1766–1780*, ed. Harold Adams Innis; and vol. 2, *1780–1789*, ed. D.C. Harvey and Charles Bruce Fergusson (T: CS 1948, 1961). A good discussion of privateering and its overall effect on the Nova Scotia economy is Julian Gwyn, 'Economic Fluctuations in Wartime Nova Scotia, 1755–1815,' in M. Conrad, ed., *Making Adjustments*.

The next major military confrontation involving Canada was the War of 1812, which produced some of Canada's earliest chauvinistic rhetoric, both at the time and afterwards. Students are forewarned. At the same time the sheer bulk (and frequent overstatements) of older literature combined with the relative lack of much recent study means that many topics in the War of 1812 deserve a re-evaluation; this area is a superb one for student essays. Useful bibliographies are Dwight La Vern Smith, ed., *The War of 1812: An Annotated Bibliography* (NY: Garland 1985), and John C. Fredriksen, ed., *Free Trade and Sailors' Rights: A Bibliography of the War of 1812* (rev. ed., Westport, CT: Greenwood Press 1985). Collections of documents are to be found in: E.A. Cruikshank, ed., *Documentary History of the Campaign upon the Niagara Frontier, 1812–1814*, 9 vols. (Welland, Ont.: Lundy's Lane Historical Society 1896–1908); Joseph Greusel, ed., 'Copies of Papers on File in the Dominion Archives at Ottawa, Canada, Pertaining to the Relations of the British Government with the United States during the Period of the War of 1812,' *Michigan Historical Collections* 15 (1909): 1–745; Cruikshank, ed., *Documents Relating to the Invasion of Canada and the Surrender of Detroit, 1812*, Public Archives of Canada Publication no. 7 (O: Government Printing Bureau 1912); and William Wood, ed., *Select British Documents of the Canadian War of 1812*, 3 vols. in 4 (T: CS 1920–8).

General overviews of this war include Harry L. Coles, *The War of 1812* (Chicago, IL: University of Chicago Press 1965); J.M. Hitsman, *The Incredible War of 1812: A Military History* (T: UTP 1965); Reginald Horsman, *The War of 1812* (NY: Knopf 1969); John K. Mahon, *The War of 1812* (Gainesville, FL: University of Florida Press 1972); Pierre Berton, *The Invasion of Canada, 1812–1813* and *Flames across the Border, 1813–1814* (T: M&S 1980–1); and G.F.G. Stanley, *The War of 1812: Land Operations* (T: MAC/

National Museums of Canada 1983). Coles and Horsman offer the American perspective, which argues that the American declaration of war was legitimate and the conduct of the war sensible if flawed. Berton overstates the contrary Canadian case. An overview of the naval situation is available in Gerald S. Graham, *Sea Power and British North America, 1783–1820: A Study in British Colonial Policy* (1941; repr. NY: Greenwood Press 1968). Christopher D. Hall places the North American struggle in its global context in *British Strategy in the Napoleonic War, 1803–15* (Manchester, Eng.: Manchester University Press 1992).

Much of the tension between Great Britain and the United States between the end of the American Revolution and the War of 1812 revolved around the military posts of the Old Northwest, which Britain surrendered along with the territory in 1783 but refused to abandon. An old but still-useful approach to this quagmire is A.L. Burt, *The United States, Great Britain, and British North America: From the Revolution to the Establishment of Peace after the War of 1812* (T: RP 1940). R. Horsman has written three works bearing on the issue: *Expansion and American Indian Policy, 1783–1812* (East Lansing, MI: Michigan State University Press 1967), *The Frontier in the Formative Years, 1783–1815* (NY: HRW 1970), and *The Diplomacy of the New Republic, 1776–1815* (Arlington Heights, IL: H. Davidson 1985). A highly critical assessment of British policy is given in J. Leitch Wright, Jr, *Britain and the American Frontier, 1783–1815* (Athens, GA: University of Georgia Press 1975).

Caught between American and British designs, the Native peoples of the Old Northwest sought room for independent manoeuvre. The best survey of the problem is Colin G. Calloway, *Crown and Calumet: British-Indian Relations, 1783–1815* (Norman, OK: University of Oklahoma Press 1987), to which now must be added G.E. Dowd, *A Spirited Resistance*, R. White, *The Middle Ground*, and R.S. Allen, *His Majesty's Indian Allies*. P.S. Schmalz provides an analysis of Native reactions in Upper Canada in *The Ojibwa of Southern Ontario*, and G.F.G. Stanley, 'The Indians in the War of 1812,' *CHR* 31/2 (June 1950): 145–65, is still worth consulting. The most important Native leader to emerge during the war was Tecumseh, whose life has taken on mythic qualities. There are a number of biographies and related works: R. David Edmunds, *Tecumseh and the Quest for Indian Leadership* (Boston, MA: Little, Brown 1984), and his biography of Tecumseh's half-brother Tenskwatawa, *The Shawnee Prophet* (Lincoln, NE: University of Nebraska Press 1983); John Sugden, *Tecumseh's Last Stand* (Norman, OK: University of Oklahoma Press 1985); and Allan W. Eckert, *A Sorrow in Our Heart: The Life of Tecumseh* (T: Bantam Books 1992). Especially good is the

entry for Tecumseh by Herbert C.W. Goltz in *DCB*, vol. 5, which summa-
rizes his unpublished thesis. The fashioning of legend is the subject of Carl
F. Klinck, ed., *Tecumseh: Fact and Fiction in Early Records* (1961; 2nd ed., O:
Tecumseh 1978).

Tecumseh was not the only legend produced by the War of 1812. The
reputation of Sir Isaac Brock, the martyred hero of Queenston Heights, for
example, rivals that of his Native ally. Lady Matilda Edgar, *General Brock*
(T: Morang 1904), is typical of early hagiography, but C.P. Stacey's entry
for Brock in *DCB*, vol. 5, is a dose of cold water. A similarly famous character is Laura Secord (Ingersoll), handled most judiciously by Ruth McKenzie
in *Laura Secord: The Legend and the Lady* (T: M&S 1971) and the entry in
DCB, vol. 9 (1976). A study of a less famous but important actor is J.M.
Hitsman, 'Sir George Prevost's Conduct of the Canadian War of 1812,'
CHA AR (1962): 34–43; see too 'Sir George Prevost,' *DCB*, vol. 5. Indeed,
virtually all of the major military actors have entries in the *DCB*.

More detailed accounts of operations in Upper Canada can be found in
Morris Zaslow, ed., *The Defended Border: Upper Canada and the War of 1812*
(T: MAC 1964), a really important collection of essays that has not yet been
superseded. On Lower Canada see Michelle Guitard, *The Militia of the Battle of Châteauguay: A Social History* (O: Parks Canada 1984), which demonstrates, among other things, that French Canadians did fight against the
Americans in the War of 1812. A.S. Everest, *The War of 1812 in the Champlain Valley* (Syracuse, NY: Syracuse University Press 1981), focuses specifically on operations along the frontier between Lower Canada and New
York State, while J. Patrick Wohler examines the hero of that theatre in
Charles de Salaberry: Soldier of the Empire, Defender of Quebec (T: Dundurn
1984). The war in the West is considered in Alec R. Gilpin, *The War of
1812 in the Old Northwest* (T: RP 1958).

For the naval war consult James Barnes, *Naval Actions of the War of 1812*
(NY: Harper 1896; repr. L: Cornmarket Press 1969); C.S. Forester, *The
Age of Fighting Sail: The Story of the Naval War of 1812* (Garden City, NY:
Doubleday 1956); Hugh Francis Pullen, *The 'Shannon' and the 'Chesapeake'*
(T: M&S 1970); Edward W. Eckert, *The Navy Department in the War of
1812* (Gainesville, FL: University of Florida Press 1973); W.A.B. Douglas,
*Gunfire on the Lakes: The Naval War of 1812–1814 on the Great Lakes and
Lake Champlain* (O: National Museums of Canada 1977); William S. Dudley, ed., *The Naval War of 1812: A Documentary History*, vol. 1, *1812*; vol. 2,
1813 (Washington, DC: Naval Historical Center, Department of the Navy
1985–92); and William Jeffrey Welsh and David Curtis Skaggs, eds., *War
on the Great Lakes: Essays Commemorating the 175th Anniversary of the Battle*

of Lake Erie (Kent, OH: Kent State University Press 1991). The course of privateering can be followed in Edgar Stanton Maclay, *A History of American Privateers* (NY: D. Appleton 1924), C.H.J. Snider, *Under the Red Jack: Privateers of the Maritime Provinces of Canada in the War of 1812* (L: M. Hopkinson 1928), and Jerome R. Garitee, *The Republic's Private Navy: The American Privateering Business as Practiced by Baltimore during the War of 1812* (Middletown, CT: Mystic Seaport/Wesleyan University Press 1977).

The War of 1812 was the military high point for the Canadas and British North America, and thereafter everything was, in a sense, downhill. Despite an absence of open warfare and the Rush-Bagot agreement of 1817 limiting armaments on the Great Lakes, however, there was no absence of border tension with the Americans; this theme was developed by Colonel C.P. Stacey in his influential pamphlet *The Undefended Border: The Myth and the Reality*, CHA Historical Booklet no. 1 (O: 1953). The overall situation for this period and beyond is presented by Kenneth Bourne, *Britain and the Balance of Power in North America, 1815–1908* (L: Longmans 1967).

An unexpected series of internal events calling for military action were the Rebellions in the Canadas of 1837–8. Their military aspects are considered in two companion volumes of the Canadian War Museum Historical Publications, Elinor Kyte Senior, *Redcoats and Patriotes: The Rebellions in Lower Canada, 1837–38* (Stittsville, Ont.: Canada's Wings/National Museums of Canada 1985), and M.B. Fryer, *Volunteers & Redcoats, Raiders & Rebels: A Military History of the Rebellions in Upper Canada* (T: Dundurn 1987). Both volumes are copiously illustrated and contain good bibliographies.

The retreat of Great Britain from the defence of British North America is discussed in detail in the old but still-reliable C.P. Stacey, *Canada and the British Army, 1846–1871* (L: Longmans, Green 1936; rev. ed., T: UTP 1963). There were some interesting footnotes on the West Coast, covered in Glynn Barratt, *Russian Shadows on the British Northwest Coast of North America, 1810–1890: A Study of Rejection of Defence Responsibilities* (V: UBCP 1983), and Barry M. Gough, *Gunboat Frontier: British Maritime Authority and Northwest Coast Indians, 1846–1890* (V: UBCP 1984).

The American Civil War, 1861–5, provided another set of military threats and problems. R.W. Winks, *Canada and the United States: The Civil War Years* (1960; 2nd ed., M: Harvest House 1971), sets the general framework, while Oscar A. Kinchen, *Confederate Operations in Canada and the North* (North Quincy, MA: Christopher Publishing House 1970), focuses specifically on the Confederacy's use of Canada as a base for guerilla operations. Naval ramifications are the subject of Frank J. Merli, *Great Britain and the Confederate Navy, 1861–1865* (Bloomington, IN: Indiana University Press 1970). Especially useful is K. Bourne, 'British Preparations for War with the North, 1861–1862,' *English Historical Review* 76 (Oct. 1961): 600–32, which discusses the ambivalence of the British government toward President Abraham Lincoln's government.

The Irish Fenians represented the last real military threat to British North America prior to Confederation. General surveys of the movement and the raids it incited are Brian Jenkins, *Fenians and Anglo-American Relations during Reconstruction* (Ithaca, NY: Cornell University Press 1969), Leon O'Broin, *Fenian Fever: An Anglo-American Dilemma* (L: Chatto and Windus 1971), W.S. Neidhardt, *Fenianism in North America* (University Park, PA: Pennsylvania State University Press 1975), and Hereward Senior, *The Fenians and Canada* (T: MAC 1978). The best account of the raids themselves is now Senior, *The Last Invasion of Canada: The Fenian Raids, 1866–1870* (T: Dundurn 1991). Jeff Keshen deals with an interesting sidelight in 'Cloak and Dagger: Canada West's Secret Police, 1864–1867,' *OH* 79/4 (Dec. 1987): 353–81. An older work of much detail is Captain John A. Macdonald, *Troublous Times in Canada: A History of the Fenian Raids of 1866 and 1870* (T: Johnston 1910); Macdonald also wrote an early set of lyrics for 'O Canada.'

EXTERNAL AFFAIRS

Like the defence of British North America, its external affairs were largely conducted by the British government as part of a larger portfolio that could just as easily be labelled Anglo-American relations. The usual story of this imperial arrangement was that the mother country acted persistently in its own interests rather than in that of its colonies. The other half of the equation was that the Americans were constantly aggressive, seeking as their 'manifest destiny,' the control of entire continent from sea to sea. Much of the literature concerns itself with the diplomatic establishment in theory of the boundary between the United States and British North America, then over the actual running of the line, then over the maintenance of the 'unguarded' frontier. Anglo-American-Canadian friendship was a post-1871 creation at best, but it was written back into the earlier period, particularly at times of crisis, when amity among the neighbours was regarded as essential.

Much of the scholarship underplayed or misconceived the role of the imperial authorities, for example, Charles E. Hill, *Leading American Treaties* (NY: MAC 1922), James Morton Callahan, *American Foreign Policy in Cana-*

dian Relations (NY: MAC 1937), Edgar W. McInnis, *The Unguarded Frontier: A History of American-Canadian Relations* (Garden City, NY: Doubleday, Doran 1942), and H. George Classen, *Thrust and Counterthrust: The Genesis of the Canada–United States Boundary* (Chicago, IL: Rand McNally 1965). More particular studies of British and American relations, which pay little attention to Canada, are Harry C. Allen, *Great Britain and the United States: A History of Anglo-American Relations, 1783–1952* (L: Odhams Press 1954), and Charles S. Campbell, *From Revolution to Rapprochement: The United States and Great Britain, 1783–1900* (NY: J. Wiley 1974). From a Canadian perspective, these works have been superseded by R.C. Stuart, *United States Expansionism*, and G.T. Stewart, *The American Response to Canada*. Useful documents are contained in William R. Manning, ed., *Diplomatic Correspondence of the United States: Canadian Relations, 1784–1860*, 4 vols. (Washington, DC: Carnegie Endowment for International Peace 1940–6). Don W. Thomson, *Men and Meridians: The History of Surveying and Mapping in Canada*, vol. 1, *Prior to 1867* (O: Ministry of Supply and Services 1966), provides a general survey of boundary issues. Little of the work in this area has until recently taken Native peoples seriously as diplomatic players or as owners of the property being negotiated over, and most of it wears its national origins on its sleeve.

The boundary was a problem from the beginning, when it was contested between France and Great Britain in a series of colonial wars that ran between 1688 and 1763. A still-useful study of the last phase of the Anglo-French conflict is Max Savelle, *The Diplomatic History of the Canadian Boundary, 1749–1763* (T: RP 1940). Savelle followed this work with a larger one, *The Origins of American Diplomacy: The International History of Angloamerica, 1492–1763* (NY: MAC 1967), which even-handedly discussed not only the Anglo-French conflict but also the other European players and areas of contention. Its weakness is in its treatment of the Native peoples. Savelle produced a third book with a more United States-oriented theme in *Empires to Nations: Expansion in America, 1713–1824* (Minneapolis, MN: University of Minnesota Press 1974).

The standard study of the Peace of Paris in 1763, which transferred New France to the British, is Zenab Esmat Rashed, *The Peace of Paris, 1763* (Liverpool, Eng.: Liverpool University Press 1951). It concentrates on the diplomatic negotiations and the immediate political situation behind them. Much of the British political background for this treaty is discussed in Jack M. Sosin, *Whitehall and the Wilderness: The Middle West in British Colonial Policy, 1760–1775* (Lincoln, NE: University of Nebraska Press 1961). Sosin's work is broader than its title suggests, and revises Clarence W.

Alvord's *The Mississippi Valley in British Politics*, 2 vols. (1917; repr. NY: Russell and Russell 1959), which had insisted that desire to acquire the western territory in North America was the central feature of British policy in this period. For the effects of the peace of 1763, examine Jack P. Greene, 'The Seven Years' War and the American Revolution: The Causal Relationship Reconsidered,' *JICH* 8/2 (Jan. 1980): 85–105, and J.M. Bumsted, 'The Canada-Guadeloupe Debate and the Origins of the American Revolution,' *Man and Nature/L'homme et la nature: Proceedings of the Canadian Society for Eighteenth-Century Studies* 5 (1986): 51–62. An insightful consideration, 'Imperial Interests and the Peace of Paris (1763),' by R. Hyam, is to be found in Hyam and Ged Martin, eds., *Reappraisals in British Imperial History* (T: MAC 1975).

Whatever the relationship, the Americans rebelled against the British within a dozen years of the 1763 peace treaty. The treaty concluding the American Revolution was also signed at Paris – in 1783 – thus eternally complicating life for students of this period. The literature on this treaty is enormous, since most American scholars find in it and its negotiations the origins of American diplomacy. The classic study is Samuel Flagg Bemis, *The Diplomacy of the American Revolution* (NY: Appleton-Century 1935; repr. Bloomington IN: Indiana University Press 1957). More modern works include Richard B. Morris, *The Peacemakers: The Great Powers and American Independence* (NY: Harper and Row 1965), and Ronald Hoffman and Peter J. Albert, eds., *Peace and the Peacemakers: The Treaty of 1783* (Charlottesville, VA: U.S. Capitol Historical Society/University Press of Virginia 1986). See also Marcel Trudel, 'Le traité de 1783 laisse le Canada à l'Angleterre,' *RHAF* 3/2 (sept. 1949): 179–99.

North American diplomacy in the period between the end of the Revolution and the War of 1812 is treated in A.L. Burt, *The United States, Great Britain and British North America*; Bradford Perkins, *The First Rapprochement: England and the United States, 1795–1805* (Philadelphia, PA: University of Pennsylvania Press 1955); Perkins, *Prologue to War: England and the United States, 1805–1812* (Berkeley and Los Angeles, CA: University of California Press 1961); Charles R. Ritcheson, *Aftermath of Revolution: British Policy toward the United States, 1783–1795* (Dallas, TX: Southern Methodist University Press 1969); and John C.A. Stagg, *Mr. Madison's War: Politics, Diplomacy and Warfare in the Early American Republic, 1783–1830* (Princeton, NJ: Princeton University Press 1983). A number of studies by American scholars considering aspects of Anglo-American relations and United States foreign policy in these years are collected in Patrick C.T.

White, ed., *The Critical Years: American Foreign Policy, 1793–1823* (NY: J. Wiley 1970). For Jay's Treaty of 1794 between Britain and the United States, which dealt in part with the western posts, the standard study remains S.F. Bemis, *Jay's Treaty: A Study in Commerce and Diplomacy* (NY: MAC 1923), but also consult Jerald A. Combs, *The Jay Treaty: Political Battleground of the Founding Fathers* (Berkeley and Los Angeles, CA: University of California Press 1970), which as its title suggests concentrates on the American domestic politics of the treaty.

There is no good full-length study of the inconclusive 1814 Treaty of Ghent, which ended the War of 1812, but see Fred L. Engelman, *The Peace of Christmas Eve* (NY: Harcourt Brace and World 1962), as well as B. Perkins, *Castlereagh and Adams: England and the United States, 1812–1823* (Berkeley and Los Angeles, CA: University of California Press 1964), which also provides an overview of the subsequent negotiations that dealt with the boundary and Great Lakes disarmament. Indeed, the Great Lakes have a substantial historiography of their own, including J.M. Callahan, *The Neutrality of the American Lakes and Anglo-American Relations* (Baltimore, MD: Johns Hopkins Press 1898; repr. NY: Johnson Reprint 1973), John Watson Foster, *Limitation of Armament on the Great Lakes* (Washington, DC: Carnegie Endowment 1914), and Don C. Piper, *The International Law of the Great Lakes: A Study of Canadian–United States Co-operation* (Durham, NC: Duke University Press 1967).

Problems in Anglo-American-Canadian relations after the Convention of 1818 are summarized by K. Bourne in *Britain and the Balance of Power*, who attacks the problem from an even broader perspective (with different dates) in *The Foreign Policy of Victorian England, 1830–1902* (Oxford: Clarendon Press 1970). More detailed studies include Justin Winsor, *The Cartographical History of the North-Western Boundary Controversy between the United States and Great Britain* (Cambridge, MA: J. Wilson and Son 1887), Albert B. Corey, *The Crisis of 1830–1842 in Canadian-American Relations* (T: RP 1941), and Kenneth R. Stevens, *Border Diplomacy: The 'Caroline' and McLeod Affairs in Anglo-American-Canadian Relations, 1837–1842* (Tuscaloosa, AL: University of Alabama Press 1989). For the American side of the Maine–New Brunswick boundary dispute see Henry S. Burrage, *Maine in the Northeastern Boundary Controversy* (Portland, ME: State of Maine 1919). The resultant Webster-Ashburton Treaty, also known as the Treaty of Washington of 1842, is presented as part of the larger picture in Howard Jones, *To the Webster-Ashburton Treaty: A Study in Anglo-American Relations, 1783–1843* (Chapel Hill, NC: University of North Carolina Press 1977), which ends with it, and Wilbur D. Jones, *The American Problem in British Diplomacy, 1841–1861* (Athens, GA: University of Georgia Press 1974), which begins with it.

The next crisis between Britain and America came over Oregon. The best modern introduction to this nasty business remains Frederick Merk, *The Oregon Question: Essays in Anglo-American Diplomacy and Politics* (Cambridge, MA: Harvard University Press 1967). But see also Merk, *Albert Gallatin and the Oregon Problem: A Study in Anglo-American Diplomacy* (Cambridge, MA: Harvard University Press 1950); Norman A. Graebner, *Empire on the Pacific: A Study in American Continental Expansion* (NY: Ronald Press 1955); a critique of Graebner by Shomer S. Zwelling, *Expansion and Imperialism* (Chicago, IL: Loyola University Press 1970); David M. Pletcher, *The Diplomacy of Annexation: Texas, Oregon, and the Mexican War* (Columbia, MO: University of Missouri Press 1973); and Charles L. Sanford, ed., *Manifest Destiny and the Imperialism Question* (NY: J. Wiley 1974), an interesting collection of contemporary documents edited for students.

For the post-Oregon situation, a useful introduction is provided by Lester B. Shippee, *Canadian-American Relations, 1849–1874* (T: RP 1939). More recent research is presented by Donald F. Warner, *The Idea of Continental Union: Agitation for the Annexation of Canada to the United States, 1849–1893* (Lexington, KY: University of Kentucky Press 1960). There are a number of particular threads. One was the Reciprocity Treaty of 1854. For an American view see Charles C. Tansill, *The Canadian Reciprocity Treaty of 1854* (1922; repr. NY: AMS Press 1983). The Canadian perspective is Donald C. Masters, *The Reciprocity Treaty of 1854: Its History, Its Relation to British Colonial and Foreign Policy and to the Development of Canadian Fiscal Autonomy* (1937; repr. T: M&S 1963). Another thread was the San Juan Islands, covered in James Osborne McCabe, *The San Juan Water Boundary Question* (T: UTP 1964). For the Prairie West consult Alvin C. Gluek, Jr, *Minnesota and the Manifest Destiny of the Canadian Northwest: A Study in Canadian-American Relations* (T: UTP 1965), and Hartwell Bowsfield, ed., *The James Wickes Taylor Correspondence, 1859–1870* (Altona, Man.: Manitoba Record Society 1968), the letters of the American 'consul' in Red River. The movement of Black slaves to Canada (the Underground Railroad) is considered in a number of works, the best and most recent being Patrick Brode, *The Odyssey of John Anderson* (T: OS/UTP 1989), and Allen P. Stouffer, *The Light of Nature and the Law of God: Antislavery in Ontario, 1833–1877* (K&M: MQUP 1992).

There is a considerable literature on the crisis of the Civil War in general and the *Trent* affair of 1861 in particular. R.W. Winks, *Canada and the*

United States: The Civil War Years, provides the general framework. The *Trent* affair is best approached through Fred Landon, 'The *Trent* Affair of 1861,' *CHR* 3/1 (Mar. 1922): 48–55, which makes light of it; Evan John Simpson, *Atlantic Impact, 1861* (L: Heinemann 1952); Norman B. Ferris, *The Trent Affair: A Diplomatic Crisis* (Knoxville, TN: University of Tennessee Press 1977); and Gordon H. Warren, *Fountain of Discontent: The Trent Affair and Freedom of the Seas* (Boston, MA: Northeastern University Press 1981). Adrian Cook, *The Alabama Claims: American Politics and Anglo-American Politics, 1865–1872* (Ithaca, NY: Cornell University Press 1975), explores the consequences of one facet of British support for the South.

BRITISH NORTH AMERICA AND THE CONSTITUTION OF THE BRITISH EMPIRE

With the Conquest, Quebec entered a British empire already in operation for several centuries. The best study of the theory behind that empire remains Klaus E. Knorr, *British Colonial Theories, 1570–1850* (T: UTP 1944), but also of interest is Richard Koebner, *Empire* (NY: Universal Library 1961), an analysis of the meaning of the word from 1485. A wonderfully detailed if somewhat old-fashioned view of that empire around 1763 is to be found in Lawrence Henry Gipson, *The British Empire before the American Revolution*, 14 vols. (NY: Knopf 1936–70), with a full bibliography (circa the late 1960s) in the final volume. An overview of the century is provided in John Manning Ward, *Colonial Self-Government: The British Experience, 1759–1856* (T: UTP 1976). Still an important work, never quite superseded, for understanding the administration of the British Empire, is Leonard Woods Labaree, *Royal Government in America: A Study of the British Colonial System before 1783* (New Haven, CT: Yale University Press 1930; repr. NY: F. Ungar 1958). Equally old but reliable is Oliver M. Dickerson, *American Colonial Government, 1696–1765: A Study of the British Board of Trade in Its Relation to the American Colonies, Political, Industrial, Administrative* (1912; repr. NY: Russell and Russell 1962), which analyses the main British policy-making body of the period. Also important is L.W. Labaree, ed., *Royal Instructions to British Colonial Governors, 1670–1776*, 2 vols. (NY: Appleton-Century 1935; repr. NY: Octagon Books 1967). A brief overview of the governors is provided by W.L. Morton, 'The Local Executive in the British Empire, 1763–1828,' *English Historical Review* 78/307 (July 1963): 436–57.

The administration of those colonies that would remain loyal during the

American Rebellion was conducted, after 1763, in the context of the increasing conflict between Britain and her American colonies. In general see Sir Reginald Coupland, *The American Revolution and the British Empire* (1930; repr. NY: Russell and Russell 1965); V.T. Harlow, *The Founding of the Second British Empire, 1763–1793*, 2 vols. (L: Longmans, Green 1952–4); L.H. Gipson, *The Coming of the Revolution, 1763–1775* (NY: Harper 1954); Robert W. Tucker and David C. Hendrickson, *The Fall of the First British Empire: Origins of the War of American Independence* (Baltimore, MD: Johns Hopkins University Press 1982); and Marc Egnal, *A Mighty Empire: The Origins of the American Revolution* (Ithaca, NY: Cornell University Press 1988). Particular views of British colonial policy after 1763 are contained in Edmund S. Morgan, *The Stamp Act Crisis: Prologue to Revolution* (Chapel Hill, NC: University of North Carolina Press 1953; rev. ed., NY: Collier Books 1963), and P.D.G. Thomas, *British Politics and the Stamp Act Crisis: The First Phase of the American Revolution, 1763–1767* (Oxford: Clarendon Press 1975).

While many older works suggested some direct connection, occasionally conspiratorial, between British policy for its northernmost colonies (especially those added in 1763) and the coming of the Revolution, most scholars now agree that such policy was trying mainly to deal with peculiar local conditions and only coincidentally distressed the Americans. Such was the case with Native policy discussed in the military section, and with the Quebec Act of 1774. One of the conspiratorial type was Victor Coffin, *The Province of Quebec and the Early American Revolution* (Madison, WI: University of Wisconsin Press 1896). An alternative view is presented in Sir R. Coupland, *The Quebec Act: A Study in Statesmanship* (Oxford: Clarendon Press 1925), while H. Neatby, *The Quebec Act: Protest and Policy* (Scarborough, Ont.: PH 1972), reviews the literature and tries for a balanced view. Coupland and Neatby disagree over the role of Guy Carleton, the governor of Quebec, but agree on the local nature of the legislation. Among more recent contributions to the debate are Pierre Tousignant, 'The Integration of the Province of Quebec into the British Empire, 1763–91. Part 1, From the Royal Proclamation to the Quebec Act,' *DCB*, vol. 4, and Philip Lawson, *The Imperial Challenge: Quebec and Britain in the Age of the American Revolution* (K&M: MQUP 1989). For a general view of the Quebec Act in the context of British policy of the time see Bernard Donoughue, *British Politics and the American Revolution: The Path to War, 1773–1775* (L: MAC 1964).

A basic overview of British policy for the island of Newfoundland in the Revolutionary era can be found in C. Grant Head, *Eighteenth Century New-*

foundland: A Geographer's Perspective (T: M&S 1976). William H. Whiteley provides more detailed analyses of the era of the American Revolution in 'Governor Hugh Palliser and the Newfoundland and Labrador Fishery, 1764–1768,' *CHR* 50/2 (June 1969): 141–63, and 'James Cook and British Policy in the Newfoundland Fisheries, 1763–7,' *CHR* 54/3 (Sept. 1973): 245–72, as well as his entry 'Sir Hugh Palliser,' *DCB*, vol. 4. A useful corrective to Whiteley's emphasis on the role of Palliser is John E. Crowley, 'Empire versus Truck: The Official Interpretation of Debt and Labour in the Eighteenth-Century Newfoundland Fishery,' *CHR* 70/3 (Sept. 1989): 311–36.

The Maritime region in this period was home to two colonies, Nova Scotia and Prince Edward Island. For the latter see J.M. Bumsted, 'British Colonial Policy and the Island of St. John, 1763–1767,' *Acadiensis* 9/1 (Autumn 1979): 3–18, and his *Land, Settlement, and Politics on Eighteenth-Century Prince Edward Island* (K&M: MQUP 1987). On the former, J.B. Brebner, *The Neutral Yankees of Nova Scotia*, and W.B. Kerr, *The Maritime Provinces*, have been somewhat revised by G.A. Rawlyk, *Nova Scotia's Massachusetts* by eliminating the imperial context almost entirely.

The Pacific explorations of James Cook and others were almost totally divorced from immediate politics and events on the Atlantic Coast. Consult J.C. Beaglehole, *The Exploration of the Pacific* (3rd ed., Stanford, CA: Stanford University Press 1966) and *The Life of Captain James Cook* (Stanford, CA: Stanford University Press 1974), and his edition of *The Journals of Captain James Cook on His Voyages of Discovery*, 4 vols. (Cambridge, Eng.: Hakluyt 1955–74). Cook and the English were not alone in their Pacific interests. French activities are covered in John Dunmore, *French Explorers in the Pacific*, 2 vols. (Oxford: Clarendon Press 1965–9), Julius S. Gassner, trans., *Voyages and Adventures of La Perouse* (Honolulu, HI: University of Hawaii Press 1969), and Russell C. Shelton, *From Hudson Bay to Botany Bay: The Lost Frigates of Laperouse* (T: NC Press 1987); and Spanish activities, in Warren L. Cook, *Flood Tide of Empire: Spain and the Pacific Northwest, 1543–1819* (New Haven, CT: Yale University Press 1973), and John Kendrick, *Men with Wooden Feet: The Spanish Exploration of the Pacific Northwest* (T: NC Press 1985).

For the Americans, the British Empire ended in 1776. Whether the Empire that operated after 1776 (or 1783, when the British admitted they had lost the thirteen colonies) was different is one of those nice questions that some academics love to debate. V.T. Harlow's *The Founding of the Second British Empire* elaborated his 'The New Imperial System, 1783–1815,' in J.H. Rose et al., eds., *The Cambridge History of the British Empire*, vol. 2,

The Growth of the New Empire, 1783–1870 (Cambridge, Eng.: Cambridge University Press 1940), and staked out the territory for change. Others have preferred to emphasize continuity. Peter Marshall, 'The First and Second British Empires: A Question of Demarcation,' *History* 49 (1964): 13–23; R. Hyam, 'British Imperial Expansion in the Late Eighteenth Century [Review Article],' *Historical Journal* 10/1 (1967): 113–24; and D.L. Mackay, 'Direction and Purpose in British Imperial Policy, 1783–1801,' *Historical Journal* 17/3 (1974): 487–501, have emphasized continuity explicitly. Implicitly, J.M. Ward, in his chapter 'The British Constitution for British Colonies: Canada, 1759–1831,' in *Colonial Self-Government*, does the same, at least for Canada. Whether settlement colonies like Canada and others like India were actually part of the same empire is another question, almost asked by G. Martin in 'Was There a British Empire? [Review Article]' *Historical Journal* 15/3 (1972): 562–9.

However many empires there were, British North America was governed by the British after 1783. The best study of that administration remains Helen Taft Manning, *British Colonial Government after the American Revolution, 1782–1820* (New Haven, CT: Yale University Press 1933). Manning's work is desperately in need of revision from two perspectives: the first, she relies too heavily on the Colonial Office records and fails to examine matters from the local documents; and the second, she does not distinguish sufficiently among different patterns of administration within British North America, failing particularly to appreciate that the British did not always operate as though the North American colonies were politically mature. There were some parallels between British government in British North America and in places like Africa, India, and the West Indies, especially in the attempt before 1791 to govern Quebec from above as if it were an alien culture and in the West, where a creole-type elite came to dominate an indigenous population.

Not all policy dealt with strictly political matters, nor was it generated totally within Britain or by the government. The Church of England (Anglican Church) was both an instrument of imperial policy and an agency with other non-secular agendas, as one can see in Judith Fingard, *The Anglican Design in Loyalist Nova Scotia, 1783–1816* (L: SPCK 1972). Other studies of the Church of England, running east to west, include Thomas R. Millman and A.R. Kelley, *Atlantic Canada to 1900: A History of the Anglican Church* (T: Anglican Book Centre 1983); Brian C.U. Cuthbertson, *The First Bishop: A Biography of Charles Inglis* (H: Waegwoltic 1987); Millman, *Jacob Mountain, First Lord Bishop of Quebec: A Study in Church and State, 1793–1825* (T: UTP 1947); Curtis Fahey, *In His Name: The Anglican Experience in*

Upper Canada, 1791–1854 (O: CUP 1991); and Thomas C.B. Boon, *The Anglican Church from the Bay to the Rockies* (T: RP 1962).

The Hudson's Bay Company as a corporate monopoly also served as an agent of British imperialism in the Canadian Northwest. Indeed, before the establishment of the colony of Vancouver Island in 1849, the Northwest was not an official portfolio of the Colonial Office. John S. Galbraith, *The Hudson's Bay Company as an Imperial Factor, 1821–1869* (T: UTP 1957), provides an analysis of how this arrangement worked and was ultimately extinguished. Galbraith's volume should be supplemented by reference to the broader surveys of E.E. Rich, *History of the Hudson's Bay Company, 1670–1870*, 2 vols. (L: HBRS 1958–9; repr. 3 vols., T: M&S 1960), and *The Fur Trade and the Northwest to 1857* (T: M&S 1967). Perhaps the best overview of the company from an imperial perspective, tantalizingly brief, is 'The Hudson's Bay Company and the Fur Trade, 1670–1870,' by imperial historian G. Williams, which comprises an entire issue of *The Beaver* 314/2 (Oct. 1983). Richard I. Ruggles, *A Country So Interesting: The Hudson's Bay Company and Two Centuries of Mapping, 1670–1870* (K&M: MQUP 1990), is a wonderful presentation of the company's delineation of space.

A larger picture of administration in the mother country itself in the period is provided in Arthur Aspinall, *The Cabinet Council, 1783–1835* (L: G. Cumberledge 1952), A.H. Dodd, *The Growth of Responsible Government from James the First to Victoria* (L: Routledge & Kegan Paul 1956), and Sir Daniel Norman Chester, *The English Administrative System, 1780–1870* (Oxford: Clarendon Press 1981). For the theory of government, emphasizing the doctrine of 'mixed government' of Kings, Lords, and Commons (translated into British North America as Governor, Council, and Assembly), consult Corinne Comstock Weston, *English Constitutional Theory and the House of Lords, 1556–1832* (L: Routledge & Kegan Paul 1965). G.T. Stewart, *The Origins of Canadian Politics: A Comparative Approach* (V: UBCP 1986), provides an overview from the Canadian perspective. Introductions to colonial government at the provincial level are available in Alexander H. McLintock, *The Establishment of Constitutional Government in Newfoundland, 1783–1832: A Study of Retarded Colonisation* (L: Longmans, Green 1941), Frank MacKinnon, *The Government of Prince Edward Island* (T: UTP 1951), J. Murray Beck, *The Government of Nova Scotia* (T: UTP 1957), and Henri Brun, *La formation des institutions parlementaires québécoises, 1791–1838* (Q: PUL 1970). John Garner, *The Franchise and Politics in British North America, 1755–1867* (T: UTP 1969), is a very much more important and general book than its title suggests.

In the years immediately after the Treaty of Paris of 1783, the principal constitutional change in the North American empire was the Constitutional Act of 1791 (also known as the Canada Act). The relevant documents are reprinted in A.G. Doughty and Duncan A. McArthur, eds., *Documents Relating to the Constitutional History of Canada*, vol. 2 (1914). There is no full-length study of the Canada Act, but see A.F. Madden, '"Not for Export": The Westminster Model of Government and British Colonial Practice,' *JICH* 8/1 (Oct. 1979): 10–29. A major development of the early nineteenth century was the establishment of a Colonial Office independent of the Board of Trade, complete with a small collection of bureaucrats. A useful introduction is P.A. Buckner, 'The Colonial Office and British North America, 1801–50,' in *DCB*, vol. 8 (1985). The story of the Colonial Office creation is best told in D. Murray Young, *The Colonial Office in the Early Nineteenth Century* (L: Longmans, Green 1961). But see also Paul Knaplund, *James Stephen and the British Colonial System, 1813–1847* (Madison, WI: University of Wisconsin Press 1953), a study of the leading colonial under-secretary of the nineteenth century; Sir Charles Joseph Jeffries, *The Colonial Office* (L: Allen and Unwin 1956); R.B. Pugh, 'The Colonial Office, 1801–1925,' in E.A. Benians et al., eds., *The Cambridge History of the British Empire*, vol. 3, *The Empire Commonwealth, 1870–1919* (Cambridge, Eng: Cambridge University Press 1959); and R.C. Snelling and T.J. Barron, 'The Colonial Office and Its Permanent Officials, 1801–1914,' in Gillian Sutherland, ed., *Studies in the Growth of Nineteenth-Century Government* (L: Routledge & Kegan Paul 1972). N.D. McLachlan examines the career of the leading colonial secretary of the early period in 'Bathurst at the Colonial Office, 1812–27: A Reconnaissance,' *Historical Studies* 13/52 (Apr. 1969): 477–502.

A decent number of biographies and collections of papers of colonial governors and other officials have been published. Most of them are older and not very valuable on the imperial relationship, since they treat their subject's colonial administration in too favourable a light. A good example is S.W. Jackman, *Galloping Head: The Life of the Right Honourable Sir Francis Bond Head* (L: Phoenix House 1958). The best place to begin with colonial governors is with the *DCB*; P.A. Buckner's sketches, especially that of Sir John Harvey in volume 8, are models of modern scholarship. Of particular value for the imperial relationship (as opposed to colonial politics) are Marjory Whitelaw, ed., *The Dalhousie Journals*, 3 vols. (O: Oberon 1978–82), George Ramsay, 9th Earl of Dalhousie, serving as governor of Nova Scotia and Lower Canada; and Sir Francis Bond Head, *A Narrative* (1839), with notes by William Lyon Mackenzie, edited by S.F. Wise (T: M&S 1969). See also Mark Francis, *Governors and Settlers: Images of Authority in the British Colonies, 1820–60* (L: MAC 1992).

Much of the literature on imperialism covering the first forty years of the nineteenth century revolves around the question of British attitudes toward colonies, with some scholars seeing the origins of the movement to anti-imperialism in these years. A good if dated statement of these matters is C.A. Bodelsen, 'The English Attitude to the Colonies from the Loss of the First Empire till 1869,' in his *Studies in Mid-Victorian Imperialism* (1924; repr. L: Heinemann 1960). Did the British governments take their overseas empire sufficiently seriously? The trend certainly has been to argue that the British paid more attention to colonial affairs – and acquired more additional territory – than contemporaries had appreciated. Stimulating introductions to imperial constitutional policy and British political problems in the early years of the nineteenth century, before, during, and after the emergence of the Rebellions of 1837–8, are to be found in the work of H.T. Manning: 'The Colonial Policy of the Whig Ministers, 1830–37,' parts 1 and 2, *CHR* 33/3–4 (Sept.–Dec. 1952): 203–36, 341–68; 'Colonial Crises before the Cabinet, 1828–1835,' *Bulletin of the Institute of Historical Research* 30 (1957): 41–61; 'Who Ran the British Empire, 1830–1850?' *Journal of British Studies* 5/1 (Nov. 1965): 88–121; and her major study – still not quite replaced – *The Revolt of French Canada, 1800–1835: A Chapter in the History of the British Commonwealth* (T: MAC 1962). More recently Peter Burroughs worked over this ground in *British Attitudes towards Canada, 1822–1849* (Scarborough, Ont.: PH 1971), which attempts to summarize the literature, and *The Canadian Crisis and British Colonial Policy, 1828–1841* (T: MAC 1972). Students should also consult A.G.L. Shaw, 'British Attitudes to the Colonies, *ca.* 1820–1850,' *Journal of British Studies* 9/1 (Nov. 1969): 71–95; Philip Goldring, 'Province and Nation: Problems of Imperial Rule in Lower Canada, 1820 to 1841,' *JICH* 9/1 (Oct. 1980): 38–56; and G. Martin, 'Confederation Rejected: The British Debate on Canada, 1837–1840,' *JICH* 11/1 (Oct. 1982): 33–57.

The Rebellions of 1837–8 produced the mission and *Report* of Lord Durham. The British context is discussed by P. Burroughs in 'The Canadian Rebellions in British Politics,' in John E. Flint and G. Williams, eds., *Perspectives of Empire: Essays Presented to Gerald S. Graham* (L: Longman 1973). Durham was for more than a century one of the heroes of the British Empire in Canada, regarded as the progenitor of responsible government and Canadian federalism in his famous 1839 *Report*, published in a 'definitive' edition as Sir Charles Lucas, ed., *Lord Durham's Report on the Affairs of British North America*, 3 vols. (Oxford: Clarendon Press 1912; repr. NY: A.M. Kelley 1970), including not only the text of Durham's report but contemporary documents, such as Charles Buller's 'Sketch of Lord Durham's

Mission to Canada in 1838,' and in abridgement by Gerald M. Craig, ed., *Lord Durham's Report: An Abridgement of 'Report on the Affairs of British North America' by Lord Durham* (T: M&S 1963). For Durham's life see Chester W. New, *Lord Durham: A Biography of John George Lambton, First Earl of Durham* (Oxford: Clarendon Press 1929), abridged by H.W. McCready as *Lord Durham's Mission to Canada: An Abridgement of 'Lord Durham: A Biography of John George Lambton, First Earl of Durham' by Chester New* (T: M&S 1963). Both the abridgement of Durham's *Report* and of his biography were in some ways regrettable, since they presented Durham's time in Canada completely out of context; students should be sure to consult the originals. Useful also is Stuart J. Reid, ed., *Life and Letters of the First Earl of Durham, 1792–1840*, 2 vols. (L: 1906; repr. Oxford: Clarendon Press 1929). A more modern biography, especially good on family matters, is Leonard Cooper, *Radical Jack: The Life of John George Lambton, First Earl of Durham, 1792–1840* (L: Cresset 1959).

Generations of commentators in Canada repeated the same general tenor of comments about Durham's importance and influence, although French Canadians came not to like it. Not until G. Martin's iconoclastic little book, *The Durham Report and British Policy: A Critical Essay* (Cambridge, Eng.: Cambridge University Press 1972), was much scepticism openly expressed about his role, although John W. Cell in *British Colonial Administration in the Mid-Nineteenth Century: The Policy-Making Process* (New Haven, CT: Yale University Press 1970) had pointed the way. William Thomas, *The Philosophic Radicals: Nine Studies in Theory and Practice, 1817–1841* (Oxford: Clarendon Press 1979), took Martin's arguments of inconsequentiality to their logical conclusion, for Durham and other colonial reformers of the period. For the reasons for French-Canadian hostility see William G. Ormsby, 'Lord Durham and the Assimilation of French Canada,' in Norman Penlington, ed., *On Canada: Essays in Honour of Frank H. Underhill* (T: UTP 1971). Janet Ajzenstat, *The Political Thought of Lord Durham* (K&M: MQUP 1988), attempts to rehabilitate Durham from charges of both racism and inconsequentiality, with limited success; her argument can be found stated briefly in 'Liberalism and Assimilation: Lord Durham Reconsidered,' in Stephen Brooks, ed., *Political Thought in Canada: Contemporary Perspectives* (T: Irwin 1984). Useful works for assessing Durham's importance are W.G. Ormsby, ed., *Crisis in the Canadas, 1838–1839: The Grey Journals and Letters* (T: UTP 1964), and P. Knaplund, ed., *Letters from Lord Sydenham, Governor-General of Canada, 1839–1841, to Lord John Russell* (L: Allen and Unwin 1931). For contemporary British North American criticisms of Durham consult Sir John Beverley Robinson, *Can-*

ada and the Canada Bill (1840; repr. NY: Johnson Reprint 1967), and Thomas Chandler Haliburton, *A Reply to the Report of the Earl of Durham* (1839; repr., ed. Alfred Goldsworthy Bailey, O: Golden Dog 1976). Few women make their way into the masculine world of imperial politics before Confederation, and when they do they are usually the wives of colonial officials, such as Lady Louisa Elizabeth Grey, Countess of Durham, whose *Letters and Diaries of Lady Durham* were edited by Patricia Godsell (n.p: Oberon 1979). Fernand Ouellet's sketch of Durham (Lambton) in *DCB*, vol. 7 (1988), is interesting, as much for what it does not say as for what it does.

Lord Durham's associates (research assistants is perhaps a better term) in Canada were Charles Buller and Edward Gibbon Wakefield, both gentlemen of dubious reputations at the time, but known as colonial reformers. The *DCB* sketches for Buller, vol. 7, and Wakefield, vol. 9, are now the best places to start an examination of their careers. Wakefield's influential writings are readily available in Muriel F. Lloyd Pritchard, comp., *The Collected Works of Edward Gibbon Wakefield* (L: Collins 1968). R.S. Neale, 'Roebuck's Constitution and the Durham Proposals,' *Historical Studies; Australia and New Zealand* 14 (1971): 579–90, presents the case for another colonial reformer, Arthur Roebuck. The effect of the Canadian crisis in Parliament on the 'colonial reformers' can be followed in Joseph Hamburger, *Intellectuals in Politics: John Stuart Mill and the Philosophic Radicals* (New Haven, CT: Yale University Press 1965), P. Knaplund, *Gladstone and Britain's Imperial Policy* (1927; repr. L: Frank Cass 1966), and W. Thomas, *Philosophic Radicals*. P. Burroughs provides samples from the documents in his edition of *The Colonial Reformers and Canada, 1830–1849: Selections from Documents and Publications of the Times* (T: M&S 1969).

For many years the development of responsible government over the decade following Durham's *Report* was seen as Canada's major contribution to the British Empire and the principal development of the pre-Confederation period. Responsible government served as the link between colonial settlement and Confederation; the history of British North America built first to responsible government, and then from responsible government to Canadian nationhood. The complex links are examined in Graeme H. Patterson, 'An Enduring Canadian Myth: Responsible Government and the Family Compact,' *JCS* 12/2 (Spring 1977): 3–16, and M. Brook Taylor, *Promoters, Patriots, and Partisans: Historiography in Nineteenth-Century English Canada* (T: UTP 1989). A useful review article of works dealing with British policy is P. Burroughs, 'The Determinants of Colonial Self-Government,' *JICH* 6/3 (May 1978): 314–29. Despite the current view that the topic of colonial self-government is at best hackneyed, there are still controversies within it. The most important are discussed in P.A. Buckner, 'The Transition to Responsible Government: Some Revisions in Need of Revising,' in C.C. Eldridge, ed., *From Rebellion to Patriation*. The current protagonists are Buckner himself, whose *The Transition to Responsible Government: British Policy in British North America, 1815–1850* (Westport, CT: Greenwood Press 1985) has superseded all previous work for depth and cogency of analysis, and a variety of his colleagues whose works have already been cited, including P. Burroughs, J.M. Ward, and G. Martin. Buckner adopts a multifaceted analysis which does not fasten much on particular dates and personalities, and he is generally more sympathetic to Durham's influence. One place where Durham certainly did not triumph was in his recommendations for assimilation of French Canada, as W.G. Ormsby has shown in *The Emergence of the Federal Concept in Canada, 1839–1845* (T: UTP 1969). An overall survey of British public opinion on colonial matters after the rebellions is provided by Stanley R. Stembridge, *Parliament, the Press, and the Colonies, 1846–1880* (NY: Garland 1982).

The achievement of responsible government in the various provinces of British North America can be followed in a variety of works of varying sophistication. The best place to pick up the current research on political and constitutional developments in the Canadas is in the pages of the *DCB*, particularly in the entries 'Robert Baldwin,' vol. 8; 'James Bruce, 8th Earl of Elgin' and 'Sir Louis-Hippolyte La Fontaine,' vol. 9; and 'Sir Francis Hincks,' vol. 11 (1982). The theme of responsible government also runs through J.M.S. Careless, ed., *The Pre-Confederation Premiers: Ontario Government Leaders, 1841–1867* (T: UTP 1980), and Jacques Monet, *The Last Cannon Shot: A Study of French-Canadian Nationalism, 1837–1850* (T: UTP 1969). An excellent and accessible primary source is A.G. Doughty, ed., *The Elgin-Grey Papers, 1846–1852*, 4 vols. (O: King's Printer 1937).

The issue of responsible government is less dominant in the historiography of the Atlantic region, apart from that of the province of Nova Scotia, where it is tied up with the career of Joseph Howe. W. Ross Livingston, *Responsible Government in Nova Scotia: A Study of the Constitutional Beginnings of the British Commonwealth* (Iowa City, IA: University of Iowa Press 1930), remains the standard account for Nova Scotia, but should be supplemented by J.M. Beck, *Joseph Howe*, 2 vols. (K&M: MQUP 1982–3). See too the *DCB* entries 'James Boyle Uniacke,' vol. 8; and 'James William Johston,' vol. 10 (1972). The best place to start a study of responsible government in the neighbouring province is W.S. MacNutt, *New Brunswick: A History, 1784–1867* (T: MAC 1963), which can be followed by the *DCB* entries 'Sir Edmund Walker Head' and 'John Richard Partelow,' vol. 9; and 'Charles

Fisher' and 'Lemuel Allan Wilmot,' vol. 10. As for Prince Edward Island, there are few reliable alternatives to the *DCB*: see, in particular, the entries 'Edward Whelan,' vol. 9; and 'George Coles,' vol. 10. Finally, Gertrude E. Gunn deals with Newfoundland in *The Political History of Newfoundland, 1832–1864* (T: UTP 1966), but see also Phillip McCann, 'Culture, State Formation and the Invention of Tradition: Newfoundland, 1832–1855,' *JCS* 23/1–2 (Spring–Summer 1988): 86–103, reprinted in J.M. Bumsted, ed., *Interpreting Canada's Past*, vol. 1, *Pre-Confederation* (2nd ed., T: OUP 1993), which well demonstrates how new perspectives can invigorate an old topic.

Responsible government was not an issue in the Hudson's Bay Company territories, but imperial relations were nevertheless important for the region. The best context for the Northwest – the work itself does not discuss the region – is W.P. Morrell, *British Colonial Policy in the Mid-Victorian Age: South Africa, New Zealand, the West Indies* (Oxford: Clarendon Press 1969). On the Northwest in general see J.S. Galbraith, *The Hudson's Bay Company as an Imperial Factor*. The principal thrust of any activity at the Colonial Office – Rupert's Land was not a colony, which was the problem – was a lifelong campaign against the company's suzerainty over Rupert's Land, almost single-handedly operated by Alexander Kennedy Isbister, a mixed blood native of the region who made a successful career in Britain. Barry Cooper, *Alexander Kennedy Isbister: A Respectable Critic of the Honourable Company* (O: CUP 1988), provides a first-rate study. Other relevant sources are A.C. Gluek, Jr, 'Imperial Protection for the Trading Interests of the Hudson's Bay Company, 1857–1861,' *CHR* 37/2 (June 1956): 119–40, and P. Goldring, 'Governor Simpson's Officers: Elite Recruitment in a British Overseas Enterprise, 1834–1870,' *Prairie Forum* 10/2 (Autumn 1985): 251–81. Isbister's campaign contributed to the controversy Lewis H. Thomas documents in 'The Mid-19th Century Debate on the Future of the North West,' in J.M. Bumsted, ed., *Documentary Problems in Canadian History*, vol. 1, *Pre-Confederation* (Georgetown, Ont.: Irwin-Dorsey 1969). The consequent challenge to the Hudson's Bay Company charter combined with favourable reports from several scientific expeditions to excite both Canadian and American imperial ambitions in the region: see A.C. Gluek, Jr, *Minnesota and the Manifest Destiny of the Canadian Northwest*, and Douglas Owram, *Promise of Eden: The Canadian Expansionist Movement and the Idea of the West, 1856–1900* (T: UTP 1980).

On the Pacific Coast the 1840s saw debate over the establishment of the formal colonies of Vancouver Island and British Columbia. Once again a good place to start is J.S. Galbraith, *The Hudson's Bay Company as an Imperial Factor*, supplemented by James E. Hendrickson, 'The Constitutional

Development of Colonial Vancouver Island and British Columbia,' in W. Peter Ward and Robert A.J. McDonald, eds., *British Columbia: Historical Readings* (V: Douglas & McIntyre 1981). The issues and outcome of the challenge to the Hudson's Bay Company on the coast may be followed in P. Knaplund, 'James Stephen on Granting Vancouver Island to the Hudson's Bay Company, 1846–1848,' *BCHQ* 9 (Oct. 1945): 259–71; Knaplund, 'Letters from James Edward Fitzgerald to W.E. Gladstone concerning Vancouver Island and the Hudson's Bay Company, 1848–1850,' *BCHQ* 13 (Oct. 1949): 1–21; and J.S. Galbraith, 'James Edward Fitzgerald versus the Hudson's Bay Company: The Founding of Vancouver Island,' in *BCHQ* 16 (July–Oct. 1952): 191–207, reprinted in Dickson M. Falconer, ed., *British Columbia: Patterns in Economic, Political and Cultural Development – Selected Readings* (VI: Camosun College 1982).

The 1850s and 1860s saw constitutional discussion shift from intra- to inter-provincial development. There was talk of federation in British North America from the eighteenth century. The idea is surveyed in L.F.S. Upton, 'The Idea of Confederation, 1754–1858,' in W.L. Morton, ed., *The Shield of Achilles: Aspects of Canada in the Victorian Age* (T: M&S 1968). Other early initiatives are examined in Chester Martin, 'Sir Edmund Head's First Project of Federation, 1851,' CHA *AR* (1928): 14–28; Reginald G. Trotter, 'The British Government and the Proposal of Federation in 1858,' *CHR* 14/3 (Sept. 1933): 285–92; Alice R. Stewart, 'Sir Edmund Head's Memorandum of 1857 on Maritime Union: A Lost Confederation Document,' *CHR* 26/4 (Dec. 1945): 406–19; Bruce A. Knox, 'The British Government, Sir Edmund Head, and British North American Confederation, 1858,' *JICH* 4/2 (Jan. 1976): 206–17; G. Martin, 'Lost Confederation Initiatives, 1846–1858,' *Bulletin of Canadian Studies* 6/2 (Autumn 1983): 25–35; and Martin, 'Launching Canadian Confederation: Means to Ends, 1836–1864,' *Historical Journal* 27/3 (1984): 575–602. Sir Edmund Walker Head's career is covered in D.G.G. Kerr, *Sir Edmund Head: A Scholarly Governor* (T: UTP 1954). A useful attempt to relate imperial and colonial policy is in Peter A. Baskerville, 'Imperial Agendas and "Disloyal" Collaborators: Decolonization and the John Sanfield Macdonald Ministries, 1862–1864,' in David Keane and Colin Read, eds., *Old Ontario: Essays in Honour of J.M.S. Careless* (T: Dundurn 1990).

Britain's role in Confederation is the subject of a number of works by G. Martin, beginning with 'An Imperial Idea and Its Friends: Canadian Confederation and the British,' in Gordon Martel, ed., *Studies in British Imperial History: Essays in Honour of A.P. Thornton* (L: MAC 1986), which summarized his unpublished PhD thesis, and elaborated in *History as Science or Lit-*

erature: Explaining Canadian Confederation, 1858–67 (L: Canada House 1989), a lecture which has been reprinted in Angus D. Gilbert et al., eds., *Reappraisals in Canadian History*, vol. 1, *Pre-Confederation* (Scarborough, Ont.: PH 1993). Martin is also the editor of and contributor to *The Causes of Canadian Confederation* (F: AP 1990). Other important works are James A. Gibson, 'The Colonial Office View of Canadian Federation, 1856–1868,' *CHR* 35/4 (Dec. 1954): 279–313, and B.A. Knox, 'The Rise of Colonial Federation as an Object of British Policy, 1850–1870,' *Journal of British Studies* 11/1 (Nov. 1971): 92–112.

For the larger international picture of Confederation see W.L. Morton, 'British North America and a Continent in Dissolution, 1861–71,' *History* 47 (1962): 139–56, reprinted in J.M. Bumsted, ed., *Interpreting Canada's Past*, vol. 1, *Before Confederation* (T: OUP 1986; 2nd ed., 1993). The American connection is discussed in D.G. Creighton, 'The United States and Canadian Confederation,' *CHR* 39/3 (Sept. 1958): 209–22.

TRADE AND COMMERCE

Europe expanded its dominion around the world chiefly in the interest of trade and commerce. Even the establishment of colonies was intended primarily to provide a better means of exploiting what came to be recognized as complex natural resources, thus adding to the prosperity of the mother country. The economic system that resulted came to be known as mercantilism. As well as the works on the theory of empire noted in the previous section, the student can also profitably examine Eli F. Heckscher, *Mercantilism*, 2 vols. (2nd ed., L: Allen and Unwin 1955); Bruno Suviranta, *The Theory of the Balance of Trade in England: A Study in Mercantilism* (NY: A.M. Kelley 1967); Walter E. Minchinton, comp., *Mercantilism: System or Expediency?* (Lexington, MA: Heath 1969); D. Wadada Nabudere, *The Political Economy of Imperialism: Its Theoretical and Polemical Treatment from Mercantilist to Multilateral Imperialism* (L: Zed 1977); and Terence Wilmot Hutchison, *Before Adam Smith: The Emergence of Political Economy, 1662–1776* (Oxford: Blackwell 1988). Perhaps the most important book in recent years on eighteenth-century England is Neil McKendrick, John Brewer, and J.H. Plumb, *The Birth of a Consumer Society: The Commercialization of Eighteenth-Century England* (Bloomington, IN: Indiana University Press 1982), because its theme explains so much about the Empire.

Mercantilism came under attack from a variety of quarters in the eighteenth century. Two of the major British critics were Josiah Tucker and Adam Smith. Tucker, a much-neglected eighteenth-century political economist, always in the shadow of Smith, is the subject of Robert Livingston Schuyler, ed., *Josiah Tucker: A Selection from His Economic and Political Writings* (NY: Columbia University Press 1931), and W. George Shelton, *Dean Tucker and Eighteenth-Century Economic and Political Thought* (NY: St Martin's Press 1981). The literature on Smith is enormous. Perhaps a good place to begin is with John Cunningham Wood, ed., *Adam Smith: Critical Assessments*, 4 vols. (L: Croom Helm 1983–4), while the best biographies are E.G. West, *Adam Smith: The Man and His Works* (1969; repr. Indianapolis, IN: Liberty Press 1976), Roy H. Campbell and Andrew S. Skinner, *Adam Smith* (NY: St Martin's Press 1982), and D.D. Raphael, *Adam Smith* (Oxford: OUP 1985), in the Past Masters series. Smith's own writings are available in the definitive *Glasgow Edition of the Works and Correspondence of Adam Smith*, 6 vols. (Oxford: Clarendon Press 1976–83), complete with introductions and full scholarly apparatus. Thinkers like Tucker and Smith combined ideas of freedom of trade with critiques of overseas empires, putting both in the context not only of economic thought but of moral philosophy, as Richard F. Teichgraeber III makes clear in *'Free Trade' and Moral Philosophy: Rethinking the Sources of Adam Smith's 'Wealth of Nations'* (Durham, NC: Duke University Press 1986).

According to older conventional wisdom, British politicians and statesmen eventually caught up with this liberalist thinking, and began to consider dismantling the Empire. Detailed statements of this interpretation are to be found in R.L. Schuyler, *The Fall of the Old Colonial System* (NY: OUP 1945), and C.A. Bodelsen, *Studies in Mid-Victorian Imperialism*. While the emergence of free trade thinking in Britain is virtually unquestioned, whether such a position was necessarily 'anti-imperial' is another matter, and much debated in the literature. The fact is that after 1783 or 1815 or 1845 – whichever date is chosen – the British Empire continued to expand throughout the nineteenth century at a fairly steady rate of about (on average) 100,000 square miles per year. A good introduction is P.J. Cain, *Economic Foundations of British Overseas Expansion, 1815–1914* (L: MAC 1980), which is a historiographical essay with an appended bibliography. The student should also consult R. Koebner and Helmut D. Schmidt, *Imperialism: The Story and Significance of a Political Word, 1840–1960* (Cambridge, Eng.: Cambridge University Press 1964); D.K. Fieldhouse, *The Theory of Capitalist Imperialism* (L: Longman 1967) and his *Economics and Empire, 1830–1914* (Ithaca, NY: Cornell University Press 1973); and Bernard Semmel, *The Rise of Free Trade Imperialism: Classical Political Economy, the Empire of Free Trade, and Imperialism, 1750–1850* (Cambridge, Eng.: Cambridge University Press 1970). A good collection of articles on all sides of the debate is in A.G.L. Shaw, ed., *Great Britain and the Colonies, 1815–1865* (L: Methuen 1970).

British domestic commercial and economic policy was not necessarily always in step with imperial policy. Domestic policy can best be approached through L.M. Brown, *The Board of Trade and the Free-Trade Movement, 1830–42* (Oxford: Clarendon Press 1958), J.B. Williams, *British Commercial Policy and Trade Expansion, 1750–1850* (Oxford: Clarendon Press 1972), and B. Hilton, *Corn, Cash, Commerce: The Economic Policies of the Tory Governments, 1815–30* (NY: OUP 1977).

The subject of British overseas investment is a fascinating one. Key works include L.H. Jenks, *The Migration of British Capital to 1875* (1927; repr. L: Nelson 1963), P.L. Cottrell, *British Overseas Investment in the Nineteenth Century* (L: MAC 1975), and Michael Edelstein, *Overseas Investment in the Age of High Imperialism: The United Kingdom, 1850–1914* (NY: Columbia University Press 1982). As Canadians today fully appreciate, one need not dominate another country politically in order to control it economically, and investment is an important means of control.

It is worth noting that none of the revisionist literature on the British and free trade in the first half of the nineteenth century argues from Canadian examples; Australia, New Zealand, and the expansion of Britain into Africa, Asia, and Oceania are at issue. No scholar has really yet asked the question whether the revisionism makes any difference to our understanding of the situation in British North America, where conventional wisdom sees a shift from an imperial to a continental economy. There is no recent work that supplies a detailed overview of this subject, probably because imperial history has become so unfashionable that it cannot even generate studies desperately needed. Virtually the only general work produced in the last few years touching on these matters is Ben Forster, *A Conjunction of Interests: Business, Politics, and Tariffs, 1825–1879* (T: UTP 1986), which is internally rather than externally structured. Instead in recent years we have had particular studies of particular industries in particular regions, a part of the overall process of removing any notion of synthesis from the pre-Confederation period. Some of the older works are therefore not only still useful, but absolutely essential, especially D.G. Creighton, *The Commercial Empire of the St. Lawrence, 1760–1850* (T: RP 1937), reprinted as *The Empire of the St. Lawrence* (T: MAC 1956), in terms of its discussion of commercial matters and not its views on Canadian politics; Gilbert N. Tucker, *The Canadian Commercial Revolution, 1845–1851* (1936; repr., ed. Hugh G.J. Aitken, T: M&S 1964), in which Canada means the province; Orville J. McDiarmid, *Commercial Policy in the Canadian Economy* (Cambridge, MA: Harvard University Press 1946), in which Canada means the country; Arthur R.M. Lower, *Great Britain's Woodyard: British America and the Timber Trade, 1763–1867* (M: MQUP 1973); and Gerald Tulchinsky, *The River Barons: Montreal Businessmen and the Growth of Industry and Transportation, 1837–53* (M: UTP 1977). The imperial shift is not important to Michael Bliss, *Northern Enterprise: Five Centuries of Canadian Business* (T: M&S 1987), or, curiously enough, to R.T. Naylor, *Canada in the European Age*. *DCB* sketches of such Canadian mercantile princes as Sir Samuel Cunard (vol. 9) and Sir Hugh Allan (vol. 11) are crucial.

Particular recent studies that impinge on the so-called Commercial Revolution, by which British North America shifted from an imperial to a continental economy, include a number of works that examine the situation in an Atlantic region far more oriented to Britain than Canada: Basil Greenhill and Ann Giffard, *Westcountrymen in Prince Edward's Isle: A Fragment of the Great Migration* (T: UTP 1967); Graeme Wynn, *Timber Colony: A Historical Geography of Early Nineteenth Century New Brunswick* (T: UTP 1981); Shannon Ryan, *Fish Out of Water: The Newfoundland Saltfish Trade, 1814–1914* (SJ: BKW 1986); Eric W. Sager and Lewis R. Fischer, *Shipping and Shipbuilding in Atlantic Canada, 1820–1914*, CHA Historical Booklet no. 42 (O: 1986); Sager with Gerald E. Panting, *Maritime Capital: The Shipping Industry in Atlantic Canada, 1820–1914* (K&M: MQUP 1990); and Rosemary E. Ommer, *From Outpost to Outport: A Structural Analysis of the Jersey-Gaspé Cod Fishery, 1767–1886* (K&M: MQUP 1991).

EMIGRATION / IMMIGRATION

Perhaps nowhere is imperial history more alive, albeit under a different guise, than in the scholarship on British emigration/immigration (distinguished in terms of whether one emphasizes departure or arrival). Over the past decade, the immigration historians have increasingly gone back to study the Old World origins of their immigrants, and focused on the 'extension and evolution' of their society and culture in the North American context, often in terms of whether the motivations that sent them across the Atlantic were fulfilled. Not only has the focus of the scholarship changed in emphasizing Old World origins, but in emphasizing particular Old World origins. Most of the earlier scholarship on immigration employed an abstract category called British or discussed an abstract country called Great Britain, completing ignoring the complexities of the British situation and thus the realities of the North American experience. It in effect invented the British. In this regard students should consult the pro-vocative essay by E.J. Hobsbawm, 'Introduction: Inventing Traditions,' in Hobsbawm and Terence Ranger, eds., *The Invention of Tradition* (Cambridge, Eng.: Cambridge University Press 1983).

For the most part the older studies tend to be mainly about imperial or colonial policy and administration, rather than about actual immigrants themselves, or their adaptation to the new environment. Such older works include S.C. Johnston, *A History of Emigration from the United Kingdom to North America, 1763-1912* (L: George Routledge 1913; repr. L: Cass 1966); William A. Carrothers, *Emigration from the British Isles* (L: P.S. King 1929); Wilbur S. Shepperson, *British Emigration to North America: Projects and Opinions in the Early Victorian Period* (Minneapolis, MN: University of Minnesota Press 1957); Helen I. Cowan, *British Emigration to British North America: The First Hundred Years* (1928; rev. ed., T: UTP 1961); and Terry Coleman, *Passage to America: A History of Emigrants from Great Britain and Ireland to America in the Mid-Nineteenth Century* (L: Hutchinson 1972). Perhaps the most useful of these earlier works, full of detailed information often not well digested or presented, are two volumes by Norman Macdonald: *Canada, 1763-1841, Immigration and Settlement: The Administration of the Imperial Land Regulations* (L: Longmans, Green 1939) and *Canada: Immigration and Colonization, 1841-1903* (T: MAC 1966). Also important is Maldwyn A. Jones, 'The Background to Emigration from Great Britain in the Nineteenth Century,' *Perspectives in American History* (1973): 1–117. Two useful research tools are Jack W. Weaver, *Immigrants from Great Britain and Ireland: A Guide to Archival and Manuscript Sources in North America* (Westport, CT: Greenwood Press 1986), and Normand Robert and Michel Thibault, *Catalog of Catholic Immigrants from the British Isles before 1825* (M: Société de recherche historique Archiv-Histro 1988).

A separate literature exists on the crossing of the Atlantic. Basic works include Oliver MacDonagh, *A Pattern of Government Growth, 1800-60: The Passenger Acts and Their Enforcement* (L: MacGibbon and Kee 1961), whose study sticks much too closely to the official documents; Edwin C. Guillet, *The Great Migration: The Atlantic Crossing by Sailing-Ship since 1770* (1937; 2nd ed., T: UTP 1963); B. Greenhill, *The Great Migration: Crossing the Atlantic under Sail* (L: HMSO 1968); and Peter Dunkley, 'Emigration and the State, 1803-1842: The Nineteenth Century Revolution in Government Reconsidered,' *Historical Journal* 23/2 (1980): 353–80. Many of the early immigrants carried contagious disease, and the epidemics that became associated with them are the subject of Charles M. Godfrey, *The Cholera Epi-*

demics of Upper Canada, 1832–1866 (T: Seccombe House 1968), and Geoffrey Bilson, *A Darkened House: Cholera in Nineteenth-Century Canada* (T: UTP 1980).

Three relatively recent studies that do examine government policy are Hugh J.M. Johnston, *British Emigration Policy, 1815–1830: 'Shovelling Out Paupers'* (Oxford: Clarendon Press 1972), O. MacDonagh, ed., *Emigration in the Victorian Age: Debates on the Issue from the 19th Century Critical Journals* (Westmead, Eng.: Greg International 1973), and B. Bailyn, *Voyagers to the West: A Passage in the Peopling of America on the Eve of the Revolution* (NY: Knopf 1986). A very influential book, although about the United States rather than Canada, has been Charlotte Erickson, *Invisible Immigrants: The Adaptation of English and Scottish Immigrants in Nineteenth-Century America* (Coral Gables, FL: University of Miami Press 1972). Unfortunately, Erickson did not make as much of the distinction between English and Scottish as she might have done.

In recent years there has been a scholarly resurgence of an emphasis on the lack of cultural homogeneity of the British Isles, at least before the twentieth century, commonly referred to as the 'Four Nations Approach.' The British Isles were, after all, made up of the union of a number of quite distinctive 'nations,' most of which had their own history and culture, and which were made up of quite distinctive regions distinguished from one another by confessional creed and language. Hugh F. Kearney, *The British Isles: A History of Four Nations* (Cambridge, Eng.: Cambridge University Press 1989), reflects this new understanding, while Linda Colley, *Britons: Forging the Nation, 1707–1837* (New Haven, CT: Yale University Press 1992), highlights elements and levels of coordination.

The smallest of the four nations of Britain is Wales, usefully compared with Canada because of its bilingual and bicultural history. There are several excellent general works students can consult: David Williams, *A History of Modern Wales* (2nd ed., L: J. Murray 1977); Gwyn A. Williams, *When Was Wales? A History of the Welsh* (L: Black Raven Press 1985); and David Smith, *Wales! Wales!* (L: Allen and Unwin 1984). A helpful series of essays on modern Wales is Tony Curtis, ed., *Wales The Imagined Nation: Essays in Cultural & National Identity* (Mid Glamorgan, Wales: Poetry Wales Press 1986). Other important works which describe the social conditions of unrest that were always the background of emigration include D. Williams, *The Rebecca Riots: A Study in Agrarian Discontent* (Cardiff: University of Wales Press 1955), on the agrarian riots of 1839–44; David J.V. Jones, *Before Rebecca: Popular Protest in Wales, 1793–1835* (L: Allen Lane 1973); and G.A. Williams, *The Merthyr Rising* (L: Croom Helm 1978), a major uprising of 1831. Sir John Rhys and David Brynmor-Jones, in *The Welsh People: Chapters on Their Origin, History, Laws, Language, Literature, and Characteristics* (NY: Haskell House 1969), provide a nationalist study of Welsh culture, and G.A. Williams, ed., *The Sociology of Welsh* (Berlin: Mouton 1987), essays on the Welsh language, spoken by nearly half the Welsh, most of them from the Protestant north. An iconoclastic look at Welsh cultural nationalism is Prys Morgan, 'From a Death to a View: The Hunt for the Welsh Past in the Romantic Period,' in E.J. Hobsbawn and T. Ranger, eds., *The Invention of Tradition.*

Because the British authorities did not consider Wales a separate nation (having 'assimilated' it into England during the Middle Ages), they did not list Welsh emigrants apart from the English. Recovering a Welsh immigration to Canada has been no easy matter, but in general see Carol Bennett, *In Search of the Red Dragon: The Welsh in Canada* (Renfrew, Ont.: Juniper Books 1985), which contains a good bibliography. By far the best monograph, lovingly written and based upon much difficult research, is Peter Thomas, *Strangers from a Secret Land: The Voyages of the Brig 'Albion' and the Founding of the First Welsh Settlements in Canada* (T: UTP 1986). Thomas illustrates the difficulty of uncovering much of the Welsh immigration and settlement.

Probably the most elusive among the 'British' immigrants are not the Welsh, but the English, partly because the country is so big and contains so many regions, most of which are associated with historic counties, and partly because the English are often not regarded as ethnics. A good place to start is with the reminder of linguistic differences provided in John M. Kirk et al., *Studies in Linguistic Geography: The Dialects of English in Britain and Ireland* (L: Croom Helm 1985). A few examples of the local literature from the regions among the most common sources of emigration must suffice: for Cornwall, Martyn F. Wakelin, *Language and History in Cornwall* (Leicester, Eng.: Leicester University Press 1975); for Devon, H.P.R. Finberg, *West-country Historical Studies* (NY: A.M. Kelley 1969), and William Page, ed., *The Victoria History of the County of Devon* (Folkestone, Eng.: Dawson for the Institute of Historical Research 1975); and for Yorkshire, Sidney Pollard and Colin Holmes, eds., *Essays in the Economic and Social History of South Yorkshire* (Barnsley, Eng.: South Yorkshire County Council 1976), and K.J. Allison, *A History of the County of York, East Riding*, 4 vols. (L: OUP for the Institute of Historical Research 1969–84). London, which stands quite apart from the counties, can be approached through Rosamund Bayne-Powell, *Eighteenth-Century London Life* (L: J. Murray 1937), R.J. Mitchell and M.D.R. Leys, *A History of London Life* (L: Longmans, Green

1958), and F.H.W. Sheppard, *London: The Infernal Wen* (Berkeley and Los Angeles, CA: University of California Press 1971). As well as regional distinctions, class is also important in assessing emigration: consult Harold Perkin, *The Origins of Modern English Society, 1780–1880* (L: Routledge & Kegan Paul 1969), R.S. Neale, *Class in English History, 1680–1850* (Oxford: Blackwell 1981), Kenneth C. Phillipps, *Language and Class in Victorian England* (NY: Blackwell 1984), and Leonore Davidoff and Catherine Hall, *Family Fortunes: Men and Women of the English Middle Class, 1780–1850* (Chicago, IL: University of Chicago Press 1987).

The literature on the English in British North America is surprisingly thin on the ground. One of the best places to look is undoubtedly the *DCB*, which usually offers a place of birth and something on upbringing. Otherwise students should consult B. Greenhill and A. Giffard, *Westcountrymen in Prince Edward's Isle*; John J. Mannion, ed., *The Peopling of Newfoundland: Essays in Historical Geography* (SJ: Institute of Social and Economic Research, Memorial University of Newfoundland 1977); B. Bailyn, *Voyagers to the West*; and W. Gordon Handcock, *Soe Longe As There Comes Noe Women: Origins of English Settlement in Newfoundland* (SJ: BKW 1989).

As for the Irish, students should understand that there were at least three Irelands, plus incredibly complex relationships between Ireland and Scotland, as well as between Ireland and the British Empire. The literature is enormous and what follows is merely a selection. A sense of the land itself is provided in J.B. Whittow, *Geology and Scenery in Ireland* (Harmondsworth, Eng.: Penguin 1974), while a good introduction to the history is Louis M. Cullen, *The Emergence of Modern Ireland, 1600–1900* (NY: Holmes and Meier 1981), which contains a full bibliography. The Catholic south is the focus of Thomas Walter Freeman, *Pre-Famine Ireland: A Study in Historical Geography* (Manchester, Eng.: Manchester University Press 1957), Sean J. Connolly, *Priests and People in Pre-Famine Ireland, 1780–1845* (Dublin: Gill and McMillan 1982), and Kevin O'Neill, *Family and Farm in Pre-Famine Ireland: The Parish of Killashandra* (Madison, WI: University of Wisconsin Press 1984). Ulster in the north is the focus of Cyril Bentham Falls, *The Birth of Ulster* (L: Methuen 1973), T.W. Moody, *The Ulster Question, 1603–1973* (Dublin: Mercier Press 1974), Geoffrey Bell, *The Protestants of Ulster* (L: Pluto 1976), Anthony Terence Quincey Stewart, *The Narrow Ground: Aspects of Ulster, 1609–1969* (L: Faber and Faber 1977), and Liam Kennedy and Philip Ollerenshaw, eds., *An Economic History of Ulster, 1820–1940* (Manchester, Eng.: Manchester University Press 1985). For the Anglo-Irish, who were a social group rather than a regional one, consult Terence De Vere White, *The Anglo-Irish* (L: Gollancz 1972), N.P. Canny,

The Formation of the Old English Elite in Ireland (Dublin: National University of Ireland 1975), and J.C. Beckett, *The Anglo-Irish Tradition* (Ithaca, NY: Cornell University Press 1976). The complex relationships between Irish and Scots are tackled in James E. Handley, *The Irish in Modern Scotland* (Cork, Eire: Cork University Press 1947), M. Perceval-Maxwell, *The Scottish Migration to Ulster in the Reign of James I* (L: Routledge & Kegan Paul 1973), L.M. Cullen and T.C. Smout, eds., *Comparative Aspects of Scottish and Irish Economic and Social History, 1600–1900* (Edinburgh: J. Donald 1977), and T.M. Devine and David Dickson, eds., *Ireland and Scotland, 1600–1850: Parallels and Contrasts in Economic and Social Development* (Edinburgh: J. Donald 1983).

Much of the recent work on Irish emigration and immigration to British North America has concentrated on distinguishing the Canadian experience from the more familiar American one, on which there is an enormous literature. Traditionally, books on the American experience often have incorporated British North America into the picture automatically, and many still do, although much of the Canadian Irish immigration predates the famines of the 1840s and much of the American one postdates it. See, for example, Kerby A. Miller, *Emigrants and Exiles: Ireland and the Irish Exodus to North America* (NY: OUP 1985). A summary of the historiography of Irish Catholic immigration to Canada is provided in William M. Baker, '"God's Unfortunate People": Historiography of Irish Catholics in Nineteenth Century Canada,' in Robert O'Driscoll and Lorna Reynolds, eds., *The Untold Story: The Irish in Canada,* vol. 1 (T: Celtic Arts of Canada 1988). A recent popular survey, weak on the earlier period and the Atlantic region, as well as on Irish regional and confessional differences, is Donald MacKay, *Flight from Famine: The Coming of the Irish to Canada* (T: M&S 1990). Much better and more balanced is Cecil J. Houston and William J. Smyth, *Irish Emigration and Canadian Settlement: Patterns, Links, and Letters* (T: UTP 1990). Also useful are such recent collections of essays as Cyril J. Byrne and Margaret Harry, eds., *Talamh An Eisc: Canadian and Irish Essays* (H: Nimbus 1986), and R. O'Driscoll and L. Reynolds, eds., *The Untold Story*, which really amounts to a multi-authored history of the Irish story. The most provocative of recent revisionists of the Irish in Canada is Donald Harman Akenson, whose *Being Had: Historians, Evidence, and the Irish in North America* (Port Credit, Ont.: P.D. Meany 1985) and *Small Differences: Irish Catholics and Irish Protestants, 1815–1922: An International Perspective* (K&M: MQUP 1988) have set off several debates.

Otherwise the literature on the Canadian Irish is organized regionally, and most of the works cited have their own bibliographies. Beginning in the east see Thomas P. Power, ed., *The Irish in Atlantic Canada, 1780–1900* (F: New Ireland Press 1991), a provocative set of essays; J.J. Mannion, *Irish Settlements in Eastern Canada: A Study of Cultural Transfer and Adaptation* (T: UTP 1974); C.J. Byrne, ed., *Gentlemen-Bishops and Faction Fighters: The Letters of Bishops O'Donel, Lambert, Scallan and Other Irish Missionaries* (SJ: Jesperson Press 1984); Terrence M. Punch, *Irish Halifax: The Immigrant Generation, 1815–1859* (H: Saint Mary's University 1981); A.A. MacKenzie, *The Irish in Cape Breton* (Antigonish, NS: Formac 1979); Peter M. Toner, ed., *New Ireland Remembered: Historical Essays on the Irish in New Brunswick* (F: New Ireland Press 1988); and Brendan O'Grady, 'Where Were the Irish in 1864?' *Abegweit Review* 6/1 (Spring 1988): 157–75.

The Irish experience in central Canada is the subject of Patrick M. Redmond, *Irish Life in Rural Quebec: A History of Frampton* (Chicago, IL: Adams Press 1977); the revisionist D.H. Akenson, *The Irish in Ontario: A Study in Rural History* (K&M: MQUP 1984); Bruce S. Elliott, *Irish Migrants in the Canadas: A New Approach* (K&M: MQUP 1988), a very stimulating monograph which demonstrates how the work of genealogists can be used for immigration history; and John Willis, 'Le Québec, l'Irlande et les migrations de la grande famine: origine, contexte et dénouement,' in Marcel Bellavance, ed., *La grand mouvance* (Sillery, Que.: SPT 1990). Key to much of the Irish experience in Canada was the Orange Order, the subject of C.J. Houston and W.J. Smyth, *The Sash Canada Wore: A Historical Geography of the Orange Order in Canada* (T: UTP 1980). *Life and Adventures of Wilson Benson* (T: n.p. 1876) is an interesting autobiography by an Irish immigrant.

Finally, there is an enormous literature on Scottish emigration. Scotland is not only a country quite distinct from England, having been joined to it by the Act of Union only in 1707, but it also has a number of distinct regions, geographically, culturally, and linguistically. A sense of the region's topographical variety can be gained from J.B. Whittow, *Geology and Scenery in Scotland* (Harmondsworth, Eng.: Penguin 1977), while G. Martin and Jeffrey Simpson, in *Canada's Heritage in Scotland* (T: Dundurn 1989), discuss the historic significance of places in modern Scotland and provide a sort of historical tour guide to the country. As for the complexities of language, *The Linguistic Atlas of Scotland* will, when completed, prove invaluable: so far one volume has been published, J.Y. Mather and H.H. Speitel, eds., *The Linguistic Atlas of Scotland. Scots Section* (L: Croom Helm 1975). In the meantime, consult Angus McIntosh, *An Introduction to a Survey of Scottish Dialects* (Edinburgh: Nelson 1952). Scots is not English, though the languages share common roots, as should be clear from Mairi Robinson, ed., *The Concise Scots Dictionary* (Aberdeen, Scot.: Aberdeen University Press

1985). Gaelic, spoken chiefly north of the Highland Fault, is the focus of Charles W.J. Withers, *Gaelic in Scotland, 1698–1981: The Geographical History of a Language* (Edinburgh: J. Donald 1984).

Patrick W.J. Riley, *The Union of England and Scotland: A Study in Anglo-Scottish Politics of the Eighteenth Century* (Manchester, Eng.: Manchester University Press 1978), explains the background of the Act of Union. Among more general studies of Scottish history consult T.C. Smout, *A History of the Scottish People, 1560–1830* (L: Collins 1969); I.F. Grant, *The Economic History of Scotland* (NY: AMS Press 1976); Bruce Lenman, *An Economic History of Modern Scotland, 1660–1976* (Hamden, CT: Archon 1977); Rosalind Mitchison, *A History of Scotland* (2nd ed., L: Methuen 1982); and Smout, *A Century of the Scottish People, 1830–1950* (L: Collins 1986). Useful reference books include R.H. Campbell and J.B.A. Dow, eds., *Source Book of Scottish Economic and Social History* (Oxford: Blackwell 1968), and J.T. Coppock, *An Agricultural Atlas of Scotland* (Edinburgh: J. Donald 1976).

There is no good modern full-length study surveying either Scottish immigration to Canada or the Scots in Canada, but J.M Bumsted provides a brief overview in *The Scots in Canada*, CHA Canada's Ethnic Groups Booklet no. 1 (O: 1982). See also Stephen J. Hornsby, 'Patterns of Scottish Emigration to Canada, 1750–1870,' *Journal of Historical Geography* 18/4 (1992): 397–416. Otherwise, for general works on Scottish immigration to Canada students can turn to William Jordan Rattray, *The Scot in British North America*, 4 vols. (T: Maclear 1880–4), which is old but still reasonably reliable for its factual content; W. Stanford Reid, ed., *The Scottish Tradition in Canada* (T: M&S 1976), which contains a number of essays of variable quality; and Donald Whyte, *A Dictionary of Scottish Emigrants to Canada, before Confederation* (T: Ontario Genealogical Society 1986), which has a bibliography of genealogical sources. Frank Emmerson, *The Scots* (Tantallon, NS: Four East Publications 1987), is a brief survey of the Scots in the Maritime provinces, which includes a useful bibliography, while Douglas Campbell and R.A. MacLean, *Beyond the Atlantic Roar: A Study of the Nova Scotia Scots* (T: M&S 1974), is more substantial if narrower in focus. Gerald Redmond, *The Sporting Scots of Nineteenth-Century Canada* (Rutherford, NJ: Fairleigh Dickinson University Press 1982), demonstrates how important Scotland was to the development of sport in Canada. A very useful work, far wider in scope than its title would suggest, is Marjory Harper, *Emigration from North-East Scotland*, 2 vols. (Aberdeen, Scot.: Aberdeen University Press 1988). The first volume, subtitled *Willing Exiles*, really provides a general survey of Scottish immigration through the period of Canadian Confederation and offers a comparative view of immigration to Australasia and the Tropics as well as to British North America. Finally, students should not miss Lowland Presbyterian Thomas McCulloch's pawky classic *The Mephibosheth Stepsure Letters*, which has been edited with a substantial introduction by Gwendolyn Davies (O: CUP 1990).

Most of the recent scholarly attention has focused on the Highland Scot in Canada, who is associated with one of the most controversial topics in Scottish history – the Clearances. The Clearances, by which the Scottish landlords in the Highlands deliberately depopulated the countryside, partly to create sheep pasturage, have always been contentious. A highly stimulating and iconoclastic look at Highland 'Tartanry' is Hugh Trevor-Roper, 'The Invention of Tradition: The Highland Tradition of Scotland,' in E.J. Hobsbawm and T. Ranger, eds., *The Invention of Tradition*, which argues that most of the traditional symbols of Scotland do not have very deep roots in the nation's past. Much of the written tradition about Clearance and emigration critical of 'the lairds' can be credited to the writings of Donald MacLeod, a Strathnaver stonemason who attacked the lairds from Canadian exile in two key books: *History of the Destitution in Sutherlandshire* (Edinburgh: Chronicle Office 1841) and *Gloomy Memories in the Highlands of Scotland: A Faithful Picture of the Extirpation of the Celtic Race from the Highlands of Scotland* (T: Printed for the Author by Thompson & Co. 1857). MacLeod's views are given modern currency in John Prebble, *The Highland Clearances* (L: Secker and Warburg 1963). A more recent popular study, focusing on the folk memory, is David Craig, *On the Crofters' Trail: In Search of the Clearance Highlanders* (L: Jonathan Cape 1990).

The argument of the landlords was that the land could not sustain the population that was expanding upon it. This argument is best followed in Malcolm Gray, *The Highland Economy, 1750–1850* (Edinburgh: Oliver and Boyd 1957), A.J. Youngson, *After the Forty-five: The Economic Impact on the Scottish Highlands* (Edinburgh: Edinburgh University Press 1973), Eric Richards, *The Leviathan of Wealth: The Sutherland Fortune in the Industrial Revolution* (L: Routledge & Kegan Paul 1973), and Michael Flinn et al., *Scottish Population History: From the 17th Century to the 1930s* (Cambridge, Eng.: Cambridge University Press 1977). Richards has also contributed *A History of the Highland Clearances*, 2 vols. (L: Croom Helm 1982–5), the first volume of which is subtitled *Agrarian Transformation and the Evictions, 1746–1886*, and the second, *Emigration, Protest, Reasons*. More engaged are James Hunter, *The Making of the Crofting Community* (Edinburgh: J. Donald 1976), and T.M. Devine, *The Great Highland Famine: Hunger, Emigration, and the Scottish Highlands in the Nineteenth Century* (Edinburgh: J. Donald 1988).

Modern scholarly study of Highland immigration to British North America began with D. MacKay, *Scotland Farewell: The People of the Hector* (T: MHR 1980), which searched the Scottish records diligently and was very sympathetic to the settlers. J.M. Bumsted, *The People's Clearance: Highland Emigration to British North America, 1770–1815* (Edinburgh/W: Edinburgh University Press/UMP 1982), argued that the early emigration before 1815 was caused less by Clearance than by the free choice of the people – a point made more briefly in his 'Scottish Immigration to the Maritimes, 1770–1815: A New Look at an Old Theme,' *Acadiensis* 10/2 (Spring 1981): 65–85. Conversely, Marianne McLean maintains in *The People of Glengarry: Highlanders in Transition, 1745–1820* (K&M: MQUP 1991) that those who went to Glengarry County in Ontario were indeed cleared. As Sister Margaret MacDonell has shown in *The Emigrant Experience: Songs of Highland Emigrants in North America* (T: UTP 1982), the bards certainly believed in Clearance, but also had mixed feelings about the new land.

One of the major figures in Highland emigration is Thomas Douglas, 5th Earl of Selkirk, whose papers are presently being published as *The Collected Writings of Lord Selkirk* (W: Manitoba Record Society 1984–) under the editorship of J.M. Bumsted. The two volumes presently available not only reprint Selkirk's own writings, including his notorious *Observations on the Present State of the Highlands of Scotland, with a View of the Causes and Probable Consequences of Emigration* (1805), but also provide lengthy biographical introductions. Selkirk's Upper Canadian settlement has been studied in A.E.D. MacKenzie, *Baldoon: Lord Selkirk's Settlement in Upper Canada* (London, Ont.: Phelps 1978). Another eminent Scot, a religious leader among the many Highland Catholics, is the subject of J.E. Rea, *Bishop Alexander Macdonell and the Politics of Upper Canada* (T: Ontario Historical Society 1974). Also see A.A. Johnston, *A History of the Catholic Church in Eastern Nova Scotia*, 2 vols. (Antigonish, NS: St Francis Xavier University Press 1960–6).

In addition to immigrants from the four nations of Britain, the other major source of settlers in British North America was the United States. Although most Americans before the Civil War of 1861–5 were themselves of British origin, they were still a quite distinctive people, whose contribution to Canada is not well understood and has received little recent direct attention from Canadian scholars. The best overview probably remains Marcus Lee Hansen, *The Mingling of the Canadian and American Peoples* (New Haven, CT: Yale University Press 1940). David D. Harvey, *Americans in Canada: Migration and Settlement since 1840* (Lewiston, NY: E. Mellen Press 1991), avoids much of the influence by its late starting date.

The New Englanders who went to Nova Scotia before the American Rebellion are the subject of two recent volumes of essays edited by M. Conrad, *They Planted Well* and *Making Adjustments*.

The most famous group of American immigrants is undoubtedly the Loyalists. Neil MacKinnon opens his essay 'The Loyalists: "A Different People,"' in D. Campbell, ed., *Banked Fires: The Ethnics of Nova Scotia* (Port Credit, Ont.: Scribblers' Press 1978), with the statement 'The Loyalist experience in Nova Scotia was not an ethnic experience.' Such a disclaimer was perhaps necessary in 1978, when the variety of Loyalist backgrounds (Black, Native, Highland Scot, Hessian soldier, and so forth) was less well appreciated. But while the diversity of Loyalists remains indisputable, it would be unfortunate to forget that the majority of Loyalist refugees (as opposed to disbanded soldiers) were of American cultural background. Such problems of characterization are dealt with in J.M. Bumsted, 'Loyalists and Nationalists: An Essay on the Problem of Definition,' *Canadian Review of Studies in Nationalism* 6/2 (Fall 1979): 218–32, reprinted in Bumsted, ed., *Interpreting Canada's Past*, vol. 1, 1st ed. Bumsted also provides a guide to the substantial Loyalist historiography in *Understanding the Loyalists* (Sackville, NB: Centre for Canadian Studies, Mount Allison University 1986). Good general introductions are to be found in Wallace Brown and H. Senior, *Victorious in Defeat: The Loyalists in Canada* (T: Methuen 1984), and Christopher Moore, *The Loyalists: Revolution, Exile, Settlement* (T: MAC 1984). Among specialized studies, on ideology see Janice Potter, *The Liberty We Seek: Loyalist Ideology in Colonial New York and Massachusetts* (Cambridge, MA: Harvard University Press 1983), and on women Mary Beth Norton, 'Eighteenth-Century American Women in Peace and War: The Case of the Loyalists,' *WMQ* 3rd ser., 33/3 (July 1976): 386–409, and J. Potter-MacKinnon, *While the Women Only Wept: Loyalist Refugee Women in Eastern Ontario* (K&M: MQUP 1993).

On the so-called late Loyalists in Upper Canada, consult F. Landon, *Western Ontario and the American Frontier* (1941; repr. T: M&S 1967). One of the most hotly debated issues in early Upper Canada was the 'Alien (for which read American) Question.' It is discussed in Paul Romney, 'Re-Inventing Upper Canada: American Immigrants, Upper Canadian History, English Law, and the Alien Question,' in Roger Hall et al., eds., *Patterns of the Past: Interpreting Ontario's History* (T: Dundurn 1988). Some of the Americans were not British; see, for example, Orland Gingerich, *The Amish of Canada* (Waterloo, Ont.: Conrad Press 1972), which chronicles a religious group, part of the Mennonite community and chiefly German-speaking, that settled mainly in Waterloo County, Ontario.

While most immigrants came from the United States or the British Isles, there were small groups of others, mainly from western Europe. The Germans, for example, are the subject of Heinz Lehmann, *The German Canadians, 1750–1937: Immigration, Settlement and Culture* (SJ: Jesperson Press 1986); the Swedes, of Helge Nelson, *The Swedes and the Swedish Settlements in North America* (NY: Arno Press 1979); and the Norwegians, of Gulbarand Loken, *From Fjord to Frontier: A History of the Norwegians in Canada* (T: M&S 1980), and Orm Overland, ed., *Johan Schroder's Travels in Canada, 1863* (K&M: MQUP 1989), which contains the travel journals of a Norwegian farmer in Upper and Lower Canada. A number of Swiss also came to British North America: E.H. Bovay, *Le Canada et les Suisses, 1604–1974* (Fribourg, Ger.: Editions Universitaires 1976), is a general history, while Winthrop Pickard Bell, *The 'Foreign Protestants' and the Settlement of Nova Scotia: The History of a Piece of Arrested British Colonial Policy in the Eighteenth Century* (T: UTP 1961; repr., intro. L.D. McCann, Sackville, NB: Centre for Canadian Studies, Mount Allison University 1990), tells the story of the particularly large contingent that came to Nova Scotia in the 1760s.

There were also a small number of Jews, widely dispersed. Benjamin Sack, *History of the Jews in Canada: From the Earliest Beginnings to the Present Day*, vol. 1, *From the French Regime to the End of the Nineteenth Century* (M: Canadian Jewish Congress 1945), and Bernard L. Vigod, *The Jews in Canada*, CHA Canada's Ethnic Groups Booklet no. 7 (O: 1984), are general surveys. The significant Jewish community of Quebec in particular is the subject of David Rome, Judith Nefsky, and Paule Obermeir, *Les Juifs du Québec: bibliographie rétrospective annotée* (Q: IQRC 1981), Rome, comp., *On the Jews of Lower Canada and 1837–38* (M: National Archives, Canadian Jewish Congress 1983), and Michael Brown, *Jew or Juif? Jews, French Canadians, and Anglo-Canadians, 1759–1914* (Philadelphia, PA: Jewish Publication Society 1987).

THE TRANSFER OF BRITISH INSTITUTIONS

Despite the current unfashionableness of traditional imperial history, many scholars still study 'the extension and evolution of British institutions overseas,' albeit under a different guise. Almost any work dealing with culture (in its several meanings) in its various manifestations in the pre-Confederation period must come to terms with the problem of cultural transfer, although few do so systematically. One study that is aware of the problem is Peter Ennals and Deryck Holdsworth, 'Vernacular Architecture and the Cultural Landscape of the Maritime Provinces – A Reconnaissance,' *Acadiensis* 10/2 (Spring 1981): 86–106. Other examples will be found in the various regional chapters of this work. There is much research to be done in this area, and students can make a contribution. We will focus here on several areas that currently attract much scholarship but are traditionally neglected in standard history texts.

To begin with, the history of language usage in its various meanings is obviously an important matter for an officially bilingual and multicultural country. Long before modern language theory, those involved understood that language was an important element of imperialism, yet, except in the most elementary terms, the subject has been avoided by mainstream Canadian history. Beyond the simple question of 'which language?' are more interesting matters of pronunciation and usage. Language choices and their resultant patterns are the subject of Alva Leroy Davis, Raven I. McDavid, Jr, and Virginia G. McDavid, *A Compilation of the Work Sheets of the Linguistic Atlas of the United States and Canada and Associated Projects* (Chicago, IL: University of Chicago Press 1969), and Gaston Dulong and Gaston Bergeron, *Le parler populaire du Québec et de ses régions voisines: atlas linguistique de l'Est du Canada*, 10 vols. (Q: Gouvernement du Québec, Ministère des Communications 1980).

The broad story of the English language is told in Robert McCrum, William Cran, and Robert MacNeil, *The Story of English* (NY: Viking 1986), while the English language in Canada is the subject of Mark M. Orkin, *Speaking Canadian English: An Informal Account of the English Language in Canada* (T: General Publishing 1970); J.K. Chambers, ed., *Canadian English: Origins and Structures* (T: Methuen 1975), which includes a bibliography; Dieter Bahr, *A Bibliography of Writings on the English Language in Canada: from 1857 to 1976* (Heidelberg, Ger.: Winter 1977); and M.H. Scargill, *A Short History of Canadian English* (VI: Sono Nis Press 1977). Walter S. Avis, who devoted his scholarly life to the study of Canadian English, provides a brief overview in 'Canadian English in Its North American Context,' *Canadian Journal of Linguistics* 28/1 (Spring 1983): 3–15. An interesting example of a contemporary observer's comments is in James Taylor, *Narrative of a Voyage to, and Travels in Upper Canada, with Accounts of the Customs, Character, and Dialect of the Country* ... (Hull, Eng.: John Nicholson 1846). Several distinctive dialects of English have been recorded. Two specific examples are examined in G.M. Story, 'Newfoundland Dialect: An Historical View,' *Canadian Geographical Journal* 70/4 (Apr. 1965): 126–31, and L.M. Dickson, 'The History of Black English in Nova Scotia – A First Step,' *African Language Review* 9 (1970–1): 263–9.

A general starting-point for the study of Canada's other official language is Alfred Ewert, *The French Language* (L: Faber & Faber 1961). Robert Vigneault, ed., *Langue, littérature, culture au Canada français* (O: Editions de l'Université d'Ottawa 1977), examines the role of French in Canada as a whole; Guy Gouthillier and Jean Meynaud, comps., *Le choc des langues au Québec, 1760–1970* (M: PUQ 1972), in the province of Quebec; and Raymond Mougeon and Edouard Beniak, *Linguistic Consequences of Language Contact and Restriction: The Case of French in Ontario, Canada* (Oxford: Clarendon Press 1991), in the province of Ontario.

Gaelic, which at one point in the first half of the nineteenth century was the third most commonly spoken European language in British North America, is discussed in J.L. Campbell, 'Scottish Gaelic in Canada,' *American Speech* 11/2 (Apr. 1936): 128–36; Charles W. Dunn, *Highland Settler: A Portrait of the Scottish Gael in Nova Scotia* (T: UTP 1953); Ian Pringle, 'The Gaelic Substratum in the English of Glengarry County and Its Reflection in the Novels of Ralph Connor,' *Canadian Journal of Linguistics* 26/1 (Spring 1981): 126–40; and Gilbert Foster, *Language and Poverty: The Persistence of Scottish Gaelic in Eastern Canada* (SJ: ISER 1988). As for what happened to Irish, consult Proinsias Mac Aonghusa, 'Reflections on the Fortunes of the Irish Language in Canada ...,' in R. O'Driscoll and L. Reynolds, eds., *The Untold Story*, vol. 2 (1988). M.B. Emeneau, 'The Dialect of Lunenburg, Nova Scotia,' *Language* 11 (1935): 140–7, traces the German language in one small community. Finally, Margaret Bennett Knight, 'Scottish Gaelic, English, and French: Some Aspects of the Macaronic Tradition of the Codroy Valley, Newfoundland,' *Regional Language Studies of Newfoundland* 4 (1 May 1972): 25–30, provides an example of what happened when European languages intermixed.

The languages of Native Canadians are the subject of increasing interest. A good starting-point is Barry J. Edwards, *A Bibliographical Check-List of Canadian Indian Linguistics in the Languages Centre of Metropolitan Toronto Central Library* (T: Languages Centre, Metropolitan Toronto Library Board 1975). Thereafter consult David H. Pentland and H. Christoph Wolfart, eds., *A Bibliography of Algonquian Linguistics* (W: UMP 1982), and Wolfart, ed., *Linguistic Studies Presented to John L. Finlay* (W: Algonquian and Iroquian Linguistics 1991).

There was considerable interaction between the languages of the Europeans and those of the Native peoples. The various creole and pidgin languages resulting from the mixing of European and Native languages are discussed in Richard Rhodes, 'French Cree: A Case of Borrowing,' in William Cowan, ed., *Papers of the Eighth Algonquian Conference* (O: CUP 1977), and his 'Metchif: A Second Look,' in Cowan, ed., *Papers of the Sev-*

enteenth Algonquian Conference (O: CUP 1985); Pauline Laverdure et al., *The Michif Dictionary: Turtle Mountain Chippewa Cree* (W: Pemmican 1983); and John C. Crawford, 'What Is Michif? Language in the Métis Tradition,' in Jacqueline Peterson and Jennifer S.H. Brown, eds., *The New Peoples: Being and Becoming Métis in North America* (W: UMP 1985). Eleanor Blain, 'Speech of the Lower Red River Settlement,' in W. Cowan, ed., *Papers of the Eighteenth Algonquian Conference* (O: CUP 1987), examines Bungee (or Bungi), which was Scots Gaelic mixed with Cree and used as a second language.

Although the amount of research on Canadian English has increased dramatically since 1948, when Morton W. Bloomfield complained that the English 'spoken by some nine million people, a speech bound both historically, culturally and socially with American English, should have been studied so little by scholars,' very little of that research has been devoted to the issues raised by Bloomfield in his 'Canadian English and Its Relation to Eighteenth Century American Speech,' *Journal of English and Germanic Philology* 47 (1948): 59–67. If Bloomfield is correct that the Loyalists are responsible for American-style pronunciations, that influence may well be their most important legacy to Canada. But see also M.H. Scargill, 'The Sources of Canadian English,' in J.K. Chambers, ed., *Canadian English*, which denies the Loyalist explanation and offers other suggestions for further research. One possibility is that the English in the British Isles has changed since the eighteenth and early nineteenth centuries, while American and Canadian versions remain more true to what existed at the time of immigration.

A number of useful dictionaries on Canadian language usage have now been published. For English see John Sandilands, ed., *Western Canadian Dictionary and Phrase-Book* (W: Telegram Job Printers 1912); W.S. Avis, ed., *A Dictionary of Canadianisms on Historical Principles: Dictionary of Canadian English* (T: Gage 1967); *Dictionary of Canadian English* (T: Gage 1967); G.M. Story et al., *Dictionary of Newfoundland English* (T: UTP 1982); Lewis J. Poteet, *The South Shore Phrase Book* (Hantsport, NS: Lancelot 1983); and T.K. Pratt, *Dictionary of Prince Edward Island English* (T: UTP 1988). For French see Gilles Colpron, *Dictionnaire des anglicismes* (M: Beauchemin 1982); Sinclair Robinson, *Practical Handbook of Quebec and Acadian French* (T: Anansi 1984); Charles Dufresne, ed., *Dictionnaire de l'Amérique française: francophonie nord-américaine hors Québec* (O: PUO 1988); and Robinson and Donald Smith, eds., *Dictionary of Canadian French* (Don Mills, Ont.: Stoddart 1990).

If language has been a relatively neglected field of study by Canadian historians, the imperial history tradition always understood the importance of law and its transference from Europe to North America. Yet it, too, is a subject that has been largely ignored by mainstream Canadian historians in recent years. One searches most of the recent textbooks in Canadian history for any discussion of what the great English jurist Sir William Blackstone described as 'the mysterious science of the law,' but finds little, except perhaps in the context of early Quebec or in terms of traditional constitutional problems. A new resurgence of legal history has resurrected the subject, at least among legal historians. The astute student will note that most of the publications that follow either appear in collections of legal history or in the law journals; very little has been published in the mainstream journals of Canadian history. The special issues of legal history in Quebec are discussed by Vince Masciotra, 'Quebec Legal Historiography, 1760–1900,' *McGill Law Journal* 32/3 (1987): 712–32.

One problem discussed by legal historians is that of the reception of English statutes by the several provinces of British North America, that is, the date after which the statutes of Parliament extend to a colony only if specified; before that date, all parliamentary statutes are deemed to have force. The law has treated the matter as one of legal fiction, allowing the legislatures or the courts to declare a date for the reception of statute law. Some of the problems are outlined in Elizabeth Gaspar Brown, 'British Statutes in the Emergent Nations of North America: 1606–1949,' *American Journal of Legal History* 7 (1963): 95–136, and in her *British Statutes in American Law, 1776–1836* (Ann Arbor, MI: University of Michigan Law School 1964), which deals with the post-rebellion period. Brown's use of the term 'British Statute' in contradistinction to the Canadian 'English Statute' may be significant. A more detailed Canadian analysis is J.E. Cote, 'The Reception of English Law,' *Alberta Law Review* 15/1 (1977): 29–92. Not every province delineated reception by statute. For those which did not, the date is more problematic, as David G. Bell shows in 'A Note on the Reception of English Statutes in New Brunswick' and 'The Reception Question and the Constitutional Crisis of the 1790's in New Brunswick,' *UNB [University of New Brunswick] Law Journal* 28 (1979): 195–201; and 29 (1980): 157–72.

The fictional reception of imperial statute law only begins the process. Beyond that point colonies have to work out a legal system. One input was all sorts of imperial legal baggage. Of what that consisted at mid-eighteenth century is delineated in Thomas Garden Barnes, '"As Near As May Be Agreeable to the Laws of this Kingdom": Legal Birthright and Legal Baggage at Chebucto, 1749,' in Peter B. Waite et al., eds., *Law in a Colonial Society: The Nova Scotia Experience* (T: Carswell 1984). Jean-Maurice Brisson, *La formation d'un droit mixte: l'évolution de la procédure civile de 1774 à 1867* (M: Thémis 1986), and Evelyn Kolish, 'The Impact of the Change in Legal Metropolis on the Development of Lower Canada's Legal System,' *Canadian Journal of Law and Society* 3 (1988): 1–25, look at the situation in Quebec.

Another strand in legal history focuses on the development of a court system. See, for example, Margaret A. Banks, 'The Evolution of the Ontario Courts, 1788–1981,' and William N.T. Wylie, 'Instruments of Commerce and Authority: The Civil Courts in Upper Canada, 1789–1812,' both in David H. Flaherty, ed., *Essays in the History of Canadian Law*, vol. 2 (T: OS 1983). A number of contemporary observations on the developing legal system in Nova Scotia have been reprinted by Barry Cahill: see his 'James Monk's "Observations on the Courts of Law in Nova Scotia," 1775'; 'Richard Gibbons' "Review" of the Administration of Justice in Nova Scotia, 1774'; and 'Henry Dundas' Plan for Reforming the Judicature of British North America, 1792,' *UNB Law Journal* 36 (1987): 131–45; 37 (1988): 34–58; and 39 (1990): 158–70. Consult also Cahill, *'Bleak House* Revisited: The Records and Papers of the Court of Chancery of Nova Scotia, 1751–1855,' *Archivaria* 29/1 (Winter 1989–90): 149–167, which points out the distinctiveness of Chancery's equity jurisdiction and – in Nova Scotia – its Irish rather than English model.

The literature on the law and the courts in Quebec is particularly rich. Among older works students should consult Pierre-Georges Roy, 'L'organisation judiciaire de la province de Québec sous le Régime anglais,' in his *Les juges de la province de Québec* (Q: Archives de Québec 1933), and H. Neatby, *The Administration of Justice under the Quebec Act* (L: OUP 1937). More recently, E. Kolish has published 'L'introduction de la faillite au Bas-Canada: conflit social ou national?' *RHAF* 40/2 (automne 1986): 215–35; 'Imprisonment for Debt in Lower Canada, 1791–1840,' *McGill Law Journal* 32/3 (1987): 602–35; and 'Some Aspects of Civil Litigation in Lower Canada, 1785–1825: Towards the Use of Court Records for Canadian Social History,' *CHR* 70/3 (Sept. 1989): 337–65.

Various provinces also introduced secular divorce courts, following American colonial models and eschewing British practice. Good studies are Kimberley Smith Maynard, 'Divorce in Nova Scotia, 1750–1890,' in Philip Girard and Jim Phillips, eds., *Essays in the History of Canadian Law*, vol. 3, *Nova Scotia* (T: OS 1990), and Wendy Owen and J.M. Bumsted, 'Divorce in a Small Province: A History of Divorce on Prince Edward Island from 1833,' *Acadiensis* 20/2 (Spring 1991): 86–104. Child custody is the subject of Constance Backhouse, 'Shifting Patterns in Nineteenth-Century Canadian

Custody Law,' in D.H. Flaherty, ed., *Essays in the History of Canadian Law*, vol. 1 (T: OS 1981), and Rebecca Veinott, 'Child Custody and Divorce: A Nova Scotia Study, 1866–1910,' in P. Girard and J. Phillips, eds., *Essays in the History of Canadian Law*, vol. 3. Backhouse is also author of *Petticoats and Prejudice: Women and Law in Nineteenth-Century Canada* (T: OS/Women's Press 1991), which confines itself to case studies.

The complex relationship between law and society is only just now receiving the attention it deserves. Students can start with W. Wesley Pue and Barry Wright, eds., *Canadian Perspectives on Law and Society: Issues in Legal History* (O: CUP 1988). Russell C. Smandych, Catherine J. Matthews, and Sandra J. Cox, eds., *Canadian Criminal Justice History: An Annotated Bibliography* (T: UTP 1987), supplies a guide to the subliterature on crime and punishment, and R.C. Macleod, ed., *Lawful Authority: Readings on the History of Criminal Justice in Canada* (T: CCP 1988), an introduction to the literature itself. More ambitious is D. Owen Carrigan's attempt to provide a survey in *Crime and Punishment in Canada: A History* (T: M&S 1991). More specialized studies include Peter McGahan, *Crime and Policing in Maritime Canada: Chapters from the Urban Records* (F: Goose Lane 1988), and J.M. Beattie, *Attitudes towards Crime and Punishment in Upper Canada, 1830–1850: A Documentary Study* (T: Centre of Criminology, University of Toronto 1977). A mini-controversy has developed over the nature of Quebec criminal law, the discussion going well beyond H. Neatby, *The Administration of Justice under the Quebec Act*. On the one side are André Morel, 'La réception du droit criminel anglais au Québec (1760–1892),' *Revue juridique Thémis* 13 (1978): 449–541, and Douglas Hay, 'The Meanings of the Criminal Law in Quebec, 1764–1774,' in Louis A. Knafla, ed., *Crime and Criminal Justice in Europe and Canada* (Waterloo, Ont.: Wilfrid Laurier University Press 1981), both arguing for considerable English impact; on the other, Jean-Marie Fecteau, 'Régulation sociale et répression de la déviance au Bas-Canada au tournant du 19e siècle (1791–1815),' *RHAF* 38/4 (printemps 1985): 499–522, which argues an internal dynamic. Fecteau has recently consolidated his work in *Un nouvel ordre des choses: la pauvreté, le crime et l'Etat au Québec, de la fin du XVIIIe siècle à 1840* (M: VLB Editeur 1989).

Whatever law was developed east of the Lakes, it was subject to a reforming current in the mid-nineteenth century. Studies of mid-Victorian legal reform include: John D. Blackwell, 'William Hume Blake and the Judicature Acts of 1849: The Process of Legal Reform at Mid-Century in Upper Canada,' in D.H. Flaherty, ed., *Essays in the History of Canadian Law*, vol. 1; John W. Cairns, 'Employment in the *Civil Code of Lower Canada*: Tradition and Political Economy in Legal Clarification and Reform,' *McGill Law*

Journal 32/3 (1987): 673–711; P. Girard, 'Married Women's Property, Chancery Abolition, and Insolvency Law: Law Reform in Nova Scotia, 1820–1867,' in Girard and J. Phillips, eds., *Essays in the History of Canadian Law*, vol. 3; and G. Blaine Baker, 'Law Practice and Statecraft in Mid-Nineteenth-Century Montreal: The Torrance-Morris Firm, 1848 to 1868,' in Carol Wilton, ed., *Essays in the History of Canadian Law*, vol. 4, *Beyond the Law: Lawyers and Business in Canada, 1830 to 1930* (T: OS 1990).

The Northwest, which had no official colonies before 1849, was a special problem, discussed in part by Hamar Foster, 'Long-Distance Justice: The Criminal Jurisdiction of Canadian Courts West of the Canadas, 1763–1859,' *American Journal of Legal History* 34/1 (Jan. 1990): 1–48. The act of Parliament transferring criminal justice to the Canadas in 1803 is the subject of Arthur S. Morton, 'The Canada Jurisdiction Act (1803) and the North-West,' *TRSC* ser. 3, 32 (1938), sec. ii, 121–37. Lord Selkirk's legal problems as a result of this statute are reported in Gene Gressley, 'Lord Selkirk and the Canadian Courts,' *North Dakota History* 24 (1957): 89–105. Whether the statute applied to the Native peoples was another matter, however. Thomas Flanagan, 'From Indian Rights to Aboriginal Rights,' in L.A. Knafla, ed., *Law and Justice in a New Land: Essays in Western Canadian Legal History* (T: Carswell 1986), provides an introduction to aboriginal rights, but also see H. Foster, 'The Saanichton Bay Marina Case: Imperial Law, Colonial History and Competing Theories of Aboriginal Title,' *University of British Columbia Law Review* 23/3 (1989): 629–50. Rupert's Land eventually got some courts, which are the subject of Kathryn M. Bindon, 'Hudson Bay Company Law: Adam Thom and the Institution of Order in Rupert's Land, 1839–54,' in D.H. Flaherty, ed., *Essays in the History of Canadian Law*, vol. 1. Also consult Roy St George Stubbs, *Four Recorders of Rupert's Land: A Brief Survey of the Hudson's Bay Company Courts of Rupert's Land* (W: Peguis 1967), and Dale Gibson and Lee Gibson, *Substantial Justice: Law and Lawyers in Manitoba, 1670–1970* (W: Peguis 1972).

Finally, students can approach the development of a legal system on the Pacific Coast through H. Foster, 'Shooting the Elephant: Historians and the Problem of Frontier Lawlessness,' in Richard Eales and David Sullivan, eds., *The Political Context of Law: Proceedings of the Seventh British Legal History Conference, Canterbury, 1985* (L: Hambledon Press 1987), and his 'English Law, British Columbia: Establishing Legal Institutions West of the Rockies,' University of Manitoba Canadian Legal History Project, Working Paper Series (1992): 1–68. See also B.M. Gough, 'Keeping British Columbia British: The Law-and-Order Question on a Gold Mining Frontier,' *Huntington Library Quarterly* 38/3 (May 1975): 269–80, and David

Ricardo Williams, 'The Administration of Criminal and Civil Justice in the Mining Camps and Frontier Communities of British Columbia,' in L.A. Knafla, ed. *Law and Justice*, reprinted in J.M. Bumsted, ed., *Interpreting Canada's Past*, vol. 1, 2nd ed. A larger perspective is provided by John McLaren et al., eds., *Law for the Elephant, Law for the Beaver: Essays in the Legal History of the North American West* (R: CPRC 1992).

CONCLUSION

What this chapter has attempted to demonstrate is that the imperial context of British North America, especially between 1763 and 1867, is a highly complex subject. While topics in colonial government, imperial policy, and constitutional niceties have more than a vaguely traditional ring to them, research and writing on such matters still goes on, although Canadian historiography has often gone too far in its rejection of an imperial past. A good many relatively unexplored questions, moreover, still lurk in the thickets of imperialism, particularly on the cultural and legal side. The early history of Canadian law is only in the opening stages of being completely rewritten, and the serious cultural study of British North America beyond the obvious has only begun. Neither legal nor cultural history for the period before Confederation can possibly be written except from some sort of imperial perspective, and when these subjects have been fully explored, it seems safe to prophesy that British North America will appear a far different collection of provinces/colonies than is presently the case.

Contributors

RALPH T. PASTORE is an Associate Professor in the Department of History and Archaeology Unit, Memorial University of Newfoundland, St John's. He has a special interest in the ethnohistory and archaeology of the Native peoples of the Atlantic region and is the author of *Shanawdithit's People: The Archaeology of the Beothuks* (SJ: Atlantic Archaeology 1992).

THOMAS WIEN is an Assistant Professor in the Département d'histoire, Université de Montréal. He has published articles on the history of early rural Canada and the multifaceted trade linking Native peoples, Canadians, and Europeans in the eighteenth century, and is currently working on a critical edition of the writings of Jean-François Gaultier, *médecin du roi*.

BARRY MOODY is an Associate Professor in the Department of History, Acadia University, Wolfville, Nova Scotia. He has a special interest in the colonial period of Acadian Nova Scotia, with a focus on the New England Planters. He is a frequent contributor to the *Dictionary of Canadian Biography* and has published in the fields of Planter studies, Maritime Baptist history, and Canadian intellectual history.

JAMES H. LAMBERT is an archivist at the Division des archives de l'Université Laval, Quebec, and has published several articles in the field of archival studies. Formerly manuscript editor with the *Dictionnaire biographique du Canada*, at Université Laval, he wrote and edited numerous biographies of figures from Lower Canada. He has published several articles on the religious history of that colony and is currently preparing a biography of Joseph-Octave Plessis.

BRYAN D. PALMER is a Professor in the Department of History, Queen's University, Kingston, Ontario, where he teaches social and working-class history. He is the author of a number of books, including *Descent into Discourse: The Reification of Language and the Writing of Social History* (Philadelphia, PA: Temple University Press 1990), *Working-Class Experience: Rethinking the History of Canadian Labour, 1800–1991* (T: M&S 1992), and, his most recent, *Capitalism Comes to the Backcountry: The Goodyear Invasion of Napanee* (T: Between the Lines 1994). He is currently engaged in a study of Upper Canada in the 1830s.

IAN ROSS ROBERTSON is an Associate Professor in the Department of History, Scarborough College, University of Toronto. His research interests are Atlantic Canada and Canadian intellectual history. Most of his recent publications concern the Prince Edward Island land question.

OLAF UWE JANZEN is an Associate Professor in the Department of History, Sir Wilfred Grenfell College, Memorial University of Newfoundland, Corner Brook. He has an interest in eighteenth-century maritime, colonial, and naval history, and has recently published several articles in these fields. Dr Janzen is vice-president of both the Canadian Nautical Research Society and the International Maritime Economic History Association.

KERRY ABEL is an Associate Professor in the Department of History, Carleton University, Ottawa. She has a special interest in the social history of the Canadian North and recently published *Drum Songs: Glimpses of Dene History* (K&M: MQUP 1993).

TINA LOO is an Assistant Professor in the Department of History, Simon Fraser University, Burnaby, British Columbia. She has an interest in social and cultural history, particularly the social history of the law. Her book *Making Law, Order, and Authority in British Columbia, 1821–1871* will be published shortly.

J.M. BUMSTED is a Professor in the Department of History, University of Manitoba, and a Fellow of St John's College. He is the author of *Land, Settlement, and Politics on Eighteenth-Century Prince Edward Island* (K&M: MQUP 1987), winner of the Dafoe Book Prize. More recently he has published *The Peoples of Canada* (T: Oxford University Press 1992), a two-volume survey of Canadian history, and *The Manitoba Flood of 1950: An*

Illustrated History (W: 1993). He regards himself as a historian of both the British Empire and of Canada.

M. BROOK TAYLOR is an Associate Professor in the Department of History, Mount Saint Vincent University, Halifax, Nova Scotia, and the author of *Promoters, Patriots, and Partisans: Historiography in Nineteenth-Century English Canada* (T: UTP 1989). He has an interest in Canadian intellectual and cultural history as well as the field of Maritime studies.

Author Index

Abel, Kerry 342, 345
Abella, Irving Martin 230
Acheson, T.W. 194, 244, 254, 265
Acton, Janice 216
Adair, E.R. 59
Adams, Blaine 90
Adams, W. Peter 202
Adilman, Tamara 385
Ahlin, J.H. 403
Aitchinson, J.H. 230
Aitken, Barbara B. 188
Aitken, Hugh G.J. 190, 193, 195, 254, 427
Ajzenstat, Janet 163, 232, 420
Akenson, Donald Harman 142, 189, 203–4, 209, 213, 218, 224, 433, 434
Akins, Thomas Beamish 99
Akrigg, G.P.V. 359
Akrigg, Helen B. 359
Albert, Peter J. 410
Alexander, Anne 281
Alexander, David 257, 310–11, 318
Allaire, Gratien 61
Allard, Michel 70–1
Allardyce, Gilbert 264
Allen, Harry C. 409
Allen, Richard 342

Allen, Robert S. 8, 199, 201, 402, 405
Alline, Henry 110
Allison, K.J. 431
Allison, Susan 385
Allodi, Mary 177
Alsop, James D. 97, 306
Altman, Ida 53
Altman, Morris 64
Alvord, Clarence W. 409–10
Alyluia, Jeanne 84
Anderson, Bern 369
Anderson, David 323
Anderson, Fred 74
Anderson, James 389
Anderson, Karen 66
Anderson, R.C. 15
Anderson, Romola 15
Andrews, Clarence L. 365
Andrews, Kenneth R. 17, 293
Anfinson, John 331
Angus, Margaret 221–2
Antler, Steven 312
Antmann, Willy 179
Archer, Christon I. 365–6, 369
Archer, S.A. 343–4
Armstrong, Frederick H. 187, 188,

193, 194, 204, 208, 209, 210, 211, 214, 223, 224, 230, 231
Armstrong, Joe C.W. 80
Armstrong, Maurice W. 106, 109
Armstrong, Robert 64, 124, 132, 133
Arnup, Katherine 68
Arora, Ved 326
Arsenault, Bona 101
Arsenault, Fernand 86
Arsenault, Georges 87–8, 250, 276
Arseneault, Jeanne 83
Arthur, Elizabeth 209, 225
Arthur, Sir George 229
Artibise, Alan F.J. 113, 142, 154, 168, 188
Aspinall, Arthur 417
Aubert de Gaspé, Philippe-Joseph 142, 176
Aubin, Paul 36, 113
Audet, Bernard 63
Audet, Louis-Philippe 67, 180, 224, 317
Audet, Pierre-E. 166
Austen, Barbara E. 54
Avis, Walter S. 440, 442
Axtell, James 23, 66, 69
Ayyar, A.V. Venkatarama 368

Babcock, Robert H. 265
Babitch, Rose Mary 83
Baboyant, Marie 65
Baccigalupo, Alain 165
Back, George 334
Backhouse, Constance 146–7, 217, 251, 444–5
Baehre, Rainer 220
Baglole, Harry 268, 269–70, 271–2
Bahn, Paul 3
Bahr, Dieter 440

Bailey, Alfred Goldsworthy 28, 46, 50, 94, 267, 277, 421
Baillargeon, Georges 127
Baillargeon, Noël 170, 181
Baillie-Grohmann, William Adolph 356, 393
Bailyn, Bernard 107, 396, 430, 432
Baker, Frank 106
Baker, G. Blaine 166, 167, 224, 446
Baker, Melvin 318–19
Baker, Raymond F. 90
Baker, William M. 248, 267, 433
Bakker, Peter 28
Baksh, Ishmael 317
Balcom, B.A. 93, 257
Baldwin, Douglas 268, 275
Baldwin, Joyce 212
Baldwin, R.M. 212
Ball, Christine 217
Ball, Georgiana 374
Balthazar, Louis 158, 164
Banfield, A.W.F. 11
Banks, Sir Joseph 298, 321
Banks, Margaret A. 444
Barbaud, Philippe 67
Barbeau, Marius 347
Barbier, Jacques A. 123
Bardet, Jean-Pierre 56
Baribeau, Claude 128
Barkham, Selma 22, 25, 286, 321
Barkley, Frances Hornby 367
Barkley, Murray 244
Barman, Jean 69, 357, 358, 361, 388
Barnes, James 406
Barnes, Thomas Garden 97, 100, 443
Barratt, Glynn 365, 407
Barron, F. Laurie 94–5, 199
Barron, T.J. 418
Barry, Francine 66

Bartels, Dennis A. 305
Barthelemy de Saizieu, Tiphaine 131
Bartolli, Tomas 368
Barton, Kenneth James 89
Basdeo, S. 256
Baskerville, Peter A. 146, 193, 194, 195–6, 424
Bates, Hilary 189
Bayfield, Henry Wolsey 180
Bayly, C.A. 395–6
Bayne-Powell, Rosamund 431
Beaglehole, J.C. 309, 366, 415
Beamish, Derek 312
Beattie, J.M. 220, 445
Beattie, Owen 335
Beatty, Betsy 152
Beaudoin, Réjean 176
Beaudoin, Thérèse 144
Beaulieu, Alain 43, 69
Beaulieu, André 115, 116, 177
Beaulieu, Jacqueline 148
Beauregard, Marthe F. 55
Beaver, Herbert 376
Beck, J. Murray 97, 103, 259, 277, 417, 422
Beckett, J.C. 433
Bédard, Hélène 148
Bédard, Marc-André 165
Beer, Donald R. 212
Begg, Alexander 353
Behiels, Michael D. 119
Béland, Madeleine 68
Béland, Mario 177
Bélanger, Diane 170
Bélanger, Jules 155
Bélanger, René 22, 286
Bélisle, Jean 177
Bell, David G. 110, 243, 443
Bell, David V.J. 200–1
Bell, Geoffrey 432

Bell, K.N. 399
Bell, Marilyn 272
Bell, Michael 287
Bell, Winthrop Pickard 99, 439
Bellavance, Marcel 140, 152, 165, 434
Bellomo, J. Jerald 220
Belshaw, John Douglas 381–2
Bemis, Samuel Flagg 410, 411
Benes, Peter 53, 54, 63
Beniak, Edouard 441
Benians, E.A. 418
Bennett, Carol 431
Benoît, Michèle 178
Benson, Adolph B. 42
Benson, Eugene 81
Benson, Wilson 434
Bercuson, David J. 403
Berger, Carl 47, 118, 186, 190, 192, 210, 229, 236, 330–1, 353, 361, 394
Berger, Thomas R. 102
Bergeron, Gaston 440
Bergeron, Lise 151
Bergeron, Yves 155
Bernard, Jacques 21
Bernard, Jean-Paul 163, 165
Bernatchez, Ginette 174
Bernier, Gérald 113, 121–2, 123, 127, 134, 141, 158, 160, 161, 183
Bernier, Jacques 156
Berton, Pierre 226, 404–5
Bervin, George 134, 140–1, 142, 154–5
Bescoby, Isabel 388, 391
Béthune, Guy 42
Betts, G.M. 230
Beutler, Corinne 127, 130, 132, 133, 134
Beverley, James 110
Bideaux, Michel 9, 21

Biggar, Henry Percival 9, 18, 19, 21, 25, 27, 29, 42, 60, 81
Biggs, C. Lesley 218
Bilak, Daniel A. 205
Bilson, Geoffrey 157, 221, 265, 430
Bindon, Kathryn M. 349, 446
Binford, Lewis R. 12
Bischoff, Peter 143, 214
Bishop, Charles A. 23, 60, 197, 337, 374
Bishop, Morris 80
Bishop, Olga 188
Bittermann, Rusty 258, 262–3, 272
Black, R.M. 173
Black, Samuel 334–5, 374
Blackwell, John D. 220, 221, 445
Blain, Eleanor 442
Blain, Jean 47
Blanchard, J.-Henri 87
Blanchette, Jean-François 84–5
Blanco, Richard L. 400
Bleasdale, Ruth 199, 214
Bliss, Michael 134, 140, 194, 254, 428
Bloch, Gerald 205
Blondin, George 333, 346
Bloomfield, Elizabeth 207
Bloomfield, L. 347
Bloomfield, Morton W. 442
Bloomfield, Valerie 398
Blue, G.V. 367
Boas, Franz 344, 364
Bodelsen, C.A. 419, 426
Bogaard, Paul A. 260
Boily, Raymond 143
Boily, Robert 113, 127, 141, 158
Boivin, Aurélien 179
Boivin, Henri-Bernard 170
Boleda, Mario 52, 57
Bolger, Francis W.P. 87, 268, 272, 278
Bolotenko, George 115

Bolt, Clarence 387
Bolus, Malvina 340
Bompas, Charlotte Selina 343–4
Bompas, William Carpenter 343
Bonenfant, Jean-Charles 165
Boon, Thomas C.B. 342, 417
Bosa, Réal 170
Bosher, John F. 61, 71
Bothwell, Robert 186
Bouchard, Gérard 48, 53, 64–5, 125, 126, 127, 128–9, 130, 133, 135, 150, 151
Bouchard, René 83
Bouchard, Russel 151
Boucher, Jacques 127
Boucher, Neil 99, 102
Boucher, Philip P. 125
Boucher, Pierre 42
Bouchette, Joseph 115
Boulle, Pierre-H. 159
Bourassa-Trépanier, Juliette 179
Bourne, Kenneth 407, 408, 411
Bourque, Bruce J. 28, 94
Bourque, Gilles 121, 141
Bourque, Hélène 178
Bourque, Mario 147
Bovay, E.H. 439
Bowen, Lynne 381
Bowen, William A. 377
Bowler, R. Arthur 226, 401
Bowman, James 358
Bowsfield, Hartwell 327, 373, 377, 412
Boxer, C.R. 19
Boyce, Betsy 232
Boyce, Gerald E. 209
Boyd, Robert T. 370
Bradbury, Bettina 65, 66, 129, 143, 146, 147, 172, 217
Bradley, James W. 50
Bradley, Mary 108

Braithwaite, Jean 368
Brass, Eleanor 347
Brasseaux, Carl A. 77, 101–2, 250
Brasser, Ted J. 22, 351
Braudel, Fernand 15
Brault, J.-R. 155, 178
Brebner, John Bartlet 79, 83, 84, 96, 98, 100, 102–3, 108, 396, 402–3, 415
Brewer, John 425
Brice-Bennett, Carol 12, 322–3
Brière, Jean-François 58, 288, 289, 306
Brierley, Jane 142
Brightman, Robert 346
Brisson, Jean-Maurice 166, 443–4
Brisson, Réal N. 64, 154–5
Brock, Daniel J. 209
Brode, Patrick 207, 212, 412
Brodeur, Raymond 171
Brookes, Alan A. 261
Brookes, Ian 10
Brooks, Katherine J. 86
Brooks, Stephen 420
Brown, (Robert) Craig 39, 230, 397
Brown, Elizabeth Gaspar 443
Brown, Jennifer S.H. 50, 55, 339, 346, 347–8, 351, 375, 442
Brown, Lucy M. 397, 427
Brown, Michael 153, 439
Brown, Robert 382
Brown, Thomas E. 222
Brown, Vera Lee 307
Brown, Wallace 152, 201, 242, 245, 438
Bruce, James, 8th Earl of Elgin 229, 422
Brun, Henri 160, 417
Brunet, Manon 173, 175
Brunet, Michel 119, 159, 400
Brunger, Alan G. 203

Brym, Robert J. 312
Brynmor-Jones, David 431
Buckley, Thomas C. 340
Buckner, Phillip A. 78, 162, 163, 164, 230, 237, 239, 246, 248, 254, 259, 276, 279, 283, 314, 395, 418, 422
Budd, Rev. Henry 343
Budgel, Richard 304
Buggey, Susan 262
Buller, Charles 419–20, 421
Bumsted, J.M. xv, 52, 54, 56, 59, 80, 81, 90, 103, 107–8, 109, 110, 152, 202, 206, 211, 218, 225, 226, 242, 245, 246, 247, 252, 264, 269, 270, 271, 275, 314, 340, 352–3, 368, 383, 403, 410, 415, 423, 425, 435, 437, 438, 444, 447
Buono, Yolande 115
Burch, Ernest S., Jr 11
Burger, Baudouin 176
Burgess, Joanne 37, 144, 155
Burley, David V. 28, 371
Burnet, Jean 202, 218
Burnett, Frederick C. 110
Burns, George 93
Burns, R.J. 211
Burpee, Lawrence J. 256, 340, 341
Burrage, Henry S. 411
Burroughs, Peter 162, 163, 227, 230, 419, 421, 422
Burt, Alfred LeRoy 159, 400, 405, 410
Burt, Sandra 216
Bushby, Arthur Thomas 384
Buss, Helen M. 218
Buszek, Beatrice Ross 242
Butler, William F. 336
Byrne, Cyril J. 246, 247, 291, 297, 300–1, 312, 316, 433, 434

Caamaño, Jacinto 369

Cadigan, Sean 297, 299
Cage, R.A. 81
Cahill, Barry 444
Cain, P.J. 426
Cairns, John W. 445
Calder, Angus 395
Callahan, James Morton 408–9, 411
Callahan, North 401
Calloway, Colin G. 73, 198, 405
Calman, D. 224
Calvin, D.D. 193
Cameron, Christina 178
Cameron, James M. 202
Cameron, Wendy 202, 203
Campbell, Anita 98
Campbell, Carol 107
Campbell, Charles S. 409
Campbell, Douglas 108, 247, 249, 250, 435, 438
Campbell, Gail G. 251, 253, 266, 267
Campbell, J.L. 441
Campbell, Joan Bourque 84
Campbell, Marjorie Freeman 209
Campbell, Roy H. 426, 435
Campbell, Terry 317
Campeau, Lucien 19, 42
Candow, James E. 103, 308, 311
Canny, Nicholas P. 396, 432–3
Cantin, Christiane 148
Cardin, Martine 130
Cardinal, Claudette 113
Careless, J.M.S. xiv, 164, 185, 186, 208, 210, 212, 229, 233–4, 235, 330, 361, 382, 422
Carey, S.H.D. 380
Carle, Paul 180
Carlos, Ann 136, 194
Caron, Diane 136
Caron, Robert 178
Caron-Houle, Françoise 41

Carrier, Maurice 179
Carrière, Gaston 342, 343
Carrigan, D. Owen 116, 445
Carrothers, William A. 429
Carter-Edwards, Dennis 220
Cartier, Jacques 9, 21, 25, 27, 29
Cartwright, George 321
Casgrain, Henri-Raymond 42
Castonguay, Daniel 59
Castonguay, Jacques 142
Caulier, Brigitte 70, 172
Cell, Gillian T. 21, 26, 286, 288, 293, 294
Cell, John W. 420
Cellard, André 68, 157
Chabot, Marc 181
Chabot, Richard 128, 131, 169
Chabot, Victorin 68
Chadwick, St John 284
Chaiton, Alf 222, 228
Chalmers, John 318
Chambers, J.K. 440, 442
Champagne, Joseph-Etienne 342
Champlain, Samuel de 42, 81
Champness, W. 389
Chapdelaine, Claude 13, 29
Chapman, J.K. 266, 277
Charbonneau, André 65, 73, 154
Charbonneau, Hubert 52, 55, 56, 57, 67, 149
Chard, Donald F. 90
Charland, Jean-Pierre 181
Charlevoix, Pierre-François-Xavier de 42
Chartrand, Luc 67–8, 179
Chaussé, Gilles 169
Cheshire, Neil 25
Chester, Sir Daniel Norman 417
Chiappelli, Fredi 14, 15, 18, 19, 21
Chittenden, Hiram Martin 387

Choquette, Leslie P. 53
Christensen, Ruth M. 300
Christianson, David J. 85
Christie, Ian R. 397
Christie, Laird 55
Cinq-Mars, François 141
Cinq-Mars, Marcelle 152–3
Cipolla, Carlo M. 15
Clairmont, Donald 249
Clark, Andrew Hill 79, 82, 87, 92–3,
    96, 255, 268
Clark, Donald W. 13
Clark, Malcolm, Jr 377
Clark, S.D. xiv, 360–1, 388
Clark, William Bell 310, 403
Clarke, Ernest A. 109, 403
Clarke, John 204–5
Clarkson, Leslie A. 17
Classen, H. George 409
Cleland, Charles E. 58
Clement, Michel 157
Clermont, Norman 11, 13, 25, 27, 29
Cliche, Marie-Aimée 66, 70, 72, 150
Clifton, James A. 199
Cloutier, Nicole 68
Clow, Michael 254
Coakley, Thomas 294
Coates, Colin 72
Coates, Kenneth S. 326, 332, 344
Coburn, David 389
Cochetière, Jacques 124
Codignola, Luca 86, 168, 294
Cody, Hiram A. 343
Coffin, Victor 414
Cogar, William B. 309
Cogswell, Fred 260
Cohen, Marjorie Griffin 216
Cole, Douglas 363
Cole, Sally C. 285
Coleman, Emma Lewis 54

Coleman, Terry 429
Coles, Harry L. 404–5
Colley, Linda 430
Colnett, James 368
Colpron, Gilles 442
Colvile, Eden 354
Combe, William 368
Combs, Jerald A. 411
Comeau, R. 119
Condemine, Odette 176
Condon, Ann Gorman 243–4
Connolly, Sean J. 432
Conrad, Glenn E. 77
Conrad, Margaret 79, 95, 100, 103,
    108, 110, 234–5, 252, 253–4, 402,
    403, 404, 438
Conway, Alan 385
Cook, Adrian 413
Cook, James 366–7, 415
Cook, Ramsay 9, 21, 27, 29, 53, 80,
    116, 185, 187, 216, 277, 331, 353
Cook, Terry 201, 230
Cook, Warren L. 365, 369, 415
Cooke, Alan 14, 333
Cooper, Barry 349, 423
Cooper, Carol 386
Cooper, Elizabeth 228
Cooper, Leonard 420
Copp, W.R. 256
Coppock, J.T. 435
Corey, Albert B. 231, 411
Cornell, Paul G. 164, 229, 234
Cornwallis, Kinahan 389
Cosbie, W.G. 221
Cote, J.E. 443
Côté, Louis-Marie 36, 113
Cottrell, P.L. 427
Coupal, Jean-Paul 116
Coupland, Sir Reginald 414
Courcy, Raymond 146, 171

Courville, Serge 65, 123–4, 124–5, 126–7, 128, 132, 135, 138, 141, 150, 151, 152
Cousins, John 269
Coutts, Robert 342
Couture, Claude 123
Couturier, Jacques Paul 172, 251, 276
Cowan, Helen I. 152, 202, 429
Cowan, William 28, 44, 60, 95, 149, 304, 441–2
Cox, Bruce 348
Cox, Ross 371
Cox, Sandra J. 445
Craig, Béatrice 125, 129, 264, 265
Craig, David 436
Craig, Gerald M. 186, 206, 229, 230, 232, 420
Cramer, Richard S. 376
Cran, William 440
Craven, Paul 139, 196, 215
Crawford, John C. 351, 442
Creese, Gillian 388
Creighton, Donald Grant xiv, 118, 120, 123, 133, 140, 190, 212, 231–2, 234, 330, 331, 361, 396, 425, 427
Crémazie, Octave 176
Crepeau, Andrée 85
Croix, Alain 69
Cronin, Kay 387
Crosby, Alfred W. 15–16
Crosby, Thomas 387
Cross, D. Suzanne 146
Cross, Michael S. 65, 143, 192, 211, 213, 214, 216, 230, 232
Crowe, Keith 344
Crowhurst, R. Patrick 307, 320–1
Crowley, John E. 298–9, 302, 415
Crowley, Terence (Terry) A. 72, 89, 92, 166, 206

Cruikshank, Ernest A. 201, 226, 229, 401, 404
Cruikshank, Julie 333, 346
Cruikshank, Ken 194
Cullen, Louis M. 432, 433
Cullen, Mary 373
Cumming, William Patterson 14
Currie, A.W. 193
Curtis, Bruce 222–3, 235
Curtis, Dennis 220
Curtis, Tony 430
Cuthbertson, Brian C.U. 244–5, 261, 416
Cutter, Donald C. 369

Dahl, Edward H. 87
Dahlie, Jorgen 211
Daigle, Jean 54, 82, 250
Dalhousie, Earl of. See Ramsay, George
Dall, W.H. 336
D'Allaire, Micheline 70, 71, 170
Damas, David 7, 11, 12, 24, 345
Daniels, John D. 51
Danylewycz, Marta 146, 171, 224
Darling, David 363
Darroch, A. Gordon 203, 205, 206, 214–15
Davidoff, Leonore 432
Davidson, Donald C. 372–3
Davidson, Heather 105
Davies, Glanville 308
Davies, Gwendolyn 242, 252, 260, 436
Davies, R. Trevor 20
Davies, Richard A. 260
Davis, Alva Leroy 440
Davis, John 18
Davis, Ralph 15, 285
Davison, James D. 253

Dawson, Joan 82, 87
Day, Alan E. 8
Day, Douglas 247, 258
Day, Gordon M. 55
Debien, Gabriel 53, 101
De Braekeleer, Marc 151
De Brou, David 161
Dechêne, Louise 47, 50–1, 53, 56, 60–1, 62–3, 65, 127, 128, 131, 137, 138, 149, 154, 321, 322, 340
Dee, H.D. 374
DeForest, Louis Effingham 91
De Jong, Nicolas 87
Delâge, Denys 40–1, 54
De Lottinville, Peter 319
Dempsey, Hugh 343
Denison, Merrill 140, 194
Denniston, Glenda 11
Denny, Alice 395
Denys, Nicolas 81
Dépatie, Sylvie 62, 65, 127–8
Desbarats, Catherine 48, 124
Deschênes, Jean-Guy 38, 147
Desilets, Andrée 142
Desjardins, Bertrand 55
Desjardins, Pauline 155
Deslandres, Dominique 69, 70
Desloges, Yvon 67, 73, 154, 179
Desmarais, Guy 130
De Smet, Pierre-Jean 387
Desrosiers, Claude 130, 135
Desrosiers, Léo-Paul 46
Desrosiers, Yvon 170
Desserud, Donald 108, 402
Dessureault, Christian 63, 125, 127–8, 130, 131
Deveau, J. Alphonse 83
Devine, T.M. 433, 436
Dewar, Kenneth C. 233
Diamond, Sigmund 64

Dickason, Olive Patricia xv, 20, 40, 70, 94, 147, 197, 332–3, 344, 348
Dickerson, Oliver M. 413
Dickin, Emily F. 377
Dickin, Samuel N. 377
Dickinson, John A. 36, 39, 63, 67, 72, 73, 122, 130
Dickson, David 433
Dickson, L.M. 440
Dickson, R.J. 107
Diffie, Bailey W. 19
Dilley, Robert S. 206
Dimand, Robert W. 205
Dionne, René 175
DiStefano, Lynne D. 225
Dobyns, Henry F. 24, 51
Dodd, A.H. 417
Dolan, Claire 126
Dollier de Casson, François 65
Dominique, Richard 38, 147
Donkin, Kate 201–2
Donnelly, Alton S. 365
Donnelly, F.K. 231
Donoughue, Bernard 414
Donovan, Kenneth 89, 92, 247, 260, 263, 289
Dorland, Arthur G. 227
Doucet, Michael J. 207, 211, 215
Doucette, Leonard E. 176
Doughty, Arthur George 42, 74, 158, 229, 334, 398, 418, 422
Douglas, R. Alan 212
Douglas, Robert 340
Douglas, Thomas, 5th Earl of Selkirk 270, 327, 437
Douglas, W.A.B. 406
Dow, J.B.A. 435
Dowd, Gregory Evans 198, 400, 405
Down, Edith E. 388–9
Down, Mary Margaret 388

Downey, Fairfax 88
Downie, William 389
Drolet, Antonio 67
Dubé, Jean-Claude 71–2
Dubeau-Legentil, René 171
Dubuc, Alfred 47, 120, 140, 141
Duchaussois, Pierre 342
Duchesne, Raymond 179, 180
Duckworth, Harry 341
Dudley, William S. 406
Duff, Wilson 359, 363–4, 381
Duffus, Allan F. 105
Duffy, Dennis 201
Duffy, Michael 290
Dufour, Andrée 181
Dufour, Pierre 139
Dufresne, Charles 442
Duguay, Geneviève 155
Dull, Jonathan 307
Dulong, Gaston 440
Dumais, Pierre 27
Dumont, Fernand 161, 171, 173
Dumont, Micheline 39, 66, 67, 145, 146
Duncan, Janice K. 380
Duncan, Kenneth 203
Dundas, Henry, 1st Viscount Melville 444
Dunham, Aileen 229
Dunkley, Peter 429
Dunlop, William 212
Dunmore, John 415
Dunn, Brenda 82, 85
Dunn, Charles W. 247, 441
Dupâquier, Jacques 52
Dupont, Jean-Claude 64, 144
Dupont, Louis 124
Du Pont Duvivier, François 98
Durham, Earl of. See Lambton, John George

Dussault, Gabriel 171
Dyck, Ian 13
Dyer, Gwynne 399–400

Eady, Ronald J. 232
Eales, Richard 446
Earl, D.W.L. 211, 230
Easterbrook, W.T. 190, 232, 254
Eber, Dorothy Harley 344
Eccles, W.J. 36, 39, 40, 59, 62, 71, 74, 337
Eckert, Allan W. 405
Eckert, Edward W. 406
Edelstein, Michael 427
Edgar, Lady Matilda 406
Edmunds, R. David 198, 405
Edwards, Barry J. 441
Edwards, G. Thomas 372, 377
Edwards, Owen 108
Egnal, Marc 414
Eid, Leroy V. 73
Eldridge, C.C. 395, 396, 422
Elgee, William H. 228
Elgin, Earl of. See Bruce, James
Elias, Peter Douglas 345
Ella, Martha Cheney 377
Elliot, Robert S. 104
Elliott, Bruce S. 152, 204, 209, 434
Elliott, Gordon R. 392
Elliott, John Huxtable 15, 20
Elliott, Shirley B. 77
Ells, Margaret 244
Emeneau, M.B. 441
Emmerson, Frank 435
Engelbrecht, William 29
Engelman, Fred L. 411
English, Christopher 301
Engstrand, Iris Higbie Wilson 366, 369
Ennals, Peter 105, 262, 439–40

Ens, Gerhard 350
Epp, Henry T. 13
Erickson, Charlotte 430
Ermatinger, Charles Oakes Zaccheus 212
Errington, Jane 201, 216, 226
Espesset (Espessat?), Hélène 141, 142
Evans, G.N.D. 271
Everest, Allan S. 401, 406
Ewart, Alfred 441

Fagan, Brian 332
Fahey, Curtis 228, 416–17
Fahmy-Eid, Nadia 66, 67, 146, 169
Faibisy, John Dewar 404
Fairchild, Byron 91
Fairley, Margaret 230–1
Falardeau, Jean-Charles 173
Falconer, Dickson M. 360, 378, 424
Falls, Cyril Bentham 432
Faragher, John Mack 377
Faribault, Marthe 67
Faulkner, Alaric 84
Faulkner, Gretchen 84
Fauteux, Joseph-Noël 63
Fecteau, Jean-Marie 122, 143, 157, 166, 167, 445
Fedorak, Charles John 391
Fellman, Anita Clair 61, 66, 252
Fenton, William N. 43
Ferguson, Barry 331, 342
Ferguson, Robert 98
Fergusson, Charles Bruce 97, 100, 404
Ferland, Jacques 142
Fernando, Tissa 211
Ferretti, Lucia 155, 172
Ferris, Norman B. 413
Field, Richard Henning 100, 104
Fieldhouse, D.K. 426
Filion, Louise 49

Filshie, Margaret A. 104
Filteau, Gérard 163
Finberg, H.P.R. 431
Fingard, Judith 143, 154, 219–20, 241, 256, 261, 265, 318, 416
Finlay, John L. 162, 396
Finn, Gérard 86
Firth, Edith G. 187, 208, 227, 230
Fischer, Lewis R. 109, 255, 274, 312, 428
Fisher, Raymond H. 365
Fisher, Robin 366, 368, 369, 370, 374, 381, 382, 383, 385–6
Fisk, A. 310
Fitzgerald, James Edward 378
Fitzgerald, Owen 88
Fitzgerald, William R. 31
Fitzhugh, William W. 12, 24
Fladmark, Knut R. 13, 363, 373
Flaherty, David H. 215, 217, 221, 224, 349, 444, 445, 446
Flanagan, Thomas 446
Fleck, Donald H. 99
Flenley, Ralph 65
Flinn, Michael 436
Flint, John E. 419
Flynn, James G. 310
Folan, W.J. 368
Foner, Philip S. 380
Forester, C.S. 406
Forsey, Eugene 213
Forster, Ben 164, 195, 196, 254, 427
Fortier, John 88
Fortin, Claire-Andrée 143
Fortin, Gérard L. 148
Foster, Gilbert 441
Foster, Hamar 375–6, 446
Foster, John E. 347, 348
Foster, John Watson 411
Fournier, Hannah 81

Fournier, Marcel 156, 179–80
Fowler, Marion 218
Francis, Daniel 59, 136, 147, 148–9, 275, 333, 339
Francis, Mark 162, 230, 418
Francis, R. Douglas 48, 99, 103, 122, 269, 278, 333, 350, 353
Frank, David 78, 239, 283
Franklin, Sir John 335
Franklin, Wayne 14
Fraser, Allan M. 294, 307, 316
Fraser, Robert L. 216, 221
Fraser, Simon 371
Fredriksen, John C. 404
Freeman, Donald B. 59, 338
Freeman, Milton M.R. 12
Freeman, Thomas Walter 432
Frégault, Guy 40, 50, 60, 71
Freitas, Chris de 203
French, Goldwin S. 106, 227, 228
Frenette, Jacques 148
Friesen, Gerald 326, 349
Friesen, Jean 358, 391
Friesen, John 318
Frost, Stanley Brice 181–2
Frostin, Charles 70
Fry, Bruce W. 89
Frye, R.P. 350
Fryer, Mary Beacock 226, 400, 401, 402, 407
Fuson, Paul 18
Fyers, Evan 309
Fyson, Donald 143–4

Gaboury, Jean-Paul 118
Gad, Gunter 225
Gadoury, Lorraine 56, 57, 66, 130, 142
Gaffield, Chad 155, 222, 223, 224
Gagan, David 204–5, 206, 207–8, 210, 211, 212, 234

Gagan, Rosemary R. 145
Gagnon, France 151
Gagnon, François-Marc 68, 69, 70
Gagnon, Hervé 180
Gagnon, Robert 142
Gagnon, Serge 46–7, 116, 117, 120, 147, 169, 171, 172, 394
Gair, Reavley 267
Galarneau, Claude 161, 170, 174, 181
Galarneau, France 161
Galaup, Jean-François de, Comte de Lapérouse 415
Galbraith, John S. 337, 373, 377, 378, 417, 423, 424
Gallagher, John 395
Gallichan, Gilles 174
Ganong, William Francis 8, 17, 81
Gardner, James S. 10
Gardner, Robert G. 106
Garitee, Jerome R. 407
Garneau, François-Xavier 117, 119
Garner, John 103, 229, 417
Garon, André 160
Garrad, Charles 30, 31
Gassner, Julius S. 415
Gates, Charles M. 357
Gates, Lillian F. 201, 231
Gaudette, Jean 101
Gaudreau, Guy 138
Gaultier de Varennes et de La Véren-drye, Pierre 340
Gauvreau, Danielle 56, 66, 147
Gauvreau, Michael 229
Gay, Daniel 153
Gelfand, Toby 68
Gentilcore, R. Louis 37, 187, 201–2
Gérin-Lajoie, Antoine 176
German, Tony 400
Gerriets, Marilyn 257
Getty, Ian A.L. 48, 197, 199, 342

Gibbons, Richard 444
Gibbs, Elizabeth (Nish) 158
Gibson, Dale 375, 446
Gibson, James A. 425
Gibson, James R. 365, 367, 370, 373, 376, 391
Gibson, Lee 446
Gidney, R.D. 222, 223
Giffard, Ann 273, 274, 428, 432
Gilbert, Angus D. 56, 100, 123, 217–18, 220, 252, 339, 340, 425
Gilbert, Louis 31
Gilbert, William 303
Gilchrist, John 285
Gillespie, Beryl C. 12
Gillis, Robert Peter 192
Gillis, Sandra J. 138, 192
Gilmore, Myron P. 18, 21
Gilmour, J.M. 196
Gilpin, Alec R. 406
Gilroy, Marion 242
Gingerich, Orland 438
Gingras, Yves 156, 179
Gipson, Lawrence Henry 413, 414
Girard, Camil 155
Girard, Marcel 351
Girard, Philip 97, 444, 445, 446
Glass, D.V. 56
Glazebrook, G.P. de T. 140, 193, 208, 230
Glover, Richard 335, 371
Gluek, Alvin C., Jr 354, 412, 423
Godfrey, Charles M. 221, 429–30
Godfrey, Stuart R. 318
Godfrey, W. Earl 11
Godfrey, William G. 90, 238, 245, 266, 276, 278
Godsell, Patricia 421
Goheen, Peter G. 177, 196, 208
Goldin, Claudia 194

Goldring, Philip 344, 419, 423
Goltz, Herbert C.W. 406
Gonzalez, Ellice B. 95
Goodfellow, J.C. 388
Goodwin, Craufurd D.W. 195
Goodwin, Daniel C. 77
Gossage, Peter 147, 150
Gosselin, Auguste 70
Goubert, Pierre 40
Gouger, Lina 52, 55
Gough, Barry M. 55, 361, 366, 371, 373, 376, 379, 381, 383, 384, 386, 407, 446
Gould, Jean 359
Goulet, Denis 156
Gourlay, Robert Fleming 205
Gouthillier, Guy 441
Gowans, Alan 105
Goy, Joseph 53, 56, 70, 124, 126, 127, 128, 129, 130, 131, 133, 134, 135, 137
Graebner, Norman A. 412
Graff, Harvey J. 215, 220
Graham, Allan 269
Graham, Elizabeth 199
Graham, Gerald S. 254, 305–6, 308, 405
Graham, William Hugh 209, 212
Granatstein, J.L. 397
Grandbois, Maryse 155
Grant, Gail Cuthbert 145
Grant, I.F. 435
Grant, John Webster 69, 86, 106, 199, 228, 262, 300, 342, 386
Grant, William Lawson 81, 282, 301
Gratton, Roger 178
Gray, John Morgan 352
Gray, Malcolm 436
Graymont, Barbara 198, 402
Green, Gretchen 218

Greene, Jack P. 410
Greenhill, Basil 273, 274, 428, 429, 432
Greenhous, Brereton 265
Greenlaw, Jane 173
Greenwood, F. Murray 164, 167
Greer, Allan 57, 63, 67, 90, 127, 135, 137, 146, 147, 163, 164, 166, 167, 181, 187, 193, 195, 213, 216, 230, 235, 279
Greiger, John 335
Grenier, Robert 22, 286
Grenon, Michel 159
Gressley, Gene 446
Greusel, Joseph 404
Grey, Lady Louisa Elizabeth, Countess of Durham 421
Griffin-Allwood, Philip G.A. 77
Griffiths, Naomi E.S. 54, 81, 82, 83, 98-9, 100, 101, 249-50, 251
Gringe, Donald A., Jr 402
Grisé, Jacques 168
Grouard, E.-J.-B.-M. 343
Groulx, Lionel 117-18, 119
Groves, Paul A. 40
Grumet, Robert Steven 359
Guay, Donald 179
Guest, Dennis 219
Guildford, Janet 253
Guillaume, Pierre 146, 170, 171
Guillemette, André 52
Guillet, Edwin C. 193, 202, 209, 231, 429
Guillod, Harry 389
Guitard, Michelle 161, 406
Gundy, H. Pearson 211
Gunn, Gertrude E. 313, 423
Gunther, Erna 364
Guyotjeannin, Olivier 289
Gwyn, Julian 91, 107, 140, 257-8, 404

Hafen, LeRoy R. 372
Haines, Francis 12
Hakluyt, Richard 8-9, 18, 24
Hale, Linda 358
Haliburton, Thomas Chandler 260, 421
Hall, Catherine 432
Hall, Christopher D. 405
Hall, Roger 187, 191, 196, 204, 215, 225, 233, 438
Hall, Tony 200
Halpenny, Francess G. 187
Hamburger, Joseph 421
Hamelin, Jean 50, 114, 115, 124, 131, 169, 170, 177
Hamell, George R. 23, 69
Hamil, Frederick Coyne 202, 209, 212, 230
Hamilton, Roberta 47
Hamilton, Scott 371
Hamilton, William B. 241, 317
Hammond, Lorne 374
Handcock, W. Gordon 291-2, 296, 298, 309, 317, 432
Handley, James E. 433
Hanham, H.J. 397
Hanington, J. Brian 85
Hanna, David B. 155
Hansen, Denise 84, 98
Hansen, Marcus Lee 437
Hanzeli, Victor Egon 67
Harbec, Hélène 77
Hardwick, Francis 371
Hardy, Jean-Pierre 64, 142, 143, 144, 145
Hardy, René 156, 169, 171
Hare, F. Kenneth 10
Hare, John 65, 114, 115, 154, 160, 161
Hargrave, Letitia 341
Hargrove, Richard J. 401

Harlow, Vincent Todd 399, 414, 415–16

Harmon, Daniel Williams 371–2

Harney, Robert F. 208

Harper, J. Russell 177, 335–6

Harper, Marjory 435–6

Harris, Donald A. 373

Harris, R. Cole 6, 37, 40, 52, 62, 82, 114, 132, 149, 187, 191, 202, 203, 242, 254, 281, 332, 357, 360, 383, 400

Harrison, Julia D. 69, 241

Harrisse, Henry 17, 19

Harry, Margaret 246, 291, 297, 312, 433

Hart, George E. 261

Hartlen, Gary 107

Hartz, Louis B. 200

Harvey, Daniel Cobb 87, 103, 237, 247, 256, 259–60, 271, 278, 403, 404

Harvey, David D. 437

Harvey, Fernand 116

Harvey, Louis-Georges 161

Haslach, Robert D. 307

Hatch, Robert McConnell 159, 401

Havard, Gilles 73

Hay, Douglas 167, 445

Hayes, Charles F., III 31

Hayman, John 382

Hazlitt, William Carew 389

Head, C. Grant 37, 192, 287, 290, 295, 296, 297, 414–15

Head, Francis Bond 418

Healey, W.J. 354

Heap, Margaret 143

Hearne, Samuel 335

Hébert, Léo-Paul 55, 149, 170

Hébert, Robert 115

Heckscher, Eli F. 425

Heidenreich, Conrad E. 10, 11, 30, 37, 49, 54, 55, 61, 87

Helleiner, Frederick M. 202

Helm, June 7, 10–11, 12, 13, 31, 38, 49, 54, 345, 363

Helmcken, John Sebastian 379, 391–2

Henderson, Elmes 208

Henderson, J.L.H. 228

Hendrickson, David C. 414

Hendrickson, James E. 358, 377, 423–4

Henige, David 24

Henripin, Jacques 56, 149

Henry, John Frazier 364

Heron, Craig 213, 214, 215

Hewes, Gordon W. 12

Hewitt, Martin 267, 275

Hewlett, Edward S. 383

Hickerson, Harold 50

Higham, Robert 306

Hill, Beth 367, 384

Hill, Charles E. 408

Hiller, James K. 284, 297, 299, 306, 311, 316, 322

Hillier, John 312

Hillmer, Norman 397

Hilton, B. 427

Hitsman, J. Mackay 226, 310, 399, 404, 406

Hobsbawm, Eric J. 396, 429, 431, 436

Hodgetts, J.E. 165, 199, 229

Hodgins, Bruce W. 212

Hodgins, John George 225

Hoffman, Bernard G. 8, 17, 20

Hoffman, Ronald 109, 410

Holdsworth, Deryck 105, 225, 262, 439–40

Holland, Clive 14, 333

Holman, Harry 274

Holmes, Colin 431

Hood, Robert 335
Hoover, Alan L. 359
Hopkins, Elizabeth 218
Horn, James 53
Hornby, Jim 249
Hornsby, Stephen J. 103, 247, 257,
    258, 262, 435
Hornstein, Sari 307
Horsman, Reginald 404–5
Hoskins, R.G. 194
Hoskins, W.G. 17
Hou, Charles 391
Houston, C. Stuart 335
Houston, Cecil J. 152, 204, 433, 434
Houston, Susan E. 220, 222, 223
Howard, Richard P. 225
Howay, Frederic William 367, 368,
    380, 384, 389–90
Howe, Joseph 251, 259
Howell, Colin 299
Howison, John 206
Howley, James P. 25–6, 303
Hudon, Christine 169
Hulton, Paul 19
Humphreys, John 295
Hunt, George T. 72
Hunt, Wayne A. 259
Hunter, A.F. 229
Hunter, James 436
Hussey, John A. 373
Hutchinson, G.M. 343
Hutchison, Rosemary 92
Hutchison, Terence Wilmot 425
Huttenback, Robert A. 206–7
Huyda, Richard J. 336
Hyam, Ronald 395, 410, 416
Hynes, Gisa I. 82

Igartua, José E. 57, 61, 124, 136
Ingram, George C. 373

Ingstad, Anne Stine 16
Ingstad, Helge 16
Innis, Harold Adams xiv, 21, 58–9, 92,
    118, 122–3, 137, 190, 191, 285, 287,
    288, 290, 329–30, 331, 337, 361–2,
    404
Innis, Mary Q. 21, 191, 196, 285
Inwood, Kris 106, 265
Ireland, John. See Magill, M.L.
Ireland, William E. 378, 382, 390,
    391–2
Irvine, Dallas D. 307
Irving, Washington 372
Isham, James 341
Ivison, Stuart 227

Jackman, S.W. 212, 418
Jackson, Eric 230
Jacob, Yves 21
Jaenen, Cornelius J. 36, 55, 69, 70, 73,
    86, 94
James, Edwin 354
James, W.J. 403
Jameson, Anna B. (née Murphy) 206,
    218
Jamieson, Alan 288
Jamieson, J.B. 29
Janzen, Olaf Uwe 296–7, 305, 307–8,
    309–10, 319, 403
Jarrell, Richard A. 156, 179–80
Jaumain, Serge 135
Jean, Claire 170
Jean, Michèle 145
Jeffries, Sir Charles Joseph 418
Jenkins, Brian 408
Jenks, L.H. 427
Jenness, Diamond 197, 364
Jennings, Francis 73, 148, 400
Jérémie, Nicolas 340
Jessett, Thomas E. 376, 388

Jetté, René 37

Jewitt, John Rodgers 369

Johansen, Dorothy O. 357, 377

Johnson, A.M. 334, 341

Johnson, Edward Philip 385

Johnson, F. Henry 388

Johnson, J.K. 184, 187, 188, 194, 202, 205, 209, 210–11, 211–12, 219, 229, 232

Johnson, Leo A. 199–200, 204, 209, 214, 216

Johnson, R. Byron 389

Johnson, Sir William 43

Johnson-Dean, Christina B. 385

Johnston, A.A. 437

Johnston, A.J.B. 90, 91, 92, 93, 262

Johnston, Basil 346, 347

Johnston, Charles M. 198, 209–10, 402

Johnston, Hugh J.M. 152, 202, 210, 366, 368, 430

Johnston, S.C. 429

Johnston, W.S. 210

Johnstone, H.F.V. 312

Jones, David C. 388

Jones, David J.V. 430

Jones, Dorothy V. 400

Jones, Elizabeth 80

Jones, Frederick 315, 316, 317, 318

Jones, George Stephen 147

Jones, Gwyn 16

Jones, Howard 411

Jones, Maldwyn A. 429

Jones, R.L. 191

Jones, Wilbur D. 412

Joulia, Dominique 129

Judah, Charles Burnet, Jr 288

Judd, Carol M. 60, 331, 338, 340, 367, 374

Kallmann, Helmut 68, 178–9

Kalm, Pehr (Peter) 42

Kane, Paul 355–6

Kaplan, Susan A. 24

Karamanski, Theodore J. 334, 372

Karr, Clarence G. 202, 384

Katz, Michael B. 204, 207–8, 209, 210, 211, 219, 222

Kay, Jeanne 51–2

Kealey, Gregory S. 65, 142, 196, 214, 215, 232

Keane, David 187, 195, 200, 205, 206, 210, 224, 225, 229, 233, 424

Kearney, Hugh F. 430

Keating, Peter 156, 157

Keefer, Janice Kulyk 260

Keefer, Thomas C. 193

Keel, Othmar 156

Keith, W.J. 206

Kelley, A.R. 416

Kellogg, Louise Phelps 42

Kelly, Kenneth 192

Kelsay, Isabel Thompson 198, 402

Kelsey, Henry 334

Kemble, John H. 381

Kendrick, John 365, 369, 415

Kennedy, John C. 323

Kennedy, Liam 432

Kennedy, W.P.M. 398

Kennett, Lee 74

Kenny, J.F. 340

Kenny, Stephen 166

Kenyon, Walter Andrew 18

Kernaghan, Lois D. 253

Kerr, D.G.G. 424

Kerr, J.B. 359

Kerr, Wilfred Brenton 298, 402, 403, 415

Keshen, Jeff 408

Kess, Cathy 381

Kesteman, Jean-Pierre 143

Kew, Michael 359
Keyes, John 138
Kidder, Frederic 403
Kilbourn, William 231
Kilian, Crawford 380
Killan, Gerald 225
Kilson, Martin L. 244
Kinchen, Oscar A. 231, 407
King, A.F. 320
Kinsman, Gary 216
Kirk, John M. 431
Klassen, Henry C. 141
Klinck, Carl F. 198, 206, 212, 260, 406
Knafla, Louis A. 167, 383, 445, 446, 447
Knaplund, Paul 378, 418, 420, 421, 424
Knecht, R.J. 20
Knight, James 340
Knight, Margaret Bennett 441
Knight, Rolph 386
Knorr, Klaus E. 413
Knowlan, Anne McIntyre 358
Knox, Bruce A. 424, 425
Knox, John 74
Koebner, Richard 413, 426
Kolish, Evelyn 135, 161, 166–7, 444
Kottak, Conrad Phillip 4
Krech, Shepard, III 7, 23, 38, 60, 149, 338, 374
Kulisek, L.L. 199
Kupp, Jan 287

Labaree, Leonard Woods 413
Laberge, Alain 53, 58, 65, 128
Lacelle, Claudette 143
Lachance, André 65, 67, 72
La Cour, Lykke de 147, 216
Lacoursière, Jacques 122
Lacroix, Benoît 168, 171–2

Laferrière, Pierre-Julien 72
Lafitau, Joseph-François 43
Laflamme, Jean 176
Laflèche, Guy 50
Laforce, Hélène 68, 146
Laframboise, Yves 154–5
Lafrance, Jeanne 175
Lafrance, Marc 65, 67, 73, 154, 179
Laganière, André 171
Lagrave, J.-P. de 177
Lagrenade-Meunier, Monique 154–5
Lahaise, Robert 170
Lahey, Raymond J. 294, 300, 301
Laidlaw, Toni 252
Laing, Lionel H. 380
Lajeunesse, Ernest J. 55, 203
Lajeunesse, Marcel 174
Lalancette, Mario 58, 62, 127–8, 137
Lalou, Richard 57
Lamb, W. Kaye 335, 368, 369, 371–2, 373, 375, 377, 379
Lambert, James H. xv, 169, 182
Lambert, Phyllis 73
Lambert, Sheila 302
Lambton, John George, 1st Earl of Durham 184, 232, 419–22
Lamonde, Yvan 67, 165, 173, 174, 175, 181
Lamontagne, Leopold 55
Lamontagne, Sophie-Laurence 144
La Morandière, Charles de 21, 58, 287
Lanctôt, Gustave 159, 401
Landon, Fred 202, 231, 413, 438
Landry, Yves 52, 53, 55–6, 65, 67
Langdon, Stephen 213
Langhout, Rosemarie 259
Langlois, Georges 51
Lanphear, Kim M. 24

Laperrière, Guy 168
Laplante, Jacques 166
Lapointe-Roy, Huguette 170, 172
LaRocque, Emma 346
Larouche, Jeannette 151
Larouche, Léonidas 55
Larrabee, Edward McM. 89
LaRue, Richard 160
Laskin, Susan L. 74
Latham, Barbara K. 381, 385
Latta, Peter 107
Laurin, Serge 155
Lavallée, Louis 65, 72
Laverdure, Pauline 442
Lavertue, Robert 132
Lavigne, Marie 145
Lavoie, Marc 104
Lavoie, Yolande 25, 150
Lawr, D.A. 223
Lawson, Murray G. 59
Lawson, Philip 159, 414
Lay, Jackie 381
Leach, Douglas E. 74, 90
Leacock, Eleanor Burke 66
Lebel-Gagnon, Louise 169
LeBlanc, Robert 54
Leblond, Sylvio 157
Lebrun, François 126, 127, 128, 129,
    130, 132, 163
Lebrun, Richard-A. 159
Leclerc, Jean 141
Leclerc, Jean-François 72, 142
Leduc, Joanne 336, 385
Lee, David 137
Leefe, John G. 79, 404
Lefebvre, André 161, 177
Lefebvre, Jacqueline 170
Lefroy, John Henry 334
Légaré, Jacques 52, 55–6
Legault, Roch 159

Le Goff, T.J.A. 131
Lehmann, Heinz 439
LeHuenen, Joseph 286
Leighton, Douglas 199
Lein, Alexander Henry 11
Le Jeune, Paul 50
Lemieux, Denise 66, 145
Lemieux, Lucien 168
Lemieux, Vincent 161
Lemire, Maurice 67, 174, 175, 176
Lemoine, Réjean 157
Lemps, Alain Huetz de 179
Lenman, Bruce 435
Lennox, Paul Anthony 31
Léonidoff, Georges-Pierre 68, 144
Leonoff, Cyril E. 380–1
Lepage, André 137–8
Lepailleur, François-Maurice 164
Lescarbot, Marc 81
Leslie, John 199
Lessard, Claude 181
Lessard, Renald 68
Létourneau, Raymond 63
Lévesque, Andrée 145, 146
Lévis, François-Gaston de, Duc de
    Lévis 42
Levy, George 106
Lewis, Frank D. 133, 194
Lewis, Oscar 345
Lewis, Robert D. 155
Lewis, Robert M. 299
Leys, M.D.R. 431
Li, Peter S. 385
Liddell, Peter 100
Light, Beth 216–17, 224
Lillard, Charles 386
Lindsay, Charles S. 89
Linebaugh, Peter 220
Linteau, Paul-André 116, 155
Litalien, Raymonde 142, 288–9

Litalien, Rolland 170
Little, J.I. 125, 133, 138, 150
Little, Linda 319
Livingston, W. Ross 422
Lockwood, Glenn J. 203, 204, 208, 209
Loken, Gulbarand 439
Lom d'Arce, Louis-Armand de, Baron de Lahontan 43
Loo, Tina 384
Lord, Barry 177
Lord, Michel 176
Lortie, J. d'A. 176
Lotz, Jim 326
Louder, Dean 151
Louis, William Roger 395
Lounsbury, Ralph 288, 290
Love, James H. 224
Lower, Arthur J. 364
Lower, Arthur R.M. xiv, 118, 138, 184, 192, 428
Lowrey, Carol D. 212–13
Lowther, Barbara J. 358
Lucas, Sir Charles 232, 419–20
Lugrin, Nancy de Bertrand 381
Lunn, Alice Jean E. 50, 59, 61
Lussier, Antoine S. 48, 197, 199, 351, 352
Lydon, James G. 290–1
Lynch, John 20
Lysaght, A.M. 298, 321

McAndrews, J.H. 10, 48–9
Mac Aonghusa, Proinsias 441
McArthur, Duncan A. 418
MacBeath, George 79
McCabe, James Osborne 412
McCaffrey, Moira T. 27
McCalla, Douglas 191, 192, 193, 194, 195–6

McCallum, John 124, 132, 191
McCann, L.D. 99, 266, 439
McCann, Phillip 314, 315–16, 317, 318, 423
McClellan, Catharine 11, 345
McCloy, T.R. 374
McCready, H.W. 232, 420
McCreath, Peter 79
McCrum, Robert 440
McCulloch, Michael 154, 162
McCulloch, Thomas 260, 436
McCullogh, Allan B. 140
McCully, Bruce T. 97
McCusker, John J. 38, 290
McDavid, Raven I., Jr 440
McDavid, Virginia G. 440
McDiarmid, Orville J. 427–8
MacDonagh, Oliver 429, 430
Macdonald, Bertram H. 179
Macdonald, Bruce 383
Macdonald, David A. 299
MacDonald, G. Edward 274
MacDonald, Graham A. 332, 333
Macdonald, John A. 408
Macdonald, Sir John A. 229
MacDonald, M.A. 83, 104
MacDonald, Mary Lu 175
McDonald, Neil 222, 228
Macdonald, Norman 152, 202, 429
McDonald, Robert A.J. 358, 360, 361, 365, 367, 370, 377, 386, 387, 388, 424
MacDonell, Margaret 247, 437
MacDougall, Heather 221
McDougall, John 343
Macfie, Matthew 380
McGahan, Peter 445
McGee, Harold Franklin, Jr 94, 241
McGhee, Robert 12, 14, 16, 17, 24, 332

Macgillivray, Don 93, 245, 247, 257
McGillivray, Duncan 341
McGillivray, R. 210
McGillivray, Simon 341
McGinnis, Janice Dickin 157, 221
McGloin, John 387
McGowan, Mark G. 110
McGrath, Patrick 17
McGuigan, Peter 246–7, 273
McIlwraith, Thomas F. 193
MacInnes, Daniel 250
McInnis, Edgar W. 409
McInnis, R.M. (Marvin) 132, 133, 191
McIntire, C. Thomas 173
McIntosh, Angus 434
MacIntyre, Florence 92
Mackay, D.L. 416
McKay, David 366
MacKay, Donald 107, 152, 433, 437
MacKay, R.A. 306, 307
McKelvie, B.A. 381
McKendrick, Neil 425
McKenna, Katherine M.J. 217
MacKenzie, A.A. 247, 434
MacKenzie, A.E.D. 437
Mackenzie, Sir Alexander 335, 371
McKenzie, Ruth 180, 406
Mackenzie, William Lyon 230–1, 418
Mackie, Richard 378
McKillop, A.B. 200, 229, 330
McKim, William 318
MacKinnon, Frank 268, 270, 272, 278, 417
Mackinnon, I.G. 106
MacKinnon, Neil 243, 438
MacKinnon, Robert A. 258, 297
MacKinnon, Wayne E. 269
Macklem, Katherine 129
McLachlin, N.D. 418
McLaren, John 376, 386, 447

MacLauchlan, Morag 373
Maclaurin, D.L. 388
Maclay, Edgar Stanton 407
McLean, Don 352
McLean, John 341, 374
McLean, Marianne 202–3, 248, 437
MacLean, R.A. 108, 247, 435
MacLean, Terry 89
McLennan, J.S. 88
MacLeod, D. Peter 48, 52, 74
MacLeod, Donald 436
Mcleod, Malcolm 373
MacLeod, Malcolm 97, 226
MacLeod, Margaret Arnett 341, 349
Macleod, R.C. 72, 445
McLintock, Alexander H. 417
McLoughlin, John 374
McManus, Gary 281, 320
MacMechan, Archibald M. 97
McMicking, Thomas 336, 385
McMillan, Alan D. 12, 40, 197
MacMillan, Carrie 260
Macmillan, David S. 81, 134, 136, 188, 193, 256, 285, 291
McMullen, Lorraine 176
McNabb, Debra 105
McNally, David 190
McNally, Paul 89
McNaught, Kenneth 210
McNeil, Alan R. 105–6, 258
McNeil, John Robert 93
MacNeil, Robert 440
McNeill, William H. 15
McNulty, Gérard E. 31
McNutt, Steven Bligh 77
MacNutt, W.S. 79, 99, 102, 103, 239, 242, 263, 266, 271, 272, 284, 313, 402, 422
Macpherson, Alan G. 10, 296, 320
Macpherson, Ian 211

Macpherson, Joyce Brown 10
McRae, Kenneth D. 200
McSkimming, Robert J. 11
Madden, A. Frederick 399, 418
Madill, Dennis 386
Magill, M.L. 194, 195
Magnuson, Roger 67, 181
Magnusson, Magnus 16
Magsino, Romulo 317
Mahant, Edelgard E. 397
Mahon, John K. 404
Mailhot, José 148
Mailhot, Laurent 176
Maisonneuve, Daniel 151
Major, Robert 176
Makahonuk, Glen 339
Makarova, Raisa V. 365
Malcolmson, Patricia 220
Malpas, J. 320
Mancke, Elizabeth 105
Mandelbaum, David 345
Mandrou, Robert 47
Mangan, J.A. 317
Mann, Horatio 272
Manning, Helen Taft 140, 160, 416, 419
Manning, William R. 409
Mannion, John J. 203, 246, 291, 295–6, 297–8, 311, 312, 323, 432, 434
Manville, G.C. 10, 48–9
Marcil, Eileen 139
Markham, A.H. 18
Marr, William L. 190
Marsan, Jean-Claude 68, 178
Marshall, David B. 110, 229
Marshall, Ingeborg 26, 27, 303, 304, 305
Marshall, P.J. 395
Marshall, Peter 416
Marston, Thomas E. 16

Martel, Gilles 171
Martel, Gordon 424
Martell, J.S. 257
Martijn, Charles A. 13, 25, 27, 30, 58, 148, 304
Martin, Calvin 23, 60, 338
Martin, Chester 334, 424
Martin, François 152
Martin, Ged 164, 207, 216, 232, 276, 316, 410, 416, 419, 420, 422, 424–5, 434
Martin, Yves 161, 171
Martyn, J.P. 232
Masciotra, Vince 443
Mason, Philip P. 226
Massicotte, Edouard-Zotique 42
Masson, Louis-Rodrigue 341
Masters, Donald C. 195, 208, 412
Mather, J.Y. 434
Mathews, Hazel C. 401
Mathews, Robin 218
Mathieu, Jacques 36, 39, 52, 55, 61, 63, 64, 65, 113, 122, 154
Matson, R.G. 28
Matthews, Catherine J. 445
Matthews, Keith 274, 284, 287, 288, 292, 296, 301, 312, 313
Mattingly, Paul H. 222
Maud, Ralph 364
Maxwell, Moreau S. 12
Maynard, Kimberley Smith 444
Mayo, H.B. 316
Mays, Herbert 204–5
Mealing, Stanley 205
Meares, John 368
Medjuck, Sheva 253
Medley, D.J. 397
Meinig, D.W. 14
Melrose, Robert 377
Melvoin, Richard I. 74

Menard, Russell R. 290
Menzies, Archibald 369
Mercier, Lucie 145
Merk, Frederick 373, 376, 412
Merli, Frank J. 407–8
Merrell, James H. 73, 148
Messier, Jean-Jacques 36
Métayer, Maurice 347
Metcalf, George 230
Metcalfe, Alan 213
Meynaud, Jean 441
Michel, Louis 63, 128, 129, 130, 135
Middleton, Richard 74
Millar, W.P.J. 194, 222, 223
Miller, Audrey Saunders 230
Miller, Christopher L. 23
Miller, J.R. xv, 40, 59, 73, 94, 148, 197, 198, 344
Miller, Kerby A. 107, 152, 433
Miller, Virginia P. 28, 94
Millman, Thomas R. 173, 416
Milloy, John S. 345
Mills, David 201
Milobar, David 159
Mimeault, Mario 58, 137
Minchinton, Walter E. 425
Miquelon, Dale 39, 60, 61
Mishler, Craig 343
Mitchell, Elaine Allan 136
Mitchell, R.J. 431
Mitchell, Robert D. 40
Mitchinson, Wendy 157, 216, 218, 221
Mitchison, Rosalind 435
Moir, John S. 173, 198, 227, 228, 295
Mollat, Michel 58, 287
Molloy, Maureen 66
Monaghan, E. Jennifer 104
Monet, Jacques 164, 422
Monette, Michel 131
Monière, Denis 158, 162, 164, 177

Monk, James 444
Montpetit, Raymond 178
Moodie, D. Wayne 60
Moodie, Susanna (née Strickland) 206, 218
Moody, Barry 105, 110, 249, 253, 256
Moody, James 242
Moody, T.W. 432
Moogk, Peter N. 53, 64, 66, 67
Moore, Christopher 39, 91–2, 93, 201, 202, 289, 438
Moore, Elizabeth L. 43
Moore, Pat 346
Moorhead, M.L. 365
Morantz, Toby 59, 60, 71, 136, 137, 148–9, 321, 322, 339, 340
Morehouse, Frances 203
Moreira, James 257
Morel, André 72, 445
Morgan, Cecilia 216
Morgan, Edmund S. 414
Morgan, Marlena 391
Morgan, Philip D. 396
Morgan, Prys 431
Morgan, Robert J. 245, 263
Morgan, W.J. 310, 403
Morice, Adrien-Gabriel 341–2, 350, 375, 387
Morin, Jacques-Yvan 71, 158
Morin, Michel 150
Morin, Yvan 130, 175
Morison, Samuel Eliot 14, 17
Morisset, Gérard 178
Morley, William F.E. 188
Morrell, W.P. 399, 423
Morris, Audrey Y. 206, 218
Morris, Richard B. 410
Morrison, James H. 257
Morrison, Jean 341
Morrison, Kenneth M. 69, 73

Morrison, R. Bruce 40
Morrison, William R. 326, 332
Morton, Arthur S. 333–4, 337, 341, 371, 446
Morton, Desmond 213, 399
Morton, James 390
Morton, W.L. 164, 169, 227, 229, 235, 326, 330–1, 333, 348, 349, 353, 354, 413, 424, 425
Mottu-Webber, Liliane 132
Mouat, A.N. 379
Mougeon, Raymond 441
Moulton, E.C. 316
Mount, Graeme S. 397
Mousnier, Roland 71, 288
Moussette, Marcel 11, 57–8, 144
Moziño, José Mariano 369
Muggeridge, John 232
Muise, D.A. 36, 116, 184, 188, 209, 277, 322
Mulcahy, Mary Nolasco 317, 318
Mulhall, David 342–3
Mullane, George 404
Mullins, J.E. 404
Munro, James 282, 301
Munro, William Bennett 62
Murphy, Orville T. 307
Murphy, Terrence 228, 247, 262, 300–1, 316
Murray, Alexander Hunter 341
Murray, Florence B. 209
Murray, Jean 298
Murray, Keith A. 372, 383

Nabudere, D. Wadada 425
Nash, Alice N. 54
Nash, Ronald J. 28
Naylor, James 256
Naylor, R.T. 190, 396, 428
Neale, R.S. 421, 432

Neary, Peter 283, 284, 298, 311, 316
Neatby, Hilda 159, 167, 224, 400, 414, 444, 445
Neatby, Leslie H. 333, 335
Needler, George Henry 218
Nefsky, Judith 153, 439
Neidhardt, W.S. 226–7, 408
Nelles, H.V. 192, 193, 200
Nelson, George 346
Nelson, Helge 439
Nelson, Ralph C. 164
Nelson, W.H. 245
Nemec, Thomas 296, 298
Nepveu, Pierre 176
Nesbitt, Bruce 260
Nesbitt, J.K. 377
Netten, John W. 317, 318
Neufeld, E.P. 195
New, Chester W. 232, 420
Newcomb, C.F. 369
Newcombe, W.A. 369
Newell, Dianne 225
Newsome, Eric 381
Nicholas, Andrea Bear 95
Nichols, George E.E. 404
Nicholson, G.W.L. 308
Nicolai, Martin L. 74
Nish, Cameron 63, 66
Noble, Joey 220
Noble, William C. 13, 31
Noël, Danièle 173
Noël, Françoise 54, 61, 128, 173
Noel, Jan 66
Noel, S.J.R. 186, 211, 229, 234, 313
Nolan, William 291
Noppen, Luc 68, 178
Norcross, E. Blanche 373, 381, 384
Norman, Christian 193
Norrie, Kenneth xv, 124, 191, 254, 287
Norris, Darrell A. 201, 202–3

Norris, John 366
Norton, Mary Beth 438
Novick, Peter 186
Numbers, Ronald L. 68

Obermeir, Paule 153, 439
O'Brien, Patricia 319
O'Broin, Leon 408
O'Callaghan, Edmund Bailey 42
O'Connell, Philip 301
O'Dea, Agnes C. 281
O'Dea, Shane 262
O'Donnell, Brendan 153
O'Driscoll, Robert 203, 433, 441
Officer, E. Roy 102
O'Flaherty, Patrick 283, 298, 300, 313
Ogden, Peter Skene 374
O'Grady, Brendan 434
Oke, Timothy 383
Oleson, Tryggvi J. 333
Oliver, Michael 118
Olivier, Daniel 175
Ollerenshaw, Philip 432
Olsen, Mark 161
Olson, Ruth A. 217
Olson, Sherry 150
Ommer, Rosemary E. 137, 149, 257, 288, 290, 298, 299, 311, 323, 428
O'Neil, Marion 371
O'Neill, Anne 92
O'Neill, Kevin 432
O'Neill, Paul 308, 319
Orkin, Mark M. 440
Ormsby, Margaret A. 357, 373, 377, 379, 385, 391
Ormsby, William G. 232, 420, 422
Ornstein, Michael 203
Osborne, Brian S. 209
Ouellet, Fernand 48, 112, 117, 119–20, 121, 122, 123, 124, 127, 129, 130–1, 131–2, 133–4, 136–7, 138, 141, 142, 149, 160, 162, 163, 182–3, 421
Ouellet, Réal 43
Oury, Guy-Marie 169
Overland, Orm 439
Owen, Wendy 252, 340, 444
Owram, Douglas xv, 124, 191, 234, 254, 287, 336, 423

Pachai, Bridglal 249
Pagden, Anthony 396
Page, William 431
Paikowsky, Sandra 213
Paine, Robert 322
Painter, George D. 16
Palardy, Jean 68
Palliser, D.M. 17
Palmer, Bryan D. 142–3, 196, 200, 213–14, 215, 217, 220
Palmer, Howard 333, 353
Palmer, Stanley H. 18, 20
Palsson, Harmann 16
Pammett, Howard T. 203
Pannekoek, Fritz 326, 331, 339, 353
Panting, Gerald E. 255, 257, 274, 312, 319, 428
Paquet, Gilles 120–1, 123, 124, 125, 128, 129–30, 131–2, 138, 140, 141, 160, 182, 396
Paradis, André 156–7
Parent, Gilles 150
Pargellis, Stanley 397
Parizeau, Gérard 142, 162
Parker, Graham 217
Parker, W.H. 131
Parks, M.G. 251, 259, 260
Parmelee, G.W. 42
Parr, Joy 66, 203, 214, 224
Parry, J.H. 15, 20

Pastore, Ralph T. 8, 26, 49, 94, 241, 304, 305
Paterson, Donald G. 140, 190
Patterson, E. Palmer, II 387
Patterson, Gilbert C. 201
Patterson, Graeme H. 230, 421
Patterson, Robert S. 318
Payne, Michael 339–40
Pazdro, Roberta J. 385
Peake, Frank A. 343, 387
Pearl, Jonathan L. 70
Peckham, Howard Henry 400
Peel, Bruce Braden 326
Peers, Laura L. 50
Pellissier, Louis 269
Pendergast, James F. 29, 30
Penlington, Norman 420
Penney, Allen 105
Pentland, David H. 441
Pentland, H. Clare 142, 191, 195, 213, 219
Perceval-Maxwell, M. 433
Percy, Michael B. 128
Perkin, Harold 432
Perkins, Bradford 410, 411
Perkins, Simeon 107, 404
Péron, Yves 56, 149
Perron, Normand 155
Perrot, Nicolas 43
Perry, Peter 311
Peterson, Jacqueline 55, 331, 347, 348, 351, 442
Pethick, Derek 364, 369, 379
Petitot, Emile 333, 346
Petryshyn, Jaroslav 193, 208, 220, 224
Pettipas, Katherine 343
Pettipas, Leo F. 13
Pettit, Sydney G. 379, 384
Phelan, Josephine 217
Phillipps, Kenneth C. 432

Phillips, Jim 97, 444, 445, 446
Phillips, Paul 142, 191, 389
Phillips, Paul T. 394
Phillips, Ruth B. 69
Phillips, William Gregory 194
Picot-Bermond, Evelyne 321
Pierce, Richard A. 365
Pierson, Ruth 253
Pierson, Stuart 299
Pike, Warburton 336
Pinard, Guy 178
Piper, Don C. 411
Pitte, Jean-Robert 179
Piva, Michael J. 164, 195
Plamondon, Lilianne 61
Pletcher, David M. 412
Pluchon, Pierre 40
Plumb, J.H. 425
Poirier, Lucien 179
Poirier, Michel 101
Pollard, Sidney 431
Pope, Peter 299
Porter, Bernard 395
Porter, J.W. 403
Porter, John R. 144, 177–8
Portlock, Nathaniel 368
Poteet, Lewis J. 238, 442
Pothier, Bernard 98, 99
Potter (-MacKinnon), Janice 217–18, 438
Potvin, Claude 77
Pouliot, Léon 169
Pouyez, Christian 25, 150, 152
Power, Bonita 317
Power, Thomas P. 246, 272, 434
Pratt, T.K. 269, 442
Prebble, John 436
Prentice, Alison xv, 39, 60, 145, 216–17, 222, 224, 251, 252, 253
Preston, Richard A. 209, 255, 305, 321

Prevec, Rosemary 31
Price, John A. 197
Price, Lynda 153
Pringle, Ian 441
Pringle, James S. 320
Pritchard, James S. 61, 73, 134
Pritchard, Muriel F. Lloyd 421
Pronovost, Claude 135
Proulx, Gilles 64
Proulx, Jean-Pierre 22, 286, 307, 308
Proulx, Jean-René 8
Provencher, Jean 144, 154–5
Provost, Honorius 153
Prowse, Daniel W. 284
Pryke, Kenneth G. 199, 213, 263, 277
Pue, W. Wesley 167, 233, 375, 445
Pugh, Ralph Bernard 398, 418
Pullen, Hugh Francis 406
Pulling, George Christopher 303
Punch, Terrence M. 100, 434
Purdy, J.D. 223

Quaife, Milo 266
Quimby, George I. 68
Quinn, David Beers 8, 13–14, 16, 17, 18, 19, 20, 21, 27, 282, 285, 293, 294
Quintal, Claire 151–2

Racine, Denis 163
Raddall, Thomas H. 99
Radforth, Ian 147, 164, 166, 167, 187, 193, 194, 195, 216, 230, 235, 279
Raible, Chris 208
Raimo, John W. 398
Rajotte, Pierre 175
Ralston, H. Keith 358, 360, 361, 381, 382, 391
Ralston, Helen 86
Ramirez, Bruno 151

Ramsay, George, 9th Earl of Dalhousie 418
Ramsden, Peter George 29–30, 31
Rand, Silas Tertius 95, 241
Ranger, Terence 429, 431, 436
Rankin, Robert Allan 275
Ransom, Roger L. 312
Raphael, D.D. 426
Rapley, Elizabeth 70
Rashed, Zenab Esmat 409
Rasmussen, Knud 347
Ratelle, Maurice 148
Rattray, William Jordan 435
Rawlyk, George A. 77, 79, 83, 84, 90, 96, 98, 100, 103, 106, 108, 109–10, 159, 201, 239, 244, 249, 254, 256, 259–60, 266, 305, 317, 402, 415
Ray, Arthur J. 59, 60, 331, 337–8, 340, 348, 367, 374
Ray, Carl 347
Rea, J.E. 231, 437
Read, Colin 187, 195, 200, 205, 206, 210, 211, 224, 225, 229, 231, 232, 233, 424
Redish, Angela 195
Redmond, Gerald 435
Redmond, Patrick M. 434
Reeves, John 283
Reid, Dennis 68, 177, 200, 213
Reid, John G. 80, 81, 83, 99, 103, 242, 253, 276, 278–9
Reid, Philippe 161, 177
Reid, Richard M. 192, 194
Reid, Robie L. 383, 389
Reid, Stuart J. 420
Reid, W. Stanford 435
Reinders, Robert C. 207
Reinhartz, Dennis 18, 20
Reksten, Terry 382
Renaud, Paul-Emile 50

Renfrew, Colin 3
Revelle, Roger 56
Reynolds, Lorna 203, 433, 441
Reynolds, Paul R. 401
Reynolds, Stephen 368
Rhodes, Richard 441–2
Rhonda, James P. 372
Rhys, Sir John 431
Ribault, Jean-Yves 289
Rice, Richard 256
Rich, E.E. 59, 285, 334–5, 337, 339, 341, 354, 372, 373, 374, 417
Richards, Elva M. 211
Richards, Eric 436
Richards, J. Howard 11
Richards, John B. 387
Richardson, A.J.H. 178
Richardson, Alfred Talbot 387
Richardson, David 383
Richardson, John 335
Richardson, R. Alan 179
Richardson, Sidney C. 321
Richardson, William 321
Richling, Barnett 322, 323
Richter, Daniel K. 50, 54, 73, 148
Rickard, T.A. 382
Riddell, John Henry 342
Rieder, David M. 82
Rieder, Norma Gaudet 82
Riengold, Nathan 179
Riley, Patrick W.J. 435
Risk, R.C.B. 221
Ritcheson, Charles R. 410
Robbins, Douglas T. 26
Robert, Jean-Claude 37, 123–4, 127, 138, 141, 150, 155, 157
Robert, Lucie 175
Robert, Normand 52, 152, 429
Robertson, Allen B. 106, 261
Robertson, H. 256

Robertson, Ian Ross xv, 269, 272, 273, 274, 276, 278
Robertson, Marion 243
Robichaud, Léon 163
Robidoux, Réjean 174, 176
Robillard, Denise 146
Robinson, Sir John Beverley 420–1
Robinson, Mairi 434
Robinson, Ronald 395
Robinson, Sinclair 442
Roby, Yves 124, 151
Rocbert de La Morandière, Marie-Elisabeth (veuve Bégon de La Cour) 42
Roche, Daniel 40
Rockoff, Hugh 194
Roetger, Robert W. 243
Rogers, Edward S. 11, 31, 50
Rogers, Irene L. 274–5
Rogers, Norman McLeod 86
Roland, Charles G. 222
Rolde, Neil 91
Rollmann, Hans 300–1, 317
Rome, David 153, 439
Romney, Paul 200, 220–1, 231, 232–3, 438
Rompkey, Ronald 99
Ronda, James P. 372
Rooke, Patricia T. 220
Roos, Arnold E. 156, 180
Rose, J. Holland 395, 415–16
Ross, Alexander 353
Ross, Eric 164, 210, 336
Ross, Frank E. 376
Rosser, Fred 227
Rostlund, Erhard 11
Rotberg, Robert I. 244
Rothenberg, Marc 179
Rothney, G.O. 284, 320
Rotstein, Abraham 59, 338

Rouban, César 177
Rouillard, Jacques 36, 113, 116, 124,
    141, 158
Rouleau, Jean-Paul 171
Roulston, Pauline 203
Rousseau, François 66–7, 71, 157, 171
Rousseau, Gilles 27
Rousseau, Guildo 175
Rousseau, Jacques 42
Rousseau, Louis 170, 171
Rowe, Frederick W. 26, 284, 304, 313,
    317, 320
Roy, Jacqueline 36, 113, 115, 116
Roy, Jean-Louis 174
Roy, Muriel K. 82
Roy, Patricia E. 358, 385
Roy, Pierre-Georges 41, 43, 444
Roy, R. 152
Royce, Marion 224
Rozon, Lucie 170
Rubinger, Catherine 93
Ruddel, David-Thiery 64, 65, 139,
    142, 143, 154
Ruddock, Alwyn A. 17, 18
Rudin, Ronald 121, 140, 153
Ruelland, Jacques-G. 177
Ruggles, Richard I. 61, 336, 417
Rumilly, Robert 96, 162
Rundle, Robert Terrill 343
Russell, Bob 215
Russell, Dale 345
Russell, Peter (1733–1808) 229
Russell, Peter 330
Russell, Peter A. 192, 205
Russell, Victor L. 208, 225, 232–3
Rust, Richard Dilworth 372
Ryan, Shannon 292, 298, 310, 311, 428
Ryerson, Stanley B. 185, 231, 233–4

Sack, Benjamin 439

Sacouman, R. James 312
Sagard, Gabriel 43
Sage, Walter N. 379, 391, 392
Sager, Eric W. 255–6, 284, 312, 319,
    428
St-Georges, Lise 127, 135
St-Hilaire, Marc 150–1
Saint-Pierre, Louise 177
Saint-Pierre, Serge 154–5
Saizieu, Tiphaine Barthelemy de 131
Salagnac, Georges Cerbelaud 309
Salée, Daniel 121–2, 123, 134, 139,
    160, 183
Salmon, J.H.M. 20
Salone, Emile 50
Salusbury, John 99
Samson, Roch 137, 139
Sanderson, C.P. 229
Sandilands, John 442
Sanfilippo, Matteo 47–8
Sanford, Charles L. 412
Sanger, Chesley W. 296, 297, 311
Sanger, David 28
Sauer, Carol O. 14
Saunders, Robert E. 211
Saunders, S.A. 254
Sauvageau, Robert 98
Savelle, Max 409
Savignac, Pierre-H. 148
Savoie, Sylvie 66
Scadding, Henry 208
Scargill, M.H. 440, 442
Schalk, Randall F. 12
Schlesinger, Roger 21
Schmalz, Peter S. 73, 197, 198, 199,
    400, 405
Schmidt, Helmut D. 426
Schnell, R.L. 220
Schroder, Johan 439
Schull, Joseph 212

Schulze, David 138
Schuyler, Robert Livingston 426
Schwantes, Carlos A. 357, 372, 377
Schwartz, Herbert T. 347
Scobie, Charles H.H. 106, 262, 300
Scott, Henry E. 111
Scott, Jamie S. 110
Scott, Joan Wallach 216
Scott, Jonathan 111
Scott, Mildred Grace 11
Scott, William Beverley 11
Sealey, D. Bruce 351, 352
See, Scott W. 264, 265
Seed, Patricia 293
Séguin, Maurice 119, 127, 131
Séguin, Normand 123–4, 126, 127, 128, 129, 130, 132, 138, 141, 150, 156, 163
Séguin, Robert-Lionel 63, 133
Selesky, Harold E. 74
Selkirk, Earl of. *See* Douglas, Thomas
Selmon, Gordon 388
Semmel, Bernard 426
Semple, Neil 228–9
Senior, Elinor Kyte 163, 407
Senior, Hereward 152, 201, 204, 226–7, 242, 408, 438
Sévigny, P.-André 141
Shammas, Carole 293
Sharpe, Errol 268
Shaw, A.G.L. 419, 427
Shea, D.S. 204
Shea, John Gilmary 42
Shearer, Ronald A. 140
Sheehan, Nancy M. 388
Shelton, Russell C. 415
Shelton, W. George 391, 426
Shepherd, James F. 312
Sheppard, F.H.W. 432
Shepperson, George 108

Shepperson, Wilbur S. 429
Sherman, Robert 189
Shippee, Lester B. 412
Shomette, Donald G. 307
Shortt, Adam 99
Shortt, S.E.D. 90, 156, 221–2
Siddiq, Fazley 258
Sidler, Earl 29
Silver, Arthur I. 165
Simard, Jean 168, 171–2
Simard, Sylvain 159
Simcoe, John Graves 229
Simmons, Richard 282
Simpson, Evan John 413
Simpson, George 341, 372–3
Simpson, Jeffrey 434
Sissons, Charles Bruce 224
Skaggs, David Curtis 406–7
Skelton, R.A. 14, 16–17, 18
Skinner, Andrew S. 426
Slater, G. Hollis 379
Slattery, Brian 20
Sloan, W.A. 340
Smandych, Russell C. 445
Smith, Adam 425–6
Smith, Allan 206, 360
Smith, David 430
Smith, Donald 442
Smith, Donald B. 38, 48, 99, 103, 197, 198, 199, 269, 278, 350
Smith, Dorothy Blakey 379, 384, 389, 391
Smith, Dwight La Vern 404
Smith, James G.E. 11, 31
Smith, Justin Harvey 400–1
Smith, Myron J., Jr 403
Smith, Paul H. 401
Smith, Peter J. 164
Smith, Philip E.L. 297, 303
Smith, W.I. 276

Smith, Waldo E.L. 300
Smitheram, Verner 269, 275
Smout, T.C. 433, 435
Smyth, Donna 252
Smyth, William J. 152, 203, 204, 433, 434
Snelling, R.C. 418
Snider, C.H.J. 407
Snow, Dean R. 23, 24, 28
Soderlund, Walter C. 213
Soltow, Lee 205
Sosin, Jack M. 198, 409
Sparling, Mary 253
Speisman, Stephen A. 219
Speitel, H.H. 434
Spelt, Jacob 196, 209
Spiess, Arthur E. 11
Spigelman, Martin S. 251
Spira, Thomas 275
Splane, Richard B. 219
Spragge, George W. 225
Sprague, Douglas N. 350
Spray, William A. 241, 249, 264
Spry, Irene 335
Spurr, John 227
Stabler, Arthur P. 21
Stacey, C.P. 74, 227, 406, 407
Stager, John K. 11
Stagg, John C.A. 410
Stagg, Ronald J. 231
Stamp, Robert M. 224, 317
Standen, S. Dale 48, 71
Stanley, George F.G. 39–40, 54, 159, 161, 198, 226, 266, 334, 349–50, 354, 399, 401, 404, 405
Stanley, Laurie 262
Starkey, David J. 290, 306
Starna, William A. 73
Starr, S. Frederick 365, 391
Staton, Frances M. 114

Steegmann, A. Theodore, Jr 12, 50
Steele, Donald 320
Steele, Ian K. 73, 290
Stefansson, Vilhjalmur 18, 24, 344
Stelter, Gilbert A. 154, 188
Stembridge, Stanley R. 422
Stern, Mark J. 207
Stevens, G.R. 193–4
Stevens, James 347
Stevens, Kenneth R. 411
Stevens, Paul L. 400
Stevenson, Winona 342
Stewart, Alan 73
Stewart, Alice R. 424
Stewart, Anthony Terence Quincey 432
Stewart, Deborah 272
Stewart, E.I. 371
Stewart, Frances L. 28, 95
Stewart, Gordon T. 109, 110, 397, 402, 409, 417
Stewart, Hilary 363, 369
Stewart, J.R. 371
Stewart, John 270
Stoddart, Jennifer 145
Stone, William Leete 401, 402
Storey, Robert 214, 215
Stortz, Gerald 228, 300
Story, G.M. 22, 286, 293, 294, 440, 442
Story, Norah 103
Stouffer, Allen P. 207, 412
Strange, James 368
Strathern, Gloria M. 326, 358
Strickland, Samuel 206, 218
Strong-Boag, Veronica 61, 66, 252, 388
Stuart, Reginald C. 397, 409
Stubbs, Roy St George 446
Sturgis, James 160

Sturtevant, William C. 7, 19, 25, 38, 345, 363
Sugden, John 405
Sullivan, David 446
Sullivan, James 43
Surtees, Robert J. 38, 148, 199
Sutch, Richard 312
Sutherland, David A. 257, 259
Sutherland, Gillian 418
Sutherland, Neil 188
Suttles, Wayne 7, 11, 363, 364, 370
Suviranta, Bruno 425
Swainson, Donald 209, 216, 222, 348
Sweeny, Robert 155
Swiggett, Howard 401
Sydenham, Earl of. See Thomson, Charles Edward Poulett
Sylvain, Philippe 168, 169
Szostak, Rick 128

Taché, Alexandre-Antonin 343
Talbot, Allen G. 215
Talbot, Edward Allen 206
Talman, James J. 201, 227
Tanguay, Cyprien 37
Tanner, Adrian 338
Tanner, Helen Hornbeck 38, 51, 348
Tanner, John 354
Tansill, Charles C. 412
Tausky, Nancy Z. 225
Taylor, C. James 220
Taylor, J. Garth 24, 25, 322
Taylor, James 440
Taylor, John H. 209
Taylor, M. Brook 46–7, 117, 186, 205, 250, 260, 270, 421
Teeple, Gary 190, 204
Tehariolina, Marguerite Vincent 148
Teichgraeber, Richard F., III 426
Teit, James 364

Tellier, Sylvie 175
Temperley, Howard 201
Tennant, Paul 381, 386
Tennyson, Brian 93, 245, 247, 257, 278
Thach, Quoc Thuy 150
Therrien, Jean-Marie 71
Thevet, André 20–1
Thibault, Charlotte 135
Thibault, Claude 36, 113, 115, 397
Thibault, Michel 152, 429
Thistle, Paul 339
Thivierge, Marise 64
Thomas, Aaron 298
Thomas, Clara 218, 228
Thomas, Earle 149, 402
Thomas, Lewis G. 334
Thomas, Lewis H. 423
Thomas, Morley K. 10
Thomas, P.D.G. 414
Thomas, Peter 282, 431
Thomas, William 420, 421
Thompson, David 334, 371
Thompson, Frederic F. 300, 306
Thomson, Charles Edward Poulett, 1st Baron Sydenham 420
Thomson, Don W. 409
Thorner, Thomas 358, 389
Thornton, Patricia A. 150, 296, 323
Thorpe, Frederick J. 295
Thurlby, Malcolm 225
Thwaites, Reuben Gold 42, 43, 50, 81
Tierney, Frank M. 260
Tikhmenev, P.A. 365
Timothy, Hamilton Baird 212
Tobin, Mary A.T. 8
Tompkins, S.R. 365
Toner, Peter M. 246, 248, 434
Tooker, Elisabeth 38, 49, 69
Tourangeau, Rémi 176

Tousignant, Pierre 113, 158, 159, 160, 414

Tovell, Rosemary L. 177

Toye, William 37, 260

Tracy, Nicholas 403

Traill, Catharine Parr (née Strickland) 206, 218

Trask, Deborah 100, 104–5

Trask, Gwen G. 110

Trask, Stuart 110

Traves, Tom 139, 196, 215

Tremaine, Marie 114

Trémaudan, Auguste-Henri de 351–2

Tremblay, Robert 143

Trépanier, Guy 155

Trépanier, Monique 178

Trépanier, Pierre 180, 251

Trevor-Roper, Hugh 436

Trigger, Bruce G. 7, 11, 22–3, 29, 30, 31, 38, 40, 48, 49–50, 54, 137, 147, 321, 322, 340

Trimmer, F. Mortimer 336

Trofimenkoff, Susan Mann 118, 122, 224, 252

Trotter, Reginald G. 424

Trottier, Louise 139

Trout, E. 193

Trout, J.M. 193

Trudel, François 25, 58, 149, 321

Trudel, Jean 68, 178

Trudel, Marcel 20, 37, 38, 39, 53, 57, 60, 62, 64, 65, 153, 410

Trueman, Allan S. 389

Trump, H.J. 311

Tuck, James A. 11, 13, 22, 26, 286, 304

Tuck, Robert C. 275

Tucker, Eric 215

Tucker, Gilbert N. 195, 427

Tucker, Josiah 425–6

Tucker, Robert W. 414

Tulchinsky, Gerald 140, 153, 194, 195, 209, 220, 227, 230, 428

Tunis, Barbara R. 156

Turgeon, Laurier 21–2, 58, 287–8, 289, 321

Turner, Frederick Jackson xiv, 329, 360–1

Twomey, Richard J. 299

Tyrrell, Joseph Burr 334, 340

Ubelaker, Douglas H. 24, 51

Underhill, Frank H. 230

Upton, Leslie F.S. 26, 94, 201, 240, 304, 403, 424

Usher, Jean 387

Vachet, André 158

Vachon, André 68, 69, 71, 169

Vachon, Monique 179

Valverde, Mariana 216

Vancouver, George 369

Van Die, Marguerite 228

Van Kirk, Sylvia 60, 218, 331, 339, 351, 375, 388

Vass, Elinor 273

Vastokas, Joan M. 200

Vaucheret, E. 86

Vaughan, Alden T. 54

Vaughan, Thomas 370

Vecsey, Christopher 69, 199

Veinott, Rebecca 445

Verchere, David R. 379

Verdon, Michel 129

Vermette, Luce 63, 129, 139

Verrette, Michel 67, 181

Vesey, Maxwell 403

Vickers, J. Roderick 13

Vigneault, Robert 441

Vigneras, L.-A. 18, 19

Vigod, Bernard L. 439

Viljoen, Tina 399–400
Vincent, Sylvie 8
Vincent, Thomas B. 108, 110, 260, 267
Vincenthier, Georges 164–5
Vlach, Milada 114–15
Vogan, Nancy 104
Voisine, Nive 168, 169, 170, 171
Voyer, Simonne 179

Waddington, Alfred Penderell 389
Wade, Mark Sweeten 389
Wade, Mason 262
Wagner, W.R. 369
Waite, Peter B. 235, 276, 316, 443
Waites, K.A. 391
Wakefield, Edward Gibbon 421
Wakeline, Martyn F. 431
Walbran, John T. 359
Waldram, James B. 95
Walker, Alexander 368
Walker, Franklin A. 224
Walker, Iain C. 89
Walker, James W.StG. 48, 207, 244, 248
Walko, Michael 29
Wallace, Birgitta Linderoth 16
Wallace, Carl M. 265, 277
Wallace, Frederick William 255
Wallace, Hugh N. 334
Wallace, J.N. 340
Wallace, W. Stewart 341, 374
Waller, George M. 96
Wallerstein, Immanuel 15
Wallot, Jean-Pierre 56, 70, 113, 114, 115, 120–1, 123, 124, 125, 126, 127, 128, 129–30, 131–2, 134, 137, 138, 140, 141, 160, 161, 165–6, 172, 182–3, 396
Walton, Gary M. 312

Warburton, Rennie 389
Ward, Harry M. 40
Ward, John Manning 315, 413, 416, 422
Ward, W. Peter 147, 149, 216, 358, 360, 361, 365, 367, 370, 377, 380, 385, 386, 387, 388, 424
Warkentin, John 40, 191, 202, 254–5, 334, 357
Warner, Donald F. 278, 412
Warren, Gordon H. 413
Warrian, Peter 215
Warwick, Jack 37
Waseem, Gertrud 99–100
Washburn, Wilcomb E. 38, 367
Watelet, Hubert 126
Waters, David M. 15
Waterston, Elizabeth 115, 206
Watkins, M.H. 190–1, 232
Watkins, Ralph 73
Weale, David 268, 269, 273–4
Weaver, Jack W. 429
Weaver, John C. 209, 211, 220, 319
Webb, Robert Lloyd 382
Weinmann, Heinz 122
Weir, Thomas R. 11
Weisz, George 156
Welland, Dennis 398
Wells, Kennedy 274
Wells, Robert V. 56
Welsh, William Jeffrey 406–7
West, E.G. 426
Westfall, William 104, 168, 225, 228
Weston, Corinne Comstock 417
Wetherell, Charles 243
Whebell, C.F.J. 230
Wheelock, Angela 346
Whelan, James M. 265
Whelan, Kevin 291
Whitbourne, Sir Richard 26, 294

White, Marian E. 30
White, Patrick C.T. 270, 410–11
White, Randall 186
White, Richard 41, 59, 73, 198, 400, 405
White, Ruth L. 164
White, Terence De Vere 432
Whitehead, Margaret 387
Whitehead, Ruth Holmes 28, 95, 240–1
Whitelaw, Marjorie 418
Whitelaw, William Menzies 276
Whiteley, William H. 292, 302, 309, 321, 322, 415
Whitney, Caspar 336
Whittow, J.B. 432, 434
Whyte, Donald 435
Wickens, Bill 95
Wicks, Rene 298
Widdis, Randy William 205
Wien, Fred 249
Wien, Thomas 60, 61, 63, 132, 134
Wilhelmy, Jean-Pierre 153
Wilkinson, Anne 212
Williams, Alan F. 308
Williams, David 430
Williams, David Ricardo 382–3, 383–4, 446–7
Williams, Glyndwr 309, 364, 366, 395, 417, 419
Williams, Gwyn A. 430, 431
Williams, J.B. 427
Williams, Savanah E. 249
Williamson, H. Anthony 322
Williamson, James Alexander 18
Willis, John 142, 152, 434
Wilson, Bruce G. 115, 187, 194, 201, 402
Wilson, C.H. 285
Wilson, C. Roderick 40

Wilson, Cynthia V. 49
Wilson, David A. 245, 246, 248
Wilson, G.A. 201
Wilson, J. Donald 67, 93, 199, 223–4, 317, 388
Wilton, Carol 26, 143, 167, 221, 233, 304, 446
Winius, George D. 19
Winks, Robin W. 207, 248, 396, 407, 412–13
Winslow, John 101
Winsor, Justin 411
Winterhalder, Bruce 12
Wise, S.F. 198, 200, 201, 211, 212, 217, 228, 397, 418
Withers, Charles W.J. 435
Withey, Lynne 366
Woehrling, José 71, 158
Wohler, J. Patrick 406
Wolf, Eric 15
Wolfart, H. Christoph 441
Wolfenden, Madge 375
Wood, B. Anne 260
Wood, Clifford 281, 320
Wood, J. David 192, 201, 204
Wood, John Cunningham 426
Wood, William 226, 404
Woodcock, George 246, 351, 357
Woodman, David C. 335
Woods, Shirley E. 135
Woodward, Frances 384
Wright, Barry 167, 215, 233, 445
Wright, Esther Clark 105, 243
Wright, J. Leitch, Jr 405
Wright, James V. 10, 13, 31, 54
Wright, Mary Ellen 109, 261
Wright, Milton J. 31
Wright, Richard Thomas 385, 388
Wrinch, L.A. 373
Wrong, George M. 91

Wyczynski, Michel 91
Wyczynski, Paul 174, 176
Wylie, William N.T. 214, 221, 222, 444
Wynn, Graeme 65, 106–7, 206, 258, 263–4, 265, 268, 279, 383, 428

Youings, Joyce A. 17
Young, Brian 39, 122, 134, 141, 142, 146, 165, 167, 171
Young, D. Murray 248, 264, 418

Young, Egerton Ryerson 343
Youngson, A.J. 436

Zaslow, Morris 226, 406
Zeller, Suzanne 180, 225, 229
Zeman, Jarold K. 77
Zimmerly, David 320
Zoltvany, Yves F. 47, 71, 72
Zumkeller, Dominique 132
Zupko, Ronald 38
Zwelling, Shomer S. 412

Subject Index

Note: References to Lower Canada include Quebec and Canada East, references to Upper Canada include Canada West, and references to British Columbia include Vancouver Island.

Abenaki 55, 96; and Anglo-French rivalry 73, 96; and the fur trade 23

Acadians 81–7, 98–9; and Anglo-French rivalry 79, 81–4, 98–102; bibliography of 77; *Evangeline* myth and 100, 250; in exile 54, 77, 82, 101–2; expulsion of 82, 100–2; in Ile Royale 99; in Ile Saint-Jean 87–8; language of 442; in New Brunswick 249–51; in New France 54, 83, 101; in Nova Scotia 249–51; population of 79, 82; in Prince Edward Island 249–51, 276; return of 82, 102

Agriculture: in Acadia 79, 81–2, 85; in British Columbia 373, 381; crisis of, in Lower Canada 119–22, 123–4, 131–3, 149–50; among the Huron 49–50; among the Iroquoian 7, 11, 29; in Lower Canada 124–33, 149; among the Micmac 240; among Native peoples 60; in New Brunswick 264–5; in Newfoundland 297–8; in New France 47–8, 62–3; in the Northwest 331, 335–6, 348–9, 352–

3; in Nova Scotia 79, 98–9, 105–6, 106–7, 258, 262–3; in Prince Edward Island 79, 87–8, 268–73; and the staples thesis 191; in Upper Canada 187, 189, 191–2. *See also* Farmers; Land policy

Algonkian (Algonquian, language grouping) 4–5, 22, 31, 60, 71; Christian missions to 69; and the French 50, 60; and the fur trade 4–5, 28, 30, 50, 60, 94, 149; and the Huron 4–5; language of 441

American Revolution 400–4, 409–10, 413–15; and the Iroquois 198, 402; and Lower Canada 159, 160, 400–2, 410, 414; and the Maliseet 96; and the Micmac 96, 403; and Native peoples 400, 402, 403, 409–10; and Newfoundland 298, 307, 309–10, 403, 415; and Nova Scotia 108–9, 256, 402–4, 415; and the Ojibwa 197–8, 400; and Upper Canada 197–8

Amish, in Upper Canada 438

Anglican Church: and British colonial
policy 416–17; and British Columbia
376, 380, 387, 388; and clergy
reserves 201; and the Hudson's Bay
Company 376; in Lower Canada
173, 416; missions to Native peoples 342, 343–4, 376, 387; in New
Brunswick 261, 267; in Newfoundland 300, 315–16, 317–18; in the
Northwest 331, 342, 343–4, 353,
417; in Nova Scotia 245, 261, 416;
in Upper Canada 201, 224, 225,
227–9, 416–17
Anglo-American colonies (to 1783) 40;
and Anglo-French rivalry 73–4, 79,
80, 83, 84, 88–91, 96–102; fishery of
290–1; and Lower Canada 159, 160,
400–2, 410, 414; and Newfoundland 290–1, 307, 309–10, 403, 415;
and Nova Scotia 108–9, 402–4, 415;
political structures of 413–14; population of, compared with New
France 56. See also American Revolution; Massachusetts; New England
Anglo-French rivalry in North America
39–41, 72–4, 409–10; and the Acadians 79, 80–4, 98–102; and the
Anglo-American colonies 73–4, 79,
80, 83, 84, 88–91, 96–102; and
Christian missions 69, 86–7, 94–5;
and the fur trade 59, 94; and Ile
Saint-Jean 87–8; and Louisbourg
88–91; and Native peoples 40–1, 50,
52, 69, 72–3, 80, 86–7, 94–6; and
Newfoundland 305–10; and New
France 39–41, 42, 72–4; and Nova
Scotia 79, 96–102
Animals: beaver 60; buffalo 7, 12, 332,
348–9; of Canada 11; caribou 11,
149; Native peoples' relationship

with 11–12, 23, 60, 338, 374; sea
otter 364–5, 366, 367
Anishinabeg 48. See also Ojibwa
Anthropology: methods and scope 3–6;
and the study of the Blackfoot 345;
of the Coast Salish 364; of the
Dakota 345; of the Huron 49–50; of
the Interior Salish 364; of the Inuit
9–10, 344; of the Katzie 364; of the
Kitwancool 364; of the Lillooet
364; of the Métis 351; of Native
peoples 3–6, 7–8, 9–10, 33–6, 38, 40,
44, 46, 48–50, 337, 345–7, 359, 363–
4; of the Shuswap 364; of the Stalo
363–4; of the Thompson 364
Archaeology: methods and scope 3–6;
and the study of Acadians 84–5; of
the Algonkian 4–5, 31; of L'Anse aux
Meadows 16; of the Beothuk 26; of
Canso 98; of the Huron 4–5, 11, 30,
31, 49–50; of the Innu 12–13; of the
Inuit 10, 12–13; of Louisbourg 88–
90; of the Micmac 27–8, 94–5; of
Montreal 155; of Native peoples 3–
6, 9–10, 12–13, 14, 34–5, 68–9, 332–
3; of the Neutral 30–1; of the Petun
30–1; of the Planters 104–5; of Quebec City 154–5; of Red Bay 22, 286;
of Rocky Mountain Fort 371; of the
St Lawrence Iroquoian 5, 28–30; in
Upper Canada 225. See also Material
culture
Architecture: in Acadia 83, 85; in
Lower Canada 144, 178; in New
France 64, 68; in Nova Scotia 105,
262, 439–40; in Prince Edward
Island 274–5; religious 105, 178,
225; in Upper Canada 220, 225;
vernacular 64, 68, 83, 85, 105, 144,
178, 225, 262, 274–5, 439–40

Army, British: and the American Revolution 159, 160, 400–3; and Anglo-French rivalry 42, 73–4, 90–1, 96–7, 98, 307–10; in British Columbia 384; in British North America 399–408; and the Civil War 407–8; and the colonial militia 90–1; and the Fenian raids 226–7, 408; in Lower Canada 140, 159, 160, 161, 163, 400–2, 404–7; in the Maritime provinces 402–3, 408; in Newfoundland 307–10, 319; and the Rebellions of 1837–8 163, 226, 231–2, 407; and the Red River Resistance of 1869–70 354; spending of 140; in Upper Canada 226–7, 231–2, 404–7, 408; and the War of 1812 161, 226, 404–6

Army, French: and Anglo-French rivalry 42, 73–4, 88–91, 96–7, 98, 307–10; and the fur trade 61; in Ile Saint-Jean 87–8; at Louisbourg 88–93; in Newfoundland 307–10; in New France 53, 62, 64; relations with colonial militia 74

Art: in British Columbia 364; in Lower Canada 177–8; of the Métis 351; of Native peoples 69, 95, 200, 240–1; Native peoples depicted in 14, 18–19, 70, 336; in New France 68; in the Northwest 335–6, 351; in Nova Scotia 253, 261; of the Pacific Coast 364; religious 68, 177–8; in Upper Canada 212–13

Artisans: in Lower Canada 142–4, 178; in New France 35, 63–4; in Prince Edward Island 275; in Upper Canada 196, 213–15

Athapaskan. See Dene

Atlases: of Alberta 11; of the Great Lakes region 11, 49; of the Great Lakes region's Native peoples 38, 348; Historical Atlas of Canada 6–7, 37, 114, 187, 281, 332, 359; linguistic, of Quebec 440; linguistic, of the United States and Canada 440; of Manitoba 11; of Montreal 37; of Newfoundland 281; of New France 37; of the Northwest Coast 11; of Ontario 37; of the Quebec climate 49; of Saskatchewan 11. See also Cartography

Banks: in Lower Canada 139–40; in Prince Edward Island 275; in Upper Canada 195

Baptist Church: Baptist Heritage in Atlantic Canada series 78; bibliography of 77; in British Columbia 387; in Lower Canada 227; in Nova Scotia 106, 109–11, 249, 262; in Upper Canada 227

Basques: fishery of 21–2, 28, 285–6, 321; whaling by 22, 286; and Native peoples 22, 25, 28, 321

Beaver (tribe) 374

Beothuk 6, 22, 25–6, 302–5; Christian missions to 303; extinction of 25–6, 302–5; and the fur trade 26, 304; and the Inuit 26; and the Micmac 26, 304–5; population of 303

Birds 4, 11

Blackfoot 345

Blacks: in British Columbia 380; British policy toward 206–7; language of 440; in Lower Canada 153; in New Brunswick 244, 248–9; in New France 64; in Nova Scotia 107, 244, 248–9, 440; in Prince Edward Island 248–9; and slavery 64, 107,

153, 207, 412; in Upper Canada
206–7, 412
Britain: and the American Revolution
159, 160, 309–10, 400–4, 409–10,
413–15; and the Civil War 407–8,
412–13; and diplomatic relations
with the United States 396, 405,
407–8, 408–13; and the exploration
of North America 8–9, 13–14, 16,
17–19, 24, 25, 27, 187, 293–5, 333–6,
340–1, 364, 366–74, 415; fishery of
17, 21, 286, 287, 288, 290–9, 301–2,
305–12, 320–3; and the Napoleonic
Wars 292, 310, 405; and the Nootka
crisis 369; and the Oregon question
376–7, 412; and the San Juan boundary dispute 383, 412; and the War of
1812 161, 371, 376, 404–7, 410–11.
See also Anglo-French rivalry in
North America; Army, British; Colonial policy, British; Emigration: British, English, Irish, Scottish, Welsh;
Native relations: with the British;
Navy, British

Captives: Anglo-American 54, 354,
369; Native 5, 25; women 54
Carrier 374
Cartography: of Acadia 87; of the Canada–United States boundary 408–9,
411; of the Great Lakes region 37;
and the Hudson's Bay Company
336, 417; of Lower Canada 125,
180; Native 336; of Newfoundland
303, 309, 320; of North America 87;
of the Northwest 336, 417; of Nova
Scotia 87; sixteenth century 8, 17; of
Upper Canada 201–2; Vinland map
16–17. *See also* Atlases
Childhood: bibliography of 188; in

Lower Canada 150; in New France
66; in Prince Edward Island 275; in
Upper Canada 220, 222. *See also*
Education; Family
Christian missions: to the Algonkian
69; and Anglo-French rivalry 69,
86–7, 94–5; to the Beothuk 303; and
conversion 69, 86; to the Cree 343;
to the Dene 333, 342; and the fur
trade 322–3, 343; and the Hudson's
Bay Company 322, 343; to the
Huron 35, 43, 69; to the Inuit 321–
3; to the Iroquois 42–3, 54–5; to the
Maliseet 80, 86–7, 94–5; to the Micmac 80, 81, 86–7, 94–5; missionary
accounts of Native peoples 34, 35,
42–3, 50, 59, 81, 323, 333, 343–4,
346, 376, 387; to the Montagnais 50,
69; to Native peoples 34, 38, 42–3,
69–70, 149, 199, 341–4, 376, 386–7;
to the Neutral 35; to the Nisga 387;
to the Saulteaux 343; to the
Tsimshian 387; and women 66, 322
Climate: of Canada 10; as a discour-
agement to immigration 53; effect
of, on agriculture in New France 63;
of Quebec 49
Coast Salish 364
Colonial policy, British 394–7, 413–25,
425–8; toward Acadia/Nova Scotia
79, 80–1, 83; and the Anglican
Church 416–17; toward the Anglo-
American colonies 40; toward British Columbia 356–7, 358–9, 361,
366–7, 369, 376–80, 382–4, 390–2,
407, 412, 415, 423–4; toward British
North America 254, 394–7, 398–9,
399–408, 408–13, 413–25, 425–8;
Colonial Office and 162, 416, 417,
418, 420; and Confederation 424–5;

and Durham's *Report* 163–4, 232, 419–22; and free trade 425–7; and the Hudson's Bay Company 336, 337, 348–9, 366, 372–3, 376–80, 417, 423–4; toward Louisbourg 88–9, 93; toward Lower Canada 158–66, 407, 414, 419, 420, 422; and mercantilism 59, 425–6; toward Newfoundland 282, 288, 301–2, 305–10, 314–15, 320–1, 414–15; toward New France 73–4; toward the Northwest 417, 423; toward Nova Scotia 79, 96–101, 415; toward Prince Edward Island 269–70, 415; Second British Empire, founding of 413–14, 415–16; in the sixteenth century 8–9, 17–18; toward Upper Canada 230, 232, 407

Colonial policy, French 40; toward Acadia/Nova Scotia 79, 80–1, 82, 83, 98; toward Ile Saint-Jean 87–8; toward Louisbourg 88–9, 93; and mercantilism 288; toward New-foundland 288, 295, 305–10, 320–1; toward New France 39–40, 41–2, 60–2, 73–4; in the sixteenth century 9, 20–1

Confederation: and British colonial policy 424–5; and British Columbia 391–2; and Lower Canada 164–5; and New Brunswick 276–7; and Newfoundland 316–17; and Nova Scotia 276–8; and Prince Edward Island 276, 278; and the Roman Catholic Church 165; and Upper Canada 234–6

Congregational Church: in Lower Canada 173; in Newfoundland 300

Conquest of New France 39–40, 42, 61, 74, 136, 158–9, 409–10; historio-graphical debate over 45–8, 117–20, 123

Costume: of the Acadians 83; at Louis-bourg 92; of the Planters 104

Cree 345; Christian missions to 343; and the fur trade 148, 337–8, 345; language of 441, 442; oral traditions of 346, 347; religion of 338, 346, 347

Dakota 345

Dene (Athapaskan) 345; Christian mis-sions to 333, 342; oral traditions of 333, 345, 346; religion of 342; women 346

Disease: among the Beothuk 26; chol-era 157, 221, 265, 429–30; malaria 375; among Native peoples 4, 15–16, 23–4, 51–2, 54, 304, 370; among the St Lawrence Iroquoian 29; smallpox 93, 370

Divorce. *See* Marriage and divorce

Ecology: of Acadia/Nova Scotia 79, 80; of Alberta 11; of the Arctic 11, 12; of the Atlantic region 10, 11; of Brit-ish Columbia 11, 12; of Canada 6–7, 10–12, 48–9, 332; and early Cana-dian history 53; of the Great Lakes region 11, 49; of Huronia 11; of Manitoba 11; of Newfoundland 10; of Ontario 11, 12; of the Prairies 12; of Prince Edward Island 79, 268; of Quebec 11; of Saskatchewan 11; of the Subarctic 10–11, 12

Economy: of Acadia 79–81, 81–2, 85; of Britain 426–7; of British Colum-bia 356–7, 376, 379–82, 388, 389–90; of Louisbourg 79, 88–9, 92–3; of Lower Canada 122–41, 427–8; of

New Brunswick 254–6, 263–5, 428; of Newfoundland 285–302, 305–12, 320–3, 428; of New France 35, 39, 50, 57–64; of Nova Scotia 79, 96, 98–9, 102–3, 105–6, 106–7, 254–6, 257–8, 404; of Prince Edward Island 79, 87–8, 254–6, 268–9, 274, 428; of Upper Canada 190–6, 427–8. *See also* Agriculture; Fishery; Fur trade; Manufacturing; Mining; Shipbuilding; Shipping; Timber trade

Education: in Acadia 85; in British Columbia 388; at Louisbourg 93; in Lower Canada 146, 170, 180–2; of Native peoples 69–70, 86, 199, 223–4, 342; in New Brunswick 267; in Newfoundland 317–18; in New France 67; in the Northwest 342, 353; in Nova Scotia 260, 261; in Prince Edward Island 272, 274; and universities 181–2, 224–5, 229, 267, 274; in Upper Canada 187, 222–5, 229; and women 67, 85, 93, 104, 146, 207, 224, 252–3

Emigration
– American: to British Columbia 376–7, 380–1, 382–3, 384–5; to British North America 437–8; to Nova Scotia 79, 102–8, 438; to Upper Canada 202, 233, 438. *See also* Loyalists
– British: to British Columbia 379, 381–2, 384–5; to British North America 428–37; to Lower Canada 152–3; to Newfoundland 292–5; to North America, compared with French 53; to Nova Scotia 79, 99; policy 152, 202, 429–30; to Upper Canada 202–3, 218

– Chinese, to British Columbia 380–1, 384–5
– English: to British North America 431–2, 440, 441; to New Brunswick 245–6; to Newfoundland 295–302, 432; to Nova Scotia 107, 245–6; to Prince Edward Island 245–6, 432; to Upper Canada 202–3
– Franco-American, to the United States 151–2
– French: to Acadia 79, 80–1, 82; to Ile Saint-Jean 79, 87–8; to Louisbourg 79, 88–9, 92–3; to Newfoundland 295; to New France 52–3, 126; to North America, compared with British 53
– German: to British North America 439; to Lower Canada 153; to Nova Scotia 99–100, 439
– Hawaiian, to British Columbia 380
– Irish: to British North America 432–4, 441; to Lower Canada 152, 434; to New Brunswick 246–8, 434; to Newfoundland 295–302, 434; to Nova Scotia 107, 246–8, 434; to Prince Edward Island 246–8, 434; to Upper Canada 202–4, 434
– Japanese, to British Columbia 385
– Norwegian, to British North America 439
– Scottish: to British North America 434–7, 441; to Lower Canada 125, 150, 152, 153; to New Brunswick 247–8; to the Northwest 352–3; to Nova Scotia 79, 80, 81, 107–8, 247–8, 435, 436, 437, 441; to Prince Edward Island 247–8, 270, 437; to Upper Canada 202–3, 437
– Swedish, to British North America 439

- Swiss, to British North America 439
- Welsh, to British Columbia 385; to British North America 430–1; to New Brunswick 431

England. *See* Britain

Exploration literature: American 368, 371–2; bibliography of 8, 36–7; British 8–9, 18–19, 26, 293–4, 334–6, 366, 367–9, 370–2, 373–4, 415; European 14, 80, 282–3, 293, 334, 364; French 9, 20–1, 27, 42, 43, 70, 81, 415; Spanish 369–70

Exploration of North America 5–6, 7, 8–9, 10, 13–32, 80–1, 282, 333, 358, 364; British 8–9, 13–14, 16, 17–19, 24, 25, 27, 187, 293–5, 333–6, 340–1, 364, 366–74, 415; French 9, 13–14, 16, 20–1, 28–30, 42–3, 61, 80–1, 334, 340–1, 367, 415; Portuguese 13–14, 16, 19; pre-Columbian 13–14, 16–18; Russian 364–5; Spanish 13–14, 16, 19–20, 364, 365–6, 369–70, 415

Family: in Acadia 82, 83; in British Columbia 385; at Louisbourg 92; in Lower Canada 128–30, 143, 147, 151, 172; in Newfoundland 297; in New France 37, 55–6, 64–5, 66; in the Northwest 339–40, 351; in Nova Scotia 98, 105; in Prince Edward Island 252; in Upper Canada 202–3, 204–5, 206, 207–8, 212. *See also* Childhood; Marriage and divorce

Farmers: in Acadia 79, 81–2, 85; in Lower Canada (Anglo-American) 125, 150; in Lower Canada (habitants) 123–33, 140, 150–1, 176; in Lower Canada compared with

Upper Canada 131–3, 191; in Newfoundland 297–8; in New France (habitants) 35, 50–1, 62–3; in Nova Scotia 258, 262–3; in Prince Edward Island 269–70, 271–3; in Upper Canada 191–2, 204–6, 209–10. *See also* Agriculture

Fenians 226–7, 408

Finance. *See* Banking; Money

Fish 11; salmon 12, 356, 361

Fishery 5–6, 7, 11, 21; of the Anglo-American colonies 290–1; Basque 21–2, 28, 285–6, 321; British 17, 21, 286, 287, 288, 290–9, 301–2, 305–12, 320–3; of British Columbia 361; Dutch 287; French 21–2, 58, 286, 287–9, 295, 297, 321; Great Lakes 58; at Louisbourg 93; of Lower Canada 137–8, 428; of Native peoples 11, 27, 57–8, 356, 363; of Newfoundland 21–2, 58, 280–1, 285–99, 305–12, 321, 323, 403, 414–15, 428; of New France 53, 57–8; of Nova Scotia 257; Portuguese 21, 285; of Prince Edward Island 274; Spanish 19, 21, 285–6, 307, 311; and the staples thesis 137, 280–1, 290, 312; techniques in 11, 57–8, 137–8; and the truck system 137–8, 298–9, 415; of the United States 307. *See also* Sealing; Whaling

Folklore. *See* Oral traditions

France: and the American Revolution 307; and the exploration of North America 9, 13–14, 16, 20–1, 28–30, 42–3, 61, 80–1, 334, 340–1, 367, 415; fishery of 21–2, 58, 286, 287–9, 295, 297, 321; and Lower Canada 161. *See also* Anglo-French rivalry in North America; Army, French;

Colonial policy, French; Emigration: French; Native relations: with
the French; Navy, French

Franchise: in British North America
417; in New Brunswick 251, 267; in
Nova Scotia 103; in Upper Canada
229; and women 251

French Revolution: and Lower
Canada 161; and Newfoundland
289, 292, 310

Frontier thesis xiv; and British Columbia 360–1; and Lower Canada 118;
and New France 48; and the Northwest 329; and Upper Canada 210

Fur trade: in Acadia 80, 83, 84, 85, 94–
5; and alcohol 69; and Anglo-French
rivalry 59, 94; and Christian missions 322–3, 343; and the Conquest
136; and the Hudson's Bay Company
59, 136–7, 148–9, 337–41, 343, 348–
9, 350–1, 361–2, 366, 370, 372–6,
376–7; in Lower Canada 136–7,
148–9; and Métis 331, 339–40, 348–
52; and Native peoples 4–5, 23, 24–
5, 26, 27–8, 29, 30, 50–2, 55, 59–60,
61, 94–5, 148–9, 197, 218, 304, 322–
3, 331, 337–41, 344–5, 364–76; and
Native women 60, 68–9, 95, 218,
339–40, 351, 375, 386; in New
France 55, 57, 58–62; in the Northwest 329–31, 336–41, 344–5, 348–
52; and the North West Company
136–7, 339–41, 348–9, 361–2, 370–2;
on the Pacific Coast 356–7, 359,
361–2, 364–76, 376–7; and the
Pacific Fur Company 371–2; and the
staples thesis 58–9, 329–31, 337,
361–2. See also Animals; Monopolies, trading; Native peoples: and the
nature of commodity exchange

Habitants. See Farmers

Haida 363, 365

Holland: attacks Acadia 83; attacks
Newfoundland 307; fishery of 287

Homosexuality 216

Hudson's Bay Company: agricultural
operations of 373; and British colonial policy 336, 337, 348–9, 366,
372–3, 376–80, 417, 423–4; in British Columbia 376–83, 417, 423–4;
and cartography 336, 417; and
Christian missions 322, 343; and
exploration 334, 336, 373–4; and the
fur trade 59, 136–7, 148–9, 337–41,
343, 348–9, 350–1, 361–2, 366, 370,
372–6, 376–7, 417; and the Métis
348–9, 350–1; and Native peoples
59, 148–9, 337–41, 370, 372–6; in
the Northwest 336, 337–41, 343,
348–9, 350–1, 417, 423; rivalry with
the North West Company 136–7,
340–1, 348–9, 370–2; on the Pacific
Coast 361–2, 366, 372–6; and Russia
372–3

Huron 22, 30, 49–50, 148; as agriculturalists 49–50; and the Algonkian
4–5; Christian missions to 35, 43,
69; environment of 11, 49; and the
French 30, 40–1, 42–3, 49–50, 69;
and the fur trade 4–5, 30; and the St
Lawrence Iroquoian 5, 29–30

Illegitimate birth: in New France 66,
72; in Upper Canada 216

Immigration: to Acadia 79–81, 82; to
British Columbia 376–7, 379, 380–
3, 384–5; to British North America
428–39; to Ile Saint-Jean 79, 87–8;
to Louisbourg 79, 88–9, 92–3; to
Lower Canada 125, 150, 152–3, 434;

to New Brunswick 242–8, 431, 434; to Newfoundland 295–302, 323, 432, 434; to New France 50–7, 67; to North America 53; to the Northwest 352–3; to Nova Scotia 79, 80, 81, 99–100, 102–8, 242–8, 434, 435, 436, 437, 438, 439, 441; to Prince Edward Island 242, 245–8, 270, 432, 434, 437; to Upper Canada 187, 198, 200–4, 217–18, 233, 429–30, 434, 437, 438. *See also* Emigration

Indentured servitude 53

Infanticide: in Lower Canada 146–7, 150; in New France 72; in Nova Scotia 261

Innu 12–13, 22. *See also* Montagnais

Interior Salish 364. *See also* Okanagan

Inuit 9–10, 12–13, 22, 24–5, 344; and the Basques 25, 321; and the Beothuk 26; and the British 19, 24–5, 344; Christian missions to 321–3; fishery of 58; and the French 25, 58, 321; and the fur trade 24–5, 149, 322–3; and the Norse 24, 333; oral traditions of 335, 344, 347; religion of 323; women 322

Iroquoian (language grouping): as agriculturalists 7, 11, 29; slavery among 73. *See also* Iroquois; Ontario Iroquoian; St Lawrence Iroquoian

Iroquois 50; and the American Revolution 148, 198, 400, 402; and Anglo-French rivalry 50, 72–3; Christian missions to 42–3, 54–5; covenant chain 73, 148; as Loyalists 198, 218; and the Ojibwa 73; population of 54–5; and the St Lawrence Iroquoian 29; and treaties 148

Jesuits: in Acadia 80, 81; *Relations* 35, 42, 50, 81. *See also* Christian missions; Roman Catholic Church

Jews: in British Columbia 380–1; in British North America 439; in Lower Canada 153, 439

Justice, the administration of: in British Columbia 375–6; 378, 379, 382–3, 383–4, 446–7; in British North America 444–7; in Lower Canada 166–8, 443, 445–6; in Newfoundland 301–2; in New France 72; in the Northwest 349, 446; in Nova Scotia 97–8, 261, 444; in Prince Ed-ward Island 271; in Upper Canada 220–1, 444, 445–6. *See also* Law

Katzie 364

Kitwancool 364

Kwakiutl 363

Land policy: in Acadia 79; in Lower Canada 152; in the Northwest 349–50; in Nova Scotia 103, 105; in Prince Edward Island 79; in Upper Canada 201–2, 204–6. *See also* Seigneurial system

Language: Acadian French 442; Black 440; English 83, 173, 269, 431, 440, 441, 442; French 67, 173, 440–1, 442; German 441; Irish 441; linguistic atlas of Quebec 440; linguistic atlas of the United States and Canada 440; Métis 351; of Native peoples 3, 6, 7, 67, 267, 347, 362–3, 441–2; pidgin 28, 351, 441–2; Scots 434–5, 441; slang 67; Welsh 431

Laurentian thesis xiv; and Lower Canada 118, 122–3, 133–4; and the Northwest 330–1; and the Pacific Coast 361; and Upper Canada 190–1

Law: bankruptcy 135; British 443; in British Columbia 446–7; in British North America 444–7; business 167, 221; *coutume de Paris* 72; international, and the Great Lakes 411; labour 143, 215; in Lower Canada 135, 143, 146–7, 166–8, 443–4, 445–6; in New Brunswick 443; in New France 72; in the Northwest 446; in Nova Scotia 443, 444, 445, 446; in Prince Edward Island 444; in Upper Canada 215, 217, 220–1, 233, 445–6; and women 146–7, 217, 251, 261, 444–5, 446. *See also* Justice, the administration of

Libraries: in Lower Canada 174–5; in New France 67

Lillooet 364

Literacy: at Louisbourg 93; in Lower Canada 181; in New England 104; in Newfoundland 318; in New France 67; in Prince Edward Island 272; in Upper Canada 215

Literature (fiction and non-fiction): in Acadia 80–1; in Lower Canada 114–15, 117–18, 142, 173–6; in New Brunswick 252, 267; in Newfoundland 283–4; in New France 37, 67; in Nova Scotia 108, 242, 252, 259–61; in Prince Edward Island 247, 252, 269, 270; in Upper Canada 186, 201, 205–6, 218. *See also* Exploration literature; Sermon literature; Travel literature

Loyalists 438; in the American Revolution 401–2; Black 244; in Cape Breton 242, 245; definition of 242, 438; language of 438; in Lower Canada 152; Native 198, 218, 402; in New Brunswick 242–5; in Nova Scotia

242–5, 438; in Prince Edward Island 242, 245; in Upper Canada 187, 198, 200–2, 217–18, 401–2, 438; women 217–18, 242, 438

Maliseet (Malecite) 22, 94–6; and the Acadians 94; and the American Revolution 96, 403; and Anglo-French rivalry 80, 86–7, 94–6; art of 241; Christian missions to 80, 86–7, 94–5; and the fur trade 94; New Brunswick policy toward 240–1; Nova Scotia policy toward 94–5, 240–1; and treaties 95

Manufacturing: domestic 139; iron 63–4, 139; in Lower Canada 138–9; in New France 63–4; and railways 139, 196; textiles 139, 194; in Upper Canada 187, 194–6. *See also* Shipbuilding

Marriage and divorce: in Acadia 82, 83; in Anglo-American colonies 56; at Louisbourg 93; in Lower Canada 130, 131, 146–7, 172; in New France 37, 66; in Nova Scotia 444–5; in Prince Edward Island 444; in Upper Canada 216, 217

Massachusetts: and Acadia 79, 83, 84; and Anglo-French rivalry 79, 83, 84, 88–91, 96–102; and Louisbourg 88–91; militia 74; and Nova Scotia 79, 96–109, 402

Material culture: of artisans in New France 64; of habitants 63, 144–5; of Lower Canada 144–5; of the Lunenburg Germans 100; methods and scope 144; of the Micmac 240; of Native peoples 363; of the Planters 104–5; of the working class 144–5. *See also* Archaeology

Medicine: in Acadia 85; and hospitals 70–1, 93, 221–2; at Louisbourg 93; in Lower Canada 156–8; in Newfoundland 319; in New France 68, 70–1; in the Northwest 353; in Nova Scotia 253; in Upper Canada 218, 221–2

Mental health: in Lower Canada 157; in the Maritime provinces 275; in Newfoundland 319; in New France 68; and psychiatry 157, 222; in Upper Canada 218, 221–2

Merchants: Acadian 250; British 291–2, 298–9, 301, 306, 311–12, 367–8; in British Columbia 361, 367–8, 382; French 61, 297; at Louisbourg 93; in Lower Canada 118, 119–21, 130, 133–41, 152–3, 361, 428; in New Brunswick 264, 265; in Newfoundland 291–2, 296–7, 301, 312, 313–15; in New France 35, 50–1, 57, 60–1, 63–4; in the Northwest 353; in Nova Scotia 98, 253, 257–8; in Prince Edward Island 273; Russian 365; Scottish 81, 134, 256, 291; in Upper Canada 193–5. See also Monopolies, trading

Methodist Church: in British Columbia 387; missions to Native peoples 303, 342, 387; in New Brunswick 261–2; in Newfoundland 300, 303; in Nova Scotia 106, 261–2; in Upper Canada 222, 224, 227–9

Métis: definition of 347–8; and the fur trade 331, 339–40, 348–52; genesis 55; and the Hudson's Bay Company 348–9, 350–1; language of 351, 441–2; and Native peoples 348; in the Northwest 331, 339–40, 347–52; and the North West Company 348–

9; and the Red River Resistance of 1869–70 349–50, 353, 354; and the Red River settlement 349–51, 353; women 339–40, 351

Metropolitan thesis xiv; and the Northwest 329, 330–1; and Upper Canada 210

Micmac 22, 27–8, 94–6, 148; and Acadians 94; as agriculturalists 240; and the American Revolution 96, 403; and Anglo-French rivalry 80, 86–7, 94–6; art of 95, 240–1; and the Beothuk 26, 304–5; Christian missions to 80, 81, 86–7, 94–5; fishery of 27, 58; and the fur trade 27–8, 94–5; material culture of 240; New Brunswick policy toward 240–1; in Newfoundland 304–5; Nova Scotia policy toward 94–5, 240–1; oral traditions of 95, 241; population of 28, 94; Prince Edward Island policy toward 240, 269; and treaties 95; women 95, 241

Midwifery: in New France 68; in Nova Scotia 253; in Upper Canada 218

Militia: of the Anglo-American colonies 74, 90–1, 96–7, 101; of British Columbia 381; in British North America 399–400; of Lower Canada 159, 161, 163, 406; of New France 73–4; of Upper Canada 226, 231–2, 406

Mining: in British Columbia 356–7, 360–1, 379–82, 382–5, 388–91; in Newfoundland 320; in Nova Scotia 257; in Upper Canada 225

Miscegenation 55. See also Métis

Mississauga 197–9

Money: in Lower Canada 139–40; in

New France 38; in Nova Scotia 99; in Upper Canada 195

Monopolies, trading: in Acadia 80, 81, 83; in Newfoundland 293–5; in New France 39, 60. *See also* Hudson's Bay Company

Montagnais 22, 25, 50; Christian missions to 50, 69; and the fur trade 59, 148; and reserves 148

Moravian Brethren: missions to Native peoples 321–3; in Newfoundland 320, 321–3

Music: of Highland Scots 247; hymnody 104, 110; in Lower Canada 178–9; in New France 68; in Nova Scotia 104, 110; in Prince Edward Island 269

Napoleonic Wars: and Britain 405; and Newfoundland 292, 310

Native peoples 40, 197; as agriculturalists 7, 11, 29, 49–50, 60, 240; and alcohol 69, 199; and the American Revolution 96, 197–8, 400, 402, 403, 409–10; and Anglo-French rivalry 40–1, 50, 52, 69, 72–3, 80, 86–7, 94–6; animals, relationship with 11–12, 23, 60, 338, 374; art of 69, 95, 200, 240–1; art, depicted in 14, 18–19, 70, 336; colonial policies toward 94–5, 147–9, 199–200, 240–1, 269, 381, 382–3, 385–6; diseases among 4, 15–16, 23–4, 26, 29, 51–2, 54, 304, 370; education of 69–70, 86, 199, 223–4, 342; fishery of 11, 27, 57–8, 356, 363; historiography of 3–6, 30–1, 33–6, 38, 46, 48, 59–60, 74–5, 94, 241; languages of 3, 6, 7, 28, 67, 267, 347, 362–3, 441–2; Loyalists 198, 218, 402; material culture of 240;

363; and the nature of commodity exchange 22–3, 59–60, 68–9, 148–9, 337–9, 344; oral traditions of 35, 48, 95, 197, 241, 333, 335, 344, 345, 346–7; political structures of 6, 71, 362–3; population of 7, 10, 23–4, 26, 28, 51–2, 54–5, 94, 303, 332, 362, 370; religion of 7, 23, 69, 199, 323, 332, 338–9, 342, 346–7; and reserves 54, 148, 199, 241; slavery among 73; and sovereignty, concepts of 73; treaties and 73, 95, 148, 197–9, 381, 386, 400; and the War of 1812 198, 226, 404–6, 410–11; women 5, 25, 39, 60, 66, 68–9, 95, 218, 241, 303, 322, 339–40, 346, 347, 375, 386. *See also* Anthropology; Archaeology; Christian missions; Fur trade; Native peoples of the Arctic, of the Northeast, of the Northwest Coast, of the Plains, of the Plateau, of the Subarctic; Native relations; *names of individual tribes and language groupings*

Native peoples of the Arctic 7, 11–12, 344, 345–6; bibliography of 8, 9; in the precontact period 12, 332. *See also* Inuit

Native peoples of the Northeast 7, 11–12, 38, 40–1, 49, 54–5, 69; bibliography of 8, 9, 38, 44; historical atlas of 38, 51; in the precontact period 13. *See also* Abenaki; Beothuk; Huron; Iroquois; Maliseet; Micmac; Mississauga; Neutral; Ojibwa; Ontario Iroquoian; Passamaquoddy; Petun; St Lawrence Iroquoian

Native peoples of the Northwest Coast 7, 12, 362–4; bibliography of 359; fishery of 356, 363; languages of 362–3; material culture of 363; population of 362, 370; in the pre-contact period 13, 362–4. *See also* Coast Salish; Haida; Katzie; Kitwancool; Kwakiutl; Nisga; Nootka; Stalo; Tsimshian

Native peoples of the Plains 7, 12, 344–5, 347; in the precontact period 13, 332–3. *See also* Blackfoot; Cree; Dakota; Ojibwa; Saulteaux

Native peoples of the Plateau 363–4. *See also* Carrier; Interior Salish; Lillooet; Okanagan; Shuswap; Thompson

Native peoples of the Subarctic 7, 11–12, 38, 49, 54, 344–6, 363; bibliography of 8, 9, 38; in the precontact period 13. *See also* Beaver; Cree; Dene; Innu; Montagnais

Native relations
– with the Basques: in Newfoundland 321; in the sixteenth century 22, 25, 28
– with the British: in Acadia/Nova Scotia 80, 94–6; in the Great Lakes region 40–1, 49–50, 58–9, 69, 73, 148–9, 400, 402, 404–6, 409–10; in Lower Canada 148–9; in New-foundland 302–5, 321–3; in the Northwest 337–47; in Nova Scotia 94–6, 403; on the Pacific Coast 367–9, 370, 371, 374–6, 385–6; in the sixteenth century 8–9, 17–19, 22–6; in Upper Canada 197–9, 226
– with Europeans 38; in Acadia 80, 94; in Newfoundland 302–3; in the sixteenth century 5–6, 8, 14, 18–19, 22–3, 25
– with the French: in Acadia/Nova

Scotia 80, 86–7, 94–6; in the Great Lakes region 40–1, 42–3, 49–50, 52, 58–60, 68–9, 72–3; in Newfoundland 321; in New France 38, 54–5, 58, 66, 69–70; in the Northwest 337–47; in the sixteenth century 9, 20–1, 22–5, 27, 28–30
– with the Russians, on the Pacific Coast 365, 370
– with the Spanish, on the Pacific Coast 365, 369–70
– with the United States: in the Great Lakes region 198, 225–6, 400, 402, 404–6, 409–10; on the Pacific Coast 367–9, 370, 371–2, 386

Navigation, art of 10; Norse 14; on the St Lawrence River 141; in the sixteenth century 14, 15

Navy, British: and the American Revolution 403–4; and Anglo-French rivalry 91, 305–10; and British Columbia 380, 384; and British North America 399–408; and the Civil War 407–8; and the Maritime provinces 403–4, 406–7; and New-foundland 299–300, 305–10, 403; and the Northwest 334; and the Pacific Coast 376, 379, 407; and the War of 1812 404–7

Navy, French 73, 91, 98, 307, 309

Neutral 30–1, 35

New England: and Acadia 79, 80, 81, 83, 84; and Anglo-French rivalry 79, 80, 83, 84, 88–91, 96–102; and Louisbourg 88–91, 92–3; militia 74; and Newfoundland 290–1; and Nova Scotia 79, 96–109

Newspapers: in British Columbia 380; in Lower Canada 115, 161, 176–7; in Nova Scotia 251, 259; and the

telegraph 177; in Upper Canada
226, 231

Nisga 387

Nobles, in New France 35, 57, 66

Nootka 365

Norse: exploration of and settlements
in North America 7, 13–14, 16–17,
333; and the Inuit 24, 333

North West Company: and exploration
370–2; and the fur trade 339–41,
348–9, 361–2, 370–2; and the Métis
348–9; and Native peoples 339–41,
370–2; on the Pacific Coast 361–2,
370–2; rivalry with the Hudson's Bay
Company 136–7, 340–1, 348–9,
370–2

Northwest passage, search for 13–14,
18, 333–5, 366; bibliography of 8

Odawa 48. *See also* Ojibwa

Ojibwa 50, 197; and the American
Revolution 197–8, 400; and Anglo-
French rivalry 73; bibliography of
38; and the British 197–9; and the fur
trade 197, 337; and the Iroquois 73;
oral traditions of 48, 197; religion of
69, 199, 346; and treaties 198–9; and
the War of 1812 198, 405

Okanagan 374

Ontario Iroquoian 22, 30–1. *See also*
Huron; Neutral; Petun

Oral traditions: of Lower Canada 179;
of Native peoples 35, 48, 95, 197,
241, 333, 335, 344, 345, 346–7

Orange Order: in British North
America 434; in New Brunswick
265; in Upper Canada 204

Passamaquoddy 240

Patronage: in Lower Canada 140; in

New Brunswick 264; in New France
71–2; in Nova Scotia 244

Petun 30–1

Photography, in the Northwest 336

Planters 79, 102–8, 402–3, 438; bibliography of 77; Planters Study Committee 78–9, 102

Police: in Lower Canada 154, 166; in
the Maritime provinces 445; in
Newfoundland 318–19; in New
France 72

Political parties: in British Columbia
379; Canadian party 162; Clear
Grits 234; Constitutional party 162;
Escheat party 271–2; in Lower Canada 161–5; Loyal Electors 271; in
New Brunswick 266; in Nova Scotia
103; Patriote party 161–3; in Prince
Edward Island 271–4; *Rouge* party
165; in Upper Canada 229, 234

Political structures: of Acadia 79, 80,
85; of the Anglo-American colonies
413–14; of Britain 417, 418; of British Columbia 358, 377–80, 382–4,
390–2, 423–4; of British North
America 413–25; church relations
with 47, 70, 86, 103, 165, 201, 224,
227, 274, 315–16; and Confederation
164–5, 234–6, 276–8, 316–17, 391–2,
424–5; and Durham's *Report* 163–4;
and elites (compacts) 141–2, 161–3,
164–5, 193, 199, 200–2, 205, 210–13,
217–18, 224, 226, 230, 232–3, 257–8,
259, 266–7, 271–2, 313–15, 379–80,
390; of Lower Canada 158–66, 414,
417–18, 422; of Native peoples 6,
71, 362–3; of New Brunswick 243–4,
264, 265–7, 276–7, 422–3; of
Newfoundland 301–2, 312–17, 414–
15, 417, 423; of New France 39–40,

41–2, 47, 71–2; of Nova Scotia 97–9, 102–3, 103–4, 244–5, 258–9, 263, 276–8, 415, 417, 422; of Prince Edward Island 245, 268–74, 276, 278, 415, 417, 423; and reform movements 212, 230–1, 232–3, 259, 266, 271–2, 313–15; of Upper Canada 186–7, 200–2, 205, 210–12, 216, 217–18, 220–1, 229–36, 422. *See also* Franchise; Patronage; Political parties

Popular disturbances: in Acadia 81; in Lower Canada 143, 166; in New Brunswick 264, 265; in New France 72; in Prince Edward Island 272, 273, 274; Red River Resistance of 1869–70 349–50, 353, 354; in Upper Canada 187, 214, 215, 217, 219, 220, 230, 233. *See also* Rebellions of 1837–8

Population: of Acadia 79, 82; bibliography of 43; of British Columbia 379; of France 52; of Lower Canada 149–53; of Native peoples 7, 10, 23–4, 26, 28, 51–2, 54–5, 94, 303, 332, 362, 370; of New Brunswick 265; of New France 50–7, 73; of New France compared with Anglo-American colonies 56; of Nova Scotia 79, 96, 103, 107; of Upper Canada 187. *See also* Disease; Emigration; Immigration

Portugal: colonial policy of 19; and the exploration of North America 13–14, 16, 19; fishery of 21, 285

Poverty: in Lower Canada 143–4; in New Brunswick 261, 265; in Newfoundland 318; in Nova Scotia 258, 261, 263; in Upper Canada 219–20

Presbyterian Church: in British Columbia 388; in Lower Canada 173; in the Northwest 353; in Nova Scotia 106, 262, 436; in Prince Edward Island 273–4; in Upper Canada 228

Protestant churches: in British Columbia 380; in Lower Canada 172–3; missions to Native peoples 199; missions to Roman Catholics 173; in Newfoundland 299–300, 303; in Upper Canada 227–9. *See also* Amish; Anglican; Baptist; Congregational; Methodist; Moravian Brethren; Presbyterian; Quakers

Public administration: of British Columbia 391; of the British Empire 162, 413, 416, 417, 418, 420; of Lower Canada 140, 164, 165; of New France 41–2, 71; of Nova Scotia 259; of Upper Canada 195, 199, 215, 219–20, 222–3, 229. *See also* Justice, the administration of; Patronage; Political structures

Quakers: in Nova Scotia 106; in Upper Canada 224, 227

Railways: in Lower Canada 139, 140–1; as manufacturers 139, 196; in New Brunswick 265, 277; in Nova Scotia 259; in Upper Canada 193–4, 196, 215; workers on 142–3, 215

Rebellions of 1837–8: in Lower Canada 131–3, 146, 161–4, 407, 411, 419; in Upper Canada 187, 226, 231–2, 407, 411, 419; women's role in 146

Reserves, Indian: in Lower Canada 148; in New Brunswick 241; in New

France 54; in Upper Canada 199.
See also Native peoples: colonial policies toward

Riots. *See* Popular disturbances

Roman Catholic Church: in Acadia 80,
81, 82, 85–7; and Anglo-French
rivalry 86–7, 94–5; and art 68, 177–
8; and British Columbia 386–7, 388–
9; and Confederation 165; French
background of, in New France 70;
and the Hudson's Bay Company
343; on Ile Saint-Jean 88; at Louisbourg 92, 93; in Lower Canada 134,
146, 150, 165, 168–72, 177–8, 179;
missions to Native peoples 34, 35,
38, 42–3, 50, 54–5, 69–70, 80, 81,
86–7, 94–5, 149, 199, 333, 341–3,
386–7; in New Brunswick 250; in
Newfoundland 294, 299–301, 315–
16, 317–18; in New France 47, 70–
1, 72; in the Northwest 333, 341–3,
353; in Nova Scotia 250, 262, 437;
in Prince Edward Island 274; and
ultramontanism 165, 169, 179; in
Upper Canada 224, 227–8, 437; and
women in religious orders 70–1, 93,
146, 150, 170–1, 253, 342, 353,
388–9

Russia: and the exploration of North
America 364–5; and the fur trade
359, 364–5, 366, 367, 370, 372–3;
and Native peoples 365, 370; on the
Pacific Coast 359, 364–5, 366, 367,
370, 372–3

St Lawrence Iroquoian 22, 28–30; disappearance of 5, 28–30

Saulteaux 343, 354

Science: in Lower Canada 179–80; in
New Brunswick 267; in Newfound-

land 320; in New France 67–8; in
Nova Scotia 260; Spanish 366; in
Upper Canada 225, 229

Sealing, in Newfoundland 297, 311

Seigneurial system: in Acadia 79, 84,
85; courts of 72; in Lower Canada
124–5, 137, 138–9, 141–2; in New
France 39, 48, 62–3, 64, 72

Sermon literature 90, 110, 171, 228

Seven Years' War 39–40, 42, 52, 53,
73–4

Shipbuilding: in Atlantic Canada 255,
312, 428; in Lower Canada 139; in
New France 63–4; in Nova Scotia
257; in Prince Edward Island 269,
273, 274

Shipping: in Atlantic Canada 255–6,
312, 428; in British Columbia 389;
French colonial 61; in Newfoundland 312; in Nova Scotia 257; in
Prince Edward Island 273, 274, 425

Shuswap 364

Slavery: and antislavery 207, 249, 412;
escaped slaves 207, 248, 412; in
Lower Canada 153; among Native
peoples 73; in New France 64; in
Nova Scotia 107; in Upper Canada
206–7

Sovereignty, concepts of: French 20,
73; Native 73

Spain: colonial policy of 20; and the
exploration of North America 13–
14, 16, 19–20, 364, 365–6, 369–70,
415; fishery of 19, 21, 285–6, 307,
311; imperial policy of 93; and
Native peoples 365, 369–70; and the
Nootka crisis 369; on the Pacific
Coast 359, 364, 365–6, 369–70

Stalo 364

Staples thesis xiv, 290; and Lower Can-

ada 118, 122–4, 137; and Newfoundland 280–1, 290, 312; and
New France 58–9; and the Northwest 329–31, 337; and the Pacific
Coast 361–2; and Upper Canada
190–1, 192, 193

Tariffs: and British North America
164, 195, 254, 427–8; and free trade
425–6; and mercantilism 59, 288,
290, 425–6; and the Reciprocity
Treaty of 1854 164, 195, 254, 412
Theatre: in Acadia 80–1; in Lower
Canada 176
Thompson (tribe) 364
Timber trade: in British Columbia
356–7, 390; in British North Amer-
ica 428; in Lower Canada 138; in
New Brunswick 263–4, 266, 428;
and the staples thesis 192; in Upper
Canada 192–3
Transportation: in British Columbia
372, 373; canals 141, 193; in Lower
Canada 140–1, 428; ships 10, 14,
15, 16, 140–1, 193, 372, 373; in
Upper Canada 187, 192–4. See also
Railways
Travel literature: of Acadia 77; bibliog-
raphy of 36–7, 77, 115, 206; of Brit-
ish Columbia 356, 382, 389;
French 42; of Lower Canada 115,
439; of Newfoundland 282–3, 298,
321; of New France 36–7, 42; of the
Northwest 336; Norwegian 439; of
Nova Scotia 259; of Prince Edward
Island 270; Swedish 42; of Upper
Canada 205–6, 439, 440. See also
Exploration literature
Treaties and Native peoples 73, 95,
148, 197–9, 381, 386, 400

Tsimshian 7, 364, 387

United States: and British Columbia
357, 359, 376–7, 382–3, 391, 412;
and British North America 396–7,
404–8, 408–13; and the Civil War
407–8, 412–13; and Confederation
425; and diplomatic relations with
Britain 396, 405, 407–8, 408–13;
escaped slaves from 207, 248, 412;
fishery of 307; and Franco-American
immigration 151–2; and the fur
trade 367–9, 371–2; and Lower
Canada 165–6, 175, 404–8; and the
Maritime provinces 255, 406–8; and
Native peoples in the Great Lakes
region 198, 225–6, 400, 402, 404–6,
409–10; and Native peoples on the
Pacific Coast 367–9, 370, 371–2,
386; and Newfoundland 307, 309–
10; and the Northwest 354, 412,
423; and the Oregon question 376–
7, 412; and the Rebellions of 1837–
8 231–2, 407, 411; and the Reciprocity Treaty of 1854 164, 195,
254, 412; and the San Juan boundary
dispute 383, 412; and Upper Canada
202, 233, 404–8, 411, 412; and the
War of 1812 161, 198, 225–6, 371,
376, 404–7, 410–11
Urban centres: bibliography of 188;
Charlottetown 274–5; Halifax 99,
262; Hamilton 196, 204, 209, 211,
215; Kingston 189, 194, 208–9, 211,
220, 221–2, 226; in Lower Canada
153–5; Montreal 37, 42, 50–1, 56,
65, 68, 73, 125, 127, 133–6, 140–1,
142, 143–4, 146, 155, 178; in New
France 56, 65; Quebec City 56, 65,
68, 73, 134–6, 140–1, 144, 149, 154–

5, 178; Saint John 265; St John's 308, 318–19; Toronto (York) 194, 196, 208, 211, 214–15, 217, 219–20, 221, 225, 231, 232–3; in Upper Canada 208–9, 210; Vancouver 358, 383; Victoria 376–7, 379–80

War of 1812 404–7, 410–11; and British Columbia 371, 376; and Lower Canada 161, 404–7; and the Maritime provinces 256, 406–7; and Native peoples 198, 226, 404–6, 410–11; and Newfoundland 310; and Upper Canada 198, 225–6, 404–7
Weights and measures, in New France 38
West Indies: trade with Newfoundland 299; trade with New France 61; trade with Nova Scotia 256, 257
Whaling: Basque 22, 286; of British Columbia 382; European 13; of Newfoundland 285, 286, 311; of New France 58; of the Northwest 344; on the Pacific Coast 382; Scottish 311
Women: in Acadia 83, 85; artists 253; authors 108, 176, 206, 218, 252; in British Columbia 359, 367, 377, 381, 385, 388–9; in business 61, 85, 250, 251, 253; captives 54; and childbirth 60, 68, 218; diaries of 252, 367, 377, 385; and domestic manufacturing 139, 216; and domestic service 143; and education 67, 85, 93, 104, 146, 207, 224, 252–3,

342, 353, 388–9; and the franchise 251; and the law 146–7, 217, 251, 261, 444–5, 446; at Louisbourg 93; in Lower Canada 122, 139, 143, 145–7; Loyalists 217–18, 242, 438; and marriage and divorce 66, 93, 146–7, 216, 217, 444–5; and medicine 218, 253, 353; and mental health 218; midwives 68, 218, 253; in New Brunswick 251–4; in New France 39, 42, 53, 61, 66, 72; in the Northwest 341, 343–4, 351, 353, 354; in Nova Scotia 108, 251–4, 261, 444–5, 446; in Prince Edward Island 251–4, 270, 444; in the Rebellions of 1837–8 146; in religious orders 70–1, 93, 146, 150, 170–1, 253, 342, 353, 388–9; in Upper Canada 206, 215–19, 406, 438; in the War of 1812 406; working class 143, 146, 216–17, 385
Women, Native 39, 60, 66, 95, 303; artists 241; captives 5, 25; and Christian missions 66, 322; Loyalists 218; oral traditions of 346, 347; role of, in the fur trade 60, 68–9, 95, 218, 339–40, 351, 375, 386
Working class: in British Columbia 381–2, 385, 389–90; Irish 142–3, 213, 219; and the law 143, 215; in Lower Canada 142–4; in the Maritime provinces 256; material culture of 144–5; in Newfoundland 319; in New France 63–4; and strikes 143, 187, 214; in Upper Canada 187, 196, 213–15, 219; women 143, 146, 216–17, 385

2934